AF901966

Eastern Wines on Western Tables

Mnemosyne Supplements

HISTORY AND ARCHAEOLOGY
OF CLASSICAL ANTIQUITY

Series Editor

Jonathan M. Hall (*University of Chicago*)

Associate Editors

Jan Paul Crielaard (*Vrije Universiteit Amsterdam*)
Benet Salway (*University College London*)

VOLUME 435

The titles published in this series are listed at *brill.com/mns-haca*

Eastern Wines on Western Tables

Consumption, Trade and Economy in Ancient Italy

by

Paulina Komar

BRILL

LEIDEN | BOSTON

Cover illustration: Black-figure Attic crater, 6th c. BC (National Museum in Warsaw, with permission. Inventory number 142345)

Library of Congress Cataloging-in-Publication Data

Names: Komar, Paulina, author.
Title: Eastern wines on western tables : consumption, trade and economy in ancient Italy / by Paulina Komar.
Description: Leiden ; Boston : Brill, 2020. | Series: Mnemosyne supplements, history and archaeology of classical antiquity, 2352-8656 ; volume 435 | Includes bibliographical references and index.
Identifiers: LCCN 2020028141 (print) | LCCN 2020028142 (ebook) | ISBN 9789004433700 (hardback) | ISBN 9789004433762 (ebook)
Subjects: LCSH: Wine industry–Italy–History–To 476. | Wine and wine making–History–To 476. | Rome (Italy)–Commerce–Middle East–History–To 476. | Middle East–Commerce–Rome (Italy)–History–To 476. | Rome (Italy)–Antiquities.
Classification: LCC HD9385.I82 K66 2020 (print) | LCC HD9385.I82 (ebook) | DDC 338.4/766320937–dc23
LC record available at https://lccn.loc.gov/2020028141
LC ebook record available at https://lccn.loc.gov/2020028142

Typeface for the Latin, Greek, and Cyrillic scripts: "Brill". See and download: brill.com/brill-typeface.

ISSN 2352-8656
ISBN 978-90-04-43370-0 (hardback)
ISBN 978-90-04-43376-2 (e-book)

Copyright 2021 by Koninklijke Brill NV, Leiden, The Netherlands.
Koninklijke Brill NV incorporates the imprints Brill, Brill Hes & De Graaf, Brill Nijhoff, Brill Rodopi, Brill Sense, Hotei Publishing, mentis Verlag, Verlag Ferdinand Schöningh and Wilhelm Fink Verlag.
All rights reserved. No part of this publication may be reproduced, translated, stored in a retrieval system, or transmitted in any form or by any means, electronic, mechanical, photocopying, recording or otherwise, without prior written permission from the publisher. Requests for re-use and/or translations must be addressed to Koninklijke Brill NV via brill.com or copyright.com.

This book is printed on acid-free paper and produced in a sustainable manner.

To all my friends and my daughter Emily

... hic totus volo rideat libellus et sit nequior omnibus libellis, qui vino madeat nec erubescat.

But I wish the present little book to laugh from one end to the other, and to be more free in its language than any of my books; to be redolent of wine.

MART. XI 15

•••

... πλὴν τῆς ἐν οἴνῳ βασάνου καὶ παιδιᾶς, τίνα ἔχομεν ἡδονὴν εἰπεῖν ἔμμετρον μᾶλλον

... what more suitable pleasure can we mention than wine with its playful testing—provided that it is employed at all carefully

PLATO, *Laws* 1.649d–e

∵

Contents

Acknowledgements

First of all, this work, which originated as a PhD thesis, would not exist if not for the project "The Eastern Mediterranean from the 4th century BC until Late Antiquity" created by Prof. K. Nawotka (University of Wrocław) and realised within the International Ph.D. Projects Programme of the Foundation for Polish Science.[1] I will now take the opportunity to thank the people who helped me while I was writing this book, of whom there are many. My PhD would not have been completed without the constant advice and guidance I received from Prof. A. Łoś, the best PhD thesis supervisor ever. I also owe a huge debt of gratitude to Dr. Z. Archibald, who helped me solve many problems during my stay in Liverpool. I would not have been able to write Chapter 3 if I did not have access to the libraries of the École française de Rome and the Deutsches Archäologisches Institut. My stay in Rome was possible thanks to Prof. C. Virlouvet and I am sincerely grateful to her. I would also like to thank Dr. G. Rizzo, who patiently answered my questions regarding ancient amphoras. Discussions with scholars from Aix-en-Provence, especially with Prof. A. Tchernia allowed me to avoid mistakes concerning certain aspects of ancient wines. I am also grateful to Prof. M.-B. Carre, thanks to whom I was able to spend some time at the library of the Centre Camille Jullian in Aix-en-Provence.

This book would not be finished if it were not for my postdoctoral internship at the Jagiellonian University in Krakow financed from the National Science Centre,[2] which allowed me to transform my PhD into a proper book, broadening the scope of research considerably. I am truly grateful to the Institute of Archaeology at the Jagiellonian University for providing me with suitable working conditions, and to prof. E. Papuci-Władyka, my internship supervisor, for her help in dealing with all the bureaucracy at the University, and for providing me with a warm welcome to the Department of Classical Archaeology.

The amphora illustrations presented in Appendix 3 were taken from the University of Southampton's website—Archaeology Data Service[3] and have been reproduced here with the kind permission of Dr. D. Williams. The illustrations

1 Within the framework of the International Ph.D. Projects Programme of the Foundation for Polish Science co-financed by the European Union, Regional Development Fund, within the frameworks of Measure 1.2 "Strengthening the Human Potential within the Science Sector" of the Innovative Economy Operational Programme.

2 Awarded as a part of placement funding for postdoctoral internships, based on decision No. DEC-2015/16/S/HS3/00098.

3 University of Southampton (2014) Roman Amphorae: a digital resource [data-set]. York: Archaeology Data Service [distributor] https://doi.org/10.5284/1028192.

were redrawn to meet printing standards by M. Marciniak, whom I would also like to thank. Additionally, I would like to thank the National Museum in Warsaw for allowing me to use an illustration of one of their Attic black-figure craters on the front cover.[4] Moreover, I would like to express my gratitude to the reviewer of this book, whose invaluable guidance enabled me to bring my work more up to date.

Finally, I would like to thank all my colleagues from the project "The Eastern Mediterranean …", especially Dominika, Asia and Marek, for making my PhD studies one of the best periods of my life. I am also very grateful to Lee Richards who corrected a lot of my still slightly 'Pidgin-English' and made this book more understandable. And last but definitely not least, I want to thank Maciek M., who was always there when I needed him and helped me through all the crises and moments of doubt. And Emily, you little monster, I am also grateful to you that you liked your nursery.

4 Inventory number: 142345.

Figures and Tables

Figures

Tables

In Search of Lost Wines: Perspectives and Limits

> ... *volgoque veritas iam attributa vino est.*
>
> ... and truth has come to be proverbially credited to wine.
>
> PLIN. *HN* XIV 14

There is no doubt that wine was one of the main consumption goods in the Mediterranean during antiquity. Considering that the wine intake of the average Roman adult male was probably between 0,5–1 litre per day,[1] production and trade of this beverage must have been significant from an economic point of view. Wines were produced in Italy, but they were also imported from all over the Mediterranean, especially the Eastern part, which throughout antiquity provided the most popular beverages. The aim of this book is to present a broad view of the consumption and trading of Eastern wines in Italy, which is likely to shed light on more general social, cultural and economic dilemmas that have long puzzled scholars.

This book is the first comprehensive and interdisciplinary study of Eastern Mediterranean wines that were imported to Italy. By combining the most important and relevant sources that provide evidence regarding this matter (i.e. the literary, archaeological and epigraphic evidence that is usually attributed to individual scientific disciplines), I can consider the subject from many different, and at times new angles, and hence avoid those frequent distortions which occur when only one type of evidence is analysed. Furthermore, the book adopts a diachronic perspective that concerns a very long period, from the 8th/7th c. BC until the end of antiquity. The term 'Eastern Mediterranean (or simply Eastern) wines' used in this book is to be understood as referring to products that were originally produced in the Aegean area, western Asia Minor, Cyprus, Cilicia, Levant, Egypt and the Black Sea region. The book shows the role that these imports played with regard to the origins of viticulture and winemaking in Italy, and how they shaped the Roman taste for wines. Also, it provides the first comprehensive analysis of all Greek and Latin literature

1 Tchernia 1986, 23–26.

© KONINKLIJKE BRILL NV, LEIDEN, 2021 | DOI:10.1163/9789004433762_002

concerning Eastern Mediterranean wines, including *tituli picti* that were found upon wine containers discovered in Italy. The evidence was analysed using the common classical philological perspective, but uniquely with regard to ancient wines, a modern oenological approach was also adopted, which enabled a better understanding of the characteristics of ancient wines. Additionally, a synthesis of wine amphoras discovered in the central and northern part of Italy (both Tyrrhenian and Adriatic) was carried out, which not only enabled the scale of importations to be estimated, but was also used to trace geographical and chronological variations in consumption patterns.

Last but not least, this study raises and attempts to clarify a number of issues that for decades have plagued the debate about the nature of the Roman economy. Their roots belong to the old dispute between the so-called 'primitivists' (or 'substantivists') and 'modernists' (or 'formalists'), which started obviously with famous and groundbreaking *The Ancient Economy* by Moses Finley. I will not dwell here on the formation of the debate, which has already been adequately framed.[2] Currently, it seems that the argument is being won by 'modernists', especially in the Anglophone world; however, the ghost of Finley still haunts the works of R. Saller, P. Bang,[3] and to a certain degree some concepts of A. Tchernia and J. Remesal Rodriguez.[4] Nevertheless, the old 'modernist' vs. 'primitivist' dispute has deviated onto a new path, where the matter of the market and growth seem to be most important. Therefore, this book will refer to four issues, which continue to be a bone of contention:

1. The role of trade

It was long assumed that trade did not play an important part in the agriculture-based Roman economy and that it was limited to luxury items. This led to the conclusion that most of the Roman Mediterranean was self-sufficient in terms of staple goods and therefore it was only military settlements and big 'consumer cities' such as Rome, Carthage and Alexandria that relied on a significant amount of imported staple commodities. This view has recently been brought back into favour by P. Bang, albeit in a slightly modified version.[5] Although archaeologists continue to provide evidence suggesting that trade was ubiquitous and enormous in volume, it is impossible to estimate this volume and hence prove that the role of the trade in ancient economy was significant. It

2 E.g. Morris 1999; Bang 1997; 2008, 17–60; Saller 2005.
3 Saller 2005; Bang 1997; 2008; Bang, Ikeguchi 2017.
4 Tchernia 2011; Remesal Rodríguez 2008.
5 Bang 2008.

may come as a surprise that even though hundreds of archaeological reports analysed thousands of transport containers discovered all over the Mediterranean, no one has so far really disproved the assumption that trade only involved 'fame regional wines', whilst *vin ordinaire* was normally produced at home.[6] This book disproves such opinion, as this scenario ceased to exist after the early stages of Roman civilisation. Starting from the late Republican, and especially during the early Imperial age, most wines imported from the East were intended for common consumption, and were not viewed as famous, luxury drinks. Moreover, as demonstrated by the synthesis of wine containers in Italy, these wines were imported in enormous quantities not only by Rome, but also by smaller centres, such as Pompeii, Naples, Padua, Oderzo, Verona, Polesine.

2. The social position of traders

The elites were not directly involved in long-distance trade, meaning that those who did deal with it were of a lower social standing, which according to 'primitivists' indicates that trade played a limited role in the ancient economy.[7] However, onomastic and prosopographic studies of the names of Baetican olive oil traders show that certain *negotiatores* were highly regarded socially, were wealthy enough to perform acts of euergetism and were often associated with prominent elite families.[8] A thorough analysis of the names of those involved in the trading of Eastern wines presented in this book allows for similar conclusions, suggesting that traders could amass considerable wealth and hold important positions within their local community. Even though traders were predominantly freedmen, some of their names suggest a connection to noble families, which strengthens the supposition that elites were involved with trade, albeit indirectly, through their former slaves.

3. The existence of economic growth

The existence, or rather the size and nature of economic growth during antiquity is another current scientific dilemma. It was long assumed that no significant growth was possible in pre-modern economies due to the low number of consumers, the high transportation costs, and the assumption that those who possessed the resources were not particularly interested in increasing

6 Finley 1999, 133.
7 Finley 1999, 35–61.
8 Chic García 1987, 251; 1993, 9, 19–20; Remesal Rodríguez 2000; 2004.

productivity.[9] This view has recently been challenged thanks to closer analyses of archaeological data. Different categories of archaeological evidence (for example, shipwrecks, animal bones, water mills, wine and olive presses, femur length, human stature, wood deposits in Germany etc.) have been used as proxies for the condition of the Roman economy by, *inter alia*, W. Jongman, G. Kron, W. Scheidel and A. Wilson.[10] These proxies suggests that aggregated growth may be observed in the economy of the Roman Empire between the late Republic and the 2nd c. AD,[11] while some studies even suggest that this growth might have had an intensive character.[12] However, the nature and scale of the growth is still a subject of scientific debate, which is currently concentrated around three models devised by scholars. The first assumes that any possible growth was moderate (max. 0,1% per year) and temporary, and was soon checked by the increase in population (Malthusian pressure). This model results from Finley's vision of the economy and is currently upheld by Saller, and to a certain degree by Bang.[13] The second, the so called 'one-off' growth, was proposed by Scheidel, who argued that unsustainable growth took place during the final years of the Republic, which was due to Mediterranean unification and state formation under Rome. Roman society (not only the elites) gained access to material resources, which in turn led to a rise in real income instead of contributing to demographic growth, which would have occurred if the wars of the last two centuries had not resulted in population contraction.[14] The last and most optimistic model presumes that the growth was sustainable and ended during either the second half of the 2nd c. AD or in the 3rd c. AD due to exogenous shocks or the erroneous politics of the later emperors, who ignored economic laws.[15]

The fiercest battle has been fought between the supporters of the second and the third model, with the latter taking the lead thanks to new analyses of lead pollution in Greenland ice cores. Precisely dated, sub-annual measurements of lead pollution, as well as atmospheric modelling dated between 1100 BC and 800 AD demonstrated a correlation between European lead emissions and historical events. For example, emissions started to rise accordingly with Phoenician expansion, intensified coeval with Carthaginian and Roman mining activities in Spain and reached their peak during the early empire.

9 Finley 1999, 83–84; Pekáry 1981.
10 E.g. Jongman 2007 a, b; 2009; 2014; Kron 2005; 2014, Scheidel 2009; Wilson 2009 a, b; 2014.
11 Scheidel 2009; Wilson 2009 a, b.
12 Jongman 2009; 2014; Kron 2005; 2008; 2014.
13 Finley 1999; Saller 2005; Bang 2008, especially 122–127.
14 Scheidel 2007b, 332–346; 2009, 46–70.
15 Temin 2013, 220–239; Silver 2007, 191–252, especially 236–239.

They fell during the periods which coincide with the plagues of the 2nd and 3rd c. AD.[16] Although this evidence tips the balance in favour of sustainable growth, it is not conclusive, as other types of archaeological evidence are rather ambiguous.[17] Furthermore, the issue regarding the existence of intensive (*per capita*) growth in the Roman period remains open. Some scholars emphasise a general well-being and social prosperity,[18] while others point out that living conditions of most of Roman society were in fact far from perfect.[19] Archaeology has so far provided contradictory data in this matter. For example, it has been observed that human stature usually correlates positively with overall well-being and a high consumption of proteins,[20] and that human height may be estimated on the basis of femur length. The study of femur length suggests that the Romans were tallest between the 1st and early 2nd c. AD, whilst after 150 AD a sharp and constant fall in human height began.[21] However, other studies of human stature, which present geographically disaggregated data provide different results,[22] whereas a comparison of femur length in a broader perspective shows that people were taller during the Iron Age and post-Roman times than during the Roman period,[23] which suggests that the Roman Empire was not exactly the land of milk and honey.

It is, therefore, obvious that more clarification is required regarding Roman economic growth and this book contributes to the understanding of this matter. The amount of imported Eastern Mediterranean wines grew between the Augustan age and the 3rd c. AD, which may serve as another proxy that confirms growth. Given that most of these wines were drunk by commoners, it is inconceivable that their quality of life was in some way reduced, when one considers that they were able to afford a growing number of imported goods. Also, if the elites accumulated capital and all the imports were in fact to satisfy their conspicuous consumption, as the heirs of 'primitivist' theory still maintain, we would only expect to find high percentages of imports in Rome, as well as in Ostia and Puteoli, which supplied the capital. However, high percentages of Eastern Mediterranean wine containers were also found in small centres, such as Naples, Padua, Verona and especially Polesine.

---

16 McConnell et al. 2018, http://www.pnas.org/content/early/2018/05/08/1721818115/tab-figures-data, accessed 15.05.2018.

17 Wilson 2009a, 213–249; 2009b, 71–82; 2014, 133–152.

18 Kron 2008; 2012; 2014; Jongman 2007b; 2009; 2014.

19 Scheidel 2006a, b.

20 Kron 2005, 70–71.

21 Jongman 2007b, 608–609; 2007a, 194, graph 7.

22 Wilson 2014, 156.

23 Harper 2017, 77, fig. 3.3.

4. Market forces or state directives

The 'primitive' vs. 'modernist' dispute has in recent years been "*replaced by, or perhaps merely recast as, a disagreement about the importance of market-driven and predation-driven transfers*".[24] P. Temin postulated that numerous Roman commercial interactions should be classified as market transactions, governed by prices that could respond freely to changing conditions, and that their number was high enough to construct a market economy. Prices, for example, were highest in Rome (the main consumption centre) and were negatively correlated with distances from Rome, which indicates unified monetary integration across the Mediterranean. Wages behaved similarly, increasing, for example, after the Antonine plague, when manpower declined. Moreover, a vigorous banking system allowed for commercial investment in long-distance trade and technological improvements to be undertaken.[25] Temin's works, however, were severely criticised, for example by A. Tchernia and G. Bransbourg, as being based on a very small and extremely questionable data sample, as well as demonstrating dubious methodology (e.g. the distance from Rome to Madrid was given in a straight line and used as the approximate distance between Rome and Lusitania). Also, Temin's assumption that prices of consumption goods should fall inversely to the distance from the main consumption centre was rejected, mostly due to the fact that the development of prices depends on various factors, such as for example state interference, which played a crucial part in the setting of prices for grain traded to Rome.[26] Nevertheless, Bransbourg and Tchernia admitted that the Roman economy did display a certain degree of market integration, particularly in the areas of certain sea trade routes and the great river valleys. Other regions, however, remained in their view largely isolated due to geographical obstacles and the high cost of overland transport.[27] These scholars seem to sympathise with Bang's opinion that the Roman economy resembled a bazaar rather than a market. One of the main arguments against market integration in antiquity was the limited ability to spread and share information. Due to this lack of information areas which possessed surpluses were unable to organise timely shipment to places where shortages occurred. Even if it was possible to organise the transport, it would be slow and vulnerable to numerous obstacles and probably would not arrive on time, especially between November and March when the Mediterranean

24 Scheidel 2014, 27.
25 Temin 2001; 2006; 2012; 2013; Kessler, Temin 2005.
26 Tchernia 2011, 101–108, n. 2; Bransbourg 2012.
27 Bransbourg 2012, 209; Tchernia 2016, 72–96.

was considered *mare clausum*.[28] According to Bang, this lack of information and the ensuing unpredictability of supply and demand characterises a bazaar economy. A consequence of which is that bazaar prices are volatile and the "*integration of market is low and fragile*". At the same time, ancient trade was dominated by large numbers of small traders, which did not promote integration.[29] Bang's critics, Silver in particular, argue that he underestimated the integration of the Roman market, ignoring the fact that volatility of prices may be governed by surplus and shortage. Moreover, small enterprises, having only a couple of employees, also characterise the modern economy, which indubitably is a market economy. Other counterarguments include evidence that cashless transfers existed in Rome, as well as evidence for a strong market interdependence.[30] However, the greatest weakness of Bang's model lies in his ignorance of archaeological evidence. Therefore, it may surprise that there has so far been only one attempt to use archaeological data to question the bazaar hypothesis. MERCURY, a computational model of the distribution of Eastern Sigillata, undertaken by T. Brughmans and J. Poblome, has shown a higher degree of integration within the Roman market than was postulated by Bang. The observed distribution of this type of pottery agrees with a computer model that assumes a high proportion of inter-site connections and hence high integration.[31] However, tableware rarely constituted the main cargo of commercial exchanges, which were concentrated mainly on foodstuffs. Therefore, even though the study of Brughmans and Poblome provides an important argument for the supporters of the 'market economy' model, it is not enough to warrant rejection of the 'bazaar model'.

This book adds further argument in favour of the market economy model by comparing the share of Eastern Mediterranean wine imports with the transport cost provided by ORBIS: The Stanford Geospatial Network Model of the Roman World, a computer-based model of transport conditions in the Roman Empire, produced by scholars from Stanford University. As suggested by the analysis of prices in Diocletian's Edict on Maximum Prices distance had little to do with transport costs, which were governed by the duration of the journey.[32] ORBIS reconstructs the duration and hence the financial cost of travel in antiquity by simulating movements along water and land routes of the Roman communi-

28 Hopkins 2017, 281; Bang 2008, 4, 131–136.
29 Bang 2008, 4, 131–201.
30 Silver 2009, 425–426; Cic. *Leg. Man.* 7.19.
31 Brughmans, Poblome 2016.
32 Arnaud 2007, 334; Scheidel 2013.

cation network.[33] The comparison of eastern wine amphora distribution with transport costs shows that between the 1st c. BC and the 3rd c. AD the cost of transportation was the most important factor that governed the trade of Eastern wines, and only those that ensured the most favourable profit to cost ratio were imported to Italy. However, a considerable change can be observed during late antiquity, which agrees with the assumption that coerced transfers played a more significant part in commercial activity during the final centuries of the Roman Empire.

As demonstrated above, there are many aspects of the Roman economy that need further investigation and/or clarification. The gaps and doubts result from certain imperfections of archaeological evidence (series or numbers are not robust enough, they are often biased and do not allow to estimate absolute values) and the fact that data from a limited geographical area was sometimes used to support general conclusions. Another problem lies in the fact that a number of previous studies regarding the nature of the Roman economy intended to show a general picture, which resulted in treating Roman Empire as a monolithic entity, without considering the fact that different areas might have had their own pace of development. Now it is obvious that economic development was not equal throughout the empire. Therefore, in this book I would like to propose a slightly different approach to the study of the Roman economy: I will select one area (Italy) and one subject only (i.e. Eastern Mediterranean wines); I will analyse it thoroughly using all the available sources, my conclusions will then be compared to existing theoretical models. Hopefully, the conclusions drawn from analysing the consumption and distribution patterns of Eastern wines in Italy will further our understanding of the general nature of the Roman, or rather Italian, economy.

1 History of Investigations

It is impossible to mention all the publications that concern or touch upon the subject of ancient wines from the Eastern Mediterranean. This is due to the fact that the sources providing information in this matter belong to different scientific disciplines, thus previous studies were for a long time concentrated on three separate issues: amphoras, stamps (with emphasis placed on their chronologies) and finally, literature regarding the characteristics of wines. Con-

33 ORBIS/Understanding, http://orbis.stanford.edu.

sequently, a great number of works regarding wine amphora forms, including containers from the Eastern Mediterranean, their typologies, origins and contents were developed.[34] As well as archaeological and archaeometric study of wine amphoras, epigraphic research of amphora inscriptions was carried out, which as a matter of fact, started even earlier than the amphora research. Works by V. Grace were pioneering in this matter,[35] but soon other scientists started to pay more attention to amphora stamps and compile corpuses of their forms.[36] Grace was also the first to notice the importance of amphoras as evidence for wine trade in the monograph *Amphoras and the Ancient Wine Trade*, published in 1961.

Along with the archaeological and epigraphic research, analyses of Greek and Latin texts that mention wines were carried out. However, many of these publications resemble short syntheses that present the subject of wines from the Eastern Mediterranean in an encyclopaedic way without developing it, or indeed drawing any conclusions. Moreover, the literary evidence is not always thoroughly analysed, as only the most popular ancient authors are usually considered. Finally, it seems that most of the works limit their interest to wines from the Aegean region, while neglecting other products from the Eastern Mediterranean that were less prominent in ancient literature.[37]

More complex, multidisciplinary approaches to the subject of wine started around 1986 when two important works were published. *Le vin de l'Italie romain. Essai d'histoire économique d'après les amphores* by A. Tchernia,[38] which concerned wines that were produced on the Apennine Peninsula as well as those that were imported from the provinces. It concentrated on the early Roman period (between the 2nd c. BC and the 2nd c. AD) and is considered to be the pioneering study with regard to seeing amphoras as important indicators of the condition of the ancient economy. Two subsections of this book concern wines from the Eastern Mediterranean: *Les bons vins et les autres: qualité et rang sociale* and *Les importations de vins grecs*. Since the main aim of this publication was to present the whole spectrum of wines that were consumed

34 It is impossible to enumerate all the works. The following are the most relevant: Panella 1974–1975; Clinkenbeard 1982; Whitbread 1995; Dupont 1998; Papuci-Władyka 1998; 1999; Reynolds 2005; 2008; Pieri 2007; Opait 2010.

35 Grace 1985.

36 For Rhodian stamp chronology see: Finkielsztejn 1995; 2001a, b; 2004a, b; Matera 2014. Thasian: Garlan 1982; 1988; 1993a, b; 2000; 2004. For stamps discovered during Polish excavations in Myrmekion, Alexandria, Tell-Atrib and Nea Paphos see: Sztetyłło 1960; 1963; 1965; 1966 a, b; 1975; 1976; 1978; 1983; 1984; 1990; 1992; 1998; 2000; 2010.

37 García Soler 1996a, b; 1999; 2001; 2002; Brock, Wirtjes 2000; Dalby 2003; Cerchiai 2013.

38 Tchernia 1986.

in Italy and the economic implications of the wine trade, the subject of the Eastern wines could not be fully developed, and is limited to the most famous products of Greek vineyards. Therefore, my book will fill the gap by considering all the wines imported to Italy from the Eastern Mediterranean. It will also provide a more diachronic perspective, spanning from the Archaic to the late Roman times. However, it will view the wine trade from an Italian perspective (like the approach adopted by A. Tchernia), and introduce an interdisciplinary approach to the subject.

Recherches sur les amphores grecques, edited by J.-Y. Empereur and Y. Garlan[39] was the second important work published in 1986 and was a milestone in the development of research on Greek containers. The broad scope of this publication, which regards all issues related to Greek transport jars dated between the Archaic and the Roman period, includes evidence of their production, typologies, imitations and distribution, as well as information concerning stamps and other inscriptions. Two articles from the *Recherches ...* are of particular importance from the perspective of understanding the consumption of Eastern Mediterranean in Italy. The first is a study by F. Salviat entitled *Le vin de Thasos, amphores, vin et sources ecrites*,[40] which explores the issue of the production of wine on Thasos. This study is also based on literary, archaeological and epigraphic evidence. However, the scope of this article is limited to the production of Thasian wine on the island itself, without considering its export and consumption beyond its homeland. The second is *Oriente ed Occidente. I considerazioni su alcune anfore "egee" di età imperiale a Ostia* by Panella. This paper is devoted to the Aegean containers dated to Imperial times that were found in *Terme del Nuotatore* in Ostia.[41] This was the first study that presented and analysed the percentages of Aegean and Oriental amphoras that were found in Italy and hence attempted to estimate the scale of their importations.

Cretan wine and amphoras have few secrets left thanks to A. Marangou-Lerat's *Le vin et les amphores de Crete: De l'epoque classique a l'epoque imperiale*,[42] in which the author focused mainly on Cretan amphora workshops and the typology of wine containers that were produced on the island. This allowed the identification of Cretan amphoras among the containers that were called

39 Empereur, Garlan 1986.

40 Salviat 1986. It should be noted that Salviat devoted a few other publications to Eastern Mediterranean wines and vines. These texts partly concern characteristics of *crus* that were drunk by the Romans, but they also focus on other wines, such as e.g. Mendean or Maroneian, that were not imported to Italy in the Roman Age, see Salviat 1993; 2013a.

41 Panella 1986.

42 Marangou-Lerat 1995.

Schoene-Mau VIII, X and XXXVI, as well as Dressel 43, discovered above all in Rome and the 'Vesuvian Cities'. The study was an important step forward in recognition of wine amphoras from the Eastern Mediterranean. The book by Marangou-Lerat also analyses literary and epigraphic evidence regarding Cretan wine, as well as providing statistics concerning percentages of amphoras produced on Crete in different archaeological contexts.

Although this publication is crucial from an archaeological point of view, it does not offer a historical or economic perspective. My research deals with similar categories of evidence, but concentrates more on historical and economic issues. And, by adopting a broader time scope and concentrating on more varieties of wines, I can show the development of economic phenomena over time, whilst also allowing for a more global perspective to be taken.

An important work concerning the origins of viticulture and winemaking in Italy was published in 2012 by A. Ciacci, P. Rendini and A. Zifferero.[43] *Archeologia della vite e del vino in Toscana e nel Lazio: dalle tecniche dell'indagine archeologica alle prospettive della biologia molecolare* presents a history of viticulture and winemaking in Etruria, from the Middle Bronze Age to modern times, which was compiled using a combination of archaeological, historical, chemical, botanical and genetic analyses. This multidisciplinary research favours the local development of viticulture and winemaking in Italy, at the same time reducing the impact from the East, especially during the period of Greek colonisation. This publication allowed me to reconsider the traditional role of the Greeks and the Phoenicians in the development of viticulture and wine production on the Apennine Peninsula. As shown in my book, they did not introduce vine and wine to the inhabitants of Italy; but their role did include the dissemination of new techniques and the introduction of new vine varieties. They were also responsible for the intensification in Italian wine production and the beginning of wine exportations. Thus, the encounter with Eastern wines was an important spur for the economic development of winemaking in Italy.

As far as wine characteristics are concerned, the study by S. Kourakou-Dragona entitled *La vigne et le vin dans le monde grec ancien*[44] is very interesting, as its author is not a researcher in classical antiquity, but a chemist and oenologist with an antiquarian interest. Knowing precisely how wine is made and being aware of the pros and cons of Greek viticulture, Kourakou-Dragona provides a new reading of ancient texts. Her oenological approach

43 Ciacci, Rendini, Zifferero 2012.

44 Kourakou-Dragona 2013.

allowed her to go far beyond classical philology, and thus she was able (through her unique and new interpretation of several epithets found in literary sources that described the characteristics of wines) to recreate the real production processes and tastes of ancient wines.

As a matter of fact, I try to follow this path in my own analyses of wine characteristics (Chapter 2), asking, for example, what processes might have been responsible for the yellow colour of wine, or why *Chian saprón* (σαπρός—rotten, putrid) was in fact among the tastiest and most highly praised wines. However, instead of concentrating on the most important features of Greek wines (as in Kourakou-Dragona's publication), I try to analyse the characteristics of all beverages from the Eastern Mediterranean, considering not only literature, but also epigraphy. Nevertheless, I must admit that ancient written sources provide the most abundant information regarding Aegean wines and a lot of this information has already been analysed by S. Kourakou-Dragona.

It is also worth mentioning the recently published *ΟΙΝΟΣ: production and import of wine in Graeco-Roman Egypt* by D. Dzierzbicka, which considers wine and its role in the economic development of Egypt during the Greco-Roman period.[45] It demonstrates where and how wine was manufactured, as well as how it was distributed after it left the winery, paying particular attention to the people who were involved in wine production. Moreover, it shows which wines were imported to Egypt from other parts of the Mediterranean and tries to trace the mechanisms and channels of their distribution. Dzierzbicka had the opportunity to analyse papyri, a category of evidence hardly known beyond Egypt, and she emphasises the significance of wine production and importations for the Egyptian economy. However, she does not address issues regarding the global economy under Roman rule, which are present in my book.

Finally, the works of G. Rizzo should be mentioned as a considerable part of the evidence used in Chapter 3 is provided by his thorough analyses of thousands of amphora fragments that were found in Rome[46] and in *Terme del Nuotatore* in Ostia.[47] Without this evidence the synthesis of wine amphoras presented in this book would be considerably less informative.

To summarise, there are publications that consider (to varying degrees) the subject of wines from the Eastern Mediterranean. However, they concentrate on one type of wine only (e.g. Thasian or Cretan) or on one category of sources (only literature or only amphoras). Moreover, no attempt has so far been made

---

45 Dzierzbicka 2018.

46 Rizzo 2003.

47 Panella, Rizzo 2014.

to show the scale of the consumption of Eastern wines in general, or the consumption of particular *crus* in Italy. This means that there has so far been no comprehensive monograph which adopts a multidisciplinary approach, an approach which would enable the subject to be viewed from a broader perspective of the economic history. This book will attempt to fill that gap.

2 Sources and Methodology

The study of classical antiquity is a frustrating scientific discipline, as generally the sources available to classical scholars are fragmentary and imperfect. Many literary texts have not survived, or they have survived as copies or as fragments in other works. Also, the authors are not all credible, especially when they refer to the remote past. Archaeology in turn gives us objects, which must be thoroughly studied before they can be used as evidence towards solving general historical dilemmas. Finally, amphora epigraphy lacks 'eloquence'. Therefore, it is necessary to address the most important problems one may encounter while dealing with these categories of sources, as well as demonstrating when they provide strong and useful evidence.

2.1 *Ancient Literature*

Greek and Latin texts mainly provide us with information concerning the characteristics of wines, such as age, colour, taste, fame and other qualities, while from time to time they also mention who drank them and on what occasions. Textual evidence is obviously also helpful in establishing the chronology of the production and consumption of wines. Unfortunately, the vast majority of ancient texts come from between the 3rd c. BC and the 3rd c. AD. Therefore, those authors that refer to the times of Romulus and Numa must be treated with great caution as they often provide us with scraps of myths, legends and personal imagination rather than with historical truth. Nonetheless, they cannot be entirely omitted, therefore the literary sources used in this book that regard the origins of Rome are compared with other types of evidence, such as archaeological, archaeobotanical, and genetic. Also, late Roman literature often copies previous works, while certain authors use terms that have long been out of use simply to showcase their erudition. Consequently, all chronologies based on literature should be compared with archaeological data.

The works analysed in this book are of a diverse nature, including *belles lettres*, which combine poetry and drama, as well as texts of a more scientific nature, such as medical, agricultural and 'encyclopaedic' writings. As it is impossible to describe in detail every single work or author that mentions wines from the Eastern Mediterranean, I will concentrate on those that provide us with the most abundant or pivotal information. The catalogue of Greek and Latin literary evidence is presented in Appendix 1.

Plautus' *Fabulae palatae* (written between c. 205 and 184 BC) are the earliest Latin texts mentioning Eastern Mediterranean wines; however, many of them are copies or adaptations of Greek works by Menander, Diphilus, Philemon or Demophilus.[48] This raises the question of whether Plautus provides us with reliable evidence regarding wine consumption in Italy, as it cannot be excluded that he simply copied the names of Greek wines from the comedies upon which he based his works. Nevertheless, E. Skwara, a specialist in ancient comedies who has translated many of Plautus' works, argues that he did not use foreign terms that might have been unknown to his audience.[49] This suggests that the Romans were probably familiar with the wines that appear in Plautus' plays and given that they were able to laugh at some of their peculiarities, they must have had knowledge not only of the literary *topos*, but also of how the wines really tasted. Since archaeological and epigraphic evidence confirms that importations of wines from the Eastern Mediterranean to Italy were contemporary with Plautus' comedies,[50] it is abundantly clear that these wines were present on Italian markets and that most Romans knew their main characteristics.[51]

Late Republican and early Imperial Latin poets, such as Vergil, Horace and Ovid, cannot be suspected of copying the work of others. It is true that Horace studied at Athens, which might have influenced his poems; however, they are so '*Roman in spirit*'[52] that it is doubtful they would present a reality other than that of Roman elite circles. At the same time, Vergil derived his technical knowledge from an agricultural text by Varro (116–27 BC), which, like the agricultural works by Cato (234–149 BC) and Columella (1st c. AD), is a practical manual concerning the subject of husbandry based upon the author's first-hand experience. All these agricultural treatises are very reliable sources regarding ancient wines. Cato, for example, spent his youth on his father's farm in Reate in the Sabine country, whilst in his later years he owned large slave labour plantations. Varro addressed his *Res Rusticae* to his wife, Fundania, probably to give her some agricultural guidance, as she had just purchased a farm.[53] Also,

48 *OCD* under 'Plautus'; Skwara 2002, 9–11.
49 Skwara 2005, 53–55.
50 See Chapter 1, Sections 3 and 5.
51 Prof. Skwara agreed with this theory in a personal conversation.
52 Benett 1987, VII–XI.
53 Hooper 2006, IX–XVIII.

Columella, who wrote the most systematic extant Roman agricultural manual, had experience in running a farm.[54]

Pliny the Elder's *Natural History*, an encyclopaedia of all contemporary knowledge,[55] devotes the whole of book XIV to vines and wines. On the one hand, it is an uncritical compilation of facts, sensational curiosities, myths and legends taken from the works of others, to which Pliny added his own observations. On the other hand, *Natural History* is a valuable document that highlights a growth (through the use of systematic nomenclature and classification) in the human understanding of the environment.[56] It is almost certain that Pliny based his hierarchy of wines, which will be frequently referred to in this book, upon reliable sources, such as Sextius Niger, a Roman writer on pharmacology who lived under Augustus and Tiberius, as well as Asclepiades of Bithynia, a physician active between 124 (or 129) and 40 BC.[57] Therefore, book XIV provides us with reliable information regarding wines that were known in the Roman world not only in the second half of the 1st c. AD, but it also considers the times of the late Republic. Fortunately, Pliny seems to be quite helpful in distinguishing between facts contemporary to his life and those that regarded previous centuries through his use of past tense when referring to things that no longer existed.

Medical writings are in general the most reliable sources regarding the qualities of wines. This is due to the fact that ancient physicians had to be very precise when making medicines or recommending certain beverages to their patients as remedies. The earliest medical text, the *Hippocratic Corpus*, is composed of works by various authors associated with the Coan and Cnidian school of ancient Greek medicine. The texts are mostly dated to the Classical period, but writings from the Hellenistic period as well as texts from the 1st and 2nd c. AD[58] also appear. The books that mention wines from the Eastern Mediterranean (*Diseases* and *Internal Affections*) most probably originated about 400 BC and were influenced by the Cnidian school.[59]

De materia medica by Dioscorides Pedanius (1st c. AD) is another important source regarding the study of the characteristics of Eastern Mediterranean wines. Dioscorides was born in Anazarbus in Cilicia and he travelled to the Greek mainland, Crete, Egypt, and Petra to collect information about the

54 *OCD* under 'Columella, Lucius Junius Moderatus'.
55 *OCD* under 'Pliny the Elder'; Rackham 1979, VII.
56 Doody 2010, 26–27; Rackham 1979, IX–X.
57 Tchernia 1997, 1247–1248.
58 Lloyd 1978, 9–12.
59 Potter, Smith 1988, IX–XI; Jouanna 1992, 102.

medicinal uses of various products. His medical knowledge is mostly of an empiric nature,[60] but in certain cases he might have used other sources, for example texts from the Alexandrian Library to which he had access. Therefore, the reliability of the 5th part of *De materia medica* (c. 64 or 77 AD) that is devoted to ancient wines should not be questioned.[61]

Our knowledge of ancient wines, however, owes its largest debt to Galen (129–late 2nd c. AD). Born in Pergamum, where he spent most of his life, Galen travelled around the Eastern Mediterranean, visiting Smyrna, Palestine, Corinth, Trace, Macedonia, Cyprus and Alexandria, and in his later years he settled in Rome.[62] The *Galenic Corpus* is a mixture of original knowledge and facts drawn from previous works (not always medical). In the corpus there are traces of the influence of, *inter alia*, Plato, Aristotle, writers from the Stoic school, and of course Hippocrates. However, there is no doubt that Galen was much more than a compiler of other people's work, as many observations, experiments and reflections are indubitably his own.[63] Wines appear in his works as ingredients of medicines or regimens, with those produced in Italy and western Asia Minor (including the adjacent Aegean islands) being particularly recommended. Considering that Galen lived for a long time in both areas and hence knew empirically typical foodstuffs, we may suspect that the wines he mentioned were available at the market and consumed by the 2nd c. AD inhabitants of these regions. He confirms this assumption in *De metodo medendi* XII 4,[64] mentioning that he describes Asian and Greek wines, because in these areas Italian beverages were not commonly present. It should be noted that most of Galen's works are composed almost exclusively of his own observations and advice, when he did refer to prescriptions or recommendations of others, he mentioned them, as for example in *De compositione medicamentorum secundum locos/genera*. Thanks to this habit we know that his sources lived predominantly between the 2nd c. BC and the 2nd c. AD. Interestingly they all mention the same types of Eastern wines, which means that these wines were continuously produced between the 2nd c. BC and the time of Galen. Later physicians, such as Oribasius, Aetius, or Paulus of Aegina were typical compilers, who based their writings upon previous medical works.[65] *Synopsis* by Oribasius was written in order to popularise Galen's works, which

60 *OCD* under 'Dioscorides (2)'.
61 Osbaldeston 2000, XX.
62 Hankinson 2009, 1–5; Grant 2000, 2–3.
63 Brock 1916, XXIV–XXV.
64 Gal. *MM*. 10.832–833K.
65 *OCD* under 'Aëtius (2)' and 'Paul (of *Aegina)'.

means that even though the work was created in the 4th c. AD, it resembles the reality of the 2nd c. AD.[66] Therefore, later medical writings cannot be treated as reliable evidence for the consumption of Eastern Mediterranean wines.

A mine of information about ancient wines, predominantly from Greek lands, is provided by Athenaeus' *Deipnosophistai* (*Deipnosophists* or *The banquet of the learned*). Athenaeus was born in Naucratis in Egypt and he flourished at the end of the 2nd and the beginning of the 3rd c. AD. Unfortunately, we do not know much about his life, since his work is the only source that provides us with information regarding this matter.[67] The exact date of the origin of *Deipnosophistai* is uncertain. However, if the Ulpian in his dialogue is modelled on Ulpian of Tyre, the lawyer who was murdered in 228 AD, we may suppose that at least a part of the book must have been written not long after this date. The book is heterogeneous in style and subject, and concerns a broad spectrum of matters associated predominantly with dining, but also with music, songs, dances, games, courtesans and luxury. It is composed of 15 books, the first two being a treasure trove of knowledge about Eastern Mediterranean wines. Unfortunately, they have been preserved only as epitomes. It is necessary to emphasise that *Deipnosophists* is largely composed of quotations from earlier authors, most of them being Greek Middle and New Comedy writers;[68] however, numerous medical works dated between the 5th and 1st c. BC were also quoted.[69] Therefore, Athenaeus' work does not reflect the reality of the 2nd/3rd c. AD as most of it concerns wines that were produced and consumed during the Classical and Hellenistic periods. A detailed chronological list of authors quoted by Athenaeus, and the names of wines that they referred to is presented in Appendix 2.

As mentioned earlier, my approach to literary evidence does not only assume the traditional perspective of Classical philology, but it also applies modern oenological knowledge regarding wine fermentation. This approach, as proven by Kourakou-Dragona, sheds new light on ancient texts.

2.2 *Amphoras*

Amphoras, ancient containers that were used to transport and store various products (predominantly liquids such as wine, olive oil and fish sauces),[70] are

---

66 Brock 1916, XIX.

67 Gulick 1927, VIII.

68 Gulick 1927, VIII–XV; OCD (4th ed.) under 'Athenaeus' (1).

69 Flemming 2000, 476.

70 Finkielsztejn 2002, 228.

the main source that allows the scale of importations of Eastern Mediterranean wines to Italy to be estimated. They are also useful in establishing chronologies, as well as providing important evidence regarding the origins of foreign wine consumption in Italy during the Archaic age. They have been appreciated as a useful source for the study of consumption and trade in antiquity since the 1970's,[71] but certain questions regarding their use still remain unclear.

2.2.1 Primary Commodity or Multi-Purpose Containers?

There is no agreement regarding the connection between the shape of an amphora and its content. Theoretically, most archaeologists who specialise in the pre-1st c. BC Eastern Mediterranean region argue that amphoras were multi-purpose containers and that it is hardly possible to connect the shape of a vessel with a particular content.[72] In practice, a review of published research concerning Greek amphoras dated between the 5th and 3rd c. BC showed that 95% of publications assumed that there was a link between the amphora shape and its content.[73] On the other hand, scholars who devote their work primarily to the Western Mediterranean, or to the Eastern part after the 1st c. BC, assume that there was a primary commodity associated with each amphora type. This theory is based on evidence derived from *tituli picti*, literary sources and iconographic references (usually coin devices that supposedly linked a city with its most important trading product)[74] and assumes that the package should indicate a certain content, because commercial success depended not only on the quality of the product but also on its advertising.[75] This book adopts a primary content approach, even though it was questioned by certain scholars. Their arguments, however, always refer to pre-Roman times, and there has so far been no evidence suggesting a lack of Roman standardisation with regard to amphoras and their content. J. Lund and V. Gabrielsen observed that in pre-Roman times there were many types of amphoras that were used to transport wine, while the containers associated with olive oil and fish sauces were very scarce, even though these commodities were also transported on a considerable scale.[76] However, fish salting factories were insignificant before 100 BC

71 Gras 1985, 272–273.
72 Lawall 2011, 23.
73 Foley et al. 2012, 391 n. 1.
74 Lawall 2011, 23.
75 Pieri 2005, 68.
76 Lawall 2011, 24; Lund 2004, 212; Lund, Gabrielsen 2005, 166 and *passim*.

(they became popular during the early Imperial age),[77] which means that the scale of the garum trade was considerably less significant in pre-Roman times, and hence the development of garum amphoras may have been limited. At the same time, inscriptions like μέλιτος θάσιον or οἴνου θάσια that are found in Egyptian papyri referring to a jar of Thasian honey and jars of Thasian wine may, according to certain scholars, be evidence that amphoras were used to carry diversified contents.[78] However, it is not certain whether names like θάσιον, κνίδιον, λέσβιον, χῖον, ῥοδιακόν/ῥόδιον were geographical terms, as they may refer to measures of volume or be identifiers of reused foreign jars (or their local imitations). Even if they do refer to jars, are these jars all the same type, are they amphoras? Finally, if Thasos and Chios exported honey and vinegar in their amphoras would this be considered as mass exportation? Given that vinegar and honey are usually used in modest quantities, it seems that even if they were exported in amphoras, the percentage of wine containers would still be considerably higher than the proportion of amphoras that carried other contents.

Another argument against amphoras as multi-purpose containers is provided by the fact that certain types of African amphoras almost always contain pitch lining, while others do not. Given that resin dissolves in olive oil, while remaining intact when in contact with wine or fish sauce, we may conclude that the shape-content relation of at least certain groups of containers should be taken for granted.[79] Similarly, we should not expect a diversified content to appear in jars that originated in regions that produced a surplus in only one commercial commodity. For example, if literary and epigraphic evidence confirms that Rhodes was famous exclusively for wine production, we can easily accept that wine was a primary content of Rhodian amphoras. However, it should be noted that wine was a more 'interesting' product than other goods, and thus might appear more frequently in written sources.[80]

2.2.2 Reuse—Exception or Rule?

Another problem regarding amphoras lies in the fact that they might have been reused as storage or even transport containers for other products.[81] A docu-

77 Wilson 2007, http://oxrep.classics.ox.ac.uk/working%20papers/quantification_fishsalting_infrastructure_capacity_roman_world/, accessed 28.01.2019.

78 Lawall 2011, 24–25; Kruit, Worp 2000, 75–97.

79 Bonifay 2017, 331–332.

80 Lawall 2011, 26.

81 Lawall 2011, 30.

ment from Zenon's archive, dated to the mid-3rd c. BC, mentions an assemblage of almost 3000 amphoras (this includes vessels from Chios, Kourion, Paphos and Paros) being collected as empties for refilling at a winery. Similarly, a Thasian amphora dated no later than 500 BC ended up at the Athenian Agora in a context that was closed in the mid-5th c. AD, which indicates that it must have been used for a long time.[82] There is no consensus among scholars regarding the reuse of olive oil amphoras. Lawall claims that they could not store other commodities, which is indicated by the existence of *Monte Testaccio* in Rome, a huge mound consisting of broken olive oil containers.[83] On the other hand, T. Peña argues that oil and fish containers might have been reused to transport wine,[84] providing us with an abundance of evidence for the reuse of many amphora types that were discovered in the Vesuvian cities.[85] This evidence suggests that foreign amphoras were often used to transport or store local products. However, it seems inconceivable that Cretan wine amphoras for example, were reused to transport Spanish garum. This means that each wine amphora from the Eastern Mediterranean that has been found in Italy was once used to transport products from the East. The Grado shipwreck, found near Aquileia, carrying 150 Aegean (Knossos 19—usually considered as a wine container) and 200 African (Africana I—commonly classified as an oil jar) amphoras filled with salted fish, is the only Roman-age wreck that provides indubitable evidence for the reuse of amphoras as packaging containers. Peña and Abdelhamid provide evidence for a further 18 wrecks that carried amphoras, which might have been used to transport or store a secondary commodity.[86] Even if we add together all the known shipwrecks that might have transported reused amphoras (including 10 dated to the Roman times: El Sec, Sud-Caveaux 1, Maïre A, Grado, Cala Culip 4, San Rossore B, Procchio, Plemmirio B, Cabrera III and Dor D),[87] these 19 wrecks still only represent a tiny percentage of the total number of 565 shipwrecks that are known to have carried amphoras.[88] The actual reuse rate is a mere 3,36 %, which means that 96,94 % of amphoras found in shipwrecks probably carried a primary commod-

82 Kruit, Worp 2000, 86–87; Lawall 2011, 31.

83 Lawall 2011, 32.

84 Peña 2007, 70, 75.

85 Peña 2007, 82–97.

86 Peña 2007, 73–76; Abdelhamid 2013, 93–99.

87 Non-Roman wrecks include: Uluburun, Giglio, Coltellazzo A, Tektaş Burnu, Saint-Gervais 2, Yassi Ada B, Serçe Limanı.

88 The Oxford Roman Economy Project, Shipwreck Database: http://oxrep.classics.ox.ac.uk/databases/shipwrecks_database/, accessed 4.06.2018.

ity. Thus, the reusing of amphoras does not appear to be significant at all and hence they may be seen as reliable sources for studying ancient commercial exchange.

2.2.3 Identifying the Origin of Amphoras

Since most amphora types were produced within limited geographical areas, their provenance may be established on the basis of their forms, clay matrix and admixtures. As a result of morphological and archaeometric studies, the geographic origins of most Archaic, Classical, Hellenistic and Roman amphora types have already been determined, but there are still a few Eastern Mediterranean forms of unknown provenance. This refers in particular to containers that were discovered in the Vesuvian cities and classified by R. Schoene and A. Mau as type XLI, as well as LRA1 and Kapitän 1 and 2.

The Eastern origin of Schoene-Mau XLI containers was suggested due to their morphology and the Greek *tituli* that have been found upon certain vessels,[89] but no exact provenance has so far been suggested. Similarly, most researchers agree that Kapitän 1 and 2 containers produced between the 2nd and the 4th c. AD were used to transport wine;[90] however, their exact origin remains disputable. According to Hayes and Panella, macroscopic analyses of their clay suggest an Aegean provenance.[91] This is confirmed by the presence of chrome and nickel in certain fragments.[92] According to P. Dyczek, these minerals may indicate various production centres, including Rhodes, the western shores of Asia Minor or even Syria.[93] Typologically, these containers are similar to Chian amphoras[94] or Cilician Pompeii V.[95] Their fabrics suggest that they might have been produced around Ephesus, Cos,[96] Samos[97] and Rhodes.[98] Peña argues that Kapitän 2 was "*probably a wine container from western Anatolia, including the Ephesus area*". His conclusion is based upon the small dimensions of these jars, their granitic macro grain component and the fact that

---

89 Panella 1986, 617–618; Bragantini, Cipriano, Improta 1991, 92.
90 For example Panella 1972, 93; 1973, 599; Lemaître 2000, 476; Martin 2000, 429.
91 Panella 1986, 631.
92 Empereur, Picon 1989, 233.
93 Dyczek 2001, 141.
94 Dyczek 2001, 263.
95 Majcherek 2007, 17 n. 45.
96 Panella 1986, 617.
97 Grace 1971, 72 n. 51.
98 However, not a single fragment of Kapitän 2 was found in any of the 20 pottery workshops they investigated on Rhodes, see Empereur, Picon 1989, 233.

a small vessel containing *caroenum Maeonium* was mentioned in a papyrus dated to the 3rd AD.[99] Fabric analysis carried out by Bezeczky in his recent study of amphoras from Ephesus suggested that buff colour Kapitän 2 may have been produced in the Cayster Valley, as well as in the region of Ephesus (Samos can also be considered).[100] Alternatively, Kapitän 1 resemble the class of amphoras that were produced on Lesbos in the 4th c. BC. Thus, they might have been manufactured on this island or in its vicinity. Since the fabric of Kapitän 1 is indistinguishable from the fabric of Kapitän 2 and considering that the two types are often attested together, Bezeczky presumes that they have similar provenance.[101] On the other hand, according to P. Reynolds the fabric of Kapitän 2 is similar to the fabric of the Zeest 72 and Zeest 80 groups, as well as to certain amphoras from Sinope that are dated to the 5th c. BC. Therefore, it is more likely that they derive from the Black Sea region, possibly Crimea.[102] Notwithstanding the fact that it is impossible to pinpoint the exact provenance of these amphoras, it is almost certain that they carried wine from the Eastern Mediterranean.

The so-called Late Roman Amphora 1 was initially produced in Cilicia at the end of the 3rd and during the first half of the 4th c. AD, but subsequently its production spread to other regions and several chronological variants evolved between the late 4th and the 7th c. AD.[103] The manufacture of LRA1 along the coast of Lycia, Pamphylia, north Syria, Cilicia, as well as on Cos, Rhodes and Cyprus is confirmed by the discoveries of amphora workshops, which were found during surface survey.[104] However, Riley's analyses also suggest Lesbos and Euboea as possible production places, while a *titulus pictus* on a container from Milan mentions Chios.[105] In addition, Cretan or Pontic imitations cannot be excluded.[106] Although it is impossible to distinguish the exact production place, it is certain that LRA1 originated in the Eastern Mediterranean.

99 Peña 1999, 84.
100 Bezeczky 2013, 149.
101 Peña 1999, 86.
102 Reynolds 2010, 90.
103 Bezeczky 2013, 158–159.
104 Opait 2010, 1015–1017; Empereur, Picon 1989, 237, 241–242; Bezeczky 2013, 159; Didioumi 2014, 170–171.
105 Riley 1981, 116; Auriemma 2007, 148, n. 1391.
106 Auriemma 2007, 149; Arthur 1998, 170.

2.2.4 Identifying the Content of Amphoras

Theories regarding amphora content are often based upon literary, epigraphic and/or archaeological evidence. Ancient texts often mention the main production/export goods of certain regions. Therefore, if a region produced amphoras as well as a liquid of some kind (for example wine, olive oil or garum), it is almost certain that the amphoras were used to transport this commodity. Furthermore, amphoras are sometimes covered with *tituli picti* or *graffiti* that are often associated with their content. The same refers to amphora stamps that included devices such as olives or grapes, which were presumably connected to the content. Finally, archaeological research provides evidence such as the shape of a container, the shape of its rim, analyses of the rests of any preserved content (if available), as well as informing us of the existence of coating on the internal part of the vessel. Resin-coating was usually applied to wine amphoras and it was probably used to keep liquid from soaking into the porous clay of the container.[107] Moreover, resin had preservative properties and could help with wine conservation by protecting the content of the vessel from oxidation, which could easily turn wine into vinegar.[108] In the case of olive oil, resin or pitch would easily dissolve and could modify the taste of the product, so pitch lining should be avoided in olive oil containers.[109] Nonetheless, recent chemical studies suggest that pitch could have also been used in olive oil amphoras, but there is no visible sign of its use since it decomposes and is absorbed by the pores of the vessel over time.[110] Therefore, the presence (or absence) of a visible pitch coating is significant in terms of distinguishing the primary content of amphoras. Finally, when remains of the content are preserved, which is rather rare, it is possible to perform chemical analyses. If traces of tartaric acid are discovered through such analyses the vessel almost certainly contained wine.[111]

Thanks to literature, epigraphy, traces of resin, and in certain cases chemical studies, there is little doubt that Archaic and Classical containers from Thasos, Mende, Lesbos, Chios, Peparethos, and Clazomenae, as well as Corinthian B and Solokha I (Peparethos II) amphoras, were used to transport wine.[112] The same refers to Hellenistic and Roman Rhodian, Coan, Cnidian, Cretan and Ana-

107 Koehler 1981, 452.

108 Sacchetti 2013, 37; Brun 2003, 68–69, 102–103.

109 Sacchetti 2013, 28; Peña 2007, 69.

110 See the study of Garnier 2007; Romanus et al. 2009; Bonifay 2017, 331–332.

111 McGovern, Michel 1996, 58.

112 Koehler 1981, 452; Doulgéri-Intzessiloglou, Garlan 1990; Lawall 2000, 18, 32 n. 20–21; Sez-

tolian vessels.[113] However, a few more words are necessary to clarify the doubts regarding the so-called Late Roman Amphoras 1 and 2.

Most of the examples of LRA1 that have been analysed had a resin or pitch-lining, which is typical of wine amphoras.[114] Considering the production area, these amphoras might have been used to transport Rhodian wine,[115] as well as Coan, Cypriot and Cilician. However, *tituli picti* attested on LRA1 examples discovered in Ballana in Egypt mention only olives, or olive oil.[116] The analysis of the residues found in LRA1 that were discovered in Florence proved that certain vessels might have contained wine, whereas others transported vegetable oil and animal fats.[117] A number of inscriptions on LRA1 refer to *artabae*, which led Emery and Kirwan to suggest that they might have carried grain, which is unlikely according to Riley, due to their wide distribution in the primary grain producing areas, such as Cyrenaica and Carthage.[118] Riley, moreover, noticed two variants (large and small) of LRA1, and proposed a hypothesis, according to which the larger vessels contained olive oil, whilst the smaller ones were used to transport wine.[119] Given that it is difficult to distinguish between the two variants while dealing only with fragments of the vessels, this hypothesis cannot be verified.[120] Nonetheless, if olive oil was indeed carried these vessels should not have been found in large quantities in north Africa, a major oil producing region during the late Roman period. Moreover, religious inscriptions on certain examples of LRA1 suggest that they carried wine.[121] D. Van Limbergen's estimations regarding wine and oil production and their consumption in northern Syria, a region that served as one of main producers of LRA1, indicate that wine, rather than olive oil, was more likely the product being exported.[122] This suggests that wine was indeed a more probable content of LRA1 jars, or at least those that were produced near Antioch. Similarly, given its long-standing

gin 2004, 178; Sacchetti 2013, 27, 64, 75, 80, 98–102. However, according to Dupont 1998, 162, certain Lesbian amphoras might have been used to transport olive oil.

113 Marangou-Lerat 1995; Rizzo 2003; Bertoldi 2012, 132, 140; Bezeczky 2013, 40, 53, 66, 80; Robinson 1959, 17.

114 Peña 2007, 69.

115 Pieri 2007, 613.

116 Williams 2005, 616–617. It should be noted that according to Peña the appearance of *tituli picti* is often evidence that an amphora has been reused to transport or store a different commodity than its original primary content, see Peña 2007, 70, 75 and *passim*.

117 Pecci, Salvini, Cantini 2010, 367, tab. 2.

118 Riley 1979, 215.

119 Riley 1979, 213–216.

120 Pacetti 1995, 274; Bonifay, Villedieu 1989, 25.

121 Williams 2005, 617.

122 Van Limbergen 2015, 183.

tradition of making Rhodian, Coan, Cypriot and Cilician wines, it is unlikely that these regions suddenly switched to olive oil. Therefore, this book categorises LRA1 as wine amphoras.

At the same time, LRA2 is excluded from this category as it is more probable that this form was designed for transporting olive oil. This amphora type is related to Dressel 24, which was probably its predecessor. Dressel 24 served for oil transport, as is suggested by *dipinti* of *oleum* that were found on two amphoras, one from Romula in Dacia and the other from *Monte Testaccio* in Rome.[123] The presence of these jars in Monte Testaccio, a famous waste heap of olive oil containers, around the mid-3rd c. AD is also telling.[124] Both Dressel 24 and LRA2 were produced on Chios; however, the latter might have also been manufactured in Argos[125] and on Samos.[126] Other possible (but so far unconfirmed) production places include Cnidus and even the Black Sea region,[127] as well as Cos and Crete during the 5th c. AD.[128] Pieri suggests that wine was the content of LRA2,[129] because Sidonius Apollinaris around 460 AD mentioned wine from Chios,[130] which seems to be rather weak evidence. However, certain specimens of LRA2, such as those discovered in Chalkidiki, Tomis, Gaul and in the Yassi Ada II wreck contained traces of pitch. Grape seeds were attested inside a few LRA2 from the Yassi Ada II wreck, but *tituli picti* on five other examples suggest that they carried olive oil or olives.[131] Given that evidence regarding this amphora type is ambiguous, it has not been considered in this book.

To sum up, even though there are still some gaps in amphora research, they have already been studied well enough to serve as evidence for the consumption of Eastern Mediterranean wines in Italy. Nothing suggests that during the Roman age the same types of containers were used to transport various commodities over long distances, while their local reuse should not affect the patterns of importations. At the same time, the origin and content of most amphora forms, those from the Eastern Mediterranean in particular, has been established. Appendix 3 demonstrates the list of wine amphoras considered in this study.

123 Opait 2007, 629, 633.
124 Reynolds 2010a, 28.
125 Pieri 2002, 130.
126 Pieri 2005, 91.
127 Bezeczky 2013, 161.
128 Reynolds 2010, 95.
129 Pieri 2002, 130. A similar opinion was expressed by Arthur 1998, 169, due to the possibility that this amphora was produced on Chios.
130 *Carm.* XVII, MGH *Auct. Antiquiss.* VIII, 242.
131 Pieri 2005, 93; Van Alfen 1996, 202.

2.3 *Tituli picti*

The Latin term '*tituli picti*' or Italian '*dipinti*' denotes a vast category of inscriptions that were painted on various surfaces for diverse purposes. The inscriptions painted on amphoras had a mostly commercial character and they may be seen as packaging labels providing information about the names of traders or producers, as well as about the characteristics of the product carried inside the transport containers.[132] The vast majority of these inscriptions come from the Vesuvian cities and most of them are dated to the 1st c. AD, just before the eruption of Vesuvius.

Most of the Vesuvian *tituli picti* on amphoras are published in the 4th volume of *Corpus Inscriptionum Latinarum* and its supplements. In some of the cases facsimiles are provided, but the majority are transcribed and as such are not free from mistakes. This is due to the fact that *dipinti* are often poorly preserved and are largely composed of cryptic abbreviations, or they are simply incomplete, hence their interpretation sometimes resembles pure guesswork rather than scientific investigation. This renders their transcription, expansion, and interpretation problematic. Moreover, since *tituli picti* tend to disappear over time, it is often impossible to verify whether they had been transcribed correctly, therefore *CIL* remains the only source of evidence for many of them.[133] As if it was not complicated enough, many inscriptions concern the secondary content of the jars and not the primary product for which they were designed.[134] Therefore, not every *titulus* on imported amphora is associated with a foreign commodity; sometimes it concerns a local product that was packaged in a foreign container. Occasionally, it is possible to distinguish *dipinti* that should be associated with the secondary content. However, in the cases where only a name or abbreviated *tria nomina* are given, we can never be certain whether they concern the traders of the primary or rather the secondary content. In such cases we can follow a colour pattern that was observed regarding Spanish amphoras, in which black inscriptions are often associated with wholesale traders and hence with the primary content, whereas red inscriptions are more likely to regard local traders and can at times be interpreted as being connected with the reuse of containers.[135]

Although the evidence seems feeble, we should not be too pessimistic about the use of amphora epigraphy. Marangou-Lerat's study of the inscriptions on

132 Peña 2007, 26.
133 Panella, 1974–1975, 151–165; Marangou-Lerat 1995, 130; Łoś 2005, 85.
134 For the reuse of amphoras see Peña 2007, 82–97.
135 Łoś 1997, 64.

Cretan amphoras proved that most of them concerned Cretan *passum*, and hence we may assume that only a small percentage of all inscriptions regard the secondary content of amphoras. Moreover, a standardisation of their colour is also helpful in this matter.

3 Pros and Cons of an Interdisciplinary Approach

The combination of literary, epigraphic and archaeological sources when reconstructing the past has many advantages, as these categories of evidence "*represent different facets of the same historic society, and they both complement and corroborate one another. Any serious critical investigation of early Roman history must make full use of both types of material in order to produce an integrated reconstruction that must answer to the demand of internal consistency and coherence*".[136] Even so, multidisciplinary approaches are not free from certain flaws. For example, archaeology provides answers to completely different questions than literary sources, which means that combining the information provided by these two categories of evidence is controversial. Each category should be interpreted according to its own rules, but interdisciplinarity often tends to over-interpret archaeological material or to treat it as an illustration of literary tradition.[137] The interpretations of material remains are often derived from ancient written sources, but there is no way of avoiding this,[138] unless we see literary and archaeological evidence as interrogating rather than interpreting each other.[139]

4 Synopsis

4.1 *Chapter 1:* Temetum *contra* vinum*: the Role of Wines from the Eastern Mediterranean in the Origins of Viticulture and Winemaking in Italy*

The first chapter demonstrates the origins of viticulture and winemaking in Italy, with particular emphasis being placed on the beginnings of the consumption of Eastern wines on the Apennine Peninsula and their role in the local development of viticultural techniques and vine varieties. This chapter also

136 Cornell 1986, 67–68.
137 Poucet 1985, 125; Cornell 1995, 29; Smith 2005, 92.
138 Riva 2010a, 2.
139 Allison 2001, 185.

shows that Eastern wines were consumed in Italy between the Archaic period and the 5th c. BC, a gap in the evidence then occurs until the end of the 3rd c. BC, when consumption again expanded. A chronology of the consumption of different types of Eastern wines in Italy is also investigated in this chapter.

4.2 *Chapter 2:* **De gustibus disputandum est**—*'Fame' or Ordinary Wines?*

The second chapter is devoted to the characteristics of wine in terms such as colour, age, taste and ranking (quality). First of all, the typical features of ancient wines in general are sketched; individual types of beverages from the Eastern Mediterranean are looked at in detail later on. The chapter also attempts to explain why the Romans imported particular Eastern wines and tries to distinguish between those beverages that were considered high-quality and the more common products.

An oenological approach was adopted when researching the ancient literary and epigraphic evidence, which means that the Greek and Latin written sources were used only as a starting point with regard to understanding the production processes of different wines. This approach resulted in the discovery that the best *crus* from the Eastern Mediterranean, namely Chian, Thasian and Lesbian, tasted like modern French *vins jaunes* or *vins de voile*, or a Spanish sherry of the *fino* variety. This taste, caused by a compound called sotolon, is described as similar to curry or roasted walnuts. It was obtained thanks to a special production process that included partial oxidation of the beverage. It seems that the Romans sought this taste when making their best *crus*, which highlights the considerable impact that Eastern Mediterranean wines had on Roman wine production.

The conclusions drawn from this chapter indicate that both high-end and common beverages (with a considerable preponderance of the latter) were exported to Italy from the Eastern Mediterranean. This falsifies Finley's statement, according to which trade was limited to famous regional wines. Famous aristocratic drinks did indeed reach Italy during the Archaic and Republican periods, but with the advent of the empire importations of lower quality beverages ensued.

4.3 *Chapter 3: Mass or Limited? Wine Importations to Italy*

This chapter shows the scale of the consumption of wines from the Eastern Mediterranean in Italy, comparing percentages of eastern wine amphoras with percentages of wine containers from other parts of the Mediterranean. Furthermore, by analysing amphora percentages I will try to distinguish which Eastern Mediterranean areas were the most important with regard to exports to Italy and why. I will also investigate the chronological and geographical variations concerning eastern wine importations to Rome, Ostia, Campania and the north Adriatic region.

The chapter demonstrates that importations of Eastern Mediterranean wines were huge in volume and that the Aegean region provided the bulk of them. Also, no considerable difference was observed between percentages of Eastern imports in Rome and those in small Campanian or Adriatic towns. This contradicts the viewpoint that most of the Mediterranean was self-sufficient in terms of foodstuffs and only the major cities needed mass importations of staple goods.

Furthermore, the patterns of wine importations to Italy were compared with ORBIS: the Stanford Geospatial model of the Roman world, which provides a map of approximated transport costs in the Roman Empire. It appears that up to the 3rd c. AD Italy imported mostly Aegean wines, whose transportation costs were very low. At the same time, places where transportation costs were considerably more expensive, such as Cyprus, Cilicia and the Levant were generally ignored. This suggests that profit was the motivating factor that governed early Roman trade, which if proven to be true supports the market economy model.

4.4 *Chapter 4: Aristocratic Luxuries or Mass Beverages?*

Chapter 4 is devoted to the consumers of Eastern wines and answers the question whether these wines were imported for the elites or the commoners. It develops and tries to falsify the conclusions that were drawn from previous analyses of written sources and amphora percentages. For example, ancient literature suggests that wines from Thasos, Lesbos and Chios were high-end products consumed by the elites. Similarly, they are very rare in the archaeological record, besides the archaic graves of the Etruscan aristocracy. Can we therefore assume that they were aristocratic luxuries? The anthropological definition of a luxury has been used to clarify this matter. At the same time, Cretan, Rhodian and Coan wines were not highly regarded by Greek or Latin poets, additionally, their amphoras are more commonly found in Pompeian taverns and the houses of poor people, rather than in local aristocratic residences. This places more emphasis on the conclusion that these wines were middle or low-quality beverages.

It seems that luxuries from the East were imported to Italy during the late Republican age, but when Roman viticulture blossomed the elites turned their heads towards local products, with importations being dominated by goods intended for common consumption.

4.5 *Chapter 5: Petty Traders or Wealthy Wholesalers? Who Imported Wines to Italy?*

This chapter deals with the actual people who were involved with the production, transportation and commerce of Eastern wines to Italy. Evidence for this is provided through prosopographic and socio-onomastic analyses of their names, which were preserved in *tituli picti* on containers discovered in the 'Vesuvian cities'. *Tituli picti* on wine containers from the Eastern Mediterranean (besides Cretan) have not yet been thoroughly analysed and this book is the first publication to present such a study. After investigating the ethnic origin and social status of the traders of Coan, Rhodian, Cilician and other Eastern wines, it was revealed that Italian freedmen who were associated with prominent families were predominant. This suggests (but unfortunately does not prove) that the wealthiest families were indirectly linked with trade, for example by financially assisting their former slaves with their commercial enterprises. Moreover, certain traders enjoyed prominent positions within the local community and were also quite wealthy, which shows that their business provided a viable source of profit and social promotion, and was by no means an insignificant branch of the Roman economy.

4.6 *Chapter 6: Twilight or Bloom? Eastern Wines during Late Antiquity*

The last chapter is devoted to wines from the Eastern Mediterranean during late antiquity. Again, it is based almost exclusively on amphora studies as this is the only category of evidence for this period; later Roman literature often copies the early Roman authors and amphora epigraphy is almost non-existent. Analyses of the amphoras demonstrate that there was a change in Eastern wine importations during late antiquity. For example, south Aegean amphoras were predominant in pottery assemblages during the Principate, yet they appear rarely in late Roman Italy, when it is Oriental containers (which were extremely scarce before the 3rd c. AD) that are the most numerous. The cost of importing from Cyprus, Cilicia and especially the Levant was high, so the popularity of wines from these regions cannot be explained by market forces. Conversely, it suggests that there was a change in the nature of the Roman economy and that coerced (probably by the state or church) trade occurred more frequently than free market exchange.

4.7 *Conclusions*

This section provides a recapitulation of the most important discoveries presented in this work, as well as demonstrating how they contribute to the long-lasting discussion regarding the nature of the Roman economy, which today constitutes the recently formed scientific battlefield which pits supporters of the idea that there was considerable growth and a market economy, against those who contest it. The discovery that it was not only Rome, but also smaller Italian urban centres that imported wine in large quantities, and that these wines were destined for common people, shows that trade played a much more significant role in the Roman economy than previously thought. This conclusion is supported by the analysis of the social position of the traders, who were by no means petty retailers earning just enough to survive. Contrarily, they were quite wealthy, well-established within their local community, and often associated with prominent families. At the same time, it seems inconceivable that wine imports from the Eastern Mediterranean between the 1st c. BC and 2nd c. AD could increase if population growth in this area resulted in pauperisation. Hence, the occurrence of *per capita* economic growth in this period is highly probable. Finally, it has been proven that up to the 3rd c. AD wine was imported almost exclusively from the areas that had the lowest transportation costs; however, from the 4th century onward this factor became insignificant. Therefore, we may assume that market forces played a much bigger role in the economy of the early empire than coerced transfers, whilst during late antiquity the situation was reversed.

CHAPTER 1

Vinum contra *temetum*: the Role of Wines from the Eastern Mediterranean in the Origins of Viticulture and Winemaking in Italy

ἔνθα τε κάλλιστος πότος ἀνδράσι γίνεται οἴνου

Here men get the greatest good from drinking wine
ATH. *Deipn.* 36d

Before describing the consumption of Eastern Mediterranean wines and its possible impact on the economy of Italy, it is necessary to understand the origins of winemaking on the Apennine Peninsula. This is an important issue, because for a long time the origins of winemaking in Italy were attributed somewhere between the Mycenaean era and the period of Greek colonisation.[1] However, due to the scarcity of evidence from before the 8th c. BC, it seemed justified to claim that the Greeks or the Phoenicians brought both viticulture and winemaking to Italy soon after the foundation of the first colonies in the southern part of the Apennine Peninsula, or slightly earlier, during the first reconnaissances of the West by the Euboeans in the 9th/8th c. BC.[2] According to this idea, wines from the Eastern Mediterranean were known to the inhabitants of Italy from the beginning of their adventure with the beverages made from fermented grapes. However, in light of new evidence, the origins of viticulture as well as the production and consumption of wine on the Apennine Peninsula seem much more complex.

It is possible to confirm that viticulture and wine production existed when both archaeobotanical and archaeological evidence is present. The archaeobotanical data confirms the cultivation of the vine, while the archaeological

1 Delpino 2007, 136.
2 Delpino 2007, 136; Unwin 1993, 82; Cristofani 1991, 70. The role of the Phoenicians was noticed by Rathje 1995; Spanò Giammellaro 2000.

© KONINKLIJKE BRILL NV, LEIDEN, 2021 | DOI:10.1163/9789004433762_003

material, such as wine presses, drinking cups and storage jars, provides evidence of wine production and consumption. Traces of tartaric acid inside of these vessels reinforce their association with wine. However, in the case of Italy, the evidence for the origin of viticulture and winemaking is rather fragmentary. There is evidence for the domestication of *vitis vinifera* and viticulture, but this does not necessarily indicate the presence of winemaking, as it cannot be excluded that the cultivation was solely intended for the purpose of consuming the fruits. On the other hand, archaeological evidence that may indicate foreign wine consumption is present, but the drinking of foreign wine has nothing to do with the local production of such a beverage. It should also be noted that there are big differences in the state of research on the origins of cultivated vine and winemaking in various areas of Italy. Recently, special attention has been paid to Etruria, where new data has come to light, mostly thanks to the project VINUM.[3] However, the areas of Latium and Campania remain in the dark, which means that there is only circumstantial evidence available to recreate the Roman origins of viticulture and winemaking.

This chapter presents genetic and archaeobotanical data regarding the domestication of the vine on the Apennine Peninsula, which sheds new light on the historical and linguistic evidence for the production of wine and hence allows for a different interpretation regarding the role played by Eastern Mediterranean wines to be formulated. It seems that both the process of domesticating the vine and wine production had local origins; however, the contact with Greek and Phoenician wines brought new elements to Italian viticulture and changed the model of the consumption of wine. Moreover, this contact also encouraged the growth and development of the central Tyrrhenian part of the Apennine Peninsula.

1 From *vitis sylvestris* to *vitis domestica*

It had been assumed for a long time that there was one centre that was involved with the domestication of *vitis*, which was attributed to the Transcaucasian region. However, recent biomolecular studies of both wild and domesticated populations of this plant in the Mediterranean suggest that domestication might have taken place independently in various areas.[4] This raises the question of whether the inhabitants of Italy encountered the vine in a form that was

---

3 Ciacci, Rendini, Zifferero 2007; 2012.
4 Fiorentino 2011, 15–16.

already domesticated and cultivated, or whether they influenced this process. Moreover, it is necessary to show when the cultivation of vine in Italy began.

The evidence for the domestication of *vitis vinifera* is provided mostly by archaeobotanical, palynological and genetic analyses. The archaeobotanical evidence is based above all on the morphological examination of grape seeds, which allows us to determine whether they are wild or domesticated. The seeds of wild grapes can be distinguished from cultivated grapes by the difference in their shape—they are rounder and have relatively short beaks.[5] The use of the Stumer index, which is a width/length ratio, enables the grape seeds to be divided into three groups: wild, domesticated and intermediate.[6] Although this method has been criticised by various scholars as being not entirely credible,[7] it is still one of the most important tools that can be used while studying the origins of vine cultivation.[8]

Palynology does not provide direct information about the domestication of *vitis*; however, the amount and the context of the vine pollen are significant in this matter. For example, wild vine species produce considerably more pollen, which is due to the fact that in their populations, masculine plants are predominant.[9] Furthermore, pollen of other plants is helpful in recognising the type of ancient environment in which they grew. For example, when vine pollen is accompanied by pollen of willow and/or alder it indicates that it must have grown in a humid environment, which is the optimal habitat for *vitis sylvestris*. Conversely, *vitis sativa* prefers drained surroundings, which are favourable neither for willow nor for alder.[10]

Finally, genetic studies allow us to find traces of human influence on the vine. Moreover, analysis of plant's DNA may show its relationship to other populations of this genre and may also enable us to identify its processes of hybridisation.[11]

Wild vine was present in the Italian landscape as early as in the Middle Pleistocene.[12] Moreover, the seeds of wild grapes have been attested in anthropological contexts, which may be dated as far back as the Mesolithic Period.[13]

5 Zohary 1996, 27.
6 Lentini 2009, 62.
7 Mariotti Lippi, Mori Secci, Bellini 2012, 119.
8 This method is credible when the sample of grape seeds is large and when the pips are not carbonised, see Thurmond 2017, 8.
9 Mariotti Lippi, Mori Secci, Bellini 2012, 120; Aranguren et al. 2012, 129.
10 Mariotti Lippi, Mori Secci, Bellini 2012, 120.
11 Giannace 2010, 81.
12 Costantini, Costantini Biasini 1999, 177.
13 Delpino 2007, 134; 2012, 190.

From the ancient Neolithic there is evidence that the fruits of *vitis vinifera sylvestris* were consumed by people inhabiting the Apennine Peninsula. Wild grape seeds dated to this period have been found in human settlement contexts, *inter alia*, in Cava Barbieri a Pienza, Podere Casanuova, Pontedera, Monte Cetona,[14] La Marmotta, San Marco di Gubbio, Rivaltella, Monte Covolo in north central Italy, as well as in Torre Canne and Grotta dell'Uzzo in the south of the Apennine Peninsula.[15] Moreover, grape seeds dated to the Neolithic and which present intermediate morphological characteristics (between wild and domesticated forms) have been discovered in the southern part of Italy, in the area of Bari (Scamuso, Cala Colombo, Madonna delle Grazie).[16] This may indicate human interference in the spontaneous growth of *vitis*. Grape fermentation in this area might have been known as early as the 4th millennium BC, as studies of organic residues on pottery jars from Monte Kronio on Sicily suggest. One of these jars contained tartaric acid and its salts, which develop naturally during wine fermentation.[17]

In central and northern Italy, the first traces of human influence on the vine are dated to the Bronze Age. The analysis of vine pollen from the area of Lago di Massaciuccoli (modern Tuscany) dated to the Early Bronze Age has shown a considerable concentration of *vitis* in areas of human settlement. This settlement was characterised by a reduction of its wooded area, which is the natural environment for *vitis sylvestris*.[18] This may suggest incidental diffusion of the wild vine, which grew out of the seeds that had been thrown away onto a refuse heap or via intentional human interference with the natural habitat of this plant.

Seeds from cultivated grapes are also first attested in Italy during the Bronze Age,[19] with a silo in San Lorenzo a Greve (Firenze) providing 929 grape seeds and 300 fragments which are dated to 3270+/-50 BP (1 sigma 1616–1464 BC; 2 sigma 1684–1430 BC). Their morphological characteristics varied, and the discovery included seeds from each stage of the domestication process (wild-intermediate-domesticated). This discovery may indicate that people in the Middle Bronze Age took care of *vitis*, for example by spreading and transplanting it.[20] However, this does not necessarily indicate the cultivation of the vine

14 Mariotti Lippi, Mori Secci, Bellini 2012, 120–121.
15 Costantini, Costantini Biasini 1999, 178, tab. 5.
16 Costantini, Costantini Biasini 1999, 180.
17 Tanasi 2017, 142–147.
18 Aranguren et al. 2007, 89.
19 Forni 2007, 73.
20 Aranguren et al. 2007, 93–95.

or the existence of a new, domesticated form of *vitis*, since the seeds of domesticated grapes might have been of a foreign origin. The foreign origin is suggested by the fact that the environment of San Lorenzo a Greve is not very favourable for the cultivation of vines. On the contrary, it is optimal for the diffusion of its wild variety.[21]

The earliest evidence for systematical harvesting of grapes comes from the Late Bronze Age. A considerable amount of grape seeds, both wild and domesticated, have been attested in Chiusi in an organic waste context. Furthermore, in Livorno-Stagno, 4555 grape seeds were found, one-sixth of which were domesticated.[22] Cultivated grape seeds have also been attested in Tarquinia and Gran Carro, dated to the Late Bronze Age and the Early Iron Age respectively.[23] These discoveries indicate that local populations were engaged in grape picking and might have started the process of *vitis* domestication (or rather paradomestication[24]). There is no doubt that grape seeds discovered in Pizzica Pantanello in Magna Graecia dated to the 9th c. BC were of a domesticated vine variety, which confirms that viticulture was practiced by local populations well before the founding of Greek colonies.[25] Furthermore, since almost all the seeds that have been attested in Italy, which date to after the 9th/8th c. BC, have the characteristics of domesticated grapes, it seems that in the Iron Age the vine was widely cultivated on the Apennine Peninsula.[26]

Therefore, it seems that the process of vine domestication in southern Italy should be dated to the 3rd and the 2nd millennium BC,[27] whereas in the north-central part it occurred later, most probably at the end of the 2nd/beginning of the 1st millennium BC.[28] However, it should be noted that although the change in seed shape may indicate the beginning of cultivation (for example in plant selection), it may also signify the introduction of an already selected vine from a different geographical area.[29] Therefore, it is unclear whether the domestication of the vine was a local process or was due to foreign influences. In this context it seems interesting that the discovery of the grape seeds from San Lorenzo a Greve does not resemble the Gaussian distribution. This suggests that various populations of *vitis vinifera* must have been present. Moreover, a

---

21 Mariotti Lippi, Mori Secci, Bellini 2012, 122; Aranguren et al. 2012, 129.
22 Delpino 2007, 135.
23 Delpino 2012, 190.
24 On the concept of paradomestication see Forni 2012, 102–107.
25 Thurmond 2017, 38.
26 Costantini, Costantini Biasini 1999, 181.
27 Forni 2007, 71.
28 Forni 2007, 72; Cianferoni 2007, 19; 2012, 30.
29 Mariotti Lippi, Mori Secci 2007, 85–86; Aranguren et al. 2007, 89–90, 95.

rather small percentage of vine pollen was attested at this settlement, which may indicate that this plant was not diffused within close proximity to the site.[30]

The results of the analysis of the morphological characteristics of grape seeds from the Neolithic village of La Marmotta (Rome) may be meaningful here. According to M. Rottoli, they demonstrate a strong convergence of characters with the other wild vines that have been attested in Italy that are dated to the Neolithic and the Bronze Age. However, they are completely different from the cultivated forms of *vitis* that appeared later in Italy.[31] This may suggest a foreign influence on vine domestication on the Apennine Peninsula. At the same time, the analysis of the morphological characteristics of grape seeds that have been found in modern Tuscany shows that they differ from the seeds of the wild grapes, but they are also different from the domestic grape seeds that are dated to the Iron Age.[32] This, however, may be explained by the 19th c. plague of phylloxera which destroyed a considerable number of European vines, resulting in new foreign vine species being introduced to recreate the viticulture.

On the other hand, a theory regarding the local domestication of *vitis* has recently been supported by the genetic analysis of species of modern wild vine carried out within the project VINUM. A DNA study of modern *vitis sylvestris* proved that specimens that grew near inhabited areas in antiquity differ from those that were found in uninhabited contexts. In addition, the population of wild vine attested in inhabited regions contained more female and hermaphrodite specimens, whereas in the natural environment males should predominate. This indicates that people influenced the wild vine, e.g. by protecting it and selecting female and hermaphrodite plants (over males that do not bring fruit), as early as in the Bronze Age.[33] Moreover, two specimens of *vitis sylvestris* from the area of Ghiacco Forte presented a genetic resemblance to vines that are cultivated today. This clearly indicates that the domestication of *vitis* in certain parts of Etruria had local origins.[34]

The hypothesis regarding local domestication of the vine in Italy is confirmed by the analysis of the agricultural techniques that were used by the ancient populations. Sereni noted that the Etruscans used the technique of high-training (vines supported on trees—*alberate*), whereas low-training

30 Aranguren et al. 2012, 129.
31 Rottoli 1993, 313.
32 Aranguren et al. 2007, 89–90.
33 Imazio et al. 2012, 618–620.
34 Ciacci 2010, 75.

(vines supported on sticks) was typical of the Greeks.[35] What is even more significant is that up until the beginning of the 19th c. there were different names attributed to vine in Italy, according to how they were cultivated. The term *vinea* designated vines that were low-trained, whereas *alberate* plants were called *arbustum*.[36] The existence of the high training system in Etruria, Latium and in the Etruscan areas of Campania until at least the 4th c. BC[37] may be seen as further proof of the pre-Greek origins of Italian viticulture. What about the production of wine?

2 Wine: A Local Invention or a Foreign Influence?

According to G. Forni, the process of domestication was autonomous in Italy,[38] but the introduction of viticulture probably started when the region was under the influence of the Aegean populations.[39] In the Minoan culture, *vitis* was domesticated at the beginning of the Bronze Age[40] and the first wine (retsina), identified by P. McGovern, was discovered in *pithoi* from Myrthos in the south of Crete, dated to ca. 2200 BC.[41] Moreover, linear B tablets indicate that the Mycenaean culture was also familiar with wine.[42] Is it then possible that it was the Mycenaeans who introduced wine to the inhabitants of Italy?

Between the 16th and the 11th c. BC numerous Mycenaean influences in the form of imported pottery that was connected mostly with the drinking and storage of wine may be observed in southern Italy and Sicily, most of which are dated to the 14th and the 13th c. BC.[43] In southern Italy, Mycenaean pottery (including amphoras) has been attested in Apulia (Gulf of Taranto), Calabria, Basilicata and Campania and as far north as Vivara, in the Bay of Naples.[44] Also, Mycenaean vessels, such as *kylikes*, goblets and amphoras, were discovered in

35 Sereni 1964, 128–131; Cerchiai 2013, 277. It seems that high-training was also practiced in the Near East, as is suggested by iconographic evidence from Niniva, see Spanò Giammellaro 2000, 52. Therefore, it cannot be excluded that this practice came to Italy with the Phoenicians.

36 Basile 2010, 98.

37 According to Volpe 2009, 373, the technique disappeared around this period.

38 Forni 2007, 73.

39 Piccoli 2004, 5; Sereni 1964, 76–78; Forni 2007, 74.

40 Brun 2004, 71–72.

41 McGovern 2003, 247–250.

42 Brun 2004, 80; Sereni 1964, 82–85.

43 La Torre 2011, 12–22.

44 Ridgway 1992, 4–7; Gras 1985, 256. However, the content of the Mycenaean amphoras is unknown; wine is as likely as olive oil.

funerary contexts in the Aeolian Islands and in south-eastern Sicily, particularly in the area of the Thapsos culture around Syracuse.[45] It is also worth noting that some contacts with the Mycenaean world were attested in north-western Italy, but they do not seem to have been associated with wine.[46]

The evidence mentioned above suggests that Aegean merchants might have imported wine to southern Italy during the Bronze Age. However, it is still unclear whether they also introduced the technique of winemaking. Moreover, it seems that the contacts with the Mycenaeans were mainly limited to the southern part of Italy and to the coastal region of the central area of the Apennine Peninsula. Finally, it is important to emphasise the lack of any vessels that may be associated with wine drinking between the 11th and the 9th c. BC in Italy.[47] This may indicate that even if the consumption and production of wine was known, these activities gradually ceased when contact with the Mycenaeans began to diminish. Therefore, even if we accept the theory that *vitis vinifera* was already cultivated and that the local populations were familiar with imported wine thanks to the contact with the Mycenaeans, there is no evidence for the continuity of its consumption.

Nevertheless, the high number of grape seeds from Livorno-Stagno (Late Bronze Age) might suggest that they were the rests from wine pressing.[48] Moreover, at every site where grape seeds were found, archaeobotanical rests of cornel were also attested. This plant does not have much nutritional value, but its berries can easily be fermented into alcohol.[49] Consequently, the rests of cornel should not be interpreted as simple aliments. On the contrary, they imply that the Late Bronze Age inhabitants of modern Tuscany knew how to make alcoholic beverages. In the same way, it cannot be excluded that they were also familiar with the fermentation of grape juice. It is certain that the tradition of making fermented beverages from cornel did not become extinct with the beginning of wine production, as a cornel press dated to the 6th c. BC has been discovered at an Etruscan factory in Pian d'Alma.[50]

The earliest evidence for grape wine production has been confirmed in Poggiomarino (Campania). Here, a considerable amount of stacked grapes, grape

45 Leighton 1999, 170–172.

46 Piccoli 2004, 6.

47 La Torre 2011, 15; Cianferoni 2007, 19.

48 Delpino 2007, 135. This author also demonstrates other calculations, which showed that after the production of 100 litres of wine, the remaining number of seeds should vary between 210,680 and 1,280,000 seeds, depending on the use of wild or domesticated grapes.

49 Mariotti Lippi, Mori Secci, Bellini 2012, 122; Aranguren et al. 2012, 128.

50 Mariotti Lippi, Mori Secci, Bellini 2012, 122.

stems and seeds (most of them being the domesticated variety) were found, together with fragments of *vitis* stems that were supposedly pruned. The context may suggest that Poggiomarino was a place where wine was pressed. Moreover, nine wooden discs that were found together with the archaeobotanical rests were interpreted as elements of a wine press. However, by the means of dendrochronological analysis, the discovery was dated to 905/864 BC.[51] Since all other installations for the pressing of grapes that have so far been attested on the Apennine Peninsula are dated significantly later, this interpretation seems rather improbable.[52] Nonetheless, Poggiomarino may be seen as a place of wine production and this confirms that this activity existed in Italy before the advent of Greek colonisation.[53] Unfortunately, it is impossible to say whether this proves the origins of local winemaking, because the pre-colonial Euboean influence cannot be excluded in this case.[54]

From the 9th c. BC, archaeological evidence related to wine production in Etruria becomes more abundant. First of all, there is tableware that is associated with the consumption of wine, which was produced locally, but had no local antecedents, which suggests that it was freely inspired by Greek pottery. Among these vessels are krater-shaped vases (*vasi crateriformi*) and amphora-kraters (*anfore-crateri*) found together with other utensils for serving liquids. They were discovered in funerary contexts in Tarquinia and are dated to the last decades of the 9th c. BC (phase IB–C of the Advanced Villanovian Period) and to 780–769 BC (phase IIA).[55] Furthermore, at the beginning of the Iron Age and maybe as far back as the end of the Bronze Age, the inhabitants of Etruria used billhooks (*pennati*), which were cutting tools that were commonly used for viticulture.[56] Based on this data, F. Delpino argues that wine production was known in Etruria and in other areas of central and south Italy before Greek colonisation began, and that it was probably influenced by contacts with the East during the Bronze Age.[57] However, the presence of the vessels connected with wine drinking in Etruria does not necessarily infer that wine was being consumed. This is due to the fact that the original function of a certain object is not always maintained. Therefore, it is possible that kraters in Etruria were

51 Cicirelli et al. 2008, 574–575.
52 Cicirelli, Albore Livadie 2008, 479; The earliest wine presses are dated to the 6th (Punta Chiarito, Pithecussai) and 5th c. BC (Villa dell'Auditorium, Roma); Foxhall 2011, 36.
53 Cicirelli et al. 2008, 574–575.
54 Sourisseau 2011, 155.
55 Delpino 2007, 138–139; 2012, 192–193.
56 Delpino 1997, 186–190; 2012, 192.
57 Delpino 1997, 187–188; 2007, 137–141; 2012, 196.

used in a different way than in Greek culture. Instead of serving sympotic purposes they might have been connected with funerary practices. Moreover, even if they were associated with the drinking of alcohol, this does not necessarily mean the drinking of wine.[58] For example, there is evidence from Spain that kraters were used for the drinking of beer.[59] Therefore, according to P. Ruby, the Tarquinian kraters should be seen as nothing more than elements of gift exchange and the circulation of prestige goods. The fact that they were imitations of Greek vessels does not contradict this theory, because the production of imitations infers an understanding and control of the technology that was required to produce such objects. Moreover, imitation itself can also be a symbol of prestige.[60]

Nonetheless, the kraters from Tarquinia are not the only vessels which may indicate that the Etruscans used wine and that this usage was independent from Greek practices. M. Torelli argues that certain ceremonial practices associated with the use of wine existed in Etruria before the introduction of the Greek symposion. He draws our attention to the two types of vessels that were typical of Etruscan and Latin traditions and did not originate in the Greek world. A small cup called *capeduncola*, that had a curved handle ending in a flat spatula, as well as *anforetta a spirale* have long been used by the Etruscans, from the Early Iron Age until the 6th c. BC. There is also the *kyathos*, a goblet with one high handle. This vessel is of Etruscan origin and its evolution may be traced back to the Late Bronze Age. According to Torelli, the above-mentioned pottery forms should be associated with *temetum*, a Latin (and probably also Etruscan) wine that was known in Italy earlier than the Greek οἶνος. It might have been a local invention or an inheritance that was continued after contact with the Mycenaeans in the Bronze Age. This wine also had its own ceremonies, which might have been developed as early as the end of the Bronze Age.[61]

According to V. Bertoldi, *temetum* originally referred to an alcoholic beverage made from sorb (*sorbus aucuparia*), which in the dialects of Lombardy and Piedmont is called *temel, tumel* or *temar*. Moreover, he associates the root *temer* with the word *tamaro*, which means *vitis sylvestris* in the modern Tuscan dialect. Latin sources mention a number of alcoholic beverages, including types made of dogwood, raspberry, cherry, blackcurrant, elderberry and figs.

---

58 Ruby 1993, 801, 805–809.
59 Sáez Fernández 2001, 114.
60 Ruby 1993, 818–820.
61 Torelli 2000a, 93–100.

However, the beverage made of fermented grapes became the most popular and the word *temetum* at a certain point started to designate grape wine.[62] A. Ciacci suggests that *temetum* was later associated with fine, imported wines. Under Greek influences the use of this word ceased, and *vinum* started to designate the alcoholic beverage made from fermented grape juice.[63] However, the root word *temet* survived in Latin in the adjectives *temulentus* and *abstemius*, which referred to the state of intoxication.

In this context one should not omit linguistic theories regarding the origins of the word *vinum*. According to M. Cristofani, the Etruscan *vinum* derives from *"lingue dell'area tiberina"*,[64] which means that it is a local term, similarly to *temetum*. On the contrary, L. Agostiniani derives it from the Greek οἶνος and claims that the Latin *vinum* has roots in this Etruscan term.[65] Although the Greek origin of the Etruscan term *vinum* is more commonly accepted, C. De Simone criticises Agostiniani, who in his opinion did not prove that in the Etruscan language *voi* changed to *vi*. Furthermore, he points out that 'wine' is a 'travelling word' (*parola viaggiante*) that always has various variants, which do not necessary obey the rules of etymology. He emphasises that similar terms can be also attested in Mycenaean languages as well as in Asia Minor, and that the word 'wine' has resembling forms in all the Italian dialects.[66] This means that the term *vinum* should be considered as 'Mediterranean' and that it is impossible to relate its variants in any rigorous way.

It is worth mentioning that almost all the evidence suggesting that wine might have been made in Italy before the period of Greek colonisation comes from Etruria. Given that one could assume that wine 'came' to Italy with the Etruscans, the issue of the origin of the Etruscan culture cannot be entirely omitted. Generally, two major theories concerning the origin of the Etruscans were proposed. The first, called autochthonic, assumed that they were native people who lived in central Italy before the Indo-Europeans came to this territory. The second postulated that the *Tyrrhenoi* originated somewhere in the Near East and came to central Italy probably during the Iron Age.[67] In the 1930's

62 Bertoldi 1942, 165–169.

63 Ciacci 2010, 77.

64 Cristofani 1991, 70. It was first attested in the Faliscan inscription dated to the 7th c. BC (CIE 8079). According to this author, although *vinum* was a word that belonged to the local culture in Latium, in the culture of drinking it was hellenised.

65 Agostiniani 2000, 106–108.

66 De Simone 2011, 475–477. Similarities between the terms that describe wine have already been mentioned by Sereni 1964, 82–83.

67 According to the less popular 'allochthonic' hypothesis the Etruscans came from the Alpine region.

M. Pallottino postulated that it is wrong to look at the Etruscan culture through the lens of the above-mentioned approaches and presented a theory regarding the formation of this culture, in which both foreign and local elements took part.[68] Genetic studies from the first decade of this century reopened the discussion concerning the origin of the Etruscans, suggesting their eastern provenance.[69] However, the most recent DNA investigations demonstrate that even though there was a post-Neolithic genetic input from the Near East in the present-day population of Tuscany,[70] the inhabitants of Asia Minor and Etruria shared a common ancestor more than 5000 years ago.[71] Although the reliability of the genetic analyses in this matter has been questioned,[72] for the time being it should be accepted that there is no argument in favour of an Etruscan migration from the Near East during the Iron Age. Therefore, the Etruscans could not have been those who brought wine to the Apennine Peninsula.

At this point we could ask the question: when did the Romans start to drink wine? The earliest archaeological evidence that can help answer this query comes from the 7th c. BC. Cultivated vine seeds dated to the first half of the 7th c. BC have been attested in graves I and K at the Roman Forum. These graves also contained *olle d'impasto*, which were vessels that are usually associated with wine. In addition, in grave K the grape seeds were present inside a bronze basin. Similar bronze basins have been attested in various places in Italy and they were often found together with Etruscan *kantharoi* and amphoras, which may suggest that they were associated with wine. There is also one grave in Gabii that contained an almost identical funerary assemblage as the graves from the Roman Forum. The only differences being that it contained a Phoenician amphora and no grape seeds. According to Gras, these discoveries suggest that

---

68 Pallottino 1968, 52–91.

69 Vernesi et al. 2004; Achilli et al. 2007.

70 Achilli et al. 2007, 767. This is suggested by the frequency of the haplogroupes HV, R0a, U7, and U3 in mt DNA that is shared between the modern inhabitants of Italy (especially those from Murlo) and Near Eastern populations.

71 Ghirotto et. al. 2013, http://www.plosone.org/article/info%3Adoi%2F10.1371%2Fjournal.pone.0055519. Accessed 3.12.2014.

72 E.g. Malyarchuk, Rogozin 2004, 923 point out that the ancient DNA samples may often be contaminated by post-mortem mutations. Moreover, the ancient DNA was taken mostly from aristocratic graves, which means that it represents only a small group of the Etruscan population. In addition, the study of mtDNA provides us with no useful information if the foreign agent came to Italy in male form only (invaders or traders). Finally, in order to check whether the Etruscans might have come from the East the DNA of Bronze Age peoples from Anatolia should be studied, rather than modern Turks.

imported wine was an impulse that prompted viticulture in Latium and that the Romans learned how to cultivate vine from the Etruscans or the Phoenicians.[73]

Literary evidence attributes the beginnings of winemaking and vine cultivation to Numa Pompilius, the second king of Rome. According to Plutarch, Numa, who was of Sabine origin, forbade making libations of wine made from unpruned vine.[74] Pliny confirmed this, adding that Numa prohibited sprinkling wine on the funeral pyre, and that Romulus made libations using milk.[75] G. Piccaluga's interpretation of these fragments suggests that Numa might have introduced wine into Roman religious rites and also encouraged the cultivation of *vitis vinifera*.[76] Worth mentioning here is the story about Mezentius, the Etruscan king from Caere, who agreed to fight against the Latins upon the condition that he would receive all the wine that was in their territory.[77] According to the literary tradition, Numa lived at the turn of the 8th and the 7th c. BC and ruled between 715 and 672 BC. Thus, the literary tradition corroborates the archaeological discoveries from the graves at the Forum. What is more, Pliny interprets the prohibition of the use of wine made from unpruned vines as an encouragement to prune the vine. In this case, the production of wine made from pruned *vitis*, and not the production of wine itself, could be interpreted as a new technology. According to Torelli, Numa's laws that were associated with wine may reflect the process of the change from local wine (*temetum*) to Greek (*vinum*), that progressively came to Etruria and Latium after the initial contact with the Euboeans in the 9th c. BC.[78] It is, however, interesting that literary tradition connects Numa with the prohibition of wine sprinkling on the funeral pyre, because cremation was rare at the time of Numa, as this practice was abandoned during the last decades of the 9th c. BC. This could indicate that the prohibition attributed to Numa did in fact occur earlier than in the 7th c. BC.[79] The information that Romulus made libations with milk does not exclude the existence of wine and its use for other purposes. As a matter of fact, Pliny mentions that wine was taboo for women in archaic Rome under Romulus.[80] Although it is not possible to say that wine indeed existed in the times of Romulus (which, moreover, cannot be dated precisely), the archaic taboo on

73 Gras 1983, 1069–1070; 1985, 368–370.
74 Plut. *Numa* 14.3.
75 Plin. *HN* XIV 88.
76 Piccaluga 1962, 101–103.
77 Plin. *HN* XIV 88.
78 Torelli 2000b, 147–149.
79 Delpino 2007, 135–136.
80 Plin. *HN* XIV 89.

women drinking wine may suggest the presence of local wine drinking traditions. Therefore, it is clear that this subject requires further investigation.

The prohibition is mentioned by various authors; however, some of them state that only certain alcohol beverages were banned, not wine in general, and that breaking the ban was severely punished, equal to adultery.[81] The most detailed description is provided by Aulus Gellius, who quotes, *inter alia*, Cato's '*On the dowry*'. This is also the most credible testimony, given that Cato was famous for his conservatism and his guarding of old Roman traditions; thus, if anyone was to provide reliable information regarding the remote past, it was the author of *De Agri Cultura*.[82] According to this testimony women "*lived an abstemious life*", which means that they did not drink *temetum*. However, they could consume *lora* (a drink that was obtained through the fermentation of water and the remnants that were left after the squeezing of grapes), *passum* (raisin wine) and *murrina* (wine flavoured with myrrh and other spices), or other sweet wines.[83] It is notable that the word *temetum* (not *vinum*), was used here, similarly as in Pliny's description of the ban. Both authors explain the meaning of *temetum*, which indicates that it was an old term not in use any more during the 1st c. AD There were various interpretations of this prohibition,[84] but the one proposed by M. Gras seems to be the most convincing. He noticed that wine amphoras as well as other banquet utensils were found in both male and female graves at the necropoleis of Castel di Decima and Laurentina dated to the Archaic period, which suggests that women used wine.[85] However, wines that could be consumed by women, such as *passum* and *defrutum*, were also considered inappropriate for libations. Therefore, Roman women were probably not allowed to drink the sacred wine that was used during religious rituals.[86] This prohibition must have disappeared between the 8th and the 5th c. BC, since it does not appear in the Law of the Twelve Tables.[87] This agrees with the studies of O. de Cazanove, according to whom the Romans distinguished wine for Jupiter from the wine for Liber Pater, who was later identified with Dionysus and Bacchus. The first was a pure, new wine that had no admixtures and was suitable for religious rituals,[88] in contrast to imported Greek or Phoenician beverages and the aforementioned *lora*,

81 D.H. II 25, 6; Plin. *HN* XIV 89–90; Plut. *Comp.Lyc.Num.* 3. 5.
82 Hooper 1934, IX–XIII.
83 *NA* X 23.
84 Noailles 1948; Durry 1955; Bettini 1995.
85 Gras 1983, 1069.
86 Gras 1983, 1071.
87 Gras 1985, 382.
88 De Cazanove 1988, 255–256.

murrina, passum and *defrutum*. The pure wine that was used for religious rituals could be identified with *temetum*, a sacred drink that was forbidden to women. Therefore, *temetum* would be something distinct from *vinum* and thus subject to different laws and customs than those that accompanied wine, which had originated in Greek tradition. This dualism between *temetum* (local) and *vinum* (foreign) resembles the one between the high-training of *arbustum* (Etruscan) and low-training of *vinea* (Greek). Moreover, it seems that the taboo concerning women and wine was abandoned when foreign wines started to be imported to Rome. This could be another argument in favour of local wine (*temetum*) being produced in Italy, before the Greeks arrived.

In summary, it seems possible that wine was introduced into Italy in the Bronze Age by the Mycenaeans. It was almost certainly produced locally during the 9th c. BC, but it was not a large-scale project. However, we still do not know if the evidence regarding 9th c. BC local wine production should be seen as a continuation of the Mycenaean influences or rather as an independent Italian discovery. It cannot be excluded that primitive viticulture and winemaking existed in Italy between the Mycenaean times and the 9th c. BC. Considering that its production was probably very primitive and limited, this could account for the fact that there are no signs of winemaking in the archaeological record during this period. With the Greek and Phoenician influences, the Italians (now the Etruscans and the Romans) would again get in touch with wine, learning new ways concerning its production and usage.

The impact of the colonists on Italian viticulture and winemaking is manifested in various ways. First of all, it seems that through contact with the Aegean, new species of vine appeared in Italy. These vine species, called *Graeculae*, are mentioned by ancient writers such as Pliny and Columella.[89] Moreover, foreign influence on Italian *vitis* is suggested by the shape of the seeds from La Marmotta (*supra*) and through the analysis of vine germplasm.[90] For example, 42 samples of vine from Valle d'Albenga showed considerable genetic variations, which suggests that crossbreeding took place.[91] This is confirmed by the fact that the Tyrrhenian vine called *Ansonica* is genetically similar to the Sicilian vine as well as to Greek species, such as *Rhoditis* and *Sideritis*, which grew mainly on Aegean islands, particularly Euboea.[92] Furthermore, the development of agricultural techniques in Italy was probably also influenced through relations with the Aegean or the Phoenicians. It seems that the pruning

89 Plin. *HN* XIV 25; *Rust.* III 2, 1, 24, 28.
90 Ciacci, Zifferero 2007, 262; Del Re 2012, 690.
91 Zifferero 2010b, 86.
92 Ciacci 2010, 78.

of *vitis* might have been one of them and that the contacts with the Greeks from the south of Italy or with the Phoenicians provided an impulse for spreading this technology.[93] Vegetative reproduction of the vine may be another foreign influence. During the genetic studies carried out within the VINUM project no identical individuals of *vitis vinifera* were found. This suggests that generative reproduction must have been practiced by the inhabitants of Italy.[94] Finally, there was the introduction of the low-training of vines supported by a vine-pole. This technique was widespread in Greek-inhabited areas, and it is confirmed as being used in Roman territories starting from the 4th c. BC. It became an alternative to the Etruscan high-training method, which was based on a tree trunk.[95] It is worth mentioning that vineyards in Pompeii were organised in the same way as vineyards on Rhodes, as the distances between the plants were the same,[96] which may be another Greek influence on Roman viticulture.

Concluding, it seems that in Italy, foreign viticulture and winemaking overlapped the existing local vine cultivation and wine production.[97] Under Greek and Phoenician influence, making and drinking wine became more popular and widespread among the inhabitants of the Apennine Peninsula, who learnt about new vine species and viticultural techniques. The settlers from the East also brought their own wines with them.

3 The Beginnings of the Consumption of Wines from the Eastern Mediterranean

It seems that wines from the Eastern Mediterranean appeared in Italy almost as early as the first colonists had settled in the south of the Apennine Peninsula. Greek and Phoenician wine production would also shortly start in the West. Since it is not always certain whether Phoenician amphoras found in Italy were produced in the Eastern or the Western part of the Mediterranean, I will concentrate here on Aegean containers, which indubitably came from the East. The earliest, dated to the 8th c. BC, were Corinthian A jars found in Greek colonies in Campania, Magna Graecia and Sicily. However, it is uncer-

93 See Spanò Giammellaro 2000, 52 for the pruning of *vitis* in the Near East.
94 Imazio et al. 2012, 620.
95 Sereni 1964, 129. The Phoenicians probably used a similar techniques, see Spanò Giammellaro 2000, 52.
96 Salviat 1993, 158–159.
97 Delpino 2007, 142; Forni 2012, 113.

tain whether these amphoras carried wine or olive oil. A wide range of Aegean containers from Attica, Corinth, Clazomenae, Lesbos, Chios, Mende, Thasos, Samos and Miletus, as well as Solokha I containers that probably originated in Peparethos, started to appear in Etruria during the 7th c. BC, and in the Po Valley from the 6th c. BC. These amphora types were widely attested throughout Italy until the 5th c. BC,[98] when Corinthian B amphoras produced in Corcyra began to dominate pottery assemblages in Italy.[99]

Aegean wine jars were the most commonly attested in Etruscan graves, because they often served as funerary offerings. However, a considerable number of amphoras, including Aegean, Etruscan, Marsilian, *Ionico-Massaliotic* and Phoenician, were also found in the sacred area in Gravisca. Most of them (more than 90%) were dated to the 6th c. BC, whereas the rest came from the 5th c. BC. Among the Aegean containers that were attested in Gravisca there were: Chian (15) Lesbian (6), Clazomenian (6), Samian (49), Milesian (5), Corinthian A (31) and B (25), 'à la brosse' (20) and Laconian (5).[100] Numerous Greek amphoras were also attested in Pyrgi, in different contexts: in the suburban sanctuary of Leucotea, in a residential area and in the waters of the harbour. Corinthian A (9), Lesbian (3), Samian (2), Milesian (4–5) and Corinthian B (5), all dated to the 6th and the 5th c. BC, were found together with Marsilian and *Ionico-Massaliotic* vessels, whereas no Phoenician and only one Etruscan amphora were recognised.[101] In addition, archaic Aegean containers dated to the 6th–5th c. BC, including Corinthian A, Chian, Samian and 'à la brosse' were discovered in the emporium of Vulci—Regisvilla.[102]

Although there is no consensus regarding the content of all the archaic amphoras from the Aegean, it seems almost certain that the containers produced on Chios, Lesbos, Thasos, Peparethos and in Mende, as well as Corinthian B vessels from Corcyra, carried wine.[103] Therefore, the Etruscan consumption of Aegean wines in the Archaic and early Classical period (between the 8th and the 5th c. BC) seems indubitable. The discovery of other vessels asso-

98 Albore Livadie 1985, 138–145; Di Sandro 1981, 11–12; Marangou-Lerat 2000, 72; Slaska 1985, 19–21; Ciampoltrini, Rendini 2012, 396; Sacchetti 2013, 28–31, 64–65, 75–76, 80–81, 93–95, 101–102; Doulgèri-Intzessiloglou, Garlan 1990, 388.

99 Sacchetti 2013, 37–38.

100 Slaska 1978, 228–230; 1985, 19–20. The estimated number of vessels was given in parentheses.

101 Colonna 1985, 6–14. However, there were other amphoras made from local clay, thus the number of Etruscan vessels should probably be higher.

102 Morselli, Tortorici 1985, 31–34.

103 Koehler 1981, 452; Doulgéri-Intzessiloglou, Garlan 1990; Lawall 2000, 18, 32 n. 20–21; Sezgin 2004, 178; Sacchetti 2013, 27, 64, 75, 80, 98–102.

ciated with the consumption of wine, as well as wall-paintings from certain graves clearly demonstrate that the Etruscans not only drank Aegean wines, but also adopted certain aspects of Greek life, such as practicing the symposion.[104] At the same time, the evidence regarding Roman interest in Eastern Mediterranean wines is rather ambiguous. Very few fragments of Aegean amphoras dated to the Archaic period have so far been found in Roman Latium. In the three Roman necropoleis of Ficana, Laurentina and Castel di Decima, except for one fragment of Corinthian A type, all the amphoras were west Phoenician types.[105] Other fragments of Corinthian A amphoras were found in Roman suburbs, at the Villa dell'Auditorium[106] and on the Palatine Hill, where a single fragment of a container from the island of Chios was discovered.[107] This is all the known evidence of Aegean amphoras from the region inhabited by the Romans that can be dated to the Archaic age.[108] However, the discoveries from certain residential areas that might contain fragments of Aegean amphoras have yet to be fully investigated.[109] Even so, it seems that there is too little evidence to argue that the Romans consumed Eastern wines during the Archaic period.

On the other hand, the lack of consumption of Aegean wines in Roman Latium would be rather strange in comparison with the Etruscan area. However, it cannot be excluded that Rome was first influenced by the Phoenicians from Sardinia, which is suggested by the findings of Phoenician amphoras in this region.[110] The Romans did not have direct contact with the Greeks, as the Etruscans did in the territory of Campania. Moreover, the Romans in the Archaic age did not have ports and thus were probably supplied through the Etruscan ports at Pyrgi and Gravisca.[111] Greek pottery often reached Latium in company with Etruscan *buccero* vessels.[112] This suggests that since ports were the places where interactions with other cultures were the most developed, foreign influences appeared later within the Roman sphere than they did with the Etruscans. The difference between the Etruscan and Latin communities is visible in funerary assemblages. For example, during the third quarter of the 8th c.

104 Bartoloni 2007, 153.
105 Gras 1983, 1068; Bartoloni 2002, 58 these amphoras are sometimes accompanied by tripod bowls, which were typical Phoenician vessels; Sacchetti 2013, 30.
106 Di Giuseppe 2006a 207, tab. 20; 2006b, 400.
107 Sacchetti 2013, 76; Zevi 1985, 119.
108 Up to the end of 2014.
109 Sacchetti 2013, 30.
110 See above.
111 Smith 1998, 34.
112 Beijer 1995, 62.

BC at least 10 % of the tombs in the necropolis of Quattro Fontanili in Veii contain complete sets of equipment and a wagon/chariot, which means that they were warrior burials. At the same time, in Castel di Decima, Osteria dell'Osa and in Rome the percentage of similar graves is lower than 1%. Moreover, in Etruria personal ornaments from the graves are generally more luxurious.[113] Considering that the number of Aegean amphoras in Etruscan cemeteries and emporia was not very high and that imported wine amphoras were attested almost exclusively in elite burials in Vulci,[114] it was assumed that wine drinking was a privilege of the Etruscan aristocracy.[115] Since funerary offerings suggest that Roman elites were poorer than their Etruscan counterparts, one may assume that they simply could not afford considerable quantities of foreign wine imports. However, recent research conducted on wine drinking equipment in Etruria does not associate it solely with the aristocracy.[116] Nevertheless, it is worth considering whether the Romans were interested in Aegean wines. During the time of the arrival of the Greeks and their ideology in Italy, Etruria was composed of big agglomerations, which had developed in the previous century. At the same time, there were many small settlements in Latium that had recently been reoccupied and were situated close to one another. The lack of fortifications around the Etruscan centres, contrary to the settlements in Latium that were fortified from the beginning, suggests that the situation south of the Tiber might have been less stable and society might have been less developed. According to G. Bartoloni, archaic Latium was still a lineage community, whereas in Etruria a social hierarchy had been developed.[117] This might have had an impact on the diffusion of Greek influence between the two areas.

Notwithstanding the above-mentioned differences in the development of the Romans and the Etruscans, the cultural framework in Latium started to change from the end of the 8th c. BC and funerary equipment from this region began to resemble Etruscan grave offerings, which indicates that there was a social and cultural change similar to that in Etruria.[118] Greek vessels associated with the consumption of wine, such as *krateroi, kylikes, oinochoai* and *skyphoi*, which can be dated to the late 8th and the 7th c. BC have been found in both funerary and residential contexts in Latium;[119] although until 650 BC they are

113 Bartoloni 1987, 46–47.
114 Rizzo 1990, 27–28.
115 Cianferoni 2012, 31.
116 Kreindler 2015.
117 Bartoloni 1987, 37–38, 47.
118 Bartoloni 1987, 48. For discoveries of sympotic pottery in Etruscan graves see Bartoloni, Acconcia, Kortenaar 2012.
119 La Rocca 1977, 375–389.

considerably less numerous than in Etruria and Campania.[120] Moreover, banquet tableware was also attested in archaic residences. It is worth noting that the famous set of banqueting dishes, decorated using the red impasto technique and dated to the second half of the 7th and the beginning of the 6th c. BC, was discovered in Ficana. The set consisted of four *holmoi* and around forty vessels that were used for pouring, mixing and drinking wine.[121] The presence of Greek vessels in archaic Roman tombs may suggest that Greek wines were consumed during this period and that the elites of Latium, similarly to their neighbours from Etruria, adopted certain aspects of the Greek symposion. Alternatively, they may be seen as elements of aristocratic gift-giving or signs of prestige, without having anything to do with the beverage.[122] However, the banqueting service from Ficana, composed mostly of local vessels, confirms the existence of aristocratic banquets in Latium, a practice very similar to Homeric banquets.[123] Therefore, the theory that suggests that Greek vessels did indeed have sympotic purposes, instead of simply being objects of prestige, seems justified. Furthermore, a passage from Pliny's *Natural History* and archaeological evidence from the graves on Forum, which have already been mentioned in this chapter, suggest that the Romans might have started to cultivate *vitis* in a Greek way during the times of Numa.[124] The construction of the *Regia* is also attributed to Numa by Roman literary tradition. This place resembles the Etruscan palace in Murlo, where the famous banquet scene was depicted. Also, the Romans were convinced that Numa was under the particular protection of the Nymph Egeria, who, among other things, miraculously refurnished his house to make it suitable for a banquet. If, as Zaccaria Ruggiu suggests, the *Regia* was indeed a place for Roman archaic banquets,[125] the presence of the symposion in Latium, at least from the end of the 8th c. BC leaves little doubt. Is it therefore possible that Greek sympotic vessels were just prestige objects that were ritually deposited in the graves, with no other function? If not, is it possible that the Romans used Greek vessels for the drinking of Phoenician or Etruscan wines only? Although it seems impossible to give a definitive answer to the question of whether the Romans consumed Eastern

120 Beijer 1995, 57–62.

121 Zaccaria Ruggiu 2003, 254–255.

122 Ruby 1993, 823.

123 Zaccaria Ruggiu 2003, 255–256.

124 This means with the use of pruning. However, it was still *vitis alberata*, of suggested Etruscan origin, and not a low-trained vine. For more on this subject see Sereni 1964, 128–131.

125 Zaccaria Ruggiu 2003, 230–231. Another supposed banquet room that probably served for a Homeric banquet in the Archaic Period (the end of the 7th or the beginning of the 6th c. BC) was attested in *Casa sulla Sacra Via*, see Zaccaria Ruggiu 2003, 248.

wines in the Archaic period, the available data does not permit one to exclude such a possibility. First of all, Aegean amphoras, even though extremely scarce, are present in Latium. Secondly, Greek vessels that were used for wine drinking are attested in Roman tombs dated to the Archaic period. Thirdly, architecture and pottery suggest that banqueting was not unknown to the Roman aristocracy. Finally, literary evidence suggests that there were Greek technological influences on Roman viticulture, which is confirmed by the DNA analysis.[126]

To sum up, the Etruscans certainly drank Eastern Mediterranean wines during the Archaic age and the same is possible for the Romans. However, evidence for Roman consumption of Eastern wines is vague and not conclusive.

4 The Economic Transformation of Italy during the 5th and 4th c. BC

There are very few fragments of eastern amphoras found in Italy dated to the early Republic. They include two fragments of Corinthian A and four of Corinthian B containers from the 6th or 5th c. BC, as well as one fragment each of Samian and Mendean amphoras dated to the 5th c. BC. Fragments of 'Chian' vessels dated between the 5th and the 4th c. BC most probably belong to the so-called 'Pseudo-Chian', which were in fact produced in south Italy and Sicily and classified later as MGS II by Vandermersch.[127] A number of fragments, discovered in the Temple of Castor and Pollux in the *Forum Romanum*, and consisting of four fragments of SOS (600–500 BC), one fragment of Corinthian A, A′ and B (600–300 BC), three fragments of Samian (550–490 BC) and one fragment from Mende (500–400 BC), might have also been used in Italy during the Republican age.[128] This rarity of Aegean wine imports during the 4th and 3rd c. BC may reflect that the importations of Eastern wines did not continue after the Archaic age and stopped sometime during the 5th c. BC. However, the scarcity of evidence may also be due to other reasons. First of all, we should keep in mind that most of the amphoras from the Archaic period were found in funerary contexts. However, the practice of depositing pottery and other items as funerary offerings was abandoned during the second half of the 6th and throughout the 5th c. BC. At the same time, amphoras discovered in residential areas are often fragmentary, which makes their identification more

126 See part 2 of this chapter.
127 Di Sandro 1981, 5–11; Vandermersch 1994, 67; Sourisseau 2011, 192.
128 Slej 2008, 204–208. The so-called 'Pseudo-Chian' or '*Ionico-Massaliotic*' and *Massaliotic* amphoras were also attested.

difficult.[129] On the other hand, there are very few material remains from Rome that can be dated to the 5th c. BC besides imported Attic pottery, whose numbers declined abruptly after 500 BC and almost disappeared around 450 BC. It should be noted that this decline is considerably sharper in Rome than in the case of the Etruscan cities, where a similar trend can be observed.[130] Furthermore, archaeological evidence for banqueting practices in the form of architectonic decorations depicting feasts also disappeared around the end of the 6th c. BC. In addition, there were no banqueting spaces in Roman houses (or other buildings) that are dated between this period and the 2nd c. BC. This may be seen as a result of social and political changes associated with the end of the monarchy and the beginning of the Republic. The organisation based upon *sodales*, in which fellow members of a fraternity gathered around the prince, changed into the aristocratic *isonomia* and reciprocal relations between client and patron, which in turn left no space for sympotic practices.[131]

Eastern Mediterranean wines, however, contrary to what was often postulated by earlier scholars,[132] were not associated exclusively with aristocratic banqueting;[133] thus, social transformation cannot have been the only factor that influenced their consumption in Italy. It seems that with the development of Italian wine production, especially in Etruria and Magna Graecia, foreign imports were no longer necessary, and appeared only occasionally. Therefore, the arrival of Eastern wines to Italy during the Archaic age, together with new viticultural varieties and technologies, spurred the development in local wine production and exportation, which soon eclipsed importations from the East.

4.1 *Etruscan Wine Production and Export*

The development of wine production in Etruria, which was intended not only for local consumption but also as an export product, had already begun at the end of the 8th c. BC when amphoras started to be produced in this region. They had Phoenician shapes, but petrographic analyses suggest that apart from Carthage, Sardinia, and Pithecussai, they were also produced in Etruria. An 8th c. BC container discovered in Vulci is among the earliest examples.[134] We know very little about the production of Phoenician-type containers in Etruria, but

129 Sacchetti 2013, 11.
130 Cornell 1986, 67–68.
131 Zaccaria Ruggiu 2003, 382–382.
132 Starting with Pallottino 1968.
133 As demonstrated by Kreindler 2015.
134 Delpino 2007, 136–137, after Pettaco 2003, 46.

it probably existed on a small scale. Moreover, it is not clear whether they were Etruscan imitations of western Punic vessels, or products that were manufactured in Punic workshops located in Etruria.[135]

Original Etruscan amphora production started around 630 BC and lasted until the 4th c. BC.[136] The Etruscan manufacturers were inspired by the Phoenicians and thus they produced similar shaped containers.[137] Two typologies of transport jars produced in Etruria have been proposed. The first was elaborated in 1974 by F. and M. Py, who based their studies mostly on vessels that had been found in southern Gaul.[138] Nine years later, in 1983, M. Slaska and M. Gras established another typology thanks to analyses of containers discovered in southern Etruria.[139] Etruscan amphoras may in general be divided into two main categories: flat-bottomed and pointed-bottomed jars produced in Vulci and in Caere respectively.[140] However, clay analysis indicates that the production of transport containers, especially of the pointed-bottom type, also took place in other centres,[141] albeit on a smaller scale. Among these centres Tarquinia, Sant'Antonio in the Albenga Valley and Doganella are worth mentioning, the latter being the only site where amphora kilns have been attested.[142] The so-called 'Tollan' amphoras (discovered in the necropolis of Tolli, where they served as urns for ashes) should also be included in the spectrum of Etruscan transport containers. Their exact place of production is still unknown, but their distribution has been confirmed in the territory of ancient Chiusi.[143]

It is almost certain that Etruscan amphoras served for the transport and storage of wine. The analysis of the contents of flat-bottomed jars discovered in Magliano-Poggio Bacchino, Firenze, and in Populonia-Cala del Piccione that was carried out by the *Instituto del C.N.R. per le Tecnologie applicate ai Beni Culturali* produced negative results for cereals and oils, but they did show the presence of tannins.[144] Tollan jars often contained traces of pitch,[145] which also indicates wine as a content, but it should be noted that an Etruscan amphora

135 Gras 1985, 327. About the possible influences between various amphora types see Pettaco 2003.
136 Perkins 2012, 414–415; Bats 2012, 377.
137 Gras 1985, 290.
138 Py and Py 1974, 141–254; Py 1985.
139 Gras 1985, 333; Bats 2012, 377.
140 Bats 2012, 377.
141 These analyses were made by Sourisseau 1997; Bats 2012, 377.
142 Bruni 2005; Perkins 2012, 419–420; Perkins, Walker 1990, 41–45, 53–54, 121, fig. 20.
143 Paolucci 2006, 420.
144 Nardi, Pandolfini 1985, 61–62.
145 Paolucci 2006, 420.

found in an archaic wreck in Isola del Giglio was full of olive pips.[146] Nevertheless, non-amphora evidence for winemaking in Etruria is abundant. For example, the intensive vine cultivation that occurred it the territory of modern Tuscany dates back to the 6th c. BC. Archaeological research in Valle d'Albenga has recently brought to light evidence for the existence of Etruscan vineyards (which most probably adopted the low-training technique) in Magliano in Toscana (Grosetto), with some being attested in the areas of ancient cemeteries. The grave discoveries suggest the end of the 6th and the beginning of the 5th c. BC as the *terminus post quem* for the vineyards.[147] Furthermore, during excavations at Podere Tartuchino in the upper Albenga Valley, around 40 km north-west from Vulci, remnants interpreted as a wine press were discovered. They consisted of a large *pithos* set into the floor that probably had a pine resin interior coating (chemical analysis identified traces of lipids deriving from pine resin), two stone footings, and a wooden post. Other fragments of large ceramic jars together with another complete *pithos* have been attested in another supposed wine pressing room at the site. The association of *pithoi* with wine is suggested by their resin coating, as well as the fact that they are similar to Middle Minoan vessels from Knossos that bore the graffito 'wine'. Large ceramic *pithoi* were attested in various farms in the Albenga Valley, which suggests the existence of other places of wine production in this region. The supposed wine press from Podere Tartuchino was dated between the second half of the 6th c. BC and the 5th c. BC, which makes it the earliest evidence for the pressing of grapes in Italy. Similar simple arrangements for the pressing of grapes are represented on Attic black-figure pottery dated to the 6th c. BC.[148]

According to Gras, the distribution of Etruscan amphoras suggests that the flat-bottomed jars were designed to store and transport wine locally between short distances, whilst pointed-bottomed vessels were designed to serve as containers for maritime transport, for example to southern Gaul.[149] The exportation of Etruscan wines to Latium, Campania, Sardinia, Corsica, Sicily, Liguria and maybe also to Carthage, occurred simultaneously with their production.[150] In Sicily they were attested in contexts dated between the late 7th and mid-6th c. BC in all the important Greek settlements, including Camarina, Megara Hyblaea, Lipari, Messina, Milazzo, Naxos, Himera and Selinunte. However, they were quite scarce and were far outnumbered by Greek containers. In Punic

146 Bound 1985, 67.
147 Marianelli, Rendini 2012, 403–407, 409, 411.
148 Perkins, Attolini 1992, 108–111, 120–122; Perkins 2012, 417–419.
149 Gras 1985, 333, 336.
150 For the distribution of Etruscan amphoras see: Cibecchini 2006; Cianferoni 2012, 31.

centres, such as Motya or Palermo, Etruscan amphora imports are rare.[151] They have been attested in small quantities in Sardinia and North Africa, but in these regions wine amphoras and tableware were not very popular, in comparison with perfume oils, which were particularly common in Carthage.[152]

A considerable number of Etruscan amphoras, dated from the end of the 7th c. BC and through the 6th c. BC, have been attested west of the Apennine Peninsula for example in ancient shipwrecks in the area of the Gulf of Lion (Antibes, Ecueil de Miet 3, Bon-Porté 1, Grand Ribaud F), as well as at numerous settlements (e.g. Empúries, Pech Maho, Montlaurès, Agde, Bessan, Lattes, Tonnerre I, La Liquière, Saint Blaisse, Marseilles etc.).[153] Gaul was the main, but not the only western destination for Etruscan wine. It was also exported to Spain, which is confirmed by the findings of Etruscan amphoras dated between the end of the 7th and the beginning of the 5th c. BC in Emporion[154] and other sites in Catalonia,[155] in Huelva, Cerro del Villar, Malaga, Villaricos, Fonteta and Cabanyal-Malvarossa.[156] It is possible that the foundation of Emporion around 575 BC was associated with Etruscan wine exportations.[157] However, it should be noted that the number of Etruscan amphoras in Spain is considerably lower than in Gaul.[158]

As suggested by the amphora distribution, Etruscan wine production was developed enough not only to satisfy the local Italian demand, but also to supply foreign 'markets'. The Etruscans started to export wine after being influenced by the Phoenicians and Greeks, and for more than a century there were eastern and western wine trades that existed simultaneously. It seems, however, that demand for Etruscan wine decreased when the inhabitants of southern Gaul started to produce their own wine. For example, Massalia was among the main consumption centres of Etruscan wines during the 6th c. BC,[159] but when this Greek colony started its own viticultural activity, percentages of Etruscan amphoras attested in the south of Gaul decreased.[160] The limited export of Etruscan wines continued throughout the 5th c. BC and eventually ceased in

151 Albanese Procelli 2017, 1657–1661.
152 Dietler 2010, 194.
153 For more details see: Bats 2012, 378–384; Duval 2006; Dedet, Py 2006, 123–126.
154 Santmartí i Grego et al. 1991, 84–85; Aquilé et al. 2006, 181–185.
155 Sanmartí, Asensio, Martín 2006, 196.
156 Colonna 2006, 12–13; Botto, Vives-Ferrándiz 2006, 122, 125, 128–129, 140–141, 181, 182, 190, fig. 15, 21, 25, 45.
157 Bats 2012, 386.
158 Sanmartí, Asensio, Martín 2006, 193–196; Morel 1981, 472.
159 Bats 2012, 385.
160 Py 1985, 84–85.

the first half of the 4th c. BC.[161] Similarly, wines from the Aegean, which were present in Marseille during the first half of the 6th c. BC, began to disappear gradually after 540/530 BC, being replaced with Marsilian varieties.[162] It seems that during the 5th c. BC, trade between Marseille and its neighbouring settlements replaced trade between Marseille and Etruria,[163] as well as between Marseille and the Eastern Mediterranean. A similar pattern may be observed in Spain: during the 7th and 6th c. BC Etruscan amphoras were very frequent, but their numbers started to decrease gradually during the late 6th c. BC and continued to diminish throughout the 5th c. BC, which correlates with the increase in *Massaliote* amphoras.[164] Does this mean that wine production in Marseille ousted Etruscan wine? Bats associated it with the reorganisation of trade in the Tyrrhenian after the battle of Alalia in 535 BC.[165] Dietler, however, argues that Etruscan amphoras started to disappear from Gaul before the indigenous production of wine flourished, and suggests that the end of Etruscan exportation should rather be associated with political instability in Etruria during the 6th c. BC, or with the actions of pirates from Liguria, who forced trade routes to be realigned.[166] Nevertheless, the situation in Gaul and Spain regarding Etruscan and Marsilian wine is similar to the situation in Italy with Aegean and Etruscan wines, that is, when local production was increased, the number of imports decreased. As long as the Etruscans were sending their wines to Gaul and Spain, Aegean importations were welcomed in Italy. However, during the 5th c. BC Gaul and Spain turned towards Massalia, leaving more Etruscan wine available on the Apennine Peninsula. Moreover, from the end of the 5th c. BC a new competitor for Eastern wines appeared—south-Italian wines transported in the so-called Greco-Italic amphoras.

4.2 *Domination of South-Italian Wines and Greco-Italic Amphoras*

It has previously been mentioned that wine was most probably known in Italy before the era of Greek colonisation, not only in Etruria, but also in Magna Graecia and Sicily. The *Odyssey* mentions the 'wine of Cyclopes' from this territory,[167] which according to Vandermersch was probably a locally produced alcohol beverage made from wild grapes.[168] Greek writers poetically called

161 Bats 2012, 383–384.
162 Bats 1998, 619–620.
163 Dietler 2010, 7.
164 Santmartí i Grego et al. 1991, 86–87; Bats 1998, 622–623.
165 Bats 1998, 626–628.
166 Dietler 2010, 197.
167 *Od.* IX 110, 357–358.
168 Vandermersch 1994, 25.

parts of Lucania and Bruttium Οἰνωτρία,[169] which may be translated as 'the land of the vine pole', which suggests that viticulture was common in this area. According to Vandermersch, the turning point in viticulture and wine-making in south Italy and Sicily was associated with the beginnings of Greek settlement and the diffusion of Aegean vines such as *Aminaios* and *Byblinos*. From the 6th c. BC Sybaris produced amphoras similar to Attic SOS containers, while vineries in Naxos and Sybaris were already comparable to Aegean examples.[170] The end of Etruscan amphora production during the 4th c. BC, along with the development of the so-called Greco-Italic containers may be seen as an important moment regarding the history of wine in Magna Graecia and Sicily. The earliest examples of Greco-Italic containers, the so-called MGS III, come from Bruttium and Lucania and date to the end of the 5th c. BC. Their production continued throughout the next hundred years, when other types appeared. Before the mid-3rd c. BC Greco-Italic containers were made in Etruria and Campania, while shortly after the mid-3rd c. BC they were produced in Latium and along the central Adriatic coast, which meant that throughout the 3rd and 2nd c. BC they dominated amphora production on the Apennine Peninsula.[171]

Vandermersch distinguished six types of Greco-Italic containers:

- MGS I—produced between 450–350 BC most probably around Thouroi and Metapontum.
- MGS II—manufactured within a triangular area between Naples, Heraclea, Lucania and Agrigentum.
- MGS III—produced from the end of the 5th c. BC to c. 250 BC and found especially in Bruttium, Lucania and NE Sicily, though the exact production place remains unknown.
- MGS IV—made between 400 and c. 280 BC in an area surrounded by Poseidonia-Tarentum-Agrigentum and distributed mainly in eastern Sicily, the Aeolian Islands, Bruttium, Tyrrhenian Lucania and south Campania.
- MGS V—produced in Campania from around the mid-4th c. BC until the First Punic War, especially in the Gulf of Naples, around Tarentum, and in central and eastern Sicily.
- MGS VI—their production in Sicily, Magna Graecia and Campania began a couple of decades before the Second Punic War.[172]

169 Antiochos *FGrHist* III 555.

170 Vandermersch 1994, 26.

171 Lyding-Will 1982, 340; Vandermersch 1994, 70–72; Paczyńska 2002; 2003; Cipriano, Mazzocchin 2017, 40, fig. 1.

172 Vandermersch 1994, 59–92.

Ancient literature also provides evidence for wine production in Magna Graecia and Sicily starting from the 5th c. BC. The comic poet Platon (5th/4th c. BC) mentioned *Kapnias* wine, the best of which was made in Beneventum in Campania.[173] Its fame was so great at that time that it reached Athens. According to Hippys of Rhegion (5th c. BC?), Biblian wine was introduced to Sicily by Pollis of Argos,[174] while Policlet of Larissa (4th c. BC) mentions the existence of a large winery at the House of Tellias in Agrigentum. This is confirmed by Diodorus of Sicily's statement that the area was favourable for vine cultivation, as well as by his description of wine-making utensils at the house of Tellias from the 5th c. BC.[175] Timaeus of Tauromenium (4th/3rd c. BC) might have been the source for Strabo's description of both Thurian wine and the sweet, wholesome wine from Lagaria, which could be further confirmation that wine was produced in south Italy at that time.[176] Finally, Leonidas of Tarentum mentions the existence of viticulture and winemaking around the city during the first half of the 3rd c. BC.[177] When Cato wrote his famous *De agricultura*, Sicilian and south Italian wines, such as *Murgentinum, Eugeneum, Aminnium* and *Lucanum* were famous and popular in Italy,[178] and from this time on they were often mentioned in Greek and Latin writings.[179]

Furthermore, epigraphy provides us with information regarding vine cultivation around both Heraclea and Morgantina (or Kamarina) during the late 4th and early 3rd c. BC;[180] wine presses were also found in Morgantina.[181] Hellenistic amphora stamps mention *Mamertinos* and Νάξιος, but one should remember that the area of Naxos was already an important centre of viticulture during the 6th and 5th c. BC.[182] Wine-making utensils, such as *pithoi* and presses dated to the 4th c. BC were found in a few Sicilian settlements, for example in Contrada Priorato and Montegiordano,[183] which suggests that during this period winemaking was a very common activity. Archaeobotany provides evidence for

173 Ath. *Deipn.* 31e.
174 Ath. *Deipn.* 31b.
175 Diod. XI 25, 5; XIII 83, 3.
176 Strab. VI 1, 14; Vandermersch 1994, 29.
177 Anth. VI 44; VI 300; VII 731.
178 *De agr.* 6, 4.
179 Vandermersch 1994, 29–30.
180 IG XIV 645 I 114; 123; 146–148; 169–170; II 40; 43–45; 54; 60; 68; 77; 83; 87; 90; 94; 96; 101; 103; 109.
181 Manganaro 1989, 193, 203–205, 215.
182 Vandermersch 1994, 34.
183 Vandermersch 1994, 99–100.

vine cultivation in Basilicata between the Archaic age and the mid-4th c. BC,[184] which also occurred in Sicily (Roccagloriosa) during the 4th and 3rd c. BC.[185]

This evidence should leave no doubt that Sicily and south Italy enjoyed a developed, large scale wine industry. The wine was not only consumed locally, but was also transported to different parts of Italy as suggested by MGS amphora findings, which also confirm that it was exported overseas to north Africa, Catalonia, the Balearic Islands, south Gaul, the Aegean region and the Eastern Mediterranean.[186] If Etruria and Magna Graecia produced wine on a large scale, one would also expect to find evidence confirming winemaking in Latium. However, in this case the sources appear to be slightly disappointing.

4.3 *Roman Wine Production during the Early Republic?*

Literary tradition suggests that wine production in Latium was already quite developed during (or even earlier than) the 5th c. BC. Dionysius of Halicarnassus (1st c. BC) mentioned the presence of vineyards in Latium during the reign of Tarquinius Priscus (616–579 BC)[187] and claimed that the Gauls who had plundered the Alban district had got drunk by drinking unmixed wine.[188] Similar information regarding the Gauls, as well as the Sabines who attacked Rome at the end of the 5th c. BC, is provided by Livy,[189] according to whom they ate so much food and drank so much wine that many of them were unable to run away from the Romans. Vandermersch sees these testimonies as evidence that wine production started quite early in Latium,[190] but other scholars regard them with scepticism, arguing that production of the renowned Alban wine was established during the 2nd c. BC, not earlier.[191]

It is possible, of course, that Livy and Dionysius of Halicarnassus might have attributed certain elements from their own reality to previous times, but there is also Sopator[192] and the comic poet Platon,[193] who provide us with first-hand information regarding wine (*kapneios* and Tyrrhenian) during the 4th c. BC in areas which were to become Roman during the subsequent century. Given that

184 Costantini, Costantini Biasini 2012, 137.
185 Vandermersch 1994, 37.
186 Vandermersch 1994, 123–147.
187 D.H. III 70.
188 D.H. XIV 8 (12).
189 Livy II 26, 3; V 44, 5–6.
190 Vandermersch 2001, 160.
191 Tchernia 1986, 57; Purcell 1985, 16.
192 Ath. *Deipn.* 702b.
193 Ath. *Deipn.* 31e.

there is evidence suggesting wine production in Etruria and Latium during the Archaic age,[194] we should agree that the hypothesis regarding early wine production cannot be simply rejected. There should be little doubt that vineyards in the Falernian district were developed, and that wine was already being made around Capua during the First Punic War, as suggested by Livy.[195] Archaeology confirms the early presence of vineyards in Latium, with examples dating from the 6th/5th c. BC until the late Republican age, the earliest of which were situated in the *ager Ficulensis*. Vineyards dated before the mid-3rd c. BC were attested in Tor Pagnotta, while those in Castellucio probably date to the 4th–3rd c. BC.[196] At the same time, intensified agricultural activity in areas suitable for viticulture is suggested by the settlement pattern in different areas of Latium and Campania. Also, the so-called proto-villas might have already existed during the 3rd c. BC, for example in Tor Bella Monaca. Additionally, inland settlements such as Pesco Morello in Cercemaggiore had facilities that were already being used for wine production during the 4th c. BC. In most of these areas viticulture and winemaking were also confirmed during the Roman age.[197]

Although no amphora workshops dated to the 4th or 3rd c. BC have so far been discovered in Latium, containers similar to the Greco-Italic forms MGS III and V are often found together with locally produced pottery. Moreover, during the late 4th and 3rd c. BC the manufacture of MGS II–V between Capua and the Gulf of Naples is confirmed. Vandermersch argues that these transport containers, which he classifies as Roman mid-Republican amphoras (RMR), provide evidence for developed wine production in Latium and Campania during the 4th c. BC. It is worth mentioning that starting from the second half of the 3rd c. BC stamps using the Latin alphabet and Latin names appear on these containers. RMR amphoras have also been found in Sicily, north Africa and in southern Gaul, which suggests that wine was exported from Latium.[198]

To further confirm the presence of early Roman winemaking, it would be ideal to find the remains of wine pressing facilities. Although *palmenti*, the primitive wine pressing vats, appeared in Sicily and Magna Graecia during the Hellenistic age, they were unknown in Latium and Campania until the late Republic.[199] However, it cannot be excluded that the earliest forms of wine pressing in Latium took place in wooden or other perishable containers, rather

194 Vandermersch 2001, 165–166 and above in this chapter.
195 Livy XXII 13–15; XXIII 18, 11–12.
196 Calci, Sorella 1995; Vandermersch 2001, 166–167.
197 Vandermersch 2001, 166–168.
198 Vandermersch 2001, 170–175, and fig. 1.
199 Masi 2012, 587.

than in rock-curved basins, thus the lack of *palmenti* does not necessarily exclude 3rd or even 4th c. BC wine production.

To sum up, there is plenty of evidence to suggest that wine was produced by the Etruscans and the western Greeks from the 5th c. BC onwards. Moreover, simultaneous Roman wine production seems plausible. This would explain why eastern Greek wine importations became less frequent, or even disappeared completely during this period, as they were not required when local, Italian wines blossomed. Wine production in Italy then intensified during the period of Roman domination, which coincided with the 'new age' of Eastern wine importations, which started around the end of the 3rd and the beginning of the 2nd c. BC. The earliest wine amphora stamps from the East discovered in Etruria, Latium and Campania were dated to the end of the 3rd c. BC.[200] Moreover, there is literary evidence in the form of Plautus' comedies, dated to the turn of the 3rd and the beginning of the 2nd c. BC, that mentions the consumption of Aegean wines in Rome.[201] From this time on, sources confirming the drinking of wines from the Eastern Mediterranean in Italy are abundant.

5 Eastern Wines in Italy: Types and Chronology

One may ask what types of Eastern Mediterranean wines were imported to Italy, as well as whether there was any difference in their chronological distribution. Combining the literary, archaeological and epigraphic evidence will be helpful in this matter. The first step is to identify the regions of the Eastern Mediterranean that exported wines to Italy.

5.1 *Types of Eastern Mediterranean Wines in Italy*

Latin authors talk frequently about wines from Chios, Lesbos, Thasos, Rhodes, Cos and Crete. Moreover, they mention: Lefkadian,[202] Ephesian, Cnidian, Mysian, Myconian, Mesogitic,[203] Tmolian[204] (from the area of Mount Mesogis and

200 Taylor 1957, 134; Laforgia 1980–1981, 217; Bevilacqua 1994, 463; Tilloca 2001, 245–247; American School of Classical Studies at Athens, Archives in the Blegen Library, Virginia R. Grace Papers.

201 Pl. *Curc.* 78; *Poen.* 699; *Rud.* 588.

202 Pl. *Poen.* 699; Plin. *HN* XIV 76.

203 Plin. *HN* XIV 74–76; Strab. XIV 1, 15.

204 Plin. *HN* XIV 74; Vitr. VIII 3, 12; Ov. *Fast.* II 313; Strab. XIV 1, 15.

Mount Tmolus in Lydia), Catacecaumenitan (from Maeonia),[205] Maroneian,[206] Ismarian[207] from Thrace, and Pramnian from the area of Smyrna,[208] as well as those from Sicyon, Cyprus, Hippodamas, Mystus, Peparethos (modern Skopelus), Telmesus (Asia Minor), Petra, Apamea,[209] Beirut, Tyre, Tripoli, Sebennys (Egypt), Euboea (*Oreticum*),[210] Sarepta,[211] Arcadia, Achaia,[212] and finally the Black Sea area (Naspercene).[213] Greek sources inform us that wine was also produced in Corinth, Mende, Amphipolis, Akanthos (the area of Mount Athos),[214] Phlius,[215] Laconia,[216] Oisyme (Thracia),[217] Asia (Aegeate and Perperine),[218] Egypt (including Taeniotic wine and wine from Lake Mareotis, Tebaid, the Arsinoite Nome in the Faiyum and Antylla near Alexandria),[219] Syria (Chalybon),[220] Libya (Pedonia)[221] and finally, to complete the list, the Greek sources refer to wines from Euboea,[222] Samos,[223] Corcyra, Zakynthos, Myndos, Halicarnassus,[224] Naxos and Skiathos.[225] Moreover, they mention Psithian, Pramnian and Bibline wine,[226] but these names probably refer to the variety of grapes from which the beverage was made.[227]

However, not all these wines were imported to Italy. Some of them were simply mentioned once by Latin authors, such as Pliny, which cannot be used as evidence for their importations, as it only shows that the Romans knew that

205 Vitr. VIII 3, 12; Plin. *HN* XIV 75; Strab. XIV 1, 15.
206 Plin. *HN* XIV 53; Tib. IV 1, 57.
207 Prop. II 33, 31–32; Verg. *Georg.* II 37–38.
208 Plin. *HN* XIV 54.
209 According to Dalby 2003, 54, Pliny meant Apamea Myrlea in Bithynia, not the Syrian city.
210 Plin. *HN* XIV 74–76.
211 Venantius Fortunatus, *Vita S. Martini* II 80–82; MGH *Auct. Antiquiss.* VIII, 242.
212 Plin. *HN* XIV 116–117.
213 Plin. *HN* XIV 76.
214 Ath. *Deipn.* 30e–f; Salviat 2013a, 72–79, 89.
215 Ath. *Deipn.* 27d.
216 Ath. *Deipn.* 31d.
217 Ath. *Deipn.* 31b.
218 Gal. *San.Tue.* 6.337K; *Bon.Mal.Suc.* 6.800–801K; *MM.* 10.833–834K.
219 Strab XVII 1, 14; 1, 35; Ath. *Deipn.* 33d–f.
220 Ath. *Deipn.* 28d.
221 Strab XVII 1.14.
222 Ath. *Deipn.* 30f.
223 Strab. XIV 1, 15.
224 Ath. *Deipn.* 33b.
225 Strattis, fr. 64 K.-A.; Eupolis fr. 271 K.-A. = Ath. *Deipn.* 30f, 52d; García Soler 2002, 58–59.
226 Ath. *Deipn.* 28f, 30b, 31a.
227 For example, Bibline wine was made from the vine variety called Biblinos, that was probably of Phoenician origin, see Salviat 2013a, 81–82.

these wines existed. For example, Maroneian and Pramnian wines that were celebrated in the Homeric Age, were, according to Pliny, still produced in the 1st c. AD. Nevertheless, it seems that they were not imported to Italy, because while looking for information about wine from Maroneia, Pliny had to rely on the testimony of the consul Mucianus, who visited this region and tried the wine.[228] Other beverages, such as Corinthian, Corcyrean, Mendean and Peparethian, were imported to Italy during the Archaic and Classical period, which is indicated by the discoveries of amphoras from these areas in Etruria. However, it seems that they were no longer imported in the Hellenistic and Roman age.

Literary evidence indicates that the Romans were familiar with wines from Chios, Lesbos, Thasos, Crete, Cos, Rhodes, Lefkada, Mt. Tmolus and Clazomenae. At the same time, amphora findings confirm that wines from Chios, Cos, Rhodes, Crete, Sicyon and Cnidus were imported to Italy.[229] The discoveries of container types Agora F65–66, and their later variant called LRA3, suggest that wines from Asia Minor (e.g. Ephesian, Tmolian or Clazomenian) were also drunk by the Romans. However, we cannot be certain what product these amphoras actually transported, moreover, it cannot be excluded that all Asian wines were transported in the same type of container.

Furthermore, Kapitän 1 and 2 amphoras are also attested in Italy, but their origin is so far unknown. They were probably used to transport Anatolian or Aegean wines, but wines from the Black Sea region cannot be excluded. Amphora findings from the Roman Imperial and late Roman period confirm importations of wines from Cyprus (Agora G199/Schoene-Mau XXVII–XXVIII), Cilicia (Agora G198/Schoene-Mau XIII, Agora M54, Schoene-Mau V and Agora G199/Schoene-Mau XXVII–XXVIII), Egypt (AE3, LRA7), the Levant (Kingsholm 117, LRA1, LRA4, LRA5–6) and the southern coastal regions of the Black Sea (SI type from Heracleia Pontica and SIII type from Sinope, Zeest 94?). To sum up, we may say that the Romans imported wines from the Aegean (Thasian, Lesbian, Coan, Cnidian, Rhodian, Cretan, Chian, Sicyonian), Lefkada, western Asia Minor (Tmolian and most likely Clazomenian and Ephesian), Cyprus, Cilicia, Syria, Egypt and the southern coasts of the Black Sea. It is notable that there is no evidence for wine imports from eastern Anatolia, Libya or the northern Black Sea region. Moreover, during the Imperial age, importations of wines from the Ionian islands and the Peloponnese are not confirmed in the archaeological material. However, it is difficult to ascertain whether this lack of evi-

228 Plin. *HN* XIV 53–54.
229 Albiach et al. 2008, 261.

dence does indeed signify a lack of importations, especially when one considers that a lot more research is required regarding the exact origin and content of containers from the Black Sea area.

5.2 *Chronology of the Consumption of Eastern Mediterranean Wines in Italy*

The next issue that should be addressed regards the start and longevity of eastern wine consumption by the Italians. It has already been mentioned that the earliest indubitable evidence for the drinking of Aegean wines by the Romans comes from the middle Republican period. The comedies of Plautus dated to the turn of the 3rd and the 2nd c. BC confirm the consumption of wines from Chios, Lesbos, Thasos and Lefkada,[230] as well as others that were mixed with seawater.[231] In the 2nd c. BC Cato the Elder provided recipes for making Greek wines, Coan in particular, whilst Varro stated that during the 1st c. BC the Romans imported wines from Chios and Cos.[232] Moreover, in *De Lingua Latina* Varro uses the words "… *alii generis enim vinum quod Chio, aliud quod Lesbo* …",[233] while explaining the intricacies of *pluralis* in Latin. This means that his readers must have been familiar with the taste of these wines, otherwise the example would be pointless. Therefore, we may assume that Lesbian wine was also imported during this period. The consumption of Chian and Lesbian wine is confirmed by various 1st c. BC Latin poets. Ariusian wine, that was produced in the north-western part of Chios, appears in Vergil's *Eclogues*[234] and in *Elegiae* by Tibullus.[235] Wine from this island is also often mentioned by Horace,[236] once in company with wine from Lesbos.[237] In addition, the Lesbian variety called *Protropos* appears in Vitruvius' *De architectura*, together with Tmolian and Catacecaumenitan wines.[238] Furthermore, Vergil in his *Georgics* enumerates various eastern vines, such as Thasian, Lesbian, Tmolian, Rhodian and Psinthian,[239] while Albius Tibullus refers to vine/wine from Maroneia.[240] This could be further confirmation that wines made from these varieties were known in Italy.

230 Pl. *Poen.* 699–700; *Curc.* 78–79.
231 Pl. *Rud.* 588–590.
232 *Rust.* II preface.
233 *Ling.* IX 40.
234 *Ecl.* 5, 71.
235 Tib. II 1.
236 *Carm.* III 19, 5; *Serm.* I 10; II 3; II 8.
237 *Epod.* 9.
238 Vitr. VIII 3, 12.
239 *Georg.* II 94–100.
240 Tib. IV 1, 57 (III 7).

The works of Columella (dated to the 1st c. AD) do not focus upon particular types of wines, but they do provide us with a general recipe for making Greek wines,[241] as well as confirming that Rome imported beverages from this area.[242] Other 1st c. authors are more precise. Martial devoted one of his *Epigrams* to wine from Crete,[243] whereas Scribonius Largus, a court physician of the emperor Claudius, often used Chian when composing his medicines. In one case he recommended drinking Chian and Lesbian.[244] Finally, there is Pliny the Elder, whose 14th book of his *Natural History* is a mine of information about ancient wines. One chapter of this book is devoted to the classification of *vina transmarina*. At the beginning he mentions Chian, Lesbian and Thasian, which are also described in the part that presents Italian and foreign *crus*.[245] According to this author, Erasistratus, a physician, added Lesbian to the same group as Thasian and Chian about four hundred and fifty years after the foundation of Rome, which means around the 3rd c. BC. If we consider that at the end of this century these wines appear in Plautus' comedies, it seems possible that the Romans started to drink them not long after the establishment of the hierarchy of *crus* in the Greek world. We learn from Pliny that *vina transmarina* were still being consumed when the Romans started their own oenological production with the so-called Opimian wine, named after Lucius Opimius, the consul in 121 BC. Greek wines were certainly in use in 89 BC, when the sumptuary law regulating their price was established.[246] This is confirmed by Diodorus, who says that after the Civil Wars young men drank Chian and that a jar of this wine cost 100 drachmas. The use of Chian, Lesbian and Thasian lasted "*ad uvos usque nostros*", according to Pliny.[247] Although it is impossible to give the exact date here, it should be mentioned that Pliny based his hierarchy of wines upon Sextius Niger, a Roman writer on pharmacology during the reign of Augustus and Tiberius. Moreover, Asclepiades of Bithynia, a physician who lived between 124 (or 129) and 40 BC might have been the inspiration for the list.[248] Therefore, the mid-1st c. BC or the beginning of the 1st c. AD could be the time of the grandfathers that Pliny referred to.

241 *Rust.* XII 37.
242 *Rust.* I preface 20.
243 Mart. XIII 106.
244 Scrib. 26; 36; 126; 165, 170.
245 Plin. *HN* XIV 73–76; XIV 94–97.
246 Plin. *HN* XIV 95–96.
247 Plin. *HN* XIV 95.
248 Tchernia 1997, 1247–1248.

Pliny also enumerates other wines that were probably imported to Rome, such as Clazomenian, Tmolian, Sicyonian and Cnidian. The presence of these wines is also suggested by other writings and/or amphora discoveries, such as those from *Casa di Ariadna* in Pompeii.[249] Moreover, Pliny mentioned Catacecaumenitan, Mesogitic, Ephesian and Pramnian wine from Smyrna.[250] It is possible that these beverages should also be added to the list of imports from western Asia Minor that were transported in Agora F65–66 containers; however, there is no evidence that could confirm this theory. A similar situation exists in the case of Lefkadian and Peparethian wines that, according to Pliny, were recommended to king Ptolemy by Apollodorus at a time when Italian vintages were unknown.[251] However, again, there is no evidence to suggest that they were consumed in Italy during the 1st c. AD. Furthermore, *Historia Naturalis* mentions Rhodian, Coan and Cretan wines,[252] whose consumption in Italy between the end of the 3rd c. BC (late 1st c. BC in the case of Cretan) and the mid-3rd c. AD is confirmed through archaeological evidence.[253] Imported amphoras from Cilicia and Cyprus found in Rome, Ostia and Pompeii indicate that wines from these areas reached Italy not only during the 1st c. AD, as Pliny's work suggests,[254] but throughout the early Roman Imperial age, same as importations from Beirut, Tyre and Egypt. However, no early imperial wine containers suggest that wine from Apamea, which appears in Pliny's list, was imported to Italy.

After the 1st c. AD Eastern Mediterranean wines were rarely mentioned by Latin authors. According to Fronto, Cretan was one of the cheapest imports during the 2nd c. AD.[255] At the same time, Aulus Gellius wrote about wines from Lesbos and Rhodes. However, the story concerns the choosing of a successor by Aristotle—Theophrastus from Lesbos or Eudemus from Rhodes—thus it was probably meant to represent the reality of 4th c. BC Greece, not 2nd c. AD Rome. There is also evidence from a couple of Latin agricultural writers which have been preserved to our times in *Geoponica*.[256] Florentinus, writing in the 3rd c. AD, provided a recipe for making Thasian wine, while Vindanionius Anatolius Berytius (4th c. AD) described how to prepare Coan wine. These

249 Where fragments of Cnidian and Sicyonian transport jars were discovered, see Albiach et al. 2008, 261, fig. 8.

250 Plin. *HN* XIV 73–75.

251 Plin. *HN* XIV 76.

252 Plin. *HN* XIV 78–79, 81.

253 See below.

254 Plin. *HN* XIV 74, 81.

255 Fronto, *De eloq.* I, 4.

256 *Geoponica* VIII 23, 24.

fragments are problematic however, because we do not know whether they are original texts or copies from earlier agricultural writings. Therefore, they cannot be treated as reliable evidence for the consumption of Coan and Thasian wines during the 3rd and 4th c. AD. One may put more trust in Venantius Fortunatus, who in the 6th c. AD described the life of Saint Martin (4th c. AD), where he mentioned wines from Crete, Samos, Colophon, Cyprus, Gaza, and Seraptis (Sarepta).[257] In a poem by Sidonius Apollinaris, dated c. 460 AD, a similar set of wines were described, i.e. wines from Chios, Gaza and Sarepta.[258] Considering that after Pliny literature was silent about Chian wine, we may wonder whether the information about it in Sidonius' song reflects reality, or whether it is a show of erudition by the author. However, other wines that were mentioned by Venantius and Sidonius might have been imported to Italy. Levantine wines also appear in other late Roman and Byzantine sources, such as Corippus' *De laudibus Iustini Augusti*, which describes a banquet of Justin II, where wines from Gaza, Sarepta, Ascalon, Tyre, Cyprus, Memphis and Meroe were served.[259] Moreover, importations of Levantine, as well as Samian and Cypriot wines, are confirmed by discoveries of amphoras. This suggests that certain Aegean, Anatolian and Cypriot wines were still known in the western Mediterranean during the 5th c. AD, and that they were drunk together with Palestinian vintages.

The written sources should be analysed alongside the data obtained from the archaeological material, which means amphoras and their stamps. Rhodian amphora stamps are the most numerous. They have been discovered in both the urban and extra-urban territory of Populonia where they date from the end of the 3rd to the beginning of the 1st c. BC (when the custom of stamping these amphoras ended).[260] Also, 60 stamps of Rhodian origin were found in Cosa, they date from the late 3rd c. BC to before 40 AD, and were accompanied by two stamps from Cos (dated to the 2nd c. BC and after 50 BC) and one from Chios (the late 2nd or early 1st c. BC).[261] Furthermore, 12 Rhodian stamps and one Coan amphora dated to the period between the end of the 3rd and the second half of the 2nd c. BC were found in the eastern necropolis of Falerii Novi.[262] Most of the Rhodian stamps from Alba Fucens (21 out of

257 *Vita S. Martini* II 80–82.
258 MGH *Auct. Antiquiss.* VIII, 242.
259 Corippus, *Laudem Justini Augusti Minoris* 3. 86–88.
260 Tilloca 2001, 245–247.
261 Taylor 1957, 134; American School of Classical Studies at Athens, Archives in the Blegen Library, Virginia R. Grace Papers.
262 Bevilacqua 1994, 463.

23) were dated to the late 2nd c. BC.[263] Three Rhodian stamps that are dated between 220–180 BC and the late 2nd c. BC were found in Luni.[264] In addition, six Rhodian stamps from Ostia have been published; however, their dating has not been established.[265] Other Rhodian stamps of unknown dating have also been found in Bolsena, Praeneste and Velletri. Aegean stamps were also discovered in Campania and their dating is similar to those from Latium and Etruria. For example, 15 Rhodian and two Cnidian stamps dated to the third quarter of the 2nd c. BC were found in the Basilica in Pompeii.[266] There was also a discovery of 32 Rhodian and four Cnidian stamps dated to the 2nd c. BC, that were discovered in *Casa di Ariadna* and *pars occidentalis* (VII 2),[267] while in Puteoli, three Rhodian stamps (one of them dated to 220–180 BC) have been attested in the Temple of Augustus.[268] It is worth mentioning that Aegean wine amphora stamps were also discovered in Suessa (3 Rhodian), Senigallia (1 Rhodian) and Ancona (at least 3 Rhodian and 1 Cnidian) in the Adriatic part of Italy. Rhodian stamps were found in many other sites in this region (for example in Ascoli Piceno, Ca' Magelli, Panzano, Piacenza, Cesena, Rimini, Bedriacum, Lodi, Cremona, Verona, Milano, Aquileia, Samnium, Daunia and Ascoli Satriano); a few examples date to the end of the 3rd c. BC, but most are dated to the 2nd c. BC.[269] In summary, Rhodian stamps are attested in Italy in the period between the 3rd and the 1st c. BC, Cnidian examples are dated to the 2nd c. BC, whilst those from Cos are dated between the 2nd and the 1st c. BC. The only stamp from Chios that has so far been attested is dated to around the turn of the 2nd and the 1st c. BC.[270]

The analysis of non-stamped containers does not change the picture regarding the importations of Eastern Mediterranean wines. One of the earliest assemblages that included imported amphoras was attested in the eastern *Sub-*

263 American School of Classical Studies at Athens, Archives in the Blegen Library, Virginia R. Grace Papers; De Visscher et al. 1955, 93.

264 Lusuardi Siena 1977, 233–234.

265 Paribeni 1914, 442.

266 Tchernia 1986, 103.

267 Pascual Berlanga, Ribera i Lacomba, Finkielsztejn 2008, 509–513.

268 Laforgia 1980–1981, 217.

269 Mazzeo Saracino 1997, 152–154; Baldacci 1972, 104; Biondani 1998, 63; Marengo, Paci 2008, 314–316.

270 There are two inscriptions interpreted as *Ar(visium)* that were discovered on two amphoras found in *Via Ostiense* in Rome that may suggest that Chian wine was consumed in the city around 97 BC, see CIL XV 4537 and 4538. However, as these *tituli* were abbreviated, uncertainty remains regarding any proposed interpretation(s). Moreover, they were written on containers that were identified as Dressel 1, see Panella 1992, 188, tab. 2.

urbium, where three chronological contexts were distinguished: *Viale della Serenissima*, dated to the late 2nd and the early 1st c. BC; a cistern dated to the Augustan period, but filled with material from the 2nd and the 1st c. BC; and *Quarto del Cappello da Prete*, dated to the Augustan-Tiberian age. *Viale della Serenissima* provided a small number of eastern containers which were poorly identified, but it seems that they might have come from Rhodes or Chios. These forms, as well as others from Ikos, Cos? (Dressel 5) and Asia Minor (Agora F65–66) are attested in the context dated to the turn of the 1st c. BC/1st c. AD.[271] The dating of Cretan, Rhodian and Dressel 5 (Coan?) containers attested in *Foro di Cesare* is similar.[272] Also, Aegean containers (probably one Chian and one Cnidian) from the late 1st c. BC were discovered in the House of the Porch in Ostia.[273] During recent excavations in *Horti Lamiani* Rhodian, Coan, Cnidian and Chian amphoras dated to the first half of the 1st c. BC have been found.[274] Finally, 2nd and 1st c. BC amphoras from Cos, Rhodes, Cnidus and Sicyon were discovered in *Casa di Ariadna* in Pompeii,[275] while during the 1st c. AD Cretan amphoras appeared in this context.[276] Cypriot, Cilician, Egyptian and Syro-Palestinian amphoras first appeared during the second half of the 1st c. AD in *Via Nova* and *Meta Sudans* in Rome.[277] Therefore, there is archaeological evidence that confirms that wines from Rhodes were imported to Italy during the 3rd c. BC, whereas wines from Chios, Cos, Sicyon and Cnidus appeared in this region during the 2nd c. BC. These imports were followed by wines form Crete and Asia Minor during the Augustan period, with wines from Cyprus, Cilicia, Levant and Egypt appearing after 50 AD. Now it is time to consider how long these importations lasted.

It seems that Chian wines were not imported to Italy after the 1st c. AD, but even when they were being imported discoveries of amphoras from this island are rare. One Chian container was found in the stores of Trajan's Markets in Rome, one fragment was discovered in *Necropoli di Porto in Isola Sacra*, whilst two were attested in Ostia (*Terme del Nuotatore*).[278] In Herculaneum, an

271 Caspio et al. 2009, 482, 486–487, fig. 35.

272 Zampini 2010, 321–333.

273 Boersma, Yntema, Van der Werff 1986, 108–109.

274 Ferrandes 2014, 364. Unfortunately, their exact numbers were not given; however, it was estimated that 12 % of all amphoras from this context were Aegeo-Oriental wine containers.

275 Albiach et al. 2008, 261, fig. 8.

276 Pascual Berlanga, Ribera i Lacomba, Finkielsztejn 2008, 509–511, 513–515.

277 Rizzo 2003, 146, tab. 26b.

278 Palma, Panella 1967–1968, 100.

amphora with the *titulus pictus* 'Chium' was discovered,[279] but it might have been deciphered erroneously. The correct reading is probably 'Choum', which means Coan. The latest is the dating of a Chian amphora fragment from *Vigna Barberini*, which was found in the layer from the Flavian period.[280]

Starting from the Augustan age and throughout the early Imperial period similar assemblages of eastern containers were attested in Italy. They were composed of predominantly Cretan, Rhodian, Coan, Cnidian and Anatolian (Agora F65–66) amphoras, which were sometimes accompanied by Cypriot, Cilician, Syrian or Egyptian containers. Imports from the Black Sea region rarely appeared.[281] The situation changed during the 3rd c. AD. In *Rione Terra* (Puteoli) Cnidian and Cretan amphoras were attested, as well as examples from Asia Minor. There were, however, neither Coan nor Rhodian containers, whereas Kapitän 2 did appear.[282] Similarly, in a 3rd c. AD deposit from *Porticus Aemilia* Cretan as well as Kapitän 1 and 2 containers were discovered, but none from the south-eastern Aegean.[283] In the early 3rd c. AD layers of the House of the Fishes (Ostia), Rhodian and Coan amphoras were still attested; however, only Cretan and Agora F65–66 jars appear in the late 3rd century context. Between the late 2nd and the 4th c. AD, amphora forms Kapitän 1 and 2 are attested frequently, regardless of the site.[284] Therefore, it is possible to argue that importations of Coan and Rhodian wines stopped around the end of the 2nd c. AD or early 3rd c. AD, when new unidentified kinds appeared. Wines from Crete were still drunk in Italy during the 3rd c. AD, but their containers do not appear in archaeological contexts dated later than that. Instead, examples of LRA1 that were produced in the south Aegean, Cyprus, Cilicia and Syria are widely attested on the Apennine Peninsula, together with the late Anatolian wine jar called LRA3. It cannot therefore be excluded that Italy still imported wines from Cos, Rhodes and Crete. However, since it is not always possible to distinguish the exact production place of LRA1 amphoras, or even

279 CIL IV 10722.

280 Rizzo 2003, 164, tab. 27c. This amphora might be residual. There were also 6 other fragments, which could have been of Chian origin, but due to their small size this attribution was not certain.

281 See for example Hesnard 1980; Garcea, Miraglia, Soricelli 1983–1984; Bragantini, Cipriano, Improta 1991; Miniero 1999; Marucci 2006; Zevi et al. 2004–2005; Ferrandes 2008; Bertoldi 2010; 2011a, b; Nocera 2013; Rinaldi 2006; 2013; Rizzo 2014.

282 De Filippo 2014, 336–339, fig. 1.

283 Contino, D'Alessandro 2014, 325–326.

284 One fragment from a Rhodian container that was attested in this context was probably residual, see Zevi et al. 2004–2005, 161–163, 178–179, 200–201, 214–215, tab. 3.6.12, 3.7.3, 3.8.12, 3.9.11.

TABLE 1 Eastern Mediterranean wines in Italy: literary evidence vs. amphoras

Date	Literary evidence (Latin writers)	Amphoras or stamps attested in Italy
3rd/2nd c. BC	Chian, Lesbian, Thasian, Lefkadian	Rhodian
2nd c. BC	Coan	Rhodian, Cnidian, Coan
2nd/1st c. BC		Chian
1st c. BC	Chian, Lesbian, Coan?, Tmolian?, Maroneian?, Rhodian	Rhodian, Cnidian, Coan, Chian, Cretan, Sicyonian, Agora F65–66
1st c. AD	Cretan, Rhodian, Coan, Cnidian, Tmolian, Clazomenian, Cypriot, Cilician, Egyptian, Syrian, Chian?	Rhodian, Cnidian, Coan, Cretan, Chian, Agora F65–66, Schoene-Mau XLI, Cilician, Syro-Palestinian
2nd c. AD	Rhodian, Cretan	Rhodian, Cnidian, Coan, Cretan, Agora F65–66, Kapitän 1 and 2
3rd c. AD	Thasian? (Latin author preserved in Greek Geoponica)	Cnidian, Cretan, Kapitän 1 and 2, Agora F65–66/LRA3, Cilician
4th c. AD	Coan? (Latin author preserved in Greek Geoponica), from Antioch	Kapitän 1 and 2, LRA1, LRA3, LRA4
5th c. AD	Chian?, Gazan, Sareptan	LRA3, LRA1, LRA4, LRA5–6, Agora M273, Agora M334, Samos Cistern Type
6th c. AD	Samian, Cypriot, Gazan, Sareptan, wine from Ascalon, Tyre and Memphis; Cretan?, Cnidian?	LRA3, LRA1, LRA4, LRA5–6, LRA7, Agora M273, Agora M334, Samos Cistern Type

their content,[285] the evidence for such importations seems rather vague. At the same time, there is no doubt that importations of Levantine wines (especially Palestinian) increased from the 4th c. AD onward and lasted until the end of antiquity.

Table 1 displays the above-mentioned information in an organised format. It presents a comparison between the literary and the archaeological evidence regarding the importations of Eastern Mediterranean wines to Italy by identifying what wines were mentioned by Latin writers, and the types of amphoras that were discovered on the Apennine Peninsula.[286]

285 See Introduction.

286 Question marks in the table denote that the wine might have been consumed in Italy, but the fragment is not explicit regarding this matter.

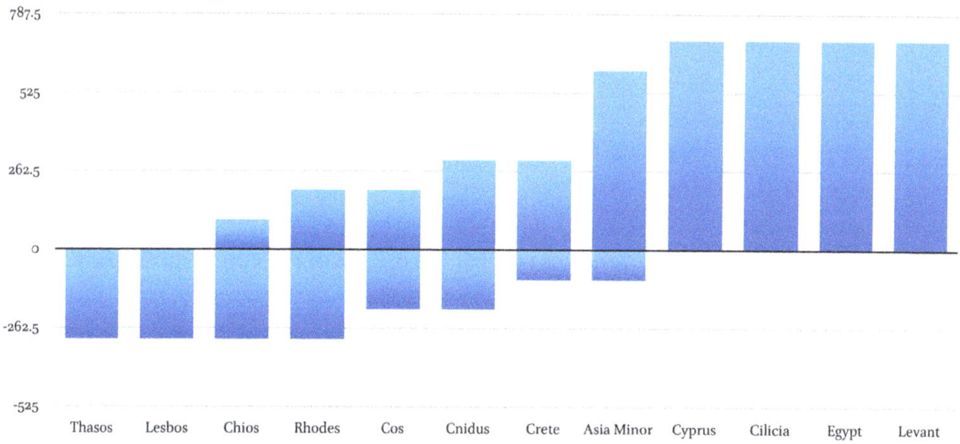

FIGURE 1 Chronology of the consumption of main Eastern wines in Italy

The chronological pattern of importations of Eastern Mediterranean wines to Italy may also be presented in graph form (Fig. 1). On the basis of literature and amphora findings it is possible to argue that wines from Lesbos and Thasos were known in Rome during the middle or late Republican period. They were consumed together with Chian wine that was present on Roman markets probably until the second half of the 1st c. AD. Wines from Rhodes, Cos and Cnidus were drunk by the Romans between the 3rd/2nd c. BC and the 3rd c. AD. Cretan wine appeared during the Augustan age and it was present on Roman tables until at least the end of the 3rd c. AD. During the Imperial period the Romans also imported wines from Asia Minor, such as Tmolian and Clazomenian, as well as Cypriot, Cilician, Egyptian and Syro-Palestinian wines. Products from the Black Sea area appeared in Italy rather occasionally. To summarise, it seems that the Romans started to drink Aegean wines from both the northern and southern part of the region during the middle Republican age. However, towards the end of the Republic they stopped importing north-Aegean beverages. Subsequently, wines from Crete and Asia Minor appeared on the Apennine Peninsula. It seems however, that the south-Aegean area, together with the western coastal areas of Anatolia became the most important sources of wine to the Romans in the early and middle Imperial period. This changed during late antiquity when importations from Palestine increased, while south-Aegean imports ceased.[287] The discoveries of late

287 The exception to this being Samian wine, which was not popular during the Imperial period.

amphoras (LRA1, LRA3 and Samos Cistern Type) suggest that wines from the Eastern Mediterranean continued to be imported to Italy as late as the 7th c. AD.[288]

6 Conclusions

In order to sum up the complex issue of the origins of the consumption of Eastern Mediterranean wines in Italy it is necessary to emphasise the most important conclusions. First of all, contrary to what was postulated by a number of scholars, Greek and Phoenician colonists from the 8th and 7th c. BC were not responsible for the introduction of viticulture and winemaking on the Apennine Peninsula. Local origins of vine cultivation and wine production dated between the Late Bronze and the beginning of the Iron Age seem more probable, though the Mycenaean influence cannot be ignored. Until the encounter with Eastern Mediterranean importations, wine was produced in Italy on a limited scale, maybe exclusively as a sacred drink. Then, as a consequence of the impact that the Greeks and Phoenicians had on the local Italian population, wine consumption became more popular during the second half of the 8th and through the 7th c. BC. The newcomers from the East brought new vine varieties and new viticultural techniques to Italy, as well as introducing the practice of banqueting. This boosted the development of Italian viticulture, particularly in the Etruscan and south-Italian regions. Etruria soon started to produce wine on a wide scale and began to export it to the West, which resulted in the economic, and possibly the social, transformation of the region. Similarly, when Greek colonies in Magna Graecia and Sicily started to produce wines to be exported, importations from the East were no longer necessary, as the demand could be satisfied using Italian-made products.

During the Archaic age the Etruscan elites, along with other members of society, indubitably drank Aegean wines during their symposia, using imported and locally imitated sympotic tableware. However, the evidence regarding Roman consumption of imported Eastern Mediterranean wines during this age is not conclusive. The earliest clear and secure evidence for Roman consumption of Eastern wines comes from the end of the 3rd c. BC. From this time until the end of antiquity, or even longer, the East supplied Italy with wines, which is

288 For example, Agora 273/Cistern Type amphoras were found in Italy, *inter alia*, in Rome, Naples, Puzzuoli, Cumae and Salerno see Arthur 1990, 281, 284–285, 288. For the latest examples of type LRA1, which have been found in Crypta Balbi in Rome, see Saguì, Manacorda 1995, 125, fig. 4.

suggested by literary, archaeological and epigraphic sources. The Aegean area provided the widest variety of wines until the 3rd c. AD, while after this date the Levant took priority.

Taking into account that the Greeks and Phoenicians had nothing to do with the introduction of wine to Italy, and that it is not certain whether the Romans were already familiar with wines from the East during the Archaic age, one may ask why the Romans started to drink Eastern wines at the end of the 3rd c. BC. In addition, they continued to import them during the Imperial age, at a time when Italian wines were widely produced and exported. Did this have something to do with the particular taste of Eastern wines? Analysing the characteristics of wines from the Eastern Mediterranean may help us to answer these questions.

CHAPTER 2

De gustibus disputandum est—'Fame' or Ordinary Wines?

Potavi modo consulare vinum.
quaeris, quam vetus atque liberale?
prisco consule conditum: sed ipse,
qui ponebat, erat, Severe, consul.

I have just drunk some consular wine.
You ask how old and how generous?
It was bottled in the consul's own year;
and he who gave it me, Severus, was that consul himself.

MART. VII 79

Many years ago, M. Finley in his revolutionary *The Ancient Economy* stated that in antiquity, while there was "*the important foreign trade in fame regional wines, vin ordinaire was normally produced at home*".[1] He referred to Athens, not to Rome, but the polis was used as an example for describing more general economic mechanisms during antiquity. This statement suggests that only high-quality and famous vintages were important objects of trade, while lower quality and common wines were not produced for export, or that the scale of their trading was not significant. No study has so far explicitly tested this statement, therefore, one of the purposes of this chapter is to verify whether it is true for *vina transmarina* in Roman Italy.

The chapter concentrates on the organoleptic characteristics and medical properties of Eastern Mediterranean wines that were consumed in Italy during the Roman age and attempts to define their 'status' within the hierarchy of imported beverages. This will establish whether they were 'fame regional wines' or rather '*vins ordinaires*'. Moreover, the chapter aims to define what

1 Finley 1999, 133.

© KONINKLIJKE BRILL NV, LEIDEN, 2021 | DOI:10.1163/9789004433762_004

qualities made ancient wines high-ranking. At first, the general characteristics of ancient wines are demonstrated. This helps our understanding of ancient wine production in general and also highlights any differences between Eastern Mediterranean wines and standard beverages. Subsequently, and based upon the literary and epigraphic evidence, the characteristics of different Eastern Mediterranean imports are presented.

1 In Search of Lost Tastes—Wines in Classical Antiquity

It is necessary to devote a few words to the general characteristics of wines in antiquity before describing in detail the Eastern Mediterranean wines that were consumed in Italy. This is due to the fact that if we want to detect peculiarities of *vina transmarina* we must first understand how the Greeks and Romans approached wine, which was rather different to today. Therefore, an understanding of the terminology used by Classical authors is required in order to familiarise ourselves with the qualities of Eastern Mediterranean wines. In order to achieve this familiarisation I will characterise ancient wines in respect of their colour, age, taste and strength, and finally, their consistency.

1.1 *Colour*

Nowadays we generally distinguish three types of wines: white, rosé and red. The so-called *vins jaunes* that are traditionally made in the Jura region in eastern France, are well known almost only to connoisseurs. However, people in classical antiquity could easily identify at least four colours of wine. Pliny the Elder enumerates *albus* (white), *fulvus* (deep yellow, reddish yellow, gold-coloured, tawny), *sanguineus* (red, bloody) and *niger* (black).[2] Numerous Greek sources also highlight similar divisions, with Mnesitheus of Athens (writing in the early 4th c. BC and quoted by Athenaeus) distinguishing μέλας (black), λευκός (white) and κιρρός (orange-tawny),[3] while Galen adds ξανθός (yellow) and ερυθρός (red).[4] It seems, however, that it is possible to use ξανθός and κιρρός interchangeably,[5] which means that both the Greeks and the Romans knew of white, yellow, red and black wines.[6] Nonetheless, M. Bouvier argues that people

2 Plin. *HN* XIV 80.
3 Ath. *Deipn.* 32e.
4 *Hipp. De vict. acut. comm.* 15.627K.
5 Gal. *San.Tu.* 6.335K.
6 Seltman 1957, 139 says that the Greeks knew of three colours, as both ερυθρός and μέλας were equivalents of the Latin *sanguineus*, but his explanation is not convincing.

in classical antiquity distinguished five colours of wine: white, yellow, grey or rosé, red and black. According to this author, white wines were the most popular, he adds that the general production process involved in creating this variety did not differ significantly from the one that we know today.[7] At this point a short digression should be made to clarify what is meant when referring to 'a white wine' today. White wines are made by pressing the juice out of the grapes so that the process of fermentation excludes their skin and seeds, which are the main sources of anthocyanins and tannins. These biomolecules are responsible for the red colour of wine as well as for its bitter and acid taste, which can be eliminated by oxidation after a long maturation process.[8] According to Bouvier, the yellow or amber coloured beverage was a product of the fermentation of raisins, whereas when the grapes were fermented for some time with their skins, grey or rosé wine was made. Red wine was produced using grapes with naturally coloured pulp or by leaving the grapes with their skins attached during the whole fermentation process. Finally, black wine was either very old or made from the raisins of red grapes,[9] which suggests that the Greek term μέλας and the Latin term *niger* may be attributed both to red wine and to the beverage that was originally white, but which became darker during the maturation process.[10]

As a matter of fact, the identification of black wine as an old beverage was first suggested by Tchernia. He noted that Falernian wine, which was often described as white or yellow, became brown or even black with time.[11] This darkening process, which is due to the oxidation of various components of white wine, may also be observed in the case of modern white wines.[12] On the contrary, red wines become lighter with time, taking on brick and amber hues. This is due to the fact that pigmented tannins precipitate as sediments over time, depleting the wine of pigment.[13] Therefore, old red wine cannot be called 'black'.

Bouvier's explanation regarding wine colours in antiquity needs further examination. This is necessary as the grey/rosé wine he refers to is mentioned neither in Greek nor in Latin texts. In modern wine nomenclature, *vin gris* is a white wine that is made of red grapes, whereas rosé can be obtained when

7 Bouvier 2000, 118.
8 Unwin 1991, 29, 44.
9 Bouvier 2000, 119.
10 Dalby 2003, 353.
11 Tchernia 1986, 343; Tchernia, Brun 1999, 133; Tchernia 2001, 128–129.
12 Tchernia, Brun 1999, 132–133, fig. 173.
13 Robinson 2006, 189 under 'colour of wine'.

the must is macerated for a short time.[14] Therefore, it is probable that Bouvier translated gris/rosé as the Latin *fulvus* or Greek κιρρός, because he was looking from a contemporary wine-making perspective. These words, however, should be seen as meaning dark yellow or orange. Tchernia noted that in a warm climate grape skins often became porous, which facilitated the liberation of anthocyanins and their infiltration into the must. This process was increased by pressing.[15] Therefore, it is possible that *fulvus* and κιρρός do not necessarily mean only wine made of raisins, or grapes that had fermented for some time with their skins. They may also describe wine that was macerated without contact with grape skins (which means white in modern terminology), which was 'contaminated' by anthocyanins. Moreover, it is also probable that this was the colour of a beverage that matured for a considerable period, but was not very old. Galen mentioned that there was no white wine that had warming properties, because white and dry wines became κιρρότεροί. He gave Caecubian as an example of a white wine that became the colour of fire with time.[16] It seems notable that the best Eastern wines from the Hellenistic age were described as κιρροὶ and παλαιοί,[17] which means that the yellow/orange-tawny colour should be associated with the wine's age. Therefore, in terms of wine the word κιρρός should be understood as a white and matured beverage.

1.2 *Age*

This raises another important question; what did 'old wine' mean to the ancient Greeks and Romans? This issue has also been raised by Tchernia, who noted that old wines were more appreciated by the Romans. He claims that in antiquity both young and old wines were drunk; however, the definition of the latter was different from what it is today. According to Ulpian, *Vetus accipietur, quod non est novum: id est et anni prioris vinum appellatione veteris continebitur.*[18] Therefore, we may suppose that wine from the previous year would be labelled in antiquity as old.[19] Nonetheless, there are inscriptions on amphoras indicating that people in classical antiquity knew wines that were much older than a year.[20] Moreover, according to Pliny, all the wines from beyond the sea were

14 Robinson 2006, 593 under 'rosé wine-making', 749 under 'vin gris'. Blending a small amount of finished red wine to a finished white wine is another method for making rosé.
15 Tchernia 1990, 66.
16 Gal. *MM.* 10.834K.
17 Orib. *Col. Med.* v 6, 45; Gal. *Comp. Med. Loc.* 13.513K.
18 Just. *Dig.* XXXIII 6, 11.
19 Tchernia 1986, 29.
20 Tchernia 1986, 30.

in the middle of their maturity at around 6 or 7 years old.[21] Finally, the list of Italian wines provided by Athenaeus, mentions beverages that were between 5 and 25 years old.[22] For example, *Falernum* was sufficiently aged for drinking after ten years, but it was really good when it was more than 15 but less than 20 years old. Similarly, Alban wine was best after 15 years, while Sorrentine needed maturation for 25 years. When it exceeded this age it could cause headaches and affect the nervous system. However, there were wines that were over 100 years old! Although it seems improbable, Pliny claims that wine made during the consulate of Opimius (121 BC) was still accessible in the third quarter of the 1st c. AD. Even though it was bitter, rough in taste and had the consistency of honey, it was used in small quantities to season certain thin wines and could be drunk when mixed with a considerable quantity of water.[23] Cicero mentions Opimian as well as an even older wine that was made in 160 BC during the consulship of Anicius, suggesting that both were available on the market. The latter however, even though it was expensive, was, according to Cicero, unpalatable and scarcely tolerable.[24] Juvenal mentions wine from the times of the Social Wars, whereas Martial refers to drinking wines that were stored during the reign of Numa, as well as Massic that was made before the Romans introduced the consulship.[25] Although the author of the *Epigrams* certainly exaggerates, mocking at Roman desire for old vintages, we may say that the ancient Greeks and Romans were able to drink very old beverages and that they knew efficient conservation methods. Moreover, these texts suggest that wines of a considerable age were more appreciated than younger varieties.

It was possible to store wine for long periods due to the fact that the Greeks and Romans, unlike people from the Middle Ages until Pasteur's time, used amphoras—containers less permeable than barrels. Moreover, both amphoras and *dolia* were covered with resin or pitch that had sterilising and preserving properties. Thanks to these innovations people in classical antiquity could enjoy the taste of a mature wine.[26] Even though it is impossible to give the exact age of an 'old wine', there is no doubt that it must have been a beverage of several years vintage.

21 Plin. *HN* XIV 78.

22 Ath. *Deipn.* 26d–27d.

23 Plin. *HN* XIV 55 and 95. It should also be noted that Velleius (II 7, 5) contradicts Pliny's words, suggesting that Opimian should no longer have been available during the consulship of M. Vinicius (30 AD). However, B. Baldwin (1967, p. 175) is convinced that the author of *Natural History* is a more reliable source in this matter.

24 Cic. *Brut.* 287.

25 Juv. V 30–31; Mart. III 62; XIII 111.

26 Tchernia 1986, 30–31.

1.3 *Taste and Strength*

It is worth mentioning that wines in antiquity were probably stronger than they are today. The general alcohol content in wine may vary between 11 and 17 percent, depending on the amount of sugar and the variety of yeast. Most of the yeast disappears when the ABV (alcohol by volume) percentage is above 16–17; however, certain species die when the ABV content is around 11 percent. Nowadays certain varieties of yeast are specially selected, and the process of fermentation and the alcoholic content are carefully controlled. That is why most dry wines contain between 12 and 14 percent of alcohol.[27] However, people in antiquity did not specifically select the yeast, and they were unable to effectively measure the alcoholic content. Moreover, they generally used very sweet grape varieties. Consequently, their wines usually contained 15–16 percent of alcohol.[28] Similarly, modern beverages made of very sweet or late harvested grapes are stronger than the average wine. It should be noted that old wines in antiquity were probably stronger than new beverages, due to water evaporating during the long maturation process.[29]

As yeast dies when the concentration of alcohol rises, in the case of very sweet grapes part of the sugar is left unfermented. This happens when the grapes are highly ripe or even shrivelled and their sugar content is above 30 percent. This is how sweet wines are actually made.[30] Considering the fact that Mediterranean vine varieties produced very sweet grapes, it is possible that it was easier to make sweet wine in antiquity. However, Kourakou-Dragona claims that in antiquity only those beverages made from sun-dried grapes were sweet. Moreover, she noted that when the percentage of sugar in the must becomes high, alcoholic fermentation slows down or even stops. Therefore, ancient wines made from sun-dried grapes whose sugar content was very high might have been low-alcoholic beverages. On the contrary, the alcoholic content of dry wines might have been high.[31]

It should be noted that sweet wines of the type *passito* (Latin *passum*), which were made of grapes that were dried after picking, had higher than usual levels of acidity. This was associated with the dehydration of grapes. A good level of acidity increases the freshness and fruitiness of wine and protects it from bacteria. Therefore, we may say that sweet wines in antiquity were more likely to endure long-distance journeys. Moreover, high acidity influences the colour

27 Unwin 1991, 38–39.
28 Alcock 2006, 93.
29 Tchernia, Brun 1999, 142–145.
30 Dalby 2000, 138; Singleton 1996, 73.
31 Kourakou-Dragona 2013, 5–8.

of wine, thus the lower the pH the redder (less blue) the wines. In the case of white wines high acidity prevents them from turning brown, which is a consequence of polymerisation of phenolics.[32] Therefore, we could say that white wines that were made of dried grapes would generally not turn dark with time.

Bouvier claims that most ancient wines were sweet,[33] which seems wrong considering what has just been discussed. This characteristic was indeed popular, but sweetness was not a general feature of all ancient vintages. This opinion results probably from the confusion surrounding the Greek terms γλυκύς and ἡδύς, which were often translated into English in the same way, that is to say 'sweet'. As far as the former goes, such a translation is correct. However, in the case of the latter we should understand it not as sweet because of the high sugar content, but rather as pleasant due to the lack of acidity.[34] As a matter of fact, in Greek and Roman writings wines called αὐστηρός, *austerus*, which is usually translated as dry, as well as αὔταρκες, that may be semi-dry or semi-sweet were also present.[35] According to Brock and Wirtjes, dry in an unpleasant sense was described as πικρός or δριμύς.[36] However, Tchernia suggests that the word δριμύς describes the spicy taste similar to modern maderised wines or the so-called *vins de voile*. The Romans obtained this particular taste by adding fenugreek to the must during the process of fermentation.[37] This was a deliberate action, thus, δριμύς wine was not too dry or too bitter, but pleasant in taste and much desired. In summary, it seems that people in classical antiquity knew a wide range of wines, apart from sweet beverages.

1.4 *Consistency*

It is worth mentioning that some Greek and Roman alcoholic drinks resembled modern aperitifs more than wines.[38] This is due to the fact that they were flavoured with different spices and aromatic herbs, such as nard, iris, fenugreek, nuts, earth almond, camel grass, myrrh, reed, cinnamon and saffron.[39] They drank absinth wine (*absinthites, absinthianum*), rose wine (*rosatum*), violet wine (*violacium*) and pepper wine (*vina condita, piperata*).[40] Some of these *addenda* may seem strange, but at least they all have a vegetable origin, and

32 Robinson 2006, 238.
33 Bouvier 2000, 118.
34 Ridgeway, Wilkins 1890, 969; Seltman 1957, 141; Dalby 2003, 359.
35 Ridgeway, Wilkins 1890, 969.
36 Brock, Wirtjes 2000, 459.
37 Tchernia 1998, 55–57; Tchernia, Brun 1999, 139–140.
38 Tchernia 1990, 68.
39 Tchernia 1990, 68; André 1981, 167.
40 André 1981, 166–167.

thus they seem edible. However, the Greeks and the Romans went further when seasoning their wines. For example, Pliny says that:

> *Graecia argilla aut marmore aut sale aut mari lenitatem excitat, Italiae pars aliqua crapulana pice, ac resina condire musta volgare ei est provinciisque finitimis. nonnusquam prioris vini faece acetove condiunt.*[41]
>
> In Greece, on the other hand, they enliven the smoothness of their wines with potter's earth or marble dust or salt or sea-water, while in some parts of Italy they use resinous pitch for this purpose, and it is the general practice both there and in the neighbouring provinces to season must with resin; in some places they use the lees of older wine or else vinegar for seasoning.[42]

This means that people in classical antiquity added gypsum, clay, marble, sea-water resin and pitch to their wines. Moreover, ash and charcoal were also popular admixtures.[43] As evidence of these practices we may evoke today's Greek *retsina* that is made by adding Aleppo pine resin to the must during the process of fermentation.[44] Its taste, obtained by this traditional method of production, is, to put it mildly, rather peculiar. The purpose of adding the above-mentioned substances was to make the wine more palatable and/or to enable the wine to preserve for a long time. For example, gypsum or lime could soften a beverage that was too hard, whereas the admixture of resin could subdue its harshness as well as improving the bouquet and conservation.[45] Wine with gypsum was, curiously, seen as suitable against poisonings.[46] As a matter of fact, gypsum/plaster are still used in wine production today, an example being Spanish Jerez (Xerez, Sherry) which is treated with gypsum to improve its colour due to its low acidity. This admixture also has preservative powers and gives the wine its character.[47] Modern use of resin has similar purposes. For example, gum acacia, a natural resin, can stabilise pigments in red wines.[48] Sulphur dioxide and bentonite are among the mineral substances that are added to wine today. The former has preservative powers as it prevents the activity of

41 Plin. *HN* XIV 120.
42 Translated by H. Rackham, Loeb Classical Library.
43 Bouvier 2000, 120; Ridgeway, Wilkins 1890, 966; Plin. *HN* XIV 126.
44 Robinson 2006, 569, under 'retsina'.
45 Alcock 2006, 94; Plin. *HN* XIV 120 and 125.
46 Dsc. *Mat.Med.* V 9 MGO.
47 Tchernia, Brun 1999, 116; Thurmond 2017, 186.
48 Robinson 2006, 568–569.

certain yeast, enzymes and bacteria, and hence inhibits oxidation.[49] The latter is used for the purpose of wine clarification, since it removes proteins and terpenols.[50] The Romans used both; the clay mentioned by Pliny might have simply been bentonite. However, sulphur dioxide was not added by the Romans to the must—they cleaned amphoras, *dolia* and other wine jars with burning sulphur fumes in order to inhibit the growth of yeasts and bacteria.[51]

The last admixture that should be described in more detail is seawater. The practice of adding seawater to the must was typical of certain Greek wines. Plautus laughs at it saying: *quasi vinis Graecis Neptunus nobis suffudit mare*,[52] whereas Cato mentions adding salt or seawater in all recipes for making wines *alla greca*. This may be the reason why André claims that this admixture was characteristic of Greek wines in general.[53] Pliny provides an anecdote regarding the origins of this custom. According to the story, it arose from the thievish practices of a slave who was substituting the wine that he had sold with seawater.[54] It is more probable, however, that the idea of adding seawater to wine was accidental and related to the production of amphoras. B. Clinkenbeard noted that modern potters on Lesbos add salt to the clay to increase its cohesion by promoting electrostatic attraction between the molecules without making it stiffer. The amount of sodium in ancient Lesbian amphoras is much larger than the average. Since tests did not prove the absorption of sodium from the soil in which the amphoras were buried, it seems probable that its high amount in Lesbian amphoras may indicate that the ancient potters also added seawater to the clay.[55] Consequently, it would be salt that was originally present in the pottery that influenced the taste of wine.

The method of adding seawater to the must or keeping vessels with must in the sea (and obtaining the wine called θαλασσίτες) was widespread among the ancient Greeks, especially in the south-eastern part of the Aegean and on the coasts of Asia Minor. It was also attested in Greece as late as in the first half of the 20th century.[56] As a matter of fact, salt continues to be used for the purpose of wine stabilisation and clarification.[57] The Romans also knew of this practice,

49 Unwin 1991, 40.
50 Lambri et al. 2012, 5–8.
51 Romano, Suzzi 1993, 374; Thurmond 2006, 146.
52 Pl. *Rud.* 588.
53 André 1981, 165.
54 Plin. *HN* XIV 78.
55 Clinkenbeard 1982, 262.
56 Matthaiou 1992–1998, 572–573.
57 Thurmond 2017, 184.

as Cato and Columella recommended adding grilled salt to wine.[58] The latter mentioned that salt acted against the mustiness or 'ropiness' of wine (*mucor*).[59] Nonetheless, the reasoning behind this practice remains unclear. Pliny suggests that seawater accelerated the process of maturity,[60] while Athenaeus mentioned that seawater added to wine made it sweet/pleasant (ἡδὺν γὰρ εἶναι τὸν οἶνον παρεγχέω μένης θαλάσσης).[61] Seawater acted as a preservative according to Columella and Plutarchus.[62] According to Mnesitheus of Athens, wines that were carefully mixed with seawater did not cause nausea and helped in the process of digestion.[63] Modern scholars give various explanations. According to one theory, the seasoning of must with seawater was in order to complete fermentation and improve the taste of wine.[64] Alternatively, there is an idea that it could increase acidity and hence kill bacteria.[65] It is also probable that pouring seawater on grapes could accelerate the dehydration process as well as eliminating certain types of yeast or bacteria.[66]

This subject was developed in detail by Tchernia and Kourakou-Dragona. The first researcher made wine according to a recipe of Columella, in which grilled salt was recommended as one of ingredients that should be added to the must in the process of fermentation. Moreover, he noted that according to French wine makers from the 19th century, salt might have reduced the solubility of albumins in wine. Therefore, sodium chloride might have served for the purpose of wine clarification.[67] The Greek chemist and oenologist, Kourakou-Dragona, explained that salt preserved weak and watery wines that were made of vines that grew in fertile soils. These vines had many grapes; however, these grapes had a low sugar content and hence produced wines with low alcohol percentages. Due to their weakness these wines could not survive long transportation. However, seawater could deactivate oxidative enzymes and hence stop fermentation. Thanks to this phenomenon these wines could stand long journeys. As a matter of fact, long maturation acted in their favour as they should be kept for at least a couple of years before consumption. Furthermore, salt helped preserve the colour of wine. According to Kourakou-Dragona, white

58 Cato *Agr.* 24, 105, 112; Col. *R.R.* XII 23, 3.
59 Col. *R.R.* XII 23, 3; Thurmond 2017, 183–184.
60 Plin. *HN* XIV 78.
61 Ath. *Deipn.* 26b.
62 Col. *R.R.* XII, 23, 3; Plut. *Moralia*, 914e.
63 Ath. *Deipn.* 32e.
64 Matthaiou 1992–1998, 573.
65 García Soler 1996b, 231.
66 Salviat 1986, 173.
67 Tchernia, Brun 1999, 114.

wine with an admixture of seawater did not turn dark with time. Finally, it helped in wine clarification, since it could liquidate proteins.[68]

Ancient wine could be described as λεπτός or παχύς. However, it is not clear what the Greek writers understood by these adjectives in terms of wine. In translations of the former the word 'thin' is frequently used, but the Liddell-Scott dictionary suggests 'light', as an interpretation of λεπτός when associated with wine. Other possible translations include delicate, subtle, refined and weak. In the medical works of Oribasius and Galen, λεπτός is often associated with the colour of wine—yellow wines (κιρροί, ξανθοί) are described as λεπτοί. People in antiquity thought that wines of this colour were heating, diuretic, digestive and 'inflaming the head' (τὴν κεφαλὴν ποιεῖ διάπυρον).[69] However, sweet white wines, though the most nutritious of all, were not easily digested. They could disturb the intestines, but were less inebriating.[70] Is it then possible that λεπτός in terms of wine means weak/light in the sense of alcohol content? This is rather unlikely, as, if this was the case, then the adjective ἀσθενής would be used, or ἄτονος, which according to Brock and Wirtjes should be understood as 'low in alcohol'.[71] Moreover, in such a case this wine would not 'inflame the head'. Another alternative is that it means rather light, as in easily digested. This again seems rather improbable, taking into account that sweet, white wines were not digestive varieties. According to Dalby, λεπτός correlates with the translucence,[72] whereas Brock and Wirtjes argue that it determines the consistency of wine, or, as we would say nowadays, its weight or body.[73] The last hypothesis seems the most probable, as the antonym of λεπτός is παχύς and its substantive, πάχος, when associated with liquids, also describes their consistency. Nonetheless, this concept could be developed. Considering that παχύς in the case of 'the sea' should be attributed to its saltiness, a similar attribution seems probable in the case of wine. Therefore, παχύς would be a beverage with some sort of admixture (for example seawater), whereas λεπτός would be neat. This hypothesis will be further developed after a detailed analysis of the characteristics of Eastern Mediterranean wines that were consumed in Roman Italy.

---

68 Kourakou-Dragona 2013, 123–124, 127, 133–134. Thurmond 2017, 183 also suggests that salt was *"particularly helpful in weak musts such as those from rain-diluted grapes"*.

69 Ath. *Deipn.* 32c.

70 Dsc. *Mat. Med.* V 9 MGO.

71 Brock, Wirtjes 2000, 457.

72 Dalby 2003, 359.

73 Brock, Wirtjes 2000, 456–458.

In conclusion, it is possible to say that people in classical antiquity demonstrated advanced oenological knowledge. They were able to prepare sweet and dry varieties of red and white wines. Also, they knew how to produce both high-alcoholic and low-alcoholic beverages. Moreover, both the Greeks and the Romans knew of many admixtures that could improve the colour, as well as the taste and consistency of wine. Finally, ancient wines could preserve for a long time thanks to diverse methods used during their conservation. However, there is nothing that suggests any difference between Eastern and Roman wines in general. It is true that the former were particularly famous for their admixture of seawater, but the Romans also added salt to wines. What was so special about wines from the Eastern Mediterranean?

2 Republican Wines of Some Repute

Although generally it is said that *de gustibus non est disputandum*, the main purpose of this chapter is to discuss Roman tastes in Eastern Mediterranean wines. It has been established in the previous chapter that the Romans certainly drank wines from Chios, Lesbos, Thasos, Cos, Rhodes, Cnidus, Sicyon, Lefkada, Crete, Cyprus, Cilicia, Syro-Palestine, Egypt, the southern Black Sea region and western Asia Minor. In the latter area at least five types of wines were produced: Tmolian, Clazomenian, Mesogitic, Ephesian and *pramnian* from Smyrna, but it is impossible to confirm whether all were imported to Italy. Aegean wines were already present in Italy during the Republican period, whereas imports from Anatolia, Cyprus, Cilicia, the Levant, Egypt and the Black Sea area appeared in the Imperial period.

Greek and Latin literature provides us with an abundance of information concerning wines from the Aegean region and it seems that all products imported from this area were of some repute. Some of them were real luxuries. At the same time, imports during the Imperial era were common and popular, but few enjoyed a particular reputation. During the Republic the Italians knew of, and enjoyed wines imported from Chios, Lesbos, Thasos, Cos, Rhodes, Cnidus and Lefkada.

2.1 *Chian*

The product from the vineyards of Chios was rated as being among the best foreign wines in Italy.[74] The wine was produced in Ariusium, the central dis-

---

74 Plin. *HN* XIV 73.

trict of the island,[75] as well as on its southern promontory at Phanae,[76] and was made from vine typical of Chios.[77] Chian wine was held in high esteem and was famous among both the Romans and Greeks. For example, Plautus, who entirely ignored Italian wines, mentioned Chian in his plays.[78] Moreover, it was often cited in a positive context by Horace,[79] while Galen saw it as the best of the Asian wines, together with Lesbian and Tmolian.[80]

It is worth mentioning that according to Theopompus, the Chians were the first people to make μέλανα οἶνον.[81] Sciortino interprets these words as an indication that red wine was made on the island.[82] However, this statement does not seem justified in the light of other literary sources. According to Galen and Oribasius, Chian was οἶνος ὁ ξανθός or κιῤῥός and διαυγής.[83] This means that according to our standards it would be described as a white and translucent beverage that matured for a considerable time.

Pomponius Porphyrio describes Chian as *dulce*.[84] Moreover, it is always among γλυκεῖς in Galen.[85] On the contrary, Aetius writes that Chian can be replaced by ἢ ἑτέρῳ αὐστηρῷ παλαιῷ ('the other dry and old') in certain prescriptions.[86] This suggests that the island of Chios produced various types of wine. Oribasius mentions οἶνος Χίος αὐστηρός, γλυκύς and αὔταρκες.[87] Athenaeus provides similar information, probably taken from 4th c. BC medical texts. According to this, there were three species of the beverage from Arousia: αὐστηρός, γλυκάζων and αὐτόκρατος. The first was a dry variety that was pleasant, nutritious and more diuretic, whereas the second was sweeter, nutritious, filling and could soften the bowels. Αὐτόκρατος was something between αὐστηρός and γλυκάζων and shared the characteristics of both.[88]

It is worth noting that Oribasius and Aetius mention that wine from Chios was old and had a pleasant aroma.[89] Plautus writing about Chian, Lesbian,

75 Plin. *HN* XIV 73; Strab. XIV 1, 35; Hdn. 31, 292.
76 Verg. *Georg.* II 98.
77 Plin. *HN* XIV 25.
78 Pl. *Curc.* 78; *Poen.* 699.
79 Hor. *Carm.* III 19, 5.
80 Gal. *San.Tu.* 6.275K.
81 Ath. *Deipn.* 26c.
82 Sciortino 2012, 165.
83 Gal. *Comp. Med. Loc.* 13.513K; *Vict. At.* 94; Orib. *Syn.* IV 3, 1; *Col. Med.* III 4, 1; V 6, 31; V 6, 45.
84 *Hor. Serm. Comm.* I 10.
85 *Vict. At.* 93–94.
86 Aet. VII 112, 34 and 47.
87 Orib. *Syn.*III 136; III 160; IV 3.1; *Col. Med.* V 6, 31; V 6, 45.
88 Ath. *Deipn.* 33f.
89 Orib. *Col. Med.* V 6, 45; Aet. VII 45, 59; VII 112, 34 and 47.

Thasian and Lefkadian wines, calls them old and toothless (*'vetustate vino edentulo aetatem'*).[90] According to Arnott, *edentulo* should be understood as 'mellowed by age',[91] thus, old and mature. Philyllius mentions Χῖον σαπρόν,[92] whereas Hermippos suggests that there was a wine called σαπρίαν that was characterised by its delightful aroma of roses, violets and hyacinths.[93] According to Salviat, this information refers to a variety of wine from Chios.[94] The terms σαπρός and σαπρίας generally mean rotten, putrid or old in the negative sense, whereas in terms of wine they are translated as old and mellow. According to Dalby, this epithet may describe wine that was made of grapes that were attacked by a noble rot.[95] However, there is no evidence that could confirm this theory. In Alexis' *Orchestris* σαπρός describes 'toothless' wine,[96] which means that this epithet should be associated with the age of wine rather than with the state of grapes.[97] Kourakou-Dragona claims that it is impossible to make wine from grapes that were attacked by *Botrytis* without the use of sulphur dioxide. Since there is no evidence that people in classical antiquity added this compound to wine, the hypothesis that was proposed by Dalby should be rejected. At the same time, she argues that the word ἀνθοσμίας does not mean 'redolent of flowers' as it is generally translated. She relates it with *fleur de vin*, which means a white film of yeast that may appear on the surface of wine.[98] A film of yeasts is also mentioned in *Geoponica* as ἄνθος, whereas Pliny and Columella call it *flos vini*.[99] These yeasts,[100] known as *flor* in the production of *fino* sherry, are also typical of French *vin de voile* and are formed when wine is matured for a couple of years in wooden casks that are not completely full. This enables oxidation and the formation of certain molecules, such as sotolon, which are responsible for the specific taste of these wines, which has been compared to that of fresh bread, curry or walnuts.[101] According to Kourakou-Dragona, the

---

90 Pl. *Poen.* 699–700.

91 Arnott 1970, 47.

92 Phil. Fr. 23 (24) = Ath. *Deipn.* 31a.

93 Herm. Fr. 77(82) = Ath. *Deipn.* 29e.

94 Salviat 2013b, 128.

95 Dalby 1997, 101.

96 Meineke, *FCG* III 459f = Kock, *CAF* II 358f.

97 This identification is also supported by García Soler 1999, 402.

98 Kourakou-Dragona 2013, 65–70. García Soler 2001, 259 and 2002, 54–55 proposes the same interpretation.

99 *Geopon.* VII 15, 6; Plin. *HN* XIV 136; Col. *R.R.* XII 30.

100 Four types of yeasts produce *flor* that is responsible for a desirable taste of wine, which means *Saccharomyces beticus, S. montuliensis, S. cheresiensis, and S. rouxii,* see Thurmond 2017, 176.

101 Robinson 2006, 750.

terms σαπρός and σαπρίας cannot be identified. The first should be associated with the film of yeast, whereas the second refers to wine that is decomposed by acidification. Contrary to other scholars, such as Salviat and García Soler, she rejects the testimony by Hermippos, arguing that it does not refer to Chian, but to some unnamed wine. Moreover, she thinks that it is satiric—Hermippos simply mocks connoisseurs who exaggerated the aromatic qualities of wines that matured under *flor*.[102] Therefore, Chian was not σαπρίας and this epithet cannot be understood as a positive quality in terms of wine. Chian was σαπρός, which means wine characterised by the specific taste of sotolon that was obtained during its long maturation under *flor*. This is interesting since the experiment by Tchernia proved that the Romans appreciated this taste, since they added fenugreek to their wines—one of very few plants that contain sotolon.[103]

Furthermore, wine from Chios was ἀθάλασσος[104] or, as Horace calls it, *maris expers*,[105] which means that it was not mixed with seawater. Nevertheless, it might have been seasoned with spices, since it had to be filtered before drinking.[106] Unfortunately, we do not know if any herbs or other substances were added to improve its taste. The only example of a Chian condiment that appeared in the texts was honey—it was called honey-sweetened (μελιχρότερος) in *Greek Anthology*.[107] Curiously, according to Dioscorides, Chian wine with honey was sometimes used to make certain kinds of perfume.[108]

The qualities of the wine from Chios were probably similar to the Italian *Falernum*, since in medical prescriptions the two may be used interchangeably.[109] This is not surprising considering the fact that they were both regarded as 'top' beverages. Falernian was considered as the best of the Italian wines, whilst Chian was the leader of the Greek *crus*.[110] However, there was a small difference between them. According to Dioscorides, wine from Chios was gentler than the Italian *grands crus*, as well as Sicilian and Istrian wines.[111]

102 Kourakou-Dragona 2013, 88–89.
103 Tchernia 1998, 506; Tchernia, Brun 1999, 126.
104 Dsc. *Mat. Med.*, V 11 MGO; Gal. *Ant.*14.162K; Aet. VII 112, 47 and 51–52; Paul. Aeg. *Epit. Med.* VII 16, 7.
105 Hor. *Serm.* II 15.
106 Ath. *Deipn.* 28d.
107 *GA* XII 108, 1–2.
108 Dsc. *Mat. Med.* I 131 MGO.
109 Orib. *Syn.* III 131; Paulus, *Epit. Med.* VII 16, 7.
110 Hor. *Serm.* II 3, 115–118.
111 Dsc. *Mat. Med.* V 10 MGO.

2.2 *Lesbian*

Lesbian wine was considered to be excellent and it seems that its qualities were similar to the wine from Chios. It was featured among the best drinks since the times of (and upon the authority of) the famous physician, Erasistratus (304–250 BC).[112] Horace mentions it together with Chian and Caecuban,[113] which was one of the best Italian *crus* in the 1st c. BC. Lesbian may be called the second-best Eastern wine in Rome. However, it seems that it was valued even more than Chian by the Greeks. Callimachus called it 'nectar of the flower of wine' (πολὺς δὲ Λεσβίης ἄωτον νέκταρ οἰνάνθης ἄγων),[114] whilst Longus described it as 'the best of wines, redolent of flowers' (ἀνθοσμίας οἶνος Λέσβιος, ποθῆναι κάλλιστος οἶνος).[115] Also, Clearchus argued that there was no wine sweeter/nicer than Lesbian (οὐκ ἔστιν ἄλλος οἶνος ἡδίων πιεῖν). Finally, Archestratus, who was considered to be an expert in the field of feasts, compared the taste of Lesbian wine with ambrosia, stating that it was definitely better than Thasian and Phoenician wines.[116]

We should now ask what qualities made Lesbian wine so special? First of all, it was an old beverage[117] characterised by a sweet (εὔπνους) aroma.[118] Secondly, its colour was usually described as λευκός, ξανθός or κιρρός and διαυγής, similarly to Chian.[119] Therefore, according to our standards it would be an old, white and translucent beverage. Finally, Dioscorides says that Lesbian was αὐστηρός;[120] however, according to Galen and Oribasius, it was γλυκύς.[121] Thus, we may presume that the island of Lesbos produced both dry and sweet wines. This is confirmed by Galen, who mentions three Lesbian cities that were particularly famous for winemaking, namely Mytilene, Eresos and Mithymna. The sweetest and the most fragrant was the wine from Mithymna. The beverage from Eresos was slightly less sweet, while the Mytilenian variety had the lowest sugar content. All these Lesbian wines were κιρροί, εὐώδεις and astringent, but not

112 Plin. *HN* XIV 73.
113 Hor. *Epod.* 9.
114 *AP* XIII 9.
115 Longus IV 10, 3, 5.
116 Ath. *Deipn.* 29c.
117 Ath. *Deipn.* 28f and 29b; Plaut. *Poen.* 699–700.
118 Clem. Al. *Paed.* II 2, 30, 2.
119 Orib. *Syn.* IV 3, 1; *Col. Med.* V 6, 31; V 6, 45; Gal. *Comp.Med.Loc.* 13.513K; *MM.* 10.835K; *Vict. At.* 94; Dsc. *Mat. Med.* V 11 MGO. It should be noted that λέσβια Αἰθιόπια was attested twice on a Ptolemaic papyrus PSI V 535 (r1, 29 and r2, 43), once associated with olive oil and once with wine. The latter might have referred to the colour of wine, but Kruit, Worp 2000, 88 related it to the colour of the jar—Lesbian amphoras came in two colours, grey and red.
120 Dsc. *Mat. Med.* V 11 MGO.
121 Gal. *MM.* 10.832–833K; *Vict. At.* 94; Orib. *Col. Med.* III 4, 1; V 6, 31.

thick.[122] Galen always called Lesbian wine λεπτός (thin, weak),[123] while Horace described it as *innocens*,[124] probably for those who have drunk it in excess. We could, therefore, associate the Greek term λεπτός with the Latin *innocens*, but according to Galen wines that were κιρροί and εὐώδεις (Lesbian among them) could inflame headaches.[125] Consequently, the statement that wine from Lesbos was light because drinking it did not cause serious discomfort the next day seems unjustified.

Notwithstanding, it is again possible to associate λεπτός with ἀθάλασσος. The lack of a salty admixture was one of the characteristics of Lesbian wine according to Dioscorides.[126] Galen confirms this, adding that it would be damaging for Lesbian wine if it was mixed with seawater.[127] Therefore, it is possible to draw a conclusion that Lesbian, like Chian, was light/thin because it was not adulterated. On the other hand, according to Pliny, *Lesbium sponte naturae suae mare sapit.*[128] This passage was interpreted by Whitbread as evidence that seawater was added to Lesbian wine.[129] However, Pliny says that wine from Lesbos naturally tasted of seawater. Does this mean that Lesbian wine was salty? This seems improbable considering the fact that the poets often praised it for its sweetness. Therefore, there must be some other quality hidden beyond Pliny's words, maybe they refer to the fact that salt was added to the clay of Lesbian transport amphoras.[130]

Salviat noticed another interesting characteristic of Lesbian wine, suggesting that its taste might have been similar to modern sherry or French *vin de voile* or *vin jaune*. A passage from Archestratus preserved in *Deipnosophists* mentions Lesbian with ὑγρὴν χαίτην λευκῷ πεπυκασμένον ἄνθει πίνειν,[131] which is translated as "*with hoary head indeed, whose moist locks are crowned with a white bouquet*". Salviat suggests that this metaphor refers to the film of yeast that is formed on the surface of wine during its maturation.[132] Therefore, similarly to Chian, Lesbian wine would distinguish itself through its specific taste, which

122 Gal. *MM*. 10.832–833K.
123 Gal. *MM*. 10.835K; *Comp. Med. Loc.* 13.405K; *SMT* 11.604K.
124 Hor. *Carm*. I 17, 21.
125 Gal. *MM*. 10.835K.
126 Dsc. *Mat. Med.* V 11 MGO.
127 Gal. *MM*. 10.832–833K.
128 Plin. *HN* XIV 74.
129 Whitbread 1995, 155.
130 See the previous section.
131 Fr. 59 Ri = Ath. *Deipn*. 29b.
132 Salviat 1986, 179.

was similar to modern *vins de voile*. This hypothesis may be confirmed by the fact that this wine is called ἀνθοσμίας by Longus.[133]

It is worth mentioning that, apart from the wine described above, there were at least three other particular kinds of Lesbian wine, namely *protropum, pramnian* and *omphakites*. The first, mentioned by Vitruvius, is probably liquid that runs naturally out of the grapes before pressing.[134] *Omphakites* was a beverage made of sour, not fully ripe grapes that were dried in the sun.[135] Πράμνιος from Lesbos is mentioned by Ephippus, quoted by Athenaeus.[136] The exact meaning of this word is unclear, because it is sometimes used as a geographical epithet and sometimes as a designation for the type of wine or vine.[137] For example, Eparchides of Icaria, a historian who lived before the end of the 3rd c. BC and who was quoted by Athenaeus, said that Pramnian wine from Icaria was neither sweet nor rich, but rather dry, hard and strong.[138] At the same time, Dioscorides described πράμνειος as wine made of sun-dried grapes[139] (which must have been sweet), but in Galen's *Glossarium* πράμνιος is defined as a dry (αὐστηρός) and dark (μέλας) wine.[140] In *Deipnosophists* we also find information according to which *Pramnian* wine was dark and suitable for long storage (παραμόνιον).[141] Therefore, it seems that Pramnian was originally an old and dry beverage produced in the area around Mt. Pramnos on the island of Icaria. Later on, its production probably extended to other regions, which is suggested by Pliny, who mentions *pramnium* from Smyrna.[142] According to Kourakou-Dragona, *pramnios* refers to a type of wine which in Homeric times was strong, dry and red, with a high degree of tannins. This is why Homer mentioned drinking Pramnian wine with barley and grated goat cheese[143]—the bitter taste of the tannins was neutralised by proteins from these admixtures. This wine was made from a variety of grapes that was called *pramnia*. In the Roman period, white and sweet wines which were made of a new vine variety called '*psinthia*' or 'white *pramnia*' became fashionable. These wines were sometimes called *pramnian*,

---

133 Longus IV 10, 3.
134 *Vitr* VIII, 3, 12; Plin. *HN* XIV 75. For more information about *protropum* see García Soler 1999, 401–402 and Kourakou-Dragona 2013, 43–49.
135 Dsc. *Mat. Med.* V 12 MGO; see García Soler 1999, 398–399.
136 Ath. *Deipn.* 28f.
137 Ath. *Deipn.* 30e.
138 Ath. *Deipn.* 30b.
139 Dsc. *Mat. Med.* V 9 MGO.
140 Gal. *Gloss.* 19, 132, 10.
141 Ath. *Deipn.* 30e.
142 Plin. *HN* XIV 54.
143 Hom. *Il.* XI 639–641; *Od.* X 233–235.

but they had nothing to do with the *pramnian* wine from the Archaic age.[144] Therefore, Dioscorides was probably talking about 'Roman *pramnian*', a sweet white wine made from raisins, whereas the Lesbian *pramnium* mentioned by Ephippus would probably resemble wines from the Homeric age. However, we do not know whether the Romans knew of these particular kinds of Lesbian wines and their peculiar properties, and hence we may assume that Lesbian wine consumed in Italy was white and fragrant, had both sweet and dry varieties, and that it matured in a natural way without any admixtures.

2.3 *Thasian*

According to Pliny and Aelian, wine from Thasos was at the forefront of Eastern Mediterranean wines, together with Chian and Lesbian.[145] It was a luxurious beverage that was drunk not because of thirst, but due to its good taste.[146] Thasian was made from grapes of the highest quality, remarkable for their sweetness.[147] Although they were nice in taste, their cultivation in Italy was unprofitable, because they needed fertile soil. Also, they had small berries that yielded little juice.[148] This wine was noble, old[149] and probably strong, since it stayed in the head for a long time.[150] Moreover, it was very fragrant (εὐώδης).[151] Its aroma was, according to Aristophanes, nicer than the smell of perfumes,[152] whereas, Hermippos says that it resembled the fragrance of apples.[153] This is interesting, because according to Kourakou-Dragona the smell of apples is a characteristic of *vins oxidatifs*, which means those that were maderised or that matured under a film of yeast.[154] Therefore, this may be further evidence that certain Greek wines were prepared similarly to modern sherry or *vins de voile*.

Maurus Servius Honoratus describes Thasian wine as *pinguis*,[155] which may mean fat in the sense of rich and oily, as well as luxurious, or full of pitch. The colour of the wine from Thasos was μέλας,[156] thus, both white and red could be

144 Kourakou-Dragona 2013, 16–18, 20–22. For more information about *pramnian* see also García Soler 1999, 399–401.
145 Plin. *HN* XIV 73; *VH* XII 31.
146 Xen. *Sym.* 4, 41; Luc. *Amores* 27; *Epicur.* 1089C, 1097D.
147 Plin. *HN* XIV 75 and 117.
148 Verg. *Georg.* II 91; Varro, *Rust.* III 2, 24, XIV 25, XIV 39.
149 Hp. *Morb.* 22.323K; Ath. *Deipn.* 29c.
150 Aristoph. *Eccl.* 1118–1119.
151 *Paed.* II 2, 30, 2.
152 Aristoph. *Eccl.* 1118–1119.
153 *CAF* fr. 82 Kock.
154 Kourakou-Dragona 2013, 86.
155 *In Verg. Georg.* II 90.
156 *Kokalos* Fr. 350 Kock; Ath. *Deipn.* XI 478d; Aristoph. *Lys.* 193.

considered. From the context in which this wine was placed in *Lysistrata*, we may assume that it had the colour of blood, hence a red colour would be more likely, according to Salviat.[157] In such a case Thasian used by Lysistrata could not be old, but it has already been shown that age was one of the main qualities of this wine, as mentioned by Hippocrates and Archestratus (quoted in *Deipnosophists*). According to Kourakou-Dragona, during the Archaic and early Classical age most Greek wines were red.[158] Therefore, Aristophanes in *Lysistrata* may refer to the 'archaic' Thasian, while Archestratus probably describes the 'new' wine produced on the island, which was white and old. This could also explain why Theophrastus wrote that Thasian wine that had been drunk in a prytaneion on the island had a great taste, because it was mixed with wheat, flour and honey.[159] Similarly to archaic *Pramnian* it might have had a high content of tannins and hence its taste was dry and bitter, which had to be neutralised. It is worth noting that Seleucus drank Thasian in a similar way; however, he used barley instead of wheat flour.[160] This suggest that the colour of Thasian wine probably changed during the 4th c. BC. Its taste might have also changed, which is suggested by a recipe preserved in *Geoponica* attributed to Florentinus, a 3rd c. AD author on farming. According to this recipe, ripe grapes that were dried for 5 days in the sun should be used to prepare Thasian wine. They should be put into must boiled down to a half before they could be pressed.[161] Such treatment would increase the content of sugar in the must and hence sweet wine would be obtained.[162] Furthermore, the recipe from *Geoponica* recommended the admixture of seawater to the must,[163] but a decree from the island dated to the 5th c. BC condemned adding water to Thasian wine,[164] which, according to Salviat, suggests that Thasian was originally among the ἀθάλασσοι (wines not mixed with seawater).[165] As mentioned above, this admixture was not recommended for *vins de voile*; therefore, if wine from Thasos belonged to this category, it should be white, sweet and without seawater.

---

157 Aristoph. *Lys.* 193–205; Salviat 1986, 178.
158 Kourakou-Dragona 2013, 122, 124.
159 *Od.* 51; Ath. *Deipn.* 32a.
160 Ath. *Deipn.* 432bc.
161 *Geopon.* VIII 23.
162 Salviat 1986, 174.
163 *Geopon.* VIII 23.
164 *IG* XII supl. 347 II.
165 Salviat 1986, 175.

2.4 *Coan*

Cos was another Greek island that, according to Strabo, was famous for its vineyards.[166] The admixture of seawater was the main characteristic of wine from Cos, and because of this it was included among the beverages called τεθαλασσωμένοι or τεθαλάττωται.[167]

In *De Agri Cultura*, Cato provides detailed recipes for *vinum Coum*. First of all, seawater should be collected 70 days before vintage and any sediment should be removed from it. The grapes should ripen thoroughly and then be left for two days in the sun after picking. Subsequently, they should be kept in a jar with seawater for three days before they are pressed.[168] Another method of making Greek wine would be adding seawater to the must using the proportion two *quadrantals* for one *culleus*,[169] which means 52,4 l. for 524 l. Consequently, seawater would constitute one tenth of the liquid, a significant amount. In the case of being far from the seashore, wine that would be no worse than Coan could be obtained by mixing 20 *quadrantals* of must with a *modius* (8,73 l.) of salt and a *quadrantal* of fresh water. Pounded rush and calamus should be added in order to give the beverage a pleasant aroma.[170] It is worth mentioning that there is a similar recipe for making Coan wine attributed to Vindanionius Anatolius Berytius, the author of a farming manual dated to the 4th c. AD, which also preserved in *Geoponica*.[171]

Thanks to Horace and Cato we know that Coan wine was white or light yellow in colour.[172] However, Hippocrates recommends drinking Coan that is αὐστηρός and ὡς μελάντατον.[173] This means that there was a variety of wine from Cos that was dry and black. Although the expression ὡς μελάντατον is unclear, we may suppose that it indicates white, but very old Coan wine (see the case of black Falernian wine in the first part of this chapter) and should be understood as 'as old as possible'. However, Kourakou-Dragona argues that the addition of seawater influenced the colour of wine—it did not turn black with time.[174] Therefore we have two possibilities. The first is that we are dealing with a red wine from Cos. The second is that in the 5th c. BC, wine from Cos was not mixed with seawater. According to Kourakou-Dragona, the custom of adding seawa-

166 Strab. XIV 2, 19.
167 Plin. *HN* XIV 78–79; Ath. *Deipn.* 32e.
168 Cato *Agr.* 112.
169 Cato *Agr.* 24.
170 Cato *Agr.* 24, 105.
171 *Geopon.* VIII 24.
172 Hor. *Serm.* II 4, 29; Cato *Agr.* 24; Plin. *HN* XIV 78.
173 Hp. *Int.Af.* 22.474K.
174 Kourakou-Dragona 2013, 127.

ter to wine did not exist in the 5th c. BC and in this period most wines were red.[175] Therefore, it seems that the colour of wine from Cos or the process of its production changed between the 5th and the 2nd c. BC. Hippocrates might have referred to red wine that had no seawater admixture, whereas the Romans drank Coan that was white and τεθαλασσωμένος. What was the quality of this wine in the Roman age?

It seems that Coan was not as highly appreciated by the poets as Chian or Lesbian. There are no texts mentioning its delightful taste or beautiful aroma. Therefore, it is possible that its rank was not superior. However, it seems that it was not a bad wine. Strabo, for example, mentions it together with Chian and Lesbian.[176] Moreover, Cato devotes a considerable part of his work explaining how to imitate wine from Cos. Would he bother to do so if the beverage was of a poor quality? This would seem rather improbable; thus, we may suppose that the taste of Coan was pleasant. Nevertheless, it probably belonged to a different category of wines than Chian, Lesbian and Thasian.

2.5 *Rhodian*

According to Pliny, *Rhodium Coo simile est*.[177] Therefore, we may suppose that this wine was white, dry and mixed with seawater. Moreover, it was probably not among the high-end products. Wine from Rhodes was made from the grapes of a local variety called *Rhodia*, that was mentioned by Vergil, Macrobius and Columella.[178] There is no information about its exact colour. Since medical texts suggest that it could be replaced by other αὐστηρός,[179] we may suppose that it was a dry wine. However, according to Timachidas, Rhodian wine was παραπλήσιον τῷ γλεύκει, which suggests that its taste was close to sweet beverages or to the new sweet wine.[180] There is similar information in Aulus Gellius' *Attic Nights*, in which the author suggests that Aristotle considered Rhodian wine to be good, but Lesbian was sweeter/nicer (ἡδίων ὁ Λέσβιος).[181] Does this mean that the island produced both dry and sweet drinks? Although this hypothesis cannot be excluded, it seems unlikely. First of all, Aristotle's comparison served as a metaphorical recommendation of his successor, choosing Theophrastus from Lesbos over Eudemus of Rhodes. Secondly, the term

175 Kourakou-Dragona 2013, 122, 124.
176 Strab. XIV 1, 15; XV 2, 19.
177 Plin. *HN* XIV 79.
178 Verg. *Georg.* II, 102; Macrob. *Sat.* III, 20, 7; Col. *R.R.* III 2,1.
179 Gal. *Suc.* 11.738K; Paul. Aeg. *Epit. Med.* VII 25, 15.
180 Ath. *Deipn.* 31e.
181 *NA* XIII 5, 8–10.

ἡδὺς means nice rather than sweet. Therefore, it is more probable that Rhodian was dry, but also nice and pleasant to taste without any unpleasant bitterness or acidity. However, another explanation is possible. According to Kourakou-Dragona, the Greek term αὐστηρός cannot be understood as dry in a modern sense, because most ancient wines had a certain amount of residual sugar, which means that in modern terminology they would be classified as semi-dry or even semi-sweet. If Rhodian wine was similar to Coan and made of grapes that were dried in the sun for two days, it should have some residual sugar left. Finally, it should be mentioned that Rhodian was mixed with seawater, but the proportion of the admixture was lower than in the case of Coan.[182]

2.6 *Cnidian*

We do not have much information concerning wine from Cnidus. According to Strabo, Cnidian was considered to be among the exceptionally good beverages.[183] Pliny mentions that *protropum* was produced on this island. He explains in another passage that this term refers to must that flows spontaneously from the grapes before they are pressed.[184] On the other hand, Pollux claims that the word *protropum* means wine, not must. Various attempts have been undertaken by scholars to explain this term. García Soler argues that *protropum* in modern terms would be classified as "*vino generoso seco*",[185] which seems strange considering that Pliny includes it in the category of sweet wines, while in *Deipnosophists* we find information that the Mytilenians called their sweet wine *protropum*. Kourakou-Dragona provides an explanation. On the basis of testimonies by Aristotle and Hesychius as well as a passage from *Geoponica*, she formulated a hypothesis, according to which the term *protropum* referred to must, not to wine. However, people in classical antiquity saw must as young, sweet, unfermented wine. If the must was obtained from fresh grapes (and not raisins) two processes might have occurred. If it was stored below 15^0 C it would not ferment and would remain sweet ἀεί γλεῦκος. However, in higher temperatures it would ferment into dry wine.[186] While explaining the term *protropum* Pliny mentions fermentation, which suggests we should assume he meant the second option, i.e. dry wine. Nevertheless, Dioscorides includes *pro-*

182 Ath. *Deipn.* 32e; Plin. *HN* XIV, 79.
183 Strab. XIV 1, 15.
184 Plin. *HN* XIV 75, 85.
185 García Soler 1999, 401–402.
186 Kourakou-Dragona 2013, 43–44. According to Kourakou-Dragona, in antiquity it was impossible to make sweet wine from grapes that were not dried.

tropum in the category of raisin wines.[187] If must was obtained from raisins similar reactions would take place depending upon the sugar content. The must could ferment into strong dry wine; strong sweet wine; or, in cases when sugar content was very high, very sweet but low-alcohol wine.[188]

Alexander of Tralles, writing in the 6th c. AD, mentions that Cnidian wine was light/thin (λεπτός) and watery (ὑδατώδης). Also, since it could have been replaced with honeyed-water it was probably sweet.[189] However, it is impossible to verify whether late Roman Cnidian had the same characteristics as the 1st c. AD *protropum*.

2.7 *Lefkadian*

Wine from Lefkada was among the drinks that Apollodorus recommended to Ptolemy,[190] which suggests that it enjoyed a good reputation. Moreover, Plautus set it together with the best, old and renowned Greek wines, such as Chian, Lesbian and Thasian.[191] However, according to Athenaeus, Lefkadian wine was bad for the head because it contained gypsum.[192] Maybe this was the reason why the Romans no longer imported it during the Imperial age. The admixture of gypsum works well with strong wines, as well as *vins de voile*.[193] Given that all wines mentioned by Plautus in *Poenulus* might be included in these categories, it seems possible that products from Lefkada shared the same characteristics. It was, however, not as appreciated as Chian, Lesbian or Thasian, which might have been due to the admixture.

2.8 *Mendean*

A fragment from a Mendean amphora discovered in the Temple of Castor and Pollux suggests that during the 5th c. BC wine from this polis reached Italy.[194] It was white, dry and soft and as it could be drunk neat, diluting it with water was not necessary. The rank of this wine in the Greek world was similar to the products from Chios, Lesbos, and Thasos, and it held its position from the Homeric times until the Hellenistic period.[195]

187 Dsc. *Mat. Med.* V 9 MGO.
188 Kourakou-Dragona 2013, 44.
189 Alexander of Tralles, ed. Puschmann, I 335, 483; II 217.
190 Plin. *HN* XIV 76.
191 Pl. *Poen.* 699.
192 Ath. *Deipn.* 33b.
193 Kourakou-Dragona 2013, 74.
194 Slej 2008, 204–208.
195 Salviat 2013a, 91, 97–98.

3 Imperial Common Imports

With the beginning of the empire a transformation may be observed with regard to the Italian wine market. South Aegean products kept their position, but wines from Lesbos and Thasos were no longer imported, while importations of Chian ceased soon afterwards. At the same time, the range of wines in Italy was enriched by imports from Crete, western Anatolia, Cilicia, Cyprus, Syria, Egypt and a very small number of products from the Black Sea region. However, these wines seldom appear in classical literature, which suggests that they were less important and probably less highly regarded.

3.1 *Cretan*

The most abundant literary evidence concerning wine from Crete dates from the 1st to the 6th c. AD.[196] Most of these sources mention that Cretan wine was very sweet. It could replace *mulsum*, a wine mixed with honey, or even honey itself in medical prescriptions.[197] It was called '*mulsum* of the poor men' by Martial.[198] Its sweetness was obtained using late harvested grapes that were dried in the sun, which facilitated a reduction in the proportion of water. The grapes were from a local, Cretan vine, called *Kretike/Kressa*.[199] Cretan wine was known in Greece under the name of γλυκύς, whereas the Romans called it *passum*.[200]

Kourakou-Dragona analysed a few recipes concerning this type of beverage. According to her, the recipe provided by Mago[201] served for making a non-alcoholic beverage. This recipe recommended pouring must over raisins and pressing them after they have absorbed it. The content of sugar in beverages that were obtained in this way would be so high that it would make fermentation into alcohol impossible. Other recipes for *passum* provided by Columella allow for making sweet and strong wine. The first recommends keeping the grapes in the sun for three days, which would not be long enough to dry them completely. The second suggests that dry wine instead of must should be poured upon raisins. This recipe served for sweetening dry wines.[202] Unfortu-

196 For example, Juv. 15; Mart. XIII 106; Fronto, *De eloq.* I, 4 and Venantius Fortunatus, *Vita S. Martini* II 81. This is confirmed also by the amphora evidence, see Chaniotis 1988, 78.
197 Gal. *Comp. Med. Loc.* 13.30–31K.
198 Mart. XIII 106.
199 Poll. VI 82; Cl. Alex. *Pedag.* II, 2, 30.
200 Plin. *HN* XIV 81; Plb. VI (6, 2) = Ath. *Deipn.* X 440e–f.
201 Col. *R.R.* XII 31,1.
202 Kourakou-Dragona 2013, 52–53, 56.

nately, there is no text that provides information regarding the exact production process of Cretan wine. We do not even know how long the grapes were dried before pressing. Nevertheless, if we consider that it could replace wine that was mixed with honey, we could suspect that it was very sweet indeed. According to Kourakou-Dragona, Cretan wine was non-alcoholic[203] and given that Pliny includes it in a separate category called *dulcia*, and not in the category of *vina transmarina*,[204] such an interpretation cannot be excluded.

It is worth mentioning that *passum* was not the only beverage that was produced on the island of Crete. There were also white wines that tasted like old beverages,[205] as well as white and light drinks.[206] The Cretans also made θηρᾶιος (*siraeum*), which was a mild and sweet wine obtained by boiling must.[207] However, these beverages were produced for local consumption rather than for export.[208] Thus, it seems unlikely that they were imported to Italy.

3.2 *Sicyonian*

It seems that wine from Sicyon was not famous in antiquity, since it does not appear frequently in literature. Given that it was not mentioned in *The Deipnosophists*, we may presume that it was not produced or exported in the Classical age. It was known in Rome during the late Republican age, which is suggested by the discoveries of amphoras from *Casa di Ariadna* (Pompeii).[209] It might have also been imported in the early Imperial period, as Pliny includes it in his list. His opinion of Sicyonian wine was rather good, because he placed it after north Aegean as well as Tmolian and Clazomenian, but before Cnidian and Ephesian.[210] However, it had no special characteristics, as it was absent in medical writings and was also ignored by the poets.

---

203 Kourakou-Dragona 2013, 56. However, Cretan wine is also mentioned in Galen's *Commentary to Hippocrates' Acute Diseases* that was edited by Kühn, see Gal. *Hipp. Morb. Acut.* 15.861–862K, where it was called οἰνῶδες, which is usually understood as 'vin vineux', a strong wine, see Béguin 2002, 145. Nevertheless, since in Loeb and Les Belles Lettres edition of *Corpus Hippocraticum* Appendix XXXVII, 2 the word κιρρὸν is given, it seems that it was later wrongly copied as κρητικὸν. Therefore, strong Cretan wine did not exist.

204 Plin. *HN* XIV 81.

205 Pall. XI 14.

206 Gal. *Hipp. De vict. acut. comm.* 15.648K.

207 Gal. *Comp. Med. Loc.* 13.8K; 13.212K; Poll. *Onom.* VI 16–17; Plin. *HN* XIV 80.

208 Marangou-Lerat 1995, 28.

209 See Chapter 1, Section 5.

210 Plin. *HN* XIV, 75.

3.3 Tmolian and Mesogitic

Dioscorides identifies Tmolian wine with *messogites* and claims that it caused headaches.[211] However, Strabo and Pliny distinguish beverages from around Mt. Tmolus from those from the area of Mt. Mesogis.[212] Moreover, Strabo classified them as exceptionally good both for their taste and medical values. According to this author, the best variety of Mesogitic came from the city of Aroma, situated near Nysa, on the far side of the Maeander River.[213] Since G. Malinowski argues that Strabo described in detail the wines that he knew or had tasted personally,[214] the testimony of the author of *Geography* seems to be more reliable than the information from Dioscorides.

Furthermore, the good quality of wine from around Mt. Tmolus is confirmed by Galen, according to whom Tmolian was among the three best wines from Asia, together with Chian and Lesbian. It was a white wine that matured for a considerable time (κιρρός) and included both sweet and dry varieties.[215] Silius Italicus placed Tmolian together with Chian and called it *divus*,[216] while according to Maurus Servius Honoratus, this wine had an aroma of crocus.[217] Pliny, however, mentioned that the Romans did not appreciate Tmolian as wine, but they did value its sweetness and used it to sweeten dry beverages. It was also believed that this admixture could make them more mature.[218]

3.4 Clazomenian

According to Pliny, *nunc gratia ante omnia est Clazomenio, postquam parcius mari condiunt.*[219] Therefore, it seems that this beverage was one of the most popular during the 1st c. AD, when it was flavoured sparingly with seawater. On the other hand, Dioscorides claimed that it spoiled quickly and had a negative effect upon one's health, because it contained seawater.[220] This discrepancy in opinions may be explained by the fact that Dioscorides referred to 'old Clazomenian' that contained too much seawater, whereas Pliny mentioned its 'new', upgraded version.

211 Dsc. *Mat. Med.* V 10 MGO.
212 Plin. *HN* XIV, 75; Strab. XIV 1, 15.
213 Strab. XIV 1, 15 and 47.
214 Malinowski 1999, 210–211.
215 Gal. *Comp. Med. Loc.* 13.513K; *SMT* 11.604K; *De probis pravisque alimentorum succis* 6.802K; Orib. *Col. Med.* V 6, 31.
216 Sil. *Pun.* VII 209–211.
217 *In Verg. Georg.* I 56.
218 Plin. *HN* XIV 74.
219 Plin. *HN* XIV 73.
220 Dsc. *Mat. Med.* V 10 MGO.

3.5 *Ephesian*

The wine from Ephesus, called *phygelites* by Dioscorides,[221] was unhealthy, according to Pliny, since seawater and boiled must were employed to season it.[222] However, Strabo claimed that it was good,[223] while Dioscorides mentioned Ephesian among the wines without seawater.[224] Therefore, we may suppose that Pliny was wrong in his description and hence he did not actually drink this beverage. On the other hand, it may simply be an example of the Greeks and the Romans having different tastes in wine. Another explanation is that the authors were referring to different types of wines that were produced in the area of Ephesus.

3.6 *Samian*

Samian amphoras were attested in Italy during the Archaic age, but there is no evidence suggesting that they carried wine. On the contrary, Strabo informs us that the island of Samos did not produce good wine, contrary to the areas surrounding it.[225] In addition, wine from Samos did not appear in Pliny's list of foreign wines, which suggests that it was not popular during most of the Roman era. However, this probably changed during late antiquity, when Samos Cistern Type amphoras reached Italy and literature started to mention Samian wine. Nevertheless, we know very little regarding its characteristics, apart from the fact that it was a watery wine (ὑδατώδης) that was probably good enough to be served at imperial banquets.[226]

3.7 *Cypriot*

References to wine from Cyprus are not very often attested in ancient sources. Strabo says only that Cyprus was a very fertile island which produced good wine and olive oil.[227] Nevertheless, Cypriot wine had a rather good reputation—in his list of foreign wines Pliny placed it after north-Aegean, Chian, Tmolian and Clazomenian, but before many others, such as Egyptian, Syrian, Mysian, Cnidian, Ephesian and Myconian.[228] It seems significant that wine from Cyprus is absent in *The Deipnosophists* and the medical writings of both Dioscorides and Galen, which suggests that it was not a popular drink. It is true that the former

221 Dsc. *Mat. Med.* V 10 MGO.
222 Plin. *HN* XIV 75.
223 Strab. XIV 1, 15.
224 Dsc. *Mat. Med.* V 11 MGO.
225 Strab. XIV 1, 15.
226 Venantius Fortunatus, *Vita S. Martini* II 80–82; Alexander of Tralles, ed. Puschmann, I 483.
227 Strab. XIV 6, 5.
228 Plin. *HN* XIV 75.

mentioned a Cypriot beverage called κατορχίτης (or τροχίτης) οἶνος; however, it was not made of grapes, but of figs.[229] The association between Cypriot wines and figs may also be found in a poem by Palladius.[230]

3.8 *Cilician*

Xenophon in his *Anabasis* informs us that many sorts of vines grew in Cilicia and that the Cilician plains enjoyed very good agricultural conditions.[231] However, no author mentions winemaking in this region before Pliny the Elder, who states that this area produced *passum*, a raisin wine that was distinguished by its sweetness. Cilician *passum* was better than the African beverage made of sun-dried grapes, but came second after the Cretan variety, which was the most famous and popular in Rome. Cilicia also produced a wine called 'Abates', but it is doubtful that the Romans imported it, as it was 'merely a laxative'.[232]

3.9 *Biblian/Byblian*

The wine called Byblinos was, according to Salviat, made from the Byblian vine that originated in Byblos in modern Lebanon. The Bible and Egyptian papyri mention wine from Lebanon and inform us that it was a high-quality drink that was able to survive transportation to Egypt.[233] Also, the Book of Hosea suggests that Lebanese wines enjoyed good fame.[234] Wine from Byblos was also mentioned by Euripides,[235] Theocritus[236] and by numerous writers quoted by Athenaeus in *Deipnosophists*. According to Achaeus, Byblinos wine was named after the region, while Epicharmus claimed that the name derived from a mountain. The historian, Armenidas, attributed 'Byblian country' to certain parts of Thrace, especially Antisare and Oesyme,[237] but Byblian vine was also cultivated in Magna Graecia. According to the 5th c. BC writer Hippys of Rhegium, it was introduced to Syracuse from Italy by the tyrant Pollis of Argos, which suggests that the sweet wine called Pollion by the Greeks from Syracuse

229 See κατορχίτης οἶνος in Dsc. *Mat. Med.* V 41 MGO, while τροχίτης οἶνος Dsc. *Mat. Med.* V 32 (Wellmann).

230 *Anth. Gr.* IX 487.

231 Xen. *Anab.* I 2,22.

232 Ath. *Deipn.* 33b.

233 Salviat 2013b, 118–122; Kourakou-Dragona 2013, 25.

234 Hosea 14:8.

235 Eur. *Ion.* 1194–1195.

236 Theoc. 14.15. He also mentions Byblis spring, see 7.116.

237 Ath. *Deipn.* 29b–c, 31a. Greek lexicography gives the same explanation after Epicharmus, see Hesychios B 609 and *Etymologicum Magnum* 197.32.

must be Bybline.[238] Archestratus from Gela (mid-4th c. BC) praised Bybline wine and classified it as a Phoenician beverage, adding that this wine was more fragrant, but less tasty than Lesbian.[239] Phylillus suggested that like the luxurious Greek *crus*, including Chian, Lesbian, Thasian and Mendean, it did not cause headaches.[240] According to Salviat's interpretation of Hesiod, Byblinos was a good wine, made from the Byblian vine, which originated in Phoenicia, but was later exported to Thrace, Boeotia and Sicily. It was made of sun-dried grapes, therefore, it was probably a sweet, old, aromatic and strong wine, that should be diluted with a considerable amount of water.[241] Kourakou-Dragona agrees that Byblian might have been a raisin wine, but suggests that it had low alcohol content.[242]

Considering the above-mentioned testimonies, it seems logical that Byblinos was made from the vine called Byblia, which originated in modern Lebanon. This vine was spread by the Phoenicians, who from the 9th c. BC established commercial relations with Cyprus and Crete and later with the Aegean, including Thasos, Thrace and Boeotia. Subsequently, they founded Carthage, and their colonies in Sicily. This is probably how the vine reached Magna Graecia and Italy. Curiously, 'Biblinos Oenos' is still produced in Greece, in the area around Mount Pangeo, near Kawala, which is situated in the territory of ancient Thrace. This is a strong wine (its alcohol content oscillates around 13.5–14%) which is produced from an unknown local vine, the fruits of which produce high levels of acidity and tannins.[243]

3.10 *Egyptian*

Although ancient Egypt was famous for beer rather than wine, the production of the 'gift of Dionysus' also enjoyed a long-lasting tradition in the country of the pharaohs, reaching as far back as the Old Kingdom period (2575–2150 BC).[244] According to Strabo, the area around Lake Mareia, situated in the southwest of Alexandria, was the main wine-producing region in Egypt during the Greco-Roman age.[245] This wine was called Mareotic or Alexandreotic.[246]

---

238 Ath. *Deipn.* 31b.
239 Fragment preserved in Ath. *Deipn.* 29b–c.
240 Ath. *Deipn.* 31a.
241 *WD* 588–596, 609–615; Salviat 2013a, 80, 86–87. For the process of raisin-wine production see Kourakou-Dragona 2013, 35–41.
242 Kourakou-Dragona 2013, 39–41.
243 http://www.elloinos.com/greek-grapes/biblinos-oenos, accessed 17.09.2016.
244 Guasch-Jané et al. 2006, 1075.
245 Strab. XVII 1, 14.
246 Ath. *Deipn.* 33d.

In addition, wine was made in the Arsinoite Nome, in the Faiyum.[247] This literary testimony is confirmed by archaeological research, which proved that wineries existed in various parts of the Nile Valley, such as the coastal areas, the Delta, the Faiyum, Bahariya Oasis, and Upper Egypt, but they were particularly concentrated in the Mareotic region, especially along the southern shore of the lake and around Abu Mina. This was probably due to climatic conditions that were far better for viticulture than in other parts of Egypt.[248] Furthermore, papyrological evidence suggests that the areas surrounding Hermopolis and Oxyrhynchos were wine-producing centres, but no wineries have so far been attested archaeologically. Additionally, epigraphy and archaeology confirm wine production in 3rd c. AD Theadelpheia.[249]

Vergil praised the white grapes from the area of Lake Mareotis,[250] where plenty of vines grew.[251] They produced good quality wine,[252] which was consumed by the rich and famous, including Cleopatra.[253] This wine was described in *Deipnosophists* as: *"excellent; for it is white and sweet, has a fine bouquet, is easily absorbed by the body and light, does not go to the head, and is diuretic"*.[254] Taeniotic wine was also made in the area of Lake Mareotis, and according to Athenaeus was considered better than the other beverages produced in the region. It was pale in colour, aromatic and slightly astringent. Athenaeus also informs us that there were many other vines and wines in Egypt, for example the variety that was produced around the city of Antylla, as well as those made around Thebes and Coptos. The latter was thin, digestive and easily absorbed by the body, so that even people suffering from fevers could drink it without any harm.[255] Dalby interprets the Σαίτης wine mentioned in the Edict on Maximum Prices as wine from Sais, arguing that it was an expensive drink.[256] However, other sources suggest that it probably referred to wine from Setia, a favourite of Augustus, as it was mentioned among Italian vintages.[257] *Setinum* appears in works by Strabo and Pliny, while no other sources mention Saite wine.[258]

247 Strab XVII 1.35.
248 Empereur 1993, 45–46; Dzierzbicka 2005, 11–24; 2010, 127.
249 E.g. *P. Flor.* II 148 recto; Dzierzbicka 2005, 26 and 51–52.
250 Vergil, *Georg.* II 91.
251 Ath. *Deipn.* 33d.
252 Strab. XVII 1, 14.
253 Hor. *Od.* 1.37.
254 Ath. *Deipn.* 33d.
255 Ath. *Deipn.* 33e–f.
256 Dalby 2003, 130; *Diocletian's Price Edict* 2.5.
257 Kropff 1971.
258 Strab. V 3, 6; Plin. *HN* XIV 61.

It seems that Egyptian wines did not enjoy a good reputation in Italy. Martial laughed at them saying: "*Disdain not this amphora of Egyptian vinegar. It was much worse when it was wine*".[259] At the same time, Pliny ignored Mareotic wine, referring only, after Vergil, to the vine from this area. The only Egyptian wine mentioned in *Natural History* is from Sebennys and was made from three famous types of vine: the Thasian, the soot-grape and the pine-tree grape ("*Thasio, aethalo, peuce*"). In Pliny's hierarchy of foreign wines it was placed far below the best foreign *crus* (northern Aegean), ranking between Levantine and Hippodamantian wines.[260] Therefore, we may assume that even though Mareotic wines were of good quality and were held in high esteem in the Eastern Mediterranean, they were not highly regarded by the Romans.

3.11 *Syrian*

Not much scholarly attention has been paid to wines that were produced in the Levant[261]. This is surprising given that this region had a long-lasting winemaking tradition, as suggested by the fact that Canaanite jars, the earliest transport amphoras, were produced in the Levant during the mid-2nd millennium BC. Wine was carried in Canaanite amphoras as indicated by *tituli* mentioning 'honeyed wine' that appear on a number of examples[262]. The descendants of the Canaanites, the Phoenicians, continued with amphora and wine production, but we know very little about the characteristics of the wines that they made, apart from the fact that Byblian wine probably originated there. However, there is evidence regarding wines that were produced by their neighbours, such as the Assyrians and Hittites. For example, cuneiform tablets from Nimrud dated to the early 1st millennium BC reveal that Assyria produced sweet/good white wines, bitter wines, strong wines, and early wines[263]. At the same time, the Hittites might have made raisin wine[264]. The Phoenicians were probably familiar with this type of wine, since Mago the Carthaginian provided us with a recipe for the preparation of *passum*, as it was called in Latin[265]. Moreover, literary testimonies suggest that Greek Byblian wine, which had a Phoenician origin, was made from raisins. Salviat attributed a Phoenician origin to certain Greek wines, such as Byblinos, Chian, Maroneian and Thracian, on the basis of

259 Martial XIII 122: *Amphora Niliaci non sit tibi vilis aceti: Esset cum vinum, vilior illa fuit.*
260 Plin. *HN* XIV 39 and 74.
261 See e.g. Leonard 1996; Powell 1996.
262 Grace 1979, 67.
263 Stronach 1996, 180.
264 Gorny 1996, 136–137, 147–158.
265 This was copied by Columella, see *R.R.* XII 31,1.

a passage from Achilles Tatius[266]. Thus, it cannot be excluded that the Phoenicians produced wines similar to Greek. It is worth mentioning that the Greek word κάδος, which means 'a wine jar' or denotes a liquid measure, comes from the Phoenician *kd*, which shows certain links between Greek and Phoenician winemaking[267].

Roman era sources mention Syrian wines[268] from Chalybon, Tyre, Sarepta, Berytus (Laodicea), Damascus and Antioch.[269] Chalybon (Chelbon, Khelbon, modern Aleppo) was situated in north-east Syria and produced wines as early as the Persian times. This beverage was first mentioned by Strabo, who suggested that it was a luxury drink.[270] It seems that it might have been produced west of modern Aleppo and north of Apamea, in the area covering the Gebels il A'la, Halaqa, Sheih Barakat and Siman, including Gebels Zawiyé Wastani and Doueilli, where numerous presses were attested.[271] Posidonius, quoted by Athenaeus, confirmed that Persian kings drank Chalybonian wine, but he claimed that this beverage was made in Damascus, where the Persians planted vine.[272] We may therefore assume that Damascus produced wine that bore the same characteristics as Chalybonian, or that they made beverages from the same vine variety. Nevertheless, it cannot be excluded that Posidonius (even though he was from Apamea in Syria) was mistaken, and that Damascus was only involved in the trade of wine from the area of modern Aleppo, where wine trading is confirmed by the Bible.[273] It is interesting that most modern Lebanese wineries are situated in the Beqaa Valley,[274] which abuts Syria (including the Damascus area) from the east. At the same time, the coastline to the west of the Beqaa Valley contains numerous ancient Phoenician ports, such as Byblos, Tyre and Sidon. Pliny informs us about wines from Beirut and Tyre, which in his hierarchy appear after north Aegean, Cypriot, Tmolian, Tripolitan and Lycian (Telmesus) beverages, but before Egyptian, Carian and Ephesian.[275]

266 Salviat 2013b, 118–119, 121.

267 Heltzer 1993, 51.

268 Hor. *Od.* 1.31.

269 Plin. *HN* XIV 74; Strab. XV 3, 22; XVI 2, 9; Libanius, *Orations* 11, 20; Mart. IV 46; Venantius Fortunatus, *Vita S. Martini* II 80–82, MGH *Auct. Antiquiss.* VIII, 242; Alexander of Tralles, ed. Puschmann, I 335, 483; II 217, 325, 327, 407, 421, 457, 485, 495.

270 Strab. XV 3, 22.

271 Van Limbergen 2015, 171; Callot 1984. However, it remains uncertain how many of these presses served for wine production.

272 Ath. *Deipn.* 28d = Poseidonios F155 Jacoby.

273 Ezekiel 27.18.

274 Robinson 2006, 398, under 'Lebanon'.

275 Plin. *HN* XIV 74.

Late antique sources provide us with some information regarding the characteristics of these wines. According to Alexander of Tralles, wine from Tyre was good for medical purposes when it was old.[276] Sidonius Apollinaris and Venantius Fortunatus, mention also wine from Sarepta, which, according to Alexander of Tralles, was thin (λεπτός), watery (ὑδατώδης) and recommended in medicine when not very old.[277] Wine from Laodicea was among the strongest beverages.[278] Finally, according to Libanius, Antioch was a wine-producing centre, but we know nothing about the qualities of the drinks that were produced there.[279] Nonetheless, the presence of LRA1 amphora production centred around Antioch[280] suggests that during late antiquity this region might have been an important wine-making area. It is also possible that Antioch was a reloading point, where wine produced in Syria's interior was transferred into amphoras and then shipped to external markets from Seleucia Pieria.

3.12 *Palestinian*

According to Corippus, the 6th c. AD poet, the area of Palestine produced white, sweet and light wines,[281] which became popular during late antiquity. A number of wine presses, as well as Christian sources, confirm the production of wine in Palestine, especially around Gaza.[282] Thanks to Gregory of Tours, we know that Gazan wine was strong.[283] This wine was also mentioned around 460 AD by Sidonius Apollinaris, together with Chian and Falernian, which were the best *crus* of the Hellenistic and early Roman period.[284] This, as well as the fact that it was served at the funerary banquet of Justinian organised by Justin II,[285] suggests that it was a high-quality drink. Alexander of Tralles provides us with information regarding wine from Ascalon. It was watery (ὑδατώδης) and good for medical purposes, when matured for a considerable time.[286] Literary evidence also suggests that Gaza and Ascalon "*export an excellent wine all over Syria and Egypt*".[287] There is, however, no confirmation that these wines

276 Alexander of Tralles, ed. Puschmann, II 457.
277 Alexander of Tralles, ed. Puschmann, I 335, 483; II 217.
278 Gregory of Tours, *Hist. Fran.* VII 29.
279 Libanius, *Orations* 11, 20.
280 Van Limbergen 2015, 170.
281 Corippus, *In Laud. Just.* 3.87–88.
282 Mayerson 1985.
283 Gregory of Tours, *Hist. Fran.* VII 29.
284 *Carmina* XVII 15 = MGH *Auct. Antiquiss.* VIII 242.
285 Corippus, *In Laud. Just.* 3.87–88.
286 Alexander of Tralles, ed. Puschmann, I 335, 483; II 457.
287 *Expositio Totius Mundi et Gentium* 29. About wine from Gaza and Ascalon see also Alexander of Tralles, ed. Puschmann I 419; II 53, 353, 393, 411, 457, 539.

were regarded as 'excellent' by the inhabitants of Italy. Nevertheless, Gazan amphoras attested in the Western Mediterranean were often discovered in large centres or in the areas inhabited by aristocracy, which may suggest that wine that they carried was associated with the elites.[288]

3.13 *Black Sea Region*

Wines from the Black Sea area are extremely rare in Latin sources and they are almost equally neglected by Greek literature. Apart from Pliny mentioning wine from Naspercene, which was produced in Pontus probably during the Hellenistic age, nothing is known about it. Wine from Bithynia aroused more interest. Thanks to Galen, Florentinus and Alexander of Tralles we know that white and sweet wine, made from the Amineian vine (or other varieties such as Drossalide or Leucothracia) was produced in this province, *inter alia*, in the area of its capital, Nicomedia.[289] Florentinus, moreover, mentioned a mysterious wine that was called δενδρογάλ ηνος οἶνος in Bithynia, stating that it was the most appreciated wine in Heraclea Pontica.[290] We do not know, however, whether any of these wines reached Rome, as at least the product made of the Leucothracia vine was good, but not durable.[291]

Analyses of Hellenistic Sinopean and other amphora stamps suggest that agricultural products from the Black Sea region were marketed, above all, within this area—the stamps are abundant throughout the Black Sea region and at the same time they are rarely attested in the Mediterranean.[292] In the 4th c. BC Demosthenes characterised Pontic trade using the following words:

> Now, men of the jury, take thought in your own minds, whether you ever knew or heard of any people importing wine by way of trade from Pontus to Athens, and especially Coan wine. The very opposite is, of course, the case. Wine is carried to Pontus from places around us, from Peparethus, and Cos, and Thasos and Mendê, and from all sorts of other places; whereas the things imported here from Pontus are quite different.[293]

288 Pieri 2012, 38–39.

289 Gal. *MM* 10.834K; *ST* 6.337K; *BM* 6.805K; Orib. *CM* 5.6.33K; *Geopon.* 4.1.3; 5.17.3–5; Alexander of Tralles, ed. Puschmann, II 27.

290 *Geopon.* 5.2.10.

291 *Geopon.* 5.17.8.

292 Discoveries of Black Sea amphoras in the Mediterranean are scarce and largely confined to the Aegean region in the Hellenistic period. Their scope widened during the Roman age but was still not very significant. Lund 2007, 185–189.

293 *Contra Lacritum* 35. Translated by A.T. Murray.

This testimony suggests that wine production was not developed enough during the 4th c. BC for wine to be exported. The lack of literary evidence regarding wines from this region may indicate that no considerable change occured during the Roman age and that in the Imperial period Black Sea imports were not conducted on a large scale.

4 Epigraphic Enigmas

Tituli picti preserved on wine amphoras from the Eastern Mediterranean in general terms confirm what we already know from ancient literature. For example, one *titulus* informs us that a Cretan amphora contained γλυκύ οἶνον,[294] which is not surprising, because sweetness was the most distinctive feature of Cretan wine. Also, a black inscription on a Cretan container from Eleutherna provided evidence that wine from Crete was ἀθάλασσος, which means without seawater.[295] Furthermore, Schoene-Mau XII, it is Dressel 2–4, amphoras are sometimes inscribed with the Greek word λευκός.[296] Considering that they contained wine from Cos or its Italian imitation,[297] and that this wine was white according to the literary evidence, no further discussion is needed. However, numerous *dipinti* do not agree with the literary testimonies or suggest other qualities of Greek wines than those that were mentioned by ancient writers. These cases should be described in more detail and explained before drawing conclusions about the characteristics of Eastern wines that were consumed in Rome.

4.1 *Rhodian and Coan as Sweet Wines?*

Only one abbreviated *titulus* mentions wine from Rhodes: *Pass(um) Rhod(ium) |P(ubli) Coeli Galli.*[298] It was found on an amphora that was classified as Schoene-Mau VIII but was in fact a Rhodian container.[299] This jar was discovered in the House of Menander (I 10, 4) in Pompeii. Literary evidence does not mention Rhodian *passum* and this type of wine was typical of Crete and Cilicia. However, it cannot be excluded that the popularity of Cretan *passum* had an impact on Rhodian wine production. It should be mentioned that a Dressel 5

294 CIL IV 6324.
295 Marangou-Lerat 1995, 150, fig. 93 (P 106).
296 CIL IV 6454 and 9529, here it is abbreviated to ΛΕΥ.
297 Italian imitations of wine from Cos are mentioned for example by Cato *Agr.* 112.
298 CIL IV 9327.
299 Marangou-Lerat 1995, 130.

amphora that was found in Kerameikos in Athens had the *titulus* γλυκύς, which may suggest that sweet wine was its content.[300] This container, typical of the early Imperial period served for the transportation of Coan wine, which was dry, according to a 5th c. BC work by Hippocrates. Therefore, we may assume that Coan wine changed between the Classical and the Roman age. Was this also the case with Rhodian? The *titulus* is almost certainly dated not long before 79 AD and the only literary source that mentions Rhodian as dry wine is a spurious work classified as Pseudo-Galen.[301] Thus, even though we cannot precisely date this text, it seems that it should be dated to the 2nd c. AD. Therefore, the logical conclusion would be that in the early Imperial age the island of Rhodes produced both dry and sweet wines. This should not come as a surprise when we consider that Lesbian, Chian and Tmolian wine also came in both varieties.

It should be mentioned that Pompeian amphoras of the type Schoene-Mau XLII resemble Rhodian containers (Camulodunum 184). Three inscribed transport jars of this type were recorded in CIL.[302] However, only one had a legible inscription that may be associated with wine—ληναῖος, which means a wine press; the other *tituli* were illegible.

4.2 *Lefkadian or White Wine from Cos?*

There is a *titulus*: *Leuc() / vet(us) / C(ai) T() C() // κορνηλιου// Corneliu(s)*,[303] attested on a Schoene-Mau XII amphora that was discovered in an unnamed house (VI 15, 13) in Pompeii. This inscription may at first sight suggest the presence of Lefkadian wine in Pompeii. However, considering the fact that it is written in a mixture of Latin and Greek, the Greek word Leucos (but written in Latin alphabet) is also probable. Another possibility could be 'Leucocoum', which means white Coan wine.[304]

It has already been said that Lefkadian was mentioned in Poenulus by Plautus. It was described as '*vetustate vino edentulo*', which should be interpreted as mellowed by age. Therefore, it seems that literary and epigraphic evidence agrees regarding the characteristics of this wine. However, the dating is problematic—Plautus wrote in the early 2nd c. BC, whereas the Pompeian inscription is probably dated to the mid-1st c. AD. There is no other Latin author that mentions Lefkadian wine in the context of Italian consumption. Although Pliny the Elder enumerated it, he quoted Apollodorus, a mysterious physician

---

300 Bezeczky 2013, 80.
301 Ps. Gal. *De succedaneis* 19.738K.
302 CIL IV 6936, 10404, 10447.
303 CIL IV 5590.
304 Remark 1881, 21.

who in a treatise had recommended wines, including Lefkadian, to one of the Egyptian Ptolemies. All the wines were of eastern origin, since this treatise was created, according to Pliny, at a time when Italian wines were not generally known.[305] This indicates that it must have been written before the 1st c. BC or even the mid-2nd c. BC, which is when Roman wine amphoras (first Dressel 1 and later Dressel 2–4) are widely attested in the Mediterranean.[306]

Considering the above information and taking into account that no containers in which Lefkadian wine could be transported have so far been recognised, it seems more probable that the *titulus* concerns wine from Cos. However, it is impossible to say whether the inscription should be read as '*leucos vetus*' or '*Leucocoum vetus*'.[307] In the first case this would mean that the Greek word 'λευκός' (meaning white) was written in Latin and accompanied by the Latin word '*vetus*'. It should be noted that 'λευκός' written in Greek is attested on one Schoene-Mau XII amphora[308] and probably on two others.[309] On the other hand, mixed Greek-Latin inscriptions are common, but they usually regard different things, for example the type of wine is given in Latin, whereas the trader's name is in Greek. A mixed *titulus* regarding the qualities of wine would be something unusual. Therefore, the interpretation of '*Leuc*' as '*Leucocoum*' seems more probable.

4.3 *Old and Excellent Wines from Cos and Crete?*

There is an inscription that was found in a *caupona* of M. Livius Alcimus in Herculaneum saying: *Ch⟨i=O⟩um / vet(us) exc(ellens) / Hercul(ani) [L]ịvi Alci(mi)*.[310] Since the form of the amphora on which this inscription was attested was not given, and considering that the text may be read as both '*Chium*' or '*Choum*', it seems at first difficult to define whether we are dealing with wine from Chios or Cos. The term '*vetus excellens*', meaning an old, excellent wine suggests the former; however, the context in which this amphora was discovered (*caupona*) indicates the latter. Unfortunately, no other inscriptions mention wine from Chios, while the black *tituli* '*Choum vetus*' appear on at least three Schoene-Mau XII (Dressel 2–4) amphoras that were found in Pompeii.[311]

---

305 Plin. *HN* XIV 76.

306 Peacock, Williams 1986, 86–92; Bezeczky 2010, 83. For more about the chronology of Roman wines see also Tchernia 1986, 61–66.

307 'Leucocoum vetus' is mentioned by Pliny *HN* XIV 78.

308 CIL IV 6454.

309 CIL IV 9529.

310 CIL IV 10722.

311 CIL IV 5541, 9320, 9321.

Another three containers of this type carried the inscription *Coum vetus*.[312] Therefore, it seems highly probable that the wine of M. Livius Alcimus was also in fact '*Choum*'.

Another question is whether this means wine from the island of Cos or its Italian imitation. However, since there was no detailed typology of Pompeian Schoene-Mau XII (Dressel 2–4) amphoras until the study of Panella and Fano[313] appeared, it is impossible to determine whether the containers mentioned in CIL were of Italian or Aegean origin. The majority of these containers found in Pompeii were of a local, Campanian origin, but Coan amphoras are also attested in the city.[314] The Latin language used in the majority of *dipinti*, as well as the appearance of Italian names (P. Appuleius Bassus, L. Sextius Syrticus, C. Atinius) on five out of seven vessels that were inscribed with '*Coum vetus*' may indicate Italian wine production. Conversely, the Greek name Apollonios that accompanies the name of the wine in one *titulus*[315] may suggest a Greek origin for this beverage. Moreover, Łoś proved that many Italian citizens were involved in the trade of Cretan wine[316] and there is nothing to suggest that the trading of other Eastern wines was not similar. Finally, even if we assume that '*Coum*' or '*Choum vetus*' refers to an Italian imitation of Coan wine,[317] it is clear that it must have had the same characteristics as the original. Therefore, it would be white wine mixed with seawater. But was it also old?

According to literature, old age was not one of the most typical characteristics of Coan wine. Moreover, the exact age was not given in any of the inscriptions that mention '*Coum*' or '*Choum vetus*'. However, a passage from Hippocrates that recommends the drinking of Coan 'as black as possible'[318] suggests that wine from this island might have been matured for a considerable period.[319] Cato's recipe for making Coan recommended keeping it in an amphora that was kept in the sun for two years,[320] but does not mention further maturation. The case of Cretan wine is similar. Two *tituli* on Cretan amphoras indicate that old wine was kept inside them, but only one has a number that

312 CIL IV 5536–5538.
313 Panella, Fano 1977.
314 For example in *Casa di Ariadna*, see Albiach et al. 2008, 261.
315 CIL IV 05541.
316 Łoś 1997.
317 This is suggested by Van der Werff 1989, 367.
318 Hp. *Int.Af*. 22.474K.
319 See the case of black Falern in the first part of this chapter.
320 Cato *Agr*. 105.

may be interpreted as an age—IIII.[321] Four-year-old wine cannot be deemed as very old. Moreover, literature does not mention a long maturation process among the main characteristics of this wine. Therefore, the epithet 'vetus' used with Coan and Cretan in *tituli* may be seen as an advertisement, because old wines were generally more appreciated. In the case of Coan this would mean wine that matured long enough to be free from undesirable actions of seawater, which at the beginning gave wine an unpleasant scent.[322] What about the word '*excellens*'? Is it connected with the old age of wine or should it also be seen as a mere advertisement?

The adjective '*excellens*' is translated as 'towering, prominent, distinguished, superior, surpassing, excellent'. It appears on 25 amphora inscriptions in the 4th volume of *Corpus Inscriptionum Latinarum* and in seven cases is accompanied by the adjective '*vetus*'. There is wine (Cretan,[323] Coan[324] and probably Falernian[325]), *defrutum*,[326] *liquamen flos*,[327] *mola*[328] and other (not always identified) goods among the products that are accompanied by this epithet. Also, in several cases additional information was given, which can be interpreted as age, e.g. *a(nnorum) III a(nnorum)*.[329] Therefore, the link between *vetus* and *excellens* is not very strong. Moreover, wine from Crete, that was indubitably good but also an ordinary and cheap beverage, was called '*excellens*'. Furthermore, in at least 18 cases the name of the 'excellent' commodity was accompanied by the name of a tradesmen. This means that apart from the information about the content of an amphora, that simplifies and informs us of commercial activities, the names of those involved with these activities were also important. For what other reason, apart from marketing purposes, would a tradesman's name appear packaging alongside an epithet that praises the content? Therefore, it seems that *dipinti* that mentioned excellent Coan wine had nothing to do with the real qualities of this beverage. It was not superior to other wines. However, M. Livius Alcimus wanted to advertise that the wine from Cos that he was selling was the best—better than the products that were sold by other merchants.

---

321 CIL IV 5602, 5596. CIL IV 5526 almost certainly regards the secondary content and is the only example that has a consular date.

322 See Kourakou-Dragona 2013, 132–133.

323 CIL IV 05526a.

324 See above.

325 CIL IV 10724–10725. The letter C on these inscriptions was interpreted as an abbreviation for Chian wine, but this seems to be an over-interpretation.

326 CIL IV 5585, 9324.

327 CIL IV 2588 = 5716.

328 CIL IV 2604.

329 CIL IV 2636 = 5635, 2636 = 5635, 2655 = 5636, 5631, 5638, 9368.

The same thing may be said about the excellent wine from Crete. According to these advertisements, the best Cretan wine was sold by M(arcus) Stlab(orius) Nymp[hod(otus).

4.4 *Chian Wine Sold in Pompeian Taverns?*

There is only one inscription that can be associated with wine from Chios, *M(arci) M() F() / Chium*, though the reading is not certain.[330] The amphora that carries this inscription was found in building IV 17 at Herculaneum, but we know neither its form nor dating. However, considering that the building was a tavern, the context in which this amphora was found is surprising. According to the literary evidence, wine from Chios was a high-quality beverage that was probably consumed by the upper social classes. Is it possible that it was also sold in the common bars?

If the deciphering of this *titulus* as '*Chium*' is correct, it would be the only evidence for the importation of wine from Chios to the Vesuvian cities. Moreover, this inscription is similar in style to *Ch⟨i=O⟩um / vet(us) exc(ellens) / Hercul(ani) [L]ivi Alci(mi)*.[331] Therefore, it seems more probable that it should be deciphered as '*Choum*', which means Coan wine. Wine from Cos and Coan style wine that was made in Italy was a popular product in Pompeii, and since both were lower-quality beverages it should not be a surprise that they were sold in taverns.

4.5 *Red Wine from Crete?*

There are inscriptions with the letters '*rubr*' or '*r*[]*bru*' that are interpreted as '*vinum rubrum*'.[332] In some cases, '*rubr*' is accompanied by '*vet*,' which is usually read as '*vetus*'. There are also many *tituli* (and one *graffio*) that contain only the letters 'VR' or 'VI R' that are also deciphered as '*vinum rubrum*'.[333] These inscriptions are painted on the containers of the type Schoene-Mau VII, VIII, X, XI, XII and XIV. One inscription of this type that was painted on a Cretan (Schoene-Mau VIII) container: *Rubr(um) / vet(us) IIII / L(uci) A() H() ()*[334] led Marangou-Lerat to conclude that this island produced red wine.[335] However, is this conclusion correct?

330 CIL IV 10721.
331 CIL IV 10722.
332 CIL IV 2616, 5595–5600 and 5944, 9590, 10303.
333 CIL IV 9354–9366, 10304–10307, 10728.
334 CIL IV 5596.
335 Marangou-Lerat 1995, 151.

First of all, it should be mentioned that '*rubr*' can be understood not only as a designation of the colour of wine, but also as its provenance. For example, it might have been a product from Saxa Rubra (Prima Porta), a village that was situated on *Via Flamina*, north of Rome. The existence of this settlement is confirmed by literary evidence, as it is mentioned for example by Cicero, Livy and Tacitus.[336] Even though there is no evidence for wine production in this region and considering that it is improbable to import wine from the north of Rome to Campania—a region famous for wine production, it cannot be excluded. Another possibility is that '*rubr*' should be interpreted as the name *Rubrius*, which means someone from the *gens Rubria*. Finally, Cato mentions *oleas virides*, which are green olives[337] and which according to certain scholars is a better development of the abbreviation VIR.[338]

These interpretations seem more possible when we consider that ancient Latin texts never mention *vinum rubrum*. Red wine is called *sanguineus*. Of course, this may be easily explained by the nature of the inscriptions and their authors. Roman writers who created literary texts were educated people who used a different vocabulary than slaves or freedmen that were involved in the commerce of wine. However, the supposed *vinum rubrum* appears often on amphoras in which white wine was transported and on other non-wine amphora types. Apart from on Cretan amphoras, '*r*[]*bru*' also appears on container type XII—which carried wine from Cos (or its Italian imitation), and we know from the literary evidence that this wine was white. There are also abbreviations interpreted as *vinum rubrum* on Schoene-Mau VII and XIV—Spanish garum amphoras as well as on Schoene-Mau XI—Tripolitanian oil amphoras. This suggests that these *tituli* concern the secondary content of the jars and suggest their reuse; hence epigraphic evidence for the existence of red Cretan wine seems very poor.

4.6 *Spiced and Non-Grape Wines?*

Certain inscriptions suggest that Eastern wines might have been spiced with different substances, or that alcoholic beverages made of fruits other than grapes were made in the Aegean regions that were famous for their grape-wines. For example, Marangou-Lerat noticed that one *titulus* indicates that Crete produced myrtle-wine.[339] According to this author, the word '*thettalisco*' that accompanies the inscription should be interpreted as the Greek name,

---

336 Cic. *Phil.* II 31; Liv. II 49; Tac. *Hist.* III 79.
337 Cato *Agr.* 7.4.
338 Bonifay et al. 2015, 193–195.
339 CIL IV 5593.

Thettaliskos. Since M. Claudius Thettaliscos was attested on Crete, she assumes that this *titulus* concerns the primary use of this amphora and hence provides us with evidence that Crete produced myrtle-wine.[340] Although there is no literary evidence for making myrtle-wine on Crete it cannot be excluded. The only question is whether demand for this type of beverage would be so high in Italy that it had to be imported.

There is also evidence that might suggest the spicing Coan wine with different substances. An unknown amphora type that was found in Pompeii had the following black inscription: *Coum Gran( ) / of(ficina) / Romae Aterio Felici.*[341] The abbreviation at the beginning of the *titulus* is sometimes interpreted as '*Coum gran(atum)*'. Therefore, it could indicate the seasoning of Coan wine with pomegranate. However, another interpretation is possible—'*Coum Gran(ianum)*'. In this case it would refer to an imitation of Coan wine that was produced in *fundo Graniano*[342] or in *officina Grani* or *Granianum.*[343] The second part of the inscription suggests that this wine was produced in Rome and that a certain Aterius Felix was involved in its production or trading. However, importing wine from Rome to Pompeii seems pointless. Campania, and the Vesuvian region in particular, were important producers of wines that were exported to Rome, whose hinterland could not satisfy the city's demand. Therefore, it seems logical to propose another interpretation. The letters 'of' may indicate an abbreviated form of the name of a proprietor of *fundus Granianus* or a wine trader. According to this interpretation, Aterius Felix would be the recipient of this wine in Rome. This idea is confirmed by the fact that his name is written in the dative case. Therefore, the story behind this amphora would be as follows. An Italian imitation of Coan wine was produced in *fundo Graniano* and was prepared for transportation to Rome, where it was to be delivered to Aterius Felix. However, this operation was not fulfilled due to the eruption of Vesuvius. This indicates that the *titulus* concerns an Italian imitation of Coan rather than wine from the island of Cos itself. In conclusion, no matter how we develop '*Coum Gran*', the hypothesis that Coan winemakers spiced their wines with pomegranate should be excluded.

There is also a mysterious *titulus* that mentions *Coum arndua*,[344] which according to Remark should be read as *arunda*, which means a kind of reed.

340 Marangou-Lerat 1995, 141, 151.

341 CIL IV 2565.

342 Cooley and Cooley 2013, 232.

343 Remark 1881, 21.

344 CIL IV 5540.

Remark noticed that this word appears in medical texts.[345] Moreover, Cato recommends adding pounded rush and calamus into the must in his recipes for making a wine similar to Coan.[346] Therefore, the evidence for spicing Coan wine with reed seems reliable. However, according to Remark the *titulus 'Coum arunda'* concerns Coan-like wine that was produced in Italy rather than wine from the island of Cos.[347] His interpretation is highly probable, given that the inscription appears upon a Spanish Schoene-Mau VII amphora and not a Schoene-Mau XII that could be attributed to Cos. After the inscription *Coum arunda*, a Greek name appears written in Latin that is preceded with 'ab',[348] which suggests an Italian origin. This may be confirmed by the context in which the amphora was discovered—Villa Pisanella, a *villa rustica* with wine-making facilities, such as a *torcularium* with a wine press and a large court with *dolia*.[349] Therefore, this *titulus* should also be seen as evidence for the reuse of the Spanish amphora as a container for Italian imitations of Coan wine that were produced in Villa Pisanella. In such a case it would have nothing to do with the qualities of the wine from the island of Cos. Nevertheless, the scarce occurrence of the name Dorotheus or Dorotheos in Italy, as well as the lack of a *nomen gentile*, may testify against such an interpretation.

In summary, *tituli* indubitably expand our knowledge regarding the characteristics of Eastern Mediterranean wines, since they often confirm data obtained from the literary sources or provide us with additional information. However, sometimes they do not agree with literature, and hence should rather be associated with the secondary content of amphoras. This regards Latin inscriptions in particular and is probably due to the fact that the form of an amphora usually provided enough information regarding its primary content, but when a container was reused to carry a different commodity, additional information was necessary. Therefore, Latin *tituli picti* are more likely to be associated with the secondary content of amphoras than Greek inscriptions. Of course, this pattern can only be applied when no additional information (apart from the quality of the product) is given, or when the inscription is not contemporary with other attested *tituli*.

345 Remark 1881, 21.
346 Cato, *Agr.* 105.
347 Remark 1881, 21.
348 There is also a second *titulus*, written in red, composed of the letters P S G. However, even if these letters were interpreted as an abbreviated *tria nomina*, their colour suggests that the person named Publius S. G. was a trader of local products.
349 Rossiter 1981, 348, 350, 352, fig. 1.

5 Conclusions

By summarising the information provided by both the ancient literature and amphora epigraphy we may come to a few general conclusions concerning the consumption of Eastern wines in Italy. First of all, it should be emphasised that there is almost no difference in the way that the Greeks and Romans viewed these wines. For example, they both greatly appreciated imports from Chios, Lesbos and Thasos. However, it seems that the Romans preferred Chian, whilst the Greeks favoured Lesbian. Wines from Rhodes, Cos, Cnidus and Lefkada enjoyed a good reputation, but they were praised neither by Greek nor by Latin writers. Similarly, both Greek and Latin authors paid little attention to the qualities of Eastern wines imported to Italy during the Imperial period. Greek and Roman opinion only disagreed regarding Egyptian wines from Mareotis and Anatolian products from Ephesus and Clazomenae. Therefore, the conclusion may be drawn that both the Greeks and Romans had similar tastes regarding wine. Moreover, this may indicate that the Roman taste for wine, as well as its consumption, was influenced by the Greeks.

Secondly, it seems that all Eastern wines that were imported to Rome were of good quality, while some of them were even praised as real delicacies. Most of them were also useful in the field of medicine and enjoyed a good reputation amongst ancient physicians.[350] Nevertheless, it is impossible to say that all Eastern wines imported to Italy held the same rank, even wines from the same region: for example, the Aegean differed greatly. This means that García Soler's assumption that all Greek wines were viewed as luxurious commodities by the Romans, was wrong.[351] High-quality wines can be easily distinguished from those varieties that were not held in such high esteem. These high-quality beverages included Chian, Lesbian and probably Thasian. They were praised by poets and appreciated by physicians. Tmolian was appreciated by Galen for its medical properties, but its taste was probably mediocre. Wines from Cos, Rhodes, Cnidus and Lefkada were appreciated during the Republic, but in the Imperial age they were viewed the same as common imports from Crete, Asia Minor, Egypt and the Levant. These wines were pleasant in taste, but it seems that there was nothing special about them. Also, wines that were appreciated in the East were not always held in such high regard by the Romans.

It is not entirely clear which special characteristics made certain wines high-ranking. As we have already seen, the majority of Eastern wines that were

350 For a comprehensive analysis of the medical qualities of Eastern wines, see Komar 2020.
351 García Soler 1996b, 229.

imported to Italy would be classified as white wines today. This applies to Chian, Lesbian, Coan, Rhodian, Gazan, Mareotic and Bithynian wines. Red wine might have appeared in the form of Thasian, the Lesbian variety called *pramnium*, and wine from Cos that was mentioned in the *Hippocratic Corpus*, but the evidence is ambiguous. Again, García Soler's assertion that Chian, Lesbian and Thasian wines were 'vinos tintos' has no confirmation in ancient literature.[352]

Tchernia claims that almost all of the main Roman *grand crus* were white,[353] which suggests that Eastern wines did not differ considerably from other wines consumed in Italy. On the other hand, Kourakou-Dragona noted that wines in the Homeric age were predominantly red.[354] This means that the characteristics of wines changed between the Archaic and the Roman period. Considering this fact, we may tentatively suggest that both the Greeks and the Romans of the Hellenistic and the Roman era generally preferred white wines. What was the reasoning behind this? Kourakou-Dragona associates it with physicians and their recommendations.[355] Indeed, Galen favoured Chian, Lesbian and Tmolian, which were white, whereas neither he nor Dioscorides mentioned Thasian, which was most likely red. Of course, this may be due to the fact that in the 2nd c. AD the island of Thasos no longer exported wines; this, however, might have been a consequence of a lack of demand for its red wine. Is it true that the recommendations of ancient physicians favoured white wines?

According to Hippocrates, strong white wines had diuretic and laxative properties, and they were recommended for treating acute diseases. In these circumstances yellow as well as dark and dry wines might have been consumed.[356] Dioscorides stated that white wines were thin and easily digested, whereas dark varieties were thick, hard to digest, heady and fattening. He approved of yellow wines as they had middle strength, but he highlighted that "*white should be chosen both in health and sickness*". If we analyse Galen's works we see that watery white wines with no aroma were good for tackling fever, whereas sweet and dry wines that were yellow or dark were to be avoided. However, black and red wines were regarded as the most nutritious, especially when thick. White wines, even when thick, were still στρυφνοί (sour, astringent) and hence less nutritive. Moreover, red and black wines were, according to Galen,

352 García Soler 2002, 52.
353 Tchernia 1990, 65.
354 Kourakou-Dragona 2013, 103.
355 Kourakou-Dragona 2013, 124.
356 Hipp. *Acut.* 14.

good for the formation of blood.[357] Therefore, it seems that both white and red wines were considered as helpful, depending on the medical condition, which means that another, non-medical explanation for the predominance of white wines should be considered.

Compared to red varieties white wines do not contain a high proportion of tannins. Therefore, they do not need a long maturation process to eliminate the bitter taste and hence, production time is shorter.[358] This could be one of the reasons for the popularity of white wines in antiquity. Furthermore, there is no ancient text that mentions the maceration of grapes after pressing, unless it was to obtain a secondary, low-quality wine, such as *lora* (or *deuteria*).[359] *Lora* was an alcoholic beverage made by fermenting water and the remnants that were left after the grapes had been squeezed; and it was consumed by the lower classes, such as peasants or slaves.[360] Therefore, is it possible to claim that all good wines were white, whereas those of an inferior quality were red? It should be added that there was no difference in the colour of high-quality Aegean beverages and those of a lower grade. Therefore, even though it seems that the Romans indeed preferred white wines, colour was not the determining factor that afforded Chian, Lesbian and Thasian wines their great esteem. What about their sweetness?

In the first part of this chapter the popular assumption that most wines in antiquity were sweet was proven to be untrue. Moreover, there is no proof supporting Dalby's statement that all transmarine wines imported to Rome "*shared natural sweetness*".[361] There is evidence that both sweet and dry wines were imported to Rome from the Aegean. Among the first category there was certainly a raisin-wine from Crete. Chian, Lesbian, Coan and Rhodian probably had both sweet and dry varieties. Furthermore, García Soler was wrong when arguing that κιρρός "*se describe como un vino seco i se sitúa entre el tinto y el blanco*",[362] because wines of this colour, such as Chian, Lesbian and Tmolian had both sweet and dry varieties.

Nevertheless, the sweetness of wines was often praised by poets, which suggests that such wines might have been regarded as tastier. Actually, ancient physicians probably favoured sweet wines as ingredients as they made their remedies more palatable. Honey was added to dry wines that served as

357 Jouanna 1996, 424; Béguin 2002, 147.
358 Fitton Brown 1962, 194.
359 Tchernia 1990, 65; Dalby 2003, 353.
360 Amouretti 1990, 80; Tchernia 1986, 19.
361 Dalby 2000, 138.
362 García Soler 1996a, 134.

medicines in order to neutralise the bitter taste of φάρμακα according to Kourakou-Dragona, who also noted that Galen recommended using sweet wine in a prescription for a theriac, in order to improve the taste of the medicine.[363] It is worth mentioning that sweet Cretan *passum* was often recommended in respiratory medicines. According to Hippocrates, sweet wines were generally better, because they had laxative and expectorant properties, they also affected the head less than strong wines.[364] On the other hand, Chian is often recommended in pharmaceutical production, but it is not specified whether a sweet or dry variety should be used. Moreover, according to Dioscorides, new sweet wines could disturb the intestines.[365] Finally, dry wines, such as Coan and Rhodian were recommended in certain circumstances. Therefore, it cannot be proven that sweet wines performed better than dry varieties in a medical sense, but they might have been more appreciated by consumers.

People in classical antiquity knew that drying the grapes increased the sugar content of wines. According to Kourakou-Dragona, it was impossible to make a sweet wine in antiquity without the use of this practice.[366] Literary testimonies confirm that Cretan, Cilician, Coan and Thasian wines were made from sun-dried grapes. Therefore, we could assume that all sweet Greek wines that were imported to Rome were made from raisins. As a matter of fact, this was suggested by Salviat, who added that Greek wines were usually made from overripe grapes. As a result, wines that were strong (c. 16% ABV), aromatic and sweet were obtained; these wines resembled modern Muscat or Malvasia.[367] However, Coan wine could be produced after two days of grape drying, whereas the grapes used to produce Thasian wine needed five days of exposure to the sun. This means that not all wines were made of equally dried grapes and hence they probably differed in sweetness and strength. Unfortunately, there is no information regarding the production of Cretan or Cilician wines, which were typically raisin based. According to Tchernia, the process of producing sweet wines made from raisins or late harvested grapes is more difficult and there is a serious risk of spoiling.[368] Thus, the complicated production process could have been considered as a determinant of a wine's high rank. Nevertheless, this theory does not seem right if we consider Cretan *passum*, which from the 1st c. AD was particularly famous, whilst at the same time being the most popu-

363 Kourakou-Dragona 2013, 15.
364 Hipp. *Acut.* 14.
365 Dsc. *Mat. Med.* V 9 MGO.
366 Kourakou-Dragona 2013, 7.
367 Salviat 2013b, 131, 138–141.
368 Tchernia 1986, 208–209.

lar and cheapest beverage.[369] Moreover, Cilician held second place among the *vina passita* in Pliny's list,[370] and there is no literary testimony suggesting that it was a high-end beverage. However, it is meaningful that apart from Cretan and Cilician no other Eastern wine that was definitively made of sun-dried grapes and imported to Rome was ever called *passum*. Can we therefore say that Cretan and Cilician wines were specific, because they were unusually sweet? Since a very high sugar content may inhibit or stop alcohol fermentation,[371] is it possible that the popularity of these wines was due to the fact that they contained little or even no alcohol? If this was the case, they would not be wines *per se* and hence they would not contradict Tchernia's theory regarding the high-quality of raisin wines that were high-alcohol beverages.

It should be noted that the best Eastern wines, i.e. Chian, Lesbian and Thasian were often described as very fragrant. The same refers to Byblian and Phoenician wines. On the contrary, the aroma of the middle-quality beverages, such as those from Cos, Rhodes, Cnidus, Crete, Cyprus, Cilicia, Egypt and the Levant was rarely mentioned. Furthermore, all renowned wines that were imported to Rome were qualified as οἰνώδης and had to be mixed with a considerable quantity of water.[372] This means that they were strong wines. Finally, Chian, Lesbian and Thasian were often described as old. This is not surprising if we consider that for the ancient Romans all wines were considered old after one year.[373] In addition, commercial maritime expeditions used to take a considerable time, which certainly had an influence on the age of the imports. On the other hand, wines from the south-Aegean, Egypt or the Levant were never described as παλαιοί in the texts. Therefore age, or to be more precise, long maturation, could be a determinant of high quality.

Furthermore, it seems that in Rome, as well as in Greece, only those wines that matured naturally, i.e. without any admixtures, were held in high esteem. It seems that admixtures were regarded as bad, because they might have had negative effects on their consumers. For example, resinated wines, which were diuretic, aided digestion and were helpful with certain sicknesses, also caused headaches and nausea.[374] Similarly, the effect of adding gypsum to beverages could cause headaches and affect the nerves.[375] Wines with added seawater

369 Marangou-Lerat 1995, 156; Tchernia 2011, 257–258.
370 Plin. *HN* XIV 81.
371 Kourakou-Dragona 2013, 7.
372 Gal. *SMT.* 11.604K.
373 See the first part of this chapter.
374 Dsc. *Mat. Med.* V 43 MGO.
375 Dsc. *Mat. Med.* V 9 MGO.

were inflative, bad for the stomach, caused thirst and hurt the nerves. They were unsuitable for people who had recently recovered from sickness.[376] Mnesitheus of Athens is the only author who mentioned them in a better light, saying that they helped with digestion and did not cause a hangover.[377] The lack of this admixture may be the reason why Chian, Lesbian and Thasian were so highly appreciated, whereas Coan, Rhodian, Ephesian and Clazomenian (that were mixed with seawater) did not enjoy such high regard. It seems that wines that were produced without the admixture of seawater were seen as tastier and healthier, whilst τεθαλασσωμένοι, even though pleasantly tasting, did not have great reputability. This may be due to the fact that they were less healthy and that their maturation process was artificially accelerated. Moreover, the admixture of seawater might have had an impact on the consistency of wine. Unadulterated beverages, such as Chian or Lesbian, were always described as λεπτοί, which probably means 'of thin consistency'. Wines mixed with seawater (Rhodian, Coan, Ephesian, Clazomenian) did not possess this quality. Therefore, it would also be the wine's consistency, or as we would now say, its body, that separated high-quality Eastern wines from common beverages. Moreover, it seems that λεπτός (in a wine context) indicates a thin consistency because of the lack of seawater. Therefore, this adjective, while describing wine, could be understood as a synonym of ἀθάλασσος. In such case, wines from Sarepta and Cnidus should also be included in the category of wines prepared without the admixture of seawater.

It is worth mentioning that there are certain concepts regarding the seasoning of wines with seawater that need revision. First of all, according to André, Greek wines were in general often treated with seawater.[378] This is mistaken, since there were either τεθαλασσωμένοι or ἀθάλασσοι among them. Secondly, Bouvier claimed that only the admixture of seawater could stabilise wine enough to enable it to survive a transmarine journey without turning into vinegar.[379] Considering the fact that the Romans imported wines that were definitely unadulterated, such as Chian, Lesbian and Thasian, Bouvier's opinion is incorrect. We should remember that people in classical antiquity knew other methods of conservation, such as the use of pitch or resin coating in amphoras. Thus, seawater was not the only preservative. Finally, according to Bouvier, all Greek wines tasted salty to the Romans because in their recipes for wines *alla*

376 Dsc. *Mat. Med.* v 9 MGO.
377 Fr. 46 = Ath. *Deipn.* 32d.
378 André 1981, 165.
379 Bouvier 1999, 39.

greca, salt was always present.[380] In light of what has been said above this statement is unjustified. The Romans were definitely aware of the fact that certain Greek wines were *maris expers*.

Finally, it seems that wines from Chios, Lesbos and Thasos probably matured under a film of yeast, which was responsible for their specific taste. Therefore, we may suspect that the spicy taste of sotolon was among the characteristics that distinguished high-end wines from common beverages. This could also explain why these wines were not seasoned with seawater. This admixture, according to Kourakou-Dragona, could improve the taste of weak and watery wines, while in the case of *vins de voile* the addiction of gypsum would work better.[381] However, there is no evidence that gypsum was indeed added to Chian, Lesbian or Thasian. Moreover, Tchernia proposed that the taste of sotolon was probably described as δριμύς.[382] Unfortunately, neither of the north-Aegean wines was ever qualified like this. Therefore, even though the hypothesis regarding the specific production process of high-quality wines seems probable, it cannot be confirmed.

Is there any difference between Eastern Mediterranean wines that were transported to Italy and other wines produced in the East? It seems that wines that had a bad reputation, such as Corinthian, were not imported to Italy, which is not surprising. However, there were for example wines from Peparethos, Mende and Maroneia, as well as other beverages from Thrace, which had a very good reputation among the Greeks, but it seems that they were not well known in Italy. Although some of these wines were imported to the Apennine Peninsula in the Archaic period, there is no evidence for their consumption being continued after the 5th c. BC. This is curious since these wines did not differ in taste from, for example, Chian, Lesbian and Thasian. Salviat, who analysed the literary evidence regarding Thracian wines, noted that they were very sweet, aromatic and strong wines, which is why they had to be mixed with water. He compared them to modern *Jerez* or Tokaji. They were probably made of sun-dried grapes and most of them (except Mendean) were described as red (ἐρυθρός, αἶθοψ) or black.[383] Wine from Akanthos was exported to the Black Sea region in the 4th and 3rd c. BC, whereas Mendean was forgotten during the 2nd c. BC.[384] Therefore, it seems that these wines were not imported to Roman Italy as they disappeared before mass importations to Italy began.

380 Bouvier 1999, 39.
381 Kourakou-Dragona 2013, 74.
382 Tchernia, Brun 1999, 134–135.
383 Salviat 2013a, 78–80.
384 Salviat 2013a, 91, 97–98.

Moreover, Z. Archibald pointed out that in many Aegean areas (for example in Ilion, Corinth, Miletus, Samos, Ainos, Oisyme, and Samothrace) wine production satisfied the demand within their own immediate regions. Akanthos, Mende (Chalkidiki) and Peparethos (north of Euboea) exported their products on a larger scale, but only Thasos, Cos, Cnidus and Rhodes had truly large export distribution patterns.[385] This means that certain Eastern wines were never exported to Italy due to economic reasons—certain eastern regions produced too little wine to be able to export it on a large scale.

In conclusion, it is possible to state that it was indeed the taste that was responsible for the rank or status of Eastern Mediterranean wines that were consumed in Rome. The best wines were old, fragrant and not adulterated, and they probably resembled modern *vins de voile*. Nevertheless, it should be emphasised that the Romans imported both high-quality wines and more common beverages, and that the second category was much more numerous. Therefore, Finley's statement that in antiquity only "*the important foreign trade in fame regional wines*" existed, while "*vin ordinaire was normally produced at home*"[386] is unjustified. The Eastern Mediterranean wines that were imported to Rome cannot be classified as 'fame regional wines', as the majority of them were common wines. However, in order to properly assess the role that the trade in Eastern wines had with regards to the Roman economy, it is necessary to estimate the scale of their importations.

385 Archibald 2013, 199–200; Panagou 2015.
386 Finley 1999, 133.

CHAPTER 3

Mass or Limited? Wine Importations to Italy during the Early Imperial Age

> ... ὁ ἐποποιὸς τὴν μὲν πρώτην πόσιν ἀπονέμει Χάρισιν,
> Ὥραις, καὶ Διονύσῳ, τὴν δὲ δευτέραν Ἀφροδίτῃ καὶ πάλιν Διονύσῳ,
> Ὕβρει δὲ καὶ Ἄτῃ τὴν τρίτην
>
> ... the first toast to the Graces, the Hours, and Dionysus,
> the second to Aphrodite and Dionysus again,
> the third, however, to Violence and Ruin.
>
> ATH. *Deipn.* 36d

The previous chapter showed that both high and lower quality wines were imported to Italy from the Eastern Mediterranean. The next step is to check the actual share that different Eastern Mediterranean imports enjoyed with regards to consumption between the late Republican and mid-Imperial period. This will help us to understand the actual role that interregional trade played in the Roman Empire, particularly concerning staple foods. The importance of this branch of the economy was not significant according to, *inter alia*, Finley,[1] Hopkins[2] and Bang.[3] Although the role of long-distance trade of staple foods has recently been more appreciated, there is still much more to be done in this matter. Therefore, this chapter is devoted mainly to the quantities of eastern wine amphoras in Italy and aims to show the scale and the dynamics of their importations. It will demonstrate what role trade in Eastern wines played with regards to the Roman economy and how this changed throughout the centuries. For example, the increase in importations may suggest the existence of economic growth in antiquity, which if true would enrich the long-standing

1 Finley 1999.
2 Hopkins 1980, 104; 1983, 84–85. Though he admits that the volume of trade increased greatly between 200 BC and 200 AD, see Hopkins 1980, 101, 105–106.
3 Bang 2008.

© KONINKLIJKE BRILL NV, LEIDEN, 2021 | DOI:10.1163/9789004433762_005

debate in this matter. Finally, by analysing the percentages of Eastern Mediterranean wine importations compared to transport costs provided by ORBIS, it may be possible to determine whether transport costs influenced the choice of wines that were imported to Italy, and hence verify whether and to what degree market forces operated during Roman antiquity. I follow Scheidel's assumption, according to which "*The notion that market forces underpinned observed transfers can be tested by relating the distribution of provenanced trade goods to their points of origin. Thus, the extent to which the distribution patterns of such goods matched cost contours might be read as a proxy for the prevalence of market exchange, which would arguably have been more sensitive to costs than coerced transfer*".[4] This study will analyse whether the wines imported to Italy from the East match the lowest 'cost contours', which are provided by ORBIS, a computer based model of connectivity in the Roman world.[5]

Pottery assemblages are among the main sources of information regarding trade patterns and may also be useful when studying the ancient economy. However, most of the publications regarding amphoras that were attested in central Tyrrhenian Italy are in the form of archaeological reports, the scope of which are usually limited to both a specific geographical area (in most cases this was merely one site)[6] and a narrow time-frame. There are only a few syntheses that try to show more general commercial trends. For example, Panella analysed which areas supplied Rome with staple goods such as grain, olive oil, wine and fish sauces between the 1st and the 3rd c. AD.[7] The same author presented the share of Gallic wine amphoras in the wine supply to the city of Rome between the second half of the 1st and mid-2nd c. AD.[8] Furthermore, Panella and Tchernia, who combined the data from Ostia (*La Longarina*, the Baths of the Swimmer and the House of the Porch) and Rome (*Meta Sudans*, *Via Nova*, the Crypt of Saint Bonaventure, and the Temple of Magna Mater), compared proportions of Italian and provincial amphoras between 50 BC and 600 AD.[9] Finally, in 2003 Rizzo presented a study of amphoras (and other categories of pottery) from six contexts in Rome dated between 64AD and the

4 Scheidel 2014, 28.

5 ORBIS: the Stanford Geospatial model of the Roman world, ORBIS/Understanding, http://orbis.stanford.edu, accessed 11.04.2019.

6 For example from *Terme del Nuotatore* in Ostia, see Anselmino, Coletti, Ferrarini 1986; or from the Temple of Magna Mater in Rome, see Carignani, Ciotola, Pacetti 1986.

7 Panella 1985. Using data from *La Longarina*, *Terme del Nuotatore* and *Castro Pretorio*.

8 Panella 1992. Amphoras from the following contexts were considered: *Meta Sudans, Via Nova-Clivo Palatino, Via Sacra-Via Nova, Crypta Balbi, Forum Transitorium*.

9 Panella, Tchernia 2002.

late Antonine period.[10] A few comparisons between the types and percentages of amphoras found in Ostia and Rome have also been carried out. For example, C. Pavolini compared percentages of containers found in *Portus* and the *Urbs* during the Flavian and the late Imperial period,[11] while S. Zampini examined amphora percentages from *Palazzo Imperiale* and *Terme del Nuotatore* in Ostia dated to the late 2nd and the early 3rd c. AD alongside percentages of containers dated to the late 2nd c. AD from *Meta Sudans* and *Foro di Cesare* in Rome.[12] Recently, Rizzo compared the numbers of Antonine age transport jars discovered in *Terme del Nuotatore* in Ostia with findings from *Via Sacchi* (*Gianicolo*), *Foro Transitorio* and *Mercati di Traiano* in Rome.[13] However, none of these studies concentrated upon wine amphoras from the Eastern Mediterranean. Moreover, they are all limited to Rome and Ostia, ignoring Campania and the Adriatic part of Italy. Finally, only amphora assemblages that were known up to 2012 were considered, but since then a lot of new data has come to light. Therefore, this study will show the subject from a different perspective, it will adopt a broader geographic and chronological scope and take advantage of the latest archaeological data. Additionally, it will provide the first comparison of importation patterns in the Tyrrhenian and Adriatic parts of Italy.

The chronological scope of this study, which stretches from c. 100 BC to 300 AD, has been selected due to the fact that staple goods were not commonly imported to Italy before the 1st c. BC. It is true that stamps from eastern wine amphoras discovered on the Apennine Peninsula can be dated as early as the 3rd c. BC, but there are no assemblages of containers dated earlier than the late Republican period for which statistical analysis would be possible. This is probably due to the fact that Italy was for a long time rather self-sufficient in terms of most staple goods. However, its population gradually increased and became more enriched, which resulted in the growing need for more foodstuffs to be imported. The scale of these importations started to grow during the 1st c. BC, but the real boom occurred under Augustus and was probably associated with the eradication of piracy, the *Pax Romana*, and the unification of the empire, which resulted in reduced transportation costs. A consequence of which was

10 Rizzo 2003.
11 Pavolini 1996.
12 Zampini 2011. Only material dated between 160–180 AD (*Meta Sudans*) and the end of the 2nd c. AD (*Foro di Cesare*) was analysed, even though material dated to other periods was attested. The amphoras analysed by Zampini come from other levels at *Foro di Cesare* than those that will be presented in this chapter. Since Zampini provided only general percentages from *Palazzo Imperiale* and considering the preliminary nature of the statistics, this data is not included in this synthesis.
13 Rizzo 2012.

that imported goods, such as wine, olive oil and fish sauces, became common in Italy during the early Imperial period.

This chapter compares the numbers and percentages of eastern wine amphoras found in Italy with the numbers and percentages of wine containers from other areas. However, according to certain scholars it is not the number of containers, but the total volume of wine that they carried that should be considered, because amphora capacities often varied considerably.[14] Such an approach is not only more complicated, but may also provide false results, because it is impossible to judge the exact capacity of a jar on the basis of a fragment from its rim or base.[15] Luckily, the doubts regarding amphora capacities have been solved by E.C. De Sena, who has proven that the statistics do not differ considerably. Therefore, regardless of whether we consider only numbers of diagnostic fragments (i.e. rims, bases, handles) or estimate the total amount of wine (calculating the number of the amphoras multiplied by their average capacity) the results should be similar. The data may be biased only for wine from Anatolia and Calabria, as the containers from these regions were much smaller than other amphoras.[16]

Furthermore, it should be emphasised that based upon the amphora evidence, the amount of Italian wines will always be underestimated. De Sena drew attention to the fact that there is literary as well as archaeological evidence for wine production in the Roman hinterland; however, no amphoras confirm their consumption in the Eternal City. This is due to the fact that these wines were transported in perishable containers, which escape detection in modern research, or in reused amphoras.[17] De Sena's estimates regarding the percentage of wine that was produced in the hinterland and consumed in Ostia and Rome suggest that the hinterland was the main source of wine for these cities, satisfying around a third of the demand.[18] These estimates corroborate calculations that were made by A. Marzano, who tried to examine the intensity of wine and olive production in Roman *suburbium* by analysing the density

14 Wilson 2009a, 230–233.

15 Approximated capacities are known, but a number of amphora types have different variants, the capacity of which may differ considerably, see Van Alfen 1996 for the capacities of LRA1. Late Roman amphora capacities varied up to several litres within a single type, see Pieri 2012, 42.

16 De Sena 2005, 3.

17 De Sena 2005, 138–140. It is suggested that wines might have been transported in barrels (*cupae*) or wineskins (*cullei/utres*), but there is no proof for the use of wooden casks in western Italy before the early 3rd c. AD. They became common in Rome in the 3rd and 4th c. AD, see Panella, Tchernia 2002, 184.

18 De Sena 2005, 142.

of presses.[19] Therefore, we should keep in mind that the statistics provided by amphora calculations represent only a certain percentage of wine that was consumed in Rome and other centres, and they ignore beverages that were produced in the neighbouring rural areas.

The synthesis presented in this chapter comprises the proportions of amphoras that have been discovered in *Latium et Campania*, as well as in *Venetia et Histria* and *Aemilia*, see Fig. 2. It is based upon archaeological reports that provide details of transport containers found in individual archaeological contexts. Wine amphora fragments were counted together, regardless of the site, but divided into four geographical units, namely: Rome, Ostia, Campania and the Adriatic area. The particular character of each context was not taken into consideration, this was in order to obtain the most general view. Unfortunately, it was impossible to appropriate equal chronological periods for each geographical unit, but they were made as similar as possible. Five chronological periods were distinguished for Rome: the late Republican period, the Augustan age, the 1st century AD, the 2nd century AD,[20] and finally the 3rd century AD. Material from Ostia and Campania allowed for more detailed time spans to be distinguished, while amphora publications from the Adriatic area mostly divide them into early and late imperial. For the purposes of this study two diagrams were produced for each area. The first shows all Eastern Mediterranean wine amphoras combined, in comparison with wine containers from other geographical areas. The second presents percentages of amphoras from different areas of the Eastern Mediterranean, which highlights those areas that were most important with regards to supplying wine to Italy. Italian amphoras were divided simply into Tyrrhenian and Adriatic, thus avoiding more specific geographical categories such as Campanian, Vesuvian, central or north-Tyrrhenian etc., which would only complicate the general picture. The category 'Adriatic amphoras' includes the containers called Lamboglia 2, Dressel 6A, Forlimpopoli and the Adriatic version of Dressel 2–4,[21] whereas Dressel 1, Dressel 2–4 and flat-based containers from Empoli were classified as 'Tyrrhenian'.[22]

The numbers of amphoras presented in this study refer in most cases to the numbers of diagnostic fragments. In a few cases where the jars were well

19 Marzano 2013.
20 This includes the entire Trajan's age.
21 Lamboglia 2 and Dressel 6A originated in the Adriatic coast (somewhere between Brindisi and Rimini), but they were also probably produced in modern Croatia (central Dalmatian coast), see Lindhagen 2009.
22 This category also includes the so-called 'di Spello'/Ostia III 369–370/II 521 amphoras that were produced in Umbria and in other centres throughout inland central Tyrrhenian Italy, especially in the Tiber valley.

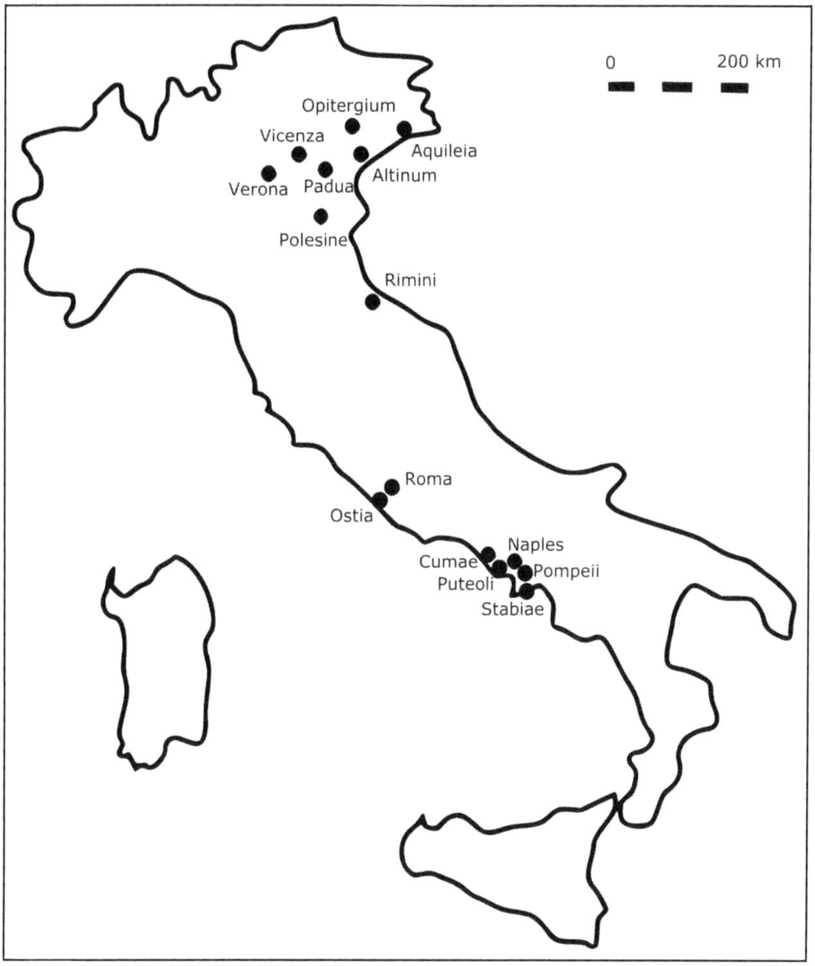

FIGURE 2 A map of sites which provided amphora assemblages considered in the synthesis

preserved, the statistics present the estimated minimal number of containers. Such an approach may result in the omission of certain amphora types that were represented only by non-diagnostic fragments, but this occurs rarely and when it does a footnote is provided containing the relevant details. The list of containers from different geographical areas considered to have carried wine is presented in Appendix 3.

1 Roma—the Eternal City

It may seem surprising, but the absence of systematic excavations and hence stratigraphic references made it impossible to trace consumption patterns in ancient Rome until the 1990's. In 1992, pottery assemblages that were attested in the Eternal City were studied and partially edited, but this included only those dated between the second half of the 1st c. AD and the first half of the 2nd c. AD (the Julio-Claudian and early Antonine dynasty). In recent years discoveries from numerous sites have been published, but apart from the works of Panella and Rizzo[23] no wider syntheses, which show changes with regards to the supply of staples, have so far been presented.

The synthesis of wine amphoras shown in this book comprises material from assemblages published up to 2015. However, not all of the assemblages could be included as a number of the archaeological reports, upon which this synthesis was based, inform us only about the types of containers that were discovered, without giving their exact numbers. Moreover, incidental findings of eastern containers, such as the Hellenistic Rhodian amphora with the stamp [Φ]ΙΛΟΚ[Ρ]ΑΤΕΣ found in *Commitium*,[24] the Rhodian transport jars attested in *Antiquario Comunale* and near *Tempio di Veiove*, as well as the probable Chian amphora from the Trajan's Markets[25] were not considered in the statistics presented below. Similarly, it was impossible to include assemblages that were not precisely dated, such as, for example, those from a necropolis under a Vatican carpark dated between the 1st and the 4th c. AD, which included one Kapitän 1 and three Cretan transport jars. Moreover, flat-bottomed amphoras, used as urns for ashes,[26] predominated in this context, which suggests that the assemblage is not representative. A wide chronological distribution—between 80 BC and 150 AD—is also the reason for excluding containers found in *Villa dell'Auditorium*.[27] There are similar problems with amphoras from the Temple of Castor and Pollux on the *Forum Romanum*, where Rhodian, Cretan, Agora F65–66 and Kapitän 1 and 2 fragments were attested, dated generally between 0–400 AD,[28] as well as with Cretan, Coan, Rhodian, Anatolian, Cypriot/Cilican

23 Panella 1992; Rizzo 2003.
24 Gjerstad 1960, 234.
25 Palma, Panella 1967–1968, 100.
26 Carre, Cipriano 2003, 204–207.
27 Di Santo 2006, 291, tab. 39 and 40, 292, tab. 41. These were found in Rooms 5 (predominantly) and 4. Greek wine containers were represented by Camulodunum 184 and Agora F65–66.
28 Slej 2008, 219–250.

and Cilician jars found in the *Porticus Aemilia* in the contexts dated generally to the Imperial age.[29] Sporadic Cretan, Rhodian, Cnidian and Pompeii 5 containers discovered in *Monte Testaccio* date to the period between 144/145 and 252 AD,[30] which does not fit into the chosen time spans. Finally, amphoras from the Baths of Trajan also had to be excluded, as diagnostic and non-diagnostic fragments were counted together. It is unfortunate that the evidence from *Terme di Traiano* had to be excluded, as the variety of eastern containers was very broad and included Rhodian, Coan, Cnidian, Cretan, Anatolian (Agora F65–66), Syrian (Kingsholm 117) and Egyptian (AE3) examples.[31] It is worth mentioning that eastern wine containers (probably Rhodian and Coan) were also found during excavations under the *Basilica San Giovani di Laterano*, but their exact provenance could not be accurately determined.[32] Moreover, Agora F65–66 as well as Kapitän 1 and 2 amphoras were discovered in *Villa della Piscina* in Centocelle, but no dates or exact numbers were given.[33] Therefore, the synthesis includes only precisely dated amphoras, the assemblages of which were randomly created and may be seen as a rather aleatory sample. The accepted material comes from 13 archaeological sites where at least 25 different archaeological contexts were distinguished, dated to between the 1st c. BC and the 3rd c. AD. These contexts include:

1. *The Forum of Caesar (Foro di Cesare)—1st c. BC*

The archaeological material from *Foro di Cesare* comes from a cistern that was constructed in the 4th c. BC. During the 1st c. BC after its cover was damaged the cistern gradually began to fill with pottery. Then, shortly before 29 BC, when the inauguration of Caesar's Forum took place, the area was obliterated due to the paving of the Forum. More than 1500 pottery fragments have been found in the cistern, 567 (36%) of which belonged to ancient containers.[34] This included 92 diagnostic fragments of wine amphoras, which belonged to at least 56 vessels.[35]

29 Contino, D'Alessandro 2014, 331, fig. 13.
30 Puig Palrem, Ruiz del Pozo 2010, 431, fig. 104; Ruiz del Pozo 2014, 573–577, 583–584, tab. 1.
31 Bertoldi 2008; 2010.
32 Spignola 1998, 98–109. Dating these containers is also problematic, thus they have been given a broad chronological timeframe of between the 1st and the 5th c. AD.
33 Infarinato 2007, 381.
34 Zampini 2010, 321–322. This article is a preliminary report that was published whilst the study was ongoing. A complete publication is planned.
35 Zampini 2010, 329–330, tab. 10.

2. *Via Sacchi, Gianicolo—Augustan period, Flavian period, late Antonine period*

Amphoras that were discovered during the construction of a car park in *Via Sacchi* in Janiculum belong to three chronological phases: the late Augustan, the Flavian, and the late Antonine age. Most of the containers dated to the Augustan period preserved almost untouched and they formed artificial terracing for the so-called '*giardino delle ollae*'. During the Flavian age the area was not in use, but around 170/180 AD it became a waste heap for amphoras.[36] The minimal number of containers was usually calculated by counting the number of rims; however, bases and handles were also considered when their numbers suggested that the estimates driven from rims were too small. Non-diagnostic fragments were taken into consideration when they indicated the presence of amphoras that were not identified by diagnostic fragments.[37] The total number of transport jars was calculated at 1811, the majority of which, namely 1587, were dated to the late Antonine age. Only 69 amphoras dated to the Flavian period, whereas 155 dated to the Augustan age. There were 85 wine amphoras from the Augustan and 49 from the Flavian periods, whilst 665 derived from the late Antonine age, making a total of 799.[38]

3. *Via Nova—Clivus Palatinus—after 64 and 70–96 AD*

The area between *Via Nova* and *Clivus Palatinus* was excavated by the *Soprintendenza Archeologica di Roma* between 1983 and 1985. These excavations demonstrated that after the fire in 64 AD, which destroyed earlier buildings, a portico with taverns was constructed along the *Clivus Palatinus*, as well as a ramp leading to the Palatine Hill. The archaeological material associated with these constructions included 343 diagnostic amphora fragments dated to 64–68 AD and 344 dated to 70–96 AD.[39]

4. *Meta Sudans—64–68, 70–80/90, 138–161 AD*

This area took its name from the monumental fountain that was constructed next to the Colosseum during the Flavian era. Part of the material, including

36 Ferrandes 2008, 247–249, 257, 259.
37 Ferrandes 2008, 247, n. 3.
38 Ferrandes 2008, 255–257, tab. 2.
39 Rizzo 2003, 7.

876 diagnostic amphora fragments, derives from when the area was levelled to facilitate the construction of the *Domus Aurea* after the fire of 64 AD. Another group, this time 455 diagnostic amphora fragments dated to the Antonine age, was associated with the construction of a sewer situated to the north-east of the yet to be built Arch of Constantine. The number of amphora fragments from this site was very high, totalling 6420.[40]

5. *The north part of the Palatine Hill—64–68, 70–90 AD and 98–117 AD*

This context comprises the area to the north of *Via Nova*, between the Arch of Titus and the House of the Vestals. Amphoras estimated at 342 on the basis of diagnostic fragments, were probably associated with the levelling of the area.[41]

6. *Crypta Balbi—80–96 AD and 98–117 AD*

Crypta Balbi comprises an architectural complex adjacent to the ancient Theatre of Balbus, where an exedra was built during the Augustan age, while in the 2nd c. AD the area was restructured and a latrine was added. Amphora fragments, including 222 diagnostic, were found in the cellars of the buildings along the *Via delle Botteghe Oscure*, which came to light in a trench situated along the external perimeter of the crypt. They are associated with the restructuration of the area dated between 80–96 AD. Another 154 amphora fragments were found in 1984 in a trench to the east of the *Conservatorio S. Catarina della Rosa*.[42]

7. *Vigna Barberini—81–96 AD*

An extremely large number of amphora fragments, 12526 in total, were discovered in the filling from a cryptoporticus in area B of the ancient *Vigna Barberini* on the Palatine Hill. The discovery was made during excavations conducted by the *École française de Rome* and the *Soprintendenza Archeologica di Roma*.[43] Diagnostic amphora fragments were calculated at 2610.[44]

---

40 Rizzo 2003, 7–10.
41 Rizzo 2003, 10–11.
42 Rizzo 2003, 12.
43 Rizzo 2003, 15–17.
44 Rizzo 2003, 165, tab. 27c.

8. *The House of Tiberius (Domus Tiberiana)*—54–235 AD

The House of Tiberius was the first imperial palace that was founded in the north-western part of the Palatine Hill. This area contained aristocratic houses during the Republican times and during the 1st c. AD emperors, such as Tiberius, Caligula and Claudius resided there. The palace was rebuilt by Nero after the fire in 64 AD and integrated into the *Domus Aurea*. Further transformations took place under Vespasian and Domitian. The latter inaugurated a second imperial palace in 92 AD and *Domus Tiberiana* probably formed a part of it. Hadrian enlarged the residence, whilst under Septimius Severus more reconstruction work was completed. Thanks to the literary evidence we know that Antoninus Pius lived there, whereas Marcus Aurelius and Commodus were brought up in *Domus Tiberiana*.[45]

The excavations conducted by the Swiss Institute of Rome between 1984 and 1987[46] uncovered 2035 amphora fragments, which constitute 18,5 % of the total ceramic material found in the *Domus*. The minimum number of containers was estimated at 330, which includes 142 wine amphoras.[47] It was possible to distinguish seven chronological periods in *Domus Tiberiana*, which stretched from before Nero's rule to the beginning of the 5th c. AD.[48] However, amphora quantifications start at Period II, the Neronian age. Eastern Mediterranean amphoras were dated to the times of Nero, Vespasian, Domitian, Hadrian and the Severan Dynasty.

9. *Aqua Marcia—1st and the beginning of the 2nd c.* AD

This amphora assemblage was found during excavations on the inner side of the Aurelian Walls, to the east of *Piazzale di Porta S. Lorenzo*.[49] The containers are dated to the 1st c. and the beginning of the 2nd c. AD. The total number of diagnostic fragments was calculated at 208, but only 177 of them were identified.[50]

45 Meylan-Krause 2002, 1.
46 Meylan-Krause 2002, 3.
47 Meylan-Krause 2002, 122, n. 415.
48 Meylan-Krause 2002, 2.
49 Volpe 1996, 15.
50 Panetta 1996. It is worth mentioning that amphoras from the Republican age were also attested at this site, but the lack of diagnostic fragments did not allow for their identification.

10. *The Forum of Nerva/Forum Transitorium—second half of the 1st c.* AD *and the 2nd c.* AD

Amphoras from the Forum of Nerva, known also as *Forum Transitorium*, come from three different areas: the south-western corner, the north-western portico and the area behind the Curia and *Basilica Aemilia*.[51] The excavations in the south-western corner of the Forum of Nerva took place in 1996–1997 and they uncovered structures belonging to a Republican *domus* that formed a part of the ancient neighbourhood of Agriletum. The area was devastated during the fire of 64 AD and filled with soil and other materials upon Nero's command. The amphoras from the filling from Room 1 and 2 date to the late 1st c. AD. Transport containers comprise 70% of the ceramic material, while their diagnostic fragments, 184 in total, were very well preserved, which facilitated their attribution. Wine amphoras predominated, reaching 79% and 56% of the total number of containers respectively.[52] Eastern amphoras, including Camulodunum 184, AC2a, AC2b, and Dressel 5 dated to the 1st c. AD were also attested in Room 3, but their exact numbers have not been published.[53]

The assemblage discovered in the north-western portico of *Forum Transitorium* comes from a 2nd c. AD sewer. It was composed of 133 diagnostic fragments of amphoras, 95 of which were identified, including 64 wine containers.[54] Also, directly behind the Curia and the *Basilica Aemilia* 1327 amphora fragments (including 426 diagnostic) dated to 81–96/98 AD were found. They were associated with the layers formed just before the inauguration of the Forum by Nerva in 98 AD, which contained waste from taverns belonging to a Macellum that was restructured under Vespasian.[55]

11. *Boccone del Povero—first half of the 2nd c.* AD

Boccone del Povero is an archaeological site situated in the ancient Roman *suburbium*, which at present belongs to *Comprensorio dell'Università degli Studi di Roma "Tor Vergata"*. It is composed of a necropolis with around 300 graves and a waste pit, both dated to the first half of the 2nd c. AD. In antiquity they belonged to a *villa rustica/suburbana*. The archaeological material, containing more than 3500 fragments of ceramic vessels (fine, kitchen and transport

51 Rizzo 2003, 12; Rinaldi 2013, 68, tab. 1; Nocera 2013, 79.
52 Rinaldi 2013, 61–63, 67–68. A Rhodian amphora was stamped with the inscription ΓΛΑ.
53 Nocera 2013, 78–79.
54 Marucci 2006, 57, 85.
55 Rizzo 2003, 12, 15.

vessels and lamps), comes from the waste pit, which also contained building materials. The number of diagnostic amphora fragments was estimated at 135 and the majority of them, namely 109, belonged to wine containers.[56]

12. *Trajan's Markets (Mercati di Traiano)—second half of the 2nd AD*

This context was originally an aristocratic household founded in the 2nd c. BC and later abandoned. Then, at the beginning of the 2nd c. AD, Trajan selected this area to be home to his forum and shopping complex. The discovered material should be dated to the late Antonine dynasty due to the closure of the complex c. 200 AD.[57]

13. *Via Marmorata*

Via Marmorata runs NW-SE through the slopes of the Aventine Hill from the Tiber to *Porta San Paolo*, and forms the eastern boarder of the modern *Quartiere Testaccio*, which in antiquity was an important place for the unloading and storage of goods. *Porticus Aemilia, Horrea Galbana*, the famous olive amphora waste heap of *Monte Testataccio*, and *Nuovo Mercato di Testaccio* (where a dump containing mostly Cretan wine amphoras was recently discovered) are all situated in the vicinity of *Via Marmorata*. The archaeological material from this context comes from excavations that took place between 2008 and 2010 that were associated with the relaying of train tracks.[58] These excavations uncovered around 3800 amphora fragments, which constitute more than 85% of all pottery found in this context. Diagnostic fragments of containers were calculated at 1180. The chronological distribution of the fragments is very broad, lasting from the Augustan age until the 7th c. AD.[59] The statistics that are presented below include 199 amphora fragments dated to the 2nd c. AD, as well as 59 that are dated to the 3rd c. AD.

It should be noted that a large number of eastern wine amphoras have recently been discovered in *Nuovo Mercato di Testaccio* on the Aventine Hill. Unfortunately, as this context cannot be compared with the others it has been excluded from the statistics, but it will be referred to in the conclusion.

56 Bertoldi 2011b, 44–45, 51–54.
57 Ceci 2006, 25.
58 Capodiferro, Quaranta 2011, 51.
59 Bertoldi 2011a, 148.

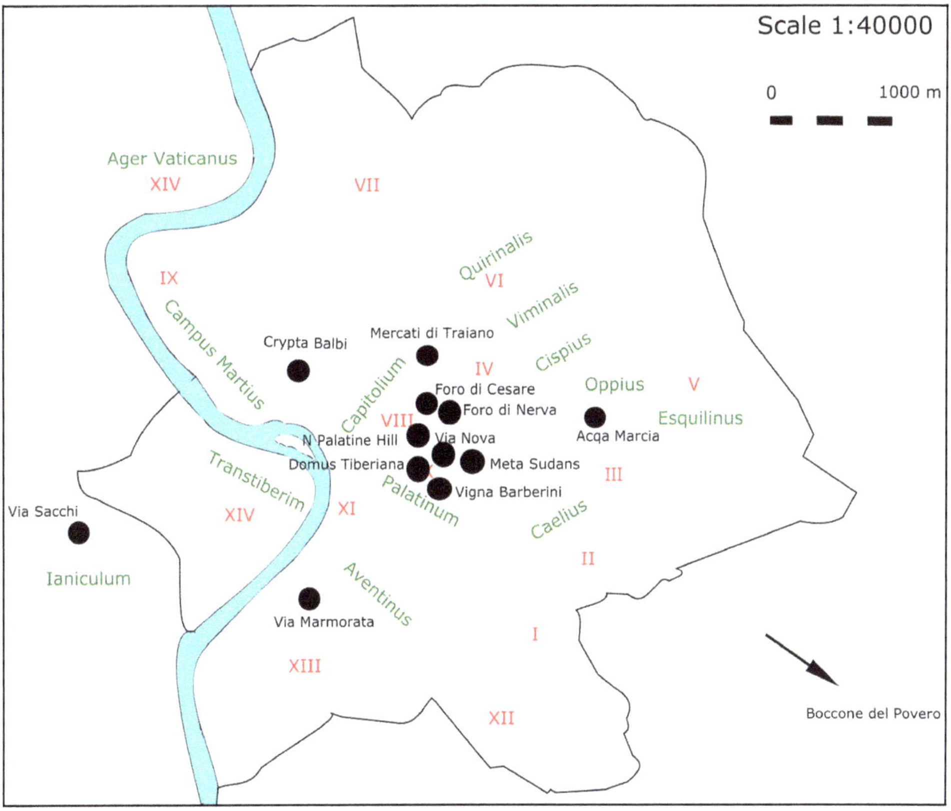

FIGURE 3 A map of amphora assemblages discovered in Rome and included in the synthesis

1.1 *Wine Importations to Rome—General Trends*

The analysis of the percentages of wine amphoras from different parts of the Mediterranean (Tab. 2, Fig. 4)[60] shows that the ratio of Eastern Mediterranean containers in Rome was always significant, since it varied between 10% and more than 50% at times. Moreover, eastern wine amphoras were always the most numerous foreign imports. This shows that the eastern part of the

60 The difference between the total numbers of wine containers and hence their percentages in this book and in my publication in SAAC from 2019 is due to the changed attribution of Schoene-Mau XV/Carrot amphora. In the paper from 2019 I classified it as wine container after Rizzo 2003, 207, tab. 33b; while in this book it is seen as a fruit container after data from Roman Amphorae: a digital resource University of Southampton, 2005 (updated 2014) https://archaeologydataservice.ac.uk/archives/view/amphora_ahrb_2005/details.cfm?id=56&CFID=b83632b1-d8f6-4a0f-9bea-1e505dcef8ba&CFTOKEN=0, accessed 8.03.2019.

TABLE 2 Provenance of wine amphoras in Rome (numbers and %)

	1st c. BC		Augustan age		1st c. AD		2nd c. AD		3rd c. AD	
Tyrrhenian	34	60,71%	30	34,88%	1524	42,17%	526	30,40%	21	31,34%
Adriatic	15	26,79%	22	26%	38	1,05%	21	1,21%	0	0%
Sicilian	0	0%	1	1,16%	154	4,26%	42	2,43%	1	1,49%
Spanish	1	1,79%	9	10,46%	346	9,57%	30	1,73%	4	5,97%
Eastern Mediterranean	6	10,71%	20	23,26%	1063	29,41%	648	37,46%	34	50,75%
Gallic	0	0%	1	1,16%	288	7,96%	242	13,99%	5	7,46%
African	0	0%	3	3,49%	201	5,56%	221	12,77%	2	2,99%
Total	**56**	**100%**	**86**	**100%**	**3614**	**100%**	**1730**	**100%**	**67**	**100%**

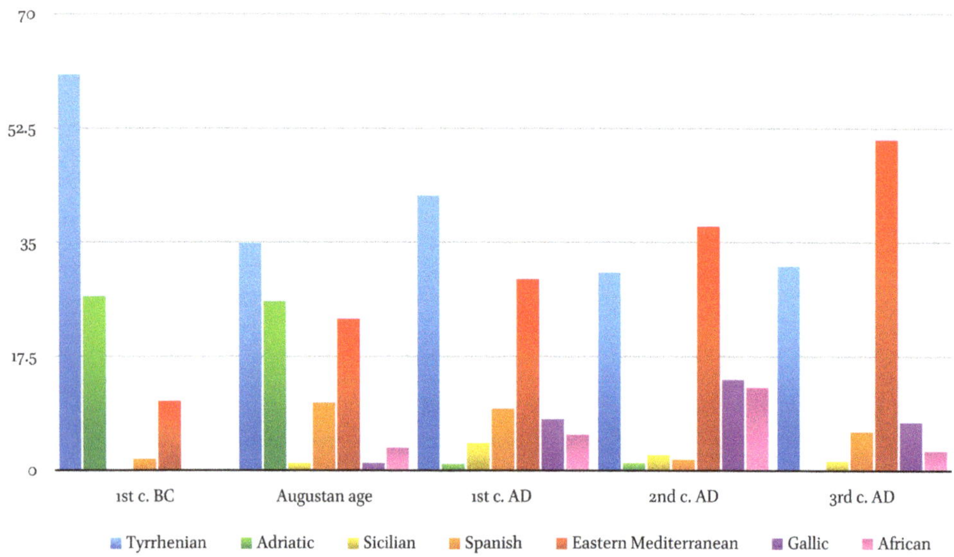

FIGURE 4 Provenance of wine amphoras in Rome (%)

Mediterranean satisfied a substantial amount of the Roman demand for wine for a very long period of time, starting from the late Republican age and lasting until the 3rd c. AD. Of course, the data for the 1st c. BC may be questioned, as it is based upon a very low number of amphora fragments, a mere 56. However, another late Republican context dated similarly to the assemblage from the Forum of Caesar has recently been discovered in *Horti Lamiani*. This provided a very high number of pottery sherds, with those belonging to transport containers reaching 2927, including 557 diagnostic examples. The percentage of Aegeo-Oriental containers was estimated at 12% of all (not only wine) amphoras, which confirms that the Eastern Mediterranean was already playing an important part in Italian wine supply during the late Republic. The other regions from where transport jars were imported, i.e. Africa and Baetica, each had only an 8% share.[61]

It was only during the late Republic and early empire that wine imports from the Eastern Mediterranean could compete with Italian wines. In the earlier periods up to the end of the 1st c. AD, eastern wine amphoras were outnumbered by Italian containers. However, gradual growth may be observed in wine importations from the Eastern Mediterranean from the 1st c. BC until the 3rd c. AD. In fact, during the 2nd and 3rd c. AD it was Eastern Mediterranean, and not Italian amphoras that were most numerous, which suggests that the Eastern Mediterranean had become Rome's most important source for wine.

Again, the 3rd c. AD sample may be questioned due to the low number of potsherds. Moreover, the data that is amphora based may be biased in favour of the Eastern Mediterranean as wooden barrels had already started to play an important part in Western Mediterranean commerce.[62] On the other hand, Reynolds noticed that ceramic assemblages dated to the 3rd c. AD are generally scarce, and that trade and the economy were regionalised during this century.[63] Therefore, the data for the 3rd c. AD, even though biased, is not utterly unrealistic. Nothing suggests that the Eastern Mediterranean lost its position as the main supplier of wine to Rome.

In summary, it is possible to state that the Romans drank Italian and Eastern Mediterranean wines above all others, which suggests that trade with the eastern part of the Mediterranean was important from an economic point of view. Thus, by no means can it be argued that the economic role of this trade was limited or insignificant.

1.2 *Eastern Mediterranean Wine Importations to Rome*

Table 3 and Figure 5 suggest that the Romans mostly imported Aegean wines, especially from Crete, Rhodes and Cos, or at least wine transported in Coan-type amphoras produced in the Aegean.[64] Anatolian wine was less popular.

61 Ferrandes 2014, 353–355, 363–364, fig. 4 and 11.
62 Tchernia 1986, 285–292; Marlière 2002; Wilson 2011a, 228–229; 2011b, 37.
63 Reynolds 2010a, 142.
64 'Cos' is in quotation marks because this category includes all Aegean amphoras of the

TABLE 3 Provenance of Eastern Mediterranean amphoras in Rome (numbers and %)

	1st c. BC		Augustan age		1st c. AD		2nd c. AD		3rd c. AD	
Rhodes	4	66,67%	9	45%	334	31,42%	93	14,35%	0	0%
Crete	1	16,67%	3	15%	392	36,88%	325	50,15%	2	5,88%
'Cos'	1	16,67%	6	30%	149	13,01%	67	10,34%	0	0%
Cnidus	0	0%	2	10%	11	1,03%	7	1,08%	0	0%
Chios	0	0%	0	0	1	0,09%	0	0%	0	0%
Anatolia	0	0%	0	0%	75	7,06%	66	10,19%	5	14,71%
Black Sea?	0	0%	0	0	0	0	1	0,15%	0	0%
Kapitän 1 and 2	0	0%	0	0%	0	0%	36	5,56%	27	79,40%
Cyprus/Cilicia	0	0%	0	0%	22	2,07%	25	3,86%	0	0%
Egypt	0	0%	0	0%	2	0,19%	4	0,62%	0	0%
Levant	0	0%	0	0%	77	7,24%	24	3,70%	0	0%
Total	**6**	100%	20	100%	1063	100%	**648**	100%	34	100%

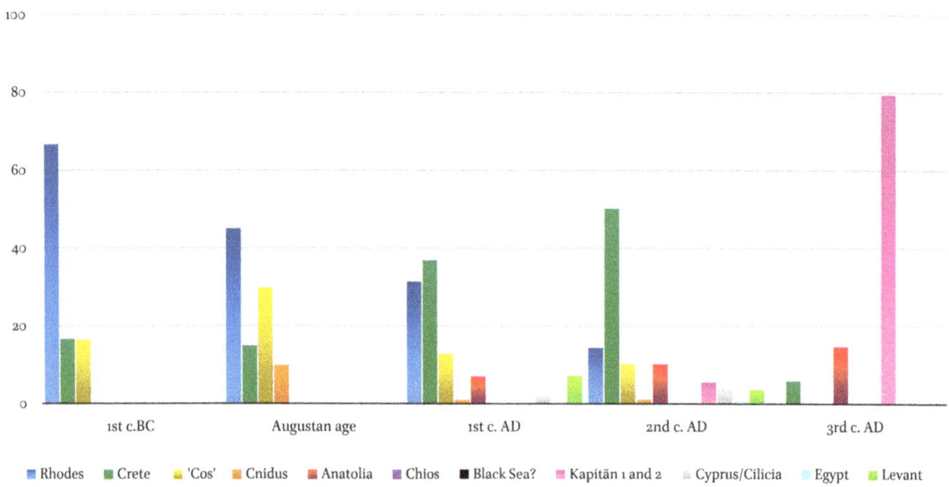

FIGURE 5 Provenance of Eastern Mediterranean wine amphoras in Rome (%)

Even though in the 2nd c. AD Anatolian amphoras shared the same percentage of the market as Coan containers, they were much smaller, thus transported

Coan type, which includes Dressel 2–4, Dressel 5, Knossos 19, Knossos 22 and Schoene-Mau XLI. However, it was not always clear whether they originated on the island of Cos or rather in other Aegean centres.

less wine. During the Augustan age Cnidian wine was ranked fourth, but lost its position during the subsequent centuries. Importations from Chios and the Black Sea region (Knossos 39)[65] are represented by only one amphora fragment. On the one hand, this may confirm the luxurious character of Chian wine as suggested by ancient literature. However, on the other hand it may show that Bithynia and Pontus were ignored by the Romans in terms of wine, which also agrees with conclusions drawn from literary evidence. Surprisingly, non-Aegean wines from the Eastern Mediterranean were rarely imported to Rome. They do appear in contexts dated to the 1st and 2nd c. AD, but their percentages never reach 8%. It seems that Egyptian wines were imported only occasionally, which might have been due to the fact that the Romans did not like the way they tasted, as Martial suggests.[66] It is, however, difficult to understand why imports from Cyprus, Cilicia, Syria and Palestine were so rare. Nevertheless, there should be no doubt that the only Eastern Mediterranean wines that counted in Rome came from the Aegean islands.

Consumption trends in Aegean wines varied depending on the period. Rhodian wine was the most popular until the 1st c. AD. Wine from Cos was also important in the earlier periods, from the 1st c. BC and throughout the Augustan age. However, during the 1st and 2nd c. AD Coan and Rhodian wines were far outnumbered by those from Crete. It seems, moreover, that the increase in the general percentage of Eastern Mediterranean wines in the 2nd c. AD is mainly due to the importations from Crete. The 3rd c. AD is the time when Kapitän 1 and 2 amphoras, that most probably come from the Aegean/Asia Minor or the Black Sea area, predominate among wine containers.

It is interesting that a Cretan amphora was attested in a context dated before 29 BC (*Foro di Cesare*), as it is generally accepted that Cretan wine started to be exported to Italy in the Augustan age.[67] This discovery suggests that these importations might have started slightly earlier. A fragment from a Chian container found in a context dated to the Imperial period is also unusual. Chian wine, similarly to Lesbian and Thasian, was mentioned frequently in the ancient texts, which suggest that the Romans drank these wines during the late Republic. This has been confirmed by the findings of Chian containers in *Horti Lamiani*, in *Suburbium* and probably also in the House of the Porch. The lack of amphoras dated to the Imperial period suggests that the north-Aegean and Chian beverages, that were imported to Italy during the Archaic and Hellenistic age, had lost their importance. Their production either stopped or was limited

---

65 A Black Sea origin of the Knossos 39 amphora is suggested by Panella, Rizzo 2014, 351.
66 Mart. XIII 122.
67 Marangou-Lerat 1995, 156.

to local markets. The discovery from *Vigna Barberini* suggests that wine importations from Chios might have lasted until the Flavian age.

To sum up, it is possible to say that in the Augustan period the Romans drank mostly Eastern Mediterranean wines from the south-eastern Aegean, Rhodian in particular. However, starting from the 1st c. AD wine from Crete became the most common. Coan, Cnidian and Anatolian wines were significant, but to a considerably lesser degree than Cretan or Rhodian, and oriental imports appeared in small quantities. Overall, it seems that the south-Aegean region was the main wine supplier to the 'Eternal City'.

2 *Campania felix*

Thanks to the eruption of Vesuvius the so-called 'Vesuvian cities' remained incredibly well preserved until our times; however, the state of research on amphoras discovered in Pompeii and Herculaneum is slightly disappointing. This is due to the fact that the first archaeologists excavating there were not particularly interested in this category of *instrumenta domestica*, unless it was inscribed. Moreover, most of the amphoras from Campania were discovered when 'amphorology' was not even in its infancy and no thought was given to amphora quantifications or archaeometric analyses. This is the reason why the share of Eastern Mediterranean wine amphoras can only be calculated for the following eight contexts, dated between the 2nd c. BC and the 3rd c. AD: *Casa di Ariadna* (Pompeii), *Palazzo Corigliano* (Naples), the House of Menander (Pompeii), *Villa San Marco* (Stabiae), *Villa di Arianna* (Stabiae), *Cratere Senga* (Puteoli), Cumae and *Rione Terra* (Puteoli). It should be mentioned that statistical analysis of pottery from the Pompeian House of the Vestals was also carried out. However, the publication does not provide us with exact numbers of amphoras, giving instead only percentages; thus, this data was not included into the synthesis presented below.[68]

1. *The House of Ariadna (Casa di Ariadna), Pompeii—2nd–1st c. BC*

The Pompeian *Casa di Ariadna* (VII 2) is a Republican *domus* where numerous containers were discovered, including 201 wine amphoras.[69] Most of them

68 De Sena, Ikäheimo 2003.

69 It is not explicit, but it seems from the context that the authors gave the estimated number of vessels or their diagnostic fragments.

were dated to the 1st c. BC;[70] however, a detailed analysis of Greek and Punic vessels has shown that most of the Rhodian stamps found in *Casa di Ariadna* and *pars occidentalis* date to the 2nd c. BC.[71]

2. *Palazzo Corigliano (Naples)—1st c. AD (before 64 AD)*

The amphoras from Palazzo Corigliano come from a ditch dated to before 64 AD. Among the 140 containers that were found in this context 35 were used to transport wine.[72] Due to the material being very well preserved, the study was based on the exact number of containers, and not just diagnostic parts.[73]

3. *House of Menander—around 79 AD*

Amphoras that were found in this aristocratic residence in Pompeii were published in the 4th volume of CIL and in a monograph devoted to the House of Menander that was printed in 2003.[74] According to the first source, 13 inscribed containers were found, including 7 that were used to transport wine. CIL mentions 3 Cretan amphoras, although one of them bore the inscription *passum Rhodium* and according to Marangou-Lerat was of Rhodian origin.[75] In addition, two Schoene-Mau XII containers with Greek *tituli* were noted in *Corpus*. These *tituli* suggest that these amphoras were of Coan/Aegean origin. The other, more recent publication shows that the House of Menander contained at least 13 wine amphoras, which included eight Italian and five Eastern Mediterranean (one Rhodian, one Coan, two Cretan, and one specimen from Cilicia). This data, which seem to be more accurate, is included in the synthesis.

4. *Villa San Marco (Stabiae)—around 79 AD*

This luxurious *villa di otium* was founded at the end of the 1st c. BC. However, most of the archaeological material that was discovered inside was probably used in 79 AD. The amphoras were originally distributed in various areas of the house; but they were later gathered in a cryptoporticus, which served as an archaeological store during the earliest excavations and was destroyed by an

70 Albiach et al. 2008, 260.
71 Pascual Berlanga, Ribera i Lacomba, Finkielsztejn 2008, 509–511.
72 Bragantini gives the number 36, but Haltern 70 is not classed as wine container.
73 Bragantini, Cipriano, Improta 1991, 88–92, 95–104.
74 Stefani 2003.
75 Marangou-Lerat 1995, 130.

earthquake in 1980. The archaeologists recovered most of the material, which included 31 wine amphoras out of 37 that were attested in the villa. Since it was impossible to give a certain provenance for one fragment of Dressel 2–4,[76] only 30 wine amphoras were taken into consideration.

5. *Villa Arianna (Stabiae)—1st c.* AD *(around 79* AD*)*

This is another luxurious *villa di otium*, similar to the House of Menander or *Villa San Marco*. A hundred amphoras were discovered in the kitchen, which suggests that they were in use at the time when Vesuvius destroyed the area. Over half of these containers were used to transport wine, with five out of these 55 wine amphoras being classified as 'anforette di area microasiatica', which probably refers to the type Agora F65–66.[77] Due to the fact that the material from *Villa Arianna*, the House of Menander and *Villa San Marco* was similarly dated, it is combined and presented as one category.

6. *Cumae—1st–2nd c.* AD[78]

The material from Cumae comes from French excavations at the necropolis known as *Mausoleo delle teste di cera*, and is dated to the end of the 1st and the first half of the 2nd c. AD. Only one fragment of Rhodian amphora was attested in the material from the first phase, for which the minimal number of containers was estimated at 43. The second phase includes at least 135 amphoras, 64 of which were wine containers. The synthesis considers only amphoras from the second phase.

7. *Cratere Senga (Puteoli)—2nd c.* AD

The material from *Cratere Senga* comes from excavations that were conducted in 1976 by the *Gruppo Archeologico Napoletano*. Amphoras were found in a very limited area of only 1 m^3. Moreover, not all fragments were recovered, since only diagnostic pieces of pottery were available for the study. Therefore, this material may not be entirely representative. Nonetheless, it is the only amphora assemblage from Campania that is published and dated to the 2nd c. AD. There

76 Miniero 1999, 323–327.
77 Federico 2013, 1739–1740, 1752, graf. IV.
78 At the time of writing this material is unpublished. I am very grateful to Dr. E. Botte for sharing this data with me.

were 63 amphoras discovered in *Cratere Senga*, 39 of which were wine containers.[79] The study was based upon the number of diagnostic fragments.

8. *Rione Terra (Puteoli)—Second Half of the 3rd c. AD.*

Rione Terra was the first urban settlement in Puteoli and it can be dated to the 2nd c. BC. Excavations were started in the early 1990's by the *Soprintendenza per i Beni Archeologici di Napoli* and are still ongoing. However, research has been conducted on amphoras that were discovered in the outlet US 6135. This context consists of containers that were found in *Taberna* 4 that was situated to the south of the cathedral. They are dated to the second half of the 3rd c. AD. The total number of amphoras was estimated at 211, among which 85 wine containers were identified.[80]

2.1 *Wine Importations to Campania—General Trends*

Table 4 and Figure 6 show the provenance of wine amphoras attested in Campania. The first thing to observe is that Eastern Mediterranean wines were the only imported beverages that counted until the 3rd c. AD, when suddenly the share of African containers grew to more than a quarter. Other imported wines such as Spanish, Gallic and Sicilian were consumed modestly. Imports from the Eastern Mediterranean were not only the most popular, they also outrivalled Italian wines that were transported in amphoras. The percentage of eastern wine containers between the 2nd/1st c. BC and the 2nd c. AD almost always exceeded 50%, reaching even 64% in Cumae. These percentages are much higher than in Rome.

The general scarcity of wine amphoras from the western provinces in Campania should not be surprising given that this area was a famous wine-producing region, but one may wonder why the percentage of Eastern Mediterranean imports was so high. This may be associated with the fact that most local wines destined for local markets were not kept in amphoras, which were used only for better quality wines and/or those that were destined for export. At the same time, Puteoli was the main Italian port for offloading cargo vessels from the Eastern Mediterranean,[81] with Rome receiving the bulk of the commodities, although some were consumed locally. This may explain the popularity of Eastern wines in Campania.

79 Garcea, Miraglia, Soricelli 1983–1984, 281–285.
80 De Filippo 2014, 335.
81 Pavolini 1996, 229–230.

TABLE 4 Provenance of wine amphoras in Campania (numbers and %)

	2nd–1st c. BC		1st c. AD (before 64 AD)		c. 79 AD		1st/2nd c. AD		2nd c. AD		3rd c. AD	
Tyrrhenian	82	40,80%	12	34,29%	54	55,67%	17	27%	17	43,59%	28	37,33%
Adriatic	12	5,97%	0	0%	0	0%	0	0%	0	0	0	0%
Sicilian	0	0%	0	0%	1	1,03%	0	0%	0	0%	0	0%
Eastern Mediterranean	106	52,74%	19	54,29%	26	26,8%	41	64,06%	22	56,41%	25	33,33%
Spanish	1	0,50%	4	11,43%	11	11,34%	5	8%	0	0	3	4,00%
Gallic	0	0%	0	0%	1	1,03%	0	0%	0	0%	0	0%
African	0	0%	0	0%	4	4,12%	1	2%	0	0%	19	25,33%
Total	201	100%	35	100%	97	100%	64	100%	39	100%	75	100%

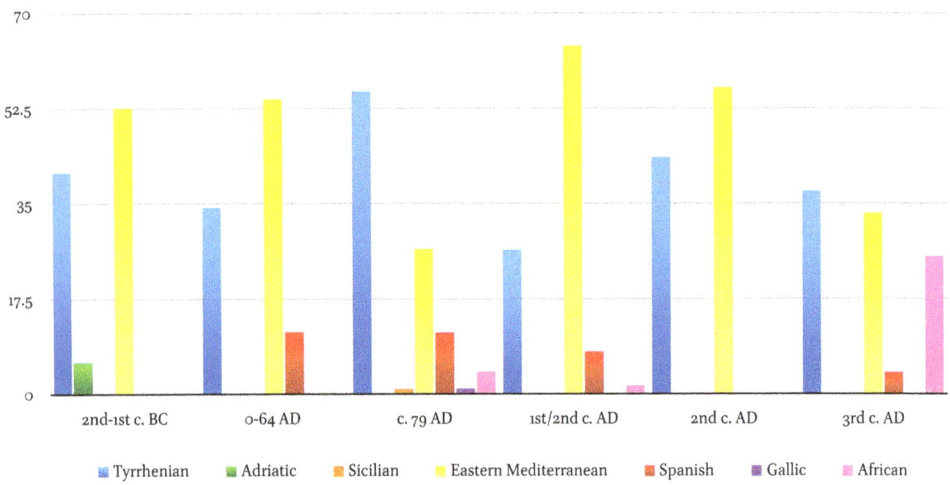

FIGURE 6 Provenance of wine amphoras in Campania (%)

Nonetheless, it should be noted that the percentages of wine amphoras from the East were very low (26,8%) in *Villa Arianna*, *Villa San Marco* and the House of Menander, where Italian containers predominated. An even lower percentage of Aegean wine amphoras, namely 11%, characterises the House of the Vestals (VI 1, 6–8, 24–26).[82] Italian wine amphoras predominated in this context, and until the half of the 1st c. AD they were almost exclusive. The name of

82 De Sena, Ikäheimo 2003, 307, tab. 3. Amphora numbers were not provided.

the house is a creation of the 18th c. tourist industry,[83] so the particular character of the building (Vestals residence) cannot be the explanation for the low percentage of eastern wine amphoras. However, all four houses were elite residences, so the differences in wine consumption patterns between the elite and common people may explain the differences in amphora statistics. This hypothesis is confirmed by the analysis of containers from *Domus Tiberiana* in Rome, which shows that the percentage of eastern wine amphoras in this imperial residence was lower than the average, varying from 17,18 % to 25 % between the 1st and 3rd c. AD,[84] whereas the average for Rome in this period ranged from 29,41 % to 50,75 % (Tab. 2). At the same time, proportions of Spanish, Gallic and African jars were higher than the average, similar to what has been observed for elite houses in Campania. Does this mean that the elites were not particularly fond of wines from the Eastern Mediterranean? Literary evidence suggests that in Imperial times Italian wines became the most famous and appreciated not only on the Apennine Peninsula, but also in the Eastern Mediterranean.[85] A positive verification of such a hypothesis would be confirmation that most Eastern Mediterranean imports were common rather than aristocratic wines.

In the publication regarding the House of the Vestals, De Sena and Ikäheimo noticed that non-Italian amphoras, apart from north-African, did not appear in Pompeii before the 1st c. AD. This led them to the conclusion that in the Republican period Pompeii was a self-sufficient town, which later became a 'consumer city'. Moreover, the authors argued that "*there is no evidence that wine was routinely imported to Italy at this time, although there may have been rare exceptions*".[86] A broader analysis of the amphora findings from Campania shows that Pompeii imported Rhodian and Coan products as early as in the 2nd and 1st c. BC. Moreover, over 50 % of the amphoras from *Casa di Ariadna* that were dated to the Republican age were imported from the Aegean region, whilst almost 6 % came from the Adriatic area. This means that at least in terms of wine, Pompeii was already more 'consumer' than self-sufficient during the late Republic. Considering that the city imported olive oil from north Africa from at least the 2nd c. BC, which is evident from De Sena and Ikäheimo's study, the self-sufficiency of Pompeii in the Republican period that was postulated seems doubtful. Moreover, the 'consumer' character of the town should also be

83 Jones, Robinson 2004, 127.
84 Based on the publication by Meylan-Krause 2002.
85 Only Italian wines were present at the Trimalchio's feast, see Petr. 21, 28, 34, 55; and at an aristocratic Athenian banquet described by Lucian *Navigium* 23. The small sample size (less than 40 amphoras) may be another explanation.
86 De Sena, Ikäheimo 2003, 305–307.

questioned, considering that it supplied Rome with wine. What is more, wines from Pompeii reached the Rhine limes, Egypt and even India,[87] which shows that judging the economy of a whole town/city on the basis of evidence from one house is not very convincing. A synthesis of findings (if possible) should be made first to observe general trends, not particular variations. De Sena and Ikäheimo proved only that the inhabitants of the House of the Vestals in the Republican age preferred local products, whereas during the Imperial period they started to consume more imported goods. The synthesis presented in this book allows us to conclude that wine importations were an important branch of the economy not only in Rome, but also in smaller centres, which falsifies the assumption that intensive trade was limited to the big cities. If this assumption were true, small Campanian towns should be more self-sufficient in terms of food, while imported amphoras should occur sporadically.

2.2 *Eastern Mediterranean Wine Imports in Campania*

Looking closely at the quantities of individual Eastern Mediterranean wines that were imported to Campania (Tab. 5 and Fig. 7) we may observe that, as in Rome, the islands of Rhodes and Crete played the most important part. Rhodes dominated during the Republican age, while Cretan amphoras became the most numerous during the 1st c. AD. This corresponds with the results of the study by Marangou-Lerat, which showed that wine from this island started to be exported on a larger scale in the Augustan period.[88]

According to F. Zevi and S. De Caro, Cretan amphoras in Pompeii were only outnumbered by Dressel 2–4 containers, which were used to transport local and regional wines, such as *Pompeianum* and *Falernum*. He associates the particular popularity of Cretan wine in Campania with the commercial relations between Cretan and Italian merchants, which were a consequence of the geographical location of the island on the main trade route connecting East and West. These relations were strengthened by Caesar's foundation of the *Colonia Julia Nobilis Knossos* and by a donation of land in the territory of Knossos to Capua, as compensation for having settled veterans on its territory by Octavian Augustus. The inscription ἐπιτυνχάνοντος (τῶν) Καμπανῶν discovered on a Cretan amphora found in Santa Maria Capua Vetere suggests that Cretan wine might have come to Campania as a part of *vectigalia* that was to be paid in kind.[89] Moreover, there were many imperial freedmen and *liberti* associated with the Cretan administration among the traders who exported wine from

87 Peacock, Williams 1986, 106.
88 Marangou-Lerat 1995, 155–156.
89 De Caro 1992/93, 309–311; Zevi 1989, 11–12.

TABLE 5 Provenance of Eastern Mediterranean wine amphoras in Campania (numbers and %)

	2nd–1st c. BC		0–64 AD		c. 79 AD		1st/2nd c. AD		2nd c. AD		3rd c. AD	
Crete	0	0%	8	42,11%	7	26,92%	15	36,59%	13	59,09%	1	4%
Rhodes	94	88,68%	3	15,79%	2	7,69%	7	17,07%	9	40,90%	0	0%
'Cos'	8	7,55%	5	26,32%	9	34,62%	1	2,44%	0	0%	0	0%
Cnidus	2	1,88%	0	0%	0	0%	7	17,07%	0	0%	9	36%
Sicyon	2	1,88%	0	0%	0	0%	0	0%	0	0%	0	0%
Anatolia	0	0%	0	0%	5	19,23%	2	4,88%	0	0%	5	20%
Kapitän 2	0	0%	0	0%	0	0%	0	0%	0	0%	2	8%
Cilicia	0	0%	3	15,79%	3	11,54%	9	21,95%	0	0	8	32%
Total	**106**	**100%**	**19**	**100%**	**26**	**100%**	**41**	**100%**	**22**	**100%**	**25**	**100%**

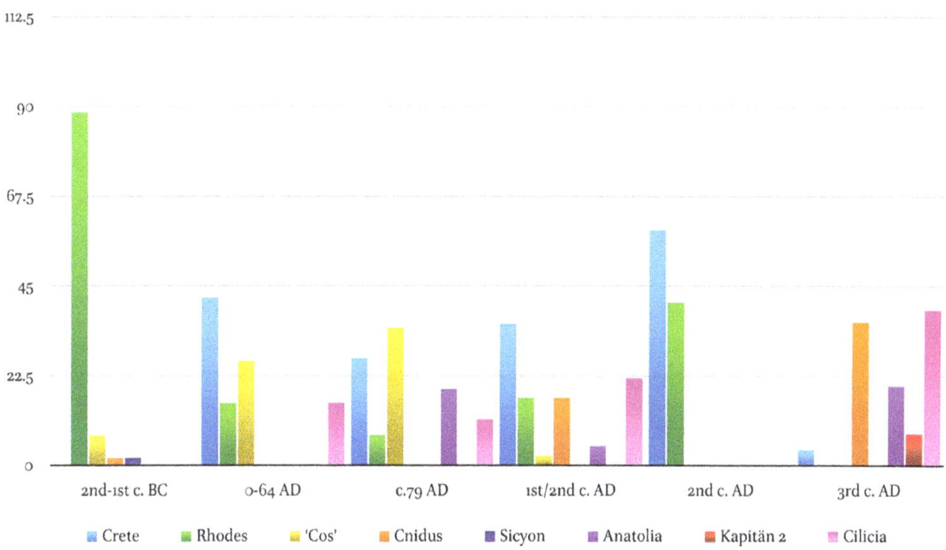

FIGURE 7 Provenance of Eastern Mediterranean wine amphoras in Campania (%)

Crete.[90] They might have used their influence to send Cretan wine to Italy on the *annona* ships when they were not fully laden, paying advantageous freight charges, or not having to pay at all.[91]

The high percentage of Cretan amphoras in Campania has also been noted by V. di Giovanni. According to his calculations, in the 1st c. AD the percentage of Cretan amphoras in *Granai del Foro* in Pompeii was comparable with wine containers of Italian origin,[92] while during the 2nd c. AD the number of Cretan wine jars reached 36,5 % of all amphoras that were discovered in *Rione Terra* and 30 % in the unedited complex of S. Patrizia in Naples.[93] Similarly to De Caro, Di Giovanni associates this phenomenon with the special relationship between Crete and Capua. He noted that Capua had a special slave, *archarius Cretae*, who was a treasurer in charge of the goods that came from the island. Moreover, according to Cassius Dion, the Capuans were still profiting from their land on Crete in the first half of the 3rd c. AD.[94]

Coan, Cnidian and later Anatolian wines were also imported, but their quantities were lower than Rhodian or Cretan, except during the 3rd c. AD. In *Palazzo Corigliano* a high percentage (almost 15 %) of Schoene-Mau XLI containers was attested. These containers resemble the so-called 'sub-Coan' type (Knossos 19) and were certainly produced in the Aegean.[95] Therefore, just like in Rome, amphoras from the Aegean region predominated in Campania. At the same time, imports from Egypt and Syro-Palestine, which were rare in the capital, were not attested at all in Campania. What may come as a surprise, however, is the high percentage of Cilician containers, which grew from almost 10 % at the first half of the 1st c. AD, to reach 32 % during the second half of the 3rd c. AD. The high percentage for the 3rd c. AD is due to the appearance of Agora M239 and proto-LRA1 amphoras, which highlights the decreasing role of the Aegean area as Italy's main wine supplier in favour of the *Oriens*.

---

90 Łoś 1995.

91 Tchernia 2011, 345–348.

92 Di Giovanni 2013, 1520.

93 Di Giovanni 2003, 88–89; Di Giovanni 2013, 1522. In the first publication the figure 36,5 % is given, whereas in the second it is c. 30 %. Given that the statistics for this deposit are yet unpublished it is impossible to verify the estimations. The 2nd c. AD deposit from *Rione Terra* should not be mistaken with the amphora assemblage from *Rione Terra* dated to the 3rd c. AD that was published by De Filippo, and has been included into the statistics that are presented in this chapter.

94 CIL X 3938 = ILS 6317, *Hist. Rom* XLIX, 14.5 after Di Giovanni 2003, 88.

95 Rizzo 2003, 155, n. 69.

3 *Portus* and Its Neighbourhood

Eastern Mediterranean wine amphoras began to appear in *Portus* from at least the 2nd or the beginning of the 1st c. BC, which is suggested by the discovery of Rhodian containers in the area of *Quatro Tempietti*.[96] Imports from Rhodes, as well as from Chios (1 fragment) and Crete (1 fragment) were also attested in *Necropoli di Porta Romana* (*Via di Hermogene*),[97] in *Magazzini agli Horrea*, in *Necropoli di Porto* (*Isola Sacra*) and in *Necropoli di Via Laurentina*, but their exact dating is not certain.[98] Aegean containers were also discovered in the *Palazzo Imperiale di Portus*, the assemblage is dated to the 3rd c. AD and consists of Rhodian (Camulodunum 184), probably Coan (Dressel 5) and Anatolian (Agora F65–66)[99] amphoras; however, their publication did not enable any meaningful statistics to be created. Deposits from other contexts in Ostia are considerably more useful in reconstructing the wine supply. These contexts are: the House of the Porch, *La Longarina*, *Binario Morto*, the House of the Fishes, the House of the Yellow Walls, *Piazzale delle Corporazioni*, *Taberna dell'Invidioso*, the Baths of the Swimmer and a surface survey in *Portus*. However, amphoras from the surface survey have been excluded from the synthesis presented in this book, due to the lack of precise dating.[100] The other contexts will now be described in more detail.

1. *House of the Porch* (*Domus del Protiro*)*—the Third Quarter of the 1st c.* BC

A small deposit in the form of a wall consisting of 76 amphoras that served for draining purposes was discovered in 1974 in the House of the Porch in Ostia. The containers, dated to the third quarter of the 1st c. BC, were well preserved. It was possible to distinguish 46 that served for the transport of wine.[101]

2. *La Longarina—50* BC*–50* AD

In 1975 a deposit of 360 amphoras was discovered at *La Longarina*, which is situated in between Ostia and *Castel Fusano*. The function of the contain-

96 Rieger 2004, 279.
97 Heinzelmann 2000, 332, 349.
98 Palma, Panella 1967–1968, 100; Heinzelmann 2000, 338, 349.
99 Zampini 2011, 94–95. It is surprising that there were no Kapitän 1 or 2 amphoras attested, since these containers are frequent in other contexts from this period.
100 Mele 2005, 235, tab. 6.19. Late imperial containers known as Kapitän 1 and 2 and LRA3 were mixed with early imperial Dressel 43 and Camulodunum 184.
101 Boersma, Yntema, Van der Werff 1986, 97, 99, 117.

ers was similar to those found at the House of the Porch—they served as drainage. These amphoras were first studied by A. Hesnard, who identified 298. Wine containers predominated (max. 181); however, 104 *garum* and 13 olive oil amphoras were also present (62 remain unidentified). They date to the beginning of the 1st c. AD.[102] In 2002, the amphoras from the *La Longarina* deposit were analysed by E. Rivello, who dated the drainage to 50 BC–50 AD.[103]

3. *Binario Morto—50 BC–50 AD*

The so-called Binario Morto is a context of 335 amphoras (including 161 wine containers) found in drainage in Ostia Antica. The area was excavated by A. Pellegrino and A. Carbonara (Ostia Antica Archaeological Park) during the construction of the east and west car parks outside Ostia Antica station (1998–1999) and the new pedestrian underpass inside (1999–2002). Funerary structures, which can be connected to the nearby Pianabella necropolis were attested in this area, as well as residential structures (most likely the pillars from a portico), and a circular ditch measuring 15 metres in diameter. The retaining wall of the ditch was covered with amphoras arranged in a double row, which probably served as a drain (the remains of a water wheel were also discovered). The amphoras date to the second half of the 1st c. BC and the first half of the 1st c. AD.[104]

4. *House of the Fishes* (Domus dei Pesci)*—the 1st c. AD—the Beginning of the 4th c. AD*

In the so-called *Domus dei Pesci* F. Zevi and his colleagues discovered almost 15.500 amphora fragments under a mosaic floor in one of the chambers. The material from this context is generally dated to between the 2nd c. BC and the beginning of the 4th c. AD,[105] but no amphora fragments dated earlier than the first half of the 1st c. AD (with the exception of Dressel 1A and Dressel 1C, which are residual) were found. The statistics presented in this chapter are

102 Hesnard 1980, 141–146, 149.
103 Rivello 2002, 438, tab. 1, 445.
104 Olcese et al. 2017, 197–199 and 201, tab. 1 and 2.
105 The chronological division of the material in the House of the Fishes is as follows: Period 1—the first half of the 1st c. AD, Period 2—the late 1st c. AD (Domitian's time), Period 3, phase 1—the beginning of the 2nd c. AD, Period 3, phase 2—the second half of the 2nd c. AD Period 3, phase 3—the beginning of the 3rd c. AD, Period 3, phase 4—the first half of the 3rd c. AD, Period 4—the end of the 3rd c. AD, Period 5—the beginning of the 4th c. AD. For archaeological findings from *Domus dei Pesci* see also Geremia Nucci, Leone 2003.

based on the archaeological report produced by F. Zevi, which was published in *Notizie degli Scavi di Antiquità*, and on the data published by Rizzo.[106] The first period corresponds with the dates from *La Longarina*, which is why the data from these contexts are combined in the statistics presented below. Amphoras dated to the beginning of the 4th c. AD were mostly residual, thus they were excluded.

5. *House of the Yellow Walls* (Casa delle Pareti Gialle)—*110–115 AD* (*layer A4*)

This is a medium-apartment house dated to the Hadrian age that forms a part of the so-called 'Garden Houses'. A deposit of amphoras was discovered under a mosaic in the central room, which belonged to an earlier structure from the Trajan period. The assemblage was published in 1970,[107] and has been recently updated by Rizzo.[108] The total number of diagnostic amphora fragments was estimated at 188, of which 72 were wine containers.

6. *Square of the Corporations* (Piazzale delle Corporazioni)—*Hadrian's Age, after 119 AD*

Amphoras from this context were discovered in the west portico of the square, under mosaics. The discovery was published in 1987,[109] and again Rizzo has provided updated amphora statistics.[110] The assemblage contained 169 diagnostic container fragments, including 48 from wine amphoras.

7. *Taberna dell'Invidioso*—*120–160 AD* (*Layer IV*)

This tavern forms a part of the thermal complex known as the Baths of the Jealous One. The material comes from the Hadrian and early Antonine age. Diagnostic amphora fragments in this context totalled 142, including 57 wine containers. The find was published by Carta in 1987 and an updated version was provided by Rizzo.[111] Surprisingly, no Eastern Mediterranean wine amphoras were attested in this tavern.

106 Zevi 2004–2005; Panella, Rizzo 2014, 439–440, tab. 31a–b.

107 Zevi, Pohl 1970, 180–188, 194, 199–201, 205–207, 216–217. Amphoras from the earlier periods were also found in the House of the Yellow Walls in layers C2, B3, B2, B1, A2 and A3, see Zevi, Pohl 1970, 92–93, 116, 126–128, 133–134, 140–141, 231–232, 234.

108 Panella, Rizzo 2014, 440, tab. 32.

109 Pohl 1987, 192–193.

110 Panella, Rizzo 2014, 440, tab. 32.

111 Carta 1987, 36–37; Panella, Rizzo 2014, 440, tab. 32.

8. *Baths of the Swimmer* (*Terme del Nuotatore*)—*Late 1st–Late 2nd c.* AD

The thermal complex commonly known as *Terme del Nuotatore*, or in English the Baths of the Swimmer, is indubitably the most famous place in Ostia in terms of amphora studies. Archaeological excavations of the complex started as early as 1966 and they lasted until 1978/1980.[112] The archaeological material was partially published under the title *Ostia I–IV*, as a part of the series *Studi Miscellanei*.[113] In 2014, *Ostia VI* was published, which is devoted, *inter alia*, to a detailed analysis of the amphoras from Area NE that were elaborated by Rizzo. This publication also presents the numbers of amphoras from Area SO (layers IV and V) and Ambiente 1 in *Terme del Nuotatore*, as well as from other contexts in Ostia such as the House of the Fishes, the House of the Yellow Walls, *Piazzale delle Corporazioni* and *Taberna dell'Invidioso*.

The Baths of the Swimmer were constructed around 70–80 AD during the early Flavian age. Most of the containers date between the Flavian age and the end of the 2nd c. AD.[114] They were grouped into four chronological periods: Period 3a (80–90 AD), Period 3b (90–120 AD), Period 4 (120–160 AD) and Period 5 (160–180/190 AD). Since these periods correspond with the chronological divisions of the material from the House of the Fishes, the House of the Yellow Walls, *Piazzale delle Corporazioni* and *Taberna dell'Invidioso*, the material from these contexts is combined in the statistics that are presented below (Tab. 6 and Fig. 8).[115]

3.1 *Wine Importations to Ostia—General Trends*

The first thing that should be observed when viewing the trends of wine importations to Ostia (Tab. 6 and Fig. 8) is that the percentages of amphoras from the Eastern Mediterranean are considerably lower than in Rome and Campania, varying between 4,7 and 23,09%. It is also interesting that these wines were apparently present in Ostia before the construction of the port by Claudius. The completion of the construction works, as well as the eruption of Vesuvius

112 Panella, Rizzo 2014, 17.

113 Carandini, Fabricotti 1967–1968; AA.VV. 1970; Carandini, Panella 1973; Carandini, Panella 1977.

114 Containers dated to the earlier periods before the construction of the thermal complex were scarce, see Panella, Rizzo 2014, 81, tab. 2.

115 Amphoras whose content is doubtful have been excluded. Only diagnostic fragments were considered apart from in Area NE of the Baths of the Swimmer, where it was possible to estimate the number of containers.

that destroyed a number of Campania vineyards, had little impact on the percentages of wine imports from the Eastern Mediterranean. These percentages grew gradually until the late Antonine age, with the most significant increases occurring between the Flavian and the Trajan age (which might have been associated with the enlargement of the *Portus*), and between the early and late Antonine period. The 3rd c. AD brought a fall in the numbers and percentages of Eastern Mediterranean amphoras found in Ostia, which contrasts with what might have been expected given the supposed spread of the use of barrels in the West.

The difference in importations from the Eastern Mediterranean between Rome and Ostia has already been noticed by C. Pavolini. However, at the time of his 1996 publication quantifications of amphoras were only available for two contexts in Rome dated to the Flavian period, namely *Forum Transitorium* and *Crypta Balbi*. Pavolini noticed that in the second half of the 1st c. AD many more Gallic containers were attested in Ostia (around 25%) than in Rome (between 2,2% and 2,7% depending on the context[116]). Contrarily, Aegeo-Oriental amphoras were very popular in the Eternal City (between 18 and almost 50%, depending on the context) and extremely rare in Ostia (0,6%).[117] Which, according to Pavolini, meant that *Portus* was not able to accommodate all the necessary supplies and thus concentrated upon importations from the western part of the Mediterranean.[118] The study that has been undertaken in this book confirms these observations, demonstrating that throughout the early empire Ostia received more wines from Gaul than it did from the whole of the Eastern Mediterranean. The capacity of *Portus* was increased after the construction of Trajan's hexagonal basin and thus it could receive more Eastern wines, but still this was too little to supply Rome.

116 All amphoras were considered, not just wine containers.

117 Pavolini 1996, 228. These figures were published in Anselmino, Coletti, Ferrarini 1986, 66, tab. 2.

118 Pavolini 1996, 229–230. Some of these commodities might have also been transported by land.

TABLE 6 Provenance of wine amphoras in Ostia (numbers and %)

	50 BC–50 AD		81–96 AD		90–120 AD		120–160 AD		160–200 AD		200–250 AD		250–300 AD	
Tyrrhenian	155	40,4%	255	33,2%	110	33%	144	25,8%	205	14,26%	45	21,84%	18	15%
Adriatic	73	19%	11	1,43%	14	4,1%	20	3,58%	208	14,46%	29	14,08%	13	11%
Sicilian	2	0,5%	62	8,06%	13	3,8%	28	5,01%	35	2,43%	6	2,91%	0	0%
Spanish	126	32,8%	91	11,8%	12	3,6%	5	0,9%	25	1,74%	8	3,88%	0	0%
Eastern Mediterranean	18	4,7%	45	5,85%	39	11,54%	78	14%	332	23,09%	40	19,42%	17	14%
African	0	0%	106	13,8%	34	10%	50	9%	137	9,53%	23	11,17%	13	11%
Gallic	10	2,6%	199	25,9%	116	34%	233	41,8%	496	34,49%	55	26,69%	60	50%
Total	**384**	100%	**769**	100%	**338**	100%	**558**	100%	**1438**	100%	**206**	100%	**121**	100%

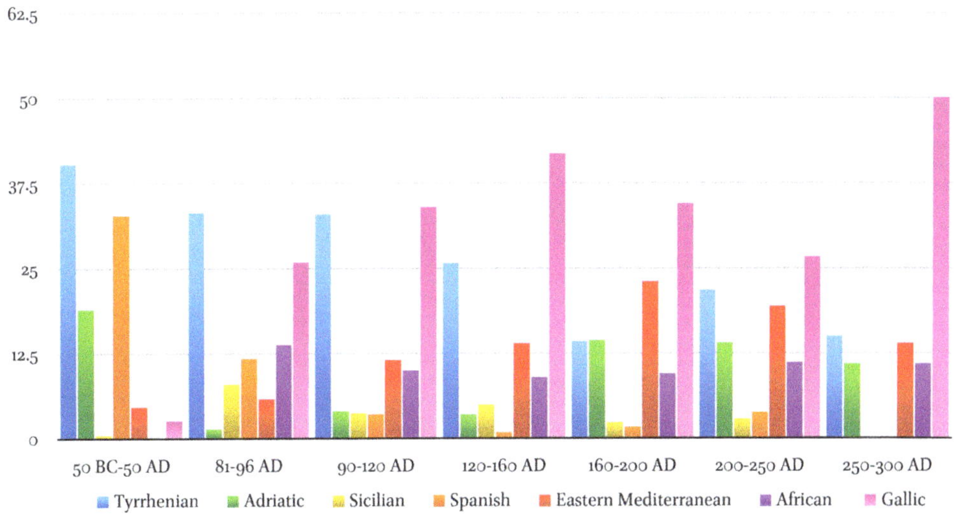

FIGURE 8 Provenance of wine amphoras in Ostia (%)

3.2 *Eastern Mediterranean Wine Importations in Ostia*

As in Rome and Campania, Aegean containers predominated among Eastern Mediterranean amphoras discovered in Ostia (Tab. 7 and Fig. 9). Moreover, the most numerous Aegean imports came from Rhodes and Crete, while 'Coan' were quite frequent until the end of the 1st c. AD. Anatolian wines were popular between 160 and 250 AD, but surprisingly, amphoras from this region were not attested during the late 3rd c. AD. Oriental imports were rather rare, while those from Egypt and the Black Sea region were almost insignificant, which agrees with the data from Rome. Similarly, as in the capital, Kapitän 1 and 2 amphoras dominated in the late 3rd c. AD assemblage and it seems that towards the end of the 3rd c. AD they were the only Aegean imports; a few fragments from Rhodian and Coan amphoras were discovered, but they might have been residual. The peaks observed in wine importations from Crete between 90–120 AD and 200–250 AD are difficult to explain as they were not observed elsewhere.

TABLE 7 Provenance of Eastern Mediterranean wine amphoras in Ostia (numbers and %)

	50 BC–50 AD		80–96 AD		90–120 AD		120–160 AD		160–200 AD		200–250 AD		250–300 AD	
Rhodes	7	39,9%	13	28,9%	6	15,4%	30	38,46%	72	21,69%	7	17,5%	1	5,88%
Crete	3	16,7%	14	31,1%	29	74,4%	29	37,18%	108	32,53%	25	62,5%	1	5,88%
'Cos'	4	22,2%	13	28,9%	1	2,56%	3	3,85%	31	9,34%	0	0%	0	0%
Cnidus	1	5,55%	2	4,44%	0	0%	2	2,56%	4	1,2%	0	0%	0	0%
Chios	1	5,55%	0	0%	0	0%	0	0%	0	0%	0	0%	0	0%
Anatolia	1	5,55%	1	2,22%	1	2,56%	6	7,69%	62	18,67%	4	10%	0	0%
Kapitän 1&2	0	0%	0	0%	0	0%	0	0%	19	5,72%	4	10%	15	88,24%
Cilicia/Cyprus	1	5,55%	1	2,22%	0	0%	4	5,13%	18	5,42%	0	0%	0	0%
Levant	0	0%	1	2,22%	2	5,13%	3	3,85%	9	2,71%	0	0%	0	0%
Egypt	0	0%	0	0%	0	0%	1	1,28%	5	1,51%	0	0%	0	0%
Black Sea	0	0%	0	0%	0	0%	0	0%	4	1,2%	0	0%	0	0%
Total	**18**	**100%**	**45**	**100%**	**39**	**100%**	**78**	**100%**	**332**	**100%**	**40**	**100%**	**17**	**100%**

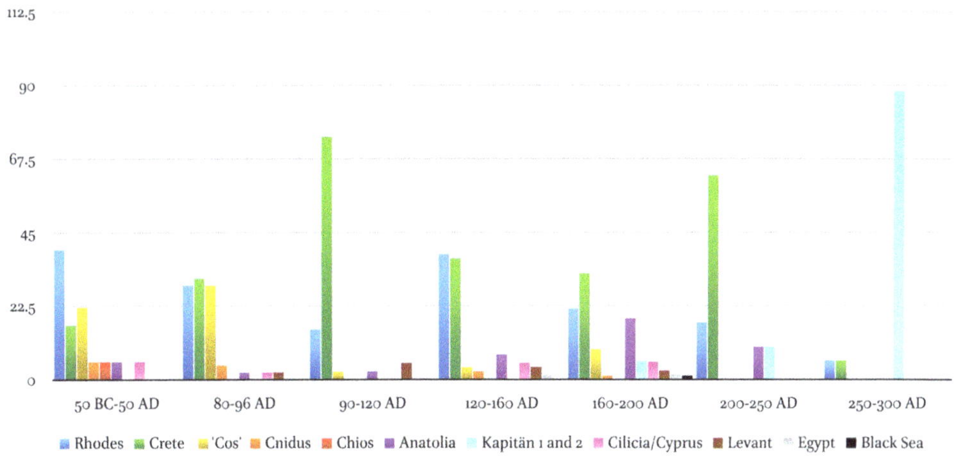

FIGURE 9 Provenance of Eastern Mediterranean wine amphoras in Ostia (%)

4 Adriatic Italy

Adriatic Italy is not as abundant in amphora assemblages as the Tyrrhenian part. Of course, amphoras are attested in almost every city, but considerable numbers of containers were only discovered in Verona, Vicenza, Padua, Oderzo, Aquileia, Altinum, Polesine and Rimini. These areas are situated on or around the *Via Postumia* and the *Via Popilia/Via Annia*, which were main Adriatic routes linking Genoa and Rimini with Aquileia. A large number of amphoras, as was typical for the northern Adriatic region, were found in ancient drainage systems, thanks to which they preserved almost complete and thus their identification poses little doubts.[119]

The synthesis does not include amphoras found in Concordia Sagittaria[120] and Caorle.[121] The publication from the first site did not provide precise numbers of the different amphora types, though it did mention that seven out of nine wine containers found in 2nd c. AD layers in *Via Fornasatta* were of 'Coan tradition', which is a very high percentage (77,78 %). In Caorle, two out of 20 late Republican amphoras originated in the East (10 %), but none were attested

119 Lunardi 1998, 37–46.

120 In Concordia two contexts were discovered: *Piazzale della Catedrale* and *Via Fornasatta*, unfortunately the publication of the former lacks exact numbers, while in *Via Fornasatta* only 9 wine containers were attested (not counting MR8), which is not enough for a synthesis, see Cipriano 2001, 194–195; Belotti 2004.

121 Only two possible Greek amphoras were discovered in Caorle, including one fragment that was uncertain.

among the 21 wine containers dated to the Principate. Thus, the very low number of transport jars attested at this site makes it non-representative. Numerous minor occasional findings could not be included in the statistics either, due to the fact that their publications concentrate on amphora types rather than their numbers.[122] Nonetheless, they do provide us with information regarding general importation trends in Eastern Mediterranean wines in the Adriatic area. According to them, the earliest foreign wines were imported to Adriatic Italy between the 4th and 2nd c. BC in Greco-Italic amphoras and most probably came from Magna Graecia and Sicily, but one should remember that these amphora types were also produced along the Adriatic coast (between Rimini and Pescara).[123] During the same period Corinthian/Corcyrean, as well as Rhodian wine containers appeared for example in Adria, though in limited quantities (5 and 2 amphora fragments respectively).[124] Hellenistic Rhodian amphoras were also found in Aquileia, in the levels dated to the 3rd and 2nd c. BC,[125] which means that wines from this island were the earliest Eastern Mediterranean imports in the area. Other Adriatic sites confirm the occasional presence of Chian and Cnidian, as well as Coan, Cretan and Rhodian amphoras, which were the most numerous and most widely distributed.[126]

The precise dating of containers was possible only for Verona and Oderzo. Publications for Altinum, Vicenza, Polesine, Padua and Rimini do not present any chronological divisions, but amphora types suggest a chronological framework between the late Republic and the 3rd c. AD. It is worth mentioning that in the case of Padua, Verona and Aquileia, archaeological material from late antiquity was also attested and will be referred to in the last chapter of this book. For now, assemblages dated between the late Republic and the Principate will be analysed.

4.1 *Altinum*

Altinum was an ancient Venetian town, which became a Roman *municipium* during the late Republic. Its role grew with the construction of the *Via Annia*, and later the *Via Claudia Augusta* which linked the Venetian Lagoon with the Danubian *limes* in Rhetia across the Alps. This geographical location made Altinum an important strategic and commercial centre in the Adriatic area. The area of the ancient Roman town of Altinum provided numerous

122 Eg. findings from Piazza Marconi in Cremona, see Nicodemo, Ravasi, Volonté 2008.
123 Cipriano, Mazzocchin 2017, 40, fig. 1.
124 Toniolo 2000, 175–176, 179.
125 Tiussi 2007, 481.
126 Auriemma, Degrassi 2015, 178; Nicodemo, Ravasi, Volonté 2008, 298.

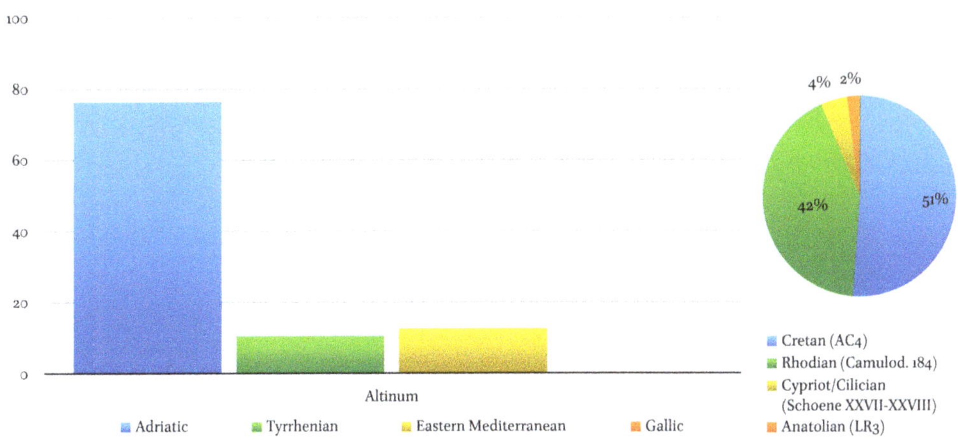

FIGURE 10 Provenance of wine amphoras in Altinum, 100 BC–300 AD (%, n = 331)

amphoras in different contexts, including: *Marcello, Vigna Bortoletto, Fornasotti, Zuccarello, Zachello, Canale Sioncello, necropoli nordest dell'Annia, necropoli "Le Bruscolade", Silone, Ca'delle Anfore*, and other occasional findings, some from an unknown context. Most amphoras were incidental discoveries or came from the tombs and various constructions within the area of the necropoleis, with drainages providing the majority. The findings from residential areas are considerably less frequent. Alessandra Toniolo's study revealed 637 diagnostic amphora fragments, which were predominantly rims and handles and were dated between the 1st c. BC and the 3rd c. AD, with a few specimens dating to late antiquity. More than half of these containers (331) were used to transport wine, and, as one may expect, most (253) were from the Adriatic area. As demonstrated by Figure 10, 35 Dressel 1 and Dressel 2–4 that were produced in Tyrrhenian Italy constituted a 10,57% share of the assemblage, which is lower than the 12,69% share of the 42 Eastern Mediterranean wine amphoras (the most common transmarine imports). Cretan amphoras (exclusively AC4/Dressel 43) were the most numerous among the eastern containers (51,11%), while second position was held by Rhodian jars (42,22%). Containers from Rhodes might have been even more numerous if we consider that there are containers named 'di tradizione rodia', which Toniolo classified as Italian imitations that transported Italian wine labelled as Rhodian,[127] which is disputable. Other Aegean jars are rare, but two fragments of Cypriot/Cilician containers were attested (4,44%), as well as a late Anatolian LR3 fragment (2,22%).

127 Toniolo 1991, 27. These amphoras were not included in the synthesis due to the uncertainty regarding their Aegean origin.

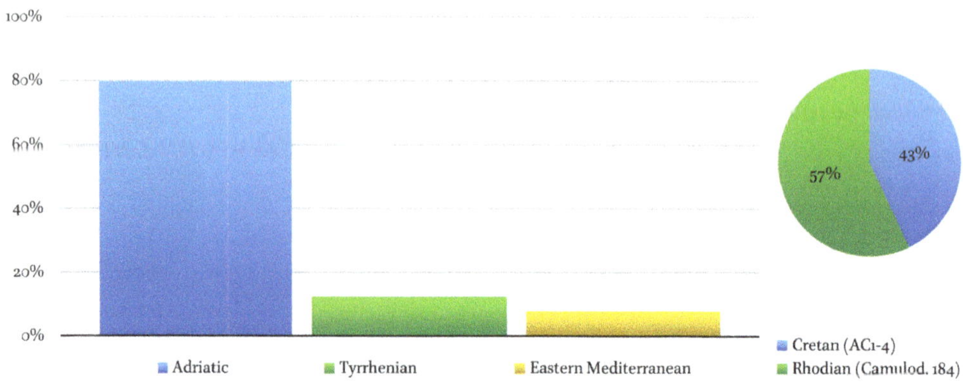

FIGURE 11 Provenance of wine amphoras in Rimini, 100 BC–300 AD (%, n = 89)

4.2 *Rimini*

Ariminium, modern Rimini, is the biggest urban centre to the south of the Po Valley. It was founded as a Roman colony in 268 BC and throughout antiquity remained an important link between the north and the south of the peninsula, it also linked Adriatic Italy with Rome after the construction of the *Via Flaminia* in 220 BC. A considerable number of amphoras, namely 222 diagnostic fragments dated between the 3rd c. BC and 5th c. AD, were discovered in *domus Romana di Palazzo Diolattevi*.[128] The following time frames were distinguished: 2nd c. BC, 100 BC–300 AD, and 300–500 AD. However, the synthesis presented in this book considers only the period 100 BC–300 AD. This is due to the fact that up to the end of the Republic only Adriatic amphoras were attested, while the number of containers for late antiquity is very low—a mere 17 (10 Oriental and 7 African spatheia). Thus, Figure 11 includes 89 wine containers dated between 100 BC–300 AD (71 Adriatic, 11 Tyrrhenian and 7 Eastern Mediterranean).

Figure 11 demonstrates that Eastern Mediterranean wines were the only foreign imports, as no Gallic, Spanish or African wine amphoras were attested. Their percentage (7,87 %), however, was not very high, and they were outnumbered by Italian Dressel 2–4 containers. Yet, it is worth mentioning that the number of Tyrrhenian jars might be overestimated, because the publication did not specify whether 11 fragments of Dressel 2–4 were of Adriatic or Tyrrhenian origin. Only Rhodian and Cretan jars were attested (4 and 3 fragments respectively).

128 Iandoli 2006, 103.

TABLE 8 Provenance of wine amphoras in Oderzo (numbers and %)

	Augustan age		0–50 AD		50–100 AD	
Adriatic	102	91,07%	49	83,05%	128	39,63%
Tyrrhenian	2	1,78%	0	0%	24	7,43%
Eastern Mediterranean	8	7,14%	10	16,95%	164	50,77%
Gallic	0	0%	0	0%	4	1,24%
Spanish	0	0%	0	0%	3	0,93%
Total	112	100%	59	100%	323	100%

4.3 *Opitergium/Oderzo*

Modern Oderzo, which once was one of the most important centres of the *Veneti*, came under the influence of Rome around the beginning of the 2nd c. BC, when the first Romans moved into the area. Soon afterwards, in 182 BC, the town was granted Latin rights, while its importance was further increased after construction of the *Via Postumia* was completed in 148 BC. In 49 BC, thanks to the *Lex de Gallia Cisalpina*, the city became a Roman *municipium* and its citizens were ascribed to the *Papiria* tribe. The etymology of its name seems significant, given that it comes from the Venetian 'opi-terg', which may be translated as 'at the market', and emphasises the role of Oderzo as an important link between the Alps and the Adriatic coast, as well as to modern *Veneto Euganeo* and *Orientale*.[129] Considerable numbers of amphoras were found in the SE necropoleis of *Via Garibaldi, Via Spine* and in *Via degli Alpini*, in numerous drains. They were dated to the Augustan age and the 1st c. AD.[130]

The percentages of amphoras in Oderzo (Fig. 12) show that importations of Eastern Mediterranean wines grew from 7,14% during the Augustan age to more than half (50,77%) in the second half of the 1st c. AD. They were the most numerous and were the only imported wines up to 50 AD, even after this date they remained the only significant imported wines as Gallic and Spanish amphoras together were estimated at less than 2,2%.

During the Augustan age all Eastern Mediterranean amphoras were of Rhodian origin; Coan started to appear after 15 AD, with Cretan appearing after 50 AD (Fig. 13). Surprisingly, the percentage of Cretan jars was low (9,62%),

129 Cipriano, Ferrarini 2001, 14.
130 Cipriano, Ferrarini 2001, 21–47 cf. Tirelli, Ferrarini, Cipriano 1998.

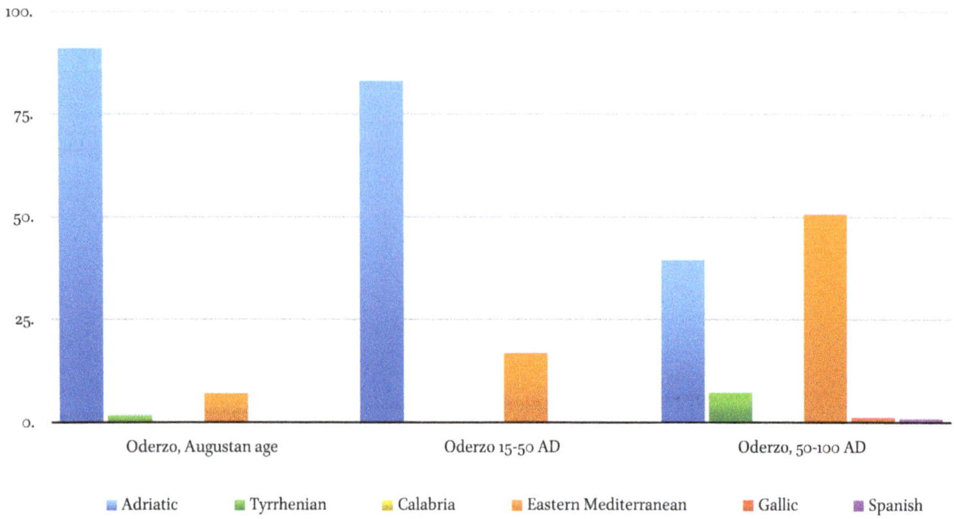

FIGURE 12 Provenance of wine amphoras in Oderzo (%, n = 494)

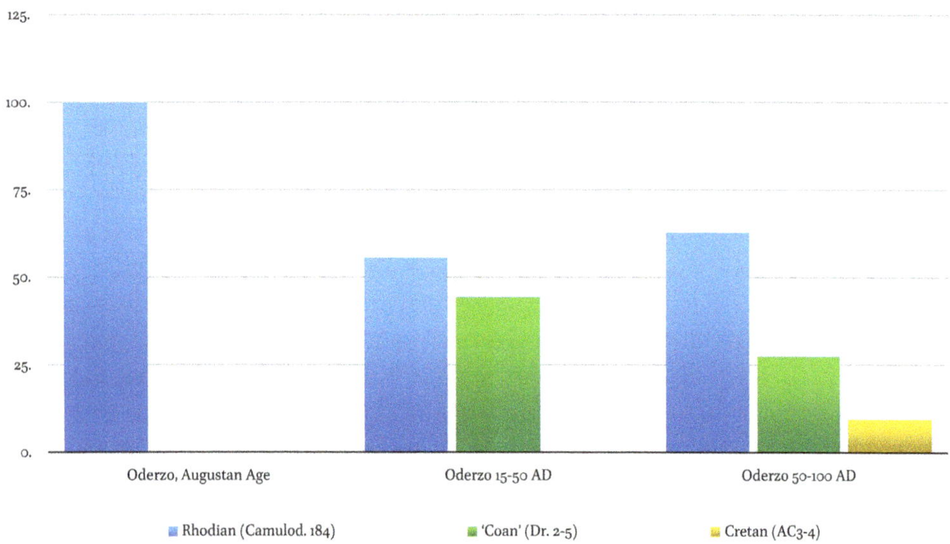

FIGURE 13 Provenance of Eastern Mediterranean wine amphoras in Oderzo (%, n = 182)

while Rhodian amphoras always provided more than half (55,56% and 62,82% respectively). Surprisingly, the percentage of wines of Coan tradition during the 1st c. AD varied between almost 30% and more than 40%.

4.4 *Padua*

'The oldest city in northern Italy' was one of the principal centres of the *Veneti*, who in the late 3rd c. BC fought together with Rome against the Gauls and Carthaginians. The Social War that began in 91 BC brought more ties between the two cities, and finally between 49 and 43 BC Padua became a Roman municipium (*Lex Julia Municipalis*), while its citizens were ascribed to the Roman tribe *Fabia*. By the end of the 1st c. BC Padua was the second wealthiest city in Italy after Rome. Amphoras were found in numerous archaeological contexts within the city, most of them, as in other parts of the Adriatic area, in ancient drainage systems. In the late Republican contexts of *piazza de Gasperi, via Trieste, via Montona, via S. Francesco/Palazzo del Bo* and *ex-Cinema Roma*, no Eastern Mediterranean containers were attested, examples of which first appeared (albeit in limited numbers—1 Rhodian and 2 unidentified) in the contexts dated to the Augustan age (*piazza Castello, via S. Pietro, via S. Francesco/Palazzo Romanin, via P. Paolo and via Umberto I*).[131]

The synthesis presented here considers the following contexts:

- *Piazza de Gasperi*—103 wine amphoras dated to the end of the 1st c. BC and mid-1st c. AD.[132]
- *Ex-cinema Roma* (17 amphoras, mid 1st c. BC, excavated in 1986), *via Manzoni*, as well as occasional finds from the area, 100 wine amphoras in total, dated between the end of the 1st c. BC and mid-1st c. AD.[133]
- *Porto Fluviale* and the area next to *Liceo Tito Livio*, 100 BC–50 AD.[134]
- *Via Gaetano, Via Boito*, 0–50 AD.[135]
- *Via P. Paoli*, Flavian age.[136]
- *Giardini dell'arena* excavated between 2004–2005—336 containers (143 for wine transport), dated from 0–150 AD.[137]
- *Via dei Salici*, 50 BC–200 AD (c. 58 wine amphoras).[138]

131 Cipriano, Mazzocchin 2011, 331–338.
132 Cipriano 1992, 55–58, 69, graf. 2.
133 Pastore 1992, 114, graf. 2.
134 Cipriano, Mazzocchin 1992, 151–153.
135 Cipriano, Mazzocchin 2011, 346–349.
136 Cipriano, Mazzocchin 2011, 351–352.
137 Mazzocchin, Rossi 2006, 12–17.
138 Mazzocchin, Tuzzato 2010, 21–29.

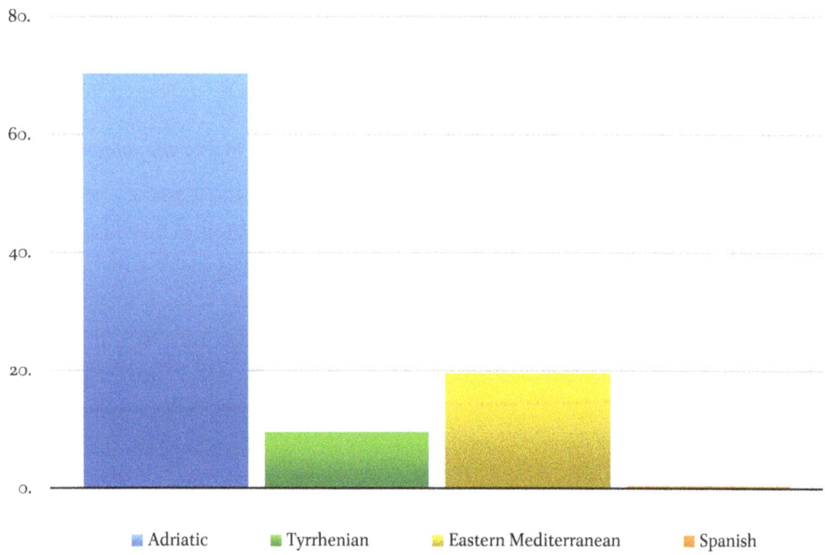

FIGURE 14 Provenance of wine amphoras in Padua (%, n = 867)

– *Via Gazzamellata* (69–96 AD), *via Beato Pellegrino* (mid-1st c. AD), *Roncaglia di Ponte San Nicoló* (0–150 AD).[139]

The synthesis excludes discoveries from the *Via Acquette* (0–50 AD) as exact numbers were not provided for most of the containers,[140] as well as those from *Colegio Ravenna* (late Republican age) as no eastern containers were attested.[141] Therefore, it comprises 867 diagnostic fragments of wine amphoras found in Padua, dated between 100 BC and 200 AD, including 610 Adriatic, 83 Tyrrhenian, 170 Eastern Mediterranean and 4 Spanish.

Figure 14 shows that Eastern Mediterranean wines were the most numerous foreign imports in Padua, reaching almost 20% of all the wines imported in amphoras. Amphoras from the East outnumbered transport jars from the Tyrrhenian part of the Apennine Peninsula, as in Oderzo and Altinum.

In Padua, only Rhodian, Cretan and Coan amphoras were attested (Fig. 15), which could be viewed as the 'standard pack' in the region. Rhodian (42,77%) predominated slightly over Cretan (37,11%), while Coan (27,13%) were the least popular. No Egyptian, Palestinian, or Cnidian amphoras were attested.

139 Cipriano, Mazzocchin, Pastore 1991; Cipriano, Mazzocchin, Pastore 1998.
140 Mazzocchin 2007b, 123, 129–130.
141 Mazzocchin 2007a, 66–72.

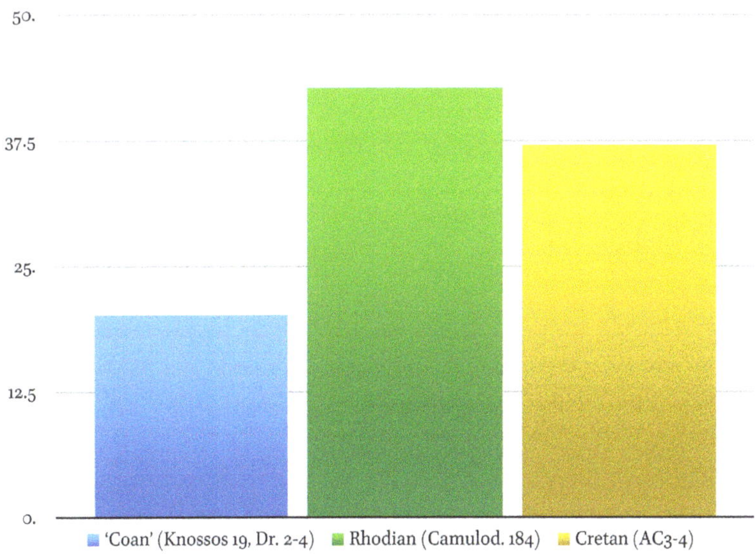

FIGURE 15 Provenance of Eastern Mediterranean wine amphoras in Padua, 100 BC–300 AD (%, n = 170)

4.5 *Polesine*

In a number of small towns and villages situated in the lower Po valley and its estuary (namely: *San Basilio, Adria, Casteguglielmo, Castelnovo Bariano, Corte Cavanella, Rovigo, Gavello, Villadose* and *S. Bellino, Trecenta*), 83 amphoras were found, dispersed in various contexts, mostly in modern residential areas. More than half of them, meaning 46, transported wine, mostly of an Adriatic origin (27 containers). Tyrrhenian amphoras were less common, as only 8 fragments were attested. Cretan jars (10) were the only non-Italian wine containers, besides a fragment of a Gallic amphora (Pelichet 47). It is possible that some African wine-jars were also present, but unfortunately the classification 'Africana grande' and 'cilindrica basso imperiale' do not allow certain attribution.[142]

Figure 16 demonstrates that more than one fifth of imports came from the Eastern Mediterranean area, and that this region was the main wine exporter for the Polesine region, more important than the Tyrrhenian coast of Italy. Curiously, all Eastern Mediterranean amphoras were from Crete.

142 Toniolo 1987, 87–128.

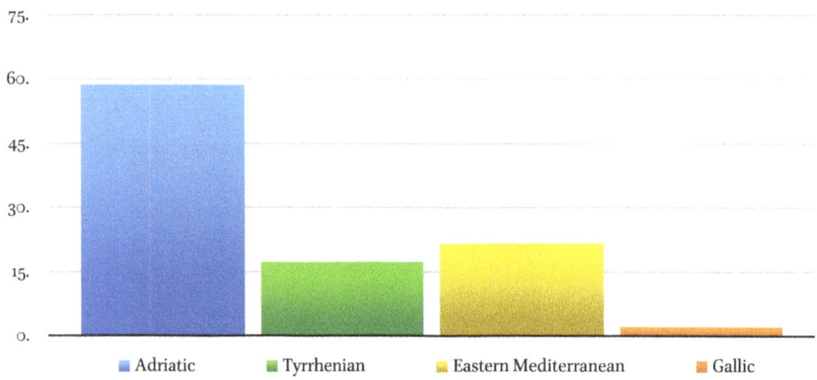

FIGURE 16 Provenance of wine amphoras in Polesine, 100 BC–300 AD (%, n = 46)

4.6 *Verona*

Verona was established as a Roman colony in 89 BC, and forty years later it was transformed into a municipium (in 49 BC) and its citizens were then ascribed to the Roman tribe *Poblilia* or *Publicia*. Several hundred amphoras were found in the city, most of them as parts of drainage systems. This study considers the following amphora assemblages:

- *Via Redentore*, eastern riverbank, 1st c. BC.[143]
- Below Wall A in *ex Campo Fiera*, western riverbank—end of the 1st c. BC–beginning of the 1st c. AD.[144]
- Ex *Convento dei Cappuccini*, next to the church of S. Francesco al Corso—324 amphoras found in 1969 and 1990, dated to the end of the 1st c. BC–beginning of 1st c. AD.[145]
- *Via Campofiore* and *Via Trezza*, to the east of the city close to *Via Postumia*, in an area that might have served as a necropolis, mid-1st c. AD.[146]

Table 9 presents exact numbers of wine amphoras from different time spans.

As with several other contexts mentioned above, Verona sees a considerable increase in the percentage of Eastern Mediterranean amphoras between the 1st c. BC and the 1st c. AD, from 0,88% to 30% respectively (Fig. 17). Moreover, they were the only significant foreign imports. Their variety until 300 AD was not wide, since only Rhodian and Cretan jars were attested (Fig. 18). The former predominated, more than doubling the number of Cretan containers.

143 Pesavento Mattioli 1999, 40–48.
144 Buchi 1973, 534–637.
145 Pesavento Mattioli 1998, 311–313.
146 Pesavento Mattioli 1998, 311–313.

TABLE 9 Provenance of wine amphoras in Verona (numbers and %)

	100 BC–50 AD		50–100 AD		100 BC–200 AD	
Adriatic	430	94,71%	15	18,75%	24	55,81%
Tyrrhenian	18	3,96%	38	47,5%	13	30,23%
Eastern Mediterranean	4	0,88%	24	30%	6	13,95%
Gallic	0	0%	0	0%	0	0%
Spanish	2	0,44%	3	3,75%	0	0%
Total	454	100%	80	100%	43	100%

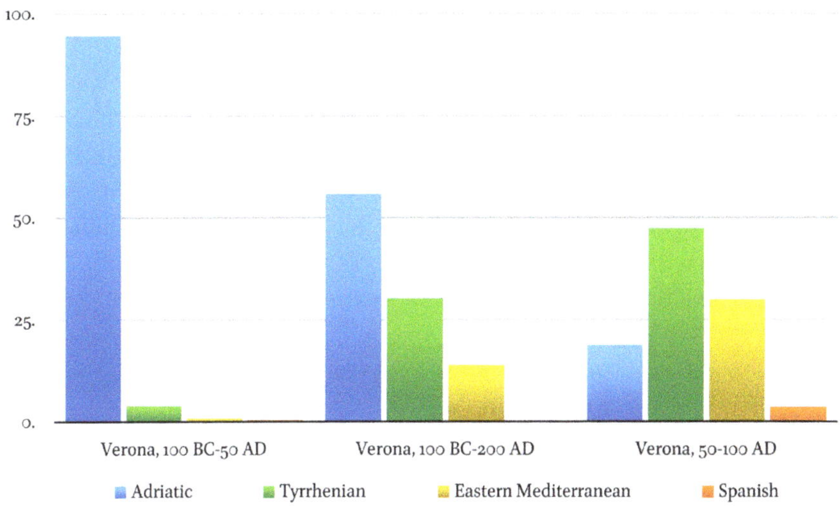

FIGURE 17 Provenance of wine amphoras in Verona (%, n = 577)

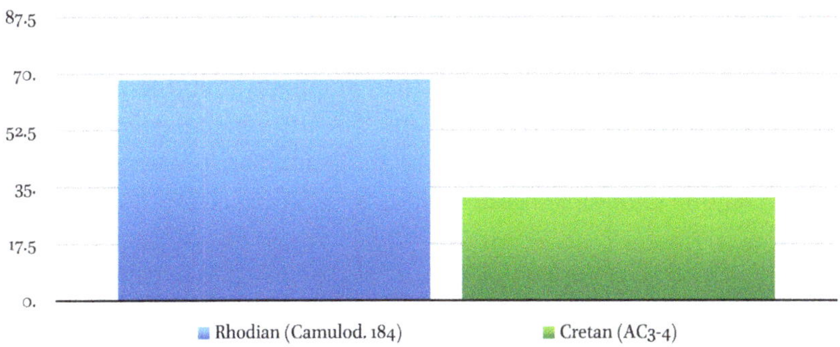

FIGURE 18 Provenance of Eastern Mediterranean wine amphoras in Verona, 100 BC–300 AD (%, n = 34)

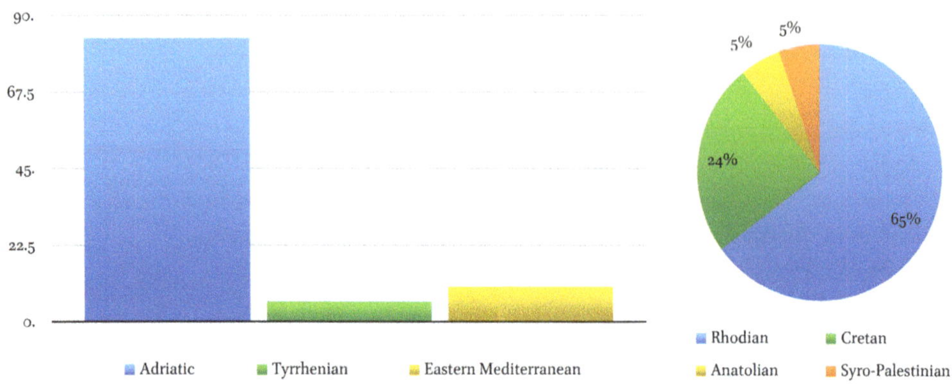

FIGURE 19 Provenance of wine amphoras in Vicenza (%, n = 345)

4.7 *Vicenza*

Ancient *Vicetia* or *Vincentia* was initially populated by the Euganei and later by the Paleo-Veneti, becoming Romanized during the 2nd c. BC. With the construction of the *Via Postumia* in 148 BC the role of the city grew significantly; its inhabitants, however, had to wait until 49 BC to receive Roman citizenship. In Vicenza, 736 amphoras have been found, including 345 wine containers, all dated between the late Republican and the Claudian age.

They were attested in the following contexts:

- *Via Cattaneo*—199 containers
- *ex convento padri camaldolesi da Rua*—9 containers
- *Campo Marzo*—102 containers
- *Pazetta S. Giacomo*—4 containers
- *Pedemuro S. Biagio*—20 containers
- *contrà della Piarda*—351 containers

The number also includes 51 containers that were found isolated in different parts of the city.[147]

In Vicenza, Eastern Mediterranean wine containers were the only foreign imports and they were more numerous than amphoras from the Tyrrhenian part of Italy (Fig. 19). Similar to Verona, Rhodian jars predominated and they were more than twice as numerous as Cretan. In addition, occasional Anatolian and Levantine imports were attested.

147 Mazzocchin 2013, 11–48, 60, 163, fig. 73 and 115.

4.8 *Aquileia*

Aquileia was the most important communication node in the Adriatic area. During the 1st c. AD and thanks to the construction of the *Via Geminia* and *Via Flavia*, Aquileia was connected to Emona across the Julian Alps, and Pula on the Istrian Peninsula. The city also received and stored commodities destined for Danubian and Transalpine provinces.[148]

Numerous amphoras have been discovered in Aquileia, but unfortunately, most of the studies concerning them have yet to be completed. This regards for example the area of *Canale Anfora*[149] a well to the south of the Forum,[150] *fondi ex Cossar*,[151] and *Porto Fluviale*.[152] Adriatic products predominated in these contexts, but it seems that in this instance they were followed by imports from the Eastern Mediterranean. However, the exact quantity of Spanish containers is unknown, as they were grouped together with Italian vessels.[153] Wine containers, especially from Rhodes (Camulod. 184), Crete (AC2 and AC4), Cos (Dressel 2–4) and Cnidus, predominated among the Eastern Mediterranean amphoras, but Cypriot/Cilician (Agora G199/MR4) and Anatolian (Agora F65–66/MR3) jars were also attested.[154] A similar set of Eastern Mediterranean wines, except for imports from Anatolia, was attested in *Via Bolivia* and the area to the East of the Forum, Cretan and Rhodian predominated reaching almost 50% and c. 35% respectively.[155] However, the publications of material from these contexts mix diagnostic with non-diagnostic fragments, making it difficult to understand what the author was referring to. Therefore, there are no graphs for Aquileia.

When summarising the data from Adriatic Italy one may conclude that Eastern Mediterranean wines were popular in various regions and not just Latium and Campania, where their importations could be a result of Rome's enormous demand for wine. During the Imperial age their percentages were also high in the north Adriatic area (between 7 and 50%), where they were the only wines imported in quantities that suggest deliberate trade (Fig. 20). Spanish and Gallic wines were extremely scarce in Adriatic Italy, which confirms the observa-

148 Carre 2007c, 623.
149 Auriemma et al. 2016, 379–403.
150 Degrassi, Maggi 2011, 261–270.
151 Dobreva 2014. A part of amphoras has been published, but their number, 22 wine containers dated at least between 100 BC–500 AD, is not representative enough to create any statistics.
152 Carre 2007a, 541, fig. 2.
153 Carre 2007b, 583–604.
154 Carre 2007b, 588–598.
155 These contexts were published in: Ceazzi, Del Brusco 2014, 943–953 and Verzár-Bass 1994.

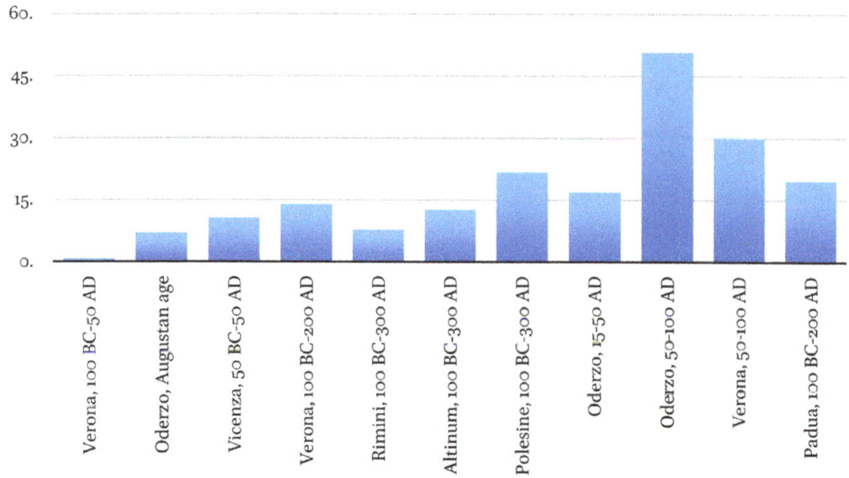

FIGURE 20 Percentages of Eastern Mediterranean wine amphoras in different contexts in Adriatic Italy

tions already made by Cacciaguerra concerning the Venetian Lagoon.[156] It is worth noting that percentages of Eastern Mediterranean wines were usually higher (apart from in Verona, Rimini and Padua) than wines produced in the Tyrrhenian part of Italy, which also shows the important role that the Eastern Mediterranean region played in supplying wine to the Adriatic area.

5 ORBIS Transport Costs and Wine Importations

A map of transport costs provided by ORBIS: The Stanford Geospatial Network Model of the Roman World is helpful in understanding the particular role that the East, or to be more precise, the Aegean region, played in supplying Italy with wine. Moreover, it is likely to provide information regarding the nature of the Roman economy. According to economic theories, if a free market existed, market forces (i.e. supply and demand) and potential profit margins would govern the trade. Considering the likelihood that transportation costs were the major determinant with regards to setting the price of basic imported consumables,[157] foodstuffs in particular, we may assume that their distribution depended upon these costs, which may be approximated thanks to ORBIS.

156 Cacciaguerra 1990, 5–7.
157 Scheidel 2014, 29.

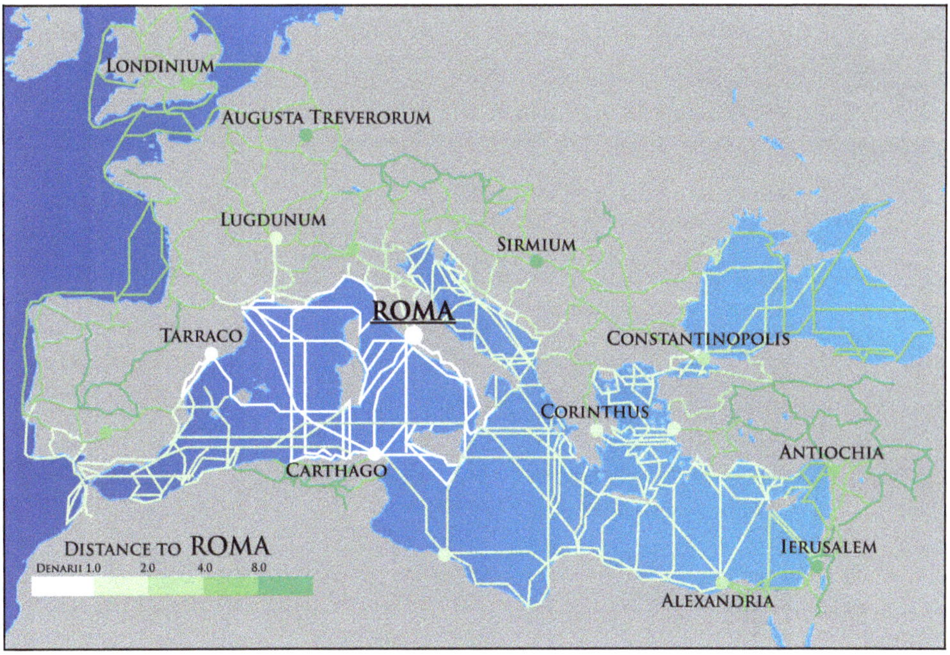

FIGURE 21 Price cost of imports to Rome according to the ORBIS model

As suggested by analysis of prices in Diocletian's Edict on Maximum Prices, distance had little to do with transport costs, which were governed by the duration of the journey.[158] By simulating movements along water and land routes within the Roman communication network, ORBIS allows to reconstruct the duration and hence the financial costs associated with travel in antiquity. At the moment ORBIS is the best-documented openly available digital resource that offers information about the transport system of the entire Roman Empire around 200 AD. Contrary to conventional maps, which fail to capture certain environmental constraints that governed the flow of goods, this model provides the time cost and financial expense associated with a wide range of different types of travel in antiquity.[159]

Figure 21 shows transport costs to Rome during summer, in the middle of the sailing season. As we can observe, it was the cheapest to import from the Tyrrhenian facade of the Apennine Peninsula, Sicily, Sardinia, Corsica, the Rhône Valley, southern Hispania Tarraconensis, southern Baetica, African coast and the Aegean region. However, importing from Lusitania, Cyprus, Cilicia, Egypt, the Levant and the Black Sea area was much more expensive. In the

158 Arnaud 2007, 334; Scheidel 2013.
159 Scheidel 2015.

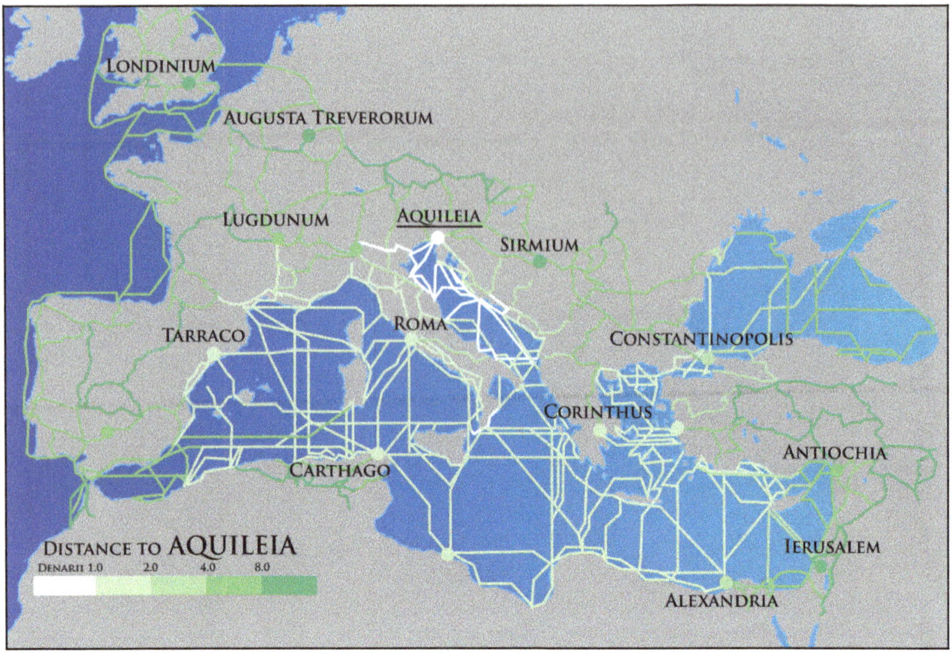

FIGURE 22 Price cost of imports to Aquileia according to the ORBIS model

case of Aquileia (Fig. 22) it was profitable to import from the Adriatic basin, the Aegean region and Africa, while transportation costs were probably an obstacle for Gallic, Baetican, Lusitanian as well as Oriental products.

The analysis of proportional share of different amphora types indicates that during the Imperial age Italy only imported wines from those areas with low transportation costs. Aegean, African, Gallic, Baetican and Tarraconesian wine amphoras are present in Rome, but Lusitanian, Egyptian, Levantine, Cypriot, Cilician and Black Sea containers are hardly attested.[160] At the same time, Aegean products are the only statistically significant wine imports in the north Adriatic part of Italy. Gallic or Baetican wine amphoras, the import of which was almost twice as expensive as the Aegean, are hardly attested. Therefore, it is reasonable to conclude that Aegean wines were so popular throughout Italy because they were not only tasty, but also cheap and easy to transport. Moreover, it seems that the price of goods, or to be more precise the transport costs, governed the trade in wines until the 3rd c. AD.

160 Amphoras from the southern Black Sea region appear sporadically in the Adriatic part of Italy, but it is unknown whether they transported wine; see Auriemma, Degrassi, Quiri 2015, 149–150.

6 Conclusions

Comparisons between amphora statistics from Rome, Campania, Ostia and north Adriatic Italy bring very interesting observations regarding the scale of the consumption of Eastern Mediterranean wines, as well as providing information regarding the process of their transportation. First of all, products from the eastern part of the Mediterranean were the most numerous imports, both in the Tyrrhenian and Adriatic parts of Italy. Their percentages sometimes even surpassed imported Italian wines,[161] especially in Campania (various contexts) and in Rome (during the 3rd c. AD). Wines from the Aegean region, such as Rhodian, Cretan and to a lesser degree Coan and Anatolian were the most popular. Cypriot/Cilician imports were rather scarce, except in Campania, where their percentages in the Imperial period reached between 10% and 32%. Other Oriental wines, such as those from the Levant and Egypt were extremely rare, as were those from the Black Sea region. It is worth mentioning that amphoras attributed to the Black Sea region are almost non-existent in Italy. They have only been attested in late 2nd c. AD layers in the Baths of the Swimmer in Ostia. Their number was estimated at 12, whereas the total number of 2nd c. AD amphoras from this context surpassed 3500.[162] Beside this, a fragment from a Knossos 39 container, which probably originated in the Black Sea area, was discovered in Rome. In the Adriatic, one example of a container attributed to Sinope was attested in Concordia Sagittaria,[163] which suggests that the Black Sea region was of no commercial importance to the Italians.

There should be no doubt that the Aegean region was the main wine supplier to Rome. However, until the early 1st c. AD in Campania, and in the second half of the century in Rome and Ostia, Rhodian wine was the first among the Aegean imports, but after that it was overtaken by Cretan wine. During the 2nd c. AD wine from Crete was the most popular of all Aegean beverages in Latium, Campania and in Adriatic Italy. Moreover, it was probably the most popular wine in the Eternal City during this period. This conclusion may be drawn due to the discovery of *Nuovo Mercato di Testaccio*, which during the 2nd c. AD served as a refuse heap for wine amphoras, Cretan in particular. The area of *Nuovo Mercato di Testaccio* belonged to the biggest late Republican and Imperial *emporion*,

161 They were probably never consumed in higher quantities than Italian wines if we add the locally produced wines that were transported in perishable containers.

162 Rizzo, Panella 2014, 409, tab. 4.

163 Belotti 2004, 80–82, fig. 17; Kassab Tezgör 2010, 169.

where *Porticus Aemilia* and three large *horrea* were constructed (*horrea Galbana, horrea Lolliana* and *horrea Seiana*).[164] The archaeological material from this context was only partially excavated and studied, which is unfortunate as this site yielded high numbers of amphora fragments. The overall proportions were calculated only for Room 1 of a storehouse. Wine amphoras were estimated at 91,5% of the total number of containers, 88,4% of which were of Eastern Mediterranean origin. Cretan amphoras predominated, since they constituted 94,7% of all oriental wine amphoras. A preliminary analysis of the amphoras from *Nuovo Mercato di Testaccio* suggests that these proportions are representative for this context in general.[165] In 2010 a preliminary report regarding Cretan amphoras from this site was published, which included 8731 fragments. These fragments represented 832 containers, including 545 dated to the first half of the 2nd century AD.[166] They correspond to 38,8% of all Cretan amphoras dated to this period and to 21,8% of all Cretan amphoras that were found in this context.[167] These data allow us to estimate that around 3817 containers from Crete were discovered in *Nuovo Mercato di Testaccio*, 1404 of which were dated to the 2nd c. AD. These numbers are unique—there is no other archaeological context where such large numbers of wine amphoras were attested. It can only be compared to the refuse heap of oil amphoras at *Monte Testaccio*. Comparisons between the numbers of Cretan containers that were attested in *Nuovo Mercato di Testaccio* and the combined numbers from other contexts (Fig. 23)[168] clearly demonstrate that the quantity of Cretan amphoras found in *Nuovo Mercato di Testaccio* is unparalleled. It is difficult to compare the proportions from this context with any other; however, it does seem that Cretan wine imports grew considerably during the 2nd c. AD. During this cen-

164 Gallone 2011, 173–176. For the port facilities in this area, see Castagnoli 1980, 36–37; Festuccia, Verde 2011, 155–156.

165 Tempesta 2011, 193–196.

166 The remaining 287 were residual and were discovered in late Imperial layers.

167 Casaramona et al. 2010, 113, 122, tab. 1.

168 The total number of Cretan amphoras from Campania, regardless of the period, is calculated using the containers registered by Marangou-Lerat 1995, 67–85 from the Vesuvian cities, numbers mentioned in the journals of previous excavations, data in CIL IV and the excavations that were conducted between 2005–2009. I am very grateful to Dr. E. Botte for sharing this information with me before it was published. The quantity of Cretan jars dated to the 2nd c. AD includes material from *Cratere Senga* and *Rione Terra* that was mentioned by Di Giovanni 2003, 88–89. The 2nd c. AD containers from *Rione Terra* were not included in the statistics that are presented in this chapter, as the exact data from this context is yet to be published. The numbers of Cretan containers in Rome and Ostia are calculated using the data mentioned in Tab. 3 and 7.

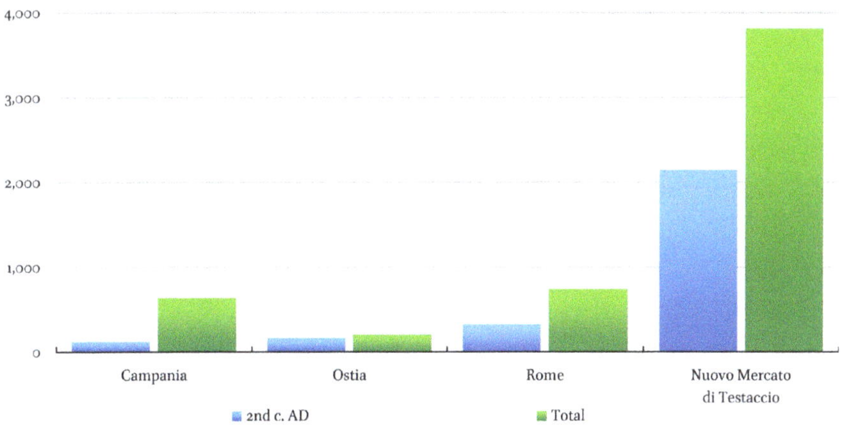

FIGURE 23 Numbers of Cretan amphoras according to the context

tury wine from Crete became the most popular wine in the Eternal City, more popular even than Italian wines transported in amphoras (Fig. 24[169]).

One may wonder whether similar refuse heaps containing other amphora types remain unexcavated, or whether the deposit from *Nuovo Mercato di Testaccio* is unique and a result of the special role that Cretan wine played with regards to the Roman demand for wine. It has already been noted that De Caro suggested that at least some Cretan wine might have come to Italy as *vectigalia* in kind.[170] Also, according to Tchernia this wine arrived in Italy on *annona* vessels and thus was free from transportation costs,[171] which resulted in its low price. One may also consider the possibility that some wine from Crete was exported to Rome in the form of a tax paid by the island in kind, similar to the way Baetican olive oil reached the German *limes*, according to J. Remesal Rodríguez.[172] Although many scholars do not agree with Remesal's theory,[173] state interference in the trade of Cretan wine would explain both its popularity and the need to create a waste heap especially for Cretan amphoras—since their content was a payment, the amount must have been precisely calculated.

Nevertheless, we should remember the privileged position that Crete and the south-eastern Aegean area held, i.e. situated on the main trade route and being frequently visited by ships transporting Egyptian grain to Italy. Due to

169 The numbers of Cretan amphoras include Nuovo Mercato di Testaccio and Tab. 3. The numbers of Italian amphoras are from Tab. 3.
170 De Caro 1992/93, 309–311.
171 Tchernia 2011, 345–348.
172 Remesal Rodríguez 1986, 111; 2008.
173 For example, Hopkins 2002, 190–232; Mattingly 1988, 52–52; Tchernia 2011, 334.

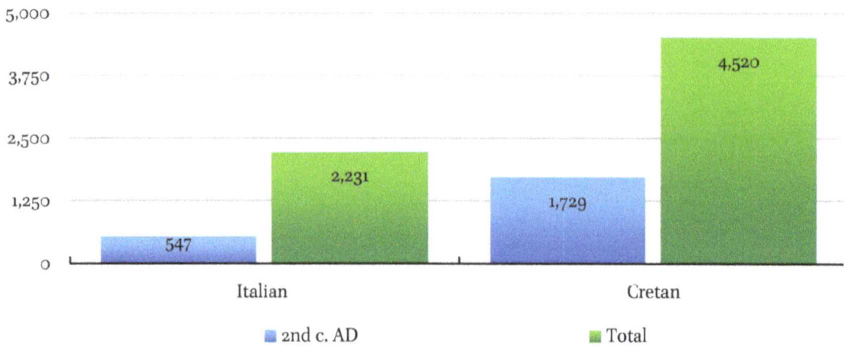

FIGURE 24 Numbers of Italian and Cretan wine containers in Rome

the tidal currents and ocean winds, ships from Alexandria could not simply sail straight to Italy, but had to sail first to the Phoenician coast and then to Rhodes (along the Lycian coast or via Cyprus), then finally onward towards Italy via the southern coast of Crete.[174] Therefore, the loading south-Aegean or west-Anatolian wines onto a ship that had probably already unloaded a consignment of Egyptian grain would seem quite reasonable.

Notwithstanding the above-mentioned possibilities, another hypothesis should be considered. Analysing the types and quantities of imported Eastern wines alongside a model provided by ORBIS that details transport costs to Rome (Fig. 21) and Aquileia (Fig. 22) in the summer season results in a very interesting convergence. During the early Imperial age Italy imported almost exclusively wines from the areas that provided low transport costs. Rome was supplied predominantly from south Gaul and Spain, northern Africa and the Aegean region, while Aquileia from the Aegean area. Oriental, Egyptian, Lusitanian, Cilician, Cypriot and Black Sea wines, the transport of which was expensive, were generally ignored both in the eastern and western part of Italy. The observed pattern of wine importations sheds new light on the nature of the Roman economy. First of all, it suggests that the cost of transport was the most important factor that governed wine trade. If state coerced transfers played the main part, as was the case with Rome's grain supply, any correlation between transportation costs and the scale of imports would go unnoticed. Therefore, this correlation indicates that market forces played an important role in the Roman economy. In other words, it seems that Temin was right when arguing that the Roman Empire had a market economy,[175] even though his argu-

174 Horden, Purcell 2000, 138; Tchernia 2016, 345–348.

175 Temin 2013.

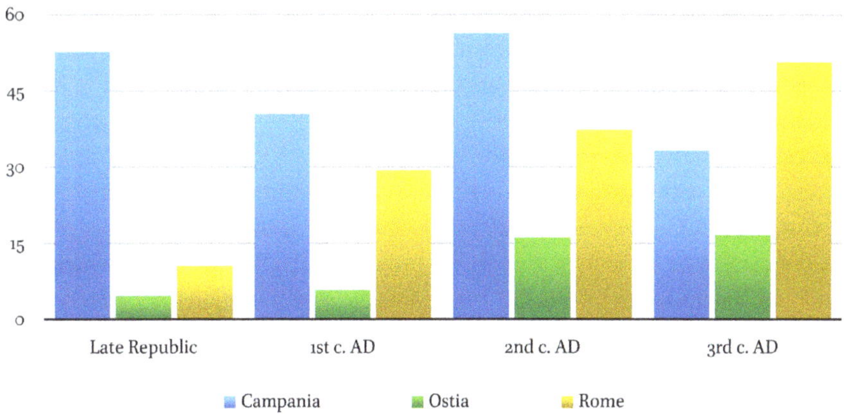

FIGURE 25 Eastern Mediterranean wine containers in Campania, Rome and Ostia (%)

ments and methodology were questioned.[176] At the same time, the study of wine importations to Italy contradicts the 'bazaar economy' model proposed by Bang,[177] at least during the early Imperial age.

Furthermore, a gradual increase in the percentages of Eastern Mediterranean wine amphoras may be observed between the 1st c. BC and the 3rd c. AD. This could be explained in two ways. On the one hand, it could mean that the Aegean region became a gradually more important wine supplier. On the other, it may simply show an increase in the use of barrels for transporting wines from the western provinces. However, there is no evidence indicating that the use of barrels was significant before the 3rd c. AD, and hence it seems more likely that the Aegean region indeed provided more wines to Italy between the 1st c. BC and the 3rd c. AD. The drop in the percentage of Eastern Mediterranean containers in Campania during the 3rd c. AD seems to correlate with an increase in the percentage of African amphoras, which may suggest that Puteoli started to receive more imports from this area.

Figure 25 leaves no doubt that up to the end of the 2nd c. AD Eastern Mediterranean imports in Campania were much more numerous than in Rome or Ostia. Eastern amphoras reached, and even exceeded 50% of all wine containers at times, which indicates the important role of Puteoli as a gateway for oriental products. At the same time, considerably less wines from the Eastern Mediterranean reached Ostia. In turn, Western Mediterranean products were much more frequent in Ostia than in Rome during the Flavian period. Accord-

176 Bransbourg 2012, http://dlib.nyu.edu/awdl/isaw/isaw-papers/3, accessed 19.03.2019.
177 Bang 2008.

ing to Pavolini, this suggested a certain specialisation of Ostia and Puteoli: the former mostly received goods from Spain and Gaul, while in the latter oriental commodities were reloaded and stored, or they were transported to Rome on small ships that could navigate the Tiber.[178] The comparison of amphora percentages confirms this hypothesis. Furthermore, it shows that the organisation of trade with the East did not change much in the 2nd c. AD, even after the enlargement of the *Portus* by Trajan, which according to many scholars resulted in the decline of the role of Puteoli.[179] However, up to the 3rd c. AD warehouses in Puteoli continued to expand, while magistrates that were associated with *annona* were present in the city until at least the 30's of the 3rd c. AD, which suggests that the economic situation of the Campanian port was rather stable.[180] Wine amphora percentages provide further evidence for the prosperity of the Campanian port. Even if more Eastern Mediterranean products started to reach Ostia at the beginning of the 2nd c. AD,[181] wine amphora percentages suggest that the reloading of Eastern wines that were destined for the Roman markets continued in Puteoli. If we consider that the decrease in the percentage of Eastern Mediterranean wine containers in Puteoli during the 3rd c. AD correlates with the increase in the proportion of African jars, we may assume that the role of Puteoli as an important port that received eastern and African products did not change considerably. Therefore, the rivalry between Ostia and Puteoli should not be considered in terms of increase and decline, but rather in terms of specialisation.

Eastern Mediterranean products also played an important part in the supply of wine to the Adriatic region, where they were the most frequent (and at times the only) imports from the provinces. Their percentages often surpassed the percentages of wines imported from the Tyrrhenian part of Italy, which clearly demonstrates that frequent imports were not only enjoyed by big cities, such as Rome, Alexandria, Ephesus and Carthage, as it was long assumed.[182] On the contrary, Aegean wines during the Imperial age provided between 7% and 50% of the wine required by small Adriatic towns and villages, which shows

178 Pavolini 1996, 229–230. Some of these commodities might have also been transported by land.

179 Maiuri 1958, 22; Annecchino 1960, 133–134 who admits that Puteoli remained an important emporium for eastern trade until the end of the Empire; De Caro 2008, 62 claims that under Commodus *classis Alexandrea* moved to Ostia.

180 D'Arms 1974; Camodeca 1994, 113; Demma 2004, 337; 2007, 112–113; Demougin 2010, 378; Tchernia 2011, 273.

181 The gradual increase of barrels being used to transport of wines from the western provinces could be another explanation.

182 Finley 1999, 123–149; Bang 2008, 142, 297–298.

that Roman commercial network must have been well developed also outside of the main commercial arteries and that the long-distance trade was vibrant and ubiquitous in ancient Italy. Moreover, there should be no doubt that wine importations to Italy had a mass character and hence the Eastern wine trade must have played an important part in the Roman economy. It is also worth emphasising that the percentages and numbers of imported Eastern Mediterranean wines grew between the Augustan age and the 2nd c. AD, which may indicate that aggregated growth, which has been postulated by certain scholars,[183] did indeed occur during this period. The popularity of Eastern, especially Aegean wines, cannot be seen simply as a result of increased demand in Rome, given that provincial, albeit densely populated parts of Italy also imported large quantities of Aegean beverages. If, as the adversaries of intensive growth assume, the elites accumulated capital and all imports were in fact to satisfy their conspicuous consumption, we would only expect to find high percentages of imports in Rome, and the ports that supplied the capital, Ostia and Puteoli. However, high percentages of Eastern Mediterranean wine containers were also found in smaller centres, such as Naples, Padua, Vicenza, Verona and especially, Polesine. Therefore, it is unlikely that these beverages reached Italy on the orders of the elite or the state. On the contrary, it seems that they were consumed predominantly by ordinary people. If such a statement is confirmed, the constant increase in Eastern Mediterranean wine importations may suggest that not only did aggregated growth occur, in Italy it might have also been intensive.

The common character of most Eastern imports, excluding north-Aegean, has already been suggested by the literary evidence. The mass importations of south-Aegean and Anatolian wines provide further support for this hypothesis. It has also been observed that few eastern wine amphoras were attested in aristocratic residences, such as *Domus Tiberiana* in Rome as well as in *Villa San Marco, Villa Arianna*, and the House of Menander in Campania. This suggests that most of the Eastern wines imported during the Imperial age were to satisfy the demands of the common people, and only north-Aegean imports during the Archaic and Republican period were viewed as aristocratic luxuries. The time has come to verify this hypothesis.

---

183 Hopkins 1980, 102–103; 2002, 190–230; De Callataÿ 2005, 361–372; Scheidel 2009, 46–70; Lo Cascio 2009, 87–106; Kron 2014, 123–146; Jongman 2006, 237–254; 2014, 169–188; 2017a, 260–268; Wilson 2007; 2009a; 2009b; 2014; McConnell et al. 2018, http://www.pnas.org/content/early/2018/05/08/1721818115/tab-figures-data, accessed 15.05.2018.

CHAPTER 4

Aristocratic Luxuries or Mass Beverages?

Nos bibimus vitro, tu murra, Pontice. Quare?
Prodat perspicuus ne duo vina calix.

We drink from glass, you from murrine, Ponticus.
For why? A transparent cup would reveal two wines.

MART. IV 85

Objects of ancient trade are usually divided into two categories: luxuries and staples. It was commonly assumed that only the latter were significant from an economic point of view, as trading in luxuries was seen as negligible and limited only to satisfy the demand of small elite circles. Although this view has been questioned and trading in luxury items has been accorded its rightful economic significance,[1] it is still important to distinguish between aristocratic luxuries and common items. This is due to the fact that one ought to understand who profited from economic growth during the Roman period. Therefore, the question of whether Eastern wines in Italy were viewed as aristocratic luxuries or mass beverages adds a further argument to the economic debate regarding the nature of Roman economic growth.

Is it possible to distinguish between aristocratic luxury wines and mass beverages? Yes, it is, and we are able to make such a distinction due to the existence of a link between social class and wine hierarchy in classical antiquity. It is obvious that the lower social classes could not afford the expensive wines that were drunk by the elite, but we also know that the rich generally did not drink plebeian wines, even in emergencies.[2] The best example that supports such a statement is provided by a rather sad anecdote concerning Mark Anthony the orator, a grandfather of the famous friend of Julius Caesar. During the period of Marius' proscriptions, Marcus Antonius (Orator) was hiding from his ene-

1 Morley 2007, 39–43.
2 Tchernia 1986, 33; 1995, 300–303.

© KONINKLIJKE BRILL NV, LEIDEN, 2021 | DOI:10.1163/9789004433762_006

mies and found shelter at the house of his friend, a plebeian. Even though this friend generally drank ordinary wine, he sent his slave to an inn for something better for his noble guest, as he did not want to serve a low-quality beverage to the famous politician. The seller, surprised by the uncommon purchase, questioned the slave, and upon learning the truth he reported it to Marius. Consequently, Mark Anthony was captured and killed. Therefore, we may say that wine cost the life of the famous orator.[3]

Returning to Eastern Mediterranean wines, were they drunk by elites or rather by common people? Would it be Mark Anthony who usually enjoyed their taste or rather his plebeian friend? Answering this question may strengthen the argument in favour of *per capita* economic growth. It has been observed that the percentages and numbers of Eastern Mediterranean wines grew between the late Republican period and the 2nd c. AD. This was indubitably a result of the population growth in Italy that has been observed during this period.[4] However, according to the Malthusian scenario, population growth should result in *per capita* income shrinking, which reduces the purchasing power of common people. Would they be able to continue buying more and more imported wines? This seems inconceivable, unless these wines were distributed by the state; however, there is no evidence for this before the late 3rd c. AD.[5] Moreover, only the inhabitants of Rome enjoyed such distributions. Therefore, it may be assumed that as long as more wines were imported to Italy, the well-being of its inhabitants did not decrease.

Identifying the consumers of Eastern Mediterranean wines is only possible after having analysed their characteristics, the quantities in which they were imported and the contexts in which their containers were found in Italy. The analysis of the literary evidence regarding the characteristics of wines that was presented in Chapter 2 showed that these beverages may be divided into at least two groups. Wines from Chios, Lesbos and Thasos enjoyed particularly good reputation among ancient authors, while the amphoras in which they were transported were discovered in Italy in limited quantities in Archaic and Republican contexts, for example in the graves of the wealthy Etruscans. This suggests that wines from these islands were luxuries available only to the aristocracy and that their consumption stopped around the Augustan age. At the same time, most of the Eastern Mediterranean wines imported dur-

3 Tchernia 1986, 33; 1995, 300–301; Plut. *Mar.* 44, 1–4.

4 Scheidel 2006b, 8–9 accessed February 2018; cf. Scheidel 2007a, 45–47; 2008, 19–30; Jongman 2005, 441–495; 2009, 124; 2014, 172; 2017b, 20, fig. 1.2; Storey and Glenn 1997, 966–978.

5 Erdkamp 2013, 267.

ing the Imperial age were not particularly praised by ancient poets. Moreover, the numbers and percentages of wine amphoras indicate that they were mass imports and were less numerous in aristocratic residences than in other contexts. Such observations suggest that these wines served for common consumption. Are these observations confirmed by further studies?

1 Luxuries for the Elite[6]

Chian, Lesbian and Thasian wines were often praised by poets because of their delightful taste and were recommended by physicians due to their medicinal values. However, is this enough to claim that they were luxurious goods? Certainly not. Luxury is a complicated concept, especially in terms of food and any consumption good needs to possess certain characteristics to be called a luxury.

1.1 *When Is Food a Luxury?*

According to *The New Oxford Dictionary of English*, 'luxury' is "*the state of great comfort and extravagant living*" or "*an inessential, desirable item which is expensive or difficult to obtain*", such as "*chocolate, scent and fizzy wine*".[7] Its definition in *The Concise Oxford Dictionary* is similar—'luxury' is explained as: "*1. choice or costly surroundings, possessions, food, etc.; luxuriousness. 2. Something desirable for comfort or enjoyment, but not indispensable. 3. Providing great comfort, expensive*".[8]

From these definitions one may deduce that a luxurious good is something that gives pleasure, which is desired, but is not essential for living. Furthermore, access to it is difficult or limited by its high price or other factors. For example, it may be very difficult to procure and/or be very labor-intensive to produce.

Morley points out that the term 'luxury' "*tends to conflate intrinsic qualities of the object in question, such as its origin, its portability and the fact that it is clearly unnecessary for sustenance, with its value in the marketplace and the identity of its ultimate consumers*".[9] According to Ch. Berry, a luxury is not simply desired, but desired widely. It must be something that a lot of people want, but only few can possess. For example, a special edition of a book designed for collectors,

6 This section in a slightly different form was previously published as a paper in Eos, see Komar 2014a.
7 Pearsal, Hanks 1998, 1103.
8 Fowler, Fowler 1995, 814.
9 Morley 2007, 40.

though rare, would not be a luxury, because it would not be widely demanded.[10] On the other hand, the inessentiality of a luxury does not mean its uselessness. A luxurious good is something related to basic needs (such as the need for food, clothes, shelter and leisure), but it is something sophisticated and refined. It must bring enjoyment apart from the simple satisfaction of basic needs. For example, bread is necessary for survival, but *fresh* bread could be seen as an indulgence.[11] Similarly, wine as a simple liquid to satisfy thirst will be a staple good, but high-quality and expensive wine could be considered a luxury. The commodity that satisfies basic needs is something that people will buy regardless of changes in prices and incomes. A luxury, however, is an item that may be easily abandoned, if its cost increases dramatically.[12]

While talking about luxury foods, the comfort and enjoyment that they bring are usually associated with their taste. It is true that luxury food should be palatable; however, it is not the only factor that can cause pleasure. It should also be noted that "*all goods carry meaning*"[13] and in the case of food this meaning, for example the prestige that its consumption suggests, may be even more important that its taste. The best example that illustrates this is an anecdote about the precious pearl that Cleopatra dissolved in a cup of wine. She drank it not because of its taste, but to prove to Mark Anthony that she could afford a more spectacular and expensive feast than the banquet that he had prepared.[14]

M. van der Veen argues that "*in terms of food, luxury usually denotes foods that are desirable or hard to obtain but not essential to human nutrition. This frequently, though not necessarily, includes exotic products, meaning foods that are unusual or desirable because of their foreign origin*".[15] This definition indicates that foreign, imported goods are often considered luxurious, but not all of them achieve this status. For example, grain imported from Egypt was definitely not a luxury for the ancient Romans. Furthermore, Van der Veen claims that luxury foods are consumed on special occasions and are often directly associated with the elites, who use them to showcase their social status and the difference between them and the masses.[16] Therefore, luxury foods are not for everyday consumption. In antiquity they were probably eaten during public feasts that accompanied religious festivals or important political events. Moreover, they

10 Berry 1994, 5.
11 Berry 1994, 11–17.
12 Douglas, Isherwood 1979, 97.
13 Douglas, Isherwood 1979, 72.
14 Plin. *HN* IX 119–121; De Garine 1976, 150–151.
15 Van der Veen 2003, 405–406.
16 Van der Veen 2003, 406.

were consumed almost exclusively by the upper social orders. Having a high price was one factor that assured an item was not commonly accessible. Moreover, in most societies there were attempts '*to limit the tendency of luxuries to become widely available*', like sumptuary laws, '*monopolising certain goods only for elite consumption*'. Consequently, the consumption of luxuries was often banned or limited by sumptuary laws or other legal restrictions.[17]

Finally, according to M. Douglas and B. Isherwood, low frequency of use is one of the characteristics of luxuries.[18] This is obviously a consequence of the features that were mentioned above. When access to a certain commodity is limited few people can consume it, and also its consumption was usually associated with special events; thus it is clear that it would not be consumed very often.

In summary, it is possible to form a list of at least five criteria that a certain food should fulfil to be called a luxury:

1. It provides pleasure, enjoyment.
2. It is inessential for survival.
3. Access to it is limited (due to foreign origin, high price, sumptuary laws etc.).
4. It is consumed by the high social strata and/or during special occasions.
5. It is used infrequently.

1.2 *It Provides Pleasure, Enjoyment*

It has already been mentioned that luxurious foods should give pleasure because of their palatable taste and/or the social meaning of their consumption. As a matter of fact, Greek poets and comedy writers very often praise the good taste and pleasant aroma of the wines from Chios, Lesbos and Thasos. For example, Callimachus calls Lesbian wine "*nectar of the flower of wine*" (πολὺς δὲ Λεσβίης ἄωτον νέκταρ οἰνάνθης ἄγων),[19] while, Longus describes it as "*the best of wines, redolent of flowers*" (ἀνθοσμίας οἶνος Λέσβιος, ποθῆναι κάλλιστος οἶνος).[20] Also, Clearchus says that there is no "*wine sweeter/nicer than Lesbian*" (οὐκ ἔστιν ἄλλος οἶνος ἡδίων πιεῖν).[21] According to Aristophanes, the fragrance of Thasian wine was nicer than the smell of perfumes,[22] while Hermippos argued that this

17 Berry 1994, 31, 76–85; Van der Veen 2003, 410.
18 Douglas, Isherwood 1979, 136.
19 *AP* XIII 9.
20 Longus IV 10, 3, 5.
21 Clearchus fr. 5 K.-A. = Ath. *Deipn.* 29c.
22 Aristoph. *Eccl.* 1118–1119.

wine, together with Chian, was the best of all.[23] The Romans held similar opinions; however, they were not so generous with their praise. Pliny says:

> *Nunc simili modo transmarina dicemus. in summa gloria post Homerica illa, de quibus supra diximus, fuere Thasium Chiumque, ex Chio quod Ariusium vocant. his addidit Lesbium Erasistrati maximi medici auctoritas, circiter* CCCCL *anno urbis Romae.*
>
> We will now in a similar manner specify the foreign wines of countries overseas. The wines held in highest esteem subsequent to the great vintages of the Homeric age about which we have spoken above were those of Thasos and Chios, and of the latter the wine called Ariusian. To these the authority of the eminent physician Erasistratus, about four hundred and fifty years after the foundation of Rome, added Lesbian.[24]

This means that from the 3rd c. BC Chian, Lesbian and Thasian were among the best foreign wines in Rome. Moreover, it seems that they were still held in high esteem when Falernian, one of the best Italian *crus*, was being produced:

> (…) *sic quoque postea diu transmarina in auctoritate fuerunt et ad avos usque nostros, quin et Falerno iam reperto, sicut apparet ex illo comico versu: Quinque Thasi vini depromam, bina Falerni.*
>
> Similarly also afterwards wines imported from oversea held the field for a long time and right down to our grandfathers' day, indeed even after Falernian had already been discovered, as appears from the one of the comedy playwright: 'I'll broach five casks of Thasian, two of Falernian'.[25]

Chian and Lesbian were mentioned in a positive context by Horace, who placed them alongside Caecuban wine, another Roman grand *cru*.[26] Moreover, the same author claimed that five-year-old boiled Chian wine was the best accompaniment to lamprey,[27] a real delicacy on Roman tables. It would be highly improbable to drink an unsavoury or common wine with such a sophisticated

23 Hermippos fr. 77 K.-A. = Ath. *Deipn.* 29f. All translations are from Loeb Classical Library, unless otherwise indicated.

24 Plin. *HN* XIV 73.

25 Plin. *HN* XIV 95.

26 Hor. *Epod.* 9, 1 and 34.

27 Hor. *Serm.* II 8, 48–49.

dish; thus, Chian must have indeed been a tasty and fancy drink. To summarise, wines from Chios, Lesbos and Thasos had a very pleasurable taste that provided enjoyment and was appreciated by both the Greeks and the Romans.

1.3 *It Is Inessential for Survival*

Although wine was one of the main consumption goods in the ancient Mediterranean region, it was not the only liquid option available. Water would be the most obvious choice to satisfy thirst. However, access to fresh unpolluted water may have been difficult, thus the consumption of light or diluted alcoholic beverages might have been the only way to guarantee protection from bacteria. This did not apply to Rome however, as from the Augustan period its inhabitants had direct access to fresh and clear water.[28] Moreover, the assortment of wines available to the Romans was very broad. Starting from the 7th/6th c. BC the Etruscans produced and exported their wines,[29] whereas large-scale Roman wine production started in the 2nd or even as early as in the 4th c. BC,[30] which means that local wines were present in Italy. Also, wines were imported from all over the Mediterranean during the Imperial period, which means that there was a wide variety of alcoholic beverages available to the Romans.[31] In addition, people in classical antiquity consumed secondary, low-quality wine-based beverages such as *lora* (or *deuteria*) and *posca*. *Lora* was made by fermenting water with the remnants of squeezed grapes, while *posca* was a mixture of water and wine that was in the process of turning to vinegar. Both of these low-quality drinks were alcoholic, and both were consumed by the poorest (peasants and slaves).[32]

Summing up, the Romans had a wide range of beverages available to them, which means that wines from Chios, Lesbos and Thasos were not essential for them to survive.

1.4 *Access to It Is Limited (Due to Foreign Origin, High Price, Sumptuary Laws etc.)*

Wines from Chios, Lesbos and Thasos were obviously foreign goods to the Romans; therefore, access to them was limited as they were not locally produced. Although, as mentioned above, not all exotic goods were luxuries, in

28 Suet. *Aug.* 42.
29 Bats 2012, 377.
30 Tchernia 1986, 57; Vandermersch 2001, 156.
31 Rizzo 2003, 203–206.
32 Amouretti 1990, 80; Dalby 2003, 270, 352–353; Tchernia 1986, 13, 19.

the case of these wines high price and the sumptuary laws related to their cost limited their accessibility.

Wine from Chios was extremely expensive in Greece—Plutarch compares its cost to that of enjoying the company of Lais (a very expensive courtesan) and mentions that this wine cost one *mina* in Athens during the time of Socrates.[33] Considering the fact that in Athens the local wine cost four drachmas per *metretes* (which is equal to around 39 l.)[34] it seems that Chian was 25 times more expensive. At the same time, Salviat mentions an inscription which indicates that an amphora (containing around 22 l.) of Chian wine cost 18 drachmas in Egypt during the mid-3rd c. BC, whereas an equal amount of Thasian wine was sold for 20 drachmas, which would buy one-fifth of a good slave.[35]

Furthermore, in 89 BC P. Licinius Crassus and L. Julius Caesar issued a sumptuary law establishing the maximum price for Greek wines as 8 asses per *quadrantal* (ca. 26,2 l.).[36] Pliny, who provides us with this information, did not specify exactly which wines were subject to this law, but the context suggests that it referred to Chian, Lesbian and Thasian. The fact that these wines were the subject of the sumptuary law means that certain attempts were made to limit their accessibility. However, what was the relative cost of these wines in comparison with other beverages? According to Varro, during the First Punic War wine was generally sold at 8 asses per *quadrantal*;[37] thus, the cost of imported beverages does not seem exaggerated according to the sumptuary law of P. Licinius Crassus and L. Julius Caesar. However, T. Frank proved that the amount of wine that Pliny was talking about was not a *quadrantal* but a *quartarius* (0.25 *sextarii*),[38] which makes more sense.[39] Therefore, a *sextarius*, which is equal to 546 ml, would cost 32 asses, meaning one amphora of Greek wine (48 *sextaria*) would cost 1536 *asses* (384 *sestertii*, 96 *denarii*). This agrees with the testimony of Diodorus of Sicily, according to which an amphora of luxurious wine was sold for a hundred drachmas.[40] Columella says that in the Roman hinterlands in the 1st c. AD the lowest price of the most ordinary wine was 300 *sester-*

33 Plut. *De tranq. anim.* 10 (= *Mor.* 470 f); *Non posse* 17 (= *Mor.* 1099a–b).

34 Ridgeway, Wilkins 1890, 968. The volume was estimated as 39,4 l. by Hultsch and 38,9 l. by Nissen.

35 Salviat 1986, 180; Salviat, Tchernia 2013, 219. For more about wine prices in Greece, see Pritchett 1956, 199–203.

36 Plin. *HN* XIV 95.

37 Varro *ap.* Plin. *HN* XVIII 17.

38 Frank 1931, 278.

39 See Dari-Mattiacci, Plisecka 2010.

40 Diod. XXXVII 3, 5.

tii per *culleus*.[41] According to R. Duncan-Jones this equates to 15 *sestertii* per amphora.[42] Therefore, imported luxurious wine in Rome was more than 25 times[43] more expensive than ordinary wine.

1.5 *It Is Consumed by the High Social Strata and/or during Special Occasions*

The high price of wines from Chios, Lesbos and Thasos was probably the reason why they were mostly consumed by the upper social classes. It seems that in Greece they were drunk by Hellenistic kings, who were famous for their sophisticated tastes and extremely sumptuous way of living. This is illustrated by an anecdote about the life of Demetrius Poliorcetes that was mentioned by Plutarch:

> πάλιν δέ ποτε πλείονας ἡμέρας ἐν πότοις γενομένου, καὶ πρόφασιν λέγοντος ὡς ῥεῦμα διοχλήσειεν αὐτόν, 'ἐπυθόμην,' φάναι τὸν Ἀντίγονον, 'ἀλλὰ πότερον Θάσιον ἢ Χῖον ἦν τὸ ῥεῦμα'.
>
> Again, on another occasion, when Demetrius had been at his revels for several days, and excused his absence by saying that he was troubled with a flux, 'So I learned,' said Antigonus, 'but was it Thasian or Chian wine that flowed?'[44]

This passage suggests that Demetrius, son of Antigonus, was a connoisseur when it came to wines from Chios and Thasos. He drank them during his revels, but it is not known if these were special occasions. However, there is evidence that Thasian and Lesbian were consumed during the marriage feast of Caranus, the king of Macedonia, which was definitely an unusual event. Atheaneus describes it as follows:

> Ἐπεὶ δὲ καὶ τούτων ἀπηλλάγημεν, ἐκλαμβάνει πάλιν ἡμᾶς θερμός τις καὶ ζωρότερος πότος, οἴνων ὄντων ἡμῖν Θασίων καὶ Μενδαίων καὶ Λεσβίων, χρυσίδων πάνυ μεγάλων ἑκάστῳ προσενεχθεισῶν. Καὶ μετὰ τὸν πότον ὑελοῦς πίναξ δίπηχύς που τὴν διάμετρον ἐν θήκῃ κατακείμενος ἀργυρᾷ πλήρης ἰχθύων ὀπτῶν

41 Col. *R.R.* III 3,10.

42 Duncan-Jones 1974, 46.

43 Tchernia 1986, 37 states that 1st c. AD Italian *grand crus* were c. 10 times more expensive than ordinary wines, while in 18th century France their cost was between 9–10 and 26 times higher, which corroborates with the calculations presented in this study.

44 Plut. *Dem.* 19, 4.

πάντα γένη συνηθροισμένων, ἅπασί τε προσεδόθη καὶ ἀργυροῦν ἀρτοφόρον ἄρτων Καππαδοκίων, ὧν τὰ μὲν ἐφάγομεν, τὰ δὲ τοῖς θεράπουσιν ἐπεδώκαμεν. Καὶ νιψάμενοι τὰς χεῖρας ἐστεφανούμεθα καὶ πάλιν στλεγγίδας ἐλάβομεν χρυσᾶς, διπλασίους τῶν πρότερον, καὶ ἄλλο διλήκυθον μύρου. Ἡσυχίας δὲ γενομένης ἐξαλλόμενος τῆς κλίνης ὁ Πρωτέας αἰτεῖ σκύφον χοαῖον καὶ πληρώσας οἴνου Θασίου ὀλίγον τι ἐπιρράνας ὕδατος ἐξέπιεν ἐπειπώ: Ὁ πλεῖστα πίνων πλεῖστα κεὐφρανθήσεται.

After we had finished with them, our attention was next engrossed in a warm and almost neat drink, the wines at our disposal being Thasian, Mendaean and Lesbian; and very large gold cups were handled to each guest. After this draught we were all presented with a crystal platter about two cubits in diameter, lying on a silver receptacle and full of a collection of all kinds of baked fish; also a silver bread-rack containing Cappadocian loaves of which we ate some and gave the rest to the slaves. Then we washed our hands and put on crowns, again receiving gold tiaras twice the size of those we had before, and another double-jar of perfume.

When all was quiet, Proteas jumped up from his couch and demanded a six-pint bowl, and filling it with Thasian wine with just a dash of water he drank it all saying ‘He that drinks most shall have least sorrow’.[45]

As befits the wedding of a king, which is not a common occasion, the environment was highly refined and fancy dishes were served on precious golden, silver and glass vessels; along with perfumes, some of these vessels were donated to the revellers. Therefore, one would assume that the wine served at such a feast, namely Thasian and Lesbian must also have been far from ordinary.

It seems that the prestige and rank of Chian, Lesbian and Thasian wines in Italy was similar. According to the archaeological evidence they were imported to Italy as early as in the 7th c. BC,[46] where they appeared in the graves of wealthy Etruscans.[47] Much later, during the 1st c. BC, wine from Chios was called ‘the wine of the rich people’ by Varro,[48] which clearly indicates that it was consumed by the upper social orders. The same author quoted by Pliny in his *Natural History* says:

---

45 Ath. *Deipn.* 29d–f.

46 Slaska 1985, 19; Sacchetti 2013, 64–65, 75–76.

47 Giannace 2010, 81; Riva 2010b, 217–218; Zifferero 2010a, 67; Cianferoni 2012, 30–31; Rizzo 1990, 27–28.

48 Varro *Sat. Men.* 104 Bücheler.

L. Lucullus puer apud patrem numquam lautum convivium vidit, in quo plus semel Graecum vinum daretur: ipse cum rediit ex Asia, milia cadum congiarium divisit amplius centum. C. Sentius, quem praetorem vidimus, Chium vinum suam domum inlatum dicebat tum primum, cum sibi cardiaco medicus dedisset: Hortensius super X cadum heredi reliquit.

When Lucius Lucullus was a boy he never saw a full-dress banquet in his father's house at which Greek wine was given more than once, but when he himself came back from Asia he distributed more than 100,000 jars in largess; also Gaius Sentius, who was praetor in our time, used to say that the first time that Chian wine entered his house was when the doctor had prescribed it for him for heartburn; but Hortensius left over ten thousand jars to his next-of-kin.[49]

This passage proves that Greek wines were drunk by noble people from the Roman aristocracy. Lucullus is a perfect example as he was an arbiter of good taste and famous for organising extremely sumptuous feasts. He also distributed Greek wines to celebrate his return from Asia. Additionally, Caesar provided Chian and Lesbian wine for the banquets that were held to celebrate his triumphs:

Quid? Non est Caesar dictator triumphi sui cena vini Falerni amphoras, Chii cados in convivial distribuit? Idem Hispaniensi triumph Chium et Falernum dedit, epulo vero in tertio consulate suo Falernum, chium, Lesbium, Mamertinum, quo tempore primum quattuor genera vini adposita constat.

And besides, did not Caesar also, when dictator, at the banquet in celebration of his triumph apportion to each table a flagon of Falernian and a jar of Chian? Caesar also gave Chian and Falernian at his triumph over Spain, but at a banquet during his third consulship he provided Falernian, Chian, Lesbian and Mamertine: this is known to be the first occasion on which four kinds of wine were served.[50]

This clearly shows that in the Republican period wines from Chios and Lesbos were drunk by outstanding Romans from the upper social strata during important public ceremonies. Moreover, this passage indicates that these wines were

49 Plin. *HN* XIV 96.
50 Plin. *HN* XIV 97.

consumed in limited quantities—only once during the feast, even in the sumptuous house of the father of Lucullus. The fact that Greek wines were not for everyday consumption may also be deduced from a passage by Pliny, who says that: "*Greek wine was so highly esteemed that only one cup was given to each guest at a banquet*".[51]

Considering the fact that wines from Chios, Lesbos and Thasos were drunk mostly by the Roman aristocracy and that their consumption was limited, it seems logical to assume that they were used infrequently, which is another characteristic of luxury goods.

1.6 *It Is Used Infrequently*

It is possible to determine how frequently wines from Chios, Lesbos and Thasos were used in Italy through amphora analysis. However, it should be noted that there is very little amphora evidence from before the reign of Augustus. According to R. Volpe, this may indicate that all imported wines were luxuries in the Republican age.[52] Since evidence from this period is limited, determining how frequently wines from Chios, Lesbos and Thasos were consumed is problematic, due to the lack of comparative material.

Nevertheless, neither Lesbian nor Thasian amphoras were attested in five late Republican amphora assemblages that were discovered in the following locations: in the Forum of Caesar,[53] the *Horti Lamiani* in Rome,[54] the *Suburbium*,[55] at the House of the Porch in Ostia[56] and in *Casa di Ariadna* in Pompeii.[57] Evidence of Chian containers includes a dubious fragment from the House of the Porch and a stamp from Cosa, as well as an unspecified number from the *Suburbium* and *Horti Lamiani*.[58]

In the Imperial age foreign commodities were mass imported, but as with the Republican period Lesbian and Thasian wines were absent in Rome's archaeological record, which contained thousands of amphora fragments. Chian fragments were discovered but were rare. One definite Chian fragment was attested in *Vigna Barberini* on the Palatine Hill, it was dated to the Flavian age and was found alongside six other fragments which may have been of Chian origin.

51 Plin. *HN* XIV 95: *tanto vero Graeco vino gratia erat, ut singulae potiones in convictu darentur*.
52 Santangeli Valenzani, Volpe 2012, 66–67; Volpe 2009, 379–381.
53 Zampini 2010, 329–330, tab. 10.
54 Ferrandes 2014, 364.
55 Caspio et al. 2009, 487, fig. 35.
56 Boersma, Yntema, Van der Werff 1986, 108–109.
57 Albiach et al. 2008, 260–261.
58 See Chapter 1.

However, these six unattributed fragments were too small to be properly recognised, and, their fabric was slightly different than that of Chian amphoras.[59] Further evidence for Chian containers includes two fragments attested in Ostia (*Terme del Nuotatore*), one fragment discovered in *Isola Sacra Necropolis*[60] and possibly an amphora from Herculaneum bearing the inscription 'Chium',[61] although it has already been mentioned that this should be read as 'Choum'. To sum up, the evidence is scarce, which suggests that wine from Chios was consumed in small quantities in Italy.

The lack of Thasian and Lesbian amphoras may indicate either a lack of their consumption, or limited consumption based on small measures. However, the use of Chian, Lesbian and Thasian is confirmed by the literary evidence, which makes the second hypothesis more likely.

In summary, ancient poets (both Greek and Roman) agree that wines from Chios, Lesbos and Thasos were palatable; thus, drinking them provided pleasure. Also, the Romans had a wide range of beverages from which to choose, therefore importing Chian, Lesbian and Thasian wines was not essential. Furthermore, high prices as well as sumptuary laws meant that access to these wines was limited, which resulted in them being consumed on special occasions only by the Greek and Roman elite. Finally, the archaeological material indicates that consumption of these wines was extremely rare. What all of this means is that Eastern Mediterranean wines from Chios, Lesbos and Thasos meet the criteria set out at the beginning of this chapter as they possessed the five characteristics that constitute luxury goods; therefore, they can indeed be called luxury items.

2 Wines for Common People

The term 'mass beverages' should be understood as middle-quality wines that were available to common people. This does not, however, mean that Eastern Mediterranean wines were accessible to all commoners. Their price in Italy was increased due to transport costs, which means that they must have been more expensive than common Italian wines. Therefore, it is hardly possible that they were consumed by the lowest social strata, who lived at or even below the subsistence level. Although Eastern Mediterranean imports were certainly

---

59 Rizzo 2003, 164, tab. 27c and personal communication.

60 Palma, Panella 1967–1968, 100. It is worth mentioning that a few Chian amphora fragments were also discovered in Paestum, see De Bonis 2008, 310.

61 See Chapter 2, Section 4.

ranked higher than modern Italian *vino della casa* or French *vin ordinaire*, the arbiters of elegance and good taste would probably not recommend them. One may therefore assume that they were mainly consumed by the middle social strata.

Modern terms like 'middle class' are used in this chapter, thus it is necessary to explain their meaning, and to justify the legitimacy of the use of sociological terminology that describes modern society while dealing with ancient populations. My view is as far removed from Finley's hypercriticism towards the concept of class,[62] as it is from Mayer's enthusiastic assumption that starting from the 1st c. BC the commercial middle classes, who had their own cultural identity, shaped the economic, societal and cultural aspects of urban life.[63] Nonetheless, no one seems to think that ancient societies in the Roman Imperial age were bipolar and formed merely of 'the rich' (or *honestiores*) and 'the poor' (or *humiliores*). It seems commonly accepted that in economic terms there were certain elements of ancient society that were not aristocratic (due to the lack of noble origin) and also not 'poor' (because of their income). Also, many scholars, after analysing domestic spaces or income distribution, provided evidence that both Greek and Roman society had 'middle classes', at least in an economic sense. The size of this group, however, remains the subject of debate.[64] Whether we use the term 'class', 'order', 'stratum' or 'status' is of little importance;[65] the point is that there was a group (or various groups) of people who lived above the subsistence level,[66] but were too poor and/or too meaningless to be classified as elite. The terms 'class' and 'stratum' will be used interchangeably as simplifications that help to describe social categories in antiquity. 'Middle class' (= middle strata) refers to people with a middle income, which excludes imperial and municipal elites (senators, equites, decurions and augustales),[67] as well as the modern understanding of 'poor people', meaning people that lived at or below the subsistence level. However, it should be emphasised that the term 'middle class' should not be seen through the lens of modern terminology.

62 Finley 1999, 44–51, he suggests 'status' instead.

63 Mayer 2012, 1–21.

64 Zanker 1998; Veyne 2000a; Scheidel 2006a; Scheidel, Friesen 2009; Mayer 2012; Kron 2014.

65 'Class', e.g. Mayer 2012; Kron 2014; 'order', 'status', e.g. Finley 1999; 'order', 'stratum', e.g. Alföldy 1991; others, e.g. 'la plèbe moyenne' Veyne 2000a. See also Łoś 1994, 284–292 for the discussion about the use of these terms and their definitions.

66 See Scheidel, Friesen 2009, who investigated elite and non-elite income. Also, Kron 2014, who uses the size and decoration of Pompeian houses to prove that mean and median incomes in the 1st c. AD Italy must have remained well above the subsistence level.

67 For more about imperial and municipal elites, see Alföldy 1991, 195–198; Łoś 1994, 293–305.

My assumption is that the consumers of Eastern Mediterranean wines that were imported to Italy during the Imperial period belonged to the 'middle class'. These were predominantly inhabitants of Italian cities (as it is quite difficult to imagine farmers who cultivated vine and produced wine being interested in buying considerable numbers of imported wines), such as successful manufacturers, craftsmen, traders, veterans, as well as low-level municipal administrators that did not belong to the elite.[68] One may also wonder whether slaves that lived in the houses of wealthy families were able to consume imported wines.

Literature does not provide us with much information regarding the consumers of mass imported Eastern Mediterranean wines, but certain clues may be found in textual evidence. Moreover, amphora statistics demonstrate the scale of the consumption of these wines, which may allow us to estimate how numerous their consumers were. The issue of the quality and ranking of wine from Rhodes has already been raised by Baldacci and Tchernia. The former claimed that Rhodian wine was *"di tipo molto ordinario, impiegato soprattutto per le truppe e destinato ad un consumo rapido: infatti non sopportava l'invecchiamento per via delle dos di acqua marina con le quali veniva spesso allungato"*. His conclusion seems to stem from the coincidental findings of a few Rhodian stamped amphoras in Cisalpina, and the fact that there were two Roman legions stationed in Cremona.[69] However, the number of stamps that were attested in the region is too low to suggest that Rhodian wine was indeed imported for consumption by common soldiers.[70] Baldacci was also wrong when arguing that seawater was the reason for the low durability of Rhodian wine. It has already been mentioned in Chapter 2 that in Roman times all transmarine wines were 6–7 years old, and that seawater was used as a preservative. In addition, in Aquileia and Ascoli Satriano, Rhodian amphoras were found in very rich graves, which would suggest that wine from this island was in fact valuable.[71]

According to Tchernia, *"Asurément ni le Rhodes ni le Cos ne sont des grands crus. Mais ce ne sont pas pour autant des vins ordinaires"*, which means that they formed a separate class, since they were seasoned with seawater. Therefore, they were not included by Pliny among *vina generosa transmarina*, even though

---

68 Certain scholars, e.g. Łoś 1994, 305 class veterans as local elites (municipal aristocracy).

69 Baldacci 1972, 105.

70 The most likely number of stamps is 10, but the exact number is unknown as the data is not explicit.

71 Mazzeo Saracino, Vergari 1997, 155.

they were not considered as bad wines.[72] Such a conclusion is confirmed by the ancient literature. Vergil mentions that wine from Rhodes was "*dis et mensis accepta secundis*",[73] which means that it was "*welcome to the gods and the banquet's second course*". Which begs the question: what type of banquet would include Rhodian wine during the 1st c. BC? The answer to which is probably those that were frequented by Vergil, who hailed from the Cisalpine *oppidum* of Mantua, whose family estate was confiscated, and who lived in Naples instead of Rome, depending on the mercy of Maecenas. Therefore, Rhodian was neither a poor nor a rich man's wine, and there is no further evidence that would suggest it was a wine that was highly appreciated. Moreover, the Greeks called it ὑπόχυτος, which is a pejorative epithet that may be translated as 'doctored'.[74] Studies of the organoleptic characteristics of wines show that the admixture of seawater was probably responsible for the fact that Rhodian wine, similarly to Coan, was less appreciated than for example Chian or Lesbian. According to Pliny, *Rhodium Coo simile est*;[75] thus, it is possible to conclude that the consumers of these wines were similar. There is no evidence for the prices of wine from Rhodes, but we do know that Coan wine was sold at half or three quarters of the price of wine from Cnidus at the beginning of the 2nd c. BC on Delos,[76] which suggests its lower quality. Moreover, Coan wine was always purchased in larger quantities than Cnidian.[77] In addition, N. Purcell claims that during the 1st c. BC the trade of Dressel 2–4 amphoras was oriented towards the needs of the Roman army.[78] Dressel 2–4 were imitations of Coan containers, and it is likely that they were used to transport wine that was similar to Coan. Considering that soldiers are usually not provided with the highest-quality products, this would be further evidence that wine from Cos was of an inferior quality and hence was probably consumed by the lower social strata. Also, the high

---

72 Tchernia 1986, 105.

73 Verg. *Georg.* II, 101–102.

74 Timachidas of Rhodes in Ath. *Deipn.* 31e.

75 Plin. *HN* XIV, 79.

76 Tchernia 1986, 105; after Larsen 1938, 392–394. There is also a Ptolemaic papyrus P.Tebt.III.2 1079 suggesting that *Knidia* cost around 270 drachmas, whereas *Rhodia* cost around 230 drachmas, see Kruit, Worp 2000, 81. This could also suggest that Cnidian wine was more expensive than Rhodian; however, this papyrus provides us with no information regarding the number of jars and does not actually confirm that wine was indeed the content. This means that this evidence is too unreliable to be considered.

77 For example, 12 jars of Cnidian and 35 jars of Coan or 10 jars of Cnidian and 35 jars of Coan, see Larsen 1938, 393.

78 Purcell 1985, 14.

numbers of Rhodian and Coan amphoras that were discovered in Italy suggest that their consumers were numerous.

Wine from Cnidus must have been better than Coan, because its price was considerably higher.[79] This may be due to the fact that it was a special wine of the *protropum* type. A similar conclusion may be drawn regarding wine from the area of Mount Tmolus. According to Galen, it was among the three best wines from Asia and was equal to Chian and Lesbian.[80] However, this is not enough to include Tmolian wine in the category of Roman aristocratic drinks, because no ancient author praised its taste highly. Moreover, Pliny stated clearly that the Romans did not appreciate Tmolian wine by itself, but it was added to improve the taste of other wines. Considering that Cypriot wine was mentioned in Pliny's list between Tmolian and Cnidian, it seems that it should be included in the same category.[81] Anatolian Agora F65–66 containers, which probably transported Tmolian wine, as well as Cnidian and Cypriot/Cilician amphoras (Schoene-Mau XXVII–XXVIII), were not very common in Italy, which suggests that wines from those regions were consumed on a smaller scale than Rhodian and Coan. Moreover, Agora F65–66 amphoras were very small—their capacity varied between 6 and 12 litres, while the average volume of other early imperial wine containers reached c. 20 litres.[82]

Cretan wine is mentioned in one of Martial's epigrams as '*mulsum* of the poor men':

> *CVI. Passum.*
> *Gnosia Minoae genuit vindemia Cretae*
> *hoc tibi, quod mulsum pauperis esse solet.*
>
> Raisin wine
> A Gnosian vintage of Minoan Crete produced this
> For you. It is wont to be the poor man's mead.[83]

79 The price of Cnidian wine on Delos at the beginning of the 2nd c. BC was between 4 and 6 drachmas, see Larsen 1938, 393, which was considerably lower than the price of Chian or Thasian in Egypt during the mid-3rd c. BC (18 and 20 drachmas respectively), see Salviat 1986, 180; Salviat, Tchernia 2013, 219, which could suggest that Cnidian was of a lower quality. However, it is not certain whether similar amounts of wine are compared. Moreover, prices might have varied considerably between Delos and Egypt. Therefore, this comparison provides no reliable evidence.

80 See Chapter 2, Section 3.

81 Plin. *HN* XIV 74.

82 Rizzo 2003, 205, tab. 32b.

83 Mart. XIII 106.

Mulsum, which is mead or honeyed wine, was probably not among the cheapest drinks. However, wine from Crete that was similar in sweetness was a beverage that even poor men could afford. Even though the 'poor' in antiquity were not necessarily people with very low incomes, but simply those that were not very rich,[84] this passage clearly states that Cretan wine was consumed by the lower social strata. However, Marangou-Lerat argues that Cretan *passum* was a good wine "*honorablement situé dans la hiérarchie des crus*", adding that Martial generally underestimated Greek wines and that Cretan is the only one to which the poet devoted an epigram.[85] His other epigrams concern the best Italian wines as well as foreign beverages from outside the Aegean. Therefore, Cretan must have been famous and popular, but would it be high-ranking? Tchernia, using as evidence a text by Fronto, claims that between the 1st and the 2nd c. AD Cretan was one of the most popular and cheapest wines, like those from Sagunto and Tarraconensis,[86] which is confirmed by amphora statistics. Therefore, it seems that this wine was ranked rather low in the hierarchy of wines, but this does not exclude its popularity among a lot of people, who especially appreciated its affordable price. Cilician *passum* held more or less the same rank as Cretan, but it was positioned second in Pliny's list.[87] Thus, if the amphora statistics confirm the popularity of Cretan wine, then they also suggest that Cilician *passum* was considerably less frequently imported. This might have been due to the fact that transporting goods from Cilicia was much more expensive than from Crete, due to the distance and the lack of special relations between Cilicia and Italy during the early Imperial age.

It is difficult to say anything about the consumers of wines from the Levant and Egypt, apart from the fact that these wines were appreciated 'at home' but neglected in Italy. Indeed, Martial was quite specific when he stated that Egyptian vinegar was better than Egyptian wine.[88] One may therefore conclude that wines from these areas were simply too bad for the Roman upper classes, and due to the transportation costs too expensive for the poor.[89]

---

84 Finley 1999, 41 explains the difference between the Greek understanding of the terms πλούσιος (rich enough to live properly on his income), πένης (had to gain a livelihood) and πτωχός (poor, beggar). For the Latin term 'pauper', which is explained in a similar way, see Veyne 2000a, 1170–1171.

85 Marangou-Lerat 1995, 16, 28.

86 Tchernia 2011, 257–258, 345–346; Fronto, *De eloq.* I, 4.

87 Plin. *HN* XIV 81.

88 Mart. XIII 122.

89 See the ORBIS model transport cost map, Fig. 21 and 22.

It is therefore possible, by using both literary and amphora evidence, to construct a hierarchy of Eastern Mediterranean wines that were imported during the Imperial age:

1. Tmolian, Cnidian, Cypriot—had special qualities and were quite expensive; nothing suggests that they were used by the elite or that they were luxurious.
2. Rhodian, Coan—were palatable, but not expensive; were ranked lower because of the admixture of seawater.
3. Cretan—was good and cheap; was very popular.
4. Cilician—was probably good but expensive due to transport costs.
5. Egyptian—was probably not appreciated by the Romans.
6. Levantine?—was either luxurious and expensive and thus imported in small quantities, or was common but quite expensive due to transport costs and thus not popular.

The contexts in which different amphoras were found may also provide information regarding the consumers of the wine that they carried. For example, discoveries in Pompeii and Herculaneum show that Cretan, Cilician and Coan wines were sold in *tabernae*,[90] which were designed for commoners rather than the upper classes.[91] On the other hand, the story regarding Mark Anthony (orator) indicates that better quality wines were also sold in such places.[92] Moreover, epigraphic evidence suggests that Edon's tavern in Pompeii served common wine together with Falern.[93] Even so, the containers transporting wine for the upper social orders should be attested more frequently in the houses of the rich than in taverns, while they should not be discovered in the houses of poor people. Therefore, an attempt has been made here to check the quantities of Eastern Mediterranean wine amphoras that were discovered in different types of residential facilities in Pompeii and Herculaneum, meaning houses, shops, workshops and taverns. The assumption is that wine amphoras from Crete, Cos, and Rhodes should predominate in the houses of common people and in taverns, while containers from Cyprus, Cilicia and Anatolia should not be found in the houses of the poor, but in houses belonging to the wealthier members of society.

For the purpose of this study, houses in Pompeii and Herculaneum were divided into four categories, according to the material status of their owners. This division is based upon classifications of Pompeian houses that were

90 Timby 2004, 385–387.
91 Wilkins, Hill 2006, 178.
92 Tchernia 1986, 33; Plut. *Mar.* 44, 1–4.
93 Tchernia 2011, 196–197; CIL IV 1679.

proposed by A. Wallace-Hadrill[94] and Łoś.[95] They both distinguished four categories of dwellings on the basis of their size, number of rooms, architectural facilities, decoration, and equipment. The first category of Łoś, namely 'aristocratic' houses, compares to Wallace-Hadrill's type 4. These are residences measuring 600–3000 m^2 that had 20 or more rooms, as well as an atrium and a peristyle. They were decorated with high-quality paintings, mosaics and sculptures and were equipped with silverware. Also, they often contained private baths.[96] The second category (Wallace-Hadrill's type 3) consists of houses measuring 300–600 m^2 that had 5–13 ground-floor rooms, as well as an atrium and a garden. They were finely decorated with paintings, mosaics and sculptures. Houses that had up to 10 rooms, but measured less than 300 m^2 were included into the next category. The third category (Wallace-Hadrill's type 2) includes dwellings with a surface area between 120 and 400 m^2 that had 2–7 ground-floor rooms and an atrium, they occasionally came with a garden and were modestly decorated. The fourth category (Wallace-Hadrill's type 1) comprises the smallest houses that had almost no decoration, this includes residences that doubled as a shop or workshop. In instances when a house's exact size, number of rooms and room designation were unknown, but the residence appeared relatively small, its decoration was used to determine which category it belonged in. If any of the dwelling's paintings were mentioned in *Pompei: pitture e mosaici*, the house was put into the third category. If the house was omitted in this publication it went into the fourth category. The fifth category of properties includes shops and workshops, whereas the numbers of amphoras discovered in taverns are presented separately.

It should be mentioned however, that many rich Pompeian houses hosted taverns or shops, the House of Amarantus (I 9, 11–12) being the best example, as in its final phase it served as a 'back office' for the tavern it hosted.[97] It was composed of two units, namely House 12 (sometimes also called the House of Q. Mestrius Maximus), which belongs in the second category, and House 11 (sometimes referred to as *Lupanar di Amarantus*), a small dwelling belonging to the fourth category. Although the House of Q. Mestrius Maximus was a wealthy residential building, its atrium served as a storage area for the wine that was served at the *caupona* of Amarantus. Therefore, Cretan (33 AC1 and 2 AC2) amphoras that were found in House 12 were in fact used by the tavern, as

---

94 Wallace-Hadrill 1994, 80–82.

95 Łoś 1991, 168.

96 The Temple of Mercury, where a number of containers were found, was also included in this category.

97 Timby 2004, 384–391.

were the nine Cretan (5 AC1 and 4 AC2), one Coan, three Aegean Dressel 2–4 and eight unidentified amphoras of Aegean provenance.[98]

Furthermore, it seems that not many Pompeian houses, even those classified as 'aristocratic', belonged to the real Roman aristocracy, like for example villas in Stabiae. Apart from the House of the Vestals (1107 m2, 30+ rooms), the House of Menander (1825 m2, 40+ rooms), and a few others, most of the wealthy residences in the city were inhabited by local, municipal elites, or by successful freedmen. The House of Ephebus, known also as the House of Cornelius Tages, provides the best example. It was placed in the first 'aristocratic' category, but was owned by a wealthy freedman, who coincidentally traded Eastern wines wholesale. The presence of Cretan wine amphoras bearing the owner's name should therefore come as no surprise, as he might have stored some of his merchandise at home. According to Kron, only 1–2% of the population of Pompeii had incomes consistent with the equestrian census (income estimated from rents),[99] and hence may be classified as the real aristocracy. Therefore, the great majority of Pompeian houses, even the wealthiest, belonged to people that were classified as 'middle class' for the purpose of this study. However, even the households of the wealthiest 2% of Pompeian society were full of slaves who drank different wines than their masters, and who also used them for culinary and/or medicinal purposes. This means that no one should be surprised that amphoras transporting common wines were discovered in the wealthiest Pompeian residences.

This study looks at amphoras that were in use around the time of Vesuvius' eruption. The House of Ariadna has been excluded from this analysis, even though numerous amphoras were found there, because these amphoras were mostly dated to the late Republican age. Most of the data used in this study comes from the 4th volume of CIL, which means that the amphoras were discovered at a time when only inscribed vessels were documented. Thus, certain 'epigraphic habits' probably influenced the numbers of amphoras that were registered.[100] However, the data from CIL is accompanied by the

98 Timby 2004, 384–391. It should be noted that an amphora similar to Kapitän 1 bore the *titulus* ΕΠΙΘΑΛΟΥ Γ ..., but, it is impossible to present any interpretation. Moreover, other levels of occupation have been distinguished in the same context. They surprisingly date back to the 6th or 5th c. BC. Among the material dated earlier than 79 AD Italian amphoras are predominant. The eastern vessels included Corinthian A, early Rhodian, AC4, Agora 137/British BIV, Dressel 5 and Kapitän 1 amphoras. The last identification seems doubtful, since the production of Kapitän amphoras is not attested before the 2nd c. AD.

99 Kron 2014, 137.

100 This means that certain types of containers might have been inscribed more frequently than others.

TABLE 10 Discoveries of Eastern Mediterranean wine amphoras in Pompeii

Category of property	Cos (including Schoene-Mau XLI)	Rhodes	Anatolia	Cnidus	Cyprus/ Cilicia (Schoene-Mau XVII–XXVIII)	Crete	Cilicia (Schoene-Mau XIII)
I	5	2	2	0	0	30	11
II	3	0	0	0	0	66	4
III	4	1	0	1	0	34	2
IV	1	0	0	0	0	17	7
Shops and workshops	1	0	0	0	0	26	3
Taverns	9	0	0	0	6	85	21
Total	23	3	2	1	6	258	48

results of recent excavations that were conducted at *Insula* I 8, the House of Menander, the House of the Vestals (context dated to between 50 and 70 AD), the House of the Four Styles,[101] *Casa del Vinario* (IX 9, 6–7) and *Officina del Garum degli Umbrici* (I 12, 8). The results of this analysis are presented in Table 10.

This analysis shows that Cretan containers were the most common in Pompeii, which agrees with the statistics that were presented in Chapter 3. Moreover, these containers appeared considerably more frequently in shops, workshops and taverns than in the houses of the Pompeian 'aristocracy', which confirms the hypothesis that this wine was drunk predominantly by people of low income such as petty traders and craftsmen. However, amphoras from Crete rarely appear in the houses of the fourth category, which indicates that the poorest were probably not able to drink it often. The distribution of Coan amphoras, even though they were much less frequent, suggests that all of Pompeian society (both rich and poor) had access to Coan wine; again, however, it was not easily affordable to those who lived in the most modest houses. Rhodian, Cnidian and Anatolian amphoras appear less frequently than Cretan or

101 Stefani 2003; Borgard, Carre, Fontaine 2007, 114; Amarger, Brun 2007, 158; De Sena, Ikäheimo, 2003, 304, tab. 1, 307, tab. 2 and 3, 317 n. 11 (approximated numbers of containers were used in this study); Peña 2007, 94–95, 101. The numbers of amphoras from *Insula* I 8 come from the French excavations conducted between 2005–2009. I am very grateful to Dr. E. Botte for sharing this information with me before it was published.

Coan, which could result from the fact that they were rarely inscribed and hence omitted from CIL. Nevertheless, publications of more recent archaeological excavations suggest that these containers did not appear in taverns, workshops and the houses of the poorest. The only Cnidian amphora was found in the third category House of the Prince of Naples (VI 15, 7–8). Moreover, a piece from an Agora F65–66 container was attested in the House of the Vestals (VI 1, 6–8, 24–26)[102] and another in insula IX 8, most probably in the House of the Centennial (that should actually be classified as a *casa signorile*) or in one of the shops surrounding it.[103] Although the sample size is very small and does not allow for any strong conclusions to be made, one may suppose that wines from Anatolia, Cnidus and Rhodes were of a better quality than Cretan. Cypriot/Cilician amphoras (Schoene-May XXVII–XXVIII) were almost equally rare, but they were discovered only in taverns, which suggests that this wine might have been a wine of the poor, similarly to Cretan. If we take a look at Cilician amphora discoveries, we may be surprised to see that they were quite numerous in the first category houses, yet scarce in the poorest properties, workshops and shops, which suggests that they were not commonly accessible. Pliny placed Cilician *passum* second after Cretan, but it is not known what criterion he used when judging the beverages. Latium and Campania were 'flooded' with cheap and hence commonly accessible imports from Crete, whereas *passum* from Cilicia probably offered a similar quality for a higher price, which resulted from the higher transport costs. This is probably the reason why the distribution of Cilician amphoras is different.

Overall, it seems that the richest inhabitants of Pompeii were not particularly interested in Eastern Mediterranean wines, since they did not consume them in very high quantities. Eastern wine amphoras were more often attested in the houses of common people, but not the poorest. Such a conclusion confirms the hypothesis that these wines were consumed by the Italian 'middle classes', i.e. the inhabitants of towns, who were rather prosperous but had nothing to do with the imperial aristocracy. It is also meaningful that amphoras which carried luxurious Eastern Mediterranean wines were absent in the Vesuvian cities, which were small towns where even elites lived differently than in Rome.

---

102 De Sena, Ikäheimo 2003, 307, tab. 3. The exact numbers were not given.

103 CIL IV 5911.

3 Conclusions

To summarise, it seems that during the late Republican period, the Eastern Mediterranean supplied Italy mostly with luxurious wines that were destined for the members of the Roman '*bonne société*', such as Chian, Lesbian and Thasian. Also, middle-quality wines from Cos, Rhodes and Cnidus were imported, although on a small scale. According to R. Volpe, scarce discoveries of foreign amphoras dated to the Republican age in general suggest that all foreign products were rare and hence they must have been expensive.[104] Therefore, during the Republic the consumers of wines from Rhodes, Cos and Cnidus probably enjoyed a higher social status. However, when importations from the provinces to Italy started to increase, these wines became accessible, and not necessarily just to the wealthy. At the same time, the consumption of luxurious Chian, Lesbian and Thasian wines among the aristocracy stopped. Therefore, it seems that around the time when common people started to consume imported wines on a larger scale, the aristocracy stopped drinking them. This suggests that the status of foreign goods changed—from being desired by many and available to few, they became widely available and ultimately degraded.[105]

This change was probably associated with the development of the production of high-quality wines in Italy. During the Imperial period, Italy already had quite a long tradition of making good wines.[106] Moreover, the Romans were no longer as delighted by Greek culture as they had been in the previous two centuries. Augustan propaganda postulated the return to ancient Roman virtues and created an image of Rome as superior to other civilisations. The emperor set trends in Rome, and Octavian Augustus favoured Setinum—a wine that was made in Latium.[107] The new Roman elite of the 1st c. AD lived during the period of Roman domination in the Mediterranean and saw no point in admiring the wines of the conquered, since their own land had long produced high-quality beverages that were even approved by emperors. Hence, imports lost their prestige. However, thanks to *Pax Romana* and the unification of the empire they became cheap to buy and because of their lower price they became more accessible, as more people could afford them. Therefore, imported wines became a common element of the Italian diet, even in small towns. Cretan wine was the most commonly available, but Rhodian, Coan, Cnidian, Anatolian, Cypriot and

---

104 Volpe 2009, 379–381; Santangeli Valenzani, Volpe 2012, 66–67.
105 Van der Veen 2003, 408–409.
106 Tchernia 1986, 34; 1997, 1249–1253.
107 Plin. *HN* XIV 61.

Cilician also reached many tables, especially those belonging to people with middling incomes, such as municipal administrators, successful traders, craftsmen and veterans. The numbers and percentages of these wine importations kept growing between the Augustan age and the 2nd c. AD, which suggests that consumer numbers also grew. If the Malthusian scenario occurred and population growth outstripped agricultural production thus reducing an individual's purchasing power, the number of imported wines should change inversely to the population growth, but proportionally to the pauperisation of this population. However, nothing like this was observed, suggesting that the quality of life of consumers of Eastern Mediterranean wines did not reduce until the end of the 2nd c. AD, which may be seen as evidence favouring the existence of intensive economic growth in Italy.

CHAPTER 5

Petty Traders or Wealthy Wholesalers? Who Imported Wines to Italy?

Sit cisterna mihi, quam vinea, malo Ravennae,
Cum possim multo vendere pluris aquam.

I'd rather have a cistern at Ravenna than a vineyard,
since I could sell water at a much better price.

Callidus inposuit nuper mihi copo Ravennae:
Cum peterem mixtum, vendidit ille merum.

A crafty innkeeper cheated me the other day at Ravenna.
I asked for wine and water, he sold me wine neat.

MART. III 56 and 57

∵

Who traded wines from the Eastern Mediterranean? This is a very important question, which may help us to understand the nature of the Roman economy. One of the arguments that diminished the role of trade in antiquity was based on the notion that the Roman elite was not particularly interested in commercial enterprises, while the traders did not enjoy important social positions. Commercial profit was neglected by the wealthy, who instead invested in landed estates, as it was the possession of land that defined social status. At the same time, wealthy freedmen and slaves were seen as exceptions to the rule. Therefore, given that there was no socially significant group that was involved with trade, it must have been marginal.[1] However, studies concerning the social status of traders do not agree with such marginalisation. For example, there were senators, albeit in limited numbers, who were involved with trade.[2] Moreover, there is plenty of evidence that suggests the elite were indirectly

1 Finley 1999, 35–61.
2 Tchernia 2011, 19–55.

© KONINKLIJKE BRILL NV, LEIDEN, 2021 | DOI:10.1163/9789004433762_007

involved with commercial activities[3] through the use of intermediaries (slaves and freedmen) who conducted commercial transactions on their behalf.[4] At the same time, there were wealthy traders in the East who might have occupied important social positions, even if it did not occur very often.[5] There is no direct evidence confirming that freedmen acted on behalf of the elite when conducting commercial transactions; however, indirect evidence suggests such a possibility.[6] It is not unreasonable to imagine former slaves setting themselves up in business after they were manumitted, using money borrowed from their former masters. If they were successful, their experience could have been used by their patrons who could then invest their money in *negocia* of their *liberti*, which ensured them risk-free profit. Tchernia argues that instead of concealing their business dealings behind slaves and freedmen, landowners "*were able to profit from the commercial enterprises they financed, often by heavily taxing these ventures through high interest rates on loans, thus avoiding the risks and constraints associated with such activities*".[7]

Studies concerning the names of traders that appeared in *tituli picti* on Baetican amphoras provide plenty of evidence regarding this matter. For example, links between producers and traders of Spanish olive oil are rare, which suggests that the manufacturers (identified in the inscriptions as δ) were usually not involved in the trading of their olive oil or fish sauces.[8] The social position of the manufacturers of Spanish olive oil was obviously high, since they were landowners. At the same time, the traders of the olive oil (identified in the inscriptions as β)[9] were predominantly Spanish freedmen. Traders of Baetican fish sauces were mostly Italian freedmen and slaves,[10] with a small number

3 D'Arms 1981; Pleket 1984.

4 Veyne 2000b, 190–192.

5 Pleket 1983; 1984.

6 Łoś 2005.

7 Tchernia 2011, 19–55; the quotation is taken from the English edition: Tchernia 2016, 10.

8 *Tituli picti* that appear on Dressel 20 amphoras were divided into four categories which represent their type and position on a container: α—numbers written on the neck, β—names in capital letters written on the upper part of the belly, γ—numbers written in the central part of the belly, δ—names written in cursive along the right handle, see Liou, Tchernia 1994, 133–134.

9 Names that appear on amphora stoppers should be associated with those involved in their transport, see Hesnard, Gianfrotta 1989, 398.

10 Étienne, Mayet 1998, 156–158; 2001, 90; 2002, 219–220, and a catalogue of names 215–218. Étienne, Mayet 2002, 219 propose that around 20–25% were of Spanish origin, whereas Łoś 2012, 105–108 thinks that although it is impossible to give exact proportions, Italians certainly predominated among traders of fish sauces. However, according to Łoś the proportion of people of Spanish origin was considerably higher among the traders of olive oil.

being freeborn.[11] It needs emphasising that some Baetican olive oil merchants were able to perform acts of euergetism, which reveals their high economic standing. They also sometimes held important social positions, while their descendants could count on social promotion, like one of *Sex. Fadius Secundus Musa's* grandsons, who achieved senatorial status.[12]

This chapter concentrates on the social position of the traders who transported wines from the Eastern Mediterranean. Its aim is to verify whether wealthy *negotiatores* or petty *venditores* were involved in the Italian wine trade, and whether they had any links to the elite. The study is based upon prosopographic and socio-onomastic analyses of the names of merchants that were found among *tituli picti* on amphoras discovered in the Vesuvian cities, mostly in Pompeii.[13] As these *tituli* served commercial purposes and were not the result of 'epigraphic habits' (as for example funerary inscriptions), the evidence they provide should be unbiased.[14] Only names appearing on Rhodian, Coan, Cnidian and Cilician amphoras will be analysed, as the inscriptions attested upon Cretan containers have already been studied by Marangou-Lerat and Łoś. At the same time, apart from Rhodian, Coan, Cnidian, Cretan and Cilician or Cypriot/Cilician, no other wine amphoras from the Eastern Mediterranean were registered in the 4th volume of CIL, which forms the basis of this study. Although the state of publication of inscriptions on amphoras in CIL is far from perfect, studies of the *tituli picti* that appear on transport containers demonstrate that they may still provide important, albeit not unquestionable evidence regarding ancient commerce.

The structure of *tituli picti* differed depending on the amphora class on which they appeared, with differences sometimes occurring even within the same class. The most eloquent, as well as the most thoroughly investigated, are inscriptions found on the Spanish olive oil amphoras classified as Dressel 20. They carried predominantly black *tituli*, among which the following four elements may be distinguished: the weight of an empty amphora, the content (olive oil) weight, the exporter's name (in the genitive case), and the names

11 Hesnard, Gianfrotta 1989, 399; Łoś 2012, 99.

12 Chic García 1987, 251; 1993, 9, 19–20; Remesal Rodríguez 2000; 2004.

13 Greek *tituli picti* that appeared on amphoras found in Rome and published in the 15th volume of CIL do not provide us with any useful evidence regarding this matter. It should be noted that a few Greek *dipinti* were also attested on amphoras that were discovered in shipwrecks found off the coast of Gaul, see e.g. Liou, Marichel 1978, 109–181; Liou 1987, 55–139; 1993, 131–148; Liou, Lequément, Desbat, 1987, 141–166; Greek containers were reloaded in Italian ports onto ships that sailed between Italy, Gaul and Spain.

14 Mouritsen 2011, 206.

of the owners/tenants of the property where the product was manufactured.[15] *Garum* amphoras (Dressel 7–11) found in Campania bore black inscriptions, but they also carried red names written in the dative case. Wine containers from Crete carried *tituli picti* in Greek or in Latin, or in both languages.[16] They concerned the origin and the qualities of the wine, the volume of a container and a date. Black names in the genitive case, associated by Marangou-Lerat with the producers of Cretan wine or wholesale traders, predominated,[17] but red names in the dative case also appeared. Łoś has proven that most of the names written in the dative case on Cretan wine and Spanish *garum* amphoras were typical of the Vesuvian area, which means that they probably belonged to regional wholesale traders, or brokers/intermediaries who bought the products from the importers in order to sell them to retailers or rich consumers. This mediation must have generated considerable profit, since there were members of the municipal elite (as well as their freedmen) among the intermediaries.[18]

It is possible to investigate the social status and ethnic origin of the traders thanks to socio-onomastic analyses of their names. Of course, these analyses do not allow definitive statements to be made, as a name cannot be treated as a certain ethnic 'marker'.[19] Nevertheless, Roman names obeyed considerably more rigid rules than Greek names, which means that Latin anthroponymy provides us with much more accurate information than the study of names, for example, in the Eastern Mediterranean. First of all, we may assume that those people whose *tria nomina* contained a Greek *cognomen* were freedmen. Of course, an eastern *cognomen* is not unquestionable evidence for a slave origin and certainly does not indicate that the holder was of an eastern provenance, as T. Frank postulated.[20] M.L. Gordon noted that Celtic names often gained a Latin look due to phonetic changes and that native names were commonly replaced by Greek and Latin names that sounded similar. Moreover, Greek slave traders gave their slaves Greek names regardless of nationality.[21] However, later studies by I. Kajanto and M. Duthoy proved that Frank was not entirely mistaken and that a name may indeed suggest social status and geographic provenance. Kajanto studied Latin and non-Latin names in a few Roman cities, noticing

15 Liou, Tchernia 1994, 133–134, 143–152.
16 Marangou-Lerat 1995, 130.
17 Marangou-Lerat 1995, 151–154. Also, Mouritsen 1988, 16 identified *tituli* in the genitive case as being associated with producers or suppliers of goods.
18 Łoś 1997, 64; 2001, 87–91; 2012, 101–102.
19 See the discussion in Porucznik, forthcoming.
20 Frank 1916, 690–693, 701–702.
21 Gordon 1924, 97, 103–104.

that parents with Greek *cognomina* used to give their children Latin names,[22] which means that a person with a Greek *cognomen* was likely to be a freedman, not a descendant of former slaves. At the same time, he observed that most *ingenui* had Latin *cognomina*, whereas *liberti* were more likely to bear a non-Latin *cognomen*. This was especially evident in the cases of former slaves from the east—around 80 % of them maintained Greek *cognomina*. Therefore, Latin and non-Latin names were linked with social position and ethnic origin.[23] Studies by Duthoy led him to similar conclusions. The percentages of *certi liberti* with Greek *cognomina* in the regions of Campania and Latium were calculated at 81,9 and 85,7 % respectively.[24] On the other hand, *ingenui* rarely carried a Greek *cognomen*.[25] Moreover, Duthoy noted that certain *cognomina Latina* are attested more frequently among freedmen than among the freeborn. This means that we may distinguish a group of *cognomina servilia*, which suggest their bearers probably had a slave origin, as well as *cognomina ingenua*, which were typical of those who were born free.[26] In short, even though names are not infallible evidence of the social status and ethnic provenance of their bearers, they allow us to draw conclusions regarding these matters that have a high degree of probability.

Furthermore, people who carried one Greek name may be identified as Greek slaves who lived in Italy, or as Greek traders who operated in the eastern part of the Mediterranean. In fact, Tchernia noted that most of the containers carrying Greek *tituli* that were found in Pompeii were of eastern origin.[27] This observation was later confirmed by the study of amphora types Schoene-Mau VIII, X and XXXVI, which appeared to be Cretan.[28] Therefore, we may presume that inscriptions written in Greek were created outside of Italy. Moreover, the analysis of the distribution of Greek names allows us to detect whether they were typical of the eastern or the western part of the Mediterranean. In the cases when a Greek name (single name only not a *tria nomina* with a Greek *cognomen*) that was popular in the eastern part of the Mediterranean was written in black in Greek, it can be presumed that the person lived in the Eastern Mediterranean and was not a Roman citizen. If a Greek name was written in red or in Latin, or if it was typical of the Western Mediterranean, it seems more

22 This observation has already been made by Frank 1916, 693 and Gordon 1931.

23 Kajanto 1968, 520–527.

24 Duthoy 1989, 185, tab. 1.

25 Duthoy 1989, 186, tab. 2. The percentage of *ingenui certi* with Greek *cognomina* for Campania is 12,8 %.

26 Duthoy 1989, 191–200.

27 Tchernia 1986, 241.

28 Marangou-Lerat 1995, 154.

likely that we are dealing with a Greek slave who lived in Italy. Latin *tria nomina* that were written in either red or black identify Italians who were probably, but not necessarily, Romans.[29] Greek *cognomina* that were used more often in the Aegean area, as well as Latin *cognomina servilia* suggest a slavish origin of their bearers, whereas Latin *cognomina ingenua* indicate a freeborn status and Italian origin. Finally, a *tria nomina* with a *cognomen* that was used above all in the Aegean region may indicate Greeks that were granted Roman citizenship.

Eastern Mediterranean wine amphoras attested in Pompeii (excluding Cretan) provided 68 names, including 43 written in Latin and 25 written in Greek. Unfortunately, information regarding the colour of the *tituli* was not always given in CIL, but at least 27 were written in black and 18 in red. The colour of the rest, excluding 3 yellow *dipinti*, is unknown. It was possible to distinguish free Roman citizens, Italian freedmen and slaves, and both free and servile Greeks among the inscriptions. However, due to many of the names being abbreviated and the lack of additional evidence, *incerti* were the most numerous category.

1 Free Romans and Local Elites

Names that can certainly be attributed to freeborn Roman citizens were not often attested on wine amphoras from the Eastern Mediterranean, but *ingenui* certainly participated in the trading of wines from Rhodes, Cos, Cilicia and Crete. For example, the inscription *Pass(um) Rhod(ium)|P(ubli) Coeli Galli*[30] was found on a Rhodian container, discovered in the stables of the House of Menander (I 10, 4) in Pompeii.[31] The name was written in black in the genitive case; thus, it is possible that P. Coelius Gallus was a *negotiator* who was involved, *inter alia*, in the trading of Rhodian wine. These *tria nomina* do not appear among other Italian inscriptions. However, *Coeli Caldi* were the most distinctive branch of the *gens Coelia* that produced a consul and a quaestor in the 1st c. BC. *Coeli* are also attested in *tituli parietarii* from Pompeii. A certain Coelius Caldus (*praenomen* not given) was mentioned in a graffito from

29 This group includes Romans who enjoyed full citizenship, as well as the so-called *Latini Juniani*, whose rights were limited. Among the long-distance wholesale traders (black inscriptions) we will probably find Roman citizens rather than *Latini Juniani*, whereas the latter were probably present among the local traders (red inscriptions). However, *tituli picti* on amphoras do not permit us to distinguish between these two categories.

30 CIL IV 9327.

31 This amphora was classified in CIL as Schoene-Mau VIII, which suggests a Cretan origin, but according to Marangou-Lerat this classification was erroneous and the amphora was from Rhodes, see Marangou-Lerat 1995, 130.

Insula I 10.[32] Another (the same?) Coelius Caldus from Pompeii supported Cuspius Pansa during the elections for the post of aedile.[33] Castrén identifies him with L. Coelius Caldus, who is known from another inscription.[34] Moreover, one P. Coelius (*cognomen* not given) was attested in a graffito on the wall of the amphitheatre in Pompeii.[35] There is also evidence from this city which may suggest that the *gens Coelia* was involved in trade. For example, an amphora of the type Schoene-Mau XIV (I 10, 4) carried the inscription: *Vi*(*num*) *r*(*ubrum*) / *in usus Coeliae Proculae*.[36] In addition, a certain Coelius with the *cognomen* 'Lesbius' was attested on a Schoene-Mau XIII amphora that was discovered in *caupona* I 7, 15.[37] According to Łoś, he was a freedman who might have been involved in wine production or trade.[38] Furthermore, P. Coelii are attested in inscriptions from outside of Pompeii, in Capua,[39] Santa Palomba[40] and Tusculum.[41] In the first case we are dealing with a freeborn person, whereas in the second with a freedman. The 2nd c. BC architrave from Tusculum gives no information regarding the social standing of the supposed P. Coelius. However, an aedile by the name of Q. Coelius Latiniensis was attested on a fountain near the architrave. The last inscription that may be associated with this *gens* comes from Puteoli and mentions Coelia Asteris, a freedwoman of Publius.[42] *Coelia* was also a prominent *gens* in Teanum Sidicium. Its members belonged to the municipal elite and held important public offices. For example, M. Coelius was a quaestor at the end of the 1st c. BC, whilst Q. Coelius Gallus held the post of duumvir in the mid-1st c. AD. L. Flavius Coelius Priscus, a duumvir and a pontifex at the end of the 2nd c. AD, can also be associated with this *gens*.[43] His daughter, Flavia Coelia Annia Argiva was *sacerdos Junonis Populonae*.[44]

---

32 CIL IV 8288.
33 CIL IV 708.
34 CIL IV 8982 graffiti from *Regio* III; Castrén 1975, 155–156.
35 CIL IV 8687.
36 CIL IV 9362. As mentioned in Chapter 2, *vir*(*ides*), which refers to green olives would be a better development of this abbreviation.
37 CIL IV 9491.
38 Łoś 1991, 73.
39 AttiAcLinc-1901-60-114, according to Claus-Slaby's epigraphic database. The original edition of this inscription could not be found.
40 The interpretation of the inscription as P. Coelius is from Claus-Slaby's database. In the original publication, AE 1974, 130, this inscription was read as L. P. Euuodius or Euhodius.
41 Gorostidi Pi 2011, 325. A name was carved on an architrave, but its reading as 'Coelius' is not certain.
42 CIL X 2314 = Sinn 185 Inscription on an urn dated to the Flavian period.
43 AE 1905, 192 after Pietruszka 2013, 158–159.
44 Pietruszka 2013, 175.

Finally, there is an inscription from Rome that indicates the involvement of the *gens Coelia* in *negotia*. Coelia Mascellina, a daughter of Cn. Coelius Mascellinus, erected a monument to her parents, where she described herself as *negotiatrix olearia ex provincia Baetica item vini* [...].[45] We do not know whether she was involved with the trading of wine from Spain or other regions; however, her name written in Latin and Greek was also attested on a bronze seal that was found on the riverbed of the Tiber, near *Cloaca Maxima*: Coeliae Cn. f. Mascellinae/ Κοιλ(ίης) Μασκελλεί/νης.[46] This indicates that the *gens Coelia* did business with the Greek world during the 1st c. BC/1st c. AD (date suggested by the presence of filiation on the seal). Therefore, our *negotiator* P. Coelius Gallus belonged to a prominent *gens* that was involved with trade. The question is whether he was a prominent member of the *gens Coelia* or one of their freedman. Considering that the *cognomen* Gallus was, according to Kajanto, carried by Roman consuls and senators,[47] it seems more likely that it belonged to the category of *cognomina ingenua*. Therefore, we may assume that P. Coelius Gallus was an important freeborn person who might have been associated with the elite. His position and that of his family in general might have been due to their commercial activities.

Another *ingenuus* who traded in old Coan wine (*Coum vetus*) was P. Appuleius Bassus, whose name (in the genitive case) appeared on a Schoene-Mau XII container written in black.[48] Schoene-Mau XII amphoras (Dressel 2–4), which are the most numerous in the Vesuvian cities, copy the Coan amphora form[49] and were produced in many different areas apart from the Aegean, including Italy, Spain and Africa. The majority of these containers found in Pompeii are of local, Campanian origin, but wine containers from Cos were also present in the city.[50] Therefore, it seems likely that Schoene-Mau XII jars that carried wine from Cos or bore Greek inscriptions did indeed originate in the East.[51] The

---

45 A photograph of the inscription was published in Panciera 1980, 244, fig. 4. Unfortunately, the dating of this monument cannot be specified; it was found reused in a tomb in a basilica dated to the Constantine period. Ferrua 1973, 69 determines the dating as '*circa del secondo secolo*'. It was thought that this inscription came from a tomb under S. Pietro, see Toynbee, Ward-Perkins 1956, 119–120.

46 CIL XV 8166.

47 Kajanto 1965, 195. The archives of *Sulpicii* mention four: C. Cestius Gallus, A. Didius Gallus, C. Pompeius Gallus and Messala Vipstanus Gallus.

48 CIL IV 5537.

49 Peacock, Williams 1986, 105–106.

50 Albiach et al. 2008, 261.

51 Tchernia 1986, 241 suggested a Greek origin for containers carrying Greek inscriptions that were found in Pompeii, which was later confirmed by Marangou-Lerat's 1995 study of amphora types Schoene-Mau VIII and X.

abbreviation PAB that was found on two Schoene-Mau XII amphoras may be interpreted as P. Appuleius Bassus.[52] According to an additional *titulus* one of the containers carried *passum lycium*, which was a sweet wine from Lycia. An eastern origin is also suggested by the Greek letters that may be interpreted as the word γλ(υκύς). Although the colour of these *tituli* is never mentioned, the different types of wines that were associated with P. Appuleius Bassus could mean that he was a *negotiator* of Eastern Mediterranean wines. The *cognomen* 'Bassus' was very popular. According to Kajanto, it was not Latin, whereas it seems that Solin includes it amongst Latin slave names.[53] However, 'Bassus' appeared as a slave name during the Republic,[54] while in the Imperial period it was often carried by prominent Romans, including consuls, a commander of the fleet, and municipal magistrates in many Italian cities, including those in Campania.[55] Therefore, we may tentatively suggest that P. Appuleius Bassus was in fact freeborn.

The case of C. Annius Maximus, attested on a Cilician container found in Insula IX 1, 2 (east of the tavern), is similar.[56] The *gens Annia* was of Etruscan origin and it was attested in Capua, Praeneste and later in Pompeii. One of its members, C. Annius Marulus, was a Pompeian duumvir.[57] Another, C. Annius Calatorius M. f. Postumus was twice a duumvir in Herculaneum during the first half of the 1st c. AD, while Annius Maximus was a duumvir in Puteoli under Tiberius.[58] The *cognomen* Maximus was one of the oldest and commonest Latin *cognomina* among the senatorial nobility and *plebs ingenua*, and hence suggests a freeborn status.[59] Therefore, it seems that C. Annius Maximus was a freeborn person from a prominent Pompeian family. This would make him another *ingenuus* that traded wine; however, it is impossible to know his exact occupation considering that the colour of the *titulus* was not given.

---

52 CIL IV 6131, 5594 = 6315. The letters P and AB in ligature, followed by a ligature of ET were also found on a stamp on an Italian amphora from Vindonissa, dated to around 50 AD, see Callender 1965, 200, no. 1274. However, it seems difficult to find any association between the *tituli* and the stamp.

53 Kajanto 1965, 244; Solin 1996, 46.

54 Gordon 1924, 96–97.

55 For example, a consul: Q. Laetanius Bassus; fleet commander: S. Lucilius Bassus; duumvirs in Capua, Venafrum and Pompeii during the reign of Augustus: Sex. Pontidius Bassus, C. Menius C. f. Ter. Bassus and Atullius C. f. Bassus; aedile in Venafrum at the beginning of the 1st c. AD; candidate for municipal magistracies in Pompeii during the Neronian Age: Cn. Audius Bassus.

56 CIL IV 5773.

57 Castrén 1975, 135.

58 Łoś 2001, 89.

59 Kajanto 1965, 104, 133; Duthoy 1989, 11, 14.

Another possible *ingenuus* that sold Cilician wine was M. Ju(lius)/Ju(nius) Ruf(us), whose name was painted in red upon a container that was discovered in the House of Fabius Amandus (I 7, 3).[60] The *cognomen* Rufus was classified by Kajanto and Duthoy as typical of freeborn people,[61] while *Junii* was a *nomen gentile* of numerous families in Latium and Campania. M. Junius was attested in a Pompeian inscription, which according to Castrén, suggests that he was a candidate for the post of quinquennalis.[62] Mouritsen, however, doubts this interpretation, suggesting that the letter 'Q' following the name could be a part of a *cognomen*.[63] In any case, M. Junius Rufus should be considered as freeborn, but he was probably not a *negotiator*. The red colour of the *titulus* suggests that he was a local or regional wine trader.

Another red *titulus*, this time bearing the name N. Fufidius Successus (in the genitive case), was attested on a Cilician Schoene-Mau XIII container that was discovered in Insula V 2.[64] Fufidius Successus was the supposed owner of a *caupona* and officina (I 8, 15–16). His property measured 175 m^2 and was composed of a bar with a back room, and a large workshop in which a kiln and plants used to produce pigments were attested. No decoration was discovered; however, further research of the site needs to be undertaken.[65] The same *tria nomina* was attested on a bronze seal that was found in the area.[66] Similar *nomina gentilia* and *cognomina* appear upon a few inscriptions from Pompeii, recommending different candidates for the post of aedile.[67] In one case, Fufidius Successus himself was a candidate.[68] According to the *Onomasticon Tullianum*, *Fufidia* was an equestrian *gens*,[69] whereas Castrén claims that it came from Arpinum, but was also attested in Campania (Puteoli and Cumae).[70] Andreau mentions Successus among the Pompeian *cognomina* which were

60 CIL IV 9543.

61 Kajanto 1965, 121; Duthoy 1989, 11, 14. Though 'Rufio' was typical of slaves, see Gordon 1924, 96.

62 Castrén 1975, 179–180, n. 4–5; CIL IV 412. M. Julius also appears in other Pompeian inscriptions, but with no additional information, see CIL IV 1440, 4429: *M(arci) Juni insula sum*, 4846, 4850, 4852.

63 Mouritsen 1988, 140.

64 CIL IV 5837.

65 Wallace-Hadrill 1996, 192.

66 NSA 1891, 169.

67 Fufidius Successus: AE 1951, 166 = CIL IV 7305c; CIL IV 7308a. Fufidius: CIL IV 4244, 4245, 7308b.

68 CIL IV 7305b.

69 *Onomasticon Tullianum* 1923, 258.

70 Castrén 1975, 169.

likely to belong to former slaves.[71] Also, Kajanto mentions that this was a participial *cognomen* that was more popular among the lower social strata.[72] This suggests that N. Fufidius Successus was a freedman, but since he stood for the post of aedile, he must have been freeborn. One may, therefore, assume that he was a descendant of *liberti*. It seems that he was a freeborn local 'businessman', whose main profit came from selling Cilican wines.

Finally, L. Sextius (or Sextilius) Syrticus may be associated with the trading of wine from Cos.[73] Two candidates for the post of duumvir with the same *cognomen* were attested during the Neronian-Flavian age in Pompeii: these were Sextius Syrticus and L. Sextilius Syrticus.[74] The *cognomen* Syrticus suggests a slavish origin,[75] and, as a matter of fact, most of the *Sextii* in Pompeii, such as L. Sextius Eros and L. Sextius Primus were freedmen, the former being a gladiator.[76] On the other hand, *Sextilii* were much more numerous in Pompeii than *Sextii*. According to Łoś, they were a prominent Pompeian family that belonged to the *ordo decurionum* from the post-Sullan to the Flavian times. Moreover, a stamp with the name Cardus Sextilius indicates that the *gens Sextilia* had *figlinae*, which means that the agricultural sector was one of the sources of their income.[77] Similarly, the *titulus* mentioning L. Sextilius Syrticus that was found on a Coan amphora could suggest that this family also profited from the wine trade. If the *nomen gentile* of our wine trader was indeed Sextilius, he could be identified with the second duumvir, since they both shared the same *praenomen*. If this is correct, it would be evidence for the direct participation of municipal elites in commercial enterprises.

2 Italian Freedmen

The names of freedmen are much more common on wine amphoras than *nomina ingenua*. A very interesting container, classified as Schoene-Mau XXXVII and bearing the inscription 'Cnidium' was discovered in Pompeii in a portico of the House of the Prince of Naples (VI 15, 8).[78] It is highly probable that this amphora was indeed from Cnidus, since wine containers from this area are

71 Andreau 1974, 286, n. 7.
72 Kajanto 1965, 93, 95.
73 CIL IV 5538.
74 CIL IV 799, 7762.
75 Łoś 1996, 208–210, 215, 231.
76 Castrén 1975, 374.
77 Łoś 1996, 129.
78 CIL IV 5535.

classified as Schoene-Mau XXXVIII, so it is possible that a minor mistake was made in the *Corpus*. This amphora carried three *tituli*, which appeared as follows:

1. painted on the neck: E (first line) M (second line) Τι Κλα (third line) Λινειкоυ (fourth line)
2. under the neck: *M Fabi Eupori* (first line) *Cnidium* (second line)
3. on the handle: *εt*\

Even though the inscriptions are not totally legible, it seems indubitable that two people, Ti. Claudius Lineikos(?)[79] and M. Fabius Eupor, were involved in this particular commercial aspect of Cnidian wine. Considering that the name M. Fabius Eupor appears in other Pompeian inscriptions, we may assume that he inhabited the town. It is possible that his name, abbreviated to M.F.E, appears in black on two Schoene-Mau XII amphoras. The first was discovered in a *biclinium* of the House of M. Loreius Tiburtinus (II 2, 2),[80] whereas the second was found in a tavern (II 5, 1[81]). This suggests that M. Fabius Eupor was also involved in the trading of Coan wine. J. Andreau calls him *negotiator vinarius*.[82] Moreover, the Greek letters Ευπο, attested on an Aegean Schoene-Mau XLI container that was discovered in the House of Poppaeus Sabinus (VI 16, 36), may be interpreted as Εὔπορος,[83] which, if associated with M. Fabius Eupor, would provide further evidence that this person traded wine on a large scale.[84]

Furthermore, M. Fabius Eupor is attested as a witness in four transactions of L. Caecilius Jucundus, a Pompeian banker.[85] According to Andreau, the witnesses in these documents were listed according to their social status.[86] Łoś

79 The name Λινειкος appears nowhere else, which means that it probably did not exist. From the way it was published in CIL we may deduce that the beginning of the word did not preserve properly, which means that maybe we should interpret it as Καλλίνικος or something similar. On the other hand, D. Publicius D. l Lin(…) was attested among Greek slave names in Rome by Solin 1996, 591. Given that it is impossible to identify the real name, this person will be referred to as Lineikos.

80 CIL IV 9444. In fact, this house belonged to D. Octavius Quartio.

81 CIL IV 9445.

82 Andreau 1974, 267.

83 CIL IV 6981.

84 Although this name is not particularly rare (according to Solin 2003 it was attested 34 times in Rome, 11 times during the 1st c. AD), it appears 11 times in Pompeii, 8 times as M. Fabius Eupor. In other cases, only the *cognomen* Eupor was given, once in Greek and twice in Latin. Since all inscriptions come from the same period and considering that the *cognomen* Eupor appears on amphoras or in taverns, it seems likely that these *tituli* referred to M. Fabius Eupor.

85 CIL IV 3340,092 = Affaires 00092, CIL IV 3340,097 = Affaires 00097, CIL IV 03340,037= Affaires 00037, CIL IV 3340,071.

86 Andreau 1974, 170–176.

assumes that people who were mentioned first, second and third enjoyed high social positions.[87] Considering that M. Fabius Eupor is often listed second (after Q. Appuleius Severus, M. Fabius Thelus or Numerius Popidius Narcissus), it is possible to argue that his social standing was high. His name suggests that he was one of numerous freedmen from the patrician *gens Fabia*, which played an important part in Pompeian trade[88]—most of the Pompeian *Fabii* were freedmen who were engaged in commercial activities.[89]

Finally, Fabius Eupor (without a *praenomen*), who was probably the same person, appears in two electoral inscriptions, in which he recommends candidates for the post of *aedile*.[90] These inscriptions are very interesting, because they provide us with information concerning the social position and occupation of Fabius Eupor. It seems that he was a political friend of C. Cuspius Pansa and M. Cerrinius Vatia. His title, *princeps libertinorum*, mentioned in one of the *tituli*, means the 'first among freedmen'. It was once interpreted as the head of the Jewish community in Pompeii.[91] However, M. Ginsburg convincingly explained that Fabius Eupor was simply a patron, or the head of a collegium of *libertini* in the city. This title, as well as the fact that his recommendations appear in several election notices suggest that he was wealthy and important.[92] Therefore, M. Fabius Eupor was a Pompeian businessman who profited from the trading of, *inter alia*, wines from the Eastern Mediterranean. There should be no doubt that he was a wealthy *negotiator*, and notwithstanding his servile origin, he also held a high position in the social hierarchy of the town.

Coelius Lesbius was also among the *negotiatores* who dealt with trade, this time in Cilician wines. His name, written in black, was found on a container discovered in a *caupona* (I 7, 15).[93] The same *cognomen* was also attested upon a Cretan amphora.[94] He was probably a freedman of the *gens Coelia*, which was also involved in the trading of Rhodian wines (see the case of Coelius Gallus). Therefore, Coelius Lesbius provides further evidence confirming that the family was related to commercial activities. Another name, again in black and this time attested on a Cilician Schoene-Mau XIII container found in the House of Julia Felix (II 4, 4), was read as Vedius Primi(genius).[95] However, if the let-

87 Łoś 1991, 163.
88 CIL V 833: *Eupor lib.*; Solin 2003, 707; Łoś 1991, 106.
89 Castrén 1975, 166; Andreau 1974, 267–268.
90 CIL IV 117 = D 06419g; CIL IV 120.
91 Ginsburg 1934, 198–199.
92 Ginsburg 1934, 199.
93 CIL IV 9491.
94 Marangou-Lerat 1995, 144.
95 CIL IV 10310.

ters accompanying the name—'Sta' were an abbreviation of *Stabianum* (which means wine from the area of Stabiae), as the authors of *CIL* suggest, we would probably be dealing with an amphora that was reused by a local merchant. On the other hand, *Stabianum* does not appear in either of the lists of Italian wines provided by Pliny and Athenaeus,[96] which makes this interpretation of 'Sta' dubious. Therefore, it is much more probable that Vedius Primi(genius) was in fact a *negotiator*. Although his name was attested in one Pompeian graffito,[97] it is impossible to say anything more about him. The *cognomen* suggests a slave origin, since most Italians carrying this name were classified as *certi liberti*.[98]

Another *negotiator*, L(ucius) A() Herme(s) appeared on a Schoene-Mau XII container discovered in the atrium of the Pompeian House of the Orchard (I 9, 5); his name was inscribed alongside the Greek letters Μομ/Παυ (written in black),[99] which suggests that the amphora originated in Cos. At the same time, the Greek *cognomen* of L. A() Hermes indicates his slavish origin. A person with the same *cognomen* and probably the same *nomen gentile*, that may be interpreted as Aur(elius), but with the *praenomen* M(arcus), is attested on at least five amphoras (Schoene-Mau IX) that were found in a tavern in Pompeii (I 9, 2). They were all written in black.[100] Moreover, the name Hermes is attested on a Schoene-Mau VII (Dressel 8) amphora that was discovered in building IX 6, 4 in Pompeii.[101] The red letters MAH upon the Schoene-Mau XII container that was discovered in a shop (or house) in Pompeii (I 6, 8–9) may also be deciphered as M. Aurelius Hermes. Therefore, it seems that Lucius Aurelius Hermes and Marcus Aurelius Hermes were involved with the retail and wholesale trade, *inter alia*, of wine from Cos. They were freedmen of the Pompeian branch of the prominent *gens Aurelia*.

Another Greek-Latin black inscription, reading Απολαμ/Vei and accompanied by the abbreviated name Sex(tus) PA( ), was found on a Schoene-Mau XII amphora in the Lupanar of Q. Mestrius Maximus (I 9, 12).[102] This place was called 'The House of Amarantus' by Della Corte due to an electoral inscription (where *Amarantus Pompeianus* recommended Q. Postumius Proculus at

---

96 Plin. *HN* XIV 61–66; Ath. *Deipn.* 26c–27d. The list provided by Athenaeus might date later than the 1st c. AD, given that it was attributed to Galen or even Athenaeus himself. However, Dalby claims that it should not be dated later than the first half of the 1st c. AD; see Dalby 2003, 357.

97 CIL IV 2413a.

98 Kajanto 1965, 134; Duthoy 1989, 11, 14.

99 CIL IV 10314.

100 CIL IV 9475.

101 CIL IV 5639.

102 CIL IV 10362. The Corpus does not specify whether Sex(tus) PA( ) was also written in black.

the post of aedile) being painted on its façade (I 9, 11).[103] Further Schoene-Mau XII/Dressel 2–4 Aegean amphoras were discovered in the garden during excavations in 1995. One bore the name *Sex Pompei Amaranti* on its neck, whereas another had *Sex Pomp* painted on its belly. Since the tavern (I 9, 11) and the house (I 9, 12) functioned together as a unit during their final years, it is likely that they were both managed (or even owned) by Sextus Pompeius Amarantus.[104] Also, the discovery of numerous Cretan amphoras at the site suggest that Sextus Pompeius Amarantus also sold Cretan wine,[105] not only Coan. However, these amphoras were gathered for reuse, which means that they were probably waiting to be refilled with local wine.[106] Sextus Pompeius Amarantus was most probably a freedman of the *gens Pompeia*, but it is impossible to specify whether he was a *negotiator* or rather a local wine seller. If he was indeed the owner of the house and the *caupona*, his estate would be quite large in size, reaching 500 m^2. His recommendation of a candidate for the post of aedile suggests that his opinion counted in the city, at least in certain circles. And, even though he was probably not as successful as M. Fabius Eupor, one should assume that he was also wealthy and prosperous.

A black *titulus* reading Αλ/Φηλikoς and written in Greek was found on a Schoene-Mau XII container from the House of Menander (I 9, 4).[107] The inscription should probably be interpreted as Al( ) Felicis, which is a genitive case of the Italian *cognomen* Felix, the most popular of all Latin slave names according to Solin.[108] Due to the black colour of the *dipinti*, Al( ) Felix may be tentatively associated with wholesale traders. Such an identification is confirmed by the fact that the *cognomen* Φηλikoς appeared on Cretan wine jars.[109]

There is a curious Greek-Latin inscription of unknown colour that reads Leuc()/vet(us)/C(ai) T() C() //Κορνελιου// Corneliu(s). It was attested on a Schoene-Mau XII amphora that was discovered in an unnamed house (VI 15,

103 CIL IV 9829a.

104 Berry 1997, 122.

105 For example, Cretan containers were found in Room 6 of House 12 (CIL IV 10285, 10435, 10437, 10440, 10453), and in the atrium of this house (10438, 10439, 10401, 10420, 10455, 10472) as well as in the *caupona* of House 11 (10322, 10359).

106 Peña 2007, 89–94.

107 CIL IV 9816.

108 Solin 1996, 680. Kajanto 1965, 134 includes it in the same category of *cognomina* as Fortunatus. Therefore, it is probably not a typical *cognomen servile*, but, as in the case of Fortunatus—see Duthoy 1989, 194—it was considerably more frequently attested among freedmen than among the freeborn.

109 CIL IV 5783, 6581–6587.

13) in Pompeii.[110] The area was predominantly of a domestic character, but the house was adjacent to a *caupona*, which could suggest that one of the people mentioned may have been an innkeeper. On the other hand, it seems logical to associate Cornelius with P. Cornelius Tages, whose name appears in the archive of C. Jucundus and on two other amphoras: an olive oil jar and a wine container of Cretan origin.[111] The latter was found in the House of Ephebus (I 7, 10–12), which belonged to P. Cornelius Tages. This was a large estate that measured more than 600 m^2 and contained more than 20 rooms, it also included a garden, bronze statues and painted decoration. P. Cornelius Tages was identified as a freedman and *negotiator vinarius* by Andreau. This identification was suggested by inscriptions on amphoras and in Jucundus' archive, as well as by the decoration of the house, which included wall paintings with oriental motifs, attributes of Mercury, and representations of Fortuna. Moreover, the date of this decoration and the structure of the house indicate that the owner must have become enriched suddenly, which may have been due to successful commercial activities.[112] *Cornelii* did not play an important part in public life in Pompeii during the first half of the 1st c. AD, but in the Neronian Age a certain C. Cornelius Macer held the office of *duovir*. However, he had a different praenomen than Tages, which suggests that they were not closely related.[113]

A red *titulus* was found on a container from an unnamed house in Pompeii (VI 16, 26). The inscription reads *Pimp Numerio Fortunato* and it is the most informative of all red Latin inscriptions found on Schoene-Mau XLI containers.[114] The same name, also written in red, but this time in Greek—Νουμεριος Φορτ(ουνατος), was found on a tavern wall in Pompeii (I 8).[115] Moreover, it was also attested on an inscription that was found in Rome,[116] but the probability that these inscriptions refer to the same person is rather low. According to Kajanto, Fortunatus was among the most popular *cognomina*;[117] however, Duthoy's study proved that it was often adopted by former slaves,[118] which means that Numerius Fortunatus was likely a freedman. The colour of the *titulus* suggests that Numerius Fortunatus was a local producer or trader. The

110 CIL IV 5590. This inscription has already been mentioned in Chapter 2, Section 4.
111 CIL IV 9437, 9493.
112 Andreau 1974, 175, 259.
113 Castrén 1975, 157–158.
114 CIL IV 6927.
115 CIL IV 7270, see also NSA 1946, 93, n. 70.
116 CIL VI 2825.
117 Kajanto 1965, 29–30.
118 Duthoy 1989, 194 sq.

question of whether he sold Greek wine or used Greek amphoras to carry his locally produced goods remains open.

An amphora with a *titulus* reading 'Choum vetus' that was found in a *caupona* (II 9) in Herculaneum also bears the inscription 'M. Livi Alcimi'.[119] The same name appears on a few other amphoras that were found in the same building, including two Schoene-Mau XIV containers.[120] We know that it was written in red on two of the discovered amphoras.[121] Unfortunately, however, the colour of the remainder was not mentioned. The appearance of his name in red may suggest that M. Livius Alcimus was a local retail trader, for example the owner of a *caupona*. Nevertheless, his name was also found on an amphora that was discovered in the House of the Fullonica (IV 5).[122] Moreover, at least four Arretine jars that were discovered in Herculaneum were inscribed with the name of M. Livius Alcimus.[123]

The Greek *cognomen* suggests that M. Livius Alcimus was a freedman of the *gens Livia*.[124] This family must have been involved in other commercial activities apart from wine trading. For example, a few freedmen of *Livii* produced transport containers, which is indicated by amphora stamps with the abbreviated form of the name (M.) Livi Ca(usori) found in the Grand Ribaud D shipwreck. According to A. Hesnard, this name appeared on numerous stamps of Pompeian Dressel 2–4 (Schoene-Mau XII) amphoras found in Pompeii, Ostia, Carthage and in Vindonissa. Another name, this time that of a certain M. Livius Quad(ratus), was attested on a Dressel 2–4 amphora discovered in villa Oplontis B, also referred to as the villa of Crassius Tertius. This amphora was among the containers that were waiting to be filled with wine when Vesuvius erupted. It should be noted that the *nomen gentile* 'Livius' originated in Latium, but it is also common in the East and in Campania, particularly in Sorrento.[125] *Livii* are not attested very often in the epigraphic material from Pompeii; instead, they appear more often in Herculaneum, where most of them used the *praenomen* Marcus. *Gens Livia* was involved in the production of wine, which is suggested by the white inscription *Timi? Livi Caesenni* that was found on a Schoene-Mau XII amphora[126]—white coloured *tituli* are likely to refer to producers.[127]

---

119 CIL IV 10722.
120 CIL IV 10784, 10787.
121 CIL IV 10785–10786.
122 CIL IV 10787.
123 CIL IV 10857–10859.
124 Duthoy 1989, 183–189.
125 Hesnard et al. 1988, 49–50.
126 CIL IV 10302.
127 Andreau 1974, 238; Łoś 1991, 67.

Moreover, a stamp reading *Abdae(i) Liviae* that was found in Pompeii[128] suggests that this family was associated with amphora production.[129] In summary, it seems possible that M. Livius Alcimus was a freedman and a local merchant, whose business involved the trading of wine and pottery during the 1st c. AD. He was associated with a prominent family, which profited from wine and amphora production.

Εὔανδρος given in the genitive case appeared on a Schoene-Mau XIII container.[130] This person could be associated with C. Atullius Evander, who lived around 54 AD and was mentioned a few times in the archive of Jucundus.[131] The name Evander, written in red, also possibly appeared on a Schoene-Mau XII wine amphora that was discovered in a Pompeian tavern (VI 16, 15). This person was probably a freedman involved in the wine business, and even though the question remains of whether he was a *negotiator* or a local dealer, it cannot be excluded that he was both, meaning that in Pompeii he sold Cilician wines under the name C. Atullius Evander, but bought the merchandise in the Eastern Mediterranean, where he went by the name Εὔανδρος.

A slave origin may also be postulated in the cases of a few other traders that were attested upon Cilician wine jars, such as Julius Hilarus and Ti. Claudius L( )?.[132] It cannot be excluded that the first should be identified as a descendant of C. Julius Hilarus, who was a *praefectus turmae* in 37 BC.[133] However, according to Castrén, most of the Pompeian *C.* and *Ti. Julii* were imperial freedmen, or their offspring.[134] The *cognomen* Hilarus, a typical *cognomen servile*, confirms that we are dealing with a freedman. Among 344 *Hilarii* of a certain social status analysed by Duthoy, 337 were *certi liberti*.[135] At the same time, Ti. Claudius L( ) does not appear in *Ordo Populusque Pompeianum*, but most of the *Ti. Claudii* attested by Castrén were freedmen. There are no clues regarding the occupation of Ti. Claudius L( ), but Julius Hilarus was probably a local salesman, considering that his name was written in red. It seems that he was involved not only with the trade of Cilician, but also of Cretan wines, since his name was also attested on a Cretan amphora.[136]

128 NSA 1939, 305.
129 Łoś 1996, 118–119, 130 n. 451.
130 CIL IV 10462.
131 CIL IV 3340.9, 10; Andreau 1974, 153, 173, 184, 323.
132 CIL IV 5803, 5848, 5852.
133 CIL IV 2437; Castrén 1975, 179, no. 14.
134 Castrén 1975, 178.
135 Duthoy 1989, 10, 14.
136 Andreau 1974, 249–250; Łoś 1997, 74; CIL IV 5852.

Members of the *gens Julia* appear upon Cilician wine amphoras at least twice more, once with the *cognomen* Drosis,[137] which was not recorded among the Pompeian *cognomina* in Castrén's work. This is a rather rare Greek name that has been attested in Athens, Aphrodisias, Perinthos, Puteoli and Naples.[138] It seems that Julia Drosis, who might have been of eastern origin, was a freedwoman of the *gens Julia*. The black colour of the *titulus* suggests that Julia Drosis was involved with the wholesale trade of Cilician wines.

There were a few Cilician wine containers that bore only abbreviations. However, some of them might have been deciphered as *tria nomina*, that were attested in other Pompeian inscriptions. One example is a red *titulus* containing the abbreviation C.I.P,[139] which could mean C. Julius Polybius or C. Julius Primigenius—both appear in the Pompeian *ordo*. Both *cognomina* indicate a slave origin,[140] which can be almost certain, considering that most of the *C. Julii* were imperial freedmen or their descendants, according to Castrén. Some of them, however, were candidates for important posts, such as duumvir or aedile, which means that freedmen descendants aspired to be municipal elites.[141] And, by selling Cilician wines locally, they were not only provided with an income, but also gained social recognition, which enhanced their prospects for social promotion.

Another member of *gens Julia* appeared in a Greek-Latin inscription on an amphora of the type Schoene-Mau XII. Unfortunately, no information is preserved in CIL regarding the place of its discovery in Pompeii. The first *titulus* (of unknown colour) may be deciphered as the Greek name Κρίτων written in the genitive case. It was accompanied by the Greek word λευκός, which may be associated with the colour of wine. Apart from this name there was also a Latin word (written in red) that may be interpreted as *princeps*, but it was written in Greek—πρινκιπας.[142] Moreover, we have an abbreviation, which is probably of a Latin *tria nomina*: C(aius) Jul(ius) Me()[143] written in red. This person may be identified as C. Julius Memor, a witness mentioned in the archive of C. Jucundus (t. 89). According to Castrén, most of the Pompeian *C. Julii* were imperial freedmen and their descendants,[144] which suggests that C. Julius Memor was probably one of them.

137 CIL IV 2649.

138 7 records in LGPN under 'Δροσίς'.

139 CIL IV 5997.

140 Polybius is of Greek provenance, whereas Primigenius was classified as a *cognomen servile* by Duthoy 1989, 14.

141 Castrén 1975, 178–179.

142 Red Greek inscriptions are generally rare; this would be one of the few exceptions.

143 CIL IV 6454.

144 Castrén 1975, 178–179.

Two Schoene-Mau XII containers were found in the atrium of a Pompeian house (I 9, 7), they bore the Greek letters λευ written in black, which may be developed as λευκός—the white colour of wine. They also included a Latin *duo nomina* in red—'Equitia Clymene'.[145] The *cognomen* may be associated with the Greek name Κλυμένη, that was attested in Greece and in Italy.[146] Therefore, we are probably dealing with a freedwoman who was involved in the wine trade. Considering that the *titulus* is red, we should identify her as a local wine seller. Another *liberta* was attested on a Schoene-Mau XIII amphora, on which a Latin *titulus* appeared that resembled the genitive form of the female name Cupronia Secunda.[147] Cupronia was a very rare *nomen gentile* that, apart from Pompeii, was attested only in Africa.[148] The lack of any additional information does not permit us to formulate any hypothesis regarding the occupation of Cupronia. The *cognomen* Secunda is as likely to be *servile* as *ingenuus*, according to Duthoy, but Kajanto claims that it was very popular among former slaves.[149] It is, thus, more probable that Cupronia Secunda was *liberta*.

Finally, it is worth mentioning a Schoene-Mau XLI amphora found in the garden of building V 3, 10 in Pompeii, which bore a Latin inscription composed of two words: *Vesoni* and *Clod*. The colour of the former was not specified, whilst the latter was written in red.[150] These words may be associated with two *nomina gentilia*: Vesonius and Clodius. The *Gens Vesonia* is attested in Pompeii. Vesonius Primus is probably the most famous member of this family. He was a mercantile freedman who lived in the House of Orpheus (VI 14, 20) and did business with L. Caecilius Jucundus. He was also an operator of a laundry that was adjacent to this house. There is a graffito bearing his name on the façade of this *fullonica*. Moreover, he appears on a wax tablet dated to 57 AD.[151] It cannot be excluded that his business had something to do with selling Eastern wines, but the evidence is too scarce to prove this hypothesis. *Clodii* are often attested in Pompeian inscriptions. According to Castrén they descend from the *scriba* A. Clodius M. f., who might have come from Rome or Puteoli. He married a heiress from the Lassi family of wine-producers, and his descendants were engaged in agricultural production.[152] Łoś mentions epigraphic evidence that indicates *Clodii* were involved in the production and trading of wine. For

145 CIL IV 9529.
146 LGPN s.v.
147 CIL IV 5817.
148 CIL VIII 5497, 18065, 18972; Castrén 1975, 160.
149 Duthoy 1989, 14; Kajanto 1965, 76–77.
150 CIL IV 5918.
151 Łoś 1996, 143; Welch 2009, 570–571.
152 Castrén 1975, 154–155.

example, an amphora that was stamped with the name *Clodia* was found in Herculaneum.[153] This name may relate to Clodia A.f., *sacerdos publica Cereris* and a daughter of A. Clodius A. f. Flaccus. He was a prominent Pompeian who belonged to the *ordo equester* and was a duumvir.[154] There are also *tituli picti* that may be interpreted as *Clod(ianum)*, *Clodian(um)*, *Clodia(num) ve(tus)* or: *Ab(!) Clodio Clemente de / superiore sine defr⟨u=I⟩to*.[155] They clearly indicate that the Pompeian *gens Clodia* was involved in the production of wine. Furthermore, there are four inscriptions that mention *Surrentinum Clodianum*.[156] One was attested on a Pompeian amphora that was discovered in Rome. Tchernia claims that all these amphoras transported wine that was produced in the Pompeian domain of *Clodii*,[157] due to his belief that *Surrentinum* represents one of their vineyards in Surrentum. On the other hand, van der Werff argues that *Surrentinum* refers to the taste of the wine rather than to its provenance.[158] According to Łoś, these data indicate that wine production was the most important source of income for *Clodii*.[159] Their name written in red upon imported amphora could indicate the reuse of the container. Another explanation is that *Clodii* were not only producers of Campanian wines, but also local distributors of foreign beverages. Since from the Julio-Claudian and Flavian periods only freedmen of this family are attested in Pompeii,[160] we may suppose that the name on the Schoene-Mau XLI container belongs to a freedman.

To sum up, there is a lot of evidence that freedmen of prominent *gentes*, such as *Julii, Livii, Coelii, Fabii, Cornelii, Pompeii, Vesonii* and *Clodii* were involved with the trading of wines from the Eastern Mediterranean. Some of these freedmen, such as M. Fabius Eupor(us), P. Cornelius Tages and Sextus Pompeius Amarantus were prominent citizens who enjoyed a good reputation among the local community. All of this means that Eastern Mediterranean wine amphoras provide further evidence that elites might have profited from trade, and that being involved in this business could accelerate social promotion.

153 IErc, 259 after Łoś 1996, 123–124, n. 406.
154 Łoś 1996, 123–124, n. 406.
155 CIL IV 2564; Panella, Fano 1977, 159; CIL IV 5574; CIL IV, 5588 after Łoś 1996, 123–124, n. 406.
156 IPI 329, 217–219; CIL XV 4592.
157 Tchernia 1979, 93–94.
158 Van der Werff 1989, 367–368.
159 Łoś 1996, 123–124, n. 406.
160 Castrén 1975, 155.

3 Free Greeks, Slaves and Greeks with Roman Citizenship

Eastern Mediterranean wine amphoras have provided us with a number of Greek names and Latin *tria nomina* written in Greek. One of these names, Tι Κλα Λινεικου, was discovered on the above-mentioned Cnidian container in the company of M. Fabius Eupor.[161] *Ti. Claudii* appear often on Cretan wine amphoras, but no *cognomen* similar to Lineikos has so far been attested. Nevertheless, considering that it was written in Greek and found on an eastern amphora, the name must have had an oriental origin. According to Marangou-Lerat, *Ti. Claudii* with Greek *cognomina* (for example Ti. Claudius Aristoteles or Ti. Claudius Epaphroditos) were Greeks who acquired Roman citizenship during the rule of the emperor Claudius.[162] However, Łoś noted that very few *cives Romani* are attested among the inhabitants of Crete in the 1st c. AD. Therefore, he thinks that it is more probable that most of these people were in fact of Italian, not of Greek origin.[163] It is difficult to say what the function of the supposed Ti. Klaudius Lineikos was in the commercial chain, because his name does not appear in other inscriptions. However, he might have been a *negotiator* who bought wines from their producers and organised their shipment to Italy. Therefore, he would be the first link in the chain concerning the distribution of Cnidian wine to Italy. Assuming that he was active in the East and considering that his *cognomen* is not typical for Greek slaves and freedmen that lived in Italy, we may speculate that he was a Greek who was granted Roman citizenship.

Another Latin name—Κλα(υδιος) Ἀρι(στοτέλης?), that was written in Greek and coloured red, has been attested on two Schoene-Mau XII and XIII amphoras that were found in a peristyle of the Lupanar of Q. Mestrius Maximus (I 9, 12).[164] Moreover, Tι. Κλαυδιος Ἀριστοτέλης appeared (in the genitive case) on at least two Cretan containers.[165] On the vessel that was found in the House of Menander (I 10, 4) it was written in black. In this case, the black inscription indicates that Κλαυδιος Ἀριστοτέλης was a *negotiator*, whereas the red coloured inscription on the Coan container is suggestive of a local trader who sold, *inter alia*, Eastern wines. Nonetheless, this case is unusual, since red Greek *tituli* are very scarce. Moreover, the *cognomen* Ἀριστοτέλης is rare in Italy, whereas it is

161 CIL IV 5535.

162 Marangou-Lerat 1995, 135, 154.

163 Łoś 1997, 67.

164 CIL IV 10441 and 10442.

165 CIL IV 9763 and Marangou-Lerat 1995, 135, 136. In the third inscription, CIL IV 9485, only the first two letters of the *cognomen* were given.

common in the Greek world. According to the *Lexicon of Greek Personal Names* (LGPN) the name was not attested in Campania, and, Solin did not record it in Rome.[166] This suggests that Τι. Κλαυδιος Ἀριστοτέλης was a Greek, probably from Crete, who was granted Roman citizenship. The question of whether he was a long-distance or a local trader remains open; however, the first option seems more probable. It is also possible that he was involved in both regional retail and large-scale maritime trading.

Greek names written in Greek may refer to either Greek slaves living in Italy, or to people living in the eastern part of the Mediterranean who were either freeborn or slaves. It is reasonable to assume that if a name was attested more often in the East, the person bearing it was likely to have lived in the Eastern Mediterranean and might have been freeborn. Conversely, if the name appeared more often in Italy, it probably referred to an Italian slave. For example, Ἀπολλώνιος is the most frequently occurring Greek name. It was written in the genitive case in Greek on a Schoene-Mau XII container that was discovered in a villa in *fundo Santini*, in the territory of Boscotrecase.[167] It also appears on two other Schoene-Mau XII amphoras that were found in Pompeii, in an unnamed house (VI 15, 8)[168] and in *Insula* IX 7. The last container also carried the inscription '*Coum vetus*'; however, it seems that it was added after the name.[169] The name Ἀπολλώνιος was also attested on a Cilician Schoene-Mau XIII wine container[170] that was discovered in a tavern (IX 6, 1) and upon an Aegean Schoene-Mau XLI wine amphora that was found in a *caupona* (V 2) in Pompeii.[171] This means that Ἀπολλώνιος was involved in the wine trade in at least three different geographical regions (Cos, Cilicia, undefined Aegean area). The name Ἀπολλώνιος was very popular in Greek-speaking regions, given that it has more than 3000 records in the LGPN, which includes over 400 records from the Aegean Islands and over 1300 from coastal Asia Minor. It was also attested in the southern part of Italy (53 times),[172] which includes 13 times in Campania (7 times in Pompeii during the 1st c. BC and the Imperial period).[173] However, it appears mostly in Latin, usually as a *cognomen*, for example Cn. Helvius Apol-

166 LGPN s.v.
167 CIL IV 6979.
168 CIL IV 5940.
169 CIL IV 5541.
170 CIL IV 6305.
171 CIL IV 6306.
172 LGPN has yet to publish Greek names from Rome and northern Italy. Solin 2003 provides us with information regarding Greek names in Rome.
173 LGPN s.v.

lonius or P. Terentius Apollonius.[174] There is only one known example of this name being written in Greek, when it appears as graffiti on the outside of a stage wall belonging to the *Theatrum Maius* in Pompeii.[175] It was very common in Rome (appearing more than 300 times), where it was written predominantly in Latin.[176] Following the conclusions of Tchernia and Marangou-Lerat regarding the Greek provenance of the amphoras that carried Greek *tituli*,[177] it seems likely that Ἀπολλώνιος, whose name was written in Greek, lived in a Greek-speaking area. This may be confirmed by the lack of a *nomen gentile*, which suggests he was not a Roman citizen. He might have been a citizen of one of Greek polis (for example Cos), or a freedman. Since in one case this name was written in black (in two other cases the colour was not noted in CIL), we may suspect that he was a *negotiator*. It seems unlikely that he was a slave, given the scale of his business. Since the containers that carried this name were found in both houses and taverns, it seems that Ἀπολλώνιος was a wholesale trader of Aegean and Cilician wines. He might have bought them from eastern producers or intermediaries and probably sold them to other merchants who distributed them in Campania. It is worth mentioning that this name written in the genitive case in Greek also appears on an amphora stopper that was found in Rome.[178] Even if it is not certain that we are dealing with the same person, it seems that the stamp may be further evidence that Ἀπολλώνιος was a wholesale trader who lived in the East. Returning to the amphora that carried the name Ἀπολλώνιος and the supposedly later *titulus* '*Coum vetus*', we may imagine that the name Ἀπολλώνιος was written by a trader who was in the process of sending wine to Italy. Subsequently, and probably at the place of distribution, a local merchant added information regarding the jar's contents.

Furthermore, the two Greek names Διοκλῆς and Διόδωρος appear in the genitive case on numerous Schoene-Mau XII and XIII amphoras, often appearing next to each other.[179] There are also two containers that bear the name Διοκλῆς, which is written in the genitive case and appears along with the name Ἀγάθη.[180] Διόδωρος could be a patronymic, whereas Ἀγάθη may be interpreted as a metronymic of Διοκλῆς. However, these names are never attested together in LGPN. Therefore, it seems more likely that they are separate names belong-

174 Castrén 1975, 190.9, 402.4.
175 CIL IV 2462.
176 Solin 2003, 294–299.
177 Tchernia 1986, 241; Marangou-Lerat 1995, 154.
178 CIL XV 4919.
179 CIL IV 2853–2866, 2867–2873, 6338–6340; CIL IV 2874–2875, 2878–2880.
180 CIL IV 2876–2877.

ing to different people. Since they appear on various types of containers that were produced in different places, such as on Cos (Schoene-Mau XII) and in Cilicia (Schoene-Mau XIII), it seems that Διοκλῆς and Διόδωρος were involved in wholesale trading of Eastern Mediterranean wines. According to W. Broekaert, the names that appear in *dipinti* found on Baetican olive oil amphoras represent business partners who shared the profits from commercial transactions.[181] Similarly, Διοκλῆς and Διόδωρος might have been *socii* in commercial enterprises. What was the relationship between them?

Διοκλῆς is a very popular name both in the Eastern Mediterranean and in Italy. However, only five out of 606 people who bore this name were attested in Campania (Nola, Misenum, Pompeii) and it was always a part of *tria nomina* that were written in Latin.[182] According to Solin, slaves or freedmen were in the majority among people named Diocles in Rome.[183] The social position of the people that bore the name Diodorus/Διόδωρος was similar,[184] as well as the geographical distribution of this name, which was often attested in Greece and Asia Minor. However, it appeared only seven times in Campania, including two records from Pompeii.[185] Therefore, it is more probable that these people were Greeks of unknown social status who lived in the Eastern Mediterranean, for example on Cos or in Cilicia, where they were involved with buying wines from producers and exporting them, *inter alia*, to Italy. However, it cannot be excluded that they were slaves who represented their Italian masters. Also, it is possible that one was a free Greek who lived in the East, while the other was a slave who represented him in Italy.

A Schoene-Mau XII amphora from the Lupanar of Q. Mestrius Maximus (I 9, 12) carried the name Εὔδημος written in black in the genitive case.[186] This name is attested neither in Campania nor in south Italy, but Solin mentions four people named Eudemus in Rome.[187] The container was discovered in a tavern owned by Sextus Pompeius Amarantus, together with numerous Cretan amphoras that bore Greek names or Latin *tria nomina* written in Greek with Greek *cognomina*. Since these were written in black, they may be attributed to *negotiatores*. It seems that the tavern of Amarantus had many suppliers, including: Καλικράτης, Τι. Κ(λαυδιυς) Ἀνεικετος, Τι. Κ(λαυδιυς) Απαπολα, Τι. Κ(λαυδιυς)

181 Broekaert 2012, 231–233.
182 LGPN s.v.
183 Solin 2003, 42–43. In Rome this name was written mostly in Latin.
184 Solin 2003, 40–41.
185 LGPN s.v.
186 CIL IV 10420.
187 LGPN s.v.; Solin 2003, 63 in one case the name was written in Greek, but it was dated to the 4th c. AD.

Αντιμι(ος), (Τι.) Κ(λαυδιυς) Ἀντίοχος and M. Π(ομπειυς) Τευπωνος. Εὔδημος was probably one of them. It seems that he lived in the Eastern Mediterranean and might have been freeborn.

Furthermore, a black *titulus* with the name Στέφανος in the genitive case was attested on a Schoene-Mau XII container from an unnamed house (II 12, 6) in Pompeii.[188] This name appears 25 times in Campania, including five times in Pompeii, but it is always a *cognomen* written in Latin.[189] Another Greek name that was written in the genitive case is Μένανδρος. It was attested on a Schoene-Mau XII amphora that was discovered in the House of Poppaeus Sabinus (VI 16, 36).[190] This name appears four times in Campania (including once in Pompeii), but is very frequent (1021) in the Eastern Mediterranean.[191] It was attested in Rome 90 times, and 34 of the people who bore it were slaves or freedmen.[192] Given that both *tituli* were written in black, it seems logical to suggest that those who bore them were wholesale traders. Since these names are more frequent in the East than in the West, we may tentatively suggest that these people operated in the Greek area, where they were responsible for purchasing wines from Greek producers and subsequently exporting them to Italy. A similar interpretation can be proposed for a Greek inscription, which resembles the genitive form of the name Ἀθηνοίτης. This name was attested once in Ephesus. This *titulus* appears on at least four Cilician amphoras,[193] once in black, which means that Ἀθηνοίτης might have been an eastern *negotiator* involved in the wholesale trading of wines. Cilician wines probably reached Ephesus, which was one of the biggest eastern ports, from where they were exported westward, for example to Italy. Another black *titulus* discovered on a Cilician Schoene-Mau XIII amphora could be interpreted as the genitive form of the Greek name Θεοδότης or Θεοδότας.[194] It was a very rare name and it was not attested in Campania. However, Theodotus appeared 45 times in Rome, and the name was carried mostly by slaves and freedmen.[195] Therefore, the question of whether he was a freeborn *negotiator* who operated in the East or rather a slave who worked in Italy remains open; however, considering the Greek letters as well as the black colour of the *titulus*, the first possibility seems more plausible.

---

188 CIL IV 10470.
189 LGPN s.v.
190 CIL IV 7002.
191 LGPN s.v. In Campania it was always given in Latin.
192 Solin 2003, 257–259.
193 CIL IV 6280–6282, 9708.
194 CIL IV 10421.
195 Solin 2003, 75–76 (under 'Theodotus').

The name Κρίτων (of unknown colour) was written in the genitive case on a Schoene-Mau XII container along with a red Latin *tria nomina* identified as C(aius) Jul(ius) Me(mor).[196] Κρίτων was very popular in the eastern part of the Mediterranean, but it did not appear in Campania, whereas in southern Italy it was rare. Solin registered five people named Criton in Rome, although in four cases it was their *cognomen*.[197] Therefore, the most reasonable interpretation of these *tituli* is that Κρίτων was a Greek trader who bought wine from Greek producers and sent them to Italy, while C(aius) Jul(ius) Me(mor), who was settled in Pompeii, received the wine and was responsible for its distribution in Campania. This duo resembles the previously referred to team of wine traders from Cnidus, i.e. Ti. Claudius Lineikos and M. Fabius Eupor.

Two Schoene-Mau XXVII amphoras bearing the Greek name Καλλίκαρπος were found in house VIII 5–6, 15. A further jar bearing the same name was discovered in another Pompeian building (IX 8).[198] The name Καλλίκαρπος was not very popular and was attested only in the East, including Cyprus and Cilicia. We may therefore assume that Καλλίκαρπος lived in the Eastern Mediterranean, from where he sent wines to Italy. Even though the colour of the inscription was not given, it seems probable that he was involved in large *negotia*.

The case of the name Ἀγάθη, attested on Schoene-Mau XII and XIII amphoras is different.[199] It appears often in Greece and in southern Italy, but it seems that it was more popular in the Western Mediterranean. For example, seven out of the 51 people who bore this name in southern Italy were attested in Campania between the 1st c. BC and the 2nd c. AD. It also appears 19 times among inscriptions from Sicily dated to the Late Imperial Age. However, it is rare in the Aegean islands (6) and in Asia Minor (6).[200] Therefore, it seems more probable that Ἀγάθη was a Greek slave who lived in Italy rather than a Greek from the Eastern Mediterranean. Solin attested this name (written mostly in Latin) in Rome 53 times, but only 14 cases distinguish the social position of the person. Slaves and freedwomen predominated, while only one freeborn Ἀγάθη is known from Rome.[201] It seems, therefore, that Ἀγάθη was a slave who lived in Italy and mediated in the wine trade. Similarly, Μηνόδοτος, who was attested on a Schoene-Mau XIII container discovered in a *triclinium* of the House of

196 CIL IV 6454.
197 LGPN s.v.; Solin 2003, 266. The fifth's *tria nomina* was in Greek.
198 CIL IV 6386–6388.
199 CIL IV 2876, 2877.
200 LGPN s.v.
201 Solin 2003, 771–772.

Lucretius, was probably also a slave.[202] This name was very common in the eastern part of the Mediterranean, particularly in Asia Minor.[203] However, it was also once attested in Pompeii in an inscription dated to the 1st c. BC or 1st c. AD.[204] Moreover, it appeared twice in Puteoli as a *cognomen* in the names: Aurelius Quirinius Me(n)odotus and P. Fabius Menodotus.[205] Considering the red colour of the *titulus* on the Cilician container we could tentatively suggest that Μηνόδοτος was a local wine salesman, which means that he was probably an eastern slave who worked in Campania.

4 *Incerti*

The category of *incerti* is the largest. It includes Greek names that were equally common in the eastern and the western part of the Mediterranean, *tria nomina* without a cognomen, as well as abbreviated and poorly preserved names. Moreover, names written in yellow were included in this category; however, inscriptions of this colour are rare. The only *titulus* associated with a name and coloured yellow could refer to the *tria nomina* M.A.V, which was painted on a Schoene-Mau XLI amphora.[206]

Another name in the *incertus* category may be interpreted as Ἀρχέλα(ος).[207] It appeared on a Schone-Mau XII amphora, but its colour is unknown. The name Ἀρχέλαος is typical of the Greek area and was attested only twice in southern Italy and Campania, but 31 times in Rome.[208] Therefore, it is difficult to propose any interpretation regarding the social position or the occupation of this trader of Coan wine. The name Ἀπελ(λῆς) appears on the same amphora type, and again the colour of the *titulus* is unknown.[209] This name only appeared in Campania twice and was always written in Latin,[210] while in Rome it was attested 29 times, almost always in Latin.[211] One could thus suppose that Ἀπελλῆς was among the traders who operated in the East; however, this name was not particularly common in that area.

202 CIL IV 2584.
203 274 records in LGPN.
204 CIL IV 1315.
205 CIL X 2149 and 2402.
206 CIL 6084.
207 CIL IV 6314 = 5941.
208 LGPN s.v.; Solin 2003, 31.
209 CIL IV 10401a.
210 LGPN s.v.
211 Solin 2003, 269. It was written in Greek twice.

The name Δίδυμος in the genitive case appeared upon two Cilician containers.[212] Even though the colour of these *dipinti* was not given, the use of Greek suggests that they were created in the Greek region. However, it should be noted that the name was also attested in Italy (in Pompeii, Puteoli, Misenum and Cumae,[213] accounting for five out of 93 records[214]). An inscription from Puteoli mentions that C. Julius Didymus was a freedman.[215] Can C. Julius Didymus from Puteoli be associated with Δίδυμος whose name appeared on a container found in Pompeii? It seems doubtful.

Διόνυσος in the nominative case appeared on a Schoene-Mau XIII amphora,[216] and possibly on another four containers of this type, as well as also probably appearing on a Schoene-Mau V.[217] It is a surprisingly rare name, which was attested only four times in LGPN,[218] and it does not appear in Campania. In Rome, a certain Q. Hebenus Q l. Dionysus from the 1st c. AD was attested.[219] Διόνυσιος/Dionysius was a much more common form, appearing a few times in Pompeii.[220] The scarcity of information does not allow us to formulate any hypothesis regarding the person who bore this name, since he could be both a slave or a freedman who acted in Italy, or a free person operating in the East.

Three Schoene-Mau XXVII amphoras, which transported wines from Cilicia and from Cyprus, were discovered in house VIII 5–6, 15 and carried the Greek name Ἀλέξανδρος in the genitive case.[221] This name, popular in the Greek world, was also common in Pompeii and other cities in Campania (Puteoli, Neapolis).[222] Therefore, it is impossible to formulate any hypothesis regarding the origin or social status of Ἀλέξανδρος.

There is another ambiguous inscription: Λύτ(τιος) μ(?) χ ω δι Ἀθηνιώνος Ἐπα(φροδείτου?) ροκουν?[223] on a Schoene-Mau XII amphora that was discovered in the area of Crapolla, in the Scafati territory near Pompeii. The colour of this *titulus* was not noted in CIL. However, if the interpretation of the first

212 CIL IV 6335–6336.

213 Didymus in red graffito—CIL IV 2319d, *Didymo sodales*—CIL IV 5274; *C. Julius Didymus lib.* I–II AD: CIL X 1878 and 3587; NSA 1893, 211.

214 LGPN s.v.

215 Didymus, spelled also as Didimus was attested in Rome, in most cases the name was carried by slaves and freedmen, see Solin 2003, 1016 (under 'Didimus').

216 CIL IV 6342.

217 CIL IV 6343–6346, 10409.

218 LGPN s.v.

219 Solin 2003, 332 (under 'Dionysus').

220 CIL IV 1041, 2021, 2966, 2974–2975, 3885.

221 CIL IV 6288–6290.

222 LGPN s.v., more than 2000 results, including more than 30 from Campania.

223 CIL IV 7000.

word as Λύττιος, which means wine from Lyttos in Crete, is correct, it should be associated with the reuse of this amphora. The phrase δι' Ἀθηνιώνος Ἐπα(φροδείτου) was attested three times on Cretan amphoras, once in black.[224] According to Marangou-Lerat, the names in the genitive case that are preceded by 'διά' should be interpreted as referring to intermediaries, who were at the service of traders. They were responsible for wine after it was bought from the producer, but before it was put into amphoras.[225] In such a case the inscription could mean that Schoene-Mau XII amphoras were occasionally reused for the transportation of wine from Crete or that this island imitated Dressel 2–4 containers. Petrographic studies that were conducted on Hellenistic amphoras that were found in Crete showed that this island imitated Coan and Rhodian types.[226] However, are such imitations probable in the Imperial age, a time when Cretan amphora types were already developed? If we reject the hypothesis that this amphora was reused, we could suppose that Ἀθηνιώνος and Ἐπαφροδειτος were involved in the transportation of wines not only from Crete, but also from Cos. One may wonder if Ἐπαφροδειτος could be associated with Epaphroditus, whose name appeared in the genitive case in Latin on a Cilician amphora discovered in the proximity of a *triclinium* of the House of Julia Felix (II 4, 12).[227] Moreover, Epaphroditus was a *cognomen* of two *liberti*, Ti. Claudius and C. Venerius,[228] the first of whom was also involved in the trading of Cretan wines.[229] Therefore, such an identification is rather doubtful. It is, however, worth mentioning that the Latin Epaphroditus was accompanied by the name P. P() Carus (written in black) on one occasion, a name which appeared twice on Cilician containers. The *cognomen* Carus was attested among Pompeian *cognomina*, but it was carried by L. Valerius.[230] Both, Carus and Epaphroditus were probably wholesale traders, which is indicated by the appearance of their names in black. The latter might have been a freedman, if we assume that Epaphroditus was a part of a *tria nomina*, but no evidence exists that could confirm such an assumption.

A black *titulus* that reads Μινουκιων,[231] which is a *genitivus pluralis* of the name Minucius, was attested on two amphoras (one Schoene-Mau XII and one

224 CIL IV 6469, 6470, 10454.
225 Marangou-Lerat 1995, 153.
226 These are the so-called East Cretan Amphoras, Type 2 and 3. Vogeikoff-Brogan, Apostolakou 2004, 417–418.
227 CIL IV 10331.
228 Castrén 1975, 251.
229 CIL IV 6408; Castrén 1975, 236.
230 Castrén 1975, 249.
231 CIL IV 9797.

unknown) that were discovered in a *caupona* (IX 9, 2) in Pompeii. Minucii are also known from other amphoras, for example Schoene-Mau VIII, X, XXXVI[232] and probably XLII,[233] as well as from two graffiti.[234] In one case we have the full name, i.e. *L(ucius) Minucius / Salvianus*. Moreover, M. Minucius Hilario was engaged in the brick industry, as his name appears on tegulae from Pompeii.[235] Łoś associated *Minucii* with M. Minucius Rufus, the proconsul of Crete and Cyrenaica in 70–71 AD, who was Italian and whose family probably conducted business on Crete. Thus, the Pompeian Minucius could be a family member or a freedman of the *Minucii*.[236] Amphoras that bore this name were found in Pompeii and in Herculaneum in at least two different taverns (II 9 and IV 14), and at the House of the Great Portal (V 35). Moreover, this name was usually written in black. Therefore, we should assume that Minucius (or *Minucii*) from Pompeii was a *negotiator*. He might have been a Cretan resident who exported wine from the island to Italy, but his social status remains uncertain.

The only *titulus pictus* found on a Cilician Schoene-Mau V container is written in black and uses the Greek alphabet,[237] but it is not entirely legible. One word may possibly be identified as Pompeius (a name given in the genitive case), which relates to the prominent *gens Pompeia*, which was even suspected of having given the city its name. Unfortunately, considering the number of this *gens* members that were attested in inscriptions, and the lack of any elements that would suggest a *nomen* or a *cognomen* in the *titulus*, it is impossible to say anything more about this person. Nevertheless, it should be noted that the use of Greek as well as the black colouring suggests that this person was a *negotiator*, who possibly resided or operated in the East.

Another Roman name written in Greek—Γέμελλο(ς),[238] was attested on a Schoene-Mau XII amphora that also carried the abbreviated *tria nomina* C.V.F. Both *tituli* were black. The abbreviation C.V.F may be developed as C. Vettius Frequens, since this name appears on other, mostly Cretan amphoras (it appears on numerous Schoene-Mau VIII vessels and one Schoene-Mau IV container).[239] The black colour suggests that Gemellus and the supposed C. Vettius

---

232 CIL IV 10793–10795.

233 CIL IV 6936. It has been noted that Schoene-Mau XLII containers might have been from Rhodes; however, in this case the attribution was dubious.

234 CIL IV 8087, 8257.

235 CIL X 8042, 74a, b.

236 Łoś 1997, 67–68.

237 CIL IV 2560.

238 CIL IV 2676. This may also be interpreted as a name of wine, cf. *gemicum eugeneum* in Cato *Agr.* 6; Plin. *HN* XIV 46; and *vites gemellae* Col. *R.R.* III 2, 10.

239 CIL IV 2671–2676. However, it is always written in red.

Frequens were *negotiatores* whose social position remains unknown. Another black *titulus* that reads 'AEQVIS' was found on a Cilician amphora discovered at the House of Menander (I 10, 4).[240] If we were to read this inscription as A. Equi(tis) S() it could refer to the *gens Equitia*, which included Equitia Clymene (who was once attested on a wine amphora).[241] Another member of this *gens*, Equitia Psamathe, was named in a Pompeian inscription which suggested she was a seller.[242] We could, therefore, tentatively suggest that the wholesale and retail aspects of the wine trade were among the areas of interest of the Pompeian *Equitii*. It was probably the occupation of freedmen associated with this family, but it is impossible to confirm whether the supposed A. Equi(tis) S() was indeed of slave origin. Similarly, an inscription of unknown colour that mentions L. Sabin(us)[243] does not allow us to formulate any hypothesis regarding the occupation of this person. Sabinus could be a *nomen gentile* or a *cognomen*. The *gens Sabinia* was attested in Pompeii, but only in the form of one representative with the *praenomen* Gaius.[244] At the same time, among inscriptions found on Spanish amphoras that were discovered in Rome a certain T. Littucius Sabinus was attested.[245] The *cognomen* Sabinus probably indicated a freeborn status.[246] Can we associate Pompeian L. Sabinus with the trader attested in Rome? Such a possibility cannot be excluded, but the scarcity of evidence makes it unlikely.

A red inscription that reads L. Muci(us) Sypo( ) was found on a Cilician amphora that was discovered in the House of the Silver Wedding (Insula V 2).[247] *Mucii*, or to be more precise *Mucii Scevolae* were an old patrician family in Rome during the 2nd and 1st c. BC. According to Castrén, Campanian *Mucii* might have been clients of this family.[248] There is no L. Mucius attested in Pompeii (a Q. Mucius—sometimes with the *cognomen* Asclepiades, and Mucius Secundus are known). However, members of this *gens* were also attested in Puteoli[249] and Capua,[250] where some of them were involved in the brick industry, for example they owned *figlinae*, given that their names appear upon tegu-

240 CIL IV 9457.
241 CIL IV 9529.
242 CIL IV 3340,43.
243 CIL IV 5889.
244 Castrén 1975, 215.
245 CIL XV 3934; Andreau 1974, 247, n. 1.
246 Pergreffi 1940, 315.
247 CIL IV 5864.
248 Castrén 1975, 192–193.
249 CIL X 2993.
250 CIL X 4227.

lae.[251] The red colour of the *titulus* found on the Cilician container suggests that one member of this *gens* might have also been involved with the wine retail trade. It is, however, impossible to say whether he was freeborn or a freedman.

There were also two Italian names, C(aius) Atinius and Augustalis, which were given in the dative case.[252] Both inscriptions were black, which means that the pattern observed for Spanish fish sauce amphoras (where inscriptions in the dative case were written in red) did not apply to Aegean wines. Although the case of the names seems unusual at first, according to Andreau, the use of the dative case should not be a surprise. He thinks that both cases (genitive and dative) could signify the same.[253] Therefore, C. Atinius and Augustalis were probably wholesale traders, since their names were written in black. However, it should be noted that the word Augustalis may refer not to the person but to the fact that he held a quasi-magistrature of *augustalis*.

Furthermore, there are abbreviations that may be associated with Latin *tria nomina*. One of them may refer to a seller of Coan wine. The letters 'A.V.S' may be deciphered as A(ulus) V(ettius) S(). This red inscription appears on three amphoras that were discovered in the same context in the *viridarium* of the House of the Pygmies in Pompeii (IX 5, 9). Two of the amphoras were of Cretan origin (Schoene-Mau VIII), while the other was a Schoene-Mau XII. And even though it is not certain that this container was produced on Cos, the fact that it was accompanied by other Greek amphoras and that the same name was attested on all three vessels suggests that it was. *Insula* 5 contains many commercial properties and there are two shops adjacent to the entrance of the House of the Pygmies. The red colour of the *dipinti*, their presence on vessels that were found in the same context, and the commercial character of the *insula* in which they were discovered suggest that the supposed A(ulus) V(ettius) S () should be treated as a local, Campanian trader. He might have been involved in the distribution of Eastern Mediterranean wines in Pompeii, for example by supplying shops and taverns or by simply selling these wines in one of the shops adjacent to the House of the Pygmies.

Another person associated with trading Coan wine, known as 'M.M.F' through an abbreviated *tria nomina*, is attested on two amphoras. The first is an unknown container that was found at a tavern (building IV 17) in Herculaneum.[254] Although this jar bears the word that was initially read as 'Chium',

251 CIL X 8042, 75a,b–76a–g.
252 CIL IV 9320, 9321.
253 Andreau 1974, 243, n. 2.
254 CIL IV 10721.

'Choum' now seems more probable.[255] Another amphora with the letters 'M.M.F', that was probably of Cretan origin, was found in Pompeii (II 1, 15).[256] In this case the supposed abbreviated *tria nomina* were painted in black. Unfortunately, it is impossible to say what names were abbreviated.[257] The association of this person with wholesale traders is suggested by the fact that the containers were found in two different towns. Moreover, in one case the letters were written in black.

Finally, it is worth mentioning that Eastern Mediterranean amphoras provided a few other inscriptions which could be abbreviated *tria nomina*, such as: C(aius) S() Man(),[258] I.P.C,[259] L.C.Ci,[260] Q.C.C,[261] M.A.M,[262] M.S.E,[263] C. Audius S( )[264] among others. However, due to the lack of additional evidence, it is impossible to glean anything from them.

5 Conclusions

In summary, 68[265] names were identified on Eastern Mediterranean wine amphoras that were discovered in the Vesuvian cities. Table 11 lists the people who were involved in the trading of Eastern Mediterranean wines, along with their possible occupation and social status. These conclusions are by no means unquestionable, given the nature of amphora inscriptions. However, they present hypotheses which seem logical based on the available evidence.

There were 19 typical Greek names, composed of one word, that were written in Greek. They may indicate slaves of Greek (albeit not exclusively) origin that lived in Italy, or freeborn Greeks who lived in the East. Most of these names were written in black, which suggests that their owners were involved with wholesale trade. In two cases (Ἀγάθη and Μηνόδοτος) it was possible to deter-

255 See Chapter 2, Section 4.
256 CIL IV 10351.
257 It cannot be associated with the stamp MMF that was found in Zugmantel and interpreted as M. M(aeni?) F(rontonis?), see Callender 1965, 188, no. 1140, because the stamp is dated later than the Pompeian inscription.
258 CIL IV 5539.
259 CIL IV 6084.
260 CIL IV 6051.
261 CIL IV 5604.
262 CIL IV 6080, 6081.
263 CIL IV 6106.
264 CIL IV 9471.
265 67 if we assume that Ἐπα(φροδείτος) and Epaphroditus were the same person.

TABLE 11 Traders of Eastern Mediterranean wines

Name	Citizenship	Social position	Colour of *titulus*	Occupation	Amphora/ wine type
P. Coelius Gallus	Italian	*ingenuus*	black	*negotiator* (*Italy*)	Rhodian
P. Appuleius Bassus	Italian	*ingenuus*	black	*negotiator* (*Italy*)	Coan
C. Annius Maximus	Italian	*ingenuus*	?	?	Schoene-Mau XIII
M. Iu(nius? -lius) Ruf(us)	Italian	*ingenuus*	red	local, Italian trader	Schoene-Mau XIII
N. Fufidius Successus	Italian	*ingenuus*	red	local, Italian trader	Schoene-Mau XIII
L. Sextius or Sextilius Syrticus	Italian	*ingenuus?*	black	*negotiator* (*Italy*)?	Coan
M. Fabius Eupor	Italian	*libertus*	?	*negotiator* (*Italy*)	Cnidian, Schoene-Mau XLI?
Coelius Lesbius	Italian	*libertus*	black	*negotiator* (*Italy*)	Schoene-Mau XIII
Ve(dius) Primi(genius)	Italian	*libertus*	black	negotiator?	Schoene-Mau XIII
L(ucius) A() Herme(s)	Italian	*libertus*	?	*negotiator* (*Italy*)?	Coan
Sextus P (ompeius) A(marantus)	Italian	*libertus*	black?	*negotiator* (*Italy*)	Coan
Al() Felix (written in Greek)	Italian	*libertus*	black	*negotiator* (*Greece*)	Coan
Cornelius (P. Cornelius Tages?)	Italian	*libertus*	?	*negotiator* (*Italy*)	Coan
Numerius Fortunatus	Italian	*libertus*	red	local, Italian trader	Schoene-Mau XLI
M. Livius Alcimus	Italian	*libertus*	red	local, Italian trader	Coan
Εὔανδρος/C. Atullius Evander?	Italian	*libertus*	black	*negotiator* and local retail trader?	Schoene-Mau XIII
Julius Hilarius	Italian	*libertus*	red	local, Italian trader	Schoene-Mau XIII
Ti. Claudius	Italian	*libertus*	?	?	Schoene-Mau XIII
Iulia Drosis	Italian	*liberta*	black	*negotiator* (*Italy*)	Schoene-Mau XIII
C·I·P· C. Julius Polybius?/ C. Julius Primigenius?	Italian	*libertus*	red	local, Italian trader	Schoene-Mau XIII

TABLE 11 Traders of Eastern Mediterranean wines (*cont.*)

Name	Citizenship	Social position	Colour of *titulus*	Occupation	Amphora/ wine type
C(aius) Jul(ius) Me(mor)	Italian	*libertus*	red	*negotiator* (*Italy*)	Coan
Equitia Clymene	Italian	*liberta*	red	local, Italian trader	Coan
Cupronia Secunda	Italian	*liberta*	?	?	Schoene-Mau XIII
Ἀγάθη	Greek?	*serva*	?	?	Coan, Schoene-Mau XIII
Μηνόδοτος	Greek?	*servus*	red	local retail trader	Schoene-Mau XIII
Vesonii	Italian	*libertus?*	red	local, Italian trader?	Schoene-Mau XLI
Clodii	Italian	*libertus?*	red	local, Italian trader?	Schoene-Mau XLI
Τι. Κλαυδιυς Λινεικος?	Roman citizen	*ingenuus?*	?	*negotiator* (*Greek*)	Cnidian
Κλα(υδιυς) Αρι(στοτελης?)	Roman citizen	*ingenuus?*	red	*negotiator* (*Italy*)	Coan, Schoene-Mau XIII
Ἀπολλώνιος	Greek	*ingenuus?*	black	*negotiator* (*Greek*)	Coan, Schoene-Mau XIII and XLI
Διοκλῆς	Greek	*ingenuus?*	?	*negotiator* (*Greek*)	Coan, Schoene-Mau XIII
Διόδωρος	Greek	*ingenuus?*	?	*negotiator* (*Greek*)	Coan, Schoene-Mau XIII
Εὔδημος	Greek	*ingenuus?*	black	*negotiator* (*Greek*)	Coan
Στέφανος	Greek	*ingenuus?*	black	*negotiator* (*Greek*)	Coan
Μένανδρος	Greek	*ingenuus?*	black	*negotiator* (*Greek*)	Coan
Ἀθηνοίτης	Greek	*ingenuus?*	black	*negotiator* (*Greek*)	Schoene-Mau XIII
Θεοδότης/Θεοδότας	Greek?	*incertus*	black	*negotiator* (Greek)?	Schoene-Mau XIII
Κρίτων	Greek	*ingenuus?*	?	*negotiator* (*Greek*)	Coan
Καλλίκαρπος	Greek	*ingenuus?*	?	*negotiator* (Greek)	Schoene-Mau XXVII
Ἀρχέλα(ος)	Greek?	*incertus*	yellow	*negotiator* (*Greek*)?	Coan

TABLE 11 Traders of Eastern Mediterranean wines (*cont.*)

Name	Citizenship	Social position	Colour of *titulus*	Occupation	Amphora/ wine type
Ἀπελ(λῆς)	Greek?	*incertus*	?	*negotiator (Greek)?*	Coan
Δίδυμος	Greek?	*incertus*	?	?	Schoene-Mau XIII
Διόνυσος? (Διόνυσιος?)	Greek?	*incertus*	?	?	Schoene-Mau XIII
Ἀλέξανδρος	Greek?	*incertus*	?	?	Schoene-Mau XXVII
Ἐπα(φροδεῖτος)	Greek?	*incertus*	?	intermediary?	Coan
Epaphroditus	Greek?	*incertus*	black	*negotiator*	Schoene-Mau XIII
P. P( ) Carus	Italian	*incertus*	black	*negotiator*	Schoene-Mau XIII
Minucius (written in Greek)	Italian	*incertus*	black	*negotiator* (*Italy*)	Coan, Schoene-Mau XIII
Pompeius (written in Greek)	Italian	*incertus*	black	*negotiator*	Schoene-Mau V
Γέμελλο(ς)	Italian	*incertus*	black	*negotiator* (*Italy*)	Coan
C. V(ettius) F(requens)	Italian	*incertus*	black	*negotiator* (*Italy*)	Coan
A. Equi(tis) S()	Italian	*incertus*	black	*negotiator*	Schoene-Mau XIII
L. Sabinus	Italian	*incertus*	?	?	Schoene-Mau XIII
A(ulus) V(ettius) S ()	Italian	*incertus*	red	local, Italian trader	Coan
M.M.F	Italian	*incertus*	black	*negotiator* (*Italy*)?	Coan
C(aius) S() Man()	Italian	*incertus*	black	*negotiator* (*Italy*)?	Coan
L. Mucius Sypo(nius)	Italian	*incertus*	red	local, Italian trader	Schoene-Mau XIII
C(aius) Atinius	Italian	*incertus*	black	*negotiator* (*Italy*)?	Coan
Augustalis	Italian	*incertus*	black	*negotiator* (*Italy*)	Coan
C(ai) T() C()	Italian?	*incertus*	?	?	Coan
L.C.Ci	Italian?	*incertus*	?	?	Schoene-Mau XLI
M.A.V	Italian?	*incertus*	yellow	?	Schoene-Mau XLI
I.P.C	Italian?	*incertus*	black	*negotiator*	Schoene-Mau XLI
M() Di Kaa	Italian?	*incertus*	red	local trader?	Schoene-Mau XLI
Q.C.C	Italian?	*incertus*	red	local trader?	Schoene-Mau XLI

TABLE 11 Traders of Eastern Mediterranean wines (*cont.*)

Name	Citizenship	Social position	Colour of *titulus*	Occupation	Amphora/ wine type
M.A.M	Italian?	*incertus*	red	local, Italian trader	Schoene-Mau XIII
C. Audius S( )	Italian?	*incertus*	red	local, Italian trader	Schoene-Mau XIII

mine that these people probably lived in Italy, which means that they were more likely slaves than freeborn. Another, named Εὔανδρος/C. Atullius Evander? was classified as a freedman. Ἀρχέλαος, Ἀπελλῆς, Δίδυμος, Διόνυσος Ἀλέξανδρος, and Ἐπα(φροδείτος) are as likely to be slaves who lived in Campania, as slaves or free Greeks who lived in the East. In nine cases the distribution of names (predominant in the Greek world, rare in Campania) as well as the fact that the inscriptions were in Greek, allow us to presume that these are the names of Greeks who lived in the East. It seems possible that their role was to buy wines from the producers or intermediaries and subsequently organise their exportation to Italy. Since slaves were not attested very often among those who were responsible for the trading of Spanish olive oil and fish sauces, it is possible to suggest analogously that the Greeks mentioned on Greek wine amphoras were freeborn.

Two more names that were written in Greek, but presented in the form of Latin *tria nomina*, appear on eastern wine amphoras that were found in the Vesuvian cities. These names are Τι. Κλαυδιυς Λινεικος? and Κλα(υδιυς) Αρι(στοτελης?) and they probably indicate Greeks who had been granted Roman citizenship. The first is likely to have operated in the East, whereas the second might have acted on Crete, or in both regions—i.e. the East and Italy, due to his name appearing in both red and black.

The other names were Latin, though four of them—Minucius, Pompeius, Gemellus and Al( ) Felix, were written in Greek. They were all inscribed in black, so they might have referred to Italian *negotiatores* who operated in the East. Other Latin names were carried by people who lived in Italy, both freeborn and freedmen. *Cognomina ingenua* allowed four freeborn traders to be distinguished, P. Coelius Gallus, P. Appuleius Bassus, C. Annius Maximus and M. Junius Rufus, who were involved with long-distance, as well as local trading of Eastern Mediterranean wines. They were members of prominent Roman families that had many municipal administration representatives in Campania. Other traders that were most probably freeborn include a local merchant

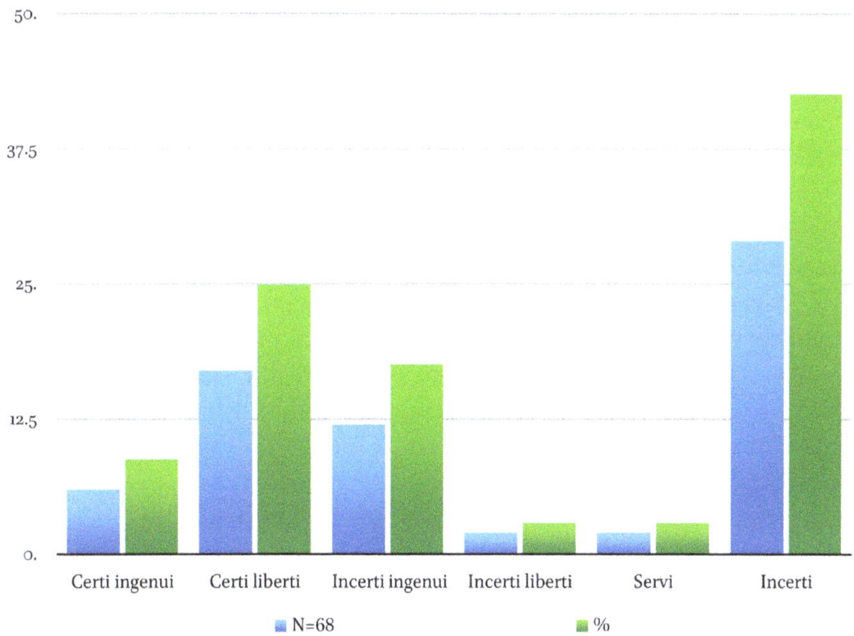

FIGURE 26 Numbers and percentages of names on Eastern Mediterranean amphoras

named N. Fufidius Successus, who was a candidate for the post of aedile, and a *negotiator* named L. Sextilius Syrticus, who was a candidate for the position of duumvir. This demonstrates that there were certain links between the municipal elite and trade, and it suggests that commercial activities were not ignored by free members of prominent Latin *gentes*.

It seems, however, that the trade in Eastern Mediterranean wines was dominated by freedmen, since *certi liberti* formed the largest group (which was composed of 17 people, or 25 % of all traders). Some of them, such as M. Fabius Eupor, M. Livius Alcimus, L. A() Hermes, Equitia Clymene, and Julia Drosis might have been of Greek/Eastern origin. This should not surprise. Łoś has proven that many Pompeian freedmen profited from commercial activities. They were not simply small and middle-sized merchants—many of them were wealthy *negotiatores* involved with the wholesale trading of foreign products.[266] Moreover, freedmen were often attested in the archives of L. Caecilius Jucundus and Sulpicii, which emphasises their importance within the Campanian business world.[267] Among the 17 freedmen traders of Eastern Mediter-

266 Łoś 1991, 102–122.

267 Mouritsen 2011, 206–207; see also Andreau 1974, 273–279.

ranean wines there were six *negotiatores* (black inscriptions) and an equal number of local merchants (red inscriptions). However, at least three more long-distance wholesale traders were identified among the *tituli* of unknown colour.

Another conclusion to be drawn is that the same people were involved in the trading of various types of Eastern Mediterranean wines. For example, Greek *negotiatores* such as Ἀπολλώνιος, Διοκλῆς and Διόδωρος were associated with the distribution of wines from Cilicia and Cos, as well as the 'Coan type' wines that were transported in Schoene-Mau XLI amphoras (in the case of Ἀπολλώνιος). Similarly, Italian *negotiatores* who imported wines did not limit their activity to one type. They were usually also associated with other Eastern wines as well as other products. M. Fabius Eupor was probably responsible for the importation and distribution of wines from Cnidus, Cos and those that were transported in Schoene-Mau XLI amphoras. P. Appuleius Bassus was involved in the trading of Coan and Lycian wines, Al ( ) Felix traded in wine from Cos and Crete, whereas *Minucii* imported beverages from Cos, Crete and Cilicia. However, the names of these traders do not appear upon containers of products other than wine, nor upon wine amphoras from different geographical regions. This indicates that a certain specialisation existed in the trading of goods that were imported to Italy. Contrarily, the names of the supposed local traders appear on several different types of containers. For example, M. Livius Alcimus was attested on a few amphora forms including Coan wine Schoene-Mau XII jars and Western Mediterranean Schoene-Mau XIV vessels, while L(ucius) A() Herme(s) appeared on a Schoene-Mau XII container and possibly on a Spanish garum Schoene-Mau VII jar.

It has already been mentioned that both the Greeks and the Romans were involved in the trading of Eastern Mediterranean wines. Nevertheless, it seems that the Romans, or at least Italians predominated. This resembles the pattern that was observed during analysis of the names of Spanish fish sauce traders by Łoś. According to him the Italians predominated among fish sauces traders, whilst Spanish merchants played an important part in the trade of olive oil in the 1st c. AD. Łoś explains this by emphasising that exportations of Spanish olive oil to Italy started in the 1st c. AD, which means that people from the Iberian Peninsula had access to this trade. Contrarily, trade in fish sauces (which already existed in the late Republican age) was dominated by the Romans and there was not much space for Spanish merchants.[268] Considering that trade in most Eastern Mediterranean wines started during the

268 Łoś 2012, 107–108.

Republican age, the predominance of Italians among eastern wine merchants should be perfectly understandable. Furthermore, we may observe a certain pattern in how trade was organised: most of the Italians were involved with the importing of wines to Italy and their distribution in Campania. At the same time, the Greeks were probably responsible for collecting wines from the producers and subsequently exporting them. This may be confirmed by the fact that sometimes two names appear on the same container, one in Greek and the other in Latin. For example, Γέμελλο(ς) was attested on a Schoene-Mau XII amphora that also carried the abbreviated *tria nomina* C.V.F, while on another Coan container the name Κρίτων was accompanied by C(aius) Jul(ius) Me(mor). The most illustrative is the example of Τι. Κλαυδιυς Λινεικος? and M. Fabius Eupor(us), attested on a Cnidian wine jar. Although males predominated among the traders, four women were also attested. They were mostly *libertae*, but one slave girl was also identified.

Finally, it should be noted that the nomina of prominent *gentes* such as Coelia, Fabia, Clodia, Vesonia, Livia, Julia, Junia, Sextilia, Equitia, Annia, and Appuleia appear among the names of traders, both freeborn and freedmen. Does this mean, as supposed by Mouritsen and D'Arms, that freedmen were often in charge of their patron's affairs, at times acting as overseas agents? This would suggest that landowners covertly participated in and profited from trade, even though it was considered as dishonourable.[269] On the other hand, independent freedmen were common in Italy.[270] Moreover, nothing suggests that M. Fabius Eupor, M. Livius Alcimus, M. Julius Memor, Julia Drosis, Equitia Clymene or any other freedman trader of Eastern Mediterranean wines executed orders on behalf of their former masters. Therefore, the question of whether freedmen acted independently, or whether their commercial activities were entwined with the world of the elite remains unanswered.

Notwithstanding, one ought to admit that it is impossible to accept that the status of traders was low and hence trade was not an important part of economy. First of all, at least four *ingenui* from prominent families were involved in the eastern wine trade. Moreover, the examples of M. Fabius Eupor, P. Cornelius Tages and Sex. Pompeius Amarantus show that freedmen who dealt with large-scale *negotia* could gain a considerable fortune and were able to achieve important positions within the city. Also, N. Fufidius Successus and L. Sextilius Syrticus were probably descendants of slaves (as suggested by *cognomina*) who continued the commercial enterprises of their ancestors, and at the same

269 Mouritsen 2011, 209–246; D'Arms 1981.

270 Garnsey 1981; D'Arms 1981, 121–148; Łoś 1991, 155–165; Andreau 1993, 188–190; Łoś 1995, 1030–1033, 1040.

time sought public office, such as aedile or duumvir. This suggests that being involved with trade could open up the path to social promotion for the children of former slaves. Similar examples are infrequent, as they are not easily traceable in the epigraphic record—most of the children of freedmen would probably change their *cognomina servilia* into something less significative.[271] Nevertheless, certain studies proved that the sons of freedmen often sought a career in municipal administration,[272] while successful merchants from Spain sometimes migrated to Rome in order to become public servants.[273] An illustrative example is also provided by an inscription on a Baetican container, which mentions *Sex. Fadius Secundus Musa*—a freedman and trader whose grandson, with the *cognomen Jucundus*, became a senator.[274] Therefore, the study presented in this chapter provides further evidence that trade was indeed an important part of the Roman economy, which influenced social dynamics. It also helps to understand why freedmen were particularly interested in risky commercial enterprises. Trade allowed successful *liberti* to make huge profits in a short space of time, money which then allowed his family to advance socially. Freedmen also knew that their former masters had, and could lend them, the capital necessary for undertaking large-scale enterprises. A freedman had much to gain and little to lose when involving himself in large-scale *negotia*. On the contrary, the elites were not directly interested in commercial investments as there was little for them to gain, whereas they had much to lose, as they were putting their fortunes and reputation on the line. At the same time, land possession offered them lower, but more steady profit. Nonetheless, they were probably eager to lend money to those who offered high returns with little risk—this is how freedmen came to dominate trade.

To sum up, even though it is impossible to state that the Pompeian elites did indeed take part in commercial activities by using slaves and freedmen, there are certain links between these two groups. Also, free people from prominent families were involved with the wine trade, while certain freedmen were quite wealthy, and their opinion mattered within their community. In addition, we know that capital from the elite facilitated the commercial transactions of freedmen, who could not only gain considerable wealth, but also improve the social status of their families, which means that social and economic status in Roman Italy was not stable, and it was not dependent solely on landed property.

271 Duthoy 1989.

272 Gordon 1931; Łoś 1991, 128 mentions C. Julius Polybius, a candidate for a duumvir who was a son of an imperial freedman.

273 Étienne, Mayet 2001.

274 Remesal Rodríguez 2004, 127.

Of course, drawing conclusions regarding the economy of the Roman Empire based upon the evidence from two small Campanian towns would be a serious mistake. Nevertheless, the evidence does show that trade was an important element of the economy, which influenced social and economic changes in the region. Therefore, this provides further evidence than the ancient economy was more modern than some might think.

CHAPTER 6

Twilight or Bloom? Eastern Mediterranean Wines in Italy during Late Antiquity

> οὐ γὰρ ἐξηνέσχετο ἰδὼν πίθον καταγνύμενον οἴνου πλέων.
> χἄτερα πόσ' ἄττ' οἴει γεγενῆσθ' ἐν τῇ πόλει; ὥστ' οὐδέποτ' ὦ δέσποιν' ἀφησόμεσθά σου.
>
> He could not bear the shock of seeing one of his casks full of wine broken. Ah! what a number of other misfortunes our city has suffered!
>
> ARISTOPH. *Peace* 704–705

∵

After the so-called Crisis of the Third Century, the New Order was established by Diocletian as a consequence of reforms that were crucial to the organisation of the empire. Although these reforms would not leave the wine trade unaffected, understanding their impact is difficult due to a considerable change in the available evidence.

1 Amphoras or Barrels?

Towards the end of the 3rd c. AD western ceramic wine containers, apart from African, disappeared from the archaeological record. At roughly the same time, from the 4th c. AD,[1] the eastern amphora forms that were known were replaced by the Late Roman Amphoras 1–7. These late containers are generally smaller than their classical predecessors (Tab. 12),[2] which may suggest a fall and split of demand for imported foodstuffs,[3] while their shape is globular rather than

1 Sometimes even earlier.

2 Tab. 12 is based on amphora capacities provided by https://archaeologydataservice.ac.uk/archives/view/amphora_ahrb_2005/details.cfm?id=8&CFID=785c66ee-febc-43b3-8daf-5006c5b4b143&CFTOKEN=0, accessed 30.01.2019; but in the case of LRA1 see Van Alfen 1996, 192–198.

3 Panella 1993, 668.

© KONINKLIJKE BRILL NV, LEIDEN, 2021 | DOI:10.1163/9789004433762_008

TABLE 12 Capacities of early and late imperial wine amphoras from the Eastern Mediterranean

Early Imperial Containers		Late Roman Containers	
Camulodunum 184	20–25 l.	LRA1	4,5–15 l.
Agora F65–66	6–12 l.	LRA3	6–12 l.
AC4	10–15 l.	LRA4	20–25 l.
Cretan (AC1-AC43)	22 l.	LRA5	20–25 l.
Dressel 2–4 Aegean	25–30 l.	LRA7	up to 10 l.
Agora G199	19–53 l.	Keay 52	12–14 l.
Dressel 2–4 Egyptian	20–25 l.	Spatheia	0,5–4 l.
Coan? (Dressel 5, Knossos 19)	c. 30 l.	Agora M273	19–25 l.
Cnidus (Mau XXXVIII)	17 l.	Samos Cistern Type	up to 10 l.
Medium	**22 l.**	**Medium**	**11 l.**

elongated (except LR7). The disappearance of western wine amphoras is usually attributed to the increased use of wooden barrels,[4] which had numerous advantages over ceramic containers. However, there has so far been no agreement regarding the scale of the use of casks, and hence the matter needs more explanation. Barrels have a better volume-to-weight ratio and can be rolled instead of carried, which makes transporting them easier than transporting amphoras. Moreover, with regards to wine production, fermentation could take place in the same container in which it was later transported, without transvasing.[5] On the other hand, barrel production is more costly and time consuming, especially if metal hoops are used. Also, wines transported in barrels do not survive as long as wines stored in amphoras, due to the porosity of wooden casks that enable the oxidation process to continue. This is why most medieval and early modern wines quickly lost their pleasant taste.[6] The invention of Port, which is a fortified wine (initially made with the addition of brandy), was to protect wines from the Douro Valley from turning into vinegar during the long-distance journey to Britain.[7] Therefore, only wines that did not need long maturation could be kept in barrels, which excluded many ancient Italian and Eastern wines that needed several or even dozens of years to mature appropriately.[8]

4 Tchernia 1986, 285–292; Marlière 2002; Wilson 2011a, 228–229; 2011b, 37.

5 Wilson 2011a, 228–229; 2011b, 37.

6 Tchernia 1986, 31.

7 Robinson 2006, 536.

8 Ath. *Deipn.* 26d–27d (the quotation is probably from Galen); Plin. *HN* 14.78; Tchernia 1986, 30.

Archaeological evidence suggests that barrels were introduced during the late 1st c. BC, initially only in Gaul and Germania, along the Rhine and the Garonne.[9] We could, therefore, easily associate barrels with river as well as land transport, where they were used for regional exchange and the supply of Roman military camps; whether they carried wine or other products (beer and vinegar have been suggested) for the troops remains obscure. The role of barrels became more significant during the 3rd c. AD and by the end of antiquity they had replaced amphoras in the western provinces.[10] The northern part of Adriatic Italy (except *Picenum*)[11] probably started to use barrels for wine exportation relatively early, which is suggested by both early imperial literature[12] and the fact that Dressel 6A amphoras disappeared during the second half of the 1st c. AD and were not replaced by another mass-produced ceramic container in the Po Valley.[13] In what is today Emilia-Romagna, however, the so-called Forlimpopoli amphoras were still being produced during the 3rd c. AD,[14] and it is generally assumed that barrels were more likely used for local and regional, not inter-regional exchange in the Adriatic area.[15] Furthermore, in the Tyrrhenian region amphoras continued to be used for local transport during the 3rd c. AD, as indicated by discoveries of Campanian Dressel 2–4 containers in Baiae.[16] Amphoras from throughout the 3rd c. AD have been found in Roman Britain and Germania during the period when barrels were supposed to have played an important role in the western wine trade (Dressel 2–4 jars were discovered near Hadrian's Wall[17] and in Gaul). It is generally assumed that the common and extensive usage of barrels was limited to certain parts of the western provinces, which included (apart from the Po Valley and Gaul) south and central Britain, Germania (mostly along the Rhine), Africa, northern Spain (albeit in limited numbers) and probably Lusitania from the 2nd c. AD.[18] It should be mentioned, however, that the remains of barrels were

9 Marlière 2002, 174–175.

10 Tchernia 1986, 285–292; Panella, Tchernia 2002, 184. Around the 1st c. AD wine was also transported in *dolia*, which were permanently installed on a ship, see Carre 2009, 290–291; Wilson 2011a, 37; 2011b, 228–229.

11 Personal information from Prof. M.-B. Carre.

12 E.g. Strab. V 1, 8 and V 1, 12.

13 Łoś, Pietruszka 2016, 525–526.

14 Cipriano, Mazzocchin 2017, 41, fig. 3 and 4.

15 Van Limbergen 2018, 218–219.

16 Łoś, Pietruszka 2016, 525. In Baiae 13% of all containers were of north Campanian origin, see Di Giovanni 2013, 1528.

17 Arthur 1995, 245; Arthur, Williams 1992, 253–254; Williams 2004, 449.

18 Marlière 2002, 174–175; Marlière and Torres Costa 2007, 95–96; Étienne and Mayet 2000, 53.

found exclusively in a narrow strip of land between Britannia and Pannonia (predominantly on the Rhine limes), as well as in four ancient shipwrecks off the coast of Britain, Gaul and north Adriatic Italy.[19] Their usage in Spain, Italy and Africa is understood exclusively on the basis of iconography and literature, but this evidence is scarce before late antiquity.[20] At the same time, numerous types of African amphoras were produced between the 4th and 7th c. AD, when iconography and literature suggest the use of wooden casks was favoured.[21] In Vindolanda, the remains of 27 barrels were attested, 26 from France (the area of Lyon) and one of local origin. Since numerous olive oil amphoras from Spain (Dressel 20)[22] were found at the site, we would also expect to find Spanish barrels, if indeed Baetica used barrels to export wine. Similarly, if barrels were preserved on the Rhine limes we should find their remains in Africa, where the climate is much more favourable for the preservation of organic material. The lack of such evidence suggests that barrels did not totally replace amphoras in the wine trade. Moreover, in the Eastern Mediterranean barrels were unlikely to have been preferred over amphoras given that this region suffered from serious deforestation.[23] As a matter of fact, amphoras survived in the East long after the Arab conquest, while their usage is confirmed as late as during the 13th c. AD. Therefore, even if barrels were widely used for long-distance wine transportation in the Western Mediterranean—which is possible but has not yet been proven—they can only affect amphora curves for Gaul and possibly the Iberian Peninsula, as no wines were imported to Italy from Germania or Britain. Since Gallic (Gauloise 1, Gauloise 4 *similis*, and Gauloise 12) and African (Dressel 30) wine amphoras, dated to the 3rd c. AD, have been found in Italy,[24] it seems that the distortion caused by using barrels was insignificant before late antiquity.

In summary, the evidence we possess so far, coupled with the perishable nature of wooden containers, does not allow us enough of an understanding of the scale of their usage. It is possible that wooden casks were used for long-distance maritime shipping of wine (and other products) and that most of the

19 McCormick 2012, 75.

20 Marlière and Torres Costa 2007, 98.

21 For example Africana 2C and D, 3A–C, and most of Keay forms, see http://archaeologydataservice.ac.uk/archives/view/amphora_ahrb_2005/cat_amph.cfm?l=A&CFID=e8256d09-6b4e-4f13-8e43-61c93e443009&CFTOKEN=0, attested 27.09.2018.

22 Marlière and Torres Costa 2005, 229–230.

23 Harris 2009, 259; 2005, 35.

24 Bonifay 2017, 334; see also http://archaeologydataservice.ac.uk/archives/view/amphora_ahrb_2005/cat_amph.cfm?l=G&CFID=b9c505ec-c151-47c8-af3e-b6261e35d483&CFTOKEN=0, accessed 3.06.2018.

wines from the Western Mediterranean (excluding African) were exported in wooden barrels. It cannot, however, be excluded that casks were more suitable for land and river transport, hence associating them with regional exchange rather than with long-distance trade would be more reasonable.

Therefore, the disappearance of western amphoras from the assemblages discovered in Italy may be explained in two ways:

1. Western products (especially wines) were no longer imported to Italy, as the Crisis of the 3rd Century influenced agricultural production and/or commercial routes, which limited western commercial activities (except African) to local and regional exchange. For example, the 4th c. AD division of the Mediterranean trade network into two parts, namely eastern and western, as well as the regionalisation of commercial activities is suggested by pottery assemblages from Beirut and Butrint.[25] A decline of the western commercial activity is also suggested by the gradual disappearance of merchant guilds in Gaul and on the Iberian peninsula, as well as the fact that the western trade was controlled by eastern merchants.[26]
2. Western products (including wines) were imported to Italy in wooden barrels instead of amphoras, which do not preserve, and hence the archaeological record does not allow us to estimate the scale of these imports. Nevertheless, it cannot be excluded that late Roman amphoras from the west have not so far been properly recognised in the archaeological record. For example, Baetican wines were exported to Gaul (attested in Lyon and Arles) in small amphoras '*a base plana*' during the early 3rd and throughout the 4th c. AD.[27] These containers have yet to be attested in other parts of the Mediterranean, but this is difficult due to their morphological similarities to Gallic wine containers, as well as to Baetican fish sauce amphoras.[28]

Whatever explanation reflects reality, we would expect to find a considerable increase in the percentages of Eastern Mediterranean wine containers between the early/mid and late Imperial period, as they were competing against less 'archaeologically visible' wine importations. Therefore, it is worth analysing the statistics to verify whether they meet these expectations. Moreover, it is also worth checking if there were any changes in terms of percentages of different types of Eastern wines imported to Italy, and especially whether the same

25 Reynolds 2010b.
26 Pieri 2012, 31, 41.
27 Reynolds 2010a, 53.
28 Reynolds 2010a, 51.

types of wines continued to be imported. Unfortunately, late imperial contexts that contain amphora assemblages are considerably less frequent than the early imperial contexts, which is why only Rome, Aquileia, Verona, Padua and Ravenna are considered.

2 Late Roman Wines in the *Urbs*

Seven late imperial amphora deposits discovered in Rome are analysed here, namely the Palatine Hill deposit (dated between 290–313 AD), *Via Marmorata* (dated between the 4th and 7th c. AD), *Domus Tiberiana* (425–625 AD),[29] *Casa delle Vestali* (Ambiente III—500–550 AD),[30] *Basilica Hilariana* (500–650 AD),[31] the Aventine Hill (c. 650 AD)[32] and *Crypta Balbi* (7th c. AD).

The Palatine Hill deposit, known in publications as the Palatine East, was recovered from the NE slope of the hill during excavations conducted by the *Soprintendenza Archeologica di Roma* and the American Academy in Rome between 1989 and 1994. It contained fragments of 203 amphoras (the estimated number of vessels), which included 91 wine containers.[33] A deposit was also found at *Casa delle Vestali*, which became a domestic area during the late 4th c. AD and was also situated on the Palatine Hill. The amphora material, excavated by the *Universitá di Roma "La Sapienza"*, came from a waste pit in the north-eastern sector of the *atrium Vestae*, and was estimated to contain 25 diagnostic fragments. The number of wine amphoras totalled 16.[34] The archaeological site of the *Domus Tiberiana*, also located on the Palatine Hill, has already been described in Chapter 3. Late Roman material, in the form of 106 containers, was found in the area of the baths situated in the NE part of the house. Wine containers, estimated at 85, predominated in the assemblage.[35] *Basilica Hilariana*, located on the Celius Hill, was founded by a pearl merchant named Publicius Hilarius as a place of the cult of Attis and Kybele, as well as being the seat of the *dendrofori* congregation during the 2nd c. AD. It was abandoned during the first half of the 5th c. AD and sub-

29 Munzi et al. 2004, 111–117, tab. 2–5.
30 Filippi et al. 2004, 174–175, tab. 4.
31 Pacetti 2004, 439–441, tab. 4 and 5; Vatta, Bertoldi 2004, 476–479, tab. 14–17.
32 Fontana et. al. 2004, 556, tab. 1.
33 The data presented here concerns material from unit A (105), elaborated by Peña 1999, 71–100.
34 Filippi et al. 2004, 164–165, 175.
35 Munzi et al. 2004, 111–117, tab. 2–5.

sequently reoccupied by small workshops, which operated in the area until the first decades of the 6th c. AD. During the second abandonment pottery waste was deposited in this context, which included amphoras. The material that was analysed as a part of this study was discovered mostly in the NE part, the central courtyard (Ambiente XVII and II respectively) and the southern area (Ambiente VI, VII, X, XII) during excavations conducted between 1987–1989 and in 1997. These contexts provided 493 diagnostic fragments of amphoras dated between 500–550 AD and 318 fragments dated between 550–650 AD. These included 293 diagnostic parts of wine containers dated between 500–550 AD and 240 dated between 550–650 AD.[36] The Aventine Hill deposit was discovered in the area of *via Sant'Alberto Magno* and *largo Arrigo VII* (saggio B) by the *Soprintendenza Archeologica di Roma* in 1989. During late antiquity a *domus signorile* existed in the area, which was abandoned in the late 7th c. AD. Amphoras, estimated at 337 diagnostic fragments, were among pottery waste that was deposited in the house during its final phase of existence. Wine amphoras were in the majority, providing 216 diagnostic fragments.[37] Finally, *Crypta Balbi* comprises an architectural complex adjacent to the ancient Theatre of Balbus. This context provided the highest number of containers, at least 1588, dated to the 7th c. AD. Most of them, 1167 in total, were classified as wine amphoras.[38]

Table 13 and Figure 27 demonstrate that percentages of Eastern Mediterranean wine containers in Rome during late antiquity were rather stable (35–40%). Contrarily to what was expected they did not grow considerably between the mid and late Imperial age, but decreased at the turn of the 3rd and 4th c. AD. However, as mentioned in Chapter 3, the sample from the early 3rd c. AD was extremely limited, thus it may not be entirely reliable. Without taking this into account, one may notice that percentages of Eastern Mediterranean wines imported to Italy between the 2nd and 7th c. AD did not change considerably and oscillated around 40%. This means that the lack of western amphoras in the archaeological evidence had no impact on the proportional share of eastern wine containers. This might suggest that Eastern Mediterranean exports had already reached their maximum during the 2nd c. AD, and that viticultural productivity in the region could not be increased. The Roman demand for wines was satisfied with importations from new regions, such as Calabria, and increased importations from Africa.

---

36 Pacetti 2004, 435, 440–441, tab. 4–5; Vatta, Bertoldi 2004, 458, 477–479, tab. 14–17.

37 Fontana et. al. 2004, 544–546, 556, tab. 1.

38 Saquì 2002. For details regarding the *Via Marmorata* deposit see Chapter 3.

TABLE 13 Provenance of wine amphoras in Rome (numbers and %)

	290–315 AD		350–550 AD		550–700 AD	
Eastern	32	35,16%	252	43,22%	706	39,90%
Italian	18	19,78%	7	1,2%	2	0,11%
Calabrian/Sicilian	41	45,05%	128	21,96%	475	26,85%
African	0	0%	196	33,62%	586	33,13%
Total	**91**	**99,99%**	**583**	**100%**	**1769**	**99,99%**

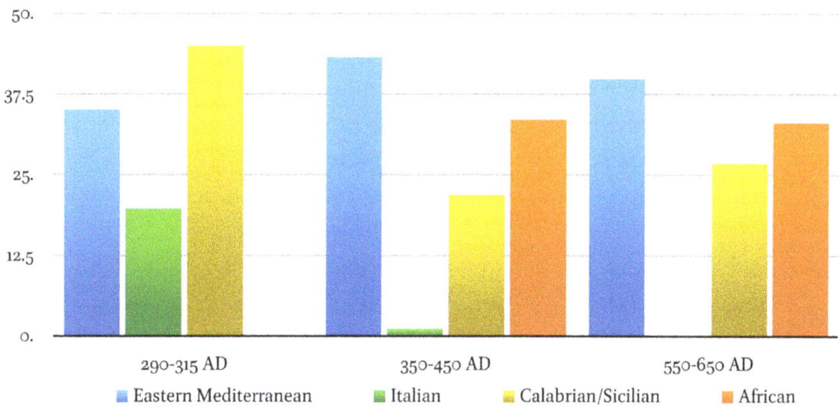

FIGURE 27 Provenance of wine amphoras in Rome (%)

It is interesting that there were no African wine amphoras discovered in the Palatine East deposit (dated between 290 and 315 AD), even though their percentages in deposits dated after 350 AD is high. African wine containers, especially during the 7th c. AD, were represented mostly by *spatheia* jars, which were not attested in unit A(105) on the Palatine Hill. Wine as a content is supposed for *Spatheion* 2 and 3 forms, but the capacity of both these jars was small (varying between 0,5 l. and 4 l.) compared to the capacity of other jars; containers from Asia Minor could carry at least 6 l., while those from the Levant could carry as much as 20–25 l. Therefore, the real volume of wines from Africa must have been at least half that of imports from the Eastern Mediterranean. Overall, it seems that from the early Imperial age until late antiquity the Eastern Mediterranean was the main wine supplier to Rome and no other region could compete with it.

However, we may notice that there has been a considerable change among Eastern wine suppliers to Rome (Tab. 14, Fig. 28). During the early Imperial age, the south-Aegean islands, particularly Crete, dominated the wine trade between Italy and the East. The 3rd c. AD saw the dominance of Kapitän 1 and 2, which might have been produced in the Aegean, in Anatolia or even in the Black Sea area.[39] However, during late antiquity, the Aegean region lost its significance, as the only Aegean wine containers imported to Rome are of the Samos Cistern Type variant, which appear rarely (between 3–14%), and were probably produced not only on Samos itself, but also in Anatolia.[40] Furthermore, from the late 4th c. AD Palestine and especially Gaza[41] entered the scene. Also, Egyptian containers started to be more popular in Italy from the 6th c. AD onward than they were during previous centuries. This pattern is confirmed by data from other contexts, which due to the state of publication, could not be included in this study,[42] namely: *Cripta di S. Bonaventura* (250–300 AD),[43] the *tabernae* next to the Temple of *Magna Mater* (trench O and A—350–400 AD, trench I and L—420–440 AD, trench P—430–475 AD),[44] *Schola Praeconum* I (425–455 AD),[45] *Schola Praeconum* II (500–550 AD),[46] *Domus de Gaudentius* (500–550 AD), *Forum Romanum* (area NE, ambiente D—600–700 AD),[47] *Crypta Balbi* (the Mithraeum—550–600 AD)[48] and *Vigna Barberini* (sector D—540/550–580/590 AD).[49] These contexts also show that during the second half of the 3rd c. AD Eastern importations in Rome were represented mostly by Kapitän 1 and 2, and Anatolian Agora 56–66/LR3 containers, while in the subsequent century their role diminished and the Oriental amphoras LRA1 and LRA4 became

39 Panella 1986, 617; Keay 1984, 137; Bezeczky 2013, 149; Reynolds 2010b, 90.

40 I classify them simply as Aegean due to the lack of reliable evidence that could disprove this theory. However, a western-Anatolian provenance has also been suggested, see Roman Amphorae: a digital resource University of Southampton, 2005 (updated 2014), https://archaeologydataservice.ac.uk/archives/view/amphora_ahrb_2005/details.cfm?id=287&CFID=f661b1c4-412b-4638-b8ef-1ef4447b09e9&CFTOKEN=0; accessed 17.05.2019.

41 Gazan amphoras (Almagro 54) were already being produced during the 2nd c. AD, but they did not appear in the West until the end of the 4th c. AD.

42 This is due to the fact that exact numbers have not been published, we only know the share they enjoyed among the total number of containers (which included non-wine carrying jars). See e.g. Carignani, Pacetti 1989b, 610–613; Remolà i Vallverdú 2000; Carsana, Del Vecchio 2010, 460–461; De Simone, Martucci 2016, 129, fig. 4; Carsana, D'Amico, Del Vecchio 2007.

43 Carignani, Pacetti 1989b, 614, tav. II.

44 Carignani, Ciotola, Pacetti 1986, 39, tab. 1. Carignani, Pacetti 1989a, 11, fig. 2; Carignani, Pacetti 1989b, 614, tav. II.

45 Whitehouse et al. 1982, 60.

46 Whitehouse et al. 1985, 178.

47 Paganelli 2004, 191, graf. 4.

48 Saguì, Coletti 2004, 244, graf. 3, 261, graf. 4, 268, graf. 5.

49 Rizzo et al. 2004, 78–79, tab. 3 and graf. 2.

more notable. From the 5th c. AD these Oriental importations continued, but they were accompanied by LRA5–6,[50] which shows the growing role of the *Oriens* in supplying wine to Rome during late antiquity. Amphora findings from Campania (Naples and Pollena Trocchia) show similar results. The layers dated to the 4th c. AD yielded AC 1 and Agora G199, as well as early forms of LRA1 and LRA3. During the subsequent centuries, LRA1, LRA3, LRA4 LRA5–6, LRA7 and Samos Cistern Type containers were attested in Naples, whereas LRA1 and LRA4 appeared in Pollena Trocchia.[51] However, it should be noted that the total percentage of Eastern Mediterranean amphoras was very low in Naples, merely 6%.[52] Considering that Aegean amphoras were considerably less numerous during late antiquity than they were during the earlier centuries of the empire, while Oriental products gained much more importance, one may conclude that late Roman commercial networks did not follow in the footsteps of their predecessors. Moreover, the disappearance of Kapitän 1 and 2 amphoras suggests that little continuity existed between the 3rd c. AD and late antiquity.

It is surprising that no jars of Cretan origin have been attested in the analysed contexts, since the island was the main wine supplier to Rome during the early Imperial age. However, it seems that Cretan wine importations to Rome stopped sometime during the 3rd c. AD, which was when Kapitän 1 and 2 amphoras appeared. Although fragments associated with AC1 found in Gortyna indicate that Crete produced ceramic transport containers in the 6th and 7th c. AD,[53] these containers are found nowhere besides Crete. It has been suggested that during the 5th c. AD, LRA2 might have also been manufactured on Crete, besides Chios, Cos,[54] Argos[55] and Samos,[56] but as mentioned above, this amphora type probably carried olive oil not wine. It seems, therefore, that from the mid-3rd and throughout the 4th c. AD Cretan amphoras were not attested in the Western Mediterranean. Fragments of late Cretan containers did appear (albeit occasionally) from the mid-5th c. AD, for example in Rome, Marseille, Tarragona. According to Reynolds this indicates a certain reestablishment of

50 Carignani, Ciotola, Pacetti 1986, 39, tab. 1; Carignani, Pacetti 1989a, 11–12, fig. 2; Carignani, Pacetti 1989b, 610–613; Remolà i Vallverdú 2000, 212–213. In *Schola Praeconum* I and II percentages of LRA3 were higher than elsewhere, see Whitehouse et al. 1982, 60; 1985, 178.

51 Arthur 1985, 250–256, tab. 16.1, 16.2 and 16.3; Carsana, Del Vecchio 2010, 460–461; De Simone, Martucci 2016, 129, fig. 4; Carsana, D'Amico, Del Vecchio 2007, 424–425.

52 Carsana, Del Vecchio 2017, 409, fig. 3.

53 Marangou-Lerat 1995, 160.

54 Reynolds 2010b, 95.

55 Pieri 2002, 130.

56 Pieri 2005, 91. Cnidus and various Black Sea regions might have also produced this container, see Bezeczky 2013, 161.

TABLE 14 Provenance of Eastern Mediterranean wine amphoras in Rome (numbers and %)

	290–315 AD		350–550 AD		550–700 AD	
Aegean	1	3,13%	3	1,19%	98	13,88%
Anatolian	6	18,75%	42	16,67%	133	18,84%
Kapitän 1 and 2	24	75%	0	0%	0	0%
LRA1	0	0%	56	22,22%	91	12,89%
Gaza (LR4)	1	3,13%	83	32,94%	149	21,1%
Palestine (LR5–6, M334)	0	0%	68	26,98%	204	28,9%
Egypt	0	0%	0	0	31	4,39%
Total	**32**	**100,01%**	**252**	**100%**	**706**	**100%**

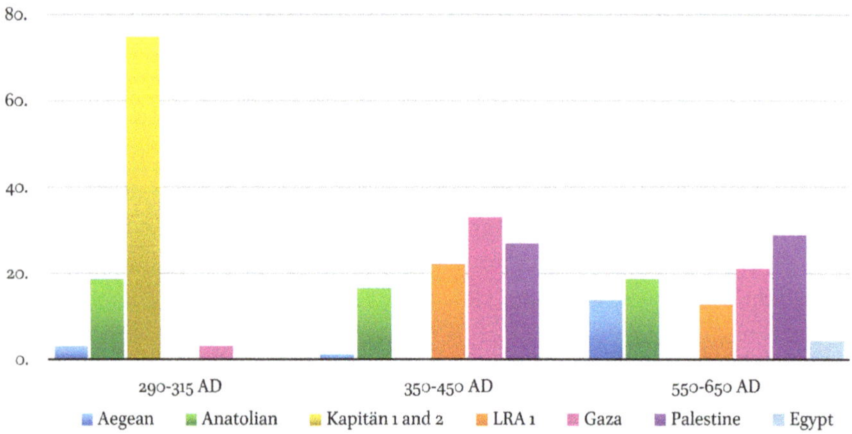

FIGURE 28 Provenance of Eastern Mediterranean wine amphoras in Rome (%)

commercial links between the island and the West.[57] Nonetheless, it should be emphasised that Cretan jars were only identified in *Magna Mater* in the context dated to the second half of the 5th c. AD in very low quantities (less than 1% of the assemblage),[58] and that they are absent in other late imperial amphora assemblages discovered in Rome.

The almost total disappearance of Cretan amphoras from Rome may be associated with the changes in *annona* provisions to Rome. From the Trajan age onward Tunisia gradually started to play a more important role in sup-

57 Reynolds 2010b, 96, 99.
58 Panella et al. 2010, 64–67.

plying Rome, which according to Reynolds had an impact on Baetican olive oil importations, which were reduced.[59] Is it therefore possible that the growing role of Tunisian grain resulted in the decrease of Egyptian importations? This decrease could be associated with the less abundant flooding of the Nile attested between 150–299 AD, which resulted in a shortage of cultivated land that made the 'river's gift' less beneficial for grain harvest.[60] If this was so, the decrease in Cretan wine importations, which owed their success on the Roman market to them being carried on *annona* ships, would be perfectly understandable. Without the diminished freight charges Cretan wine would be too expensive to be widely available, and as it was *mulsum pauperis*, it would not be popular among the wealthy. On the other hand, if surplus wine continued to be produced on the island its producers should look for new markets, but as suggested by the archaeological material nothing like this happened.[61] During the Roman age Crete did not export its goods to the East on a large scale;[62] however, it is impossible to verify whether such exports ceased due to the increase in Levantine wine production, or simply because the island was no longer able to produce a surplus.

One may wonder whether climate change impacted upon Cretan viticulture. The Cretan climate is very sensitive to variations caused by the North Atlantic Oscillation (NAO) and El Niño Southern Oscillation (ENSO),[63] while viticulture is generally a very climate-sensitive area of agriculture. The Roman Climate Optimum dated between 200 BC–200 AD might have aided the growth and development of Cretan viticulture, while the climatic instability that occurred between 200 and 400 AD[64] might have led it to ruin. However, the climatic change also influenced Palestine, where several droughts during the 3rd and early 4th c. AD were attested, but they did not lead to the destruction of viticulture. Contrarily, a humid period was attested in the region from the late 4th and 5th c. AD, which is probably one of the reasons why the area blossomed during late antiquity.[65]

Finally, it is interesting that Rome continued to import high numbers of wine amphoras, even though the population of the city contracted considerably. It is assumed that during the 2nd c. AD the city had a population of roughly one

59 Reynolds 2010a, 17.

60 McCormick 2012, 189.

61 However, Cretan amphoras dated between 525–670 AD have recently been identified in the Black Sea region, see Sazanov 2014.

62 Reynolds 2010a, 71.

63 Moody 2005, 455–459.

64 For climate changes in the Roman age see McCormick et al. 2012, 174–191.

65 McCormick 2012, 188.

million inhabitants, which decreased to 800,000 around 400 AD. The transfer of the capital to Ravenna and Constantinople as well as the Vandal raids might have resulted in the population shrinking to just 100,000 by 500 AD.[66] Other scholars are even more pessimistic, estimating the Roman population during the 5th c. AD at 350,000 and during the 6th c. AD at a mere 60,000 inhabitants,[67] or even as little as 58,000 around 419 AD.[68] Notwithstanding their drastically reduced numbers, Rome's inhabitants continued to import considerable quantities of wines from the Eastern Mediterranean, which suggests a long-lasting tradition. Also, this is further evidence that confirms these wines were popular, not aristocratic drinks, since their consumption continued when the ruling elite and the imperial court left the city.

3 Late Roman Wines in Adriatic Italy

Four cities in north-Adriatic Italy provided late Roman amphoras, namely Aquileia, Verona, Padua and Ravenna. However, since the publications of archaeological material from these sites did not allow for more narrow chronological units to be distinguished, the amphora statistics refer to the whole of late antiquity, stretching from 300 to 700 AD approximately. Therefore, even though late antiquity was not a monolithic time period, and numerous historical events probably influenced several variables concerning the pattern of wine consumption, these variables cannot be traced.

Except Ravenna, each city is represented by only one late Imperial deposit. For example, the synthesis for Aquileia comprises only the material from *Casa delle Bestie Ferite*—a late imperial aristocratic *domus* complete with mosaics and an abside. The *domus* was excavated by archaeologists from the University of Padua, who found 603 amphora fragments, including 462 diagnostic fragments, which belonged to at least 179 containers.[69] *Capitolium* in Verona provided 302 amphora fragments dated to the late Imperial age, more than

66 O'Donnel 2009, 48.
67 Durliat 1990, 117, fig. 1.
68 Russel 1958, 73.
69 Bueno, Mantovani, Novello 2012, 159–161. Containers found in late contexts at *Via Bolivia* and in the Area to the East of the Forum were excluded, as their publications often do not specify whether they refer to diagnostic or non-diagnostic fragments, see Ceazzi, Del Brusco 2014; Verzár-Bass 1991; 1994. The discovery from the area of the *Grandi Terme* was also excluded due to the preliminary state of publication, see Rubinich, Braidotti 2007. Finally, a publication of an amphora deposit found in *via dei Patriarchi* did not provide numbers of containers, see Ventura, Braidotti 2017.

half of them (164) served for wine transport.[70] At the same time, late amphoras in Padua came from *Battisero di Padova*, where 89 diagnostic amphora fragments were discovered, 29 of them belonging to wine containers.[71] Finally, a high number of containers (8200 EVE) were discovered during excavations conducted by the University of Bologna's archaeology department in the Harbour Area of Classe in Ravenna. The amphoras, including 5189 wine jars, were found in a large complex of warehouses.[72]

Table 15 and Figure 29 demonstrate that percentages of late Roman wine amphoras in Aquileia, Verona, Padua and Ravenna in general terms confirm the pattern observed in Rome. Three regions supplied Adriatic Italy with wine, namely Africa, the East and Calabria/Sicilia; the latter, however, was of little importance. At first sight African products were a much more important rival to Eastern Mediterranean wines in the Adriatic area than they were in Rome. This especially concerns Aquileia and Verona, where African wine amphora percentages exceeded more than half of all wine containers. This may be due to the fact that Aquileia was a harbour city, which received and stored commodities destined for the Danubian and Transalpine provinces.[73] It cannot thus be excluded that until 429 AD African wines reached the harbour together with African grain, the supply of which was organised by the *annona*. These products, or at least some of them, were later sent to Roman military camps in the Danubian provinces, instead of being distributed among the inhabitants of the Venetian Lagoon and the lower Po Valley. As with Cretan wine, which according to Tchernia often arrived in Rome on *annona* ships free from freight charges,[74] African wines might have enjoyed privileged transportation costs in Aquileia.

It should, however, be noted that most of the African wine jars found in these cities were of the *spatheia* type,[75] the capacity of which was at least four times smaller than that of other amphora forms (with the exception of LRA3); thus the real volume of wine imported to Aquileia from the East and from Africa might have in fact been comparable. Therefore, it is possible to conclude that Eastern Mediterranean wines were similarly popular in Rome, Verona and Aquileia, satisfying more than 40% of the demand. Their dramatic predominance in Padua (78,57%) may be due to the very small sample size (29 wine con-

70 Bruno 2008, 373–386.
71 Ganzarolli 2015, 80–127.
72 Cirelli 2014, 541, 552 fig. 9, cf. also an earlier publication in Augenti et al. 2007, 265–274, fig. 14, 17, 24 and 33.
73 Carre 2007c, 623.
74 Tchernia 2011, 345–348.
75 Larger containers, such as Africana II A and D and Agora M254 were considerably less frequent, estimated at 10 and 13 diagnostic fragments respectively.

TABLE 15 Provenance of wine amphoras in Aquileia, Verona, Padua and Ravenna (numbers and %)

	Aquileia		Verona		Padua		Ravenna	
Calabrian/Sicilian	7	2,77%	0	0%	3	10,71%	315	6,07%
Eastern	115	45,63%	66	40,74%	22	78,57%	3981	76,72%
African	130	51,58%	96	59,26%	3	10,71%	893	17,21%
Total	**252**	**99,98%**	**162**	**100%**	**28**	**100%**	**5189**	**100%**

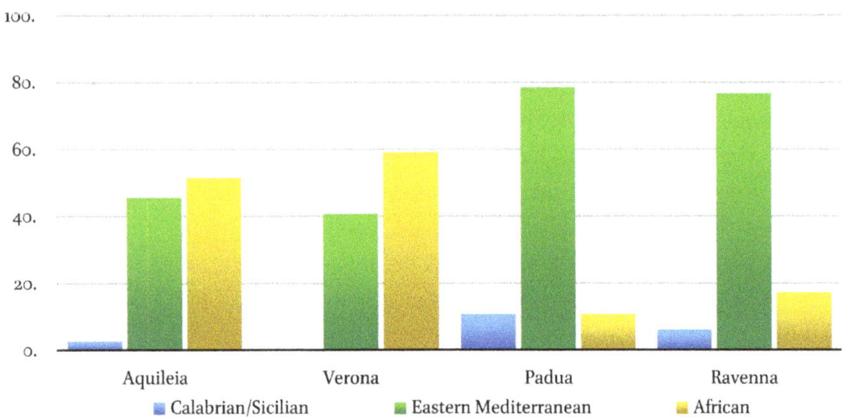

FIGURE 29 Provenance of wine amphoras in Aquileia, Verona, Padua and Ravenna (%)

tainers), which thus is likely to be biased. On the other hand, it agrees with the percentages from Ravenna, where an almost identical proportion (76,72%) of eastern wine amphoras was discovered. Considering that African wine jars in Ravenna were represented by the *spatheia* form, whose volume is limited, one may conclude that the Eastern Mediterranean was almost the exclusive source of wine for this city. However, all cylindrical African amphorae were counted together in the publication regarding the Ravenna deposit and it is unknown whether they included the forms Keay 25.1–3, which might have also transported wine.[76] Therefore, the special position of the Eastern Mediterranean in supplying Padua and Ravenna with wine is uncertain.

Table 16 and Figure 30 show that the shift from Aegean (Samos Cistern Type) to Cypriot/Cilician (LRA 1) and Gazan (LRA 4) wines that was noted in Rome

76 For the content of these amphoras see Woodworth et al. 2015.

TABLE 16 Provenance of Eastern Mediterranean wine amphoras in Aquileia, Verona, Padua and Ravenna (numbers and %)

	Aquileia		Verona		Padua		Ravenna	
Aegean	1	0,87%	0	0%	0	0%	149	3,74%
Anatolian	32	27,83%	7	10,60%	2	9,09%	980	24,62%
LRA1	52	45,22%	11	16,66%	6	27,27%	819	20,57%
Gaza	26	22,61%	48	72,73%	14	63,64%	1427	35,84%
Palestine	4	3,48%	0	0%	0	0%	552	13,87%
Egypt	0	0%	0	0%	0	0%	54	1,36%
Total	115	100,01%	66	100%	22	100%	3981	100

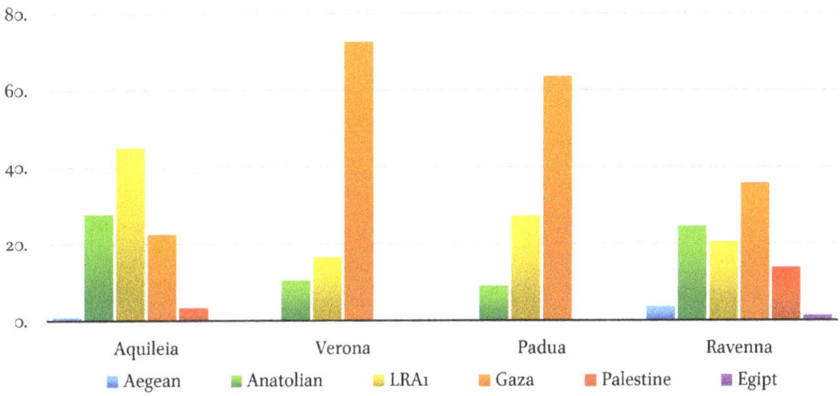

FIGURE 30 Provenance of Eastern Mediterranean wine amphoras in Aquileia, Verona, Padua and Ravenna (%)

may also be observed in the north-Adriatic region, though again we are not certain what the share of south-Aegean containers was within the total number of LRA1. In Padua and Verona neither Agora M273 nor Samos Cistern Type amphoras, which did appear in Aquileia and Ravenna, were attested. Moreover, non-Gazan amphoras from Palestine and Egypt have not so far been discovered in these cities, whilst they were also present in Aquileia and Ravenna.[77] This means that Aquileia and Ravenna enjoyed the widest range of Eastern Mediterranean wines, which must have been due to their special character. The former

77 The presence of Egyptian containers in Aquileia was confirmed by findings from *Via Bolivia*, and excavations on the eastern side of the forum, which as mentioned above, were excluded from this study.

was a large harbour city, which must have enjoyed access to more diversified products than inland sites such as Verona and Padua. Ravenna housed a seat of the imperial court for most of the 5th c. AD, which resulted in a wider variety of goods being imported to satisfy the demands of its sophisticated inhabitants. Notwithstanding these differences, studies of Eastern Mediterranean amphoras demonstrated that late antiquity saw a considerable increase in the role that Oriental wines played in Italian wine commerce, both in the Tyrrhenian and Adriatic regions.

4 ORBIS Transport Costs and Wine Importations

Looking at transport costs provided by ORBIS (Fig. 21 and 22) and wine importations to Italy during late antiquity one may be surprised that the pattern observed during the early empire changed utterly. It is true that the lack of amphoras from Gaul, Tarraconensis or Baetica may be easily explained by the supposed use of barrels for transportations of wines from these regions. However, as has been noted in the first part of this chapter, long-distance maritime transport of wines from these areas has not so far been proven, so it is equally possible that western provinces no longer exported to Italy due to political instability in the West. Africa was the exception, since during late antiquity the role of modern Tunisia in Italian supply grew considerably. However, the most notable change is observed in the importations from the East: the Aegean region lost its significance, while the role of Palestine, Cyprus and Cilicia increased significantly. This may be a surprise considering that, according to ORBIS, importing from these areas was quite expensive due to transportation costs which were twice as high as importing from the Aegean region.

According to modern economic theories, if transport costs are the main price-determining factor, this will affect the price of an expensive product proportionally less than the price of a cheap product.[78] Therefore, it might have been profitable to import high-quality or luxurious wines from the Near East to Italy, but mass beverages should be bought from those areas with low transport costs. This can be observed in Italy during the early Imperial age, which means that profitability was the main factor governing wine supply and that market forces played a crucial part in the economy of the empire until the mid-3rd c. AD. It seems, however, that after the crisis of the 3rd century price lost its leading role in organising commercial exchange, at least in the case of wines from

78 Silver 2009, 440.

the Eastern Mediterranean. Consequently, other factors, such as the orders of the state, must have started to play much more important part in long-distance wine trade. This suggests that the nature of the Roman economy after the crisis changed towards a more controlled system.

5 Conclusions

The analysis of percentages of late antique wine amphoras in Italy allows for two important conclusions to be drawn:

1. The percentages of Eastern Mediterranean wines imported to Italy did not grow between the early Imperial age and late antiquity, which means that the disappearance of western amphoras from the archaeological record had little impact on Eastern wine importations. The gap, thus, must have been filled with increased imports from Africa and Calabria/Sicily. This, however, does not mean that the volume of importations from the East remained the same between the early/mid and late Imperial age. On the contrary, given that the population of Rome contracted dramatically during late antiquity, the real volume of Eastern Mediterranean wine imports must have fallen accordingly. Even so, Eastern wines continued to be present on Roman tables when the ruling elite left the city, which indicates that the consumption of these wines was common and widespread among the lower social orders. Also, it demonstrates the important and long-lasting role that these wines played in the Roman economy.
2. There was a change from Aegean (Rhodian, Cretan and Coan) to Cilician, Cypriot and especially Levantine wines observed both in Rome and in north-Adriatic Italy during late antiquity. This is very interesting, because the areas that were marginal in terms of wine supply to Italy during the early and mid-Imperial age, became much more important during the final centuries of antiquity. It is worth mentioning that the pattern of wine importations in Italy does not differ from what we observe in different areas of the Mediterranean, where LRA1, LRA3 and LRA4 dominate amphora assemblages.[79] Cypriot and Cilician versions of LRA1 were the most numerous from the 4th until the end of the 6th c. AD in Butrint and Beirut,[80] as well as in late imperial layers in Ephesus.[81] In Alexandria

79 Reynolds 2010a, b.
80 Reynolds 2010b.
81 Komar 2016.

(Building 12, Sector G) 80% of LRA1 were of Cypriot origin, while 15% were attributed to Cilicia, which leaves little room for Aegean or Anatolian products.[82]

A quick look at the development of Palestinian, Cypriot and Cilician viticulture and wine commerce is necessary in order to have a better understanding of the increased popularity as wine suppliers these areas enjoyed during late antiquity. Palestine was producing wines from at least the Phoenician times, but these products, which were highly thought of throughout antiquity, were not exported in large quantities to the Western Mediterranean before the 4th c. AD. Between the 4th and 7th c. AD this region experienced considerable population growth, while settlement density reached levels that were unprecedented and were not seen again until the 20th century.[83] These anomalous increases were usually associated with the adoption of Christianity as the empire's main religion, and the transformation of Palestine as the Holy Land and all that entailed. It was assumed that thanks to pilgrimage and the influx of both private and public capital the province became rich, which attracted new settlers, resulting in local population growth.[84] Recently however, the role of Christianity appears to have been exaggerated, as a number of archaeological surveys suggest that both the population and the settlement started to grow during the 2nd c. AD, and that this was associated with Palestine becoming a Roman province, rather than with the expansion of Christianity.[85] On the other hand, Christians might have been more interested in consuming wines from the Holy Land, which resulted in their appearance on Italian markets. Moreover, 'holy wines' were probably most appreciated for their purpose in church services.[86] For example, Gazan amphoras are sometimes the only eastern containers discovered on western sites that had religious character.[87] Therefore, the development of Christianity might have been an element that fuelled Palestinian viticulture. At the same time, the population growth in Palestine during late antiquity ensured a workforce for the labour-intensive agricultural activities of viticulture and winemaking. Finally, pilgrims, were second most commonly attested travellers (after envoys) during early Middle Ages. However, the boundaries between pilgrims and merchants are rather fluid: pilgrims indubitably sailed aboard commercial vessels, while merchants sometimes pretended to be

---

82 All deposits from Building 12, Sector G, see Kingsley, Decker 2001, 4.
83 Bar 2004, 307; Kingsley 2001, 44.
84 Avi-Yonah 1958, 41–49.
85 Bar 2004.
86 Arthur 1998, 162; Reynolds 2010a, 84.
87 Pieri 2012, 37.

pilgrims to avoid tolls.[88] Consequently, pilgrimages might have had a positive impact on the connectivity of the Holy Land with the Western Mediterranean.

These factors, however, could not have played a key role and are not sufficient to explain the extraordinary popularity of Gazan and Palestinian wine imports in Italy. Furthermore, it is unlikely that they influenced the increase in Egyptian, Cypriot and Cilician wine importations. Cypriot prosperity during late antiquity is indicated by shipwrecks, which show that maritime trade in the southern part of the island grew considerably during the late Roman age, starting probably around the 4th c. AD. At the same time, settlement intensification in the Cypriot countryside was observed, which also suggests economic well-being. Most of the attested wrecks consisted of small ships, which indicates the existence of local and regional exchange rather than long-distance trade.[89] However, deep water surveys have not been conducted, and, considering the high percentages of Cypriot and Cilician wine amphorae in both Italy and the Eastern Mediterranean during this period, it seems that interregional long-distance trade also took place, on an intensive scale. Importations of LRA1 amphoras during the 5th and 6th c. AD in Dichin and other military sites link Cypriot wines with the *annona* supply system. This link is strengthened by the fact that in 537 AD Justinian created *quaestura exercitus*, which united the provinces of Lower Moesia and Scythia with Caria, the Cyclades and Cyprus in order to facilitate the supply of the *annona militaris* to the Lower Danube frontier garrisons.[90] At the same time, epigraphic evidence suggests that Cilician merchants in the 5th c. AD paid a lower levy than other *naukleroi*,[91] which might also suggest their association with the exchange of foodstuffs for state purposes. As a matter of fact, state shippers usually enjoyed custom-free status,[92] which made their personal commercial goods more competitive due to the lower price. Therefore, it cannot be excluded that the commercial success of Cypriot and Cilician wines was linked to the *annona*. On the one hand, they were distributed within the frame of the state supply system. On the other hand, the ships supplying the state might have carried surpluses, which were sold duty-free on the market independent from the state.

Notwithstanding these factors, the increase in importations of Oriental wines may also be associated with the changes in the organisation of the empire during late antiquity. It has been noted that the period of the late 3rd

88 McCormick 2001, 270–281.
89 Leidwanger 2013, 188–189.
90 Swan 2004, 381–382; Reynolds 2005, 577.
91 Decker 2005, 54–55.
92 McCormick 2001, 90.

and early 4th c. AD is characterised by a general scarcity of ceramic assemblages. This, together with the lack of evidence for private building activity, may be interpreted as a sign of the crisis caused by the civil wars and barbarian raids. According to Reynolds, the decrease in commercial activity during this period along with the regionalisation that followed might have been associated with political instability. In such an environment merchants lost confidence, despite Diocletian's attempts to create a New Order. Moreover, the administrative division of the empire into East and West entailed a similar regionalisation of the economy, the process of which began even earlier in the 3rd c. AD.[93] Subsequently, in 330 AD the capital was transferred from Rome to Byzantium, which during this century became a major consumption centre. Reynolds sees the growth of the role of Constantinople as the main catalyst for the development of the Levant, and other areas of the Byzantine East, but notes that Levantine trade had already intensified during the second half of the 3rd c. AD.[94] In the new capital, like in Rome, *annona civica* took care of bread distribution, which was possible thanks to the redirecting of Egyptian grain to the 'New Rome'. Moreover, several consumption goods reached Constantinople as 'taxes in kind' from *Diocesis Orientis*. In turn, *Diocesis Africae* became the sole supplier to Rome.[95] According to Pieri, a decline of production in the West as well as "*the exceptional commercial draw that Constantinople exerted in the East beginning in the mid-fourth century, prompted the emergence of new regional areas of production that had previously been largely dormant*".[96] The growth in significance of the new capital at the expense of Rome affected the major trade routes involved with the supply of grain—ships that transported grain from Alexandria no longer travelled westward via Crete, but eastward via Palestine, Syria, Cyprus and Cilicia, transporting products from these areas to Ephesus and areas further to the north and west.

Furthermore, considering the unstable situation in many western provinces during the late Roman age, it seems that large consumption centres, such as Rome, needed more supplies from the East in order to satisfy their demand for wine. This might have provided a catalyst for Eastern Mediterranean regions that previously had no western markets for their goods to increase production in order to satisfy the demand from the West. As suggested by the ORBIS model (Fig. 21), the costs involved with transporting goods from Cyprus, Cilicia, and the Levant were high, so it was probably unprofitable to export products from

93 Reynolds 2010a, 142.
94 Reynolds 2010b, 98.
95 Panella 1993, 635; Reynolds 2010a, 74.
96 Pieri 2012, 31.

these areas to Rome in large quantities, and hence they had to limit themselves to local and regional markets. However, when more ships started to transport Egyptian grain to Byzantium (instead of Rome), these areas became privileged, as they were located near to the main grain route and could more easily sell their products to the new capital. The part of Oriental production that was a surplus on ships carrying goods to Byzantium might have been sold in one of eastern ports, from where it could be later sent towards the West.

Changes that occurred in the supply of Eastern Mediterranean wine to Italy may also be associated with changes in the nature of the Roman economy. In 1985 P. Arthur noted that the distribution of Samos Cistern Type amphoras in main Byzantine *castra* and towns suggests that wines that they transported reached Italy through state directives. Moreover, the increase in percentages of African amphoras between the 4th and 5th c. AD in Naples together with a reduction in their typological diversity led him to conclude that Campania became less self-sufficient and that the Roman state started to play a more important role in regulating commerce.[97] However, he assumed that the general distribution of amphoras during the first half of the 6th c AD "*largely expresses the existence of market forces, through a complex network that involved the entire Mediterranean basin*". More limited movement of goods, which suggests the prevalence of transfers governed by institutions, has not, according to him, been observed until the end of this century.[98] In light of the evidence provided by this study, it seems that the market forces lost their leading role much earlier. While viewing the amphora statistics compared with the ORBIS model of the Roman world (Fig. 21 and 22) one will see that during the early Imperial age Italy imported wines from areas that had low transport costs, such as Baetica and Tarraconensis, south Gaul, north Africa and the Aegean region. Oriental beverages were rare in both the capital and Adriatic Italy, probably because their transportation costs were too high for profit to be made. However, soon after the Crisis of the 3rd century Italy started to import from the Eastern Mediterranean almost exclusively oriental wines, the transport cost of which (approximated by ORBIS) was high. This means that non-market factors started to play a dominant role in commercial exchange.

State interference in the commercial activities of late antique urban centres, outside of the normal profit mechanism, is postulated by a number of scholars. According to Dark, it might have been decisions made by the state that restored prosperity and ensured the well-being of the Roman economy after

97 Arthur 1985; 1998, 175; 2002, 128–130.
98 Arthur 1998, 157, 174–175.

the Crisis of the 3rd c. AD. The role of the state in organising the production and exchange of goods might have been so important that he refers to the economy during late antiquity as a 'command economy'.[99] Other scholars, however, are sceptical towards this theory, arguing rather that the late Roman economy "*comprised a series of more or less regulated regional markets in which the state intervened for its own purposes*".[100] Notwithstanding, no one really doubts that the role of the state and its influence on commercial exchange increased after Diocletian's reforms. At the same time, market forces and profit-oriented transactions must have lost their position as leading agents in commercial exchange. Obviously, these forces did not disappear completely, as there is no evidence that implies the state had total control over the production and distribution of Eastern wines or other goods.[101] However, the role of the market did diminish due to the limitations imposed by state regulations.[102] We should keep in mind that during the 3rd c. AD the grain dole was changed to bread, that permanent olive oil distributions started under Septimius Severus, and that around 270 AD Aurelian added pork and wine to the variety of goods distributed by the state.[103] In consequence, during the second half of the 4th c. AD a *canon vinarius* (a system of wine provisions to Rome) was elaborated, and this wine was sold with a 25% discount.[104] This shows that from the late 3rd c. AD there was growing state intervention in the wine business. Of course, this intervention concerns only wine supplied to Rome and Constantinople; however, these cities were the biggest Mediterranean markets. According to McCormick, the role of *annona* provisions had a crucial impact on trade organisation during late antiquity, because it "*subsidized and encouraged trade which went beyond the movement of state levies. The system reduced transport costs substantially by decreasing capital outlays for the ships in at least some cases, by diminishing risk and guaranteeing predictable business rhythms, routes, and rates (albeit lower ones) aboard ships loaded with state supplies, on which private merchandise might literally have traveled piggyback and duty-free*".[105] If, as suggested by the *Codex Theodosianus*, the prices of wines included in the *canon vinarius* were set artificially, the high transport costs associated with Oriental wines

99 Dark 2007, 3.
100 Sarris 2015, 171.
101 Kingsley 2001, 57. See also McCormick 2012 for the evidence that market conditions were present during late antiquity.
102 However, Pieri 2012 argues that the late Roman economy was 'a fundamentally commercial economy'.
103 Erdkamp 2013, 267; after Hist. Aug. *Septimius Severus* 18.3 and *Aurelian* 35.2 and 48.1.
104 Interpretation of the passage CTh 11.2.2 by Peña 1999, 173–179.
105 McCormick 2001, 87–92, quotation on page 90.

were no longer as important as they used to be, and these wines could easily travel to Italy. To sum up, the change in Eastern Mediterranean wine imports suggests the transformation of the late antique economy after the mid-3rd c. AD from a free market towards a more controlled version.

The state is one possible agent that might have maintained control; the church might have been another. This institution probably played a part in the distribution of goods from the south of the Levant to the West. Being free from *collatio lustralis*, the church could offer more favourable prices for the goods that were produced within its estates. Unfortunately, this hypothesis is unverifiable through the archaeological evidence.[106] We know, however, that the church encouraged agricultural production, including viticulture, in many areas of the Near East, as ecclesiastical institutions possessed both capital and the organised manpower necessary for such enterprises.[107] A number of wine presses found in monasteries and other church estates in Palestine suggest that the church might have been the main wine producer in this region.[108] This institution possessed enormous estates as well as a great number of servants and dependants,[109] thanks to which it was able to transport shipments of grain over long distances during times of famine.[110] Even though clerics were not allowed to act as *negotiatores*, the ban did not cover commercial activities undertaken for the benefit of either the poor or the church. There is plenty of evidence to suggest that the clergy took part in commercial exchange, and, moreover, that their position was privileged compared to ordinary traders, given that they had immunities for long distance commerce.[111] In summary, the growing role of the state, as well as the introduction of the church as a privileged agent in late Roman trade, were probable causes for the observed shift in Eastern Mediterranean wine importations to Italy, which suggests a transformation from the market economy during the early Imperial age towards regulated economy.

The development of the Levantine, Cypriot and Cilician wine trades may therefore be described as follows:

1. The incorporation of these areas into the Roman Empire provided an impulse that encouraged development and growth in production, which might have been necessary, according to Hopkins' tax and trade model.

106 Reynolds 2010a, 148; 2010b, 100.
107 Kingsley, Decker 2001, 9–11.
108 Decker 2009, 137.
109 Whittaker 1993, 169–170.
110 Whittaker 1993, 168; Reynolds 1995, 129.
111 Whittaker 1993, 169.

2. From the mid-3rd c. AD, when the Western Mediterranean experienced crises and instability, the East consolidated.
3. The 4th c. AD brought with it the growing needs of the Danubian army (enlarged by Diocletian), a change of capital city and changes to the main trading routes, as well as the development of Christianity and the supposed church investment in viticulture and wine commerce; all these factors were favourable with regards to production growth in the East and the subsequent exportation of its products.
4. State interference in commercial exchange diminished the role of transport costs as the main factor concerning trade, and hence products from distant areas could appear on markets that were inaccessible in the previous 'market economy' environments.
5. The network of commercial agents associated with the church used their privileged position to take control of the wine market, favouring products from their eastern estates. However, it remains unclear whether Aegean wines simply did not survive the competition with the Orient, or whether their production and export ceased due to other factors (e.g. climatic change), which allowed the Levant, Cyprus and Cilicia to fill the gap. Notwithstanding, during late antiquity the bloom of the *Oriens* occurred simultaneously with the twilight of the Aegean.

CONCLUSIONS

The Economics of the Wine Trade

> ἡμεῖς δ' ἐν οἴνῳ συμπόται σοφώτατοι
>
> When we are warm with wine, how wise we grow.
>
> ARISTOPH. *Lys.* 1227

∵

The search for lost wines presented in this book demonstrated that the Eastern Mediterranean area played a crucial part in the development of Italian wine history. Thanks to the contacts with the East new vine species as well as viticultural techniques reached the Apennine Peninsula. Imported wines and associated pottery were not only eagerly consumed by the archaic inhabitants of Italy, but also influenced local wine, amphora and tableware production, as well as their export. Moreover, Eastern wines were present on western tables throughout antiquity, starting from the late 8th or early 7th c. BC and lasting until at least the 7th c. AD.

The Aegean region was the main wine supplier to Italy. During the Archaic period it provided high-quality wines from Thasos, Lesbos and Chios, which were still drunk by the Romans in the late Republican age. These were old wines that matured for a long time (from several to more than 20 years) probably under a film of yeast (the so-called *flor* in Spanish). Therefore, they tasted similar to modern-day French *vins jaunes* or *vins de voile*, or the Spanish sherry *fino*. This taste is caused by a compound called sotolon and has been compared to that of curry or roasted walnuts. These wines (except Thasian) had both a sweet and dry variety and were prepared without the admixture of seawater. They were consumed by the upper social classes and may be considered as eastern luxuries that were present on western tables at the end of the Republic. Importing these wines was not meaningful in terms of the economy, but their consumption was significant from a societal viewpoint. This was due to north-Aegean wines being seen as symbols of prestige, and therefore those people who could obtain these products must have held high social positions and enjoyed luxurious lifestyles.

During the 3rd c. BC south-Aegean wines appeared, especially Coan and Rhodian. These were white wines prepared with seawater, which was added to

© KONINKLIJKE BRILL NV, LEIDEN, 2021 | DOI:10.1163/9789004433762_009

the must during the process of fermentation and acted as a preservative. However, the real boom in Eastern Mediterranean importations started with the advent of the empire. Sweet Cretan raisin-wine called *passum* ruled the market, being accompanied by *passum* from Cilicia, *protropum* from Cnidus, Clazomenian and probably Ephesian (which were τεθαλασσωμένοι), Tmolian, Cypriot, Syrian, Egyptian and maybe also Bithynian. Most of these wines did not delight the ancient poets and playwrights, because there was nothing special about them. Wines from the Black Sea region, Levant, Egypt, Cilicia and Cyprus were not very popular. Contrarily, south Aegean and western Anatolian products were imported in mass quantities, for mass consumption, by the masses. They were often sold in taverns and were found in the houses of the poor. These importations mean that the wine trade must have played an important part in the Roman economy and that it was not limited to luxury goods. Staples other than grain, for example common wines from the Eastern Mediterranean, were also transported on a large scale, and not only to major centres of consumption, such as Rome, but also to small Campanian and Adriatic towns such as Pompeii or Polesine. Furthermore, socio-onomastic and prosopographic analyses of names that were attested on wine amphoras discovered in Campania suggest that *negotiatores vinarii* could earn a substantial amount of money and become prominent among the local community. Moreover, many of the free people and freedmen who traded Eastern Mediterranean wines were associated with prominent families and local elites, which suggests that the financial capital of the elite played an important part in commercial enterprises. At the same time, being associated with commerce facilitated enrichment and promotion for a freedman, and his offspring, who could seek public office using the capital accumulated by their fathers from the wine business. Therefore, the trade in, *inter alia*, Eastern Mediterranean wines to Italy during the early Imperial age was an important factor that influenced socio-economic structures and their changes. Given the scale of the trade, as well as the social position of the traders, it is impossible to look at the wine trade as economically insignificant.

A comparison of the quantities of amphoras dated to the Republican period with those containers dated to the Imperial era suggests that there was a general increase in consumption of foreign goods in Rome. According to Volpe, during the Republic the share of all amphoras in the whole ceramic material assemblage was around 5–6% at most. Conversely, in the Imperial period the percentage is always above 30%. This means that the Roman *suburbium* probably satisfied most of the wine demand during the Republic. However, in the Imperial period importations became common, whereas a part of Italian production was dedicated to the *grands crus*.[1] It seems that before the Augustan

---

1 Santangeli Valenzani, Volpe 2012, 66–67; Volpe 2009, 379–381.

period, mass long-distance trade, in which ceramic containers were used, was not developed. Mass trade began after the conquest of Egypt and the defeat of the pirates, when *pax Romana* was established and Romans controlled the Mediterranean Sea. As a result, the prices of foreign goods declined, while the conquest of new territories resulted in the enrichment of the inhabitants of Italy. Moreover, during the late Republic and early empire the population of Italy might have grown between three and ten times.[2] The peak in the number of inhabitants took place in the 1st c. BC and/or the 1st c. AD, while the decrease started approximately during the second half of the 2nd c. AD.[3] The city of Rome itself might have experienced a growth of between 250,000 to one million during the Augustan age.[4] It was not only cities that grew: smaller settlements, for example in Etruria, also experienced significant population growth.[5] The overall population of the empire is estimated to have grown from 45 million during the Augustan age to 60 million in the late 2nd c. AD, just before the onset of the plague.[6]

A constant and considerable increase in percentages of Eastern Mediterranean wine amphoras, ranging from 10 to over 50 %, may be observed in Rome between the late Republican age and the 3rd c. AD, which falls within the period of population growth. Given that wines from the Eastern Mediterranean were the most numerous provincial imports in Rome, Campania and Adriatic Italy, sometimes even surpassing the percentages of Italian varieties, it is safe to say that the region satisfied a large part of the Italian wine demand. This means that the East was very important from an economic perspective, because it was the major wine supplier to Rome and other urban centres in Italy. Moreover, it indicates that aggregated economic growth occurred between the late Republic and the 2nd c. AD, which adds another argument to the discussion regarding the nature of the Roman economy. However, most scholars currently have reached agreement and admit that at least limited growth may be observed. The real question is whether it was just aggregated or also *per capita* growth, and whether it was sustainable or not.[7] The studies of G. Kron suggest that people in classical antiquity were better nourished than the working classes of 18th and 19th c. Europe,[8] and that the average Roman male was similar in stature to the average mid-twentieth century inhabitants of France, Spain

2 Scheidel 2006b, 8–9, accessed 1.02.2018; 2007a, 45–47; 2008, 19–30; Jongman 2005, 441–495.
3 Jongman 2009, 124.
4 Jongman 2014, 172; Storey, Glenn 1997, 966–978.
5 Jongman 2014, 172, fig. 1; 2017b, 20, fig. 1.2.
6 Bang 2008, 124; Frier 2000, 812–813.
7 Wilson 2014, 147.
8 Kron 2008; 2012.

or Northern Italy.[9] At the same time, there is a positive correlation between changes in human stature and the rate of GDP *per capita*,[10] which suggests that the occurrence of intensive growth in antiquity seems highly probable. According to Jongman, diet may reflect both extensive and intensive growth. For example, high income results in an increase in meat consumption. He points out that numbers of attested animal bones as well as sizes of animals were the largest between 100 BC and 400 AD, and that the increase in bones numbers occurred between 100 BC and 200 AD. This increase indicates consumption growth, which may in fact simply be a result of population growth. However, Jongman's calculations regarding pottery fragments from Nettuno suggest that "*population pressure did not depress the consumption of the high-income elasticity goods such as wine or fine ware, on the contrary*".[11] Even though these conclusions may be easily questioned due to them being based on a small range of data, they are small pieces of a complicated puzzle that help us to understand the nature of ancient economic growth.

The consumption of Eastern Mediterranean wines in Roman Italy may be seen as another piece of the same puzzle. Of course, this consumption *per se* is by no means strong evidence for economic growth, *per capita* growth in particular. It simply allows us to see this issue from another perspective. First of all, it demonstrates that the availability of foreign goods, Eastern wines among them, changed in Rome between the Republican and the Imperial periods. The Imperial 'middle classes' had access to products that were reserved for the aristocracy during the Republic. Moreover, the mass scale of wine imports from the Eastern Mediterranean throughout the early Imperial age demonstrates that a lot of people could afford them. Finally, since the growing population of Italy was able to consume imported wines it seems that *per capita* incomes did not decrease, as the Malthusian theory assumes. If the Malthusian pressure did occur and the standard of living in Italy did decrease, we would observe a simultaneous decrease in purchasing power and hence a fall in the numbers of imports, especially if these imports were consumed by ordinary people, who would suffer most from a fall in real wages. This study shows that nothing like this happened, at least in terms of wines imported from the Eastern Mediterranean. Moreover, it is worth mentioning that Cretan wine was particularly sweet, which means that it must have had a high calorific value. Considering that common people could easily afford this wine, we may assume that the

9 Kron 2005, 77–78.

10 Kron 2014, 129.

11 Jongman 2014, 174–175, fig. 3. The total number of amphora and fine ware fragments per period was divided by the estimated number of people.

calorific value of their diet increased when they changed, as an example, from local ordinary wine to sweet imported Cretan *passum*. This must have influenced their well-being. Considering that Cretan wine was imported in large quantities, particularly during the 2nd c. AD, one ought to admit that there is nothing to suggest an inhibition of growth before the end of the 2nd/beginning of the 3rd c. AD. Therefore, considering the evidence, the existence of sustainable intensive growth during the earliest centuries of the empire seems reasonable.

The Aegean area provided most of Italy's imported wine during the early Imperial age and probably also in the 3rd c. AD. The particular popularity of Cretan wine was associated with the shipping of grain to Rome within the *annona* framework, as the wine was probably transported free of charge on the *annona* cargo ships. At the same time, Cos and Rhodes were situated along the routes of the trading vessels that transported grain from Egypt to Rome, which might have influenced the popularity of wines from these islands. Similarly, when the role of Ephesus as the principal eastern port increased in Roman times, wines from Asia Minor started to be exported to Rome. Generally speaking, as shown by the comparison of importations with the ORBIS model, between the 1st and 3rd c. AD the Romans imported wines mostly from regions that had low transport costs. Wines from the Levant, Cyprus and Cilicia reached Italy in very small quantities. On the contrary, during late antiquity oriental imports became much more important than Aegean. Therefore, it seems that profitability was a crucial economic factor that influenced Roman choice in Eastern Mediterranean wines during the first three centuries of the empire, which means that low transport costs governed the wine trade during this period. However, during late antiquity other factors must have been involved, since the variety of Eastern Mediterranean wines imported to Italy changed completely. This conclusion provides evidence for supporters of a 'market economy' during the early Imperial age. Not only is there evidence that market forces played the most important role in wine commerce during the early empire, but there is also evidence that during late antiquity coerced transfers became much more important. The transformation took place in the 3rd c. AD, so the Crisis of the Third Century is likely to have also played a crucial part in this process.

The birth of the market economy may also be responsible for the cessation of north-Aegean wine importations to Italy. Thasos, Lesbos, and to a certain degree Chios, seemingly stopped exporting wines to Italy at roughly the same time the Italian import boom started.[12] Salviat explains the disappear-

12 For more about this see Komar 2014b.

ance of north-Aegean wines from the markets as a result of the competition from south-Aegean varieties. Lesbian and Chian exporters to a certain degree adapted to the new conditions, but Thasian products disappeared completely.[13] This hypothesis can be confirmed by archaeological evidence from the Black Sea region. It seems that the increase in the discoveries of Rhodian stamps in this area correlated with a decrease in the amount of Thasian stamps.[14] Similarly, in the Balkan region there are no Thasian amphoras after the second quarter of the 3rd c. BC, which is when Rhodian vessels began to appear in the archaeological material.[15] Therefore, the hypothesis regarding south-Aegean competition seems probable, especially if we consider that wines such as Rhodian and Coan were considerably cheaper, and that the drinking of luxurious imported wines in Rome had already lost its social significance. What mechanism lied behind this? According to C. Tzochev, if we accept that ancient trade relations operated in a profit-oriented reality, it seems that the sale of Thasian wine on Black Sea markets must have influenced the growth of wine production on the island. This increased Thasian wine supply in the Black Sea region must have caused its price to fall. Thus, selling its wine on distant markets became less profitable, which forced Thasos' wine producers to look to other markets on, and close to their island. Of course, other factors might have had an impact, such as the change in trade routes that favoured south-Aegean beverages, the decline of Athens as a commercial hub and the destruction of rural territories in the Bosporan Kingdom and Dobruja—the main sources of cereals in the region during the mid-3rd c. BC.[16] Nevertheless, the situation of Thasian wine in the Black Sea region resembles what happened in Italy. When the drinking of north-Aegean wines lost its symbolic meaning, which was associated with social status, and when cheap south-Aegean beverages appeared on Roman markets, north-Aegean islands could no longer profit from exporting their wines to the Apennine Peninsula, because the prices of imported wines decreased. During the late Republic ships transporting marble, pieces of art, and slaves from the East to Rome[17] might have easily taken north-Aegean wines onboard as additional cargo. In the Imperial age, however, these products were no longer in demand; hence, wines from Thasos and Lesbos were the only

---

13 Salviat 2013a, 99.

14 Conovici 2005, 108–111, fog. 7–9. It seems that the relative frequency of Thasian amphora eponyms in Istros, Tomis and Kallatis declined around 250–230 BC, whereas Rhodian examples increased in this period.

15 Archibald 2013, 202.

16 Tzochev 2016.

17 Tchernia 1986, 72–73. A shipwreck transporting Lamb. 2 amphoras provides evidence for this possibility.

viable cargo from this region and importing them was unprofitable. As a consequence, wine merchants from these islands must have looked to other markets, or perhaps changed their 'specialisation'. According to Kourakou-Dragona, Lesbos and Thasos started to produce olive oil,[18] which may also apply to Chios, given that amphoras from the Imperial period that are attributed to this island probably carried olive oil.[19]

To sum up, the consumption of Eastern Mediterranean wines in Italy was important from both a social and an economic perspective. These beverages influenced Roman tastes in wines and their introduction also impacted upon Italian wine production. Their consumption in the Republican age was a part of elite self-identification and was also a determinant of luxury and social prestige. In the early Imperial period, the Aegean region was Italy's most important wine supplier, satisfying its demand for mass produced beverages for commoners to consume. During this period the wine trade became a significant part of the Roman economy, as well as influencing social dynamics, at least in Campania. The consumption of Eastern Mediterranean wines may also indicate Roman economic growth and might suggest that sustainable *per capita* growth occurred in Italy between the late Republican period and the 2nd c. AD. The Roman choice in wines during the early empire suggests that market forces determined the trade of wine to Italy, while during late antiquity coerced transfers played a much more important part in commercial exchange. What all of this means is that since the wine trade was indeed important and not limited to 'fame regional wines', and since there is evidence that market forces played an important part in exchange during the early empire, and since there are signs of intensive growth between c. the 1st c. BC and 2nd c. AD, and since traders were not insignificant members of society, one should realise that any attempts to highlight the primitiveness of the Roman economy are doomed to failure, as they will always clash with the archaeological data. Therefore, the study of Eastern wines on western tables proves that the ancient Roman economy was in fact much more 'modern' than it for a long time appeared.

---

18 Kourakou-Dragona 2013, 221.

19 See amphoras Dressel 24 *similis*, for example Opait, Tsavropaulos 2011, 317; Panella, Rizzo 2014, 322.

APPENDIX 1

Catalogue of Greek and Latin Texts That Mention Wines from the Eastern Mediterranean

Greek Sources

5th c. BC

Herodotus, *Histories* II 60, 3.

5th/4th c. BC

Antisthenes, *Fragmenta varia*, fr. 117.
Hippocrates, *De affectionibus interioribus* 25, 22–23.
De affectionibus interioribus 30, 22–23.
De morbis III 17, 41–43.
Aristophanes, *Ecclesiazusae* 1116–1126.
Ecclesiazusae 1139–1143.
Lisystrata 194–197.
Plutus 1020–1021.
Fr. 545 (530)–548 (535) = Poll X 72, Lys 196.
Thesmophoriazusae, Fr. 334 (317) = Ath. *Deipn.* I 29a.
Kokalos, Fr. 350 Kock = Ath. *Deipn.* XI 478d.
Daitaleis (*Men of Dinnerville*) Fr. I 446 Kock = Ath. *Deipn.* XI 484f and 527c.
Epilycus, Fr. 7 (6) = Ath. *Deipn.* I 28e.
Xenophon, *Symposium* 4, 41.

4th c. BC

Antidotos, Fr. 4 = Ath. *Deipn.* I 28e.
Antiphanes, Fr. 238 (242) = Ath. *Deipn.* I 28f.
Leptiniskos, Fr. 138 (140) = Ath. *Deipn.* XIV 641f.
Archestratus, Fr. 59 Ri = Ath. *Deipn.* I 29b–d.
Clearchus, Fr. 5 = Ath. *Deipn.* I 28e.
Demosthenes, *Contra Lacritum* 31, 32, 35.
Ephippus, Fr. 28 (28.29) = Ath. *Deipn.* I 28f.
Eubulos, Fr. 121= Ath. *Deipn.* I 28f.
Fr. 129 (131) = Ath. *Deipn.* I 29a.
Hermippos, Fr. 77 (82) = Ath. *Deipn.* I 29e–f.
Matro of Pitane, *Convivium atticum* 109–110.

© KONINKLIJKE BRILL NV, LEIDEN, 2021 DOI:10.1163/9789004433762_010

Philyllius, Fr. 23 (24) = Ath. *Deipn.* I 31a.
Theopompus in Ath. *Deipn.* 26c.
Xenophon, *Anabasis* I 2, 22.

4th/3rd c. BC

Alexis, Fr. 276 (274)–277 (275) = Ath. *Deipn.* I 28e.
Fr. 278 (276) = Ath. *Deipn.* I 28f.
Fr. 232 (230) = Ath. *Deipn.* X 431b.
Andocides, *In Alcibiadem* 30.

3rd c. BC

Bato, Fr. 3 = Ath. *Deipn.* VII 279c.
Erasistratus, Fr. 283, 1, 5–17.
Fr. 283, 3, 6–17.
Fr. 283, 2, 1–25.
Hedylus, *Epigrams* = Ath. *Deipn.* XI 473a.
Hegesander FHG 368 = Ath. *Deipn.* IV 167e.
Hippolochus in Ath. *Deipn.* IV 129d–f.
Kallimachus, *Greek Anthology* XIII 9.
Leonidas of Tarentum, *Greek Anthology* VII 422.
Machon in Ath. *Deipn.* XIII 579f.
Posidippus, *Greek Anthology* V 183.
Theophrastus, *Research on plants*, (HP 9.18.10–11) = Ath. *Deipn.* I 31f.
Od. 51 = Ath. *Deipn.* I 32a.

2nd–1st c. BC

Posidonius, Fr. 211b, 15–20 = Diodorus Siculus, *Bibliotheca historica* XXXVII 3, 1–5.
Scholion on Aristophanes' *Wealth* 1021.
Scholion on Aristophanes' *The Acharnians* 671b–671c.
Scholion on Aristophanes' *Lysistrata* 196.
Scholion on Aristophanes' *Peace* 835–837a (F GrHist 392 t2).
Scholion on Hesiod's *Opera et dies* 588–590, 12–17.
Timachidas of Rhodes = Ath. *Deipn.* I 31e.

1st c. BC

Diodorus Siculus, *Bibliotheca historica* XXXVII 3, 1–5 (this fragment is probably taken from Posidonius 211b, 15–20).
Philodemus, *Greek Anthology* XI 34.
Poseidonios F155 Jacoby = Ath. *Deipn.* 28d.

1st c. AD

Aretaeus, *De curatione acutorum morborum* II 3, 10.
De curatione diuturnorum morborum I 5, 14.

Dioscorides, *De materia medica* I 129 = I 98 2.[1]
De materia medica I 131 = I 99, 3.
De materia medica II 141, 1 = II 171.
De materia medica V 6 = V 5, 1.
De materia medica V 9 = V 6, 4.
De materia medica V 10 = V 6, 8–9.
De materia medica V 11 = V 6, 11.
De materia medica V 12 = V 6, 14–15.
De materia medica V 85 = V 75, 11.
De materia medica II 91 = II 76, 13.
De materia medica V 82 = V 72, 2.

Strabo, *Geography* XIV 1, 15.
Geography XIV 2, 19.
Geography XIV 6, 5.
Geography XV 3, 22.
Geography XVI 2, 9.
Geography XVII 1, 14.
Geography XVII 1, 35.
Geography XVI 2, 9

1st/2nd c. AD

Archigenes, Fr. 12–13.

Dio Chrysostomus, *Orationes* 6, 12.

Plutarch, *De tranquilitate animi* 469b–c.
De tranquilitate animi 10 (= *Moralia* 470 f).
Non posse suaviter vivi secundum Epicurum 17 (= *Moralia* 1099a–b).
Alcibiades 12.
Demetrius 19, 4.

2nd c. AD

Achilles Tatius, *Clitophon and Leucippe* II 2.

Galen, *De sanitate tuenda* IV 6 = Kühn VI 275–276.
De sanitate tuenda V 5 = Kühn VI 334–335.
De sanitate tuenda V 5 = Kuhn VI 337.

---

1 The second numeration is from the edition of M. Wellman.

De probis pravisque alimentorum succis= Kühn VI 802.
De probis pravisque alimentorum succis 11 = Kühn VI 803.
De metodo medendi XII 4 = Kühn X 832–833.
De metodo medendi XII 4 = Kühn X 833–834.
De metodo medendi XII 4 = Kühn X 835–836.
Ad Galuconem de medendi methodo I 15 = Kühn XI 52.
De simplicium medicamentorum temperamentis ac facultatibus III 20 = Kühn XI 604.
De composicione medicamentorum secundum locos I 6 = Kühn XII 462.
De composicione medicamentorum secundum locos III 3 = Kühn XII 680.
De compositione medicamentorum secundum locos IV 6 = Kühn XII 728.
De composicione medicamentorum secundum locos IV 7 = Kühn XII 774.
De composicione medicamentorum secundum locos IV 7 = Kühn XII 777.
De composicione medicamentorum secundum locos V 5 = Kühn XII 867.
De compositione medicamentorum secundum locos VII 1 = Kühn XIII 3.
De compositione medicamentorum secundum locos VII 1 = Kühn XIII 8.
De compositione medicamentorum secundum locos VII 1 = Kühn XIII 11.
De compositione medicamentorum secundum locos VII 2 = Kühn XIII 15, 10–18.
De compositione medicamentorum secundum locos VII 2 = Kühn XIII 26, 5–7.
De compositione medicamentorum secundum locos VII 2 = Kühn XIII 29, 15–16.
De compositione medicamentorum secundum locos VII 2 = Kühn XIII 30–31.
De compositione medicamentorum secundum locos VII 2 = Kühn XIII 32, 7–9.
De compositione medicamentorum secundum locos VII 2 = Kühn XIII 33, 7–9.
De compositione medicamentorum secundum locos VII 2 = Kühn XIII 49, 17–50.
De compositione medicamentorum secundum locos VII 2 = Kühn XIII 52–53.
De compositione medicamentorum secundum locos VII 3 = Kühn XIII 70, 6–10.
De compositione medicamentorum secundum locos VII 3 = Kühn XIII 70.
De compositione medicamentorum secundum locos VIII 8 = Kühn XIII 212.
De compositione medicamentorum secundum locos VIII 8 = Kühn XIII 215.
De compositione medicamentorum secundum locos X 1 = Kühn XIII 323.
De compositione medicamentorum secundum locos X 3 = Kühn XIII 355–356.
De compositione medicamentorum per genera I 8 = Kühn XIII 405.
De compositione medicamentorum per genera II 10 = Kühn XIII 513–514.
De compositione medicamentorum per genera IV 1 = Kühn XIII 659.
De compositione medicamentorum per genera VII 13 = Kühn XIII 1035.
De antidotis I 5 = Kühn XIV 28–29.
De antidotis II 1 = Kühn XIV 107–108.
De antidotis II 1 = Kühn XIV 111.
De antidotis II 9 = Kühn XIV 153.
De antidotis II 10 = Kühn XIV 162.
De antidotis II 14 = Kühn XIV 185.

De antidotis II 17 = Kühn XIV 202–203.
De remediis parabilibus II 19 = Kühn XIV 454.
De remediis parabilibus II 24 = Kühn XIV 470.
De rebus boni malique VI 800–801.
In Hipp. De victu acutorum commentaria IV 73 = Kühn XV 861.
In Hippocrates de victu acutorum XV 645.
De victu attenuante 93–95.
De victu attenuante 99.
De succedaneis 15 = Kühn XIX 738.
De simplicium medicamentorum temperamentis ac facultatibus XI 648.
Herodianus, *De prosodia catholica* XXXI 292–293.
Jullius Pollux, *Onomasticon* VI 15.
Onomasticon X 72.
Longus, *Daphnis et Chloe* IV 10, 3.
Lucian of Samosata, *Verae historiae* 1, 7.
Amores 27.

3rd c. AD

Athenaeus, *Deipnosophistai* 33d–f.
Claudius Aelianus, *Varia historia* XII 31, 1–14.
Epistulae rusticae 8, 1–8.
Clemens Alexandrinus, *Paedagogus* II 2, 30, 1–3.
Philostratus, *Imagines* II 26, 4.

4th c. AD

Libanius, *Epistulae* B 151 (C 255), 10.
Declamation 1, 18.
Declamation 30, 1, 24, 1–8.
Declamation 32, 40–41.
Orations 11, 20.
Oribasius, *Eclogae medicamentorum* 73, 18–20.
Synopsis et Eustathium filium II 66, 4.
Synopsis ad Eustathium filium II 131, 1–2.
Synopsis ad Eustathium filium III 136, 1.
Synopsis ad Eustathium filium III 139, 1–2.
Synopsis ad Eustathium filium III 150, 1.
Synopsis ad Eustathium filium III 160, 1.
Synopsis ad Eustathium filium IV 3, 1 = *Libri ad Eunapium* I 20, 1 = *Collectione medicae* III 4.
Collectione medicae V 6, 30–31.
Collectione medicae V 6, 45.

Palladas in *Greek Anthology* IX 487.
John Chrysostom, *In Matthaeum homilia* 1, LVIII, p. 531.
In Matthaeum homilia 1, LVIII, p. 494.
Quintus of Smyrna, *Fall of Troy* V 348–351.
Themistius, *In Aristotelis physica paraphrasis* V (2), p. 117.

4th/5th c. AD

Nonnus of Panoplis, *Dionysiaca* XXIV 224–236.

5th/6th c. AD

Aetius, *Iatoricum* II 252, 23.
Iatoricum VII 45, 59.
Iatoricum VII 55, 65–69.
Iatoricum VII 114, 100.
Iatoricum VII 112, 34.
Iatoricum VII 112, 47.
Iatoricum VII 112, 51–52.
Iatoricum VII 112, 67.
Iatoricum II 242, 12–15.

6th/7th c. AD

Alexander of Tralles, ed. Puschmann, I 301, 335, 419, 483; II 17, 27, 53, 171, 353, 393, 217, 237, 325, 327, 331, 407, 411, 457, 421, 483, 485, 487, 495, 539.

7th c. AD

Paulus Aegineta, *Epitomae medicae* III 22, 8, 5–7 = VII 16, 57, 3–6.
Epistomae medicae III 22, 22, 7–12.
Epitomae medicae VII 11, 41, 1–5.
Epitomae medicae VII 16, 7, 1–5.
Epitomae medicae VII 16, 12, 7.
Epitomae medicae VII 25, 15.
Anxippus, Fr. 1, 17–20.
Eustachius, *Commentarii ad Homeri Il* 1, p. 102.
Commentarii ad Homeri Il 1, p. 348.
Commentarii ad Homeri Il 2, p. 164.
Commentarii ad Homeri Il 3, p. 285.

10th c. AD

Book of Suda 58, 1–10; 59, 1–3; 1276, 1–4.
Geoponica VIII 23; VIII 24.

Constantin VII Porphyrogennetos, *De virtutibus et vitis* I, p. 315.
Commentarium ad Homerii Odysseam I, p. 35.
Commentarium ad Homerii Odysseam I, p. 267.
Comment ad Homerii Iliadem III, p. 285.

11th c. AD

Michael Psellos, *Oratoria minoria* 6, 48–55.
Oratoria minoria 26, 47–52.
Poemata 22, 113t–118.

12th c. AD

Etymologicum magnum 443, 7–10.

Date Uncertain

Dionysius, *Greek Anthology* XII 108, 2.
Athenaeus, *Deipn.* I 30b, unknown quotation.
Deipn. I 32e–f.[2]
Deipn. 33b.
Deipn. II, 45e.[3]
Deipn. IV 137b.

Latin Sources

3rd/2nd c. BC

Plautus, *Curculio* 78–79.
Poenulus 699–700.
Rudens 588–590.

2nd c. BC

Cato the Elder, *De Agri Cultura* 24.
De Agri Cultura 105.
De Agri Cultura 112.
De Agri Cultura 158.

---

2 The source of the quotation is unknown, but it might be Mnesitheus of Athens or Galen, which means 4th c. BC or 2nd c. AD.

3 The source of the quotation is unknown, but it might be Hippocrates who is quoted in the next sentence.

1st c. BC

Albius Tibullus, *Elegiae* II 1.
Elegiae IV 1, 57 (III 7).
Cicero, *In Verrem* II 5, 146.
Horace, *Carmina* I 37.
Carmina III 19.
Epodon 9.
Sermones I 10.
Sermones II 3.
Sermones II 4.
Sermones II 8.
Sextus Propertius, *Elegies* II 33, 31–32.
Varro, *De Lingua Latina* IX 40.
Rerum rusticarum de agri cultura II, preface.
Vergil, *Eclogues* V 71.
Georgics II 37–38.
Georgics II 91
Georgics II 94–100.
Vitruvius Pollio, *De architectura* VIII 3, 12.

1st c. BC/1st c. AD

Cornelius Celsus, *De medicina* III 25.
De medicina III 27.
Javolenus, *From the Posthumous works of Labeo III* in *Digesta Justiniani* XXXIII 6, 16, 2.
Ovid, *Fasti* II 313.

1st c. AD

Columella, *De re rustica* I, preface 20.
De re rustica III 2, 1.
De re rustica III 2, 24.
De re rustica III 2, 28.
De re rustica XII 37.
Martial, *Epigrams* IV 46.
Epigrams XIII 106.
Epigrams XIII 122.
Pliny the Elder, *Natural History* XIV 9.
Natural History XIV 25.
Natural History XIV 39.
Natural History XIV 53–54.
Natural History XIV 73–75.

Natural History XIV 76.
Natural History XIV 77.
Natural History XIV 78–79.
Natural History XIV 81–82.
Natural History XIV 95–97.
Natural History XIV 109.
Natural History XIV 116–117.
Natural History XIV 119.
Natural History XIV 120.
Natural History XXXIV 104.
Scribonius Largus, *Compositiones* 26.
Compositiones 36.
Compositiones 126.
Compositiones 165.
Compositiones 170.

2nd c. AD

Apuleius Madaurensis, *Apologia* I 24.
Aulus Gellius, *Noctes Atticae* XIII 5.
Marcus Cornelius Fronto, *De Eloquentia* 1, 4.

5th c. AD

Saint Sidonius Apollinaris *Carmina* XVII 15 = MGH *Auct. Antiquiss.* VIII 242.

6th c. AD

Gregory of Tours, *Historia Francorum* VII 29.
Flavius Cresconius Corippus, *De laudibus Iustini Augusti* 3, 86–88.
Venantius Fortunatus, *Vita S. Martini* II 80–82.

APPENDIX 2

List of Authors That Mention Eastern Mediterranean Wines Quoted by Athenaeus

Name	Date	Types of wines mentioned
Homer	8th c. BC	From Thrace
Alcman	7th c. BC	From Sparta
Archilochus	7th c. BC	From Naxos and Ismara
Achaeus from Eretria	5th c. BC	Bybline
Armenidas	5th c. BC	Bybline
Cratinus	5th c. BC	Mendean
Hermippos	5th c. BC	Mendean, Thasian, Chian, Peparethian
Hippys of Rhegium	5th c. BC	Bybline
Aristophanes	5th/4th c. BC	Chian, Thasian, Peparethian, Pramnian
Epicharmus	5th/4th c. BC	Bybline
Epilycus	5th/4th c. BC	Chian, Thasian
Strattis	5th/4th c. BC	Skiathos
Clearchus	Second half of the 4th c. BC	Lesbian
Theopompus	Second half of the 4th c. BC	Chian
Amphis	4th c. BC	Icarian, from Akanthos
Antidotos	4th c. BC	Thasian, Lesbian
Archestratus	Mid-4th c. BC	Lesbian, Bybline, Thasian
Aristoteles	4th c. BC	Wine of Troezen
Ephippus	Mid-4th c. BC	Lesbian
Eubulus	370–360 BC	Chian, Lesbian, Thasian, Lefkadian
Phaenias of Eresus	4th c. BC	Mendean
Philyllius	4th c. BC	Lesbian, Chian, Thasian, Mendean, Bybline
Antiphanes	387–334 BC	Thasian
Alexis	4th/3rd c. BC	Thasian, Lesbian, Corinthian, Euboean

© KONINKLIJKE BRILL NV, LEIDEN, 2021 | DOI:10.1163/9789004433762_011

(*cont.*)

Name	Date	Types of wines mentioned
Eparchides	3rd c. BC	Pramnian from Icaros
Hedylus	3rd c. BC	Chian
Machon	3rd c. BC	Chian, Thasian
Theophrastus	3rd c. BC	Arcadian, Achaean, Troezenian, Thasian, Erythraean
Timachidas of Rhodes	2nd/1st c. BC	Rhodian
Didymus Chalcenterus	1st c. BC/1st c. AD	Pramnian
Alciphron of Meander	?	Pramnian from the Ephesus area
Author uncertain: Galen? Other physician? (Style similar to Galen and the context must be the 2nd c. BC or later, because Italian wines are also mentioned. However, this fragment does not appear in any of the known Galen's works)	2nd c. AD?	Myndian, Halicarnassian, Rhodian, Coan, Cnidian, Lesbian, Chian, Corcyrean, Zakynthian, Lefkadian

Catalogue of Amphoras Classified as Wine Containers Discovered in Italy between the 1st c. BC and Late Antiquity

This appendix is based on information from the University of Southampton (2014) Roman Amphorae: a digital resource [data-set]. York: Archaeology Data Service [distributor] https://doi.org/10.5284/1028192. The catalogue excludes Knossos 22 and Schoene-Mau XLI forms.

Type	Origin	Date	Shape
Eastern Mediterranean—the Aegean region			
Chian	Chios	450/430 BC–early 1st c. AD	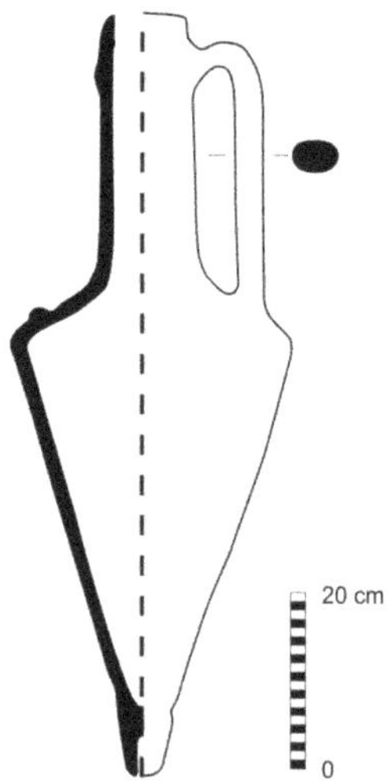

© KONINKLIJKE BRILL NV, LEIDEN, 2021 | DOI:10.1163/9789004433762_012

(*cont.*)

Type	Origin	Date	Shape
Dressel 2–4	Aegean (especially Cos), Cilicia	1st c. BC–2nd c. AD (Cilician variant 1st–2nd c. AD)	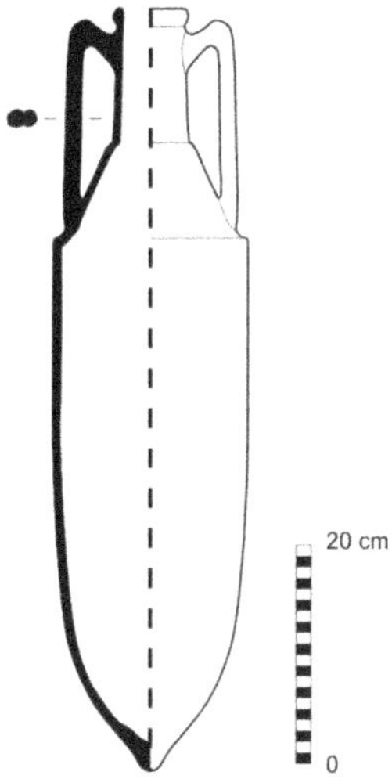
Dressel 5/ Knossos A53	Cos	1st c. BC–2nd c. AD	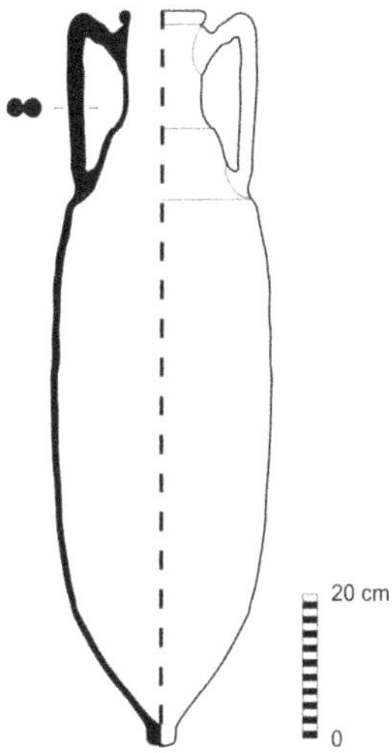

(cont.)

Type	Origin	Date	Shape
Camulodunum 184	Rhodes	Late 1st c. BC–mid-2nd c. AD	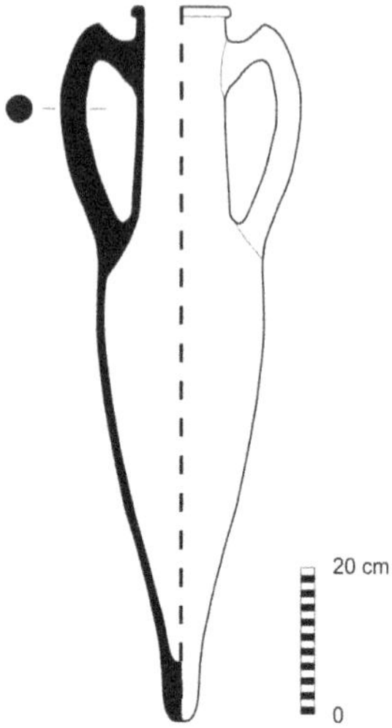
Crétoise 1 (AC1)	Crete	Early 1st to mid-4th c. AD	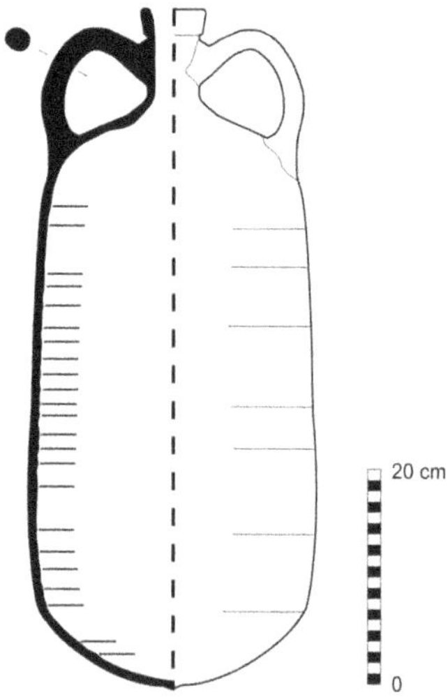

(*cont.*)

Type	Origin	Date	Shape
Crétoise 2 (AC2)	Crete	Early 1st–early 3rd c. AD	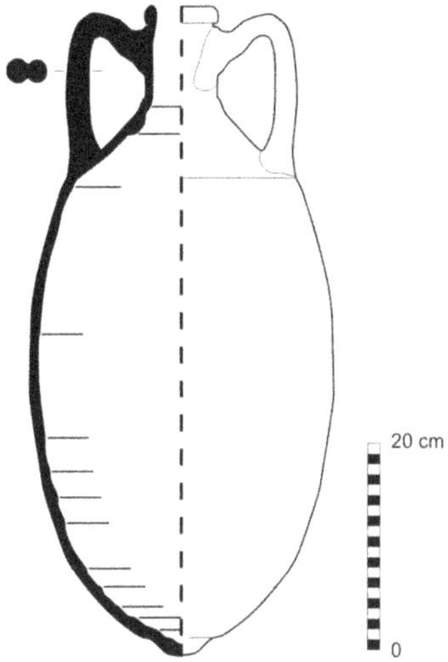
Crétoise 3 (AC3)	Crete	Early 1st–mid-3rd c. AD	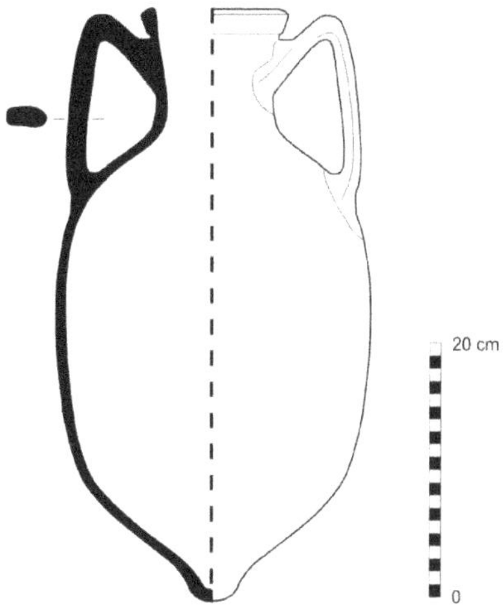

(*cont.*)

Type	Origin	Date	Shape
Crétoise 4 (Dressel 43)	Crete	Early 1st–early 3rd c. AD	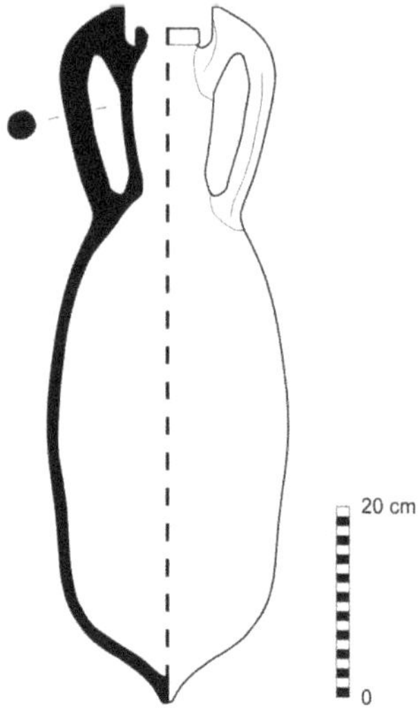
Agora F65–66	Coastal areas of Asia Minor, including the region of Ephesus	Mid-1st c. BC–4th c. AD	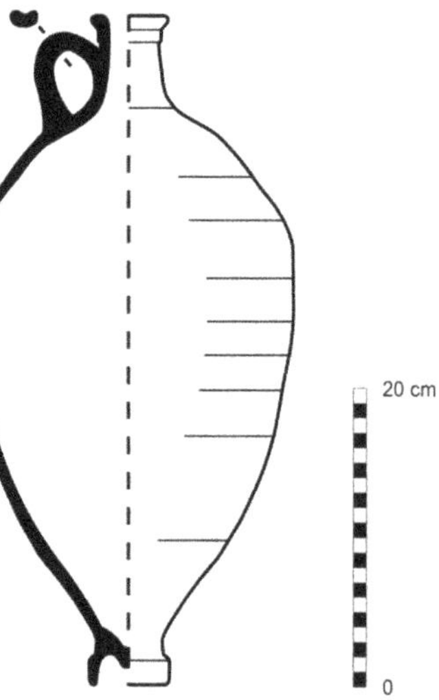

(*cont.*)

Type	Origin	Date	Shape
Schoene-Mau XXVII–XXVIII/ Agora G199	Cyprus/Cilicia	1st–4th c. AD	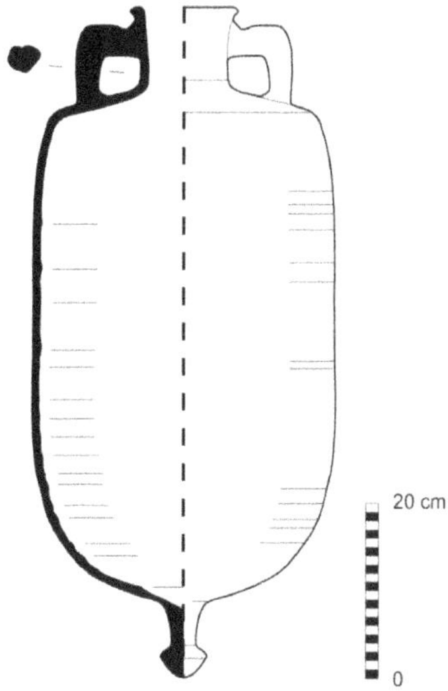
Agora G198/ Schoene-Mau XIII	Cilicia	1st–2nd c. AD	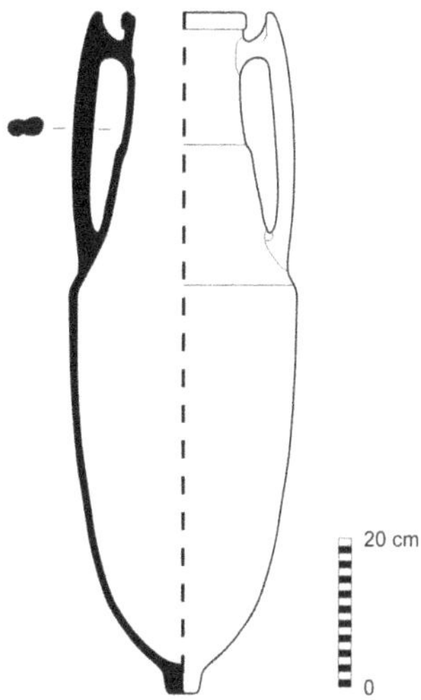

(*cont.*)

Type	Origin	Date	Shape
Agora M54	Cilicia	1st–2nd c. AD	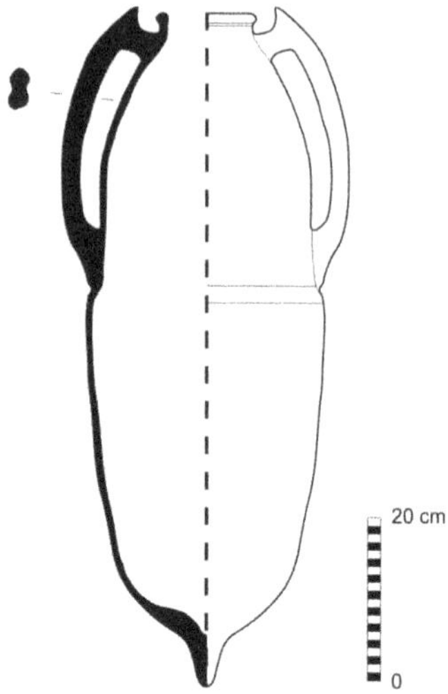
Schoene-Mau V/Pompeii 5	Cilicia	1st–mid-2nd c. AD	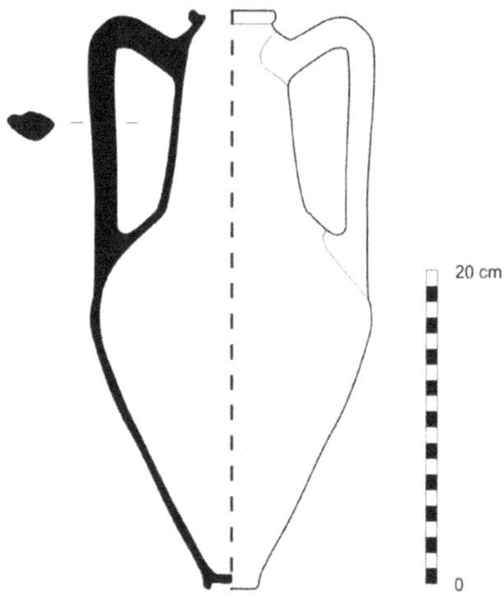

(*cont.*)

Type	Origin	Date	Shape
Eastern Mediterranean—the Levant and Egypt			
Kingsholm 117/Peacock& Williams 66	Syro-Palestine	1st c. AD	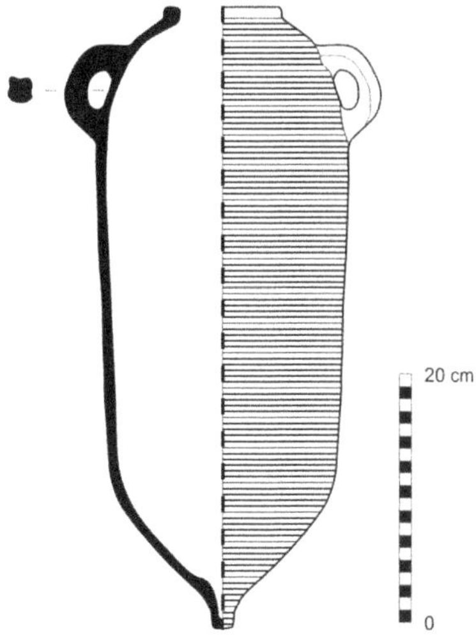
Amphore Égyptienne 1	Egypt (around the shores of Lake Mariout)	3rd c. AD	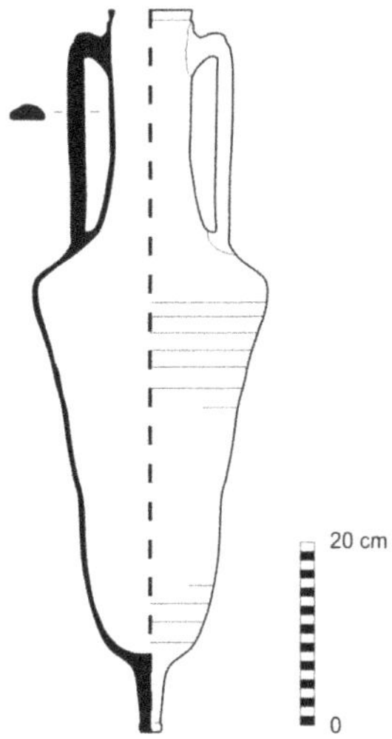

(*cont.*)

Type	Origin	Date	Shape
Amphore Égyptienne 2	Egypt (around the shores of Lake Mariout)	2nd c. AD	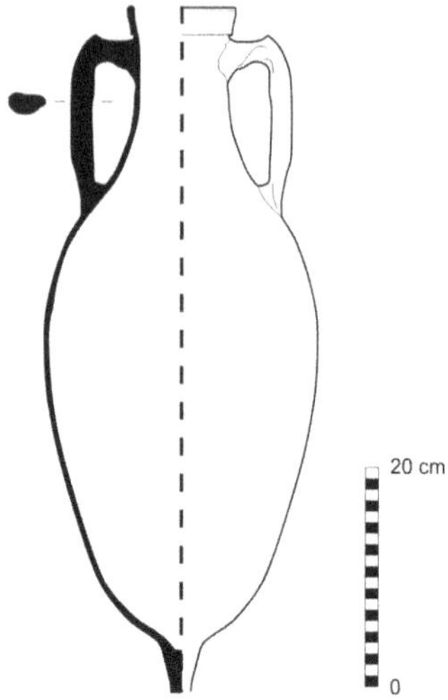
Amphore Égyptienne Bitronconique 3	Egypt (around the shores of Lake Mariout, Hermopolis Magna, in the Faiyum and at Zawyet el-Maietin)	Late 1st c. BC–5th c. AD	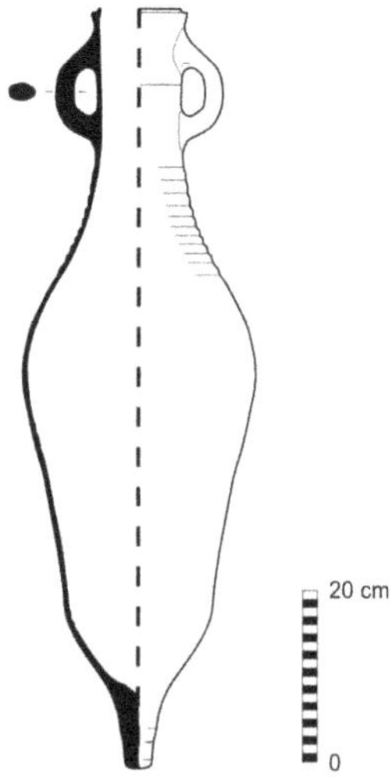

(*cont.*)

Type	Origin	Date	Shape
Late Roman amphoras from the Eastern Mediterranean			
LRA1	Cilicia and Cyprus, possibly Syria and south-Aegean	Mid-3rd–mid-7th c. AD	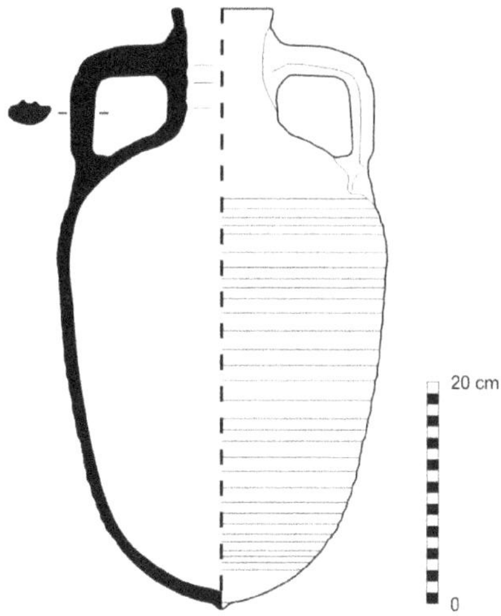
LRA3	Western Asia Minor, including Ephesus, the Meander Valley, Kusadasi, Miletus and possibly Pergamon	4th–6th c. AD	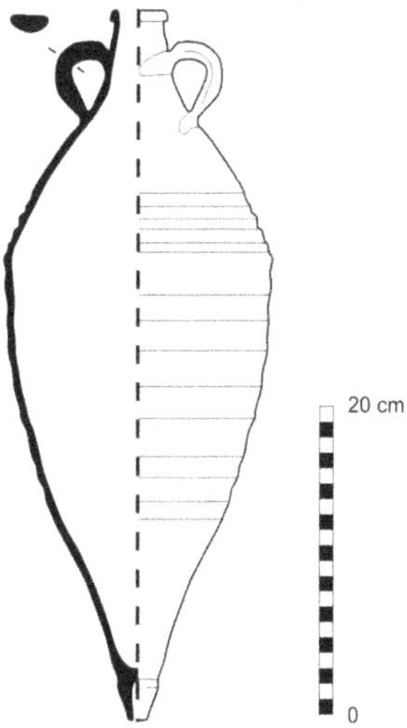

(cont.)

Type	Origin	Date	Shape
LRA4/Almagro 54	Coastal southern Palestine	4th–7th c. AD	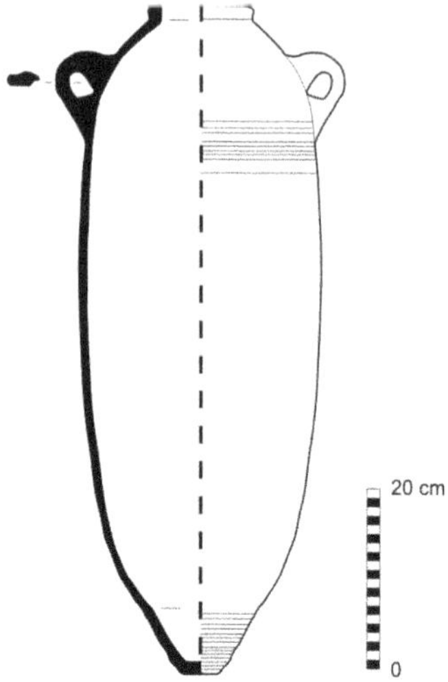
LRA5/6	Palestine, possibly North Egypt from the late 5th c. AD	1st/2nd c. AD–c. 750 AD	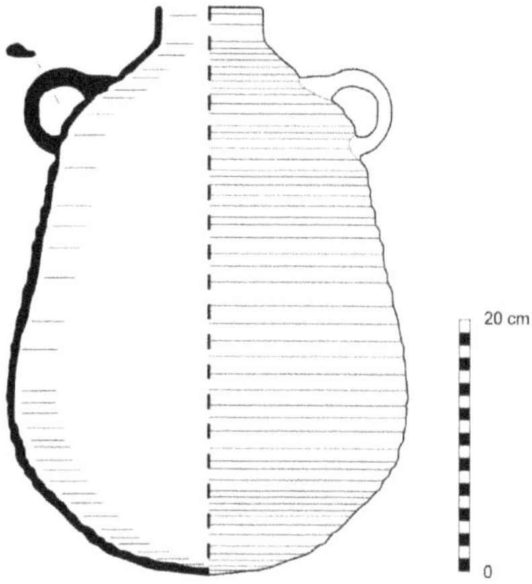

(*cont.*)

Type	Origin	Date	Shape
LRA7	Egypt (Oxyrhynchus, Hermopolis Magna, Antinoopolis, Akoris and Lake Mariout)	Late 4th–7th or 8th c. AD	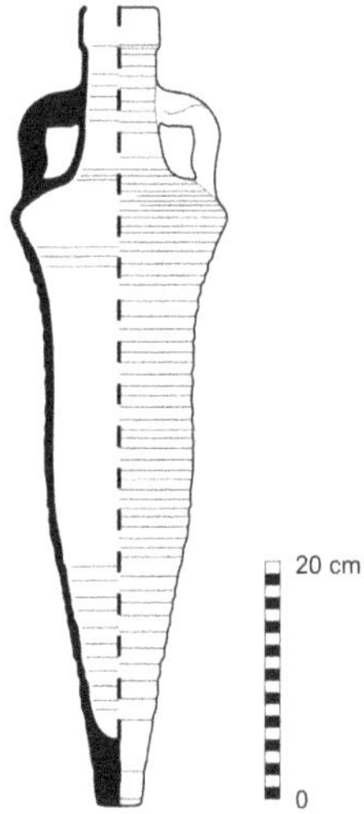
Agora M273	Eastern Mediterranean islands or mainland	4th–5th c. AD	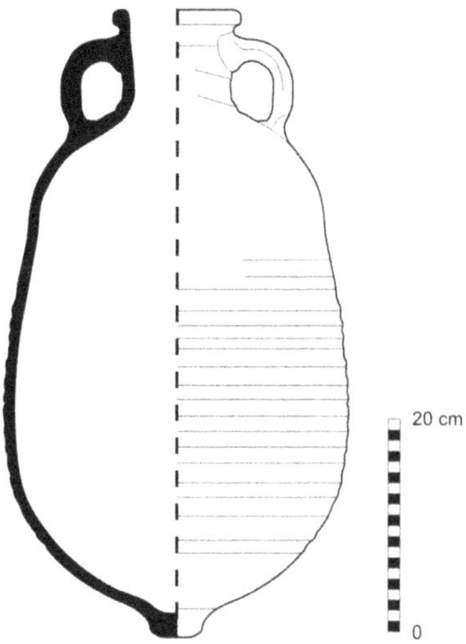

(cont.)

Type	Origin	Date	Shape
Samos Cistern Type	Samos, possibly the Turkish coast around Halicarnassus, the lower Maeander valley area and the eastern Aegean	6th–7th c. AD	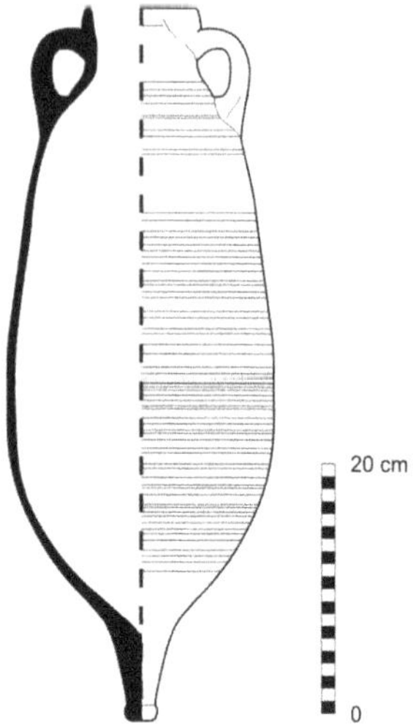
Italy			
Lamboglia 2	Adriatic coast	2nd–1st c. BC	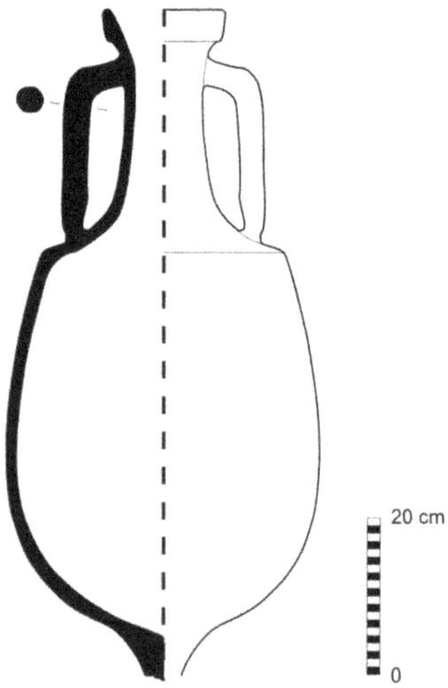

(*cont.*)

Type	Origin	Date	Shape
Dressel 6A	Adriatic coast	Late 1st c. BC–mid-1st c. AD	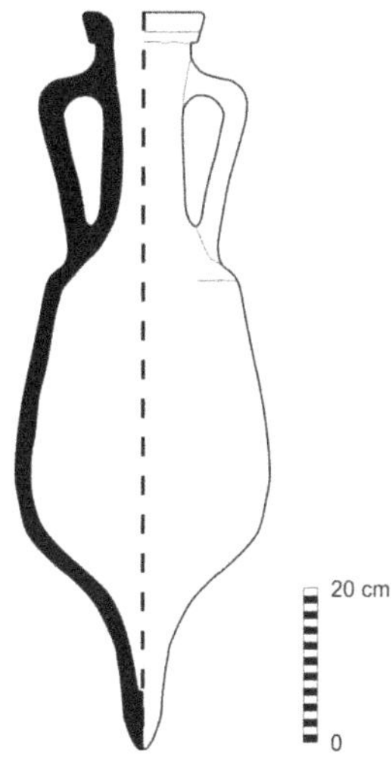
Dressel 2–4	Campania	c. 70 BC–early 3rd c. AD	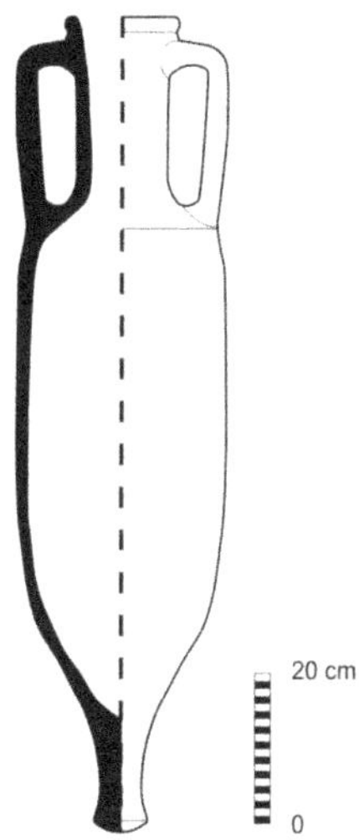

(cont.)

Type	Origin	Date	Shape
Forlimpopoli amphora	NE Italy, area of Forlimpopoli	1st c. BC–early 3rd c. AD	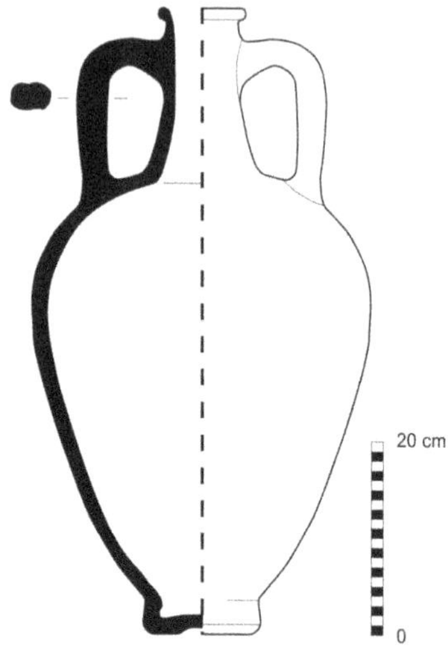
'Di Spello' amphora	Umbria, central Italy (Tiber Valley in particular)	1st–2nd c. AD	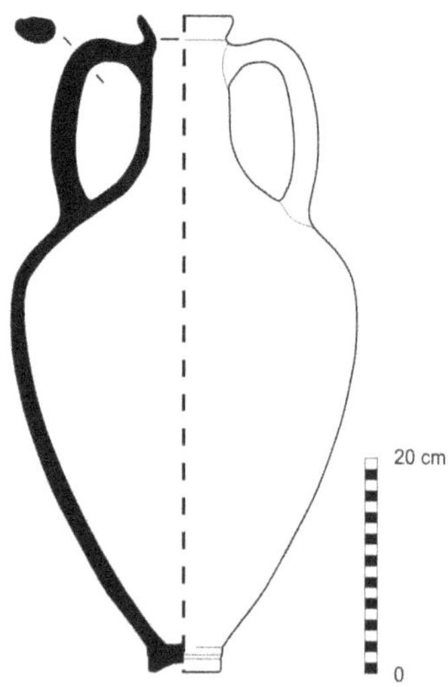

(*cont.*)

Type	Origin	Date	Shape
'Di Empoli' amphora	Arno Valley (Empoli)	2nd–5th c. AD	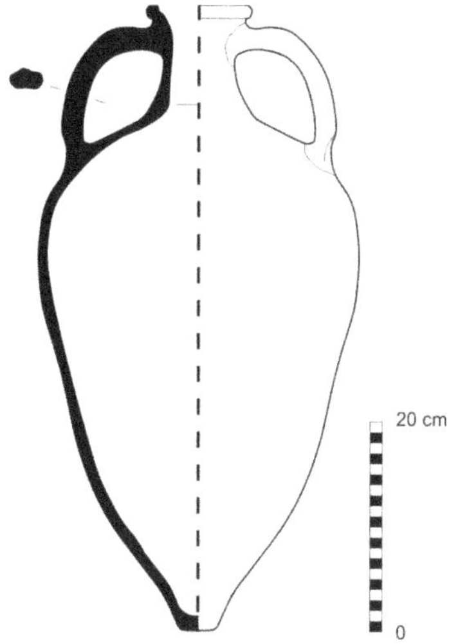
Keay 52	Calabria, possibly Sicily	4th–7th c. AD	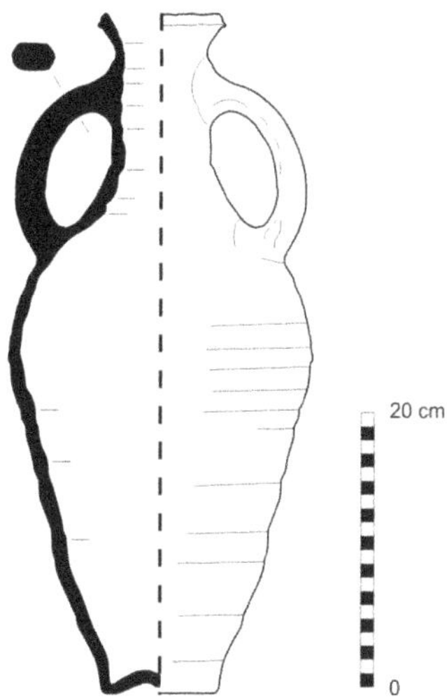

(*cont.*)

Type	Origin	Date	Shape
Gaul			
Gauloise 1	*Gallia Narbonensis*, essentially the lower Rhône Valley	1st–3rd c. AD	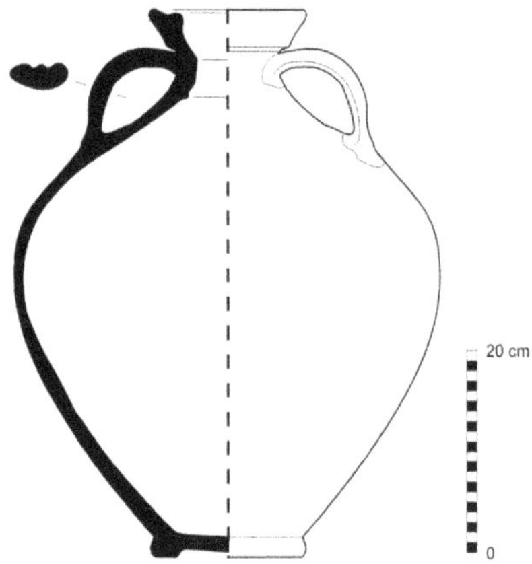
Gauloise 2	*Gallia Narbonensis* and Provence	Around 40 BC to the Augustan period	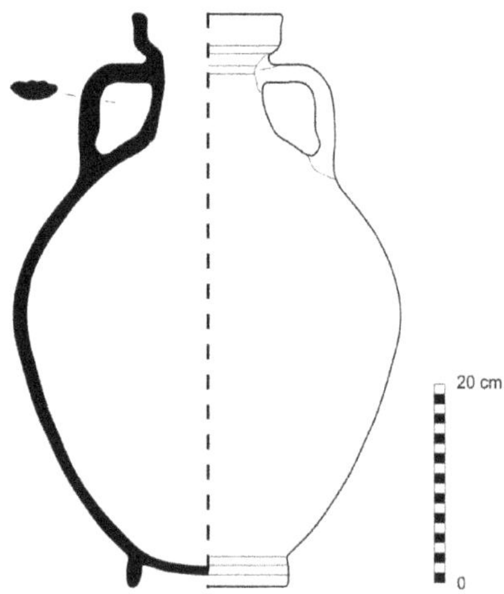

(*cont.*)

Type	Origin	Date	Shape
Gauloise 3	*Gallia Narbonensis*, Chartres, Noyon, Châlon-sur-Saône, Sens and the Bordeaux region	1st c. AD	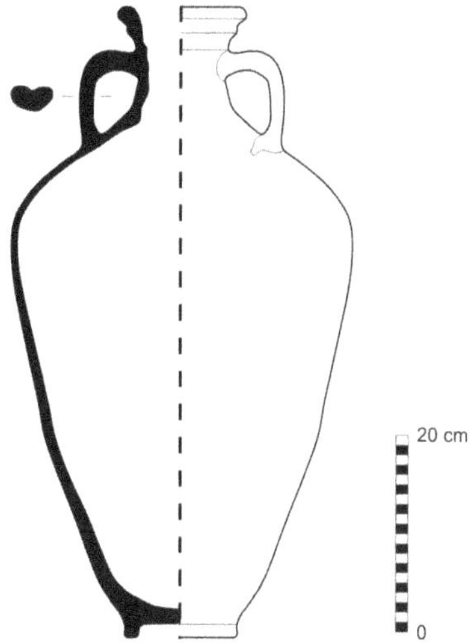
Gauloise 4	Narbonne, Languedoc, Provence	1st–3rd c. AD	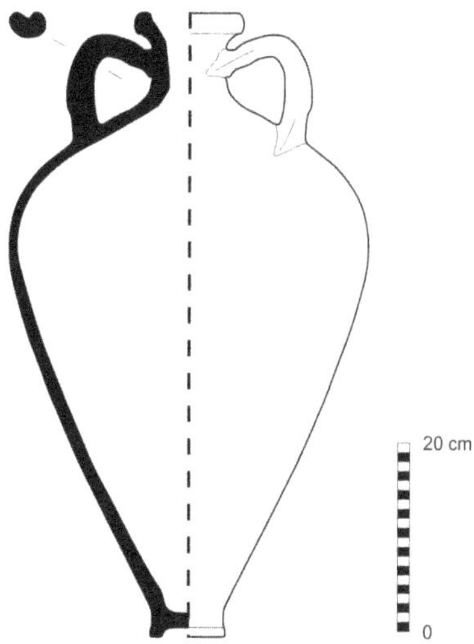

(cont.)

Type	Origin	Date	Shape
Gauloise 5	*Gallia Narbonensis* (an imitation was produced in the region of Bordeaux in Aquitaine)	1st–2nd c. AD	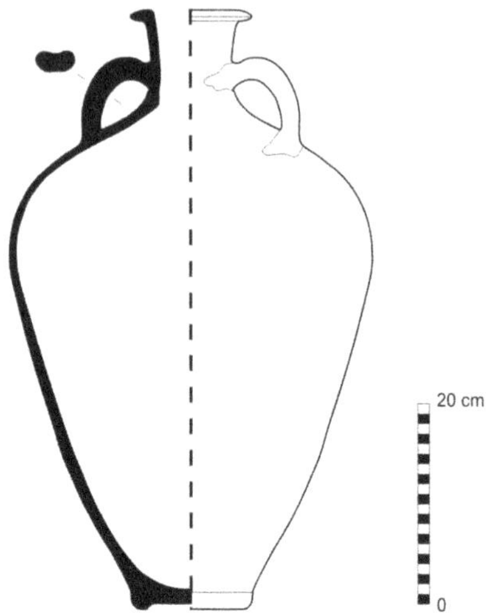
Dressel 28	Velaux, Bouches-du-Rhône, but mostly produced in Spain	1st–2nd c. AD	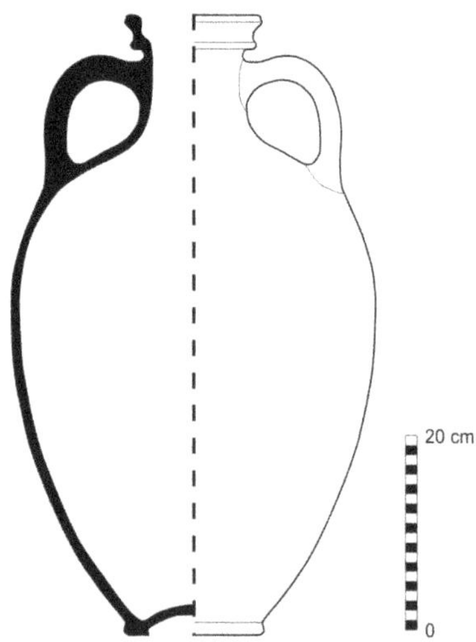

(*cont.*)

Type	Origin	Date	Shape
Africa			
Dressel 30 (Keay 1A, B and Tunisian variants)	*Mauretania Caesariensis* and the cities of *Tubusuctu*/Tiklat or *Saldae*/Bougie; Zeugitana region of Tunisia at Neapolis/Nabeul and in the Cap Bon region at El-Assa and in the Byzacena region at Salakta	3rd–4th c. AD	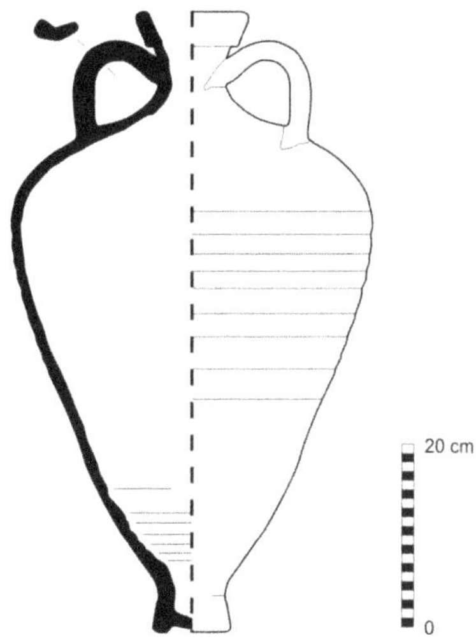
Africana IID	*Hadrumetum* in the Sahel region of Roman *Byzacena*, as well as at *Leptiminus*, *Sullecthum*, *Thaenae*, Oued El-Akarit.	3rd–4th c. AD	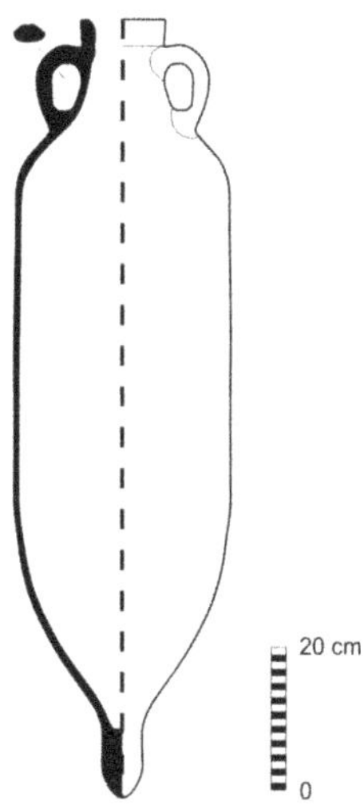

(*cont.*)

Type	Origin	Date	Shape
Africana III A	Tunisia, mainly *Zeugitana* and *Byzacena*, possibly Algeria	3rd–4th c. AD	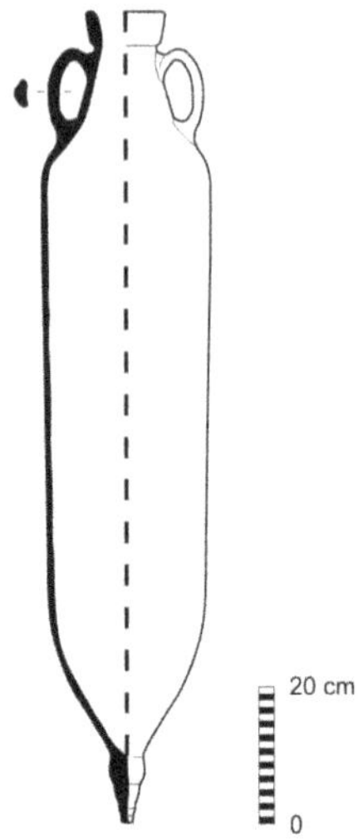
Africana IIIB	Nabeul and probably in other parts of Tunisia	4th c. AD	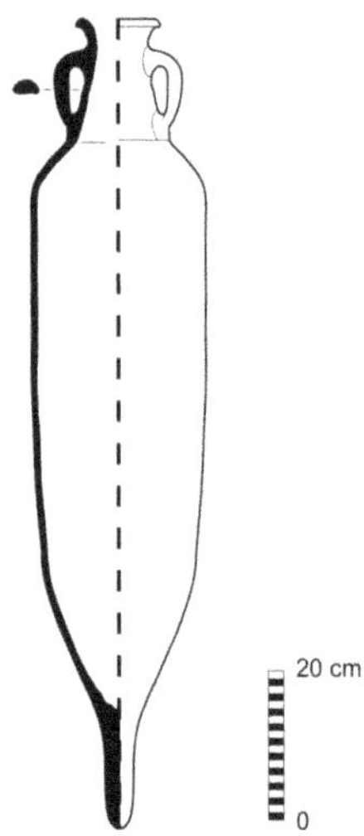

(cont.)

Type	Origin	Date	Shape
Africana IIIC	Tunisia, mainly *Zeugitana* and *Byzacena*	4th–5th c. AD	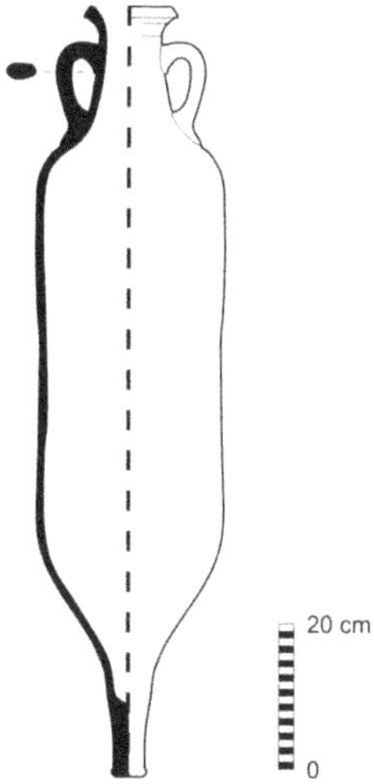
Spatheion 2	North Africa	5th–6th c. AD	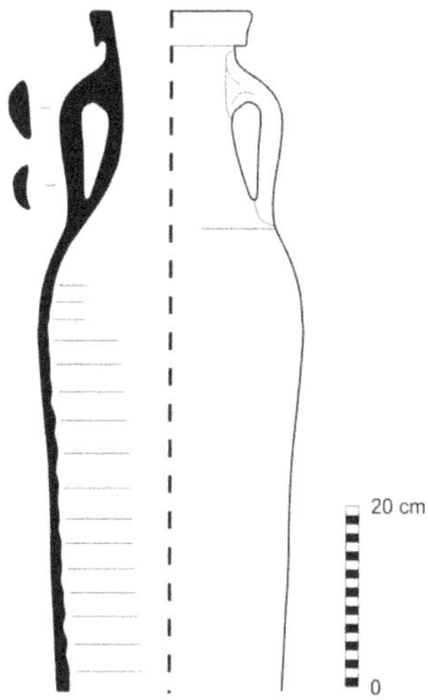

(*cont.*)

Type	Origin	Date	Shape
Spatheion 3	Variant C is attested to in the Zeugitana region at *Neapolis* and variant D in the *Byzacena* region at Moknine.	6th–8th c. AD	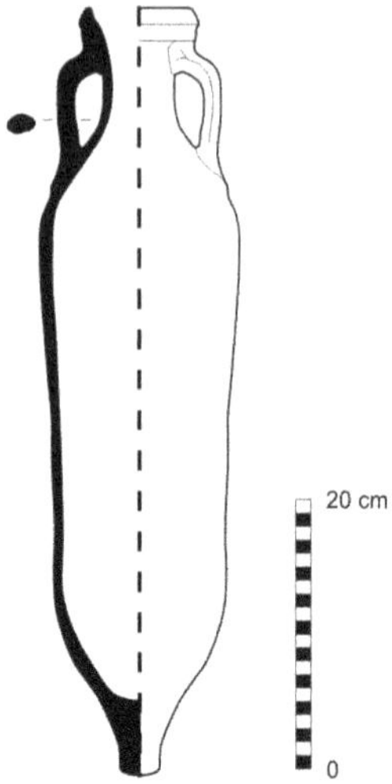
Spain			
Dressel 28	Guadalquivir valley of *Baetica*, but also produced in France	1st–2nd c. AD	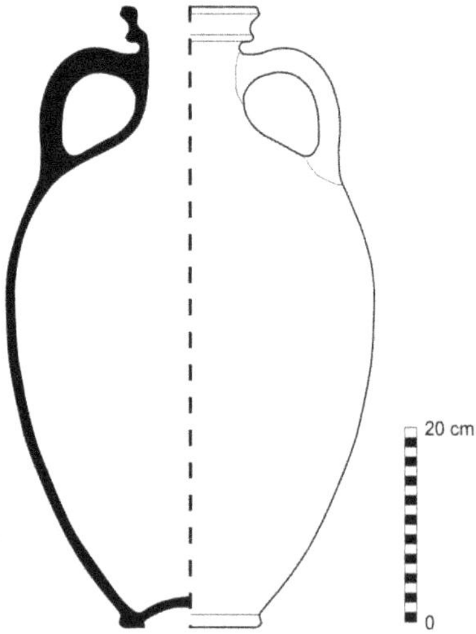

(*cont.*)

Type	Origin	Date	Shape
Dressel 2–4 Catalan	Hispania *Tarraconensis* from Tarragona to Girona.	1st c. BC–2nd c. AD	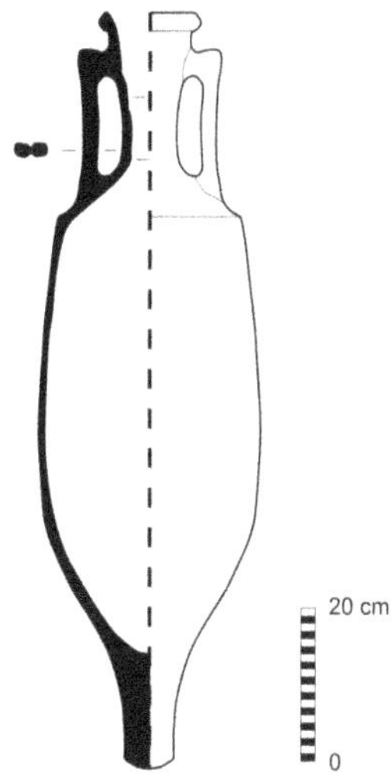
Haltern 70	*Baetica*: upper and middle Guadalquivir valley, the Marismas, and the Huelva and coastal region	1st c. BC–2nd c. AD	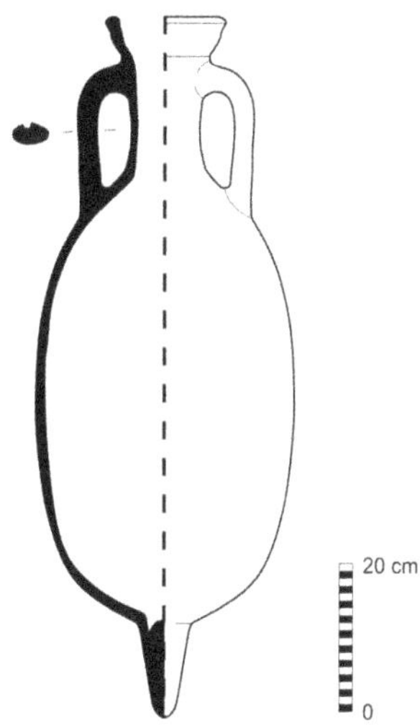

Bibliography

Abbreviations

CAF *Comicorum Atticorum fragmenta.*

CMG *Corpus Medicorum Graecorum.*

FCG *Fragmenta Comicorum Graecorum.*

FHG *Fragmenta Historicorum Graecorum*

LRCW *Late Roman coarse wares, cooking wares and amphorae in the Mediterranean.*

LGPN *A lexicon of Greek personal names*, P.M. Fraser, E. Matthews eds., Oxford /New York 1987–2010.

MDIA *Monographs of the Danish Institute at Athens.*

MGH Auct. Antiquiss. *Monumenta Germaniae historica inde ab anno Christi quingentesimo usque ad annum millesimum et quingentesimum. Auctores antiquissimi.*

MGO *Medicorum Graecorum Opera.*

OCT *Oxford Classical Texts.*

OCD *The Oxford Classical Dictionary* (4th ed.), S. Hornblower, A. Spawforth, E. Eidinow eds., Oxford 2012.

Teubner *Bibliotheca Scriptorum Graecorum et Romanorum Teubneriana.*

Journal abbreviations are according to L'Année philologique.

List of Epigraphic and Literary Sources

AE L'Année épigraphique, Paris: Presses universitaires de France.

CIL *Corpus Inscriptionum Latinarum* (Berlin-Brandenburgische Academie des Wissenschaften)

- vol. IV: *Inscriptiones parietariae Pompeianae Herculanenses Stabianae*, C. Zangemeister, R. Schoene eds., Berlin 1871.
  - Suppl. II: *Inscriptiones parietariae et vasorum fictilium*, A. Mau ed., Berlin 1909.
  - Suppl. III: *Inscriptiones Pompeianae Herculanenses parietariae et vasorum fictilium*, fasc. 1–4, M. Della Corte, P. Ciprotti eds., Berlin 1952–1970.
- vol. XV: *Inscriptiones urbis Romae Latinae. Instrumentum domesticum*, H. Dressel ed., Berlin 1891 (part 1), 1899 (part 2).

IG *Inscriptiones Graecae* (Berlin-Brandenburgische Akademie der Wissenschaften)
– vol. XII. Supplementum: *Addenda to IG XII, 2–3, 5, and 7–9*, F. Hiller von Gaertringen ed., 1939.

Aelianus, Claudius, *Varia Historia et fragmenta*, C.G. Kühn ed., Lipsiae: Teubner, 1780.

Aelianus, Claudius (transl.), *Claudius Aelianus His Various History*, T. Stanley ed., London 1665.

Aetius, *Aetii Amideni Libri medicinales*, A. Olivieri ed., (CMG VIII 1–2), Lipsiae/Berolini: Akademie-Verlag, 1935 and 1950.

Andocides, *Minor Attic Orators in two volumes* (1: Antiphon Andocides, with an English translation), K.J. Maidment ed., London: Heinemann/Cambridge, Mass.: Harvard University Press, 1968.

Apuleius of Madaura, *Opera Omnia*, G.F. Hildebrand ed., Hildesheim: G. Olms, 1968.

Apuleius of Madaura (transl.), *The Apologia and Florida of Apuleius of Madaura*, H.E. Butler ed., Oxford: Clarendon Press, 1909.

Aretaeus, *Aretaei Cappadocis Opera Omnia*, C.G. Kühn ed., (MGO XXIV), Lipsiae: officina libraria Car. Cnoblochii, 1828.

Aretaeus (transl.), *The Extant Works of Aretaeus, The Cappadocian. Aretaeus*, F. Adams ed., London 1856.

Aristophanes, *Aristophanis fabulae*, N. Wilson ed., vol. I–II, Oxford: OCT, Oxford University Press, 2007.

Athenaeus, *Athenaei Naucratitae Dipnosophistarum Libri XV*, vol. I–III, G. Kaibel ed., Lipsiae: Teubner, 1887–1890.

Cato, *M. Porci Catonis de agri cultura*, A. Mazzarino ed., Lipsiae: Teubner, 2011.

Clemens of Alexandria, *Clementis Alexandrini Paedagogus*, M. Marcovich ed., Lugduni Batavorum 2002.

Clemens of Alexandria (transl. by W. Wilson) in *Ante-Nicene fathers: the writings of the fathers down to A.D. 325*, A. Roberts, J. Donaldson eds., Peabody, Mass.: Hendrickson Publishers, 1994.

Comicorum Graecorum Fragmenta, G. Kaibel ed., Berlin 1899.

Comicorum Atticorum fragmenta, vol. I–III, T. Kock, Lipsiae: Teubner, 1880–1888.

Demosthenes, *Demosthenis Orationes*, M.R. Dilts ed., vol. I–IV, Oxford: OCT, Oxford University Press, 2002–2009.

Demosthenes (transl.), *Private orations* (with an English translation), A.T. Murray ed., London: Heinemann, 1939.

Dioscorides, *Pedanii Dioscuridis Anazarbei De materia medica libri quinque*, M. Wellmann ed., Berolini: Weidmannos, 1904–1916.

Dioscorides, *Pedanii Dioscordis Anazarbei De materia medica libri quinque*, C. Sprengel ed., (MGO XXV–XXVI), Lipsiae: Teubner, 1829–1830.

Dioscorides (transl.), *Fünf Bücher über die Heilkunde. Pedanius Dioscurides aus Anazarba*, M. Aufmesser ed., Hildesheim: Olms-Weidmann, 2002.

Dioscorides (transl.), *De materia medica by Pedanius Dioscorides*, L.Y. Beck ed., Hildesheim: Olms, 2005.

Dioscorides (transl.), *Dioscorides. De Materia Medica*, T.A. Osbaldeston ed., Johannesburg 2000.

Fragmenta Comicorum Graecorum, vol. I–V, A. Meineke ed., Berolini: G. Reimer 1839–1857.

Fronto, *M. Cornelii Frontonis epistulae*, M.P.J. van den Hout, Lugduni Batavorum: Brill, 1988.

Fragmenta Historicorum Graecorum, K.O. Müller ed., Parisiis: Editore Ambrosio Firmin Didot, 1841–1883.

Galen, *Claudii Galeni Opera Omnia*, C.G. Kühn ed., (MGO I–XX), Lipsiae: officina libraria Car. Cnoblochii, 1821–1833.

Galen, *De victu Attenuante*, K. Kalbfleisch ed., (CMG V 4,2), Lipsiae/Berolini: Teubner, 1923.

Gellius, Aulus, *A. Gellii Noctium Atticarum libri XX*, vol. II, M.J. Hertz, C. Hosius eds., Stuttgartiae: Teubner, 1981.

Hippocrates, *Magni Hippocratis Opera Omnia*, vol. I–III, C.G. Kühn ed., (MGO XXI–XXIII), Lipsiae: officina libraria Car. Cnoblochii, 1825–1827.

Hippocrates (transl.), *On Regimen in Acute Diseases*, F. Adams ed., Adelaide: The University of Adelaide Library, 2007.

Horatius Flaccus, Quintus, *Opera*, F. Klingner ed., Lipsiae: Teubner, 2012.

Libanius, *Libanii Opera*, R. Foerster ed., Lipsiae: Teubner, 1903–1927.

Libanius (transl.), *Selected Letters of Libanius from the Age of Constantinus and Julian*, S. Bradbury ed., Liverpool: Liverpool University Press, 2004.

Libanius (transl.), *Libanius: Imaginary Speeches*, D.A. Russel ed., London: Duckworth, 1996.

Longus, *Daphnis et Chloe*, M.D. Reeve ed., Lipsiae: Teubner, 2013.

Lucian, *Luciani Samosatensis opera*, K.G. Jacobitz ed., Lipsiae: Teubner, 1913.

Martial, *Epigrammata*, W.M. Lindsay ed., Oxford: OCT, 1922.

Matro of Pitane, *Matro of Pitane and the tradition of epic parody in the 4th c. BCE: text, translation and commentary*, S.D. Olson, A. Sena eds., Atlanta Ga.: Scholars Press 1999.

Oribasius, *Oribasii Collectionum medicarum reliquiae libri I–VIII*, J. Raeder ed., (CMG VI 1,1), Lipsiae/Berolini: Teubner, 1928.

Oribasius, *Oribasii Synopsis ad Eustathium*, J. Raeder ed., (CMG VI 3), Lipsiae/Berolini: Teubner, 1926.

Oribasius, *Oribasii Libri ad Eunapium*, J. Raeder ed., (CMG VI 3), Lipsiae/Berolini: Teubner, 1926.

Paulus Aegineta, *Libri*, J.L. Heiberg ed., CMG IX 1–2, Lipsiae/Berolini: Teubner, 1921 and 1924.

Plautus, *Comoediae I–II*, W.M. Lindsay ed., Oxford: OCT, 1922.

Plautus (transl.), *Curculio*, in *The complete Roman drama*, G.E. Ducworth ed., New York, 1942.

Pliny the Elder, *Naturalis historiae libri XXXVII*, vol. II, J. von Ludwig, K. Mayhoff, T. Friedrich eds., Lipsiae: Teubner, 1967–1970.

Plutarch, *Non posse suaviter vivi secundum Epicurum*, G.N. Bernardakis ed., Lipsiae: Teubner, 1895.

Plutarch, *Plutarchi Vitae parallelae*, vol. I–IV, Cl. Lindskog, K. Ziegler eds., Lipsiae: Teubner, 1914–1939.

Pollux, *Onomastikon*, I. Bekker ed., s.l. 1846.

Propertius, Sextus, *Elegiarum libri IV*, P. Fedeli ed., Lipsiae: Teubner, 2013.

Psellus, Michael, *Poemata*, L.G. Westerink ed., Lipsiae: Teubner, 1992.

Psellus, Michael, *Oratoria minora*, A.R. Littlewood ed., Lipsiae: Teubner, 2011.

Sidonius Apolinaris, *Gai Solii Apollinaris Sidonii Epistulae et carmina*, Ch. Lütjohann ed., (MGH *Auct. Antiquiss.* VIII), Berolini: Weidmannos 1887.

Scribonius Largus, *Scribonii Largi conpositiones*, G. Helmreich ed., Lipsiae: Teubner, 1887.

Strabo, *Strabonis Geographica*, vol. I–X, S.L. Radt ed. (with German translation), Göttingen: Vandenhoeck & Ruprecht, 2002–2011.

Tibullus, Albius, *Albii Tibulli aliorumque carmina*, Stuttgardiae: Teubner, 1988.

Tibullus (transl.), *Tibullus: Elegies introduction, text, translation and notes* (3rd ed.), G. Lee ed., Liverpool: F. Cairns, 1990.

Varro, *M. Terenti Varronis De lingua latina quae supersunt*, G. Goetz, F. Schöll eds., Lipsiae: Teubner, 1910.

Vergil, *P. Vergili Maronis Opera*, R.A.B. Maynors ed., Oxford: OCT, Clarendon Press, 1969.

Vitruvius, *Vitruvii de architectura libri decem*, F. Krohn ed., Lipsiae: Teubner, 1922.

Literature

AA.VV. 1970: *Ostia II. Le terme del Nuotatore. Scavo dell'ambiente I* (Studi miscellanei 16), Roma.

Abdelhamid S. 2013: 'Against the throw-away-mentality: the reuse of amphoras in ancient maritime transport', in H.P. Hahn, H. Weiss eds., *Mobility, meaning and the transformations of things*, Oxford, pp. 91–106.

Achilli A., Olivieri A., Pala M., Metspalu E., Fornarino S., Battaglia V., Accetturo M., Kutuev I., Khusnutdinova E., Pennarun E., Cerutti N., Di Gaetano C., Crobu F., Palli D., Matullo G., Santachiara-Benerecetti A.S., Cavalli-Sforza L.L., Semino O.,

Villems R., Bandelt H.J., Piazza A., Torroni A. 2007: 'Mitochondrial DNA variation of modern Tuscans supports the Near Eastern origin of Etruscans', *The American Journal of Human Genetics* 80, pp. 759–768.

Agostiniani L. 2000: 'Il vino degli Etruschi: la lingua', in C. Cremonesi, D. Tomasi eds., *L'avventura del vino nel Bacino del Mediterraneo: itinerari storici ed archeologici prima e dopo Roma* (Simposio internazionale, Conegliano, 30 settembre–2 ottobre 1998), Conegliano, pp. 103–108.

Albanese Procelli R.M. 2017: 'Sicily', in A. Naso ed., *Etruscology*, Boston/Berlin, pp. 1653–1668.

Albiach R., Ballester C., Escrivà I., Fernández A. 2008: 'Estudios estratigráficos y geofísicos entre la casa de Ariadna y el Vicolo Storto (VII, 4)', in P.G. Guzzo, M.P. Guidobaldi eds., *Nuove ricerche archeologiche nell'area vesuviana (scavi 2003–2006)*, Roma, pp. 249–264.

Albore Livadie C. 1985: *La situazione in Campania*, in AA.VV., *Il commercio Etrusco arcaico* (Atti dell'Incontro di Studio, Roma 1983), Roma, pp. 127–154.

Alcock J.P. 2006: *Food in the ancient world*, London.

Alföldy G. 1991: *Historia społeczna starożytnego Rzymu*, Poznań 1991.

Allison P.M. 2001: 'Using the material and written sources: Turn of the Millennium approaches to Roman domestic space', *AJA* 105, pp. 181–208.

Amarger M.-P., Brun J.-P. 2007: 'La forge de l'insula I, 6, 1 de Pompéi', *Quaderni di studi pompeiani* 1, pp. 147–168.

Amouretti M.-C. 1990: 'Vin, vinagre, piquette dans l'Antiquité', in G. Garrier ed., *Le Vin des Historiens* (Actes du Ier Symposium Vin et Histoire, 19–21 mai 1989), Suze-La-Rousse, pp. 75–87.

André J. 1981: *L'alimentation et la cuisine a Rome*, Paris.

Andreau J. 1974: *Les affaires de monsieur Jucundus*, Rome.

Andreau J. 1993: 'The freedmen', in A. Giardina ed., *The Romans*, Chicago, pp. 175–198.

Annecchino R. 1960: *Storia di Pozzuoli e della zona flegrea*, Pozzuoli.

Anselmino L., Coletti C.M., Ferrarini M.L. 1986: 'Ostia. Terme del Nuotatore', in A. Giardina ed., *Società romana e impero tardoantico* 3: *Le merci. Gli insiediamenti*, Roma /Bari, pp. 45–81.

Aquilé X., Castanyer P., Santos M., Tremoleda J. 2006: 'El commercio etrusco en emporion: evidencias sobre la presencia de materiales etruscos en la Palaia Polis de Empúries', in S. Gori, M.Ch. Bettini eds., *Gli Etruschi da Genova ad Ampurias* (Atti del XXIV Convegno di studi etruschi ed italici, Marseille, Lattes, 26 settembre–1 ottobre 2002), Pisa, pp. 175–192.

Aranguren B., Bellini C., Mariotti Lippi M., Mori Secci M., Pelazzi P. 2007: 'L'avvio della coltura della vite in Toscana: L'esempio di San Lorenzo a Greve (Firenze)', in A. Ciacci, P. Rendini, A. Zifferero eds., *Archeologia della Vite e del Vino in Etruria*, Siena, pp. 88–95.

Aranguren B., Bellini C., Mariotti Lippi M., Mori Secci M., Pelazzi P. 2012: 'Testimonianze dell uso della vite nell Bronzo Medio: nuovi dati da San Lorenzo a Greve (Firenze)', in A. Ciacci, P. Rendini, A. Zifferero eds., *Archeologia della vite e del vino in Toscana e nel Latium. Dalle tecniche dell'indagine archeologica alle prospettive della biologia molecolare*, Firenze, pp. 125–131.

Archibald Z.H. 2013: *Ancient economies of the Northern Aegean. Fifth to first centuries BC*, Oxford.

Arnaud P. 2007: 'Diocletian's prices edict: the prices of seaborne transport and the average duration of maritime travel', *JRA* 20, pp. 321–336.

Arnott W.G. 1970: 'Studies in Comedy, II: Toothless wine', *GRBS* 11(1), pp. 43–47.

Arthur P. 1985: 'Naples: notes on the economy of a dark age city', *Papers in Italian Archaeology IV* (BAR Int. Series 4), pp. 247–259.

Arthur P. 1990: 'Anfore dell'alto adriatico e il problema del Samos Cistern Type', *AN* 61, pp. 281–295.

Arthur P. 1995: 'Roman exports to the North. Wine in the West: a view from Campania', in J. Swaddling, S. Walker, P. Roberts eds., *Italy in Europe: economic relations 700 BC–AD 50*, London, pp. 241–251.

Arthur P. 1998: 'Eastern Mediterranean amphorae between 500 and 700: a view from Italy', in L. Saguí ed., *Ceramica in Italia: 6–7 secolo* (Atti del Convegno in onore di John W. Hayes, Roma, 11–13 maggio 1995), Firenze, pp. 157–183.

Arthur P. 2002: *Naples. From Roman town to city-state*, Rome.

Arthur P., Williams D. 1992: 'Campanian wine, Roman Britain and the third century A.D.', *JRA* 5, pp. 250–260.

Augenti A., Cirelli E., Nannetti M.C., Sabetta T., Savini E., Zantedeschi E. 2007: 'Nuovi dati archeologici dallo scavo di Classe', in S. Gelichi, C. Negrelli eds., *La circolazione delle ceramiche nell'Adriatico tra tarda antichità e altomedioevo*, Mantova, pp. 257–295.

Auriemma R. 2007: 'Anfore. Produzioni orientali', in C. Morselli ed., *Trieste antica. Lo scavo di Crosada*, Trieste, pp. 136–154.

Auriemma R., Degrassi V. 2015: 'Flussi di circolazione e redistribuzione in Adriatico tra tarda Repubblica e Impero: anfore da contesti terrestri e subacquei', in Y. Marion, F. Tassaux eds., *AdriAtlas et l'histoire de l'espace adriatique du VIe s. a.C. au VIIIe s. p.C.: actes du colloque international de Rome (4–6 novembre 2013)*, Bordeaux, pp. 453–478.

Auriemma R., Degrassi V., Quiri E. 2015: 'Eastern amphora imports in the Adriatic Sea: evidence from terrestrial and underwater contexts of the Roman Imperial age', in S. Demesticha ed., *Per terram, per mare: seaborne trade and the distribution of Roman amphorae in the Mediterranean*, Uppsala, pp. 139–160.

Auriemma R., Degrassi V., Gaddi D., Maggi P. 2016: 'Canale Anfora: uno spaccato sull'importazione di alimenti ad Aquileia tra I e III sec. d.C.', in G. Cuscito ed., *L'alimen-*

tazione nell'antichità: atti della 46. settimana di studi aquileiesi: Aquileia (14–16 maggio 2015), Trieste, pp. 379–403.

Avi-Yonah M. 1958: 'The economics of Byzantine Palestine', *Israel Exploration Journal* 8(1), pp. 39–51.

Baldacci P. 1972: 'Le principali correnti del commercio di anfore romane nella Cisalpina', in A. Forni ed., *I problemi della ceramica romana di Ravenna, della Valle Padana e dell'alto Adriatico* (Atti del Convegno Internazionale, Ravenna 1969), Bologna, pp. 103–127.

Baldwin B. 1967: 'Opimian wine', *AJPh* 88(2), pp. 173–175.

Bang P.F. 1997: 'Antiquity between "Primitivism" and "Modernism"', *Workpaper* 53–97, Centre for Cultural Research, University of Aarhus, http://www.hum.au.dk/ckulturf/pages/publications/pfb/antiquity.htm, accessed 11.04.2019.

Bang P.F. 2008: *The Roman bazaar: a comparative study of trade and markets in a tributary empire*, Cambridge.

Bang P.F., Ikeguchi M. 2017: 'Afterword to: Keith Hopkins' Models, ships and staples', in C. Kelly ed., *Sociological studies in Roman history / Keith Hopkins*, Cambridge, pp. 306–312.

Bar D. 2004: 'Population, settlement and economy in late Roman and Byzantine Palestine (70–641 AD)', *Bulletin of the School of Oriental and African Studies* 67(3), pp. 307–320.

Bartoloni G. 1987: 'Le comunità dell'Italia centrale tirrenica e la colonizzazione greca in Campania', in M. Cristofani ed., *Etruria e Lazio arcaico* (Atti dell'Incontro di studio, 10–11 novembre 1986), Roma, pp. 37–53.

Bartoloni G. 2002: 'Appunti sull'introduzione del banquetto in Lazio: la coppa del principe', in M.G. Amadasi Guzzo, M. Liverani, P. Matthiae eds., *Da Pyrgi a Mozia: studi sull'archeologia del Mediterraneo in memoria di Antonia Ciasca*, Roma, pp. 57–68.

Bartoloni G. 2007: 'Il consumo del vino nell'Italia centrale tirrenica', in A. Ciacci, P. Rendini, A. Zifferero eds., *Archeologia della Vite e del Vino in Etruria*, Siena, pp. 147–160.

Bartoloni G., Acconcia V., Kortenaar S. 2012: 'Viticoltura e consumo del vino in Etruria: la cultura materiale tra la fine dell'età del Ferro e l'Orientalizzante Antico', in A. Ciacci, P. Rendini, A. Zifferero eds., *Archeologia della vite e del vino in Toscana e nel Lazio. Dalle tecniche dell'indagine archeologica alle prospettive della biologia molecolare*, Firenze, pp. 201–275.

Basile B., Di Pasquale G., Monaco A., Vella M. 2010: 'Sopravvivenze dell'antico paesaggio della vite in Campania', in G. di Pasquale ed., *VINUM NOSTRUM: arte, scienza e miti del vino nelle civiltà del Mediterraneo antico*, Firenze, pp. 96–105.

Bats M. 1998: 'Marseille archaïque. Étrusques et Phocéens en Méditerranée nord-occidentale', *MEFRA* 110/2, pp. 609–633.

Bats M. 2012: 'L'arrivée du vin étrusque sur le litoral del Méditerranée nord-occidentale (VIe–Ve s. av. J.-C.)' in A. Ciacci, P. Rendini, A. Zifferero eds., *Archeologia della vite e del vino in Toscana e nel Lazio. Dalle tecniche dell'indagine archeologica alle prospettive della biologia molecolare*, Firenze, pp. 377–389.

Béguin D. 2002: 'Le vin médecin chez Galien', in J. Jouanna, L. Villard eds., *Vin et sante Grèce ancienne* (BCH Suppl. 40), pp. 141–154.

Beijer A.J. 1995: 'Greek and local pottery in ancient Latium. The question of Greek influence in Latium in the iron age', in M. Maaskant-Kleibrink ed., *Caeculus 2. The landscape of the Goddess*, Groningen, pp. 55–64.

Belotti Ch. 2004: *Ritrovamenti di anfore a Iulia Concordia: aspetti topografici ed economici*, Roma.

Benett C.E. 1987: *Horace. The Odes and Epodes*, Cambridge/London.

Berry Ch.J. 1994: *The idea of luxury: a conceptual and historical investigation*, Cambridge.

Berry J. 1997: 'The conditions of domestic life in Pompeii in a.d. 79: a case study of Houses 11 and 12, Insula 9, Region I', *PBSR* 65, pp. 103–125.

Bertoldi T. 2008: 'Terme di Traiano: materiali dal saggio 3M', *MEFRA* 120(2), pp. 447–467.

Bertoldi T. 2010: 'I materiali del contesto traianeo (saggio M) dallo scavo nell'angolo sud-occidentale', *BCAR* 111, pp. 307–310.

Bertoldi T. 2011a: 'Le anfore', in A. Capodiferro, P. Quaranta eds., *Alle pendici dell'Aventino. Gli scavi di Via Marmorata 2*, Roma, pp. 148–174.

Bertoldi T. 2011b: *Ceramiche comuni dal suburbio di Roma*, Roma.

Bertoldi T. 2012: *Guida alle anfore romane di età imperiale: forme, impasti e distribuzione*, Roma.

Bertoldi V. 1942: *Linguistica storica. Questioni di metodo*, Napoli.

Bettini M. 1995: 'In vino stuprum', in O. Murray, M. Tecusan eds., *In vino veritas*, London, pp. 214–237.

Bevilacqua G. 1994: 'Bolli anforari rodii da Falerii Novi', in AA.VV., *Epigrafia della produzione e della distribuzione* (Actes de la VIe Rencontre franco-italienne sur l'épigraphie du monde romain, Rome, 5–6 juin 1992), Roma, pp. 463–475.

Bezeczky T. 2010: 'Italian wine in the Eastern Mediterranean. Amphorae from Etruria, Latium, and Campania from the fourth century B.C. to the first century A.D. The Case of the Ephesian Amphorae', *Bollettino di Archeologia on line* I. Volume speciale B/B8/6, pp. 82–92, accessed 30.10.2014.

Bezeczky T. 2013: *The amphorae of Roman Ephesus*, Vienna.

Biondani F. 1998: 'Verona. Via Ponte Pietra 19. Rinvenimenti di strutture in opera reticolata', *QdAV* 14, pp. 55–66.

Boersma J., Yntema D., Van der Werff J. 1986: 'Excavations in the House of the Porch (V.II.4–5) at Ostia', *BABesch* 61, pp. 77–137.

Bonifay M. 1986: 'Observations sur les amphores tardives à Marseille d'après les fouilles de la Bourse (1980–1984)', *RAN* 19, pp. 269–301.

Bonifay M., Villedieu F. 1989: 'Importations d'amphores orientales en Gaule (ve–viie siècle)' in V. Déroche, J.M. Spieser, eds., *Recherches sur la céramique byzantine* (Actes du colloque organisé par l'École française d'Athènes et l'Université de Strasbourg II), Athènes, pp. 17–46.

Bonifay M., Piéri D. 1995: 'Amphores du ve au viie siècle à Marseille. Nouvelles données sur la typologie et le contenu', *JRA* 8, pp. 94–121.

Bonifay M., Botte E., Capelli C., Contino A., Djaoui D., Panella C., Tchernia A. 2015: 'Nouvelles hypothèses sur l'origine et le contenu des amphores africaines Ostia LIX et XXIII', *Antiquités africaines* 51, pp. 189–210.

Bonifay M. 2017: 'The distribution of African pottery under the Roman Empire', in A. Wilson, A. Bowman eds., *Trade, commerce, and the state in the Roman world*, Oxford, pp. 327–351.

Borgard P., Carre M.-B., Fontaine S.-D. 2007: 'Pompéi: un site de référence? Approche socio-économique de l'insula I 8', in L. Barnabei ed., *Contributi di archeologia vesuviana III: I culti di Pompei. Raccolta critica della documentazione*, Roma, pp. 108–116.

Botto M., Vives-Ferrándiz Sánchez J. 2006: 'Importazioni etrusche tra la Baleari e la Penisola Iberica (VIII–prima metà del V sec. A.C.)', *Annali della Fondazione per il Museo Claudio Faina* 13, pp. 117–196.

Bound M. 1985: 'Una nave mercantile di età arcaica all'Isola del Giglio', in AA.VV., *Il commercio Etrusco arcaico* (Atti dell'Incontro di Studio, Roma 1983), Roma, pp. 65–70.

Bouvier M. 2000: 'Recherches sur les goûts des vins antiques', in P. François ed., *Le vin de Rome* (Rencontres de Carcassonne 27 Juin 1998, 19 Juin 1999), Toulouse-Le Mirail, pp. 115–133.

Bragantini I., Cipriano M.T., Improta P. 1991: 'Anfore', in I. Bragantini ed., *Ricerche archeologiche a Napoli. Lo scavo di Palazzo Corigliano*, Napoli, pp. 88–103.

Bransbourg G. 2012: 'Rome and the economic integration of empire', *ISAW Working Papers 3*, http://dlib.nyu.edu/awdl/isaw/isaw-papers/3, accessed 19.03.2019.

Brock A.J. 1916: *Galen. On the natural faculties*, London/New York.

Brock R., Wirtjes H. 2000: 'Athenaeus on Greek wine', in D. Braund, J. Wilkins eds., *Athenaeus and his world: reading Greek culture in the Roman Empire*, Exeter, pp. 455–465.

Broekaert W. 2012: 'Joining forces. Commercial partnerships or societates in the early Roman Empire', *Historia* 61/2, pp. 221–253.

Brughmans T., Poblome J. 2016: 'Roman bazaar or market economy? Explaining tableware distributions through computational modelling', *Antiquity* 90, pp. 393–408.

Brun J.-P. 2003: *Le vin et l'huile dans la Méditerranée antique: Viticulture, oléiculture et procédés de fabrication*, Paris.

Brun J.-P. 2004: *Archéologie du vin et de l'huile: de la Préhistoire à l'époque hellén*, Paris.

Bruni S. 2005: 'Aspetti dell'economia di Tarquinia in età arcaica: il caso del vino', in

O. Paoletti, G. Camporeale, eds., *Dinamiche di sviluppo delle città nell'Etruria meridionale. Veio, Caere, Tarquinia, Vulci* (Atti del XXIII Convegno di Studi Etruschi e Italici, 1–6 Ottobre 2001), I–II, Pisa/Roma, pp. 383–394.

Bruno B. 2008: 'Le anfore di media e tarda età imperiale di produzione italica, egeo-orientale, ispanica e le anfore non identificate', in G. Cavalieri Manasse ed., *L'area del Capitolium di Verona: ricerche storiche e archeologiche*, Verona, pp. 373–386.

Buchi E. 1973: 'Banchi di anfore romane a Verona. Note sui commerci cisalpini', in AA.VV., *Il territorio veronese in età romana* (Convegno del 22–24 ottobre 1971), Verona, pp. 534–637.

Bueno M., Mantovani V., Novello M. 2012: 'Progetto Aquileia: Casa delle Bestie Ferite Commercio e consumo ad Aquileia. Analisi delle anfore tardoantiche alla luce di alcuni contesti', *RCRF* Acta 42, pp. 159–168.

Cacciaguerra L. 1990: *Anfore e commerci nella Venetia: dalle anfore elementi utili per la storia economica del Veneto orientale tra il 3. secolo avanti cristo e il 6. secolo dopo Cristo*, Venetia.

Calci C., Sorella R. 1995: 'Forme di paesaggio agrario nell'ager ficulensis', *Atlante Tematico di Topografia Antica* 4, pp. 117–127.

Callender M.H. 1965: *Roman amphorae with index of stamps*, London/New York/Toronto.

Callot O. 1984: *Huileries antiques de Syrie du nord*, Paris.

Camodeca G. 1994: 'Puteoli porto annonario e il commercio del grano in età imperiale', in AA.VV., *Le Ravitaillement en blé de Rome et des centres urbains des débuts de la République jusqu'au Haut-Empire* (Actes du colloque international de Naples, 14–16 Février 1991), Roma, pp. 103–128.

Capodiferro A., Quaranta P. 2011: 'Via Marmorata: un esempio di scavo urbano di emergenza', in A. Capodiferro, P. Quaranta eds., *Alle pendici dell'Aventino. Gli scavi di Via Marmorata* 2, Roma, pp. 51–53.

Carandini A., Fabricotti E. 1967–1968: *Ostia I. Le terme del Nuotatore, ambiente IV* (*Studi Miscellanei* 13), Roma.

Carandini A., Panella C. 1973: *Ostia III. Le terme del Nuotatore. Scavo degli ambienti III, VI, VII. Scavo dell'ambiente V e di un saggio nel'area SO* (*Studi miscellanei* 21), Roma.

Carandini A., Panella C. 1977: *Ostia IV. Le terme del Nuotatore. Scavo dell'ambiente XVI e dell'area XXV* (*Studi Miscellanei* 23), Roma.

Carignani A., Ciotola A., Pacetti F. 1986: 'Roma. Il contesto del tempio della Magna Mater sul Palatino', in A. Giardina ed., *Società romana e impero tardoantico III: Le merci, gli insediamenti*, Roma, pp. 27–43.

Carignani A., Pacetti F. 1989a: 'Le importazioni di anfore bizantine a Roma fra IV e V secolo: le evidenze di alcuni contesti urbani', in V. Deroche, J.-H. Spieser eds., *Recherches sur la Céramique Byzantine* (*BCH* Suppl. 18), pp. 5–16.

Carignani A., Pacetti F. 1989b: 'Anfore tardo-antiche dagli scavi del Palatino', in AA.VV.,

Amphores Romaines et Histoire Économique. Dix ans de Recherche (Actes du Colloque de Sienne 22–24 mai 1986, Collection de l' École Française de Rome 114), Roma, pp. 610–615.

Carre M.-B., Cipriano M.T. 2003: 'Le anfore della necropoli sotto l'autoparco del Vaticano', in E.M. Steinby ed., *La necropoli della via Triumphalis. Il stratto sotto l'Autoparco vaticano*, Roma, pp. 199–210.

Carre M.-B. 2007a: 'L'évolution des importations à Aquilée: Les nouvelles donnes de la fuille au nord du port fluvial. I. La periodisation', in G. Cuscito, C. Zaccharia eds., *Aquileia dalle origini alla costituzione del ducato longobardo* (*Antichità Altoadriatiche* 65), Trieste, pp. 539–546.

Carre M.-B. 2007b: 'L'évolution des importations à Aquilée. III. Les amphores orientales: données quantitatives comparées', in G. Cuscito, C. Zaccharia eds., *Aquileia dalle origini alla costituzione del ducato longobardo* (*Antichità Altoadriatiche* 65), Trieste, pp. 583–604.

Carre M.-B. 2007c: 'L'évolution des importations à Aquilée. V. Quelques réflexions sur les échanges à Aquilée', in G. Cuscito, C. Zaccharia eds., *Aquileia dalle origini alla costituzione del ducato longobardo* (*Antichità Altoadriatiche* 65), Trieste, pp. 621–632.

Carre M.-B., 2009: 'Transport en vrac', in J.-P. Brun, M. Poux, A. Tchernia eds., *Le Vin: Nectar des Dieux, Génie des Hommes*, Barcelona (2nd ed.), pp. 290–291.

Carsana V., Del Vecchio F. 2010: 'Il porto di *Neapolis* in età tardo antica: il contesto di IV secolo D.C.' in S. Menchelli, S. Santoro, M. Pasquinucci, G. Guiducci eds., *LRCW* 3 (BAR Int. Ser. 2185), Oxford, pp. 459–470.

Carsana V., Del Vecchio F. 2017: 'Le anfore di V secolo d.C. dai contesti di edifici prossimi al porto di Neapolis', in. D. Dixneuf ed., *LRCW* 5, Alexandria, pp. 407 417.

Carsana V., D'Amico V., Del Vecchio F. 2007: 'Nuovi dati ceramologici per la storia economica di Napoli tra tarda anticità ed altomedioevo', in M. Bonifay, J.-Ch. Tréglia eds., *LRCW* 2, pp. 423–437.

Carta M., 1987: 'Descrizione stratigrafica dello scavo. Materiali rinvenuti', in M. Carta, I. Pohl, F. Zevi eds., *Ostia. La taverna dell'Invidioso. Piazzale delle Corporazioni, portico Ovest: saggi sotto i mosaici* (NSA 32, suppl. 1978), pp. 19–164.

Casaramona A. et al. 2010: 'Anfore cretesi dallo scavo del Nuovo Mercato di Testaccio', *RCRF Acta* 41, pp. 113–122.

Caspio A., D'Agostini C., Molari C., Musco S., Raiano D., Rizzo G., Zabotti F. 2009: 'Riflessioni sul suburbio orientale di Roma', in V. Jolivet, C. Pavolini, M.A. Temei, R. Volpe eds., *SUBURBIUM II: Il suburbio di Roma dalla fine dell'Età monarchica alla nascita del sistema delle ville* (*V–II secolo a.C.*), Roma, pp. 455–496.

Castagnoli F., 1980: 'Installazioni portuali a Roma', in J.H. D'Arms, E.Ch. Kopff eds., *The seaborne commerce of ancient Rome: studies in archaeology and history* (MAAR 36), Rome, pp. 35–42.

Castrén P. 1975: *Ordo populusque Pompeianus. Polity and society in Roman Pompeii*, Rome.

Ceazzi A., Del Brusco A. 2014: 'La ceramica comune, la ceramica da cucina locale e importata e le anfore dallo scavo di Via Bolivia', in N. Poulou-Papadimitriou, E. Nodarou, V. Kilikoglou eds., *LCRW* 4, pp. 943–953

Ceci M. 2006: 'Un contesto medio imperiale dall'area dei Mercati di Traiano', in R. Meneghini, R. Santangeli Valenzani eds., *Roma: Lo scavo dei fori imperiali 1995–2000: i contesti ceramici*, Roma, pp. 25–56.

Cerchiai C. 2013: *Nettare di Dioniso. La vite e il vino attraverso le parole degli autori antichi*, Roma.

Chaniotis A. 1988: 'Vinum Creticum excellens. Zum Weinhandel Kretas', *MBAH* 7(1), pp. 62–89.

Chic García G. 1987: 'El commercio del aceite de la Astigi romana', *Habis* XVII, pp. 243–264.

Chic García G. 1993: 'Los Aelii en la producción y difusión del aceite bético', *MBAH* 9(2), pp. 1–22.

Ciacci A. 2010: 'La ricostruzione del paesaggio vitivinicolo antico: l'indagine sui vitigni e la circolazione varietale', in G. di Pasquale ed., *VINUM NOSTRUM: arte, scienza e miti del vino nelle civiltà del Mediterraneo antico*, Firenze, pp. 74–79.

Ciacci A., Zifferero A. 2007: *Il «Progetto VINUM». Prime considerazioni conclusive*, in A. Ciacci A., P. Rendini, A. Zifferero eds., *Archeologia della vite e del vino in Etruria*, Siena, pp. 249–272.

Ciampoltrini G., Rendini P. 2012: 'Vie e porti del vino nella valle dell'Albegna in età etrusca (VI–V secolo a.C.)', in A. Ciacci, P. Rendini, A. Zifferero eds., *Archeologia della vite e del vino in Toscana e nel Latium. Dalle tecniche dell'indagine archeologica alle prospettive della biologia molecolare*, Firenze, pp. 391–401.

Cianferoni G.C. 2007: 'La vite e il vino in Etruria: i problem aperti', in A. Ciacci, P. Rendini, A. Zifferero eds., *Archeologia della Vite e del Vino in Etruria*, Siena 2007, pp. 19–20.

Cianferoni G.C. 2012: 'La vite e il vino in Etruria: i problem aperti', in A. Ciacci, P. Rendini, A. Zifferero eds., *Archeologia della vite e del vino in Toscana e nel Latium. Dalle tecniche dell'indagine archeologica alle prospettive della biologia molecolare*, Firenze, pp. 29–31.

Cibecchini F. 2006: 'L'arcipelago toscano e l'isola d'Elba: anfore e commerci marittimi', in S. Gori, M.Ch. Bettini eds., *Gli Etruschi da Genova ad Ampurias* (Atti del XXIV Convegno di studi etruschi ed italici, Marseille, Lattes, 26 settembre–1 ottobre 2002), Pisa, pp. 535–551.

Cicirelli C., Albore-Livadie C., Costantini C., Delle Donne M. 2008: 'La vite a Poggiomarino, Longola: un contesto di vinificazione dell'Età del Ferro', in P.G. Guzzo, M.P. Guidobaldi eds., *Nuove ricerche archeologiche nell'area vesuviana (scavi 2003–2006): atti del convegno internazionale, Roma, 1–3 febbraio 2007*, Roma, pp. 574–575.

Cicirelli C., Albore Livadie C. 2008: 'Stato delle ricerche a Longola di Poggiomarino:

quadro insediamentale e problematiche', in P.G. Guzzo, M.P. Guidobaldi eds., *Nuove ricerche archeologiche nell'area vesuviana (scavi 2003–2006): atti del convegno internazionale, Roma, 1–3 febbraio 2007*, Roma, pp. 473–487.

Cipriano S. 1992: 'I depositi di Piazza De Gasperi', in S. Pesavento Mattioli, F. Cosimo Panini eds., *Anfore romane a Padova. Ritrovamenti dalla città*, Modena, pp. 55–102.

Cipriano S. 2001: 'Aspetti economici', in. L. Plesnicar Gec, G. Rosada, P. Egidi eds., *Concordia. Tremilla anni di storia*, Padova, pp. 192–196.

Cipriano S., Ferrarini F. 2001: *Le anfore romane di Opitergium*, Oderzo.

Cipriano S., Mazzocchin S. 1992: 'Anfore dalla zona del porto fluviale', in S. Pesavento Mattioli ed., *Anfore romane a Padova. Ritrovamenti dalla città*, Modena, pp. 151–160.

Cipriano S., Mazzocchin S. 2011: 'Bonifiche con anfore a Padova: note di aggiornamento alla cronologia e alla distribuzione topografica' in L. Capuis, M. Cupitò eds., *Tra protostoria e storia: studi in onore di Loredana Capuis*, Roma, pp. 331–367.

Cipriano S., Mazzocchin S. 2017: 'Western Adriatic amphorae productions: the research status', in G. Lipovac Vrkljan, I. Radić Rossi, A. Konestra eds., *ADRIAMPHORAE: Amphorae as a resource for the reconstruction of economic development in the Adriatic region in Antiquity: local production*, Zagreb, pp. 33–47.

Cipriano S., Mazzocchin S., Pastore P. 1991: 'Novità eproblemi emergenti da un recente ritrovamento di anfore romane a Padova', *QdAV* 7, pp. 163–174.

Cipriano S., Mazzocchin S., Pastore P. 1998: 'Padova. Tre casi in aree a diversa funzionalita', in S. Pesavento Mattioli ed., *Bonifiche e drenaggi con anfore in epoca romana: aspetti tecnici e topografici* (Atti del seminario di studi, Padova, 19–20 ottobre 1995, Materiali d'archeologia 3), Modena, pp. 161–174.

Cirelli E. 2014: 'Typology and diffusion of amphorae in Ravenna and Classe between the 5th and the 8th centuries AD', in N. Poulou-Papadimitrou, E. Nodarou, V. Kilikoglou eds., *LRCW* 4, pp. 541–552.

Clinkenbeard B.D. 1982: 'Lesbian wine and storage amphoras: a progress report on identification', *Hesperia* 51(3), pp. 248–268.

Colonna G. 1985: 'Anfore da trasporto arcaiche: il contributo di Pyrgi', in AA.VV., *Il commercio Etrusco arcaico* (Atti dell'Incontro di Studio, Roma 1983), Roma, pp. 5–18.

Colonna G. 2006: 'Il commercio etrusco arcaico vent'anni dopo', in G.M. Della Fina ed., *Gli Etruschi e il Mediterraneo: commerci e politica*, Roma, pp. 9–28.

Conovici N. 2005: 'The dynamics of trade in transport amphoras from Sinope, Thasos and Rhodos on the western Black Sea Coast: a comparative approach', in V. Stolba, L. Hannestad eds., *Chronologies of the Black Sea area in the period c. 400–100 BC*, Aarhus, pp. 97–117.

Contino A., D'Alessandro L. 2014: 'Materiali ceramici dagli scavi della Porticus Aemilia (Testaccio, Roma). Campagne di scavo 2011–2012', *RCFR Acta* 43, pp. 323–334.

Cooley A.E., Cooley M.G.L. 2013: *Pompeii and Herculaneum: a sourcebook*, London (2nd ed.).

Cornell T. 1986: 'The value of the literary tradition concerning Archaic Rome', in K.A. Raaflaub ed., *Social struggles in Archaic Rome*, Berkeley/Los Angeles/London, pp. 47–74.

Cornell T. 1995: *The beginnings of Rome: Italy and Rome from the Bronze Age to the Punic Wars (c. 1000–264 B.C.)*, London.

Costantini L., Costantini Biasini L., 1999: 'La viticoltura della Grecia alla Magna Grecia: la documentazione archeobotanica', in O. Failla, G. Forni eds., *Alle radici della civiltà del vino in Sicilia*, Menfi, pp. 169–192.

Costantini L., Costantini Biasini L. 2012: 'Archeologia della vitivinicoltura in Basilicata: un bilancio delle ricerche archeobotaniche a Pizzica Pantanello (Metaponto, Matera)', in A. Ciacci, P. Rendini, A. Zifferero eds., *Archeologia della vite e del vino in Toscana e nel Latium. Dalle tecniche dell'indagine archeologica alle prospettive della biologia molecolare*, Firenze, pp. 133–140.

Cristofani M. 1991: 'Vino e simposio nel mondo etrusco arcaico', in P. Scarpi ed., *Storie del vino* (Homo Edens II, Atti del Colloquio), Milan, pp. 69–76.

Dalby A. 1997: *Siren feasts: a history of food and gastronomy in Greece*, London.

Dalby A. 2000: *Empire of pleasures: luxury and indulgence in the Roman world*, London.

Dalby A. 2003: *Food in the ancient world from A to Z*, London/New York.

Dari-Mattiacci G., Plisecka A.E. 2010: 'Luxury in ancient Rome: scope, timing and enforcement of sumptuary laws', *Amsterdam Center for Law & Economics Working Paper* 3, pp. 1–26.

Dark K. 2007: 'Globalizing late antiquity: models, metaphors and the realities of long-distance trade and diplomacy', *Reading Medieval Studies* 32, pp. 3–14.

D'Arms J.H. 1974: 'Puteoli in the second century of the Roman Empire: a social and economic study', *JRS* 64, pp. 104–124.

D'Arms J.H. 1981: *Commerce and social standing in ancient Rome*, Cambridge.

Davies J.K. 2001: 'Hellenistic economies in the post-Finley era', in Z.H. Archibald, J.K. Davies, V. Gabrielsen, G.J. Oliver eds., *Hellenistic economies*, London/New York, pp. 7–44.

Debidour M. 1986: 'En classant les timbres thasiens', in J.-Y. Empereur, Y. Garlan eds., *Recherches sur les amphores grecques* (Actes du colloque international organisé par le Centre national de la recherche scientifique, l'Université de Rennes II et l'École française d'Athènes, Athènes, 10–12 septembre 1984, BCH Suppl. 13), Athens, pp. 311–334.

De Bonis R. 2008: 'La partie septentrionale de l'îlot', in I. Bragantini, R. De Bonis, A. Lemaire, R. Robert eds., *POSEIDONIA-PAESTUM V*, Rome, pp. 245–330.

De Callataÿ F. 2005: 'The Graeco-Roman economy in the super-long run: lead, copper, and shipwrecks', *JRA* 18, pp. 361–372.

De Caro S. 1992/93: 'Vino di Cnosso dei Campani: un nuovo documento epigrafico per la storia del vino cretese in età romana', *ASAtene* 70–71, pp. 307–312.

De Caro S. 2008: 'I Campi Felgrei in eta Romana', in F. Zevi ed., *Museo Archeologico dei Campi flegrei, Catalogo generale 1*, Cumae/Napoli, pp. 53–64.

De Cazanove O. 1988: 'Jupiter, Liber et le vin latin', *Rev. Hist. Rel.* 205(3), pp. 245–265.

Decker M. 2005: 'The wine trade of Cilicia in late antiquity', *ARAM Periodical* 17, pp. 51–59.

Decker M. 2009: *Tilling the hateful earth: agricultural production and trade in the late antique East*, Oxford.

Dedet B., Py M. 2006: 'Chronologie et diffusion des importations étrusques en Languedoc oriental', in S. Gori, M.Ch. Bettini eds., *Gli etruschi da Genova ad Ampurias* (Atti del 24 convegno di studi etruschi ed Italici. Marseille-Lattes, 26 settembre–1 ottobre 2002), Pisa, pp. 121–144.

De Filippo M. 2014: 'Anfore dal Rione Terra, Pozzuoli (Napoli)', *RCRF Acta* 43, pp. 335–343.

De Garine I.L. 1976: 'Food, tradition and prestige', in N. Kretchmer, H.L. Barnett eds., *Food, man and society*, New York/London, pp. 150–173.

Degrassi V., Maggi P. 2011: 'Il pozzo occidentale del foro di Aquileia. Commerci e consumi attraverso l'evidenza dei materiali di riempimento', in S. Cipriano, E. Pettenò eds., *Archeologia e tecnica dei pozzi per acqua dalla pre-protostoria all'età moderna* (atti del convegno Borgoricco, Padova, 11 dicembre 2010), Trieste, pp. 261–270.

Del Re A. 2012: 'Il «Progetto ArchoVino»: i parchi della viticoltura e i vigneti storici in Europa', in A. Ciacci, P. Rendini, A. Zifferero eds., *Archeologia della vite e del vino in Toscana e nel Latium. Dalle tecniche dell'indagine archeologica alle prospettive della biologia molecolare*, Firenze, pp. 663–682.

Delpino F. 1997: 'I Greci in Etruria prima della colonizzazione euboica. Ancora su crateri, vino, vite e pennati nell'Italia centrale protostorica', in M. Pallottino, G. Bartoloni eds., *Le necropoli arcaiche di Veio*, Roma, pp. 185–194.

Delpino F. 2007: 'Viticoltura, produzione e consume del vino nell'Etruria protostorica', in A. Ciacci P., Rendini, A. Zifferero eds., *Archeologia della Vite e del Vino in Etruria*, Siena, pp. 133–146.

Delpino F. 2012: 'Viticoltura, produzione e consume del vino nell'Etruria protostorica', in A. Ciacci P., Rendini, A. Zifferero eds., *Archeologia della vite e del vino in Toscana e nel Latium. Dalle tecniche dell'indagine archeologica alle prospettive della biologia molecolare*, Firenze, pp. 189–199.

Demma F. 2004: 'Pavimenti e mosaici dagli edifici pubblici di Pozzuoli. Materiali e contesti', in C. Angelelli ed., *Atti del IX colloquio dell'Associazione italiana per lo studio e la conservazione del mosaico (Aosta, 20–22 febbraio 2003)*, Ravenna, pp. 325–350.

Demma F. 2007: *Monumenti Pubblici di Puteoli. Per un'Archeologia dell'Architettura*, Roma.

Demougin S. 2010: 'Encore l'annone', in M. Silvestrini ed., *Le tribù romane* (Atti della XVIe Rencontre sur l'épigraphie, Bari 8–10 ottobre 2009), Roma, pp. 375–383.

De Sena E.C. 2005: 'An assessment of wine and oil production in Rome's hinterland: ceramic, literary, art historical and modern evidence', in B. Santillo Frizell, A. Klynne eds., *Roman villas around the Urbs. Interaction with landscape and environment* (Proceedings of the Conference at the Swedish Institute in Rome, September 17–18, 2004), Rome, pp. 135–149.

De Sena E.C., Ikäheimo J.P. 2003: 'Supply of amphora-borne commodities and domestic pottery in Pompeii 150 BC–AD 79: Preliminary evidence from the House of the Vestals', *European Journal of Archaeology* 6(3), pp. 301–321.

De Simone C. 2011: 'Il nome del "vino" nei dialetti dell'Italia antica', in M. Lombardo, A. Siciliano, A. Alessio eds., *La vigna di Dioniso: vite, vino e culti in Magna Grecia* (Atti del quarantanovesimo convegno di studi sulla Magna Grecia. Taranto 24–28 settembre 2009), Taranto, pp. 471–479.

De Simone G.F., Martucci C.S., 2016: 'Thirst for wine? An amphorae assemblage from Vesuvius and the problem of self-sufficiency in late antique Campania', *RCRF Acta* 44, pp. 127–135.

De Visscher F., De Ruyt F., De Laet S.J., Mertens J. eds., 'Les fouilles d' Alba Fucens (Italie Centrale) de 1951 a 1953 III', *AnClass* 24(1), pp. 51–119.

Didioumi S. 2014: 'Local pottery production in the island of Cos, Greece from the early Byzantine period. A preliminary report', in N. Poulou-Papadimitriou, E. Nodarou, V. Kilikoglou eds., *LRCW* 4, Oxford, pp. 169–180.

Dietler M. 2010: *Archaeologies of colonialism: consumption, entanglement, and violence in ancient Mediterranean France*, Berkeley.

Di Giovanni V. 2003: 'Le anfore da trasporto. L'impianto fognario sottoposto al settore ovest del decumano di via Duomo', in L. Crimaco, C. Gialanella, F. Zevi eds., *Da Puteoli a Puzzuoli. Scavi e richerche sulla rocca del Rione Terra*, Napoli, pp. 79–93.

Di Giovanni V. 2013: 'Le dinamiche degli scambi economici nella Campania in età imperiale. Circolazione delle produzioni africane: ceramiche fini, anfore da trasporto e ceramiche da cucina', in M. Bastiana Cocco, A. Gavini, A. Ibba eds., *L'Africa Romana XIX. Trasformazione dei paesaggi del potere nell'Africa settentrionale fino alla fine del mondo antico* (Collana del Dip. Storia Uiv. Sassari 43), Roma, pp. 1511–1538.

Di Giuseppe H. 2006a: 'I reperti', in A. Carandini, M.T. D'Alessio, H. Di Giuseppe eds., *La fattoria e la villa dell'Auditorium nel quartiere Flaminio di Roma*, Roma, pp. 201–211.

Di Giuseppe H. 2006b: 'Le clasi ceramiche. Periodi 3 e 4', in A. Carandini, M.T. D'Alessio, H. Di Giuseppe eds., *La fattoria e la villa dell'Auditorium nel quartiere Flaminio di Roma*, Roma, pp. 375–402.

Di Sandro N. 1981: 'Appunti sulla distribuzione delle anfore commerciali greche in Campania tra l'VIII sec. e il 273 a.C.', *AION(archeol)* 3, pp. 1–14.

Di Santo S. 2006: 'I reperti', in A. Carandini, M.T. D'Alessio, H. Di Giuseppe eds., *La fattoria e la villa dell'Auditorium nel quartiere Flaminio di Roma*, Roma, pp. 287–293.

Dobreva D. 2014: 'Verso uno studio del paesaggio economico aquileiese. Sintesi dei dati relativi ai ritrovamenti ceramici della campagna 2013', in J. Bonetto, A.R. Ghiotto eds., *Aquileia—Fondi ex Cossar. Missione archeologica 2013*, Padova, pp. 77–92.

Doody A. 2010: *Pliny's Encyclopedia. The reception of the Natural History*, Cambridge.

Douglas M., Isherwood B. 1979: *The world of goods, towards the archaeology of consumption*, London.

Doulgéri-Intzessiloglou A., Garlan Y. 1990: 'Vin et amphores de Péparéthos et d'Ikos', *BCH* 114(1), pp. 361–389.

Duncan-Jones R. 1974: *The economy of the Roman Empire: quantitative studies*, Cambridge.

Dupont P. 1998: 'Archaic Greek transport amphoras', in R.M. Cook, P. Dupont eds., *East Greek pottery*, London/New York, pp. 142–191.

Durliat J. 1990: *De la ville antique à la ville byzantine. Le problème des subsistances*, Rome.

Durry M. 1955: 'Les femmes et le vin', *REL* 33, pp. 108–113.

Duthoy R. 1989: 'Cognomen est omen? Quelques jalons pour une anthroponymie sociale du monde romain', in M.-M. Mactoux, E. Gény eds., *Mélanges Pierre Léveque* 2 (Annales Littéraires de l'Université de Besançon, Centre de Recherches d'Histoire Ancienne 82), Paris, pp. 183–205.

Duval S. 2006: 'Mobilier, céramique et commerce à destination d'habitats indigènes en Provence occidentale, du VIe s: au debut du Ve s. av. J.-C.' in S. Gori, M.Ch. Bettini eds., *Gli Etruschi da Genova ad Ampurias: atti del XXIV convegno di studi etruschi ed italici (Marseille—Lattes, 26 settembre–1 ottobre 2002)*, Pisa/Roma, pp. 103–119.

Dyczek P. 2001: *Roman amphorae of the 1st–3rd centuries AD found on the Lower Danube: Typology*, Warszawa.

Dzierzbicka D. 2005: 'Wineries in Graeco-Roman Egypt', *JJP* 35, pp. 9–89.

Dzierzbicka D. 2010: 'Wineries of the Mareotic Region', in L. Blue, E. Khalil eds., *Lake Mareotis: reconstructing the past* (Proceedings of the International Conference on the Archaeology of the Mareotic Region Held at Alexandria University, Egypt 5th–6th April 2008), Oxford, pp. 127–133.

Dzierzbicka D. 2018: *ΟΙΝΟΣ: production and import of wine in Graeco-Roman Egypt* (*JJP* Suppl. 31), Warszawa.

Empereur J.-Y. 1993: 'La production viticole dans l'Egypte ptolémaïque et romaine' in M.-C. Maouretti, J.P. Brun eds., *La production du vin et de l'huile en Méditerranée*, Athens, pp. 39–47.

Empereur J.-Y., Picon M. 1989: 'Les régions de production d'amphores impériales', in AA.VV., *Amphores romaines et histoire économique: dix ans de recherche*, Roma, pp. 223–248.

Erdkamp P. 2013: 'The food supply of the capital' in P. Erdkamp ed., *The Cambridge Companion to ancient Rome*, Cambridge, pp. 262–277.

Étienne R., Mayet F. 1998: 'Les mercatores de saumure hispanique', *MEFRA* 110(1), pp. 147–165.

Étienne R., Mayet F. 2000: *Trois clés pour l'économie de l'Hispanie romaine 1: Le vin hispanique hispanique*, Paris.

Étienne R., Mayet F. 2001: 'Les élites marchands de la péninsule Ibérique', in M. Navarro Caballero, S. Demougin eds., *Élites hispaniques*, Bordeaux, pp. 89–104.

Étienne R., Mayet F. 2002: *Trois clés pour l'économie de l'Hispanie romaine 2: Salaisons et sauces de poisson hispaniques*, Paris.

Federico R. 2013: 'La ceramica e le anfore dal deposito delle cucine della Villa di Arianna a Stabiae: un'analisi preliminare sui materiali di prima età imperiale romana, commerci e cibus', in L. Girón Anguiozar, M. Lazarich González, M. da Conceiçao Lopes eds., *Actas del I Congreso Internacional sobre Estudios Cerámicos homenaje a la Dra. Mercedes Vegas*, Cádiz, pp. 1738–1764.

Ferrandes A.F. 2008: 'I contenitori da trasporto', in F. Filippi ed., *Horti et sordes. Uno scavo alle falde del Gianicolo*, Roma, pp. 247–283.

Ferrandes A.F. 2014: 'Circolazione ceramica e approvvigionamento urbano a Roma nel I secolo a.C. Nuovi dati dall'area degli Horti Lamiani', *RCRF Acta* 43, pp. 353–366.

Ferrua A. 1973: 'Le iscrizioni pagane della catacomba di Pretestato', *RendLinc* 28, pp. 63–99.

Festuccia S., Verde G. 2011: 'Nuovo Mercato di Testaccio: storie da un cantiere', in A. Gallone, S. Zottis eds., *L'archeologia con gli occhi di Silvia* (Atti della giornata di studi per ricordare Valeria Silvia Mellace), Catania, pp. 153–168.

Filippi D. et al. 2004: 'La Casa delle Vestali: un immondezzaio di VI secolo d.C.', in L. Paroli, L. Venditelli eds., *Roma dall'antichità al medioevo, 2. Contesti tardoantichi e altomedievali*, Roma, pp. 164–179.

Finkielsztejn G. 1995: 'Chronologie basse des timbres amphoriques rhodiens et évaluation des exportations d'amphores', *ActaHyp* 6, pp. 279–296.

Finkielsztejn G. 2001a: *Chronologie détaillée et révisée des éponymes amphoriques rhodiens, de 270 à 108 av. J.-C. environ. Premier bilan* (BAR Int. Ser. 990), Oxford.

Finkielsztejn G. 2001b: 'Politique et commerce a Rhodes au IIe s. a.C.: le témoignage des exportations d'amphores', in A. Bresson, R. Descat eds., *Les cités d'Asie Mineure Occidentale au IIe siècle a.C.*, Bordeaux, pp. 181–196.

Finkielsztejn G. 2002: 'Du bon usage des amphores hellénistiques en contextes archéologiques', in P. Lévêque, J.-P. Morel eds., *Céramiques hellénistiques et romaines. Productions et diffusion en Méditerranée orientale* (*Chypre, Égypte et côte syro-palestinienne*), (Actes du colloque tenu à la Maison de l'Orient méditerranéen Jean Pouilloux du 2 au 4 mars 2000), Lyon, pp. 227–233.

Finkielsztejn G. 2004a: 'Corpus et catalogues des timbres amphoriques rhodiens', in J. Remesal Rodríguez ed., *Epigrafía anfórica* (Workshop. Barcelona, 9–10 mayo 2003), Barcelona, pp. 55–65.

Finkielsztejn G. 2004b: 'Establishing the chronology of Rhodian amphora stamps: the next steps', in J. Eiring, J. Lund eds., *Transport amphorae and trade in the Eastern*

Mediterranean (Acts of the International Colloquium at the Danish Institute at Athens, September 26–29, 2002, MDIA 5), Athens, pp. 117–121.

Finley M.I. 1999: *The ancient economy*, Berkeley (updated edition).

Fiorentino G. 2011: 'Viti e vitigni nel mondo antico: il contributo dell'archeobotanica', in M. Lombardo, A. Siciliano, A. Alessio eds., *La vigna di Dioniso: vite, vino e culti in Magna Grecia* (Atti del quarantanovesimo convegno di studi sulla Magna Grecia. Taranto 24–28 settembre 2009), Taranto, pp. 9–31.

Fitton Brown A.D. 1962: 'Black Wine', *The Classical Review New Ser.* 12(3), pp. 192–195.

Flemming R. 2000: 'The physicians at the feast. The place of medical knowledge at the Athenaeus' dinner-table', in D. Braund, J. Wilkins eds., *Athenaeus and his world: reading Greek culture in the Roman Empire*, Exeter, pp. 476–482.

Foley B.P., Hansson M.C., Kourkoumelis D.P., Theodoulou T.A. 2012: 'Aspects of ancient Greek trade re-evaluated with amphora DNA evidence', *JASc* 30, pp. 389–398.

Fontana S., Munzi M., Beolchini V., Del Vecchio F., De Luca I. 2004: 'Un contesto di VII secolo dall'Aventino', in L. Paroli, L. Venditelli eds., *Roma dall'antichità al medioevo, 2. Contesti tardoantichi e altomedievali*, Roma, pp. 544–568.

Fontana S. 2005: 'General discussion', in S. Keay, M. Millett, L. Paroli, K. Strutt eds., *Portus: an archaeological survey of the port of imperial Rome*, London, pp. 235.

Forni G. 2007: 'Quando e come sorce la viticoltura in Italia', in A. Ciacci, P. Rendini, A. Zifferero eds., *Archeologia della Vite e del Vino in Etruria*, Siena, pp. 69–81.

Forni G. 2012: 'La matrice euromediterranea della nostra viticoltura. La prospettiva pluridisciplinare', in A. Ciacci, P. Rendini, A. Zifferero eds., *Archeologia della vite e del vino in Toscana e nel Latium. Dalle tecniche dell'indagine archeologica alle prospettive della biologia molecolare*, Firenze, pp. 93–118.

Fowler H.W., Fowler F.G. eds. 1995: *The Concise Oxford Dictionary of Current English*, Oxford.

Foxhall L. 2011: 'Produzione e commercio del vino in Grecia', in M. Lombardo, A. Siciliano, A. Alessio eds., *La vigna di Dioniso: vite, vino e culti in Magna Grecia* (Atti del quarantanovesimo convegno di studi sulla Magna Grecia, Taranto 24–28 settembre 2009), Taranto, pp. 35–47.

Frank T. 1916: 'Race mixture in the Roman Empire', *The American Historical Review* 21(4), pp. 689–708.

Frank T. 1931: 'Pliny, H. N. XIV, 95, quadrantal', *AJPh* 52(3), pp. 278.

Frier B.W. 2000: 'Demography', in *The Cambridge ancient history* XI (2nd ed.), Cambridge, pp. 787–816.

Gallone A. 2011: 'Nuovo Mercato di Testaccio: lo sviluppo di un quartiere commerciale tra la trada repubblica e l'impero', in A. Gallone, S. Zottis eds., *L'archeologia con gli occhi di Silvia* (Atti della giornata di studi per ricordare Valeria Silvia Mellace), Catania, pp. 169–178.

Ganzarolli G. 2015: 'Le anfore tardoantiche e altomedievali dal contesto del Battisero di Padova', *Archeologia Veneta* 28, pp. 80–127.

Garcea F., Miraglia G., Soricelli G. 1983–1984: 'Uno scarico di materiale ceramico di età adrianeo-antonina da Cratere Senga (Puzzuoli)', *Puteoli. Studi di Storia Antica* VII–VIII, pp. 245–285.

García Soler M.J. 1996a: 'El vino en la antigua Grecia. Formas de elaboración y consumo', in J. Santos ed., *La Rioja, el vino y el Camino del Santiago*, Vitoria, pp. 133–142.

García Soler M.J. 1996b: 'El vino griego en las fuentes literarias latinas', in S. Celestino Pérez ed., *El vino en la antigüedad romana: II Simposio Arqueología del Vino*, Jeréz, pp. 227–232.

García Soler M.J. 1999: 'Algunos nombres del vino nel griego antiguo', *HABIS* 30, pp. 391–403.

García Soler M.J. 2001: 'Apuntes para un estudio sobre el vino en la comedia griega', in J. Maldonado Rosso ed., *Actas del I Simposio de la Asiciación Internacional de Historia y Civilización de la vid y el vino* 1, El Puerto de Santa María, pp. 257–263.

García Soler M.J. 2002: 'Los vinos en la comedia griega', *DUORO: Estodios&documentos* 7(13), pp. 49–64.

Garlan Y. 1982: 'Les timbres amphoriques thasiens. Bilan et perspectives de recherche', *Annales (HSS)* 37(5), pp. 837–846.

Garlan Y. 1988: *Vin et amphores de Thasos*, Paris.

Garlan Y. 1993a: 'À qui étaient destinés les timbres amphoriques grecs?', *CR Acad. Inscr.* 137(1), pp. 181–190.

Garlan Y. 1993b: *Nouvelles remarques sur la chronologie des timbres amphoriques thasiens, JS* 2, pp. 149–181.

Garlan Y. 2000: *Amphores et timbres amphoriques grecs. Entre érudition et idéologie* (Memoirés de l'académie des inscriptions et bellen-lettres 21), Paris.

Garlan Y. 2004: *La Publication des Timbres Amphoriques Grecs*, in J. Remesal Rodríguez ed., *Epigrafía anfórica* (Workshop. Barcelona, 9–10 mayo 2003), Barcelona, pp. 9–11.

Garnsey P. 1981: *Independent freedman in the economy of Roman Italy under the Principate*, Klio 63, pp. 359–371 (also published in P. Garnsey, W. Scheidel eds., *Cities, peasants and food in classical antiquity. Essays in social and economic history*, Cambridge 1998, pp. 28–44).

Geremia Nucci R., Leone A. 2003: 'Ostia. Sondaggio nella domus dei Pesci. Dati preliminari sullo scavo e sul material ceramico', *RCRF Acta* 38, pp. 63–67.

Ghirotto S., Tassi F., Fumagalli E., Colonna V., Sandionigi A., Lari M., Vai S., Petiti E., Corti G., Rizzi E., De Bellis G., Caramelli D., Barbujani G. 2013: 'Origins and Evolution of the Etruscans' mtDNA', *PLoS ONE* 8(2): e55519, https:doi:10.1371/journal.pone.0055519.

Giannace M. 2010: 'Il progetto Vinum: siti archeologici e persistenza della vite silvestre in Etruria', in G. di Pasquale ed., *VINUM NOSTRUM: arte, scienza e miti del vino nelle civiltà del Mediterraneo antico*, Firenze, pp. 80–83.

Ginsburg M.S. 1934: 'Princeps libertinorum', *Transactions and Proceedings of the American Philological Association* 65, pp. 198–206.

Gjerstad E. 1960: *Early Rome III: Fortifications, domestic architecture, sanctuaries, stratigraphic excavations*, Rome.

Gordon M.L. 1924: 'The nationality of slaves under the early Roman Empire', *JRS* 14, pp. 93–111.

Gordon M.L. 1931: 'The freedman's son in municipal life', *JRS* 21, pp. 65–77.

Gorny R.L. 1996: 'Viticulture and ancient Anatolia', in S.J. Fleming, S. Katz eds., *The origins and ancient history of wine*, New York, pp. 133–174.

Gorostidi Pi D. 2011: 'Aggiornamento del corpus epigrafico tuscolano: le iscrizioni repubblicane', in G. Ghini ed., *Lazio e Sabina 7* (Atti del Convegno: Settimo Incontro di Studi sul Lazio e Sabina), Roma, pp. 323–330.

Grace V. 1971: 'Samian Amphoras', *Hesperia* 40, pp. 52–95.

Grace V. 1979: *Amphoras and the ancient wine trade*, Princeton/New Jersey 1979.

Grace V. 1985: 'The Middle Stoa dated by amphora stamps', *Hesperia* 54(1), 1985, pp. 1–54.

Grant M. 2000: *Galen on food and diet*, London.

Gras M. 1983: 'Vin et société à Rome et dans le Latium à l'époque archaïque', in AA.VV., *Modes de contacts et processus de transformation dans les societies anciennes* (Actes du colloque de Cortone, 24–30 mai 1981), Roma, pp. 1067–1075.

Gras M. 1985: *Trafics tyrrhéniens archaïques*, Rome.

Guasch-Jané M.R., Andrés-Lacueva C., Jáuregui O., Lamuela-Raventós R.M. 2006: 'First evidence of white wine in ancient Egypt from Tutankhamun's tomb', *JASc* 33(8), pp. 1075–1080.

Gulick C.B. 1927: *Athenaeus. The Deipnosophists*, London/New York.

Hankinson R.J. 2009: 'The man and his work' in R.J. Hankinson ed., *The Cambridge Companion to Galen*, Cambridge, pp. 1–33.

Harper K. 2017: *The fate of Rome*, Princeton.

Harris W. 2005: 'The Mediterranean and ancient history', in W. Harris ed., *Rethinking the Mediterranean*, Oxford, pp. 1–42.

Harris W. 2009: 'A comment on Andrew Wilson: Approaches to quantifying Roman trade', in A. Bowman, A. Wilson eds., *Quantifying the Roman economy: methods and problems*, Oxford, pp. 259–264.

Heinzelmann M. 2000: *Die Nekropolen von Ostia* (Studien zur antiken Stadt 6), München.

Heltzer M. 1993: 'Olive oil and wine production in Phoenicia and in Mediterranean trade', in M.C. Amouretti, J.-P. Brun eds., *La production du vin et de l'huile en Mediterranee* (*BCH* Suppl. 26), Athens, pp. 49–54.

Hesnard A. 1980: 'Un dépôt augustéen d'amphores à La Longarina, Ostie' in J.H. D'Arms,

E.Ch. Kopff eds., *The seaborne commerce of ancient Rome: Studies in archaeology and history* (MAAR 36), Roma, pp. 141–156.

Hesnard A., Carre M.-B., Rival M., Dangréaux B. 1988: 'L'épave romaine Grand Ribaud D (Hyères, Var)', *Archaeonautica* 8, pp. 5–180.

Hesnard A., Gianfrotta P., 1989: 'Les bouchons d'amphore en Pouzzolane', in AA.VV., *Amphores romaines et histoire économique. Dix ans de recherche* (Actes du colloque de Sienne, 22–24 mai 1986, Publications de l'EFR 114), Roma, pp. 393–441.

Hooper W.D. 1934: *Introduction to Cato and Varro on Agriculture*, Cambridge/London.

Hooper W.D. 2006: *Marcus Porcius Cato, On Agriculture. Marcus Terentius Varro, On Agriculture*, Cambridge/London.

Hopkins K. 1980: 'Taxes and trade in the Roman Empire (200 B.C.–A.D. 400)', *JRS* 70, pp. 101–125.

Hopkins K. 1983: 'Models, ships and staples', in. P.D.A. Garnsey, C.R. Whittaker eds., *Trade and famine in classical antiquity* (Proceedings of the Cambridge Philological Society supplementary volume 8), Cambridge pp. 84–85.

Hopkins K. 2002: 'Rome, taxes, rents and trade', in W. Scheidel, S. von Reden eds., *The ancient economy*, Edinburgh, pp. 190–230 (first published in *Kodai: Journal of Ancient History* 6–7, 1995/96, pp. 41–71).

Hopkins K. 2017: *Sociological studies in Roman history*, Cambridge.

Horden P., Purcell N. 2000: *The corrupting sea: a study of Mediterranean history*, Oxford.

Iandoli M. 2006: 'Le anfore della domus Romana di Palazzo Diolattevi a Rimini: alcune riflessioni sui circuiti commerciali', in O. Mattioli, L. Braccesi eds., *Armininium. Storia e archeologia*, Roma, pp. 103–153.

Imazio S., Somaschini A., Biagini B., Grassi F., Labra M. 2012: 'Progetto VINUM: metodi di analisi del genoma e primi risultati', in A. Ciacci, P. Rendini, A. Zifferero eds., *Archeologia della vite e del vino in Toscana e nel Latium. Dalle tecniche dell'indagine archeologica alle prospettive della biologia molecolare*, Firenze, pp. 601–622.

Infarinato A. 2007: 'I materiali della fase di abbandono della Villa della Piscina: una nota preliminare', in R. Volpe ed., *Centocelle II. Roma S.D.O. Le inagini archeologiche*, Roma, pp. 381–384.

Jones R., Robinson D. 2004: 'The making of an élite house: the House of the Vestals at Pompeii', *JRA* 17, pp. 107–130.

Jongman W.M. 2005: 'The Augustan census and the population of Italy', *Athenaeum* 92, pp. 441–495.

Jongman W.M. 2006: 'The rise and fall of the Roman economy: population, rents and entitlement', in P. Bang, M. Ikeguchi, H. Ziche eds., *Ancient economies and modern methodologies. Archaeology, comparative history, models and institutions*, Bari, pp. 237–254.

Jongman W.M. 2007a: 'Gibbon was right: the decline and fall of the Roman economy', in O. Hekster, G. De Kleijn, D. Slootjes eds., *Crises and the Roman Empire*, Leiden/Boston, pp. 183–199.

Jongman W.M. 2007b.: 'The early Roman Empire: consumption', in W. Scheidel, I. Morris, R.P. Saller eds., *The Cambridge economic history of the Greco-Roman world*, Cambridge, pp. 592–618.

Jongman W.M. 2009: 'Archaeology, demography, and Roman economic growth', in A. Bowman, A. Wilson eds., *Quantifying the Roman economy: Methods and problems*, Oxford, pp. 115–126.

Jongman W.M. 2014: 'The new economic history of the Roman Empire', in F. de Callataÿ ed., *Quantifying the Greco-Roman economy and beyond*, Bari, pp. 169–188.

Jongman W.M. 2017a: 'Afterword to: Keith Hopkins, Taxes and trade in the Roman Empire (200 B.C.–AD 400)', in C. Kelly ed., *Sociological studies in Roman history / Keith Hopkins*, Cambridge, pp. 260–268.

Jongman W.M. 2017b: 'The benefits of market integration: five centuries of prosperity in Roman Italy' in T.C.A. De Haas, G.W. Tol eds., *The economic integration of Roman Italy: rural communities in a globalizing world*, Leiden/Boston, pp. 15–27.

Jouanna J. 1992: *Hippocrate*, Paris.

Jouanna J. 1996: 'Le vin et la médecine dans la Grèce ancienne', *REG* 109, pp. 410–434.

Kajanto I. 1965: *The Latin cognomina* (Societas Scientiarum Fennica, Commentationes Humanarum Litterarum 36/2), Helsinki.

Kajanto I. 1968: 'The significance of non-Latin cognomina', *LATOMUS: Revue d'études latines* 27(3), pp. 517–534.

Kassab Tezgör D. 2010: 'Le réseau commercial des amphores sinopéennes entre les IIe–IIIe s. et le VIe s. de notre ère', in. D. Kassab Tezgör, N. Inaishvili eds., *Patabs I. Production and Trade of Amphorae in the Black Sea*, Paris, pp. 167–173.

Keay S.J. 1984: *Late Roman amphorae in the Western Mediterranean: a typology and economic study: the Catalan evidence*, Oxford.

Kessler D. and Temin P. 2005: 'Money and prices in the early Roman Empire', *MIT Department of Economics Working Paper* No. 05–11, https://papers.ssrn.com/sol3/papers.cfm?abstract_id=704724, accessed 22.09.2019.

Kingsley S. 2001: 'The economic impact of the Palestinian wine trade in late antiquity', in S. Kingsley, M. Decker eds., *Economy and exchange in the East Mediterranean during late antiquity*, Oxford, pp. 44–68.

Kingsley S., Decker M. 2001: 'New Rome, new theories on inter-regional exchange. An introduction to the East Mediterranean economy in late antiquity', in S. Kingsley, M. Decker eds., *Economy and exchange in the East Mediterranean during late antiquity*, Oxford, pp. 1–27.

Koehler C.G. 1981: 'Corinthian developments in the study of trade in the fifth century', *Hesperia* 50(4), pp. 449–458.

Komar P. 2014a: 'Greek wines for the Roman elite: in search of Eastern luxuries on Western tables', *Eos* 101(2), pp. 227–244.

Komar P. 2014b: 'Consumption of Greek wines in Roman Italy—between literary and archaeological evidence', *Food & History Journal* 12(3), pp. 99–131.

Komar P. 2016: 'Wines from Cyprus and Cilicia in antiquity: taste and trade', *Electrum* 23, pp. 155–185.

Komar P. 2020: '*In vino sanitas*: medical qualities of Greek wines', *MEFRA* 132 (2), in press.

Kourakou-Dragona S. 2013: *La vigne et le vin dans le monde grec ancien*, Athènes.

Kreindler K. 2015: *Consumption and exchange in central Italy in the ninth through sixth centuries BCE*. PhD thesis, Stanford University.

Kron G. 2005: 'Anthropometry, physical anthropology and the reconstruction of ancient health, nutrition, and living standards', *Historia* 54, pp. 68–83.

Kron G. 2008: 'The much maligned peasant. Comparative perspectives on the productivity of the small farmer in classical antiquity', in L. De Ligt, S. Northwood eds., *People, land and politics. Demographic developments and the transformation of Roman Italy, 300 B.C.–A.D. 14*, Leiden, pp. 71–119.

Kron G. 2012: 'Food Production' in W. Scheidel ed., *The Cambridge Companion to the economic history of the Roman world*, Cambridge, pp. 156–174.

Kron G. 2014: 'Comparative evidence and the reconstruction of the ancient economy: Greco-Roman housing and the level and distribution of wealth and income', in F. de Callataÿ ed., *Quantifying the Greco-Roman economy and beyond* (Pragmateiai 27), Bari, pp. 123–146.

Kropff A. 1971: *An English translation of the edict on maximum prices, also known as the price edict of Diocletian*, Berlin.

Kruit N., Worp K. 2000: 'Geographical Jar Names', *Archiv für Papyrusforschung* 46, pp. 65–146.

Laforgia E. 1980–1981: 'La ceramica del Tempio di Augusto a Pozzuoli', *Puteoli. Studi di storia antica* IV–V, pp. 201–222.

Lambri M., Dordoni R., Silva A., De Faveri D.M. 2012: 'Comparing the impact of bentonite addition for both must clarification and wine fining on the chemical profile of wine from Chambave Muscat grapes', *International Journal of Food Science & Technology* 47(1), pp. 1–12.

La Rocca E., 1977: 'Importazioni greche nell'VIII sec. a.C.', *PP* 32, pp. 375–389.

Larsen J.A.O. 1938: 'Roman Greece', in T. Frank ed., *An economic survey of ancient Rome*, Baltimore, pp. 259–498.

La Torre G.F. 2011: *Sicilia e Magna Grecia. Archeologia della colonizzazione greca d'Occidente*, Bari.

Lawall M. 2000: 'Graffiti, wine selling, and the reuse of amphoras in the Athenian agora, ca. 430 to 400 B.C.', *Hesperia* 69(1), pp. 3–90.

Lawall M. 2011: 'Socio-economic conditions and the contents of amphorae', in C. Tzochev, T. Stoyanov, A. Bozkova eds., *PATABS II. Production and trade of amphorae in the Black Sea*, Sofia, pp. 23–33.

Leidwanger J. 2013: 'Amphorae and underwater survey: making sense of late Roman trade from scattered sherds and shipwrecks', in M. Lawall, J. Lund eds., *The transport amphorae and trade of Cyprus*, Aarhus, pp. 180–190.

Leighton R. 1999: *Sicily before history: an archaeological survey from the palaeolithic to the Iron Age*, London.

Lemaître S. 1997: 'L'amphore de type Agora F65–66, dite "monoansée"', in AA.VV., *SFÉCAG* (Actes du congrès du Mans, 8–11 mai 1997), Marseille, pp. 311–319.

Lentini A. 2009: 'New archaeobotanical data on the cultivation of Vitis ssp. at Pyrgos-Mavrorachi, notes of Kinyras, since 4th millennium B.C. and evidence from Erimi', AA.VV., *192 Progress in Cultural Heritage Preservation—EUROMED 2012 Cyprus Wine Museum and Department of Antiquities Museum*, Nicosia, pp. 56–73.

Leonard A. Jr. 1996: 'Canaanite jars and the late bronze age Aegeo-Levantine wine trade', in P.E. McGovern, S.J. Fleming, S.H. Katz eds., *The origins and ancient history of wine*, Amsterdam, pp. 233–254.

Lindhagen A. 2009: 'The transport amphoras Lambolgia 2 and Dressel 6A: a central Dalmatian origin?', *JRA* 22, pp. 83–108.

Liou B. 1987: 'Inscriptions faites sur amphores: Fos (suite), Marseille, Toulon, Port-la-Nautique, Arles, Saint-Martin-de-Crau, Mâcon, Calvi', *Archaeonautica* 7, pp. 55–139.

Liou B. 1993: 'Inscriptions peintes sur amphores de Narbonne (Port-la-Nautique)', *Archaeonautica* 11, pp. 131–148.

Liou B., Marichel R. 1978: 'Les inscriptions peintes sur amphores de l'anse Saint-Gervais à Fos-sur-Mer', *Archaeonautica* 2, pp. 109–181.

Liou B., Lequément R., Desbat A. 1987: 'Inscriptions peintes sur amphores: Lyon et Saint-Romain-en-Gal', *Archaeonautica* 7, pp. 141–166.

Liou B., Tchernia A. 1994: 'L'interprétation des inscriptions sur les amphores Dressel 20', in C. Nicolet, S. Panciera eds., *Epigrafia della produzione e della distribuzione* (Actes de la VIIe Rencontre franco-italienne sur l'épigraphie du monde romain, Rome, 5–6 juin 1992), Rome, pp. 133–156.

Lloyd G.E.R. 1978: *Hippocratic writings*, London.

Lo Cascio E. 2009: 'Urbanization as a proxy of demographic and economic growth', in A. Bowman, A. Wilson eds., *Quantifying the Roman economy: methods and problems*, Oxford, pp. 87–106.

Lunardi P. 1998: 'Significato e obiettivi del consolidamento dei suoli oggi e nell'antichità', in S. Pesavento Mattioli ed., *Bonifiche e drenaggi con anfore in epoca romana: aspetti tecnici e topografici* (Atti del seminario di studi, Padova 19–20 ottobre 1995), Modena, pp. 37–46.

Lund J. 2004: *Oil on the waters? Relections on the contents of Hellenistic transport ampho-*

rae from the Aegean, in J. Eiring, J. Lund eds., *Transport amphorae and trade in the Eastern Mediterranean* (Acts of the International Colloquium at the Danish Institute at Athens, September 26–29, 2002, MDIA 5), Athens, pp. 211–216.

Lund J., Gabrielsen V. 2005: 'A fishy business. Transport amphorae of the Black Sea region as a source for the trade in fish and fish products in the Classical and Hellenistic Periods', in T. Bekker-Nielsen ed., *Ancient fishing and fish processing in the Black Sea region*, Aarhus, pp. 161–170.

Lund J. 2007: 'The circulation of ceramic fine wares and transport amphorae from the Black Sea region in the Mediterranean, c. 400 BC–AD 200', in V. Gabrielsen, J. Lund eds., *The Black Sea in Antiquity. Regional and interregional economic exchanges* (Black Sea Studies 6), Aarhus, pp. 183–194.

Lusuardi Siena S. 1977: 'Anfore', in A. Frova ed., *Scavi di Luni II*, Roma, pp. 218–270.

Lyding Will E. 1982: 'Greco-Italic Amphoras', *Hesperia* 51/3, pp. 338–356.

Łoś A. 1991: *Wyzwoleńcy w Pompejach. Studium stosunków ekonomicznych w kampańskim mieście*, Wrocław.

Łoś A. 1994: 'Struktury społeczne w epoce wczesnego cesarstwa (27 p.n.e.–235 n.e.). Warstwy wyższe', in J. Wolski, T. Kotula, A. Kunisz eds., *Starożytny Rzym we współczesnych badaniach. Państwo-Społeczeństwo-Gospodarka*, Kraków, pp. 281–315.

Łoś A. 1995: 'La condition sociale des affranchis privés au Ier siècle après J.-C.', *Annales (HSS)* 5, pp. 1011–1043.

Łoś A. 1996: *"Dobrze urodzeni" i "dorobkiewicze". Studium socjologiczne elit miast kampańskich od Augusta do Domicjana*, Wrocław.

Łoś A. 1997: 'Qui exportait le vin crétois en Campanie à l'époque julio—claudienne?', *Antiquitas* 22, pp. 63–76.

Łoś A. 2000: 'Les affaires "industrielles" des élites des villes campaniennes sous les Julio-Claudiens et les Flaviens', *MEFRA* 112 (1), pp. 243–277.

Łoś A. 2005: 'Les affaires commerciales des notables municipaux. Remarques sur les »mercatores« notés dans les inscriptions amphoriques du Ier siècle après J.-C.', in A. Łoś, K. Nawotka eds., *Elite in Greek and Roman Antiquity* (Antiquitas 28), Wrocław, pp. 81–109.

Łoś A. 2012: 'Remarques sur l'origine géographique et statut socio-juridique des négociants d'huile et de saumure hispaniques', *Eos* 99(2), pp. 97–112.

Łoś A., Pietruszka W. 2016: 'Le vignoble campanien sous les Antonins', *MEFRA* 128 (2), pp. 521–558.

McGovern P.E., Michel R.H. 1996: 'The analytical and archaeological challenge of detecting ancient wine: two case studies from the ancient Near East', in P.E. McGovern, S.J. Fleming, S.H. Katz eds., *The origins and ancient history of wine*, Amsterdam, pp. 57–65.

Maiuri A. 1958: *I Campi Flegrèi: dal sepolcro di Virgilio all'antro di Cuma*, Roma (3rd ed.).

Majcherek G. 2007: 'Aegean and Asia Minor Amphorae from Marina el-Alamein', in

S. Marchand, A. Marangou eds., *Amphores d'Égypte de la Basse Époque à l'époque arabe*, Cairo, pp. 9–31.

Malinowski G. 1999: 'In vino veritas. Uzupełnienia do biografii Strabona', *Eos* 86(2), pp. 199–215.

Malyarchuk B.A., Rogozin I.B. 2004: 'On the Etruscan mitochondrial DNA contribution to modern humans', *American Journal of Human Genetics* 75, pp. 920–923.

Manganaro G. 1989: 'Casa e terra a Kamarina e Morgantina nel iii–ii sec. A.C.', *PdP* 44, pp. 189–216.

Marangou-Lerat A. 1995: *Le vin et les amphores de Crete: De l'epoque classique a l'epoque imperiale* (Etudes cretoises 30), Paris.

Marangou-Lerat A. 2000: 'Le plus agréable des vins grecs', in C. Cremonesi, D. Tomasi eds., *L'avventura del vino nel Bacino del Mediterraneo: itinerari storici ed archeologici prima e dopo Roma* (Simposio internazionale, Conegliano, 30 settembre–2 ottobre 1998), Conegliano, pp. 71–85.

Marengo S.M., Paci G. 2008: 'Per la circolazione delle anfore rodie e tardo-repubblicane in area adriatica', in P. Basso, E. Buchi eds., *Est enim ille flos Italiae: vita economica e sociale nella Cisalpina romana* (Atti delle Giornate di studio in onore di Ezio Buchi, Verona 30 nov.–1 dic. 2006), Verona, pp. 313–328.

Marianelli S., Rendini P. 2012: 'Tracce di impianti agrari a Magliano in Toscana (Grosseto)', in A. Ciacci, P. Rendini, A. Zifferero eds., *Archeologia della vite e del vino in Toscana e nel Latium. Dalle tecniche dell'indagine archeologica alle prospettive della biologia molecolare*, Firenze, pp. 403–412.

Mariotti Lippi M., Mori Secci M., Bellini C. 2012: 'L'archeobotanica, e lo studio della vite nella Preistoria in Toscana', in A. Ciacci, P. Rendini, A. Zifferero eds., *Archeologia della vite e del vino in Toscana e nel Latium. Dalle tecniche dell'indagine archeologica alle prospettive della biologia molecolare*, Firenze, pp. 119–124.

Marlière É. 2002: *L'outre et le tonneau dans l'occident romain*, Montagnac.

Marlière É., Torres Costa J. 2007: 'Transport et stockage des denrées dans l'Afrique romaine: le rôle de l'outre et du tonneau' in A. Mrabet, J. Remesal Rodríguez eds., *In Africa et in Hispania: études sur l'huile africaine*, Barcelona, 85–106.

Martin A. 2000: 'Amphorae at Olympia', *RCRF Acta* 36, pp. 427–433.

Marucci A. 2006: 'Foro Transitorio. Sistema di smaltimento delle acque del portico nord-occidentale: stratigrafia e materiali dei livelli di abbandono (fasi II e III)', in R. Meneghini, R. Santangeli Valenzani eds., *Roma. Lo scavo dei fori imperiali 1995–2000: i contesti ceramici*, Roma, pp. 57–92.

Marzano A. 2013: 'Agricultural production in the hinterland of Rome: wine and olive oil', in A. Bowman, A. Wilson eds., *The Roman agricultural economy: organisation, investment, and production*, Oxford, pp. 85–106.

Masi A. 2012: 'I palmenti come indicatori archeologici della produzione vitivinicola', in A. Ciacci, P. Rendini, A. Zifferero eds., *Archeologia della vite e del vino in Toscana e nel Latium. Dalle tecniche dell'indagine archeologica alle prospettive della biologia molecolare*, Firenze, pp. 583–590.

Matera M. 2014: *Analiza importu towarów w amforach rodyjskich na podstawie materiałów odkrytych w Tanais. Zarys kontaktów handlowych Rodos z obszarem dolnego Donu w III–I w p.n.e.* Unpublished PhD thesis, Warszawa.

Matthaiou A.P. 1992–1998: 'Οἶνος ἀθάλασσος', *Horos* 10–12, pp. 571–576.

Mattingly D.J. 1988: 'Oil for export. A comparison of Lybian, Spanish and Tunisian olive oil production in the Roman Empire', *JRA* 1, pp. 33–56.

Mayer E. 2012: *The ancient middle classes. Urban life and aesthetics in the Roman Empire, 100 BCE–250 CE*, Cambridge.

Mayerson Ph. 1985: 'The wine and vineyards of Gaza in the Byzantine period', *BASOR* 257, pp. 75–80.

Mazzeo Saracino L., Vergari M. 1997: 'Bolli d'anfora greci e romani da Suasa', *Ocnus* 5, pp. 151–172.

Mazzocchin S. 2007a: 'I materiali: il drenaggio 1', in F. Cozza, A.R. Serafini eds., *I colori della terra: storia stratificata nell'area urbana del Collegio Ravenna a Padova*, Padova, pp. 66–72.

Mazzocchin S. 2007b: 'Padova via Acquette 9: nuovi dati dal settore meridionale della citta romana', *QdAV* 23/2007, pp. 123–139.

Mazzocchin S., Rossi C. 2006: 'Un nuovo drenaggio di anfore dai Giardini dell'Arena a Padova', *Bollettino del museo civico di Padova* 95, pp. 7–43.

Mazzocchin S., Tuzzato S. 2010: 'Padova, via dei Salici. Nota preliminare su un drenaggio a sud della città romana', *QdAV* 26, pp. 21–29.

Mazzocchin S., 2013: *Vicenza. Traffici commerciali in epoca romana. I dati della anfore*, Trieste.

McConnell J.R., Wilson A.I., Stohl A., Arienzo M.M., Chellman N.J., Eckhardt S., Thompson E.M., Pollard A.M., Steffensen J.P. 2018: 'Lead pollution recorded in Greenland ice indicates European emissions tracked plagues, wars, and imperial expansion during antiquity', *PNAS* 115(22), pp. 5726–5731.

McCormick M. 2001: *Origins of the European economy: communications and commerce, A.D. 300–900*, Cambridge.

McCormick M. 2012: 'Movements and Markets in the First Millennium. Information, Containers, and Shipwreck', in. C. Morrisson ed., *Trade and markets in Byzantium*, Washington, pp. 51–98.

McCormick M., Büntgen U., Cane M.A., Cook E.R., Harper K., Huybers P., Litt T., Manning S.W., Mayewski P.A., More A.F.M., Nicolussi K., Tegel W. 2012: 'Climate change during and after the Roman Empire: reconstructing the past from scientific and historical evidence', *Journal of Interdisciplinary History* 43(2), pp. 169–220.

McGovern P. 2003: *Ancient wine: the search for the origins of viniculture*, Princeton.

Mele C. 2005: 'Amphorae', in S. Keay, M. Millett, L. Paroli, K. Strutt eds., *Portus: an archaeological survey of the port of imperial Rome*, London, pp. 223–235.

Meylan Krause M.-F. 2002: *Domus tiberiana. Analyses stratigraphiques et céramologiques* (BAR Int. Ser. 1058), Oxford.

Miniero P. 1999: 'I reperti della villa. Anfore', in A. Barbet, P. Miniero eds., *La villa San Marco a Stabia*, Naples/Rome/Pompei, pp. 323–330.

Moody J. 2005: 'Unravelling the threads: climate changes in the Late Bronze III Aegean', in A.L. D'Agata, J. Moody, E. Williams eds., *Ariadne's Threads: Connections between Crete and the Greek Mainland in Late Minoan III (LM IIIA2 to LM IIIC)*, Athens, pp. 443–470.

Morel J.P. 1981: 'Le commerce étrusque en France, en Espagne et en Afrique', in G. Camporeale ed., *L'Etruria mineraria* (Atti del XII Convegno di studi etruschi e italici, Firenze-Populonia-Piombino, 16–20 giugno 1979), Milano, pp. 463–508.

Morley N. 2007: *Trade in classical antiquity*, Cambridge.

Morris I. 1999: *Foreword to the updated edition of the ancient economy by M. Finley*, Berkeley, ix–xxxii.

Morris I., Saller R.P., Scheidel W. 2008: 'Introduction', in I. Morris, R.P. Saller, W. Scheidel eds., *The Cambridge economic history of the Greco-Roman world*, Cambridge, pp. 1–12.

Morselli Ch., Tortorici E. 1985: 'La situazione di Regisvilla', in AA.VV., *Il commercio Etrusco arcaico* (Atti dell'Incontro di Studio, Roma 1983), Roma, pp. 27–40.

Mouritsen H. 1988: *Elections, magistrates and municipal élite: studies in Pompeian epigraphy*, Roma.

Mouritsen H. 2011: *The freedman in the Roman world*, Cambridge.

Munzi M., Fontana S., De Luca I., Del Vecchio F. 2004: 'Domus Tiberiana: contesti tardoantichi dal settore nord-orientale', in L. Paroli, L. Venditelli eds., *Roma dall'antichità al medioevo, 2. Contesti tardoantichi e altomedievali*, Roma, pp. 91–128.

Nardi G., Pandolfini M. 1985: 'La diffusione delle anfore etrusche nell'Etruria settentrionale', in AA.VV., *Il commercio Etrusco arcaico* (Atti dell'Incontro di Studio, Roma 1983), Roma, pp. 41–63.

Nicodemo M., Ravasi T., Volonté M., 2008: 'Le vie delle anfore. Il commercio di derrate alimentari a Cremona attraverso i dati dello scavo di Piazza Marconi', in M. Baioni, C. Fredella eds., *Antichi commerci nella Lombardia Orientale*, Milan, pp. 285–303.

Noailles P. 1948: 'Les tabous du manage dans le droit primitif des Romains', *Fus et Jus*, Paris, pp. 1–27 (first published in Annales Sociologiques, série C, fasc. 2, 1937).

Nocera D. 2013: *Un contesto ceramico dall'ambiente 3 del Foro di Nerva*, in M. Ceci ed., *Contesti ceramici dai Fori Imperiali*, Oxford, pp. 75–85.

O'Donnell J. 2009: *The ruin of the Roman Empire*, London.

Olcese G., Cau Ontiveros M.Á., Fantuzzi L., Razza A., Surace D.M., Tsantini E. 2017: 'Le anfore del contesto della ruota idraulica di Ostia Antica: archeologia e archeometria', *Archeologia Classica* 68, pp. 197–224.

Opait A. 2007: 'From 24 to LR2?' in M. Bonifay, J.-Ch. Tréglia eds., *LRCW 2* (BAR Int. Ser. 1662), Oxford 2007, pp. 627–643.

Opait A. 2010: 'On the origin of Carthage LR Amphora 1', in S. Menchelli, S. Santoro, M. Pasquinucci, G. Guiducci eds., *LRCW* 3 (BAR Int. Ser. 2185), Oxford, pp. 1015–1022.

Opait A., Tsavropaulos A. 2011: 'Amphorae of Dressel 24 Similis Type in the Central Aegean Area (Chios-Erythrai-Kyme)', *ABSA* 106, pp. 275–323.

Pacetti F. 1995: 'Appunti su alcuni tipi di anfore orientali della prima età bizantina. Centri di produzione, contenuti, cronologia e distribuzione', in L. Quilici, S. Quilici Gigli eds., *Agricoltura e commerci nell'Italia antica*, Roma, pp. 273–294.

Pacetti F. 2004: 'Celio. *Basilica Hilariana*: scavi 1987–1988', in L. Paroli, L. Venditelli eds., *Roma dall'antichità al medioevo, 2. Contesti tardoantichi e altomedievali*, Roma, pp. 435–457.

Paczyńska K. 2002: 'Amfory grecko-italskie jako świadectwo handlu w IV i III wieku p.n.e.: typologia, produkcja, dystrybucja i sposoby oznakowania', *Światowit* 4 (45), Fasc. A, pp. 107–120.

Paczyńska K. 2003: *Rozwój handlu Italii republikańskiej w świetle produkcji i dystrybucji amfor grecko-italskich* (*IV–I wiek p.n.e.*). Unpublished PhD thesis, Warszawa.

Paganelli M. 2004: 'Area N-O del Foro Romano: l'Ambiente D nell'alto medioevo', in L. Paroli, L. Venditelli eds., *Roma dall'antichità al medioevo, 2. Contesti tardoantichi e altomedievali*, Roma, pp. 180–203.

Pallottino M. 1968: *Etruskowie* (translated by J. Maliszewska-Kowalska), Warszawa.

Palma B., Panella C. 1967–1968: 'Anfore', in A. Carandini, E. Fabricotti eds., *Ostia I. Le terme del Nuotatore, ambiente IV* (Studi Miscellanei 13), pp. 97–116.

Panagou T. 2015: 'Patterns of amphora stamp distribution. Tracking down export tendencies', in E.M. Harris, D.M. Lewis, M. Woolmer eds., *Markets, households and city-states in the ancient Greek economy*, Cambridge/New York, pp. 207–229.

Panciera S. 1980: 'Olearii', *MAAR* 36, pp. 235–250.

Panella C. 1972: 'Annotazioni in margine alle stratigrafie delle Terme Ostiensi del Nuotatore', in P. Baldacci, G. Kapitän, N. Lamboglia eds., *Recherches sur les amphores romaines* (Actes du Colloque de Rome, 4 mars 1971), Rome, pp. 69–106.

Panella C. 1973: 'Appunti su un gruppo di anfore della prima, media e tarda età Imperiale', in A. Carandini, C. Panella eds., *Ostia III. Le terme del Nuotatore. Scavo degli ambienti III, VI, VII. Scavo dell'ambiente V e di un saggio nel'area SO* (Studi miscellanei 21), pp. 460–633.

Panella C. 1974–1975: 'Per uno studio delle anfore di Pompei', *Studi Miscellanei* 22, pp. 151–165.

Panella C. 1985: 'I commerci di Roma e di Ostia in età imperiale (secoli I–III): le derrate alimentari', in AA.VV., *Misurare la terra: centuriazione e coloni nel mondo romano. Città, agricultura, commercio: materiali da Roma e dal suburbio*, Modena, pp. 180–189.

Panella C. 1986: 'Oriente et Occidente: considerazioni su alcune anfore 'egee' di età imperiale a Ostia', in J.-Y. Empereur, Y. Garlan eds., *Recherches sur les amphores grecques* (Actes du colloque international organisé par le Centre national de la recherche scientifique, l'Université de Rennes II et l'École française d'Athènes, Athènes, 10–12 septembre 1984, *BCH* Suppl. 13), Athens, pp. 609–636.

Panella C. 1992: 'Mercato di Roma e anfore galliche nella prima età imperiale', in F. Laubenheimer ed., *Les amphores e Gaule. Production, circulation*, Besançon, pp. 185–213.

Panella C. 1993: 'Merci e scambi nel Mediterraneo tardoantico', in *Storia di Roma: 3. L'età tardoantica. 2. I luoghi e le culture*, Torino, pp. 613–697.

Panella C., Fano M. 1977: 'Le anfore con anse bifide conservate a Pompei. Contributo ad una loro classificazione', in G. Valled ed., *Méthodes classiques et méthodes formelles dans l'étude des amphores* (Actes du Colloque de Rome, 27–29 mai 1974), Rome, pp. 133–164.

Panella C., Tchernia A. 2002: 'Agricultural products transported in amphorae: oil and wine', in W. Scheidel, S. von Reden eds., *The ancient economy*, Edinburgh, pp. 173–189 (first published in French as: *Produits agricoles transportés en amphores*, in *L'Italie d'Auguste a Dioclétien*, pp. 145–165).

Panella C., Coletti F., Saquí L. 2010: 'Contesti tardoantichi di Roma: una rilettura alla luce di nuovi dati', in S. Menchelli, M. Pasquinucci, S. Santoro eds., *LRCW* 3 (BAR Int. Ser. 2185), Oxford, pp. 57–78.

Panella C., Rizzo G. 2014: *Ostia VI. Le terme del Nuotatore* (*Studi miscellanei* 38), Roma.

Panetta V. 1996: 'Le anfore', in R. Volpe ed., *Aqua Marcia: Lo scavo di un tratto urbano* (Studi e materiali dei monumenti comunali di Roma), Firenze, pp. 159–180.

Paolucci G. 2006: 'Le anfore tipo 'tolle': contributo al commercio di vino nell'Etruria settentrionale interna', in G.M. Della Fina ed., *Gli Etruschi e il Mediterraneo. Commerci e politica* (Atti del XIII Convegno Internazionale di Studi sulla Storia e l'Archeologia dell'Etruria), Roma, pp. 417–432.

Papuci-Władyka E. 1998: 'Amfory typu Kos i Sub-Kos w świetle najnowszych badań', in F. Kiryk, M. Wilczyński, J. Ciecieląg eds., *Amicorum Dona. Studia dedykowane Profesorowi Stefanowi Skowronkowi w siedemdziesięciolecie urodzin*, Kraków, pp. 155–165.

Papuci-Władyka E. 1999: 'A research report on Hellenistic pottery: Cos Amphorae', *SAAC* 8, pp. 47–54.

Paribeni R. 1914: 'I quattro tempietto di Ostia', *MonAnt* 23, pp. 441–484.

Pascual Berlanga G., Ribera i Lacomba A., Finkielsztejn G. 2008: 'Las ánforas griegas y púnicas de recientes excavaciones en la regio VII de Pompeya', in J.P. Ballester, G. Pascual eds., *Comercio, redistribución y fondeaderos. La navegación a vela en el Mediterráneo* (V Jornadas de Arqueología Subacuática, Gandía 2006), Valencia, pp. 501–517.

Pastore P. 1992: 'Anfore da varie località di Padova conservate presso la Soprintendenza Archeologica per il Veneto', in S. Pesavento Mattioli ed., *Anfore romane a Padova. Ritrovamenti dalla città*, Modena, pp. 103–150.

Pavolini C. 1996: 'Mercato ostiense e mercato romano: alcuni contesti ceramici a confronto', in A. Gallina Zevi, A. Claridge eds., *Roman Ostia revisited*, London, pp. 223–242.

Peacock D.P.S., Williams D.F. 1986: *Amphorae and the Roman economy: an introductory guide*, London.

Pearsall J., Hanks P. 1998: *The New Oxford Dictionary of English*, New York.

Pecci A., Salvini L., Cantini F. 2010: 'Residue analysis of some late Roman amphora coming from the excavations of the historical centre of Florence', in S. Menchelli, S. Santoro, M. Pasquinucci, G. Guiducci eds., *LRCW* 3 (BAR Int. Ser. 2185), Oxford, pp. 363–367.

Pekáry T. 1981: 'Zur Bedeutung des Handels in der Antike', in G.A. Ritter, R. Vierhaus eds., *Aspekte der historischen Forschung in Frankreich und Deutsch*, Gottingen, pp. 30–39.

Peña J.T. 1999: *The urban economy during the Early Dominate. Pottery evidence from the Palatine Hill* (BAR Int. Ser. 784), Oxford.

Peña J.T. 2007: *Roman pottery in the archaeological record*, Cambridge.

Pergreffi O. 1940: 'Ricerche epigrafiche sui liberti', *Epigraphica* (*Riv. Ital. di Epig.*) 2, pp. 314–336.

Perkins P. 2012: 'Production and commercialization of Etruscan wine in the Albenga Valley', in A. Ciacci, P. Rendini, A. Zifferero eds., *Archeologia della vite e del vino in Toscana e nel Latium. Dalle tecniche dell'indagine archeologica alle prospettive della biologia molecolare*, Firenze, pp. 413–426.

Perkins P., Walker L. 1990: 'Survey of an Etruscan city at Doganella, in the Albegna Valley', *PBSR* 58, pp. 1–143.

Perkins P., Attolini I. 1992: 'Etruscan farm at Podere Tartuchino', *PBSR* 60, pp. 71–134.

Pesavento Mattioli S. 1998: 'I commerci di Verona e il ruolo della Via Postumia. Un aggiornamento sui dati delle anfore', in G. Sena Chiesa, E.A. Arslan eds., *Optima via. Atti del convegno internazionale di studi "Postumia. Storia e archeologia di una grande strada romana alle radici dell'Europa", Cremona 13–15 giugno 1996*, Cremona, pp. 311–313.

Pesavento Mattioli S. 1999: 'Anfore romane a Verona: nuovi rinvenimenti', *QdAV* 15, pp. 40–48.

Pettaco L. 2003: 'Anfore fenicie, anfore pithecusane, anfore etrusche: considerazioni sul modello 'tirrenico'', *Miscellanea etrusco-italica* III, pp. 37–69.

Piccaluga G. 1962: 'Numa e il vino', *SMSR* 33, pp. 99–103.

Piccoli F. 2004: *Il vino nel Nord Italia in epoca romana*, Verona.

Pieri D. 2002: 'Marchands orientaux dans l'économie occidentale de l'Antiquité tardive' in L. Rivet, M. Sciallano eds., *Vivre, produire et echanger: reflets méditerranéens, Melanges offerts a Bernard Lieu*, Montagnac, pp. 123–132.

Pieri D. 2005: *Le commerce du vin oriental: à l'époque byzantine, Ve–VIIe siècles: le témoignage des amphores en Gaule*, Beyruth.

Pieri D. 2007: 'Les centres de production d' amphores en Méditerranée orientale durant l' Antiquité tardive: quelques remarques', in M. Bonifay, J.-Ch. Tréglia eds., *LRCW* 2, Oxford, pp. 611–625.
Pieri D. 2012: 'Regional and Interregional Exchanges in the Eastern Mediterranean during the early Byzantine period' in C. Morrisson ed., *Trade and markets in Byzantium*, Washington, pp. 27–49.
Pietruszka W. 2013: *Elity miast kampańskich w okresie Antoninów i Sewerów*. Unpublished PhD thesis, Wrocław.
Pleket H.W. 1983: Urban elites and business in the Greek part of the Roman Empire, in P. Garnsey, K. Hopkin, C.R. Whittaker eds., *Trade in the ancient economy*, London, pp. 131–144.
Pleket H.W. 1984: 'Urban elites and the economy in the Greek cities of the Roman Empire', *MBAH* 3(1), pp. 3–35.
Pohl I. 1987: 'Piazzale delle Corporazioni, portico Ovest: saggi sotto i mosaici', in M. Carta, I. Pohl, F. Zevi eds., *Ostia. La taverna dell'Invidioso. Piazzale delle Corporazioni, portico Ovest: saggi sotto i mosaici* (*NSA* 32, suppl. 1978), Roma, pp. 165–443.
Porucznik J. forthcoming: *Cultural identity in the northern Black Sea area in antiquity: (de)constructing past identities*, Leuven.
Potter P., Smith W.D. 1988: *Transl. of Hippocrates VI*, London.
Poucet J. 1985: *Les origines de Rome. Tradition et histoire*, (Publications des faculties Universitaires Saint-Luis 38), Bruxelles.
Powell M.A. 1996: 'Wine and the vine in ancient Mesopotamia. The cuneiform evidence', in P.E. McGovern, S.J. Fleming, S.H. Katz eds., *The origins and ancient history of wine*, Amsterdam, pp. 97–122.
Pritchett W.K. 1956: 'The Attic Stelai, Part II', *Hesperia* 25(3), pp. 178–328.
Puig Palrem A., Ruiz del Pozo P. 2010: 'Miscelánea: las ánforas del Maditerráneo oriental, Galas, Itálicas y las otras ánforas Hispanas', in J.M.ª Blásqiez Martínez, J. Remesal Rodríguez eds., *Estudios sobre Monte Testaccio* (*Roma*) 5, Barcelona, pp. 415–438.
Purcell N. 1985: 'Wine and wealth in ancient Italy', *JRS* 75, pp. 1–19.
Py M. 1985: 'Les amphores etrusques de Gaule meridionale', in AA.VV., *Il commercio etrusco arcaico* (Atti dell'Incontro di Studio, Roma 1983), Roma, pp. 73–94.
Py F., Py M. 1974: 'Les amphores étrusques de Vaunage et de Villevieille, Gard', *MEFRA* 86, pp. 141–254.
Rackham H. 1979: *Introduction to Pliny Natural History in ten volumes*, Cambridge/London 1979.
Rathje A. 1995: 'Il banchetto in Italia centrale: quale stile di vita?', in O. Murray, M. Tecusan eds., *In vino veritas*, London, pp. 167–175.
Remark P. 1881: *De amphorarum inscriptionibus Latinis quaestiones selectee*, Bonn.
Remesal Rodríguez J. 1986: *La annona militaris y la exportacion de aceite betico a Germania*, Madrid.

Remesal Rodríguez J. 2000: 'L. Marius Phoebus mercator olei hispani ex provincia Baetica. Consideraciones en torno a los términos mercator, negotiator y diffusor olearius ex Baetica', in G. Paci ed., *Epigraphai: miscellanea epigrafica in onore di Lidio Gasperini*, Tivoli, pp. 781–797.

Remesal Rodríguez J. 2004: 'Promoción social en el mundo romano a través del comercio', in J. Remesal Rodríguez, F. Marco Simón, F. Pina Polo eds., *Vivir en tierra extraña: emigración e integración cultural en el mundo antiguo*, Barcelona, pp. 125–136.

Remesal Rodríguez J. 2008: 'Provincial interdependence in the Roman Empire: an explanatory model of Roman economy', in P.P.A. Funari, R.S. Garraffoni, B. Letalien eds., *New perspectives on the ancient world modern perceptions, ancient representations*, Oxford, pp. 155–159.

Remolà i Vallverdú J.A. 2000: *Las ánforas tardo-antiguas en Tarraco* (*Hispania Tarraconensis*), (Col.lecció Instrumenta 7, Universitat de Barcelona), Barcelona.

Reynolds P. 1995: *Trade in the Western Mediterranean AD 400–700: the ceramic evidence*, Oxford.

Reynolds P. 2005: 'Levantine amphorae from Cilicia to Gaza: a typology and analysis of regional production trends from the 1st to 7th centuries', in J.Mª. Gurt i Esparraguera, J. Buxeda i Garrigós, M.A. Cau Ontiveros eds., *LRCW* 1 (BAR Int. Ser. 1340), Oxford, pp. 563–611.

Reynolds P. 2008: 'Linear typologies and ceramic evolution', *FACTA* 2, pp. 61–87.

Reynolds P. 2010a: *Hispania and the Roman Mediterranean, AD 100–700*, London.

Reynolds P. 2010b: 'Trade networks of the East, 3rd to 7th centuries: the view from Beirut (Lebanon) and Butrint (Albania) (fine wares, amphorae and kitchen wares)', in S. Menchelli, S. Santoro, M. Pasquinucci, G. Guiducci eds., *LRCW* 3 (BAR Int. Ser. 2185), Oxford, pp. 89–114.

Reynolds P. 2018: 'The supply networks of the Roman East and West: interaction, fragmentation, and the origins of the Byzantine economy', in A. Bowman, A. Wilson eds., *Trade, commerce, and the state in the Roman world*, Oxford.

Ridgeway W., Wilkins A.S. 1890: 'Vinum', in W. Smith, W. Wayte, G.E. Marindin eds., *Dictionary of Greek and Roman Antiquities*, London, pp. 962–971.

Ridgway D. 1992: *The first Western Greeks*, Cambridge.

Rieger A.-K. 2004: *Heiligtümer in Ostia* (Studien zur antiken Stadt 8), München.

Riley J.A. 1979: 'The coarse pottery from Berenice', in J.A. Lloyd ed., *Excavations at Sidi Khrebish Benghazi* (*Berenice*) 2, Tripoli, pp. 91–467.

Riley J.A. 1981: 'The pottery from Cisterns 1977.1, 1977.2 and 1977.3', in J.H. Humprey ed., *Excavations at Carthage 1977 conducted by the University of Michigan 6*, Ann Arbor, pp. 85–122.

Rinaldi A. 2006: 'Materiali Neroniani del Foro di Nerva', in R. Meneghini, R. Santangeli Valenzani eds., *Roma: Lo scavo dei fori imperiali 1995–2000: i contesti ceramici*, Roma, pp. 5–24.

Rinaldi A. 2013: 'Contesti ceramici del Foro di Nerva dagli ambienti 1 e 2. I vasi decorate a matrice in terra sigilata italic e le anfore', in M. Ceci ed., *Contesti ceramici dai Fori Imperiali*, Oxford, pp. 61–73.

Riva C. 2010a: *The urbanisation of Etruria*, Cambridge.

Riva C. 2010b: 'Trading settlements and the materiality of wine consumption in the North Tyrrhenian Sea region', in B. Knapp, P. van Dommelen eds., *Material connections: mobility, materiality and Mediterranean identities*, London/New York, pp. 210–232.

Rivello E. 2002: 'Nuove acquisizioni sul deposito della Longarina (Ostia antica)', *MEFRA* 114(1), pp. 421–449.

Rizzo G. 2003: *Instrumenta urbis I: ceramiche fini da mensa, lucerne ed anfore a Roma nei primi due secoli dell'impero*, Roma.

Rizzo G. 2012: 'Roma e Ostia, un binomio ancora possibile? Di alcuni generi trasportati in anfora in età tardo-antonina, Rome', in S. Keay ed., *Rome, Portus and the Mediterranean*, London, pp. 87–103.

Rizzo G., Capone M., Costantini C., Gafa R., Pentricci M., Munzi M. 2004: 'Vigna Barberini, settore D, periodo IV. 540/550–580/590 d.C.', in L. Paroli, L. Venditelli eds., *Roma dall'antichità al medioevo, 2. Contesti tardoantichi e altomedievali*, Roma, pp. 72–90.

Rizzo M.A. 1990: *Le Anfore da trasporto e il commercio etrusco arcaico 1. Complessi tombali dall'Etruria meridionale*, Roma.

Robinson H.S. 1959: *Pottery of the Roman period*, Princeton.

Robinson J. 2006: *The Oxford Companion to wine*, Oxford (3rd ed.).

Rodrígues Almeida E. 1987–1988: 'Diffusores, negotiatores, mercatores olearii', *BCAR* 92, pp. 299–306.

Romano P., Suzzi G. 1993: 'Sulfur dioxide and wine micro-organisms', in G.E. Fleet ed., *Wine microbiology and biotechnology*, London, pp. 373–394.

Romanus K., Baeten J., Poblome J., Accardo S., Degryse P., Jacobs P., De Vos D., Waelkens M. 2009: 'Wine and olive oil permeation in pitched and non-pitched ceramics: relation with results from archaeological amphorae from Sagalassos, Turkey', *JASc* 36, pp. 900–909.

Rossiter J.J. 1981: 'Wine and oil processing at Roman farms in Italy', *Phoenix* 35(4), pp. 345–361.

Rothschild-Boros M.C. 1981: 'The determination of amphora contents', in G. Barker, R. Hodges eds., *Archaelogy and Italian Society* (BAR Int. Ser. 102), Oxford, pp. 79–89.

Rottoli M. 1993: ' "La Marmotta", Anguillara Sabazia (RM). Scavi 1989. Analisi paletnoobotaniche: prime risultance. Appendice 1', in M.A. Gugazzola, G. D'Eugenio, A. Pesina eds., *"La Marmotta" (Anguillara Sabazia, RM). Scavi 1989. Un abitato perilacustre di età neolitica* (Bullettino di Paletnologia Italiana 84), Roma, pp. 305–315.

Rubinich M., Braidotti E. 2007: 'Anfore dall'area delle Grandi Terme di Aquileia. Risultati preliminari', *Aquileia Nostra* 78, pp. 193–227.

Ruby P. 1993: 'Tarquinia, entre la Grèce et Sala Consilina. Éléments pour l'étude de la circulation des biens de prestige dans l'Italie centrale et méridionale protohistorique', *MEFRA* 105(2), pp. 779–832.

Ruiz del Pozo P. 2014: 'Miscelánea: Las ánforas del Mediterráneo Oriental, Galas, Itálicas y las otras ánforas hispanas', in J.M.ª Blázquez Martínez, J. Remesal Rodríguez eds., *Estudios sobre el Monte Testaccio (Roma) VI*, Barcelona, pp. 571–592.

Russell J.C. 1958: *Late ancient and medieval population*, Philadelphia.

Sacchetti F. 2013: *Les amphores grecques dans le nord de l'Italie: Echanges commerciaux entre les Apennins et les Alpes aux époques archaïque et classique*, Paris/Aix-en-Provence.

Saller R. 2005: 'Framing the debate over growth in the ancient economy', in J.G. Manning, I. Morris eds., *The ancient economy: evidence and models*, Stanford, pp. 223–238.

Salviat F. 1986: 'Le vin de Thasos. Amphores, vin et sources écrites', in J.-Y. Empereur, Y. Garlan eds., *Recherches sur les amphores grecques* (Actes du colloque international organisé par le Centre national de la recherche scientifique, l'Université de Rennes II et l'École française d'Athènes, Athènes, 10–12 septembre 1984, *BCH* Suppl. 13), Athènes, pp. 145–195.

Salviat F. 1993: 'Le vin de Rhodes et les plantations du dème d'Amos', in M.-C. Amouretti, J.-P. Brun eds., *La production du vin et de l'huile en Mediterranée* (BCH Suppl. 26), Paris, pp. 151–161.

Salviat F. 2013a: 'Vignes et vins anciens de Maronée à Mendé', in F. Salviat, A. Tchernia ed., *Vins, vignerons et buveurs de l'antiquité*, Rome, pp. 71–100 (first published in ΜΝΗΜΗ Δ. ΛΑΖΑΡΙΔΗ, Thessaloniki 1990, pp. 457–476).

Salviat F. 2013b: 'Origine orientale et diffusion des cépages grecs', in F. Salviat, A. Tchernia eds., *Vins, vignerons et buveurs de l'antiquité*, Rome, pp. 115–141.

Salviat F., Tchernia A. 2013: 'Les appellations d'origine dans l'antiquité grecque et romaine,' in F. Salviat, A. Tchernia eds., *Vins, vignerons et buveurs de l'antiquité*, Rome, pp. 217–226.

Sanmartí J., Asensio D., Martín M.A., 2006: 'Etruscan imports in the indigenous sites of Catalonia', in S. Gori, M.Ch. Bettini eds., *Gli Etruschi da Genova ad Ampurias* (Atti del XXIV Convegno di studi etruschi ed italici, Marseille, Lattes, 26 settembre–1 ottobre 2002), Pisa, pp. 193–202.

Santmartí i Grego E., Castanyer i Masoliver P., Tremoleda i Trilla J., Santos M. 1991: 'La presencia commercial etrusca en la Emporion arcaica, determinada a partir de las ánforas', in J. Remesal Rodríguez, O. Musso eds., *La presencia de material etrusco en la Península Ibérica*, Barcelona, pp. 83–94.

Santangeli Valenzani R., Volpe R. 2012: 'Paesaggi agrari della viticoltura a Roma e nel suburbium', in A. Ciacci, P. Rendini, A. Zifferero eds., *Archeologia della vite e del vino in Toscana e nel Latium. Dalle tecniche dell'indagine archeologica alle prospettive della biologia molecolare*, Firenze, pp. 61–69.

Sáez Fernández P. 2001: 'La cerveza en el mundo grecorromano. Consumo e ideología', in M. Molina ed., *La cerveza en la antigüedad*, Sevilla, pp. 109–124.

Saquì L. 2002: 'Roma, i centri privilegati e la lunga durata della tarda antichità. Dati archeologici dal deposito di 7 secolo nell'esedra della Crypta Balbi', *Archeologia Medievale* 29, pp. 7–42.

Saquì L., Manacorda D. 1995: 'L'esedra della Crypta Balbi e il monastero di S. Lorenzo in Pallacinis', *Archeologia Laziale* 12(1), pp. 121–134.

Saquì L., Coletti C.M. 2004: 'Contesti tardoantichi dall'area a S-E della Crypta Balbi', in L. Paroli, L. Venditelli eds., *Roma dall'antichità al medioevo, 2. Contesti tardoantichi e altomedievali*, Roma, pp. 242–277.

Sarris P. 2015: 'Integration and disintegration in the Late Roman economy: the role of markets, emperors, and aristocrats', in L. Leuven ed., *Local economies?: production and exchange of inland regions in late antiquity*, Leiden, pp. 167–188.

Sazanov A. 2014: 'Cretan amphorae from the northern Black Sea region: contexts, chronology, typology', in N. Poulou-Papadimitriou, E. Nodarou, V. Kilikoglou eds., *LRCW* 4, Oxford, pp. 399–409.

Scheidel W. 2006a: 'Stratification, deprivation, and quality of life', in M. Atkins, R. Osborne eds., *Poverty in the Roman world*, Cambridge, pp. 40–59.

Scheidel W. 2006b: 'Population and demography', *Princeton/Stanford Working Papers in Classics*, http://www.princeton.edu/~pswpc/pdfs/scheidel/040604.pdf, accessed February 2018.

Scheidel W. 2007a: 'Demography', in W. Scheidel, I. Morris, R. Saller eds., *The Cambridge economic history of the Greco-Roman world*, Cambridge, pp. 38–86.

Scheidel W. 2007b: 'A model of real income growth in Roman Italy', *Historia* 56, pp. 332–346.

Scheidel W. 2008: 'Roman population size: the logic of the debate' in L. de Ligt, S.J. Northwood eds., *People, land, and politics: demographic developments and the transformation of Roman Italy, 300 B.C.–A.D. 14*, Leiden, pp. 17–70.

Scheidel W. 2009: 'In search of Roman economic growth', *JRA* 22, pp. 46–70.

Scheidel W. 2013: 'Explaining the maritime freight charges in Diocletian's Prices Edict', *JRA* 26, pp. 464–468.

Scheidel W. 2014: 'The shape of the Roman world: modelling imperial connectivity', *JRA* 27, pp. 7–32.

Scheidel W. 2015: 'Orbis: the Stanford geospatial network model of the Roman World', *Princeton/Stanford Working Papers in Classics*. Available at SSRN: https://ssrn.com/abstract=2609654 or http://dx.doi.org/10.2139/ssrn.2609654, accessed 10.10.2019.

Scheidel W., Friesen S.J. 2009: 'The size of the economy and the distribution of income in the Roman Empire', *JRS* 99, pp. 61–91.

Sciortino M. 2012: 'Un nucleo inedito di anfore da trasporto dall'abitato di Spina', *LANX* 12, pp. 158–194.

Seltman C. 1957: *Wine in the ancient world*, London.

Sereni E. 1964: *Per la storia delle più antiche tecniche e della nomenclatura della vite e del vino in Italia*, Firenze.

Sezgin Y. 2004: 'Clazomenian Transport Amphorae of the Seventh and Sixth Centuries', in A. Moustaka, E. Skarlatidou, M.-C. Tzannes, Y.E. Ersoy eds., *Klazomenai, Teos and Abdera: Metropoleis and Colony* (Proceedings of the International Symposium held at the Archaeological Museum of Abdera, 20–21 October 2001), Thessaloniki, pp. 169–184.

Silver M. 2009: 'Historical otherness, the Roman bazaar, and primitivism: P.F. Bang on the Roman economy', *JRA* 22, pp. 421–443.

Singleton V.L. 1996: 'An enologist's commentary on ancient wines', in P.E. McGovern, S.J. Fleming, S.H. Katz eds., *The origins and ancient history of wine*, Amsterdam, pp. 67–77.

Skwara E. 2002: *Plaut. Komedie* 1, Warszawa.

Skwara E. 2005: 'Widz w teatrze Plauta. Charakterystyka rzymskiego odbiorcy na podstawie komedii "Bacchides"', *Meander* 60(1), pp. 48–68.

Slaska M. 1978: 'Gravisca. Le ceramiche comuni di produzione Greco-orientale', in AA.VV., *Les céramiques de la Grèce de l'Est et leur diffusion en Occident* (Actes du colloque international du Centre national de la recherche scientifique, Centre Jean Bérard, 6–9 juillet 1976), Paris, pp. 223–230.

Slaska M. 1985: 'Le anfore da trasporto a Gravisca', in AA.VV., *Il commercio Etrusco arcaico* (Atti dell'Incontro di Studio, Roma 1983), Roma, pp. 19–21.

Slej K. 2008: 'Transport Amphorae', in K. Slej, M. Cullhed eds., *The Temple of Castor and Pollux II, 2. The finds and the trenches*, Roma, pp. 201–282.

Smith Ch.J. 1998: 'Traders and artisans in archaic central Italy', in H. Parkins, Ch. Smith eds., *Trade, traders and the ancient city*, London/New York, pp. 31–51.

Smith Ch.J. 2005: 'The beginning of urbanization in Rome', in R. Osborne, B. Cunliffe eds., *Mediterranean urbanization (800–600 B.C.)*, Oxford, pp. 91–112.

Solin H. 1996: *Die stadtrömischen Sklavennamen: ein Namenbuch*, Stuttgart.

Solin H. 2003: *Die griechischen Personennamen in Rom: ein Namenbuch*, Berlin (2nd ed.).

Sonnenschein E.A. 1891: *Edition of Rudens by T. Maccius Plautus*, Oxford.

Sourisseau J.-Ch. 2011: 'La diffusion des vins grecs d'Occident du VIIIe au IVe s. av. J.-C., sources écrites et documents archéologiques', in T. Cinquantaquattro, M. Lombardo, A. Alessio eds., *La vigna di Dioniso: vite, vino e culti in Magna Grecia* (Atti del quarantanovesimo convegno di studi sulla Magna Grecia. Taranto 24–28 settembre 2009), Taranto, pp. 143–252.

Spanò Giammellaro A. 2000: *Il vino nel mondo fenicio-punico*, in C. Cremonesi, D. Tomasi eds., *L'avventura del vino nel Bacino del Mediterraneo: itinerari storici ed arche-*

ologici prima e dopo Roma (Simposio internazionale, Conegliano, 30 settembre–2 ottobre 1998), Conegliano, pp. 45–69.

Spignola G. 1998: 'Ceramica' in P. Liverani ed., *Laterano 1. Scavi sotto la Basilica di S. Giovanni in Laterano. I materiali*, Vaticano, pp. 98–109.

Stefani G. 2003: *Menander: la Casa del Menandro di Pompei*, Milano.

Storey G.R., Glenn R. 1997: 'The population of ancient Rome', *Antiquity* 71/274, pp. 966–978.

Swan V. 2004: 'Dichin (Bulgaria) and the supply of amphorae to the ower Danube in the late Roman–early Byzantine period', in J. Eiring, J. Lund eds., *Transport amphorae and trade in the Eastern Mediterranean*, Athens, pp. 371–382.

Sztetyłło Z. 1960: 'Stemplowane imadła amfor z wykopalisk polskich w Mirmeki na Krymie', *Meander* 15, pp. 382–392.

Sztetyłło Z. 1963: 'Stamped amphora handles from Polish excavations in Tell Atrib (1957–1961)', *Eos* 53, pp. 335–340.

Sztetyłło Z. 1965: 'Stemplowane imadła amfor greckich z wykopalisk polskich w Mirmeki na Krymie z 1958 roku', *Rocznik Muzeum Narodowego w Warszawie* 7, pp. 93–117.

Sztetyłło Z. 1966a: 'Quelques remarques en marge des études sur l'iconographie des timbres amphoriques grecs', in M.L. Bernhard ed., *Mélanges offerts à Kazimierz Michałowski*, Warszawa, pp. 669–674.

Sztetyłło Z. 1966b: 'Quelques problemes relatifs à l'iconographie des timbres amphoriques. La représentation de statues', *EtTrav* 3, pp. 46–80.

Sztetyłło Z. 1975: 'Timbres amphoriques grecs des fouilles polonaises à Alexandrie (1962–1972)', *EtTrav* 8, pp. 160–235.

Sztetyłło Z. 1976: *Nea Paphos 1: Les timbres céramiques 1965–1973*, Warszawa.

Sztetyłło Z. 1978: 'Timbres céramiques des fouilles polonaises à Alexandrie (1973–1974)', *EtTrav* 10, pp. 259–316.

Sztetyłło Z. 1983: *Les timbres céramiques dans la collections du Musée National de Varsovie*, Warszawa.

Sztetyłło Z. 1984: 'Timbres céramiques des fouilles polonaises à Nea Paphos en 1978', *EtTrav* 13, pp. 366–370.

Sztetyłło Z. 1990: 'Timbres céramiques des fouilles polonaises à Alexandrie (1974–1979)', *EtTrav* 14, pp. 160–212.

Sztetyłło Z. 1992: 'Timbres céramiques des fouilles polonaises à Alexandrie (1979–1982)', *EtTrav* 16, pp. 151–177.

Sztetyłło Z. 1998: 'Stemple ceramiczne z wykopalisk polskich z Nea Pafos', in W. Daszewski, H. Meyza eds., *Cypr w badaniach polskich* (Materiały z Sesji Naukowej zorganizowanej przez Centrum Archeologii Śródziemnomorskiej UW im. Prof. K. Michałowskiego, Warszawa, 24–25 luty 1995), Warszawa, pp. 111–117.

Sztetyłło Z. 2000: 'Pottery stamps. Tell Atrib 1985–1995 I', *EtTrav* 34, pp. 53–163.

Sztetyłło Z. 2010: *Pottery stamps from Nea Paphos. Excavations in 1990–2006* (Nea Paphos 6/PAM Monograph Series 2), Warszawa.

Tanasi D., Greco E., Di Tullio V., Capitani D., Gullì D., Ciliberto E. 2017: '1H-1H NMR 2D-TOCSY, ATR FT-IR and SEM-EDX for the identification of organic residues on Sicilian prehistoric pottery', *Microchemical Journal* 135, pp. 140–147.

Stronach D. 1996: 'The imagery of the wine bowl. Wine in Assyria in the early first millennium B.C.', in P.E. McGovern, S.J. Fleming, S.H. Katz eds., *The origins and ancient history of wine*, Philadelphia, pp. 175–195.

Taylor D.M. 1957: 'Cosa: black glaze pottery', *MAAR* XV, pp. 65–193.

Tchernia A. 1979: 'Il vino: produzione e commercio', in F. Zevi ed., *Pompei* 79, pp. 87–96.

Tchernia A. 1986: *Le vin de l'Italie romaine. Essai d'histoire économique d'après les amphores*, Roma.

Tchernia A. 1990: 'La vinification des Romains', in G. Garrier ed., *Le Vin des Historiens. Actes du Ier Symposium Vin et Histoire, 19–21 mai 1989*, Suze-la-Rousse, pp. 65–74.

Tchernia A. 1995: 'Le vin et l'honneur', in O. Murray, M. Tecuşan eds., *In vino veritas*, London, pp. 297–303.

Tchernia A. 1997: 'Le cercle de L. Licinius Crassus et la naissance de la hiérarchie des vins à Rome', *CRAI* 141(4), pp. 1247–1259.

Tchernia A. 1998: 'Archéologie expérimentale et goût du vin romain', in AA.VV., *El Vi a l'antiguitat: economia, producció i comerç al Mediterrani occidental: II Colloqui Internacional d'Arqueologia Romana, actes (Barcelona 6–9 de maig de 1998)*, Badalona, pp. 503–509.

Tchernia A., Brun J.-P. 1999: *Le vin romain antique*, Grenoble.

Tchernia A. 2001: 'Acre falernum: JUVÉNAL, XIII, 213–216', *RPh* 75(1), pp. 125–130.

Tchernia A. 2011: *Les Romains et le commerce*, Naples.

Tchernia A. 2016: *The Romans and trade*, Oxford.

Temin P. 2001. 'A market economy in the early Roman Empire', *JRS* 91, pp. 169–181.

Temin P. 2012: 'The contribution of economics', in. W. Scheidel ed., *The Cambridge Companion to the Roman economy*, Cambridge, pp. 45–70.

Temin P. 2013: *The Roman market economy*, Princeton/Oxford.

Tempesta C. 2011: 'Nuovo Mercato di Testaccio. Dallo scavo archeologico allo studio dei materiali. I reperti ceramici dell'ambiente I degli horrea', in A. Gallone, S. Zottis eds., *L'archeologia con gli occhi di Silvia* (Atti della giornata di studio per ricordare Valeria Silvia Mellace, Palazzo Massimo alle Terme, 7 marzo 2009, Roma), Catania, pp. 189–200.

Thurmond D.L. 2006: *A handbook of ancient food processing. For her bounty no winter*, Leiden.

Thurmond D.L. 2017: *From vines to wines in classical Rome: a handbook of viticulture and oenology in Rome and the Roman West*, Leiden/Boston.

Tilloca C. 2001: 'Bolli anforari rodii dall'Ager Populoniensis', *ArchCl* 52(2), pp. 229–254.

Timby J. 2004: 'Amphorae from excavations at Pompeii by the University of Reading', in J. Eiring, J. Lund eds., *Transport amphorae and trade in the Eastern Mediterranean*, Aarhus, pp. 383–392.

Tirelli M., Ferrarini F., Cipriano S. 1998: 'Oderzo (TV): Strutture di bonifica con anfore presso il molo fluviale e la necropoli sud-orientale', in S. Pesavento Mattioli ed., *Bonifiche e drenaggi con anfore in epoca romana: aspetti tecnici e topografici* (Atti del seminario di studi, Padova, 19–20 ottobre 1995, Materiali d'archeologia 3), Modena, pp. 135–156.

Tiussi C. 2007: 'Importazione vinaria ad Aquileia in età repubblicana. Le anfore rodie', in G. Cuscito, C. Zaccharia eds., *Aquileia dalle origini alla costituzione del ducato longobardo* (Antichità Altoadriatiche 65), Trieste, pp. 479–496.

Toniolo A. 1987: 'I contenitori da trasporto di epoca romana nel Polesine di Rovigno', *Archeologia Veneta* 10, pp. 87–128.

Toniolo A. 1991: *Le anfore di Altino*, Padova.

Toniolo A. 2000: *Le anfore di Adria: IV–II secolo a.C.*, Venezia.

Torelli M. 2000a: 'Primi apunti per un'antropologia del vino degli Etruschi', in C. Cremonesi, D. Tomasi eds., *L'avventura del vino nel Bacino del Mediterraneo: itinerari storici ed archeologici prima e dopo Roma* (Simposio internazionale, Conegliano, 30 settembre–2 ottobre 1998), Conegliano, pp. 89–100.

Torelli M. 2000b: *Gli Etruschi* (Exhibition catalogue), Milano.

Toynbee J., Ward Perkins J.B. 1956: *The Shrine of St. Peter and the Vatican excavations*, London.

Tzochev C. 2016: 'Markets, amphora trade and wine industry: the case of Thasos', in E.M. Harris, D.M. Lewis, M. Woolmer eds., *The ancient Greek economy: markets, households and city-states*, Cambridge/New York, pp. 230–253.

Unwin T. 1991: *Wine and the vine. An historical geography of viticulture and the wine trade*, London/New York.

Van Alfen P.G. 1996: 'New light on the 7th-c. Yassi Ada shipwreck: capacities and standard sizes of LRA1 amphoras', *JRA* 9, pp. 189–213.

Vandermersch C. 1994: *Vins et amphores de Grande Grèce et de Sicile IVe–III s. avant J.-C.*, Naples.

Vandermersch C. 2001: 'Aux sources du vin romain, dans le Latium et la Campania à l'époque médio-républicaine', *Ostraka* 10, pp. 157–206.

Van der Veen M. 2003: 'When is food a luxury?', *World Archaeology* 34(3), pp. 405–427.

Van der Werff J.H. 1989: 'L. Eumachi, A propos d'une marque d'amphore trouvée à Nimègue', *Berichten van de Rijksdienst voor het Oudheidkundik Bademanderzoeg Jurgang* 39, pp. 357–376.

Van Limbergen D. 2015: 'Figuring out the balance between intra-regional consumption and extra-regional export of wine and olive oil in late antique northern Syria', in A. Diler, K. Şenol, Ü. Aydinoglu eds., *Olive oil and wine production in Eastern Mediterranean in Antiquity*, Izmir, pp. 169–189.

Van Limbergen D. 2018: 'The central Adriatic wine trade of Italy revisited', *OJA* 37/2, pp. 201–226.

Vatta G., Bertoldi T. 2004: 'Celio. *Basilica Hilariana*: scavi 1997', in L. Paroli, L. Venditelli eds., *Roma dall'antichità al medioevo, 2. Contesti tardoantichi e altomedievali*, Roma, pp. 458–479.

Ventura P., Braidotti E. 2017: 'Aquileia (UD). Le anfore tardoantiche dal pozzo di via dei Patriarchi', in. D. Dixneuf ed., *LRCW* 5, Alexandria, pp. 313–330.

Vernesi C., Caramelli D., Dupanloup I., Bertorelle G., Lari M., Cappellini E., Moggi-Cecchi J., Chiarelli B., Castrì L., Casoli A., Mallegni F., Lalueza-Fox C., Barbujani G. 2004: 'The Etruscans: a population-genetic study', *The American Journal of Human Genetics* 74, pp. 694–704.

Verzár-Bass M. 1991: *Scavi ad Aquileia I, L'area a est del foro, Rapporto degli scavi 1988*, t. 1, Roma.

Verzár-Bass M. 1994: *Scavi ad Aquileia I, L'area a est del foro, Rapporto degli scavi 1989–91*, t. 2, Roma.

Veyne P. 2000a: 'La plèbe moyenne', *Annales* (*HSS*) 55, pp. 1169–1199.

Veyne P. 2000b: *La Société romaine*, Paris.

Vogeikoff-Brogan N., Apostolakou S. 2004: 'New evidence of wine production in East Crete in the Hellenistic period', in J. Eiring, J. Lund eds., *Transport amphorae and trade in the Eastern Mediterranean* (Acts of the International Colloquium at the Danish Institute at Athens, September 26–29, 2002. MDIA 5), Athens, pp. 417–427.

Volpe R. 1996: 'L'area dello scavo', in R. Volpe ed., *Aqua Marcia: Lo scavo di un tratto urbano* (Studi e materiali dei monumenti comunali di Roma), Firenze, pp. 15–18.

Volpe R. 2009: 'Vino, vigneti et anfore in Roma repubblicana', in V. Jolivet, C. Pavolini, M.A. Temei, R. Volpe eds., *SUBURBIUM II: Il suburbio di Roma dalla fine dell'Età monarchica alla nascita del sistema delle ville (V–II secolo a.C.)*, Roma, pp. 369–381.

Wallace-Hadrill A. 1994: *Houses and society in Pompeii and Herculaneum*, Princeton.

Welch K.E. 2009: 'Pompeian men and women in portrait sculpture', in P.W. Foss, J.J. Dobbins eds., *The world of Pompeii*, London/New York (2nd ed.), pp. 550–584.

Whittaker C.R. 1993: 'Late Roman trade and traders', in C.R. Whittaker ed., *Land, city and trade in the Roman Empire*, Aldershot, pp. 163–180.

Whitbread I.K. 1995: *Greek transport amphorae. A petrological and archaeological study*, Athens.

Whitehouse D., Barker G., Reece R. 1982: 'The Schola praeconum, 1. The coins, pottery, lamps and fauna', *PBSR* 50, pp. 53–101.

Whitehouse D. 1985: 'The Schola praeconum 2', *PBSR* 53, pp. 163–210.

Wilkins J.M., Hill S. 2006: *Food in the ancient world*, Malden/Oxford.

Williams D.F. 2004: 'The eruption of Vesuvius and its implications for the early Roman amphora trade with India', in J. Eiring, J. Lund eds., *Transport amphorae and trade in the Eastern Mediterranean* (Acts of the international colloquium at the Danish Institute at Athens, september 26–29, 2002), Athènes/Aarhus, pp. 441–450.

Williams D.F. 2005: 'An integrated archeometric approach to ceramic fabric recognition. A study case on LRA1', in J.Mª. Gurt i Esparraguera, J. Buxeda i Garrigós, M.A. Cau Ontiveros eds., *LRCW* 1, Oxford, pp. 613–624.

Wilson A. 2007: 'Quantification of fish-salting infrastructure capacity in the Roman world', http://oxrep.classics.ox.ac.uk/working%20papers/quantification_fishsalting_infrastructure_capacity_roman_world/, accessed 15.05.2018.

Wilson A. 2009a: 'Approaches to quantifying Roman trade', in A. Bowman, A. Wilson eds., *Quantifying the Roman economy: methods and problems*, Oxford, pp. 213–249.

Wilson A. 2009b: 'Indicators for Roman economic growth: a response to Walter Scheidel', *JRA* 22, pp. 71–82.

Wilson A. 2011a: 'The economic influence of developments in maritime technology in antiquity', in W.V. Harris, K. Iara eds., *Maritime technology in the ancient economy: ship design and navigation* (*JRA* Supp. 84), Portsmouth/Rhode Island, pp. 228–229.

Wilson A. 2011b: 'Developments in Mediterranean shipping and maritime from the Hellenistic period to AD 1000', in D. Robinson, A.I. Wilson eds., *Maritime archaeology and ancient trade in the Mediterranean*, Oxford, pp. 33–59.

Wilson A. 2014: 'Quantifying Roman economic performance by means of proxies: pitfalls and potential', in F. Callataÿ ed., *Quantifying Greco-Roman economy and beyond* (Pragmateiai 27), Bari, pp. 133–152.

Woodworth M., Bernal D., Bonifay M., De Vos D., Garnier N., Keay S., Pecci A., Poblome J., Pollard M., Richez F., Wilson A. 2015: 'The content of African Keay 25/Africana 3 amphorae: initial results of the Coronam Project', in C. Oliveira, R. Morais, A. Morillo Cerdán eds., *Archaeoanalytics. Chromatography and DNA analysis in archaeology*, Esposende, pp. 41–57.

Zaccaria Ruggiu A. 2003: *More regio vivere: il banchetto aristocratico e la casa romana di età arcaica*, Roma.

Zampini S. 2010: 'Lo scavo della cisterna del Foro di Cesare: lo studio del materiale ceramico', *Scienze dell'antichità: storia, archeologia, antropologia* 16, pp. 321–333.

Zampini S. 2011: 'La ceramica dello scavo del 2007 nel Palazzo Imperiale di Portus', in S. Keay, L. Paroli eds., *Portus and its Hinterland: Recent Archaeological Research*, London, pp. 93–99.

Zanker P. 1998: *Pompeii: private and public life*, Cambridge.

Zevi F. 1985: 'La situazione nel Lazio', in AA.VV., *Il commercio Etrusco arcaico* (Atti dell'Incontro di Studio, Roma 1983), Roma, pp. 119–125.

Zevi F. 1989: 'Introduzione', in AA.VV., *Amphores romaines et histoire économique. Dix ans de recherche* (Publications de l'École Française de Rome 114), Roma, pp. 3–19.

Zevi F., Geremia R., Leone A., Moreschini L. 2004–2005: 'OSTIA-Sondaggio stratigrafico in uno degli ambienti gella domus dei Pesci (1995 e 1996)', *NSA* 15–16, pp. 21–327.

Zevi F., Pohl I. 1970: 'Ostia. Saggi di scavo', *NSA* 24, suppl. 1, pp. 43–234.

Zifferero A. 2010a: 'Il paesaggio agrario in area tirrenica: la produzione e il commercio del vino etrusco', in G. di Pasquale ed., *VINUM NOSTRUM: arte, scienza e miti del vino nelle civiltà del Mediterraneo antico*, Firenze, pp. 66–73.

Zifferero A. 2010b: 'Il progetto ArcheoVino: vite silvestre e vitigni autoctoni nella Valle dell'Albegna', in G. di Pasquale ed., *VINUM NOSTRUM: arte, scienza e miti del vino nelle civiltà del Mediterraneo antico*, Firenze, pp. 84–89.

Zohary D. 1996: 'The domestication of the grapevine Vitis vinifera L. in the Near East', in P.E. McGovern, S.J. Fleming, S.H. Katz eds., *The origins and ancient history of wine*, Amsterdam, pp. 23–30.

Index of Ancient Sources

Index of Names and Subjects

www.ingramcontent.com/pod-product-compliance
Ingram Content Group UK Ltd.
Pitfield, Milton Keynes, MK11 3LW, UK
UKHW022224051026
15624UKWH00002B/349

9 789004 433700